To the Gates of Stalingrad

The Stalingrad Trilogy, Volume I

To the Gates of Stalingrad

Soviet-German Combat Operations, April–August 1942

David M. Glantz

with

Jonathan M. House

University Press of Kansas

© 2009 by the University Press of Kansas
All rights reserved

Published by the University Press of Kansas (Lawrence, Kansas 66045), which was
organized by the Kansas Board of Regents and is operated and funded by Emporia State
University, Fort Hays State University, Kansas State University, Pittsburg State University,
the University of Kansas, and Wichita State University

Library of Congress Cataloging-in-Publication Data

Glantz, David M.
  To the gates of Stalingrad : Soviet-German combat operations, April-August 1942 /
David M. Glantz with Jonathan M. House.
    p. cm. — (The Stalingrad trilogy ; v. 1) (Modern war studies)
  Includes bibliographical references and index.
  ISBN 978-0-7006-1630-5 (cloth : alk. paper)
  1. Stalingrad, Battle of, Volgograd, Russia, 1942–1943. 2. Soviet Union. Raboche-
Krestíianskaia Krasnaia Armiia—History—World War, 1939–1945. 3. Germany.
Heer.—History—World War, 1939–1945. I. House, Jonathan M. (Jonathan Mallory),
1950– II. Title.
  D764.3.S7G59 2009
  940.54'21747—dc22   2008049847

British Library Cataloguing-in-Publication Data is available.

Printed in the United States of America
10 9 8 7 6 5 4 3 2 1

The paper used in this publication is recycled and contains 30 percent postconsumer
waste. It is acid free and meets the minimum requirements of the American National
Standard for Permanence of Paper for Printed Library Materials Z39.48-1992.

To my daughter Susan Mangan and her husband, Darin,
for inspiring me with the wondrous gift of
my granddaughter, Elizabeth

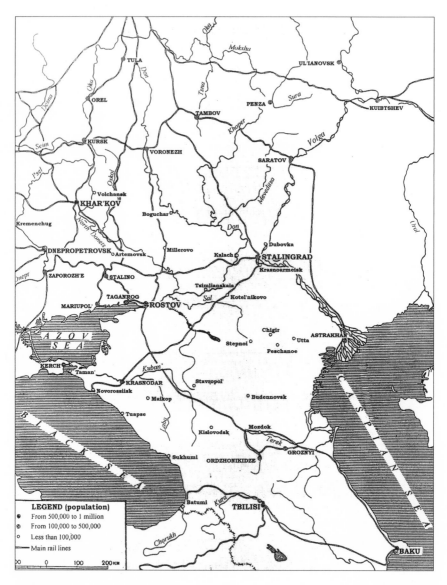

Area of military operations, April–November 1942

Contents

Maps, Tables, and Illustrations

TABLES

Photographs

Both at the time of the battle and in historical retrospective, Stalingrad has captured the imagination of millions of people. The battle has become a metaphor for the ferocity of the Soviet-German conflict and, indeed, for the devastating nature of twentieth-century warfare as a whole. Historical accounts, novels, and motion pictures have naturally focused on the namesake city of the Soviet dictator, the place where hundreds of thousands of soldiers and civilians died for control of a few square kilometers of blasted urban landscape.

Given the millions of words written on this subject in dozens of languages, a reader's first question might well be to ask whether there is anything new to say about the matter or, indeed, why the world needs yet another "Stalingrad book." The answers to these questions are that, in fact, much about the battle has been ignored or misunderstood; therefore, a new study is justified for a number of reasons.

First, this trilogy attempts to provide a comprehensive operational history of the entire German 1942 campaign and of the Soviet response to that campaign, a struggle that lasted from May 1942 until March 1943. Contrary to popular belief, the city of Stalingrad was not the original objective of this campaign; in fact, it merited only a passing reference in the original German operations order. Even after the struggle for the city had captured worldwide attention, Germany persisted in its original objective of seizing oil fields in the Caucasus region, a goal that consumed so many troops and supplies that the German attackers lacked the combat power to take and hold the city. Only by examining this campaign as a whole can one understand the battle for Stalingrad in its proper context.

Second, existing histories concentrated primarily on the fighting in Stalingrad proper without examining in detail the complex and arduous fighting that took place on German Sixth Army's "path" to the city and the incessant struggle on the flanks, particularly in the Caucasus, Voronezh, and Rzhev regions. Vital to the outcome of the campaign as a whole, this ostensibly peripheral fighting sapped the German forces' energy and resources, providing essential context for the climactic battles in the Stalingrad region in November 1942. Moreover, as this volume will demonstrate, the Soviet Union had almost exhausted the invading Sixth Army before it even reached the city proper.

Third, within the confines of the city, the course of the battle was significantly different from that described in most previous accounts. In large measure, this was due to the paucity of detailed records for the campaign. On the Soviet side, the politics of the cold war compounded the natural secrecy of the Russian State to ensure that few documents were available until the 1990s. Most historians, therefore, chose to rely upon the memoirs of Vasilii Ivanovich Chuikov, the commander of Soviet 62nd Army, who conducted the primary defense of Stalingrad. While Chuikov's memoirs were remarkably detailed and honest when they appeared in the 1960s, he had to write without complete access to, or freedom to quote from, the official Soviet records of the battle. Working largely from memory and often inaccurate intelligence reports from the period, Chuikov therefore committed several major errors in describing the locations, composition, and combat actions of the German Sixth and Soviet 62nd Armies, errors that carried over into most subsequent histories. Western sources were equally scarce, both because the Soviets captured the records and eyewitnesses of Sixth Army in 1943 and because of the chaos that descended on Germany at the end of the war two years later. Many of the classic German accounts written by Walter Goerlitz, Paul Carrell, and others, though superb efforts at the time of publication, were therefore as prone to error as were Chuikov's memoirs.

This study, by contrast, goes well beyond the traditional accounts to include two major groups of additional sources. First, we compare the daily official records of both sides, using a considerable number of primary documents. The records of the People's Commissariat of Internal Affairs, which provided Moscow with an independent and often critical view of the battle, have never been exploited before. The same applies to the records of Soviet 62nd Army and many of its subordinate divisions and brigades. Second, a number of Soviet memoirs and German divisional histories have accumulated over the past 65 years, adding greater texture and richness to earlier views of the battle. Since the 1980s, German historians have produced a superb official history of this campaign, a history that provides many details and shades of meaning that were previously unknown. Finally, an emerging generation of new Russian historians, unfettered from the restraints and shibboleths of former Soviet times, have authored fresh, detailed, and candid accounts of many aspects of the fighting.

The resulting account is so detailed and nuanced that it could not easily be contained within a single volume. Instead, the first two volumes follow the German offensive from its inception to final exhaustion and stalemate in November 1942. The rest of the story is the subject of the third volume, concentrating on the Red Army's counteroffensive on 19 November 1942, its capture of Stalingrad in early February 1943, and the German maneuver battles that temporarily restored their front lines in the late winter of 1943.

Based on these new sources, this study offers unprecedented detail and fresh perspectives, interpretations, and evaluations of the Stalingrad campaign, superseding all previous historical accounts. Both the German offensive and the Soviet defense emerge as being markedly different from our traditional understanding of the 1942 campaign.

Any research effort of this magnitude incurs obligations of gratitude for the support provided by numerous individuals and agencies. In this regard, we must particularly thank Jason Mark, both for his generous personal assistance and for the groundbreaking tactical accounts of Stalingrad published by Leaping Horseman Books in Sydney, Australia. Likewise, Michael Jones, the British author of *Stalingrad: How the Red Army Triumphed*, an insightful study of the psychology of Soviet commanders and soldiers in the battle, generously provided us with many Russian archival documents from his collection of sources. William McCrodden, who has spent a lifetime compiling detailed and definitive orders of battle for German forces during the war, shared with us the numerous draft volumes produced by his research.

Finally, we are also indebted for the usual prodigies of effort provided by the staffs of the Military History Institute in Carlisle, Pennsylvania, the Combined Arms Research Library at Fort Leavenworth, Kansas, and the Hightower Library of Gordon College in Barnesville, Georgia. As with our previous efforts, we gratefully acknowledge the crucial role Mary Ann Glantz played in editing this manuscript.

David M. Glantz   *Jonathan M. House*
Carlisle, PA   Leavenworth, KS

To the Gates of Stalingrad

Along the Sukhaia Vereika River, 23 July 1942

The Germans were closing in on Major General A. I. Liziukov from three sides. He was desperate to stop them, the only way to save the encircled half of his 2nd Tank Corps.

Three weeks before, Liziukov had been commander of 5th Tank Army, one of the Red Army's first attempts to create a large mechanized unit equivalent to a German panzer corps.[1] The headquarters of the Soviet Supreme High Command (*Stavka*) had reinforced 5th Tank Army to a total of 641 tanks and ordered it to attack southward into the flank of the new German offensive, seeking to cut off XXXXVIII Panzer Corps, whose divisions had just seized the southern Russian city of Voronezh.[2] A key city on the Don River, Voronezh was rapidly becoming a focus of struggle because it formed a natural northern anchor for the German advance eastward to Stalingrad and southward to the Caucasus. The Soviet dictator, Joseph Stalin, believed that Liziukov faced only one German panzer division and expected 5th Tank Army to chop off the spearhead of the overextended German armor before the panzers could receive reinforcement from the hard-marching infantry divisions.

But everything had gone wrong from the start. Few, if any, Soviet commanders and staff officers had the experience necessary to maneuver large mechanized formations in battle. Liziukov's army headquarters had been in existence for only six weeks, and his three subordinate tank corps, each equivalent to an armored division, had been formed only in April. The Soviets appeared incapable of coordinating three tank brigades, let alone three tank corps, in a single operation. Instead of attacking in a solid mass, the three corps had arrived on the scene and entered battle piecemeal between 6 and 10 July. Moreover, the Red soldiers found themselves opposed by two panzer divisions with 300 tanks, soon reinforced by a number of infantry divisions. Absolute German air superiority made Liziukov's task even more difficult.

Nor did his superiors help him in any way. As was its custom, the *Stavka* attempted to micromanage the battle, sending a series of specific instructions along with senior officers, including the head of all Soviet armor, to personally supervise his actions. Meanwhile a bewildering series of changes occurred in the *front*, or Soviet army group, that supervised 5th Tank Army. Frequently, the actions that the *Stavka* criticized were simply Liziukov and his subordinates obeying the instructions given by one of the three successive commanders of Briansk Front.

1

Despite these troubles, Liziukov succeeded in gaining German attention, forcing his opponents to concentrate large numbers of troops and aircraft to defend their northern flank. Yet success was invisible to Stalin, who disbanded the tank army headquarters and demoted Liziukov to tank corps commander on 15 July.

Even that had not ended the agony. Under constant hectoring from Moscow, Briansk Front continued its counterstrokes against the Germans, who by 20 July had built a solid wall of infantry divisions, backed up by 9th Panzer Division, to protect their northern flank. One of these Red counterstrokes achieved a limited penetration on 21–22 July, but this attack force, which included a rifle division and the two lead tank brigades of Liziukov's 2nd Tank Corps, was soon hemmed in on three sides by German infantry and armor.

By all accounts, Aleksandr Il'ich Liziukov had been a skillful and brave commander in 1941, becoming one of the first men recognized as a Hero of the Soviet Union because he had performed superbly during the battle for Moscow as the deputy to Lieutenant General A. A. Vlasov, commander of Western Front's 20th Army. After three weeks of failure in midsummer 1942, however, Liziukov had reached the end of his rope by 23 July. Ordered by Lieutenant General N. E. Chibisov, commander of Briansk Front's special operational group conducting the counterstroke, to locate his corps' two tank brigades encircled deep in the German rear area and lead them back to safety, Liziukov, at 0900 hours on 23 July, climbed into a KV heavy tank with his commissar. He personally directed the tank southward from his headquarters at Bol'shaia Vereika and across the Sukhaia Vereika River, seeking to break through the enemy infantry and armor to rescue his two brigades. Just short of the German defensive positions, in a patch of woods south of the village of Lebiazh'e, several hundred meters west of Hill 188.5, Liziukov's tank was immobilized by fire from an antitank gun. The stranded tank acted as a magnet for German fire, and the general ordered his crew to abandon the vehicle. Machine-gun fire wounded the driver and killed the radio operator as they bailed out of the hatches. Liziukov himself escaped from the tank but was killed instantly by artillery fire.[3]

The disjointed, uncoordinated actions of 5th Tank Army and its component corps and brigades seemed to confirm the widespread German contempt for Soviet military staff work and leadership. Yet repeated Soviet counterstrokes of this kind delayed and weakened the Germans long before they reached Stalingrad. And less than four months after Liziukov's suicide ride, the surviving Soviet tank commanders proved themselves to be more than a match for their German counterparts.

CHAPTER 1

The *Wehrmacht*

By the time Russian General Liziukov was killed on 23 July, the Red Army had been fighting the *Wehrmacht* (German Armed Forces) for 13 months. The *Wehrmacht* was close to the peak of its effectiveness when it launched Operation Barbarossa, the surprise invasion of the Soviet Union in June 1941. One hundred and fifty-two divisions, including 19 panzer (armored) and 15 motorized infantry divisions, thrust rapidly into Soviet territory, seeking to encircle their Red counterparts. The *Luftwaffe* (German air force) achieved air superiority within the first two days, supporting the panzer advance and harassing any Soviet countermoves. In a series of huge encirclements—at Minsk, Smolensk, Uman', Kiev, Viaz'ma, Melitopol', and elsewhere—almost 2 million Soviet soldiers fell into German hands. Within three months, the Germans and their allies advanced more than 1,200 kilometers, capturing many of the Soviet Union's population and industrial centers, encircling Leningrad and threatening Moscow and Rostov.

The German attack caught the Red Army at the worst possible time.[1] Four years of political purges had decapitated the Soviet officer corps; many commanders had just emerged from the Siberian prison camps when the war began, and others were still being "cleansed," or purged, from the ranks of the armed forces. The surviving officers, often commanding units far above their limited training and experience, tended to fight in predictable, stylized formations that were easy prey for the veteran Germans. Moreover, although the Soviets possessed huge mechanized and air force organizations, these formations lacked logistical systems capable of providing them with adequate fuel, ammunition, and spare parts and were equipped with a mixture of worn out, obsolescent equipment and brand new weapons whose crews had not yet learned to operate them effectively. Finally, in a desperate bid to delay the impending conflict, Stalin had forbidden his forces to take defensive precautions, allowing the Germans to catch them before they had a chance to deploy from garrisons to field positions.

Despite all these advantages, the Germans fell short of victory because they had underestimated both the magnitude of their task and the mobilization capacity of their opponents. The vast distances of European Russia placed an enormous strain on the German system of supply and maintenance. This strain was compounded by the meager Soviet transportation network, whose railroads were of a wider gauge than those of the Germans, and whose unpaved roads turned into muddy canals when it rained, consuming fuel and vehicle repair parts at three times the expected rate. The deeper the German penetrations, the more difficult became the task of resupplying the attackers.

Beset by a multitude of daunting logistical problems, beginning in mid-July 1941, German offensive operations evolved into a succession of often improvised spurts, involving advances of 110–130 kilometers within periods of roughly ten days punctuated by pauses of seven to ten days necessary to regroup and replenish the advancing forces with fuel and ammunition. Allowing for the inevitable slowdown in operational tempo occasioned by Red Army counterattacks and counterstrokes and the equally vexing intervention of bad winter weather, these logistical constraints dictated the pace of operations and, by doing so, helped deny the *Wehrmacht* victory in Operation Barbarossa.

The same long distances and primitive lines of communication meant that the German mechanized formations often outran the foot-mobile infantry and horse-drawn artillery. Each time the invaders encircled their foes the panzers were unable to contain them, waiting for the infantry to catch up. In the interim, irreplaceable Red Army commanders and staff officers, together with thousands of their men, often escaped from the weakly held pockets, joining local partisans or returning to their own lines.

These escapes compounded the second aspect of Germany's failure. At the start of the invasion, German intelligence estimated that the Red Army had approximately 200 divisions, but within six weeks the invaders had actually counted at least 360.[2] The extraordinary ability of the Soviet Union to generate huge new military formations—however poorly trained and equipped those formations might be—made the German idea of destroying the bulk of the Red Army an impossible dream. The frustrated Germans discovered that whenever they eliminated one group of Soviet soldiers another wave of defenders appeared as if from nowhere to continue the struggle.

These Soviet divisions did not defend passively but fought back at every opportunity. Frequently, the Red Army's actions were so poorly coordinated that only the front-line German troops were aware that a counterattack was under way, and German officers were unable to detect the difference between local counterattacks and intended Soviet counterstrokes or even counteroffensives. Still, such attacks exacted a stiff toll on German equipment and manpower. By 13 August 1941, after only seven weeks of fighting, the Germans had suffered 389,924 casualties—11.4 percent of their original troop strength.[3] Unlike their opponents, the Germans were woefully short of replacements for these soldiers.

By late November 1941, such losses, in conjunction with the challenges of distance and logistics, had brought the German Army to a halt, overextended and exhausted, already defeated at Rostov, stuck on the outskirts of Leningrad and just short of Moscow. Then, on 5 December the Soviet Stavka (Headquarters of the Supreme High Command) launched a series of counterattacks against the German spearheads in Moscow's suburbs, which grew in intensity into head-on counterstrokes by mid-December. Frozen in the snow and surprised by an enemy they had thought was beaten, the Germans were easy prey for the Red Army. In early January 1942, elated by their initial successes, Josef Stalin and his most effective field commander, General Georgii Konstantinovich Zhukov of the Red Army, broadened these attacks into a general offensive along virtually the entire 2,500-kilometer front, from the Baltic to the Black Sea.

In the crisis, Adolf Hitler forbade any withdrawals, ordering the threadbare German units to fight wherever they stood. A number of German generals found themselves relieved of command for pulling back to consolidate their defenses. Although Hitler had acted instinctively—almost irrationally—his rigidity proved to be the best course of action. Despite its hard-won combat experience, the battered Red Army lacked the capacity to destroy the Germans. In a confused series of battles that lasted until April 1942, the Soviets mauled their opponents and pushed them away from Moscow but could not achieve any decisive penetration to reach their objective, Smolensk. When the spring rainy period and associated flooding (*rasputitsa*) arrived, the German Army was still alive, and the front looked more like a tangled skein of yarn than a line on a map. From Leningrad in the north to the Khar'kov region in the south, a series of German and Soviet salients protruded eastward and westward into the enemy's territory. Prior to a renewed German offensive, therefore, these salients would have to be eliminated (see Map 1).

REBUILDING THE *WEHRMACHT*

When the fighting died down, both sides were at the end of their resources. The Red Army had the capacity to rebuild, but the *Wehrmacht* never recovered completely from the losses it suffered during 1941.

By 31 January 1942, the German Army in the East had suffered 917,985 casualties, in addition to 18,098 *Luftwaffe* casualties and significant losses among the armies of Germany's allies in Finland, Romania, and Hungary.[4] German matériel shortages were almost equally serious. During the first seven months of Operation Barbarossa, the Germans had lost more than 41,000 trucks and 207,000 horses, at a time when horses provided the primary mobility for artillery and supply units in most infantry divisions. The cost in artillery, antitank guns, and mortars exceeded 13,600 gun tubes, and the *Luftwaffe* had written off 4,903 aircraft as destroyed.[5] By the end of March 1942, the strength of German forces in the East had fallen from more than 3 million men in June 1941 to slightly more than 2.5 million, supported by about 3,300 tanks and assault guns.[6] After weathering its failures at Leningrad, Moscow, and Rostov and surviving the trying winter of 1941–1942 intact, the Germans considered only 8 of their 162 divisions in the East to be fully capable; the 16 panzer divisions had only 140 functioning tanks, equivalent to one full-strength division, among them.[7]

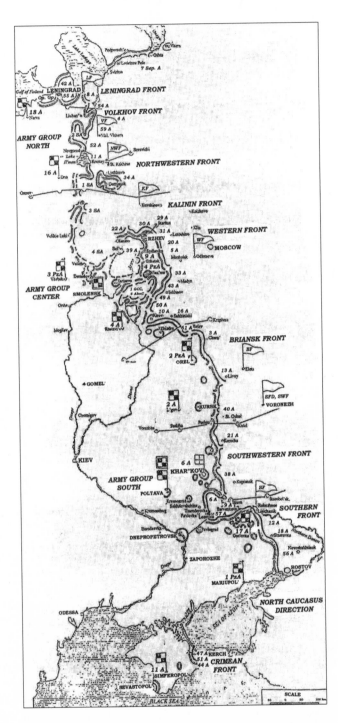

Map 1. The situation on the Soviet-German front on 1 April 1942

Throughout World War II, Germany was limited as much by raw material shortages as by enemy action. As early as November 1941, the Germans had begun to melt down church bells and textile manufacturing cylinders to obtain the copper necessary for electrical wiring and ammunition shell casings. The need for other raw materials, especially petroleum, often dictated German strategy, a reality that hit hard at Stalingrad. Without such materials, German industry would be hard-pressed to replace the lost weapons and vehicles.

To rebuild the German armies in the East required more than just raw materials, however. In December 1941, 282,300 men—including many who worked in the armaments industry—received orders to report for military service. General Georg Thomas, head of the Office of War Economy and Armaments, convinced Hitler that the nation must dedicate its remaining resources to replacing the lost equipment rather than building new formations and weapons, as was the dictator's habit. On 10 January 1942, Hitler issued an order to reorganize the armaments ministry. Top production priority went to field weapons, followed by mechanized forces and antitank guns.[8] A month later, the Führer's favorite architect, Albert Speer, became minister for armaments and war production after his predecessor died in an air crash. Although Germany's economy remained divided into various economic fiefdoms, Speer was able to increase production and conserve scarce materials by negotiating compromises among rival agencies and companies.[9]

Still, despite the efforts of Thomas and Speer, Germany was unable to restore all of its eastern forces to the strength they had enjoyed in June 1941. Put simply, Hitler the politician hesitated to impose total economic mobilization on his own populace. Instead, Germany attempted several halfway measures in 1941–1942. To replace the lost motor vehicles, the Germans conducted major efforts during November and December to commandeer civilian trucks in the occupied lands of western and central Europe. However, three-quarters of these vehicles became immobilized by parts shortages and winter weather; even those trucks that did reach the front only complicated the German maintenance and mobility problems by saddling units with a bewildering variety of vehicles.

German officials were forced to distribute their scarce reserves of personnel and equipment according to a strict set of priorities. Elite units, including the armored, motorized, and combat (Waffen) SS divisions, came first, but even they were not restored to their 1941 capabilities. In Army Group South, where the next German offensive would occur, mechanized units were supposed to reach 85 percent of their authorized strength; farther north, however, each panzer division was authorized enough armor to equip only one tank battalion rather than the two or three battalions of the previous year. The same was true even in some panzer divisions of First Panzer Army located in the south. Infantry divisions fared even worse in the distribution of resources. In Army Groups North and Center, 69 out of 75 divisions were reduced from nine to six battalions of infantry, and their artillery was cut from four guns per battery to three. These infantry divisions also had to make do with great reductions in horse and motor transportation, making it difficult to redeploy forces in response to an enemy attack.[10]

To complicate matters even further, the majority of eastern divisions were not withdrawn to the rear to rest and refit but had to reconstitute themselves while still defending a sector along the front. Thus, even before Germany's 1942 summer offensive, the typical German division was notably less capable than it had been in 1941. Only the *Luftwaffe* began the 1942 campaign at substantially the same level (2,635 aircraft in the East) that it had fielded in 1941 (2,770), and even these figures concealed a decline in the quality of German aircrews.[11]

In technical terms, then, German weapons remained essentially the same as those of 1941. The workhorse tanks of the panzer force were the *Panzerkampfwagen* (PzKpfw) III and IV medium tanks, but the lighter Panzer II was almost completely withdrawn from service in 1942. Just as many panzer divisions had to make do with foreign-model tanks in 1941, some of the newer panzer divisions had to make do with a mixture of German and captured armor. Beginning in March 1942, German factories produced the Panzer IV in the new F2 model, which included a long-barreled 75mm gun that had greater armor penetration capability. Yet this new version was still a rarity when the Germans resumed the offensive that summer.[12] The new 50mm antitank gun, intended to replace the woefully inadequate 37mm, had begun to come off the assembly line in greater numbers but was still the exception in ordinary German infantry units. Thus the armor-piercing capacity of the average German tank and antitank gun remained technically inferior to the standard Soviet medium tank, the T-34/76 (armed with a 76.2mm gun). Virtually all German commanders, however, believed that superior tactics and training would compensate for shortages in numbers and firepower.

SATELLITE ARMIES

The Germans were more confident about their own abilities than about those of their allies. Like Napoleon Bonaparte before him, Hitler had to rely on satellite armies to cover the vast expanses of European Russia. This was already true when the invasion began in 1941, when every kilometer that the Germans advanced forced them to defend on a wider and wider front. In the projected summer offensive of 1942, an Axis advance down the northeastern coast of the Black Sea and into the Caucasus would further extend the front lines and therefore increase the demand for troops.

With German forces stretched to the limit to occupy Western Europe while bleeding to conduct major offensives in the East, Germany's allies became the only source for major additional forces. The army of Finland in the north was both capable and highly motivated, but the same could not be said for the other satellite armies. Under considerable diplomatic pressure, these armies were increased to a nominal total of 52 divisions for the 1942 campaign—27 Romanian divisions (each equivalent in size to a German brigade), 13 Hungarian divisions, nine Italian divisions, two Slovak divisions, and the Spanish "Blue" Division.[13] For obvious reasons due to politics and national pride, the contributing governments insisted that these troops serve under their own corps and field army commanders. Although the Germans provided liaison officers and communications detachments to the satellite headquarters, they had to use persuasion and diplomacy to ensure cooperation from these other armies.

Few of these units had the training and equipment appropriate for the type of mechanized, maneuver warfare that decided most battles in the East. In August 1941 a Soviet ambush near Odessa had severely mauled the single Romanian armored division, which was never able to replace its obsolescent tanks.[14] The two Italian motorized divisions suffered from the same technical problems displayed by the thinly armored and underpowered Italian motor vehicles in North Africa. The remaining satellite divisions were lightly equipped cavalry and infantry formations, more suitable for rear-area security against Soviet partisans than for confronting a Red Army tank force. Although the Germans provided some capable antitank batteries to support their allies, no amount of courage could make up for their overall deficiencies in artillery and antitank firepower.

These allies did indeed have courage; despite the often contemptuous opinion of their German masters, the satellite forces contained many brave men and at least some competent soldiers. Some of these men were fanatical fascists, sent to Russia in part because they were disruptive influences at home. Others had little interest in fascism but shared the widely held belief that Soviet communism was a menace to their societies. Even the Romanian troops, whose poorly trained officers were openly abusive of their own men, demonstrated their willingness to fight but only if properly supported by heavy weapons. Therefore, when the Soviets launched their counteroffensives in late 1942 the circumstances would make resistance almost impossible. Once the winter weather and the tide of battle turned against the Axis, many of the satellite soldiers understandably declined the dubious honor of a pointless death in the snow.

THE STRATEGIC PICTURE

Prior to the 1941 invasion of Russia, Adolf Hitler had dominated Western Europe, with only Great Britain still openly at war with Nazi Germany. One year later, however, Hitler found himself fighting the two greatest industrial powers in the world—the United States and the Soviet Union—on two separate fronts. Thus, even as the German High Command prepared for a 1942 offensive in the East, it had to consider the demands of other theaters of war. Although the United States had only begun its mobilization, Hitler could not rid himself of the fear that the British, aided by the Americans, might attempt to take pressure off the Soviets by launching a limited invasion in Norway or France. In a 28 March 1942 conference on the coming campaign in the East, Hitler insisted that several high-priority units, including the *Luftwaffe*'s Hermann Göring Parachute Panzer Division and three reconstituting panzer divisions, must be stationed in the West. He also focused on the problems of supplying Field Marshal Erwin Rommel's *Afrika Korps* in North Africa. The dictator foresaw the possibility that such problems might require a major attack against the British island of Malta, which straddled the sea-lanes between Italy and North Africa.[15]

Germany's strategic position in spring 1942 was not completely negative, of course. The sudden entry of the United States into the war had given the German submarine service an unprecedented opportunity to inflict damage on merchant shipping in U.S. waters. Hitler had every reason to expect these U-boat victories would damage the U.S. and British economies and delay the deployment of U.S. forces to Europe. Yet the very complexity of the wider war—with the conflicting demands for resources for the U-boats, for North Africa, and for Western Europe—made German decision-making more difficult than it had been in 1941.

Even in the East, several options competed with the Caucasus for Hitler's attention. In the north, the besieged city of Leningrad beckoned. Capturing that great city—the birthplace of the Bolshevik Revolution—would not only give the Germans political and psychological leverage but also would allow the German and Finnish forces in the region to join together and shorten their defensive lines. With luck, an offensive in the north might cut off the Soviet arctic seaports, reducing the flow of Allied Lend-Lease supplies into the Soviet Union. In addition, all along the northern and central fronts, particularly in the Liuban' region southeast of Leningrad and the Viaz'ma region west of Moscow, large pockets of Soviet forces already encircled in the Germans' rear needed to be eliminated. Similarly, isolated German salients protruding into the Soviets' rear had to be strengthened so that German strongpoints could be reconnected into a coherent defensive line, again permitting stronger defenses with fewer forces.

South of Khar'kov, German intelligence analysts detected a concentration of enemy troops near a westward bend of the front south of Khar'kov and the Northern Donets River. This protrusion, the remnant of the Soviet Barvenkovo-Lozovaia offensive in January–February 1942, was variously known as the Izium or Barvenkovo salient. The Germans suspected, correctly, that their opponents were planning to use the Lozovaia bridgehead and Izium on the Northern Donets River, together with a smaller bridgehead they had seized on the western bank of the river east of Khar'kov, as the basis for a late spring offensive to recapture Ukraine. Therefore, prior to any general German offensive, it would be prudent to eliminate both the salient and the troop concentration it contained. The German plan for this preliminary attack was known as Operation Fridericus; on 12 May 1942, Fridericus was preempted by the anticipated Soviet offensive.

Finally, the Germans had to clear out the Crimean Peninsula before they advanced farther east. The fortified city of Sevastopol', which had repulsed all German assaults in 1941, posed multiple threats to the Germans. From its base in Sevastopol', the Red Navy's Black Sea Fleet could harass the coming German offensive all along the eastern coast of the Black Sea. In addition, the Crimea was a stationary aircraft carrier, a natural base from which the Red Air Force could attack the vital oil fields of Ploiesti, Romania.[16]

Nor was Sevastopol' the only danger in the Crimea. On 26 December 1941, the Trans-Caucasus Front's 51st and 44th Armies had surprised and embarrassed the Germans by conducting a major amphibious landing on the Kerch' Peninsula at the eastern end of the Crimea. General Erich von Manstein's combined German-Romanian Eleventh Army halted this invasion during January but lacked sufficient strength to eliminate the Soviet bridgehead. This Soviet concentration, like the garrison at Sevastopol', posed a continuing threat that had to be eliminated prior to the main summer offensive. To this end, Manstein planned Operation Trappenjagt [Bustard Hunt] to clear the Crimea in May 1942. Eleventh Army was reinforced with the largest siege weapons in the German inventory, a collection of howitzers and mortars with calibers up to 800mm. In combination with the *Luftwaffe*, these guns were expected to breach the defenses of Sevastopol' in a matter of days.

PLAN FALL BLAU

Leningrad, Viaz'ma, Izium, and the Crimea were only warm-up acts or sideshows to the main objective for 1942: the seizure of the Caucasus region and, above all, its two oil fields—the small one at Maikop and the much larger one centered around Baku, in what is now Azerbaijan. These two fields produced about 80 percent of all Soviet petroleum products, and their loss would be a serious blow to the Red Army's defense effort. More important, lack of petroleum was the single greatest limitation on the German economy and war machine. As early as October 1941, the *Wehrmacht* began to fall short of its petroleum needs and was able to complete Operation Barbarossa only by extorting more from the Romanians. By 1942 the German and Italian surface fleets were almost immobilized by lack of fuel, and the submarine forces struggled with a 50 percent reduction in supplies. Thus, Hitler and his military planners came to regard the Caucasus oil fields as the solution to most of their problems.[17]

Control of the Caucasus promised other advantages for Germany. In addition to petroleum, the region contained extensive reserves of coal, peat, manganese, and other materials. Moreover, the Caucasus was the natural gateway to the Middle East; its seizure would eliminate another major conduit for Lend-Lease aid to Moscow, the route through Iran. Some Germans even dreamed of pushing southward from the Caucasus to link up with Rommel's *Afrika Korps* in a gigantic pincer that would seize control of the vast oil reserves in the Middle East.

For all these reasons, the Caucasus, as well as Stalingrad on the Volga River, had been part of German thinking since July 1940, when Hitler initiated planning for the invasion of the Soviet Union.[18] By October 1941 prolonged Soviet resistance had forced the planners in German Army Headquarters [*Oberkommando des Heeres* or OKH] to move the date for such an operation forward into 1942. Throughout the difficult winter months of 1941–1942, Hitler frequently returned to this topic, insisting that specialized mountain formations be held ready to push through the Caucasus as early as possible the following spring.[19]

Once the winter battles came to a halt, the plan for the next campaign took final form.[20] On 29 March 1942, Colonel General [*Generaloberst*] Franz Halder, Chief of the Army General Staff, presented Hitler with the OKH draft for the summer offensive. Originally entitled Fall (Plan) Siegfried, the name had already been changed to Plan Blau (Blue), apparently because the failure of Barbarossa had made further references to mythical figures seem embarrassingly grandiose. After Hitler commented extensively on Halder's proposal, General Alfred Jodl, the operations chief of the *Wehrmacht* High Command [*Oberkommando der Wehrmacht* or OKW], Germany's joint services headquarters, revised the plan and again presented it to the dictator a week later.

The plan as written by Halder and revised by Jodl was a typical product of the German staff system: It established an overall concept of operations and responsibilities of subordinate headquarters but left many decisions concerning the execution of the campaign to field commanders, especially to the commander of Army Group South, Field Marshal [*Generalfeldmarschall*] Fedor von Bock. However, the experience of the winter campaign had fueled Hitler's confidence in his own abilities as well as his suspicions about professional soldiers. As a result, he insisted that Jodl add detailed instructions about the conduct of the campaign. The result was a cross between an operations order, military strategy, and wishful thinking.

Führer Directive (Weisung) No. 41, issued on 5 April 1942, assumed the Soviet Union had been exhausted by a year of warfare and that one additional push would rupture the Red Army while seizing the Caucasus oil fields.

> The winter battle in Russia is coming to an end. Thanks to their conspicuous bravery and selfless actions, the soldiers of the German Eastern Front have succeeded in achieving an immense success of German arms on the defense.
>
> The enemy has suffered huge losses in personnel and weaponry. Striving to exploit his imaginary initial successes, he has expended the main mass of those reserves which were earmarked for the conduct of the subsequent winter operations.
>
> As soon as the weather and terrain conditions are favorable, exploiting their superiority, the German command and forces must once again seize the initiative in their hands and impose their will on the enemy.[21]

Still, the directive tacitly recognized that no single campaign was likely to crush the Soviet Union completely, as had been the goal of Operation Barbarossa in 1941. Instead, the most Hitler could hope for was to destroy Stalin's troop units and hold the remnants of the communist regime at arm's length, pushing them eastward toward the Ural Mountains. The stated objective of the 1942 campaign was to "conclusively destroy the forces remaining at the Soviets' disposal and, insofar as possible, deprive the Russians of their important military-economic centers."[22] To this end, the Führer intended to "employ all of the forces at the disposal of the German Armed Forces and the armed forces of his allies" while "in every circumstance . . . doing all to protect our occupied territory in western and central Europe and especially the sea coast."[23] Hitler envisioned another series of encirclement battles but emphasized that these encirclements must be sealed off tightly so the Soviets did not escape to fight again.

The directive discussed all aspects of the effort in the East beginning with a renewed assault south of Leningrad (Operation *Nordlicht* [Northern Lights]) to eliminate Soviet forces encircled behind German lines the previous winter, a series of limited offensives to straighten the German lines in the central portion of the front, and operations to eliminate Soviet forces in the Crimea and around Izium on the Northern Donets River, preparatory to a full-scale invasion of the Caucasus region. Only after these operations were completed would the Germans launch the main operations for the summer, first to conquer southern Russia and the Caucasus region, and second to capture Leningrad.

The distances involved were so great and the transportation lines so tenuous that the main effort in the south would be conducted in phases, later referred to as "Blau I," "Blau II," and so on (see Map 2). Moreover, the dictator wanted to begin the summer campaign with limited, low-risk operations that would restore the confidence of his shaken troops. Despite Hitler's tendency to add details, these phases were still expressed in somewhat general terms; only later did the German field commanders assign specific tasks to the various field armies. The following section of the text, therefore, attempts to flesh out the ambiguous outline of the original plan.[24]

Blau I would begin with "an enveloping offensive or penetration toward Voronezh from the region south of Orel." Attacking from the Kursk and Belgorod regions, two large pincers of panzer and motorized forces—the northern group stronger than the southern—would thrust almost due east to capture Voronezh just east of the Don River. In the pincers' wake, part of the follow-on infantry divisions would "quickly create a stable defensive front" extending from Orel to Voronezh.[25] The objective of this phase was to establish a strong defensive line from Orel to Voronezh along the main thrust's northern flank and to encircle and destroy all Soviet forces west of Voronezh.

During Blau II, the panzer and motorized forces were to "continue the offensive from Voronezh southward along the Don River with their left wing to support the second penetration, which was to be conducted eastward roughly from

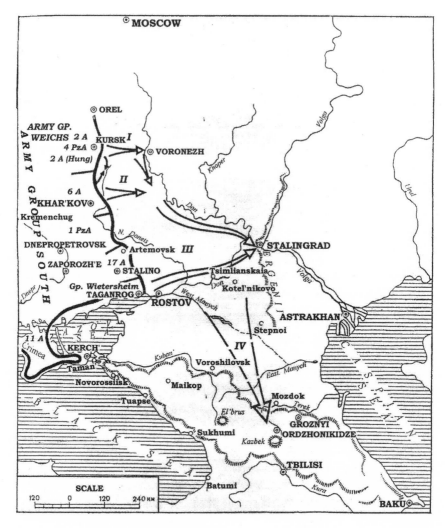

Map 2. Plan Blau according to Hitler's Directive No. 41, 5 April 1942

the Khar'kov region."[26] Thus, the same panzer and motorized forces that cleared Soviet forces from the region west of Voronezh would advance southward from the city, parallel to but on the southern bank of the Don River, to link up near Millerovo with a second German penetration originating from the vicinity of Izium on the Northern Donets River. Again, strong defensive works along the Don River were to secure the main operation's left flank while a second encirclement further reduced the Soviet defenders.

From Millerovo, Blau III called for a much deeper advance eastward along the southern bank of the Don River and then across the Don to the vicinity of Stalingrad on the Volga River. There, the German thrust would again meet a parallel advance that was to originate on the German southern flank between Artemovsk and Taganrog, seize the bridges across the Northern Donets River and the key communications junction and Don River bridges at Rostov, and continue east. This operation would give Germany control of the valuable industrial region of the Donets River Basin (Donbas). In light of later events, it is ironic that the German plan paid only scant attention to Stalingrad itself, whose seizure was certainly desirable but not vital to the campaign:

> The third attack in this scheme of operations will be so conducted that the forces thrusting down the Don can link up in the Stalingrad area with forces advancing toward the east from the Taganrog and Artemovsk regions between the lower course of the Donets [River] and Voroshilovgrad. In the end, these latter forces must link up with the panzer army advancing on Stalingrad. . . .
>
> Every effort will be made to reach Stalingrad itself, or at least to bring the city under fire from heavy artillery so that it may no longer be of any use [to the Soviets] as an industrial or communications center.[27]

Führer Directive No. 41 went on to specify supporting tasks for the *Luftwaffe* and the *Kreigsmarine* [German Navy] and to insist on absolute secrecy in preparing for the offensive. To this end, the Germans had already launched Operation *Kreml'* [Kremlin], a deception designed to play on Soviet fears that the new German offensive would focus on Moscow.[28]

Blau IV, the subsequent advance into the Caucasus, was projected in the introductory paragraphs of Directive No. 41 but was not spelled out in detail: "Initially, it is necessary to concentrate all forces at hand for the conduct of the main operation in the southern sector of the front for the destruction of the enemy west of the River Don and subsequently seize the oil region of the Caucasus and the passes through the Caucasus range."[29]

By that time, however, Germany had been planning for this operation for months, and German staff officers were well aware of Hitler's intentions. Panzer and motorized divisions would spearhead the attack except in the High Caucasus Mountains, where the German mountain troops would come into their own. Oil Brigade Caucasus, a specialized organization of more than 10,000 troops, was waiting to move into the oil fields and restore production as quickly as possible. While the German spearheads pushed rapidly southward, the satellite armies, reinforced by antitank batteries and backed by a few mobile German divisions, would protect the ever-extending Axis left flank.

Such an advance would be, to say the least, an operational and logistical challenge greater than any previous German offensive. The straight-line or air distance from Kursk to Groznyi was 760 kilometers, and the various encirclements of the plan represented a total advance of more than 1,000 kilometers. To control this sprawling operation, Hitler foresaw the need to split Bock's Army Group South into two separate entities at some point during the campaign. On 14 April, in preparation for this split, he instructed the OKH to create an additional army group headquarters under the command of Field Marshal Wilhelm List, who had conquered and occupied the Balkans in 1941.[30]

Hitler's appreciation of the need to create two army groups to conduct Plan Blau underscored the most serious potential flaw in the operational plan. While planning Operation Barbarossa more than a year before, German planners had recognized the necessity of employing a single army group along each strategic axis of advance. Because there were three such axes into the Soviet Union—the northwestern (Leningrad), western (Moscow), and southwestern (Kiev)—German planners had formed three army groups—Army Group North, Army Group Center, and Army Group South—to conduct operations along these axes. Hitler's Plan Blau, however, required Army Group South to operate along at least two strategic axes, first, toward Voronezh and Stalingrad and, second, deep into the Caucasus region. Understanding this reality but lacking sufficient forces to create a full new army group, once Blau began Hitler simply decided (artificially, it turned out) to split Army Group South into Army Groups A and B.

In addition to proving illusory, this field expedient also failed to recognize that the forces conducting Blau would, in reality, be operating along three strategic axes—along the Voronezh as well as the Stalingrad and the Caucasus axes. Although prescient enough to recognize the *Wehrmacht*'s likely overextension, Hitler failed to appreciate until it was too late how serious this overextension would become. Ultimately, when he did, the Führer reluctantly decided to employ primarily armies of his Axis allies to cover and protect this third strategic axis.[31]

AXIS FORCE DISPOSITIONS

In early April 1942, the 2.5 million German soldiers in the East, supplemented by almost 1 million troops of its axis allies, were organized into three army groups—North, Center, and South—and one separate army (see Table 1).

In addition to 2.5 million German troops, by early April the Axis host in the East counted roughly 450,000 Finnish troops and 440,000 Romanian, Hungarian, and Italian soldiers. However, because most of the Allied forces designated to participate in the summer campaign did not begin deploying eastward until late April, only a fraction of these armies was available to participate actively in combat operations before late summer.

Meanwhile, from March through June, force transfers from other army groups and the West increased Army Group South's (including Eleventh Army) strength to 71 German divisions, including 46 infantry, 4 jäger, 2 mountain,

Table 1. Axis Forces in the East, April 1942 (armies, corps, and mobile divisions and brigades)

ARMY OF LAPLAND (Colonel General Eduard Dietl)
    Mountain Corps Norway
    XXXVI Mountain Corps
    III Finnish Corps

FINNISH ARMY
    Maaselkä Group
    Aunus [Olonets] Group
    Isthmus [Karelia] Groups

ARMY GROUP NORTH (Colonel General Geog von Küchler)
    Eighteenth Army (General of Cavalry Georg Lindemann)
        I Army Corps (20th Motorized Division and 1st SS Police Motorized Division)
        XXVI Army Corps
        XXVIII Army Corps
        XXXVIII Army Corps (2nd SS Motorized Brigade)
        L Army Corps
        Reserve—12th Panzer Division
    Sixteenth Army (Colonel General Ernst Busch)
        II Army Corps (SS *Totenkopf* [Death's Head] Motorized Division)
        X Army Corps (18th Motorized Division)
        XXXIX Motorized Corps (8th Panzer Division)
    Army Group Rear Area Command North

ARMY GROUP CENTER (Field Marshal Günter von Kluge)
    Ninth Army (General of Panzer Troops Walter Model)
        VI Army Corps (7th Panzer Division)
        XXIII AC (1st Panzer Division)
        XXVII Army Corps
        XXXXI Motorized Corps (2nd Panzer Division and 36th Motorized Division)
        XXXXVI Motorized Corps (14th Motorized Division and SS *Das Reich* [The Reich]
            Motorized Division)
        LVI Motorized Corps (6th Panzer Division)
    Third Panzer Army (Colonel General Hans Reinhardt)
        LIX Army Corps
    Fourth Panzer Army (Colonel General Richard Ruoff, Colonel General Hermann Hoth in
    May)
        V Army Corps (5th Panzer Division and 3rd Motorized Division)
        VII Army Corps
        IX Army Corps
        XX Army Corps (20th Panzer Division)
    Fourth Army (Colonel General Gottfried Heinrici)
        XII Army Corps
        XIII Army Corps
        XXXXIII Army Corps
        XXXX Motorized Corps (19th Panzer Division)
    Second Panzer Army (General of Panzer Troops Rudolf Schmidt)
        XXXV Army Corps (29th Motorized Division)
        LIII Army Corps (17th Panzer Division and 25th Motorized Division)
        XXIV Motorized Corps (4th and 18th Panzer Divisions)
        XXXXVII Motorized Corps (Part, 4th Panzer Division)
    Army Group Reserve—10th and 11th Panzer Divisions
    Army Group Rear Area Command Center

ARMY GROUP SOUTH (Field Marshal Fedor von Bock)
    Second Army (Colonel General Maximilian von Weichs)
        LV Army Corps (1st SS Motorized Brigade)
        XXXXVIII Motorized Corps (9th Panzer Division and 16th Motorized Division)

(continued)

Table 1. Continued

Sixth Army (General of Panzer Troops Friedrich von Paulus)
    VIII Army Corps
    XVII Army Corps (3rd Panzer Division)
    XXIX Army Corps
    LI Army Corps
Seventeenth Army (General of Panzer Troops Hermann Hoth, Colonel General Richard
    Ruoff in June) (Grouped with First Panzer Army as Army Group [*Armeegruppe*] Kleist in
    April–May 1942)
    IV Army Corps
    XXXXIV Army Corps
    LII Army Corps
First Panzer Army (Colonel General Ewald von Kleist) (in Army Group Kleist in
    April–May 1942)
        XXXXIX Mountain Corps, Group Mackensen [III Motorized Corps] (14th Panzer
            Division)
        XIV Motorized Corps (13th and 16th Panzer Divisions, 1st SS *Leibstandarte* [Body
            Guard—LAH] Adolf Hitler and 5th SS *Wiking* [Viking] Motorized Divisions, and
            Slovak Mobile Division)
        Italian Mobile Corps
        Romanian Cavalry Corps
        Reserve—16th and 60th Motorized Divisions
Eleventh Army (Colonel General Erich von Manstein)
        XXX Army Corps
        XXXXII Army Corps
        LIV Army Corps
        Romanian Mountain Corps
        Reserve—22nd Panzer Division
Army Group Rear Area Command South
OKH Reserve South—23rd Panzer Division

ROMANIAN THIRD ARMY (General Petre Dumitrescu) (providing security along the Black Sea coast
    until July 1942) (VI Romanian Army Corps in action in May 1942)

SECOND HUNGARIAN ARMY (Colonel General Gusztav Jany) (began deploying to the east in April
    1942)
    III Army Corps
    IV Army Corps
    VII Army Corps

7 motorized (5 army and 2 SS), 9 panzer, and 3 security, with 1 SS infantry brigade (see Table 6). In addition, the 22 Hungarian, Romanian, Italian, and Slovak divisions already at the front or in the rear area, as well as other divisions promised by Germany's allies, would raise the strength of Bock's army group to a total of well more than 90 divisions. In addition to its own strength of roughly 1 million German soldiers, Army Group South could expect reinforcement by as many as 300,000 Romanian, Hungarian, and Italian soldiers.[32] In regard to its vital armored strength, although Bock's army group should have fielded a full complement of 1,900 tanks, shortages in virtually all panzer divisions reduced this figure to roughly 1,700 tanks and assault guns, including 300 obsolete Pz. II models or command tanks.

GERMAN COMMANDERS

Bock and List might be the field commanders of Adolf Hitler's army groups, but the Führer remained in overall charge. In the course of almost a decade as ruler of Germany, he had gradually assumed all key positions in the government and military high command—head of state, head of government, commander in chief of the *Wehrmacht*, and, after December 1941, commander in chief of the German Army. At one point in the 1942 campaign, Hitler even assumed (on paper) command of an army group.[33] As he intended, his occupation of these positions limited the ability of professional staff officers and commanders to coordinate with one another; they found it increasingly difficult to operate in the well-known German system of *auftragstaktik*, which established an overall mission and intent but allowed great flexibility in executing that intent. As early as January 1940, the dictator had issued a standing order that each army commander should concern himself only with his immediate objective rather than coordinating with adjacent headquarters and looking at the wider picture.[34] After repeated disagreements with his staff officers, Hitler in September 1942 dismissed Army Chief of Staff Franz Halder and replaced him with a younger, more enthusiastic, and (presumably) more subservient man, General Kurt Zeitzler.[35]

Although the OKH was nominally in charge of the German Eastern Front, all major decisions were made in the Fuehrerhauptquartier (Führer Headquarters), located first at *Wolfsschanze* [Wolf's Lair] in East Prussia and then (after 16 July 1942) at *Wehrwolf* [Werewolf] near Vinnitsa in western Ukraine. Here, Hitler held a major conference at noon and a smaller one in midevening, intervening in operations whenever he felt it necessary. Although their construction differed, each of these sites had only limited space for staff officers, so all (in East Prussia) or part (in Ukraine) of the OKH staff was located elsewhere.

Yet it would be an oversimplification to portray Hitler, at this stage of the war, as an irrational fanatic who ignored all professional military advice. In summer 1942, most senior commanders remained loyal to Hitler, even when they had increasing disagreements with him about the conduct of the war. Hitler, in turn, relied upon his military minions despite his growing sense that the traditional independence of senior officers was thwarting his wishes. German intelligence estimates supported his belief that the Soviets were on their last legs, and the basic concept, if not the exact wording, for Plan Blau originated with Halder, Jodl, and their subordinates.

Even when the dictator went against the recommendations of his subordinates, he was frequently proved to be correct, as in his famous insistence on standing firm in winter 1941–1942. Of course, such successes encouraged him to believe that standing fast was always the best solution in a crisis, a belief that would cost the Germans dearly at Stalingrad. Nevertheless, it is too convenient to absolve all the German commanders by blaming their Führer for every failure in 1942. Few senior commanders doubted their success in the coming campaign, and they differed with Hitler primarily in terms of how to achieve that success.

The senior officers Hitler chose to command the army groups designated to conduct Operation Blau were experienced generals. The most seasoned of these commanders was Field Marshal Fedor von Bock, who had already weathered a year of army group command on the German Eastern Front. He was born in 1880 as Moritz Albert Franz Friedrich Fedor von Bock, and the field marshal's father had been awarded the title of nobility for bravery displayed during the Franco-Prussian War. After serving in both infantry and General Staff posts, Bock rose quickly to command 4th Infantry Regiment in 1926, 1st Cavalry Division in 1929, 2nd Infantry Division in 1931, Eighth Army in 1938, and Army Group North, which he led in the 1939 Polish campaign. During Operation Barbarossa, Hitler granted Bock's Army Group Center the honor of spearheading the *Wehrmacht*'s advance on Moscow, a task that Bock performed with undiminished ardor. In January, after the German defeat at Moscow, Hitler chose Bock to command Army Group South (later Army Group B) and prepare it for the decisive advance on Stalingrad.[36]

Field Marshal Sigmund Wilhelm List, whom Hitler would choose to command his Army Group A in Operation Blau, was born in 1880 and graduated from the General Staff Academy in 1912. A veteran of World War I, List rose to command the Fourteenth Army in the Polish campaign and then the Twelfth Army in the French campaign (May–June 1941) and the campaign in the Balkans (April 1941). He remained the Southeastern Theater commander in the Balkans throughout 1941 and early 1942. List took command of the drive into the Caucasus while Blau I was nearing completion but before Blau II commenced.[37]

Army group commanders changed with bewildering frequency during the Stalingrad campaign, but at the next lower level—that of field army—one air commander (Richthofen) and six ground leaders—Hoth, Manstein, Kleist, and Paulus and, to a lesser extent, Weichs and Ruoff—played pivotal roles.

Colonel General Wolfram *Freiherr* von Richthofen commanded *Fliegerkorps* (air corps) VIII, a high-priority *Luftwaffe* unit that acted as a fire brigade to provide battlefield air support at the point of main German effort on the German Eastern Front during 1941–1942. He capitalized on his success in this role, rising to command Fourth *Luftflotte* (German air fleet) in June 1942. Born in 1895, Richthofen had a long career stretching back to his World War I service in the fighter squadron of his famous older cousin, the Red Baron, Manfred von Richthofen. His service in the Spanish Civil War was blemished by the notorious German air attack on the town of Guernica. Throughout the 1942 campaign, the younger Richthofen was often frustrated and impatient. In particular, he resented the fact that army commanders relied on his aircraft to blast through any Soviet resistance; to his mind, this role as handmaiden to the ground advance prevented the *Luftwaffe* from reaching the full potential of its airpower.[38]

Colonel General Hermann Hoth was one of Germany's most experienced armored tacticians. Born in 1885, he rose through the infantry's ranks to command 17th Infantry Regiment and 18th Infantry Division in the 1930s and XV Army Corps (Motorized) in the French campaign in 1940. Unlike many of his peers, he survived the 1941 crisis in which so many commanders had been dismissed. This short, almost wizened soldier led Third Panzer Group and then Seventeenth Army during Operation Barbarossa in 1941 before assuming command of Fourth Panzer Army in May 1942. In this role Hoth was instrumental in the initial advance under Blau and later helped conduct the vain efforts to relieve the surrounded forces at Stalingrad.[39]

Fritz-Erich von Manstein began the 1942 campaign as the general commanding Eleventh Army in the Crimea and ended it as the field marshal of the improvised Army Group Don that pushed the Red Army back later in winter 1942–1943. Born Erich von Lewinski in 1887, but soon named after his stepfather, Manstein, as a former Imperial Guardsman and general staff officer, was known as a strict disciplinarian with an abrasive personality. He was also one of the most brilliant planners in the German Army and was not at all modest about his abilities. This self-confident brilliance, combined with considerable enthusiasm for Hitler's policies, fueled his rapid rise from command of 5th Infantry Regiment in 1920, 18th Infantry Division in 1938, and LVI Motorized Corps in 1941 to command of an army in 1941 and army group in 1942.[40]

If Manstein had an equal in the German Army, it was probably the handsome and poised Colonel General Ewald Paul Ludwig von Kleist. Born into a long line of Prussian aristocrats and soldiers in 1881, Kleist was a committed royalist and devout Christian who never hid his distaste for Nazism. After commanding 9th Infantry Regiment and 2nd Cavalry Division in the early 1930s, Kleist was assigned to head VIII Army Corps in 1935. Although his attitudes led Hitler's regime to retire him briefly in 1938, once war began, the former cavalryman was recalled to active duty, where he demonstrated a consummate grasp of mobile warfare, rising to command Fourteenth Army's XXII Army Corps during the Polish campaign, Panzer Group Kleist during the campaign in the West, and First Panzer Group and Army during Operation Barbarossa in 1941–1942. As such, he was instrumental in defeating the Soviet offensive at Khar'kov in May. When the Soviet trap closed around Stalingrad in November, the Germans south of the encirclement were almost cut off. While Manstein fought to relieve the beleaguered city, Kleist succeeded in extricating Army Group A from the Caucasus, conducting a brilliant defense that earned him a marshal's baton.[41]

Because of his starring role in the Stalingrad tragedy, Friedrich Wilhelm Ernst Paulus became a controversial figure in German military history.[42] Born in 1890, the son of a minor civil servant, Paulus was a product of his times in imperial Germany, an intelligent workaholic from the middle class who aspired to fit into the upper-class world of the military. In 1912 Paulus acquired quasiaristocratic status by marrying a Romanian noblewoman. Tall, lean, and immaculately dressed, he appeared the model officer. By 1918 he had become a captain while serving as a staff officer at battalion and regiment level. Between the world wars, Paulus pursued the standard career of a German General Staff specialist, interrupted only twice for brief, obligatory assignments with troops. On the first occasion, he led an infantry company in the same regiment as Erwin Rommel. In 1934–1935, Lieutenant Colonel (*Oberstleutnant*) Paulus commanded the 3rd Motor Transport Battalion, the prototypical armored reconnaissance battalion for the new German panzer arm. Thereafter, he reverted to his normal role, becoming chief of staff of panzer forces in 1935, chief of staff of XVI Army Corps (Motorized) in 1938, and chief of staff of Army Group (*Heeresgruppe*) 4 in 1939.

In preparation for the 1939 invasion of Poland, then-Colonel Paulus became chief of staff for Tenth Army, commanded by Walter Reichenau. Reichenau, an early convert to Nazism, was in the midst of a meteoric career; Paulus's methodical staff work was the perfect complement to Reichenau's personal, assertive style of hands-on leadership, and the general became Paulus's patron. After the 1940 campaign, Paulus reached the penultimate position in his career field as *Oberquartiermeister* I (Deputy Chief of the General Staff) under Halder. As such, Paulus drafted the original plan for Operation Barbarossa, although he later claimed to have doubts about the outcome of the campaign.[43]

The refined, reserved Paulus was never comfortable arguing with coarser, more assertive men such as Hitler and Reichenau, but he recognized the considerable ability of such leaders, and they in turn valued his loyal service as a meticulous subordinate. Given Hitler's quest for obedient minions who would faithfully execute their Führer's orders, it was perhaps inevitable that Friedrich Paulus would receive a starring role in the new campaign. On 5 January 1942, the man who had never commanded anything larger than a battalion was promoted to full general of panzer troops and appointed to head the German Sixth Army, one of the spearheads of Plan Blau.

At the time, Reichenau was Paulus's immediate superior as commander of Army Group South. Undoubtedly, Reichenau envisioned the next campaign as an extension of their previous relationship, with Reichenau himself leading from the front while his protégé brought his usual thoroughness to the execution of Plan Blau. Within days of Paulus's appointment, however, his patron died unexpectedly after exercising in the extreme cold of Russia. Fedor von Bock, an old-school aristocrat whose professional judgment often brought him into conflict with Hitler, replaced Reichenau. Thereafter, Paulus was on his own.[44]

Maximilian *Freiherr* (Baron) von Weichs an dem Glon, commander of Second Army during the first year of the war and an *Armeegruppe* that bore his name in the initial phase of Operation Blau, was the oldest in this group of army commanders. Born in 1881, Weichs, who like so many of his fellow panzer officers began his military career as a cavalryman, rose in stature to command 18th Cavalry Regiment in 1928. After a stint in senior staff positions in the early 1930s, where he earned notoriety for his outspoken oppositions to the army's involvement in politics, Weichs, now a Major General, commanded 3rd Cavalry Division in 1933 and, after his transfer to the panzer arm, 1st Panzer Division in 1935. Thereafter, he commanded XIII Army Corps during the Polish campaign in 1939 and Second Army during the Western campaign in 1940 and the Balkans campaign in 1941. Although a late arrival in Operation Barbarossa, his Second Army earned plaudits for its vital role in encircling and destroying the Red Army's Southwestern Front at Kiev in September 1941. During this period Weichs was called the "antiaircraft general" for his imaginative employment of 88mm antiaircraft guns in a ground combat role. Although illness forced Weichs to leave his army in late November 1941, he returned to it in mid-December 1942, just in time to help contain the Red Army's winter offensive.[45]

The most junior army commander in this group was Colonel General Richard Ruoff, commander of Seventeenth Army. Born in 1893, the infantryman Ruoff served in key staff positions at corps and army level during the 1930s and commanded V Army Corps (as well as V Military District [*Wehrkreis*] in Stuttgart) during the Polish and French campaigns in 1939 and 1940. In the initial phases of Operation Barbarossa, the infantry of Ruoff's V Corps had single-handedly defeated two counterattacking Soviet mechanized corps in fierce fighting near Grodno during Army Group Center's dramatic advance on Minsk. Later, he was instrumental in destroying Red Army forces encircled in the Smolensk region. In recognition of these feats, Hitler appointed Ruoff to command Army Group Center's Fourth Panzer Army in January 1942 and Army Group South's Seventeenth Army in June. Soon after Operation Blau began, Ruoff would find himself leading Seventeenth Army deep into the sprawling region of the Caucasus Mountains.[46]

If command stability at the army level was vitally important for the *Wehrmacht* to succeed in Plan Blau, it was even more important at corps and division level in its panzer arm because, as Operation Barbarossa had confirmed, this arm provided the *Heeres* (the German Army) with virtually all of its offensive punch and defined its strategic and operational reach—the ultimate depth to which it could advance. In short, with few exceptions, the reach of German army groups and armies correlated directly with the depth to which their panzer corps and component panzer and motorized divisions could operate; they could advance as far as these corps but no farther. Therefore, logistical constraints aside, success in Plan Blau depended directly on the operational effectiveness of these panzer corps and, in turn, on the command acumen and leadership talents of their commanders, in this case seven experienced panzer generals—Wietersheim, Langermann, Stumme, Geyr, Kempf, Mackensen, and Kirchner—the respective commanders of XIV, XXIV, XXXX, XXXXVIII, III, and LVII Panzer Corps (note: the German Army designated its motorized corps as panzer corps in early summer 1942).

Like all of his fellow panzer corps commanders, the high reputation of General of Infantry Gustav Anton von Wietersheim, commander of XIV Panzer Corps in Operation Blau, was based on his stellar performance during Operation

Barbarossa, when his panzer corps had spearheaded First Panzer Group's difficult and impressive march eastward to Kiev. Born in 1884, and an infantry officer early in his military career, Wietersheim commanded 29th Infantry Division (Motorized), recognized as one of the army's finest mobile divisions, from 1936 to 1938, and earned for himself a reputation as one of the army's premier specialists in motorized operations. Rising to command XIV Army Corps (Motorized) during the Czech crisis in 1938, Wietersheim led that corps from the Polish campaign in 1939 through Operation Barbarossa, while also serving a stint as chief of staff of German forces in the West. Despite demonstrating his excellence as a panzer corps commander during Operation Barbarossa and the first two months of Operation Blau, Hitler would deny Wietersheim command of an army, probably because the corps commander had openly questioned the Führer's plan for operations in the West. Still questioning Wietersheim's reliability, Hitler relieved him of command in September 1942 and inserted General Hans Hube, commander of 16th Panzer Division.[47]

General of Panzer Troops Willibald *Freiherr* von Langermann und Erlenkamp, commander of XXIV Panzer Corps during Operation Blau, had also been a star in the Barbarossa campaign. Born in 1890, after transferring from the cavalry, Langermann rose rapidly in the ranks of the *Heeres*'s panzer arm to command the famed 29th Motorized Division under Hans Guderian's XXXXIX Army Corps in the Western campaign in 1940 and XXIV Motorized Corps' 4th Panzer Division in Operation Barbarossa. During Barbarossa, his panzer division spearheaded the dramatic advance by Guderian's Second Panzer Group to Smolensk and the group's subsequent spectacular encirclement operations at Kiev and Briansk on the road to Moscow. Rewarded for his performance in 1941, Langermann received command of XXIV Motorized (Panzer) Corps in January 1942 and remained there until his death on 2 October 1942 in the epic struggle for Stalingrad.

General of Panzer Troops Georg Stumme, commander of XXXX Panzer Corps during the first three weeks of Operation Blau, was just as talented and experienced as Wietersheim and Langermann. Born in 1886 and initially an artilleryman, Stumme rose to command 2nd Jäger (Light Infantry) Division in 1938 and, after its conversion into 7th Panzer Division the following year, led this panzer division with distinction during the Polish campaign. After relinquishing command of 7th Panzer Division to General Erwin Rommel, Stumme commanded XXXX Motorized Corps from the Western campaign in 1940 onward. During Operation Barbarossa, his motorized corps spearheaded the advance by Army Group Center's Ninth Army north of Smolensk during summer 1941 and Fourth Panzer Army's desperate but futile advance on Moscow during Operation Typhoon in the fall. In Plan Blau, Stumme's redesignated panzer corps would lead the advance of Paulus's Sixth Army to Voronezh. However, Stumme was relieved of command on 21 July 1942 and court-martialed because of the Reichel affair (an infamous security breach; see Chapter 3). He remained in Hitler's disfavor until September, when the Führer selected him to replace Rommel, who had fallen ill, as commander of Panzer Army Afrika.[48]

General of Panzer Troops Leo Dietrich Franz Geyr von Schweppenburg, who succeeded Stumme as commander of XXXX Panzer Corps on 21 July 1942 in the wake of the Reichel affair, proved more fortunate than his counterparts Wietersheim, Langermann, and Stumme. Born in 1886 and initially a cavalryman by specialty, Geyr commanded 14th Cavalry Regiment from 1931 to 1933 and served as military attaché in Brussels, London, and Prague from 1933 to 1937, where he reportedly worked effectively on behalf of the *Abwehr* [Counterintelligence]. Transferring to the panzer arm, Geyr commanded 3rd Panzer Division during the Polish campaign in 1939 and XXIV Army Corps during the Western campaign in 1940; after his corps was fully motorized in November 1940, he led it during the daring thrusts by Guderian's Second Panzer Group during the initial phases of Operation Barbarossa. Known for his audacity as a field commander, Geyr distinguished himself during the encirclement battle at Kiev in September 1941 and Guderian's trying struggle in the Tula region south of Moscow in October and November 1941.

Returning to the East in June 1942 after a brief respite in Germany, Geyr, in Operation Blau, commanded First Panzer Army's III Panzer Corps until 21 July, when in the midst of the opening phase of Blau he replaced Stumme as commander of Fourth Panzer Army's XXXX Panzer Corps. After leading that corps during its dash to the Don River east of Rostov and spearheading First Panzer Army's deep thrust into the Caucasus region, Geyr encountered misfortune in September 1942, when the Führer, dissatisfied with Army Group A's performance in the Caucasus, shook up the army's command cadre, relieving Geyr of his command.[49]

Arguably the most prominent general among this group of senior panzer leaders, General of Panzer Troops Werner Kempf, commander of XXXXVIII Panzer Corps during Operation Blau, ultimately succeeded in obtaining army command. Born in 1886, Kempf was an infantry officer who transferred to panzer forces in the late 1930s and commanded, in succession, 4th Panzer Brigade in 1937, Composite Division Kempf during the Polish campaign in 1939, 6th Panzer Division during the Western campaign in 1940, and XXXXVIII Motorized Corps during Operation Barbarossa. Kempf's panzers spearheaded XXXXI Motorized Corps' rapid advance across the Maas River in the West, and his XXXXVIII Motorized Corps led First Panzer Army in the Kiev encirclement during Barbarossa and, later, formed the linchpin between Army Group Center and Army Group South during Operation Typhoon in the fall and the difficult times of Red Army's winter offensive in 1941–1942. In Operation Blau, under control of Hoth's Fourth Panzer Army, Kempf's panzer corps led *Armeegruppe* Weichs's drive to the Don River and, still in the panzer army's vanguard, led the march that propelled the panzer army first to the lower Don River east of Rostov, then ultimately to the western bank of the Volga River at Stalingrad.[50]

General Eberhard von Mackensen, whose prowess matched that of Kempf, replaced Geyr as commander of III Panzer Corps on 21 July 1942. He commanded III Panzer Corps throughout the remainder of summer and fall 1942 and ultimately replaced Kleist as commander of First Panzer Army during the operation's waning stages. Born in 1889, Mackensen served as chief of the General Staff's Railroad Directorate in August 1939 before he was appointed chief of staff, in succession, of Field Marshal List's 5th Group of Forces in Vienna and Fourteenth and Twelfth Armies during the Polish and Balkans campaign of 1939 and 1941. He was appointed command of First Panzer Group's III Motorized Corps in Operation Barbarossa; Mackensen's forces were the first to reach the outskirts of Kiev and, subsequently, played a vital role in the Uman' and Kiev encirclements and First Panzer Army's advance through the Donbas region to Rostov-on-the-Don. He continued to lead this redesignated III Panzer Corps in Operation Blau, where his panzers would reach the outskirts of Ordzhonikidze before being forced to retreat; he replaced Kleist as First Panzer Army's commander.[51]

The least known of the six senior panzer generals participating in Operation Blau was General of Panzer Troops Friedrich Kirchner, commander of LVII Panzer Corps throughout the operation. Born in 1885 and also a cavalryman, Kirchner commanded 1st Infantry Regiment and 1st Infantry Brigade in the 1930s before transferring to the panzer forces and taking command of the famous 1st Panzer Division in 1939. He burnished his reputation, leading his 1st Panzer under XIX Army Corps' control, during the Western campaign in 1940 and spearheading the rapid advance of Army Group North's XXXXI Motorized Corps to Leningrad's suburbs during the summer phase of Operation Barbarossa. Assigned command of LVII Army Corps in November 1941, he reorganized it into a panzer corps in June 1942 and led the corps in Army Group A's advance deep into the Caucasus region, where it achieved the dubious distinction of attempting to conduct highly maneuverable armored operations in the restrictive terrain of the High Caucasus Mountains.[52]

If the success of Army Groups South, A, and B in Plan Blau depended on how effectively their constituent armies and panzer armies operated, the success of these armies, if not the army groups as a whole, depended on the tactical efficiency of their panzer and motorized divisions. In large measure, then, victory in Plan Blau rested on the shoulders of the German Army's premier tacticians, as well as the skill and acumen of the commanders of Army Group South's panzer and motorized divisions. On 28 June and thereafter, this group of elite panzer leaders included:

3rd Panzer Division—General of Panzer Troops Hermann Breith; Lieutenant General Franz Westhoven on 1 October 1942

9th Panzer Division—Lieutenant General Johannes Bässler; Major General Heinrich-Hermann von Hülsen on 27 July 1942; Lieutenant General Walter Scheller on 4 August 1942

11th Panzer Division—General of Panzer Troops Hermann Balck

13th Panzer Division—General of Panzer Troops Traugott Herr; Lieutenant General Helmut von der Chevallerie on 1 November 1942

14th Panzer Division—General of Panzer Troops Friedrich Kuhn; Major General Ferdinand Heim on 1 July 1942; Lieutenant General Hans *Freiherr* von Falkenstein on 1 November 1942

16th Panzer Division—Major General Hans-Valentin Hube; Lieutenant General Günther von Angern on 15 September 1942

22nd Panzer Division—Lieutenant General Wilhelm von Apell; Lieutenant General Hellmut von der Chevallerie on 7 October; Lieutenant General Eberhard Rodt on 1 November 1942

23rd Panzer Division—Lieutenant General Wilhelm Hans *Freiherr* von Boineburg-Lengsfeld; Major General Erwin Mack on 20 July 1942; Lieutenant General Wilhelm Hans *Freiherr* von Boineburg-Lengsfeld on 26 August 1942

24th Panzer Division—General of Panzer Troops Bruno *Ritter* von Hauenschild; Lieutenant General Arno von Lenski on 12 September 1942

3rd Motorized Division—Lieutenant General Helmuth Schlömer

16th Motorized Division—General of Panzer Troops Sigfrid Henrici

29th Motorized Division—Major General Max Fremerey; Major General Hans-Georg Leyser on 28 September 1942

60th Motorized Division—Lieutenant General Otto Kohlermann; Major General Hans-Adolf von Arensdorff in November

Grossdeutschland (Greater Germany—"GD") Motorized Division—General of Infantry Walter Hörnlein

5th SS *Wiking* ("Viking") Motorized Division—SS Lieutenant General Felix Steiner

1st SS *Leibstandarte* (Body Guard—LAH) Adolf Hitler Motorized Division—SS Lieutenant General Otto "Sepp" Dietrich

Unlike their counterparts in the Red Army, this group of panzer leaders, to a man, were experienced generals who had successfully commanded at regiment or division level during the campaigns in Poland in 1939, in the West in 1940, and Operation Barbarossa. Thoroughly imbued with the spirit of the offensive and faith in blitzkrieg as applied by the commanders of the *Wehrmacht*'s panzer groups and motorized corps from 1939 through 1941, these generals were also well aware of the unique circumstances and challenges inherent in conducting operations in the vastness of the East, a daunting theater, where military operations had proven far more difficult and trying than those conducted in the West, where blitzkrieg had been born.

Most if not all of this group of skilled panzer leaders performed well in Operation Blau, and those who survived either continued to command at the division level or rose to command corps and, in some cases, full armies. Although the

General of Panzer Troops Friedrich Paulus, commander of Sixth Army, meeting with his commanders

General of Panzer Troops Werner Kempf

Colonel General Ewald von Kleist, commander First Panzer Group

Colonel General *Freiherr* Wolfram von Richthofen, commander of Fourth Air Fleet, observing bombing strikes with General of Panzer Troop, Hans Hube, commander of 16th Panzer Division, on 22 August 1942

Field Marshal Fedor von Bock, commander Army Group Center

Colonel General Hermann Hoth, commander Third Panzer Group

biographies of many of these generals remain obscure, a few warrant further note. For example, General of Panzer Troops Hermann Breith, born in 1892, who commanded 3rd Panzer Division throughout most of Operation Blau, commanded 36th Panzer Regiment during the Polish campaign in 1939, 5th Panzer Division's 5th Panzer Brigade during the campaign in the West in 1940, and 3rd Panzer Division in October 1941, when his division fought with distinction in the struggle for the Briansk, Orel, and Tula regions. Breith commanded 3rd Panzer Division throughout all of Operation Blau.[53]

The most famous panzer general in this group was Hermann Balck, arguably one of the most capable of his generation of officers. Born in 1893, Balck commanded at company level in the cavalry during World War I and at battalion level in the 1920s and 1930s, before commanding 1st Panzer Division's 1st Infantry Regiment during the Western campaign in 1940 and 2nd Panzer Division's 2nd Panzer Regiment during the Balkan campaign in 1941. After a stint on the OKH staff during Operation Barbarossa, Balck took command of 11th Panzer Division in May 1942 and led it during Operation Blau, where his panzer division bore the brunt of the struggle with the Red Army's 5th Tank Army at Voronezh before being transferred northward to Army Group Center.[54]

Although he did not survive the war, General Hans Hube also carved out an illustrious record, particularly after replacing General Wietersheim as commander of XIV Panzer Corps in September 1942. Born in 1890, Hube lost his right arm during World War I but, despite his infirmity, rose to command 3rd

Infantry Division in 1939 and 16th Panzer Division in 1940. Spearheading First Panzer Army's thrust into the Ukraine in summer 1941, Hube's 16th Panzer Division played a pivotal role in the panzer army's encirclements at Uman' and Kiev in August and September 1941 and its struggle for Khar'kov and Rostov in October and November 1941. During Operation Blau, after his 16th Panzer Division led Sixth Army's dramatic but difficult advance across the Don River and to the Volga River north of Stalingrad in August 1942, Hitler rewarded Hube with command of XIV Panzer Corps in September.[55]

General of Panzer Troops Traugott Herr, also born in 1890, commanded 25th Infantry Division's 13th Regiment during the Polish campaign in 1939 and 66th Infantry Regiment (Motorized) during the Western campaign in 1940. After leading 13th Infantry Brigade during Operation Barbarossa, he led III Motorized Corps' 13th Panzer Division during First Panzer Army's advance to Kiev and Rostov in the summer and fall of 1941. Once again, his panzer division spearheaded III Panzer Corps' advance during Operation Blau, which propelled his division to the banks of the Terek River deep in the Caucasus region, where Herr was wounded in action and forced to depart.[56]

Still others, as was the case with General of Panzer Troops Ferdinand Heim, ultimately incurred Hitler's wrath and were relieved of command. Heim was born in 1895 and was a veteran of World War I. After Heim served with XIX Army Corps before the war and with panzer troops during prewar campaigns, his star soared during Operation Blau, when he received command of 14th Panzer Division in July 1942 and XXXXVIII Panzer Corps on 1 November 1942. However, when Heim's panzer corps failed to anticipate and defeat the Red Army's 19 November 1942 counteroffensive northwest of Stalingrad, Hitler summarily relieved him of command.[57] Hitler also sacked General of Panzer Troops Hans Boineburg-Lengsfeld as commander of 23rd Panzer Division for his division's role in the infamous Reichel affair, although he reinstated him to command the same division in August 1942.[58]

The most famous of the motorized division commanders in Operation Blau was General Walter Hörnlein, who was born in 1893 and commanded 69th Infantry Regiment in 1937 and 80th Infantry Regiment in 1939. After being promoted to colonel in 1940, Hörnlein led *Grossdeutschland* Infantry Regiment throughout Operation Barbarossa and the vastly more powerful *Grossdeutschland* Motorized Division during Operation Blau, although the OKH transferred his division northward to Army Group Center by late summer.[59]

THE GERMAN SOLDIER

Germany's soldiers, like its commanders, were a mixed bag of old professionals and new enthusiasts. After three years of uninterrupted triumph, the winter campaign of 1941–1942 cost the German Army in experience and confidence as well as in equipment. Even Adolf Hitler recognized this when he specified, in Plan Blau, that the first battles must be calculated to ensure easy victories and restore the self-confidence of the troops.

To meet the urgent need for replacements in spring 1942, infantry divisions received soldiers with as little as two months of training.[60] An army that prided itself on training and tactical skill now had to deal with half-trained recruits and subpar units. This began a deadly spiral that continued for the rest of the war: Inexperienced, partially trained soldiers were more likely to die than experienced ones, which increased the demand for replacements and forced the training base to send out men with steadily decreasing periods of training.

The high turnover in troops, with its resulting influx of younger Germans, also contributed to a trend that existed as early as 1941—what might be called the Nazification of the German Army. With certain exceptions, such as Reichenau, senior commanders were still the products of the conservative, professional army of World War I and the Weimar Republic. Increasingly, however, junior officers and the rank-and-file had grown up under the Nazi regime and often reflected Nazi attitudes.[61] Whatever the generals believed, at the small unit level, many Germans accepted the racial theories of their Führer, regarding their opponents as uncivilized subhumans. This attitude encouraged the Germans to fight with great bravery because they feared capture more than death. Yet the same belief structure had a darker side. Isolated from German society in a strange and frightening land, German soldiers were guilty of constant callousness and intermittent atrocities against Soviet civilians as well as prisoners of war.

In 1942, the German soldier was probably more competent than his Soviet counterpart, but, given the experiences of 1941, neither side needed lessons from the other about the ferocity of a struggle for survival.

CHAPTER 2

The Red Army

At the end of the long winter of 1941–1942, Josef Vissarionovich Stalin and Adolf Hitler drew similar yet contradictory conclusions about events. Each dictator had gained confidence in his own military judgment, convinced that his rigorous conduct of the defense had saved his army. Each man believed his opponents were on their last legs and that even a small amount of additional combat power during the winter battles would have brought a quick and decisive end to the war. As a consequence, Stalin, like Hitler, overestimated the time it would take his enemy to rebuild his divisions. Each man was surprised when the other proved capable of renewed offensive action in May 1942.

REBUILDING THE RED ARMY

That spring, while the *Wehrmacht* struggled to restore its existing combat units, the Red Army achieved an even greater miracle by creating new organizations from scratch, literally reinventing itself in the midst of war.[1]

The pressure of enemy invasion and conquest had smashed the Red Army's cumbersome and largely ineffective prewar force structure in late summer 1941. In response the Soviets had opted to form smaller and simpler formations and units that could be created quickly with minimal equipment.[2] The vast majority of new formations in 1941 were infantry (rifle) divisions and brigades (or demidivisions), the former with 6,000–10,000 men armed with rifles and machine guns and supported by a few guns and howitzers, and the latter with 4,000–5,000 men and even weaker artillery support. Divisions in the field fought with what they had—usually 2,500 to 5,000 men but frequently with as few as 1,000 "bayonets" (combat troops).[3] Although a few remnants of the large, prewar mechanized corps and tank divisions survived, all new tank production was funneled into forming crude tank brigades, first with a strength of 93 tanks in August 1941 and then decreasing to 67 tanks in September and 46 tanks in December, with a minimum of maintenance and support personnel. Many of these brigades died as quickly as they were formed, chewed up in the desperate winter battles of 1941–1942. Their function was to provide immediate support to the underequipped infantry rather than to maneuver as separate forces.

Soviet horse cavalry units achieved a mixed record in those same battles. Horses could move where swamps, snow, ice, and fuel shortages prevented mechanized maneuver. Because cavalry formations were relatively easier to form, and tanks were in short supply, the Soviets fielded 15 cavalry corps with two to three cavalry divisions each during the first eight months of the war and relied on these to conduct deep maneuver. Between January and May 1942, for example, Major General Pavel A. Belov had used his 1st Guards Cavalry Corps and a few separate tank battalions as the nucleus of an improvised "cavalry-mechanized group" that led a guerrilla-like existence behind the German lines 400 kilometers southwest of Moscow.[4] Yet movement across country was not the same as mobility on the battlefield. Cavalry forces like Belov's, whose heaviest weapons were their 50mm mortars, lacked the combat power to overcome German infantry divisions, however depleted and threadbare those divisions had become.

Thus, Stalin and his generals were convinced they needed larger, more capable mechanized units to fight the Germans on even terms. Fortunately, Soviet industry was up to the challenge of equipping such units. In 1941 production had fallen precipitously as complete factories were packed up and shipped eastward to avoid capture. Despite the confusion of war and the difficulty of construction in the depths of winter, by early 1942 these factories had reestablished themselves east of the Ural Mountains and were pumping out weapons at a phenomenal rate. Three thousand aircraft, 4,500 tanks, 14,000 field guns, and hundreds of thousands of other weapons came off the assembly lines between January and May.[5] In addition, limited amounts of Lend-Lease equipment began to arrive from Great Britain and the United States during late 1941; all-wheel drive trucks were particularly useful for supplying the mobile forces when they left their railroad lines behind.[6] Soviet raw materials and munitions were by no means unlimited, but the Red Army began the second year of the war with much better tools than it had possessed in 1941.

Lieutenant General of Tank Forces Iakov Nikolaevich Fedorenko, chief of the Red Army's Main Auto-Armored Directorate (GABTU), organized much of this equipment into a new generation of mechanized units. Fedorenko formed the Red Army's first four wartime tank corps, actually division-sized combined-arms mechanized forces, on 31 March 1942. Soon a steady stream of tank corps came into existence, with nine additional formations appearing in April, six in May, and so on, for a total of 28 by December.[7] Initially, these tank corps were short of specialized equipment and necessary logistical and technical support. The first four corps each consisted of two tank brigades, one motorized rifle (truck-mounted infantry) brigade, and a minimum of support units, for a total strength of 5,603 men and 100 tanks. Growing production and initial experience caused Fedorenko to add a third tank brigade and other units; by July a typical tank corps consisted of three tank brigades of 53 tanks each, the same motorized infantry brigade, and battalions of motorcycle-mounted reconnaissance troops, mortars, multiple rocket launchers (the famed *Katiushas*), and antiaircraft guns, all supported by a single combat engineer company, a transportation company, and two mobile repair units. The authorized strength of these corps ranged from

7,200 to 7,600 men and 146 to 180 tanks (30–65 heavy, 46–56 medium, and 70 light tanks), although in practice specialized equipment—radios, recovery vehicles, and the like—remained in short supply.[8]

The new tank corps performed poorly in combat during the spring and summer of 1942 because they were too weak to conduct sustained operations. Therefore, in September 1942 Fedorenko began to organize another type of formation, a mechanized corps in which truck-mounted infantry, with improved artillery and antitank support, rather than tanks, were in the majority. These mechanized corps came in three basic types so they could operate in more varied terrain. In theory, such corps consisted of a nucleus of three mechanized brigades, each with a regiment of 39 medium tanks, as well as trucked infantry, and one or two tank brigades or one or two separate tank regiments, and most of the same supporting arms found in the tank corps.[9] Thus organized, the three types of mechanized corps fielded 175, 224, or 204 tanks, respectively.

Such a mechanized corps was fully equivalent, on paper, to a panzer division; the smaller tank corps needed more infantry and artillery to defend the ground it seized but nevertheless promised to give the Red Army a level of combat power that it had previously lacked.

On 25 May 1942, the People's Commissariat of Defense [*Narodnyi Komissariat Oborony*] (NKO), or War Commissariat, which was responsible for forming and fielding new formations and units, took the next logical step, creating two experimental formations that it designated the 3rd and 5th Tank Armies. Two more tank armies (1st and 4th) took form in early July and, together with the previous two tank armies, found themselves committed to battle almost instantly. On paper, a tank army was equivalent in size to a panzer corps, giving the Red Army its first true capability for larger, operational-level mechanized maneuver. Given the immaturity of the Soviet armored force, however, it was perhaps inevitable that these tank armies would contain a hodgepodge of units with inexperienced leaders. Although there were many variations, in 1942 a tank army usually consisted of two or three tank corps, a separate tank brigade, one or more rifle (infantry) divisions, plus artillery and supporting units.[10] On occasion, this army might also include cavalry corps or divisions. The rifle elements were intended to create a penetration that could be exploited by the tank units, but the 1942 tank army as a whole had such varied levels of mobility and armored protection that it was hard-pressed to operate as a coherent unit.

Prior to Stalin's Great Purge of its officer corps from 1937 to 1941, the Red Army had developed a sophisticated concept for conducting mobile, flexible mechanized warfare at the operational and tactical levels. Fighting German panzers in 1941, however, had severely tested this theory and taught inexperienced Soviet commanders additional painful lessons about the nature of tank warfare. In theory, therefore, the Red Army understood the techniques necessary to employ its new mechanized formations effectively.

A fundamental difficulty remained, however. The NKO could find the troops and most of the equipment to form tank corps and armies, and Soviet theorists could offer an appropriate set of operational and tactical concepts. What they could not produce were experienced leaders and technicians to maneuver the tank and mechanized forces in accordance with theory. Some of the men who had survived as commanders of Red Army tank brigades in 1941 exhibited the maturity to move up to the next level as corps commanders the following spring. Yet there was no way to produce experienced commanders for the even more complex tank armies. It was equally impossible to train the communications personnel, logisticians, staff planners, and other experts necessary to translate the commander's desires into reality on the battlefield. As Liziukov's tragic performance at Voronezh demonstrated, the Red Army's tank units were not yet ready to conduct large-scale mechanized operations against their German counterparts. In fact, many of the higher-level headquarters in the conventional, infantry-heavy rifle corps, armies, and *fronts* (army groups) were equally inexperienced in the skills necessary to concentrate, supply, and direct those organizations in battle; the speed required for mechanized maneuver only complicated this weakness.

As in the German Army, the mechanized formations were made possible only by a strict set of supply priorities that relegated ordinary rifle units to last place. Except for a few favored divisions that were designated as "Guards," Soviet rifle units in 1942 remained almost unchanged from the previous year. The typical rifle division received a few more artillery pieces, and a few wounded veterans returned to duty during the spring lull, but in general a rifle division was only marginally more capable than it had been in 1941. Although strengths varied widely, a 1942 rifle division was lucky to have 7,000 effectives with limited heavy equipment.

In terms of weaponry, newly produced 45mm antitank guns were much more effective against German armor. Yet Soviet tank designs, like their German counterparts, were almost identical to those of the previous year, which meant that the Red Army retained its technical superiority. Soviet engineers did try to simplify the existing designs in order to increase production without affecting performance—and they succeeded magnificently. Thus in 1942 as in 1941, the T-34 medium tank had better armor and better armament (a 76.2mm high velocity main gun) than the German Panzer III and IV. The T-34 retained significant design problems, particularly in the layout of its turret, the quality of its gunsights, and the initial lack of radios, but its ability to operate in extreme weather with minimal maintenance made it a formidable weapon.[11] The KV-1 heavy tank, with the same main gun and even thicker armor, was almost invulnerable to anything smaller than the famous German 88mm antiaircraft gun. However, the KV-1 also had design problems that hampered its crew, and each KV-1 represented a massive investment in material and production man-hours. As a result, Fedorenko concentrated on increasing production of T-34s. Moreover, Soviet industry continued to turn out thousands of T-60 light tanks with 20mm guns. These were useful for reconnaissance but lacked the armored protection or armament to engage German panzers with any hope of success. In truth, the Soviets produced these obsolescent light tanks simply because they did not require a special tank assembly plant; they could readily be built on assembly lines used for light trucks and automobiles. Similar considerations of mass production prompted the Soviets to continue building existing artillery and antitank designs rather than fielding more capable versions.

THE STRATEGIC DEBATE

One of the enduring issues in the field of military intelligence is the relative weight given to the capabilities of an enemy versus the known or suspected intentions of that enemy. Accurate knowledge of enemy troop strengths and dispositions allows an intelligence analyst to identify the various operations that an opponent is capable of conducting. Yet such knowledge of capabilities is insufficient if the analyst is uncertain or misled as to enemy intentions. By contrast, it is easy for the analyst to delude himself that he knows the enemy's intentions and thereby to ignore any contrary evidence regarding his capabilities.

. This theoretical issue goes to the heart of the Soviet failures in 1942. Mesmerized by the desperate battles of the previous winter, Stalin and his subordinates were convinced that the next German offensive would make Moscow its primary objective, with a possible secondary offensive in the south. Soviet intelligence analysts and commanders calculated that 70 German divisions could strike from the center of the enemy front eastward toward Moscow; these analysts and commanders ignored the possibility that many of those same divisions could pivot and strike southward.[12] The Moscow defenses therefore received first priority for weapons, formations, and units, as well as the construction of defensive lines and field fortifications. It is ironic that a group of dedicated Marxists, who supposedly believed that the basis of all power lay in controlling the means of production, would focus on defending their political capital and ignore the economic value their opponent saw in the southeastern region of the Soviet Union.

Even as the guns fell silent in March, the Soviet senior leadership began planning for the next campaign. Stalin, convinced he had been within inches of victory during the winter battles, wanted to launch a new general offensive as soon as his troops had regained some strength and the spring mud had dried out. The dictator's subordinates did their best to dissuade him, particularly the chief of his General Staff, Boris Mikhailovich Shaposhnikov, his deputy chief of staff, Aleksandr Mikhailovich Vasilevsky, and the General Staff's former chief and victor at Leningrad and Moscow, Georgii Konstantinovich Zhukov. Nevertheless, the resulting Soviet strategy was almost incoherent.[13]

The chief of the Red Army General Staff, Marshal of the Soviet Union Boris Shaposhnikov, was a scholarly gentleman of 60 who served as a staff officer in the tsar's army during World War I and, after joining the Red Army in 1918, became the acknowledged father of the General Staff. A skilled General Staff officer and a preeminent theorist and military historian in his own right, Shaposhnikov "held to the officer's code of an earlier generation, something not commonly encountered among his peers."[14] As well known for his decency, independence, and candor as for his theoretical prowess, Shaposhnikov helped create the modern Red Army during the 1920s, commanding the Leningrad, Moscow, and Volga Military Districts in the 1920s and 1930s. He also contributed materially to the creation of the Red Army General Staff with his theoretical masterpiece, *The Brain of the Army*, which he wrote in 1927–1929. His feistiness and reputation as a "top-notch military commander unequaled for erudition, professional skill and intellectual development" and his love for cavalry allowed him to survive the purges of the late 1930s and become chief of the Red Army General Staff in spring 1937 and a deputy People's Commissar of Defense in August 1940.[15]

Never ideological (he didn't join the Communist Party until 1939), Shaposhnikov often disagreed with Stalin regarding Soviet defense strategy, including prewar defense planning, but he nevertheless survived, probably because Stalin respected his nonthreatening candor. Illustrating Shaposhnikov's strange relationship with Stalin, he was one of the few whom the dictator addressed by his Christian name and patronymic.

Although Shaposhnikov was discredited and removed as chief of the General Staff in early 1940 by virtue of his association with the Finnish War debacle, Stalin reappointed him in July 1941. Thereafter, he reshaped the General Staff into an organ that would achieve wartime victory. Always a moderating influence on Stalin, his influence ultimately prompted the Soviet leader to defer to General Staff leadership in the war effort. More important, Shaposhnikov was responsible for the rapid rise of Vasilevsky and N. F. Vatutin to leading positions in the Soviet war effort. In spring 1942, a severe respiratory condition, complicated by overworking, was slowly destroying Shaposhnikov's health; on 10 May he was forced to retire to the less demanding position of head of the Higher Military Academy. In the interim, he labored to persuade Stalin of the dangers of a premature offensive. Shaposhnikov was convinced, once the spring thaw ended, that the Germans would launch a new offensive; just as in the previous year, any Soviet attack must wait until this threat had expended itself on the Red Army defenses.

The 47-year-old Colonel General Aleksandr Mikhailovich Vasilevsky—Shaposhnikov's deputy, chief of operations, and handpicked successor—supported his chief's arguments, even at the risk of Stalin's displeasure. He was one of the few soldiers who enjoyed Stalin's trust, in part because he was a key staff officer who remained in Moscow during its 1941 defense, when most of the government had evacuated the city. Vasilevsky was arguably the most skilled member of the *Stavka* and second only to Zhukov as Stalin's most trusted general. A former infantry officer who did not enjoy the benefits of belonging to Stalin's cavalry clique (those who had been associated with Stalin in the 1st Cavalry Army during the Civil War), Vasilevsky advanced through merit alone and joined the General Staff after his graduation from the General Staff Academy in the semipurged class of 1937. By this time he had commanded a regiment during the 1920 Polish War and another regiment in the 48th Rifle Division in the 1920s.

Rising from colonel to colonel general in four years, Vasilevsky was Shaposhnikov's favored heir apparent as chief of the Red Army General Staff. With his chief's help, Vasilevsky became deputy chief of the Operations Directorate in May 1940, where he played a vital role in developing the Red Army's defense and mobilization plans during the last few months of peace. In the wake of the German invasion Stalin appointed Vasilevsky chief of that directorate and deputy chief of the General Staff in August 1941. While he helped plan most of the major Red Army operations in 1941 and 1942, Vasilevsky also served as Representative of the *Stavka*—a Stalin troubleshooter—during many of these operations. In October 1941, for example, he helped restore Red Army defenses west of Moscow after its disastrous defeats at Viaz'ma and Briansk, and in April and May 1942 he coordinated Northwestern Front's ill-fated attempt to liquidate German forces in the Demiansk salient.

Even though Vasilevsky could not completely dissuade Stalin from launching new attacks in the spring, the sage advice he provided probably hastened his appointment as chief of the General Staff in June 1942 and as deputy People's Commissar of Defense in October.[16] As such, Vasilevsky would play a vital role in formulating the military strategy the *Stavka* employed to counter the *Wehrmacht*'s advance to Stalingrad during the summer and fall of 1942 and would become one of the foremost architects of the subsequent Red Army victory in its counteroffensive in the region during November and December 1942.

Army General Georgii Konstantinovich Zhukov, the acknowledged savior of Leningrad and Moscow in fall 1941 at age 45, was already Stalin's favorite general by spring 1942.[17] Serving with distinction in the Red Army's cavalry forces during and after the Russian Civil War, Zhukov became a junior member of Stalin's cavalry clique and commanded, in succession, a cavalry regiment and brigade and 4th Cavalry Division before leading 1st Army Group (with 57th Special Rifle Corps) in its stunning victory over elements of the vaunted Japanese Kwantung Army at Khalkhin Gol in August 1939. In recognition of Zhukov's distinguished service, Stalin made him a Hero of the Soviet Union and appointed him commander of the Kiev Special Military District in June 1940, a post he occupied until January 1941, when he became chief of the Red Army General Staff and 1st Deputy Commissar of Defense.

A charter member of Stalin's wartime *Stavka*, Zhukov coordinated the Southwestern Front's attempted counteroffensive during the first week of the war and commanded, in succession, Reserve Front in August and September 1941, Leningrad Front in September and October 1941, Western Front from October 1941 through August 1942, and, simultaneously, the Western Main Direction from February through May 1942. As a commander, Zhukov earned lasting fame for his tenacious defense of Leningrad in September 1941 and Moscow in October and November 1941. He then planned and conducted the Red Army's counteroffensive in the Moscow region from December 1941 through April 1942; despite his single-minded but often ruthless conduct of the campaign, his forces saved Stalin's capital but failed to achieve the *Stavka*'s more ambitious strategic aims.

As Hitler's *Wehrmacht* conducted Operation Blau across southern Russia in summer 1942, Zhukov's Western Front would organize counterstroke after counterstroke to divert German attentions and forces from their primary objective in the south. After Stalin rewarded Zhukov by anointing him deputy Supreme Commander in August 1942, at the culminating point of the German Blau offensive, Zhukov would play a key role in planning the Red Army's strategic counteroffensives at Stalingrad (Operation Uranus) and in the Rzhev region (Operation Mars), during which he coordinated the operations in his Western Front and the neighboring Kalinin Front.[18]

As Stalin and his key General Staff officers discussed future military strategy in spring 1942, Zhukov understood the wisdom of what Shaposhnikov and Vasilevsky advocated. However, Zhukov was a naturally pugnacious man who was not above currying favor with his master. According to his own recollection, Zhukov warned against the danger of dissipating Soviet strength in too many local offensives. Despite such denials, it was entirely in character that Zhukov would privately encourage Stalin to contemplate limited offensive actions within the context of an overall defensive. Indeed, even Zhukov acknowledged that he may have erred in advocating a limited offensive farther north, in the Rzhev-Viaz'ma region, which he regarded as the German base for an attack on Moscow.[19]

The outcome of this strategic debate proved disastrous. In early March Stalin's initial guidance for the next campaign called for a so-called active strategic defense but directed planning for at least six local offensives, from the Crimea in the south to Leningrad in the north.[20]

While the *Stavka* continued to plan for a defensive campaign, subordinate commanders responded to Stalin's obvious preferences by developing attack options. Field commanders must have known the limitations of their own troops, yet they gave Stalin overly optimistic assessments of the proposed offensives. Nowhere was this more true than in the Southwestern Main Direction Command, one of three superheadquarters Stalin established on 10 July 1941 that were supposed to be intermediaries between the *fronts* (army groups) and the *Stavka*. In 1941–1942, the Southwestern Main Direction, which included the Southwestern and Southern Fronts, was commanded by Marshal of the Soviet Union Semen Konstantinovich Timoshenko, an aggressive warhorse whose experience in the Russian Civil War made him slow to grasp the challenges of mechanized blitzkrieg.

Far more competent than Marshals K. E. Voroshilov and S. M. Budenny, his fellow main direction commanders in 1941, Timoshenko fared little better than his colleagues. To his credit, however, unlike Voroshilov, Timoshenko had played no apparent part in the vicious repression of the Red Army officers' corps in the 1930s, and he avoided adopting the fawning attitude to Stalin characteristic of Voroshilov and so many others.[21] Timoshenko began his military career as a private in the tsar's army during World War I but joined the Red Army in 1918. During the Civil War, he commanded a cavalry regiment in the defense of Tsaritsyn (later Stalingrad), where he befriended Stalin, who was responsible for the city's defense. Paralleling Stalin's career as a commissar, he commanded 2nd Separate Cavalry Brigade and 6th and 4th Cavalry Divisions in Budenny's famed 1st Cavalry Army from 1919 to 1920, participating in the heavy fighting against White forces in southern Russia. After the war he commanded 3rd Cavalry Corps in the late 1920s, served as deputy commander of the Belorussian Military District in 1933, and commanded the North Caucasus, Khar'kov, and, finally, the Kiev Special Military Districts from 1937 to 1939 and the Ukrainian Front during its invasion of Eastern Poland in September 1939. Timoshenko's reputation soared during the Finnish War when, in the wake of the embarrassing defeats the Red Army suffered at the hands of the Finns in late 1939, he led Northwestern Front in its successful penetration of the Mannerheim Defensive Line and ended the war with no further defeats.

Appointed Commissar of Defense of the USSR at age 45 in the wake of the unsuccessful Finnish War, Timoshenko organized and carried out the massive but failed prewar military reform of the Red Army from May 1940 to the outbreak of war. When war began, Stalin appointed Timoshenko chief of the *Stavka* on 23 June 1941 and, in succession, commander of Western Front on 30 June and the Western Direction on 10 July, while retaining the marshal as his 1st Deputy Commissar of Defense.

Stoic and unflappable, Timoshenko watched almost helplessly as the *Wehrmacht*'s advancing forces dismembered and then swallowed up the three forward deployed armies of his main direction's Western Front during the first ten days of fighting. By the time German forces crossed the Dnepr River in early July, Timoshenko was wearing three hats as commander in chief of the Western Direction and commander of Western Front and the new Central Front. Although he was unable to contain the German advance short of Smolensk, in mid-July he planned and carried out a major counterstroke that forced Hitler to halt his offensive on Moscow, albeit temporarily, on 30 July. Timoshenko's forces then pummeled German defenses in the Smolensk region in late August and early September, thereby persuading Hitler to shift the axis of his main advance southward toward Kiev. Despite warnings from Zhukov, Stalin belatedly disbanded Timoshenko's Western Direction Command and dispatched the marshal southward to replace Budenny and restore order in the Southwestern Main Direction Command at the gates of Kiev.

Although Timoshenko presided over the disastrous destruction of the Red

Army's Southwestern Front at Kiev in September 1941, he continued to command the Southwestern Direction (as well as a reformed Southwestern Front) throughout fall 1941 and winter 1941–1942. During this period he organized major counteroffensives in the Rostov region in November and December 1941 and in the Izium region in January 1942. In addition to expelling German forces from Rostov, these operations carved a large salient in the German defenses on the western bank of the Northern Donets River south of Khar'kov.[22] It was this area that Stalin and Timoshenko proposed to attack in the spring, seeking to exploit perceived German weaknesses or at least to divert some of the panzer forces that, according to most Soviet commanders, were massing to attack toward Moscow.

In response to Stalin's planning guidance, in early March 1942 Timoshenko called a meeting of the Southwestern Direction's (and Southwestern Front's) Military Council, his principal assistants.[23] These included several men destined for fame: the main direction's (and Southwestern Front's) chief political officer (commissar), N. S. Khrushchev; Southwestern Front's chief of staff, Lieutenant General P. I. Bodin; and Lieutenant General I. Kh. Bagramian, who wore two hats as chief of staff of Timoshenko's main direction command and chief of operations in Bodin's *front*.

A native of Ukraine, Communist Party member since 1918, and military commissar during the Civil War, Nikita Sergeevich Khrushchev had risen from his Ukrainian roots to become 1st Secretary of the Moscow Party Committee in 1935 and, in the wake of the purges, 1st Secretary of the Ukrainian Party's Central Committee in 1938. In that capacity, the 47-year-old Khrushchev became the "member" (commissar) of the Southwestern Main Direction Command in early July 1941, surviving the multiple defeats the Southwestern Front experienced along the borders in June and early July and the disastrous encirclements at Uman' and Kiev in August and September. Emerging from these ordeals with reputations intact, Khrushchev and Timoshenko orchestrated the restoration of the Southwestern Direction's defenses in November and December 1941 and forged its victories during the winter offensive of 1941–1942.

Despite his service as commissar—a post many Red Army officers feared and despised—Khrushchev's earthy language, sharp native skills, and penchant for suffering hardships alongside his men earned the grudging respect of many Red Army soldiers. Appreciative of Khrushchev's tenacity and organizational and inspirational skills, if not his occasional ruthlessness, as the war progressed, Stalin increasingly relied on the obvious talents of his "Ukrainian commissar."

Timoshenko's chief of staff, 45-year-old Lieutenant General Ivan Khristoforovich Bagramian, was one of two ethnic Armenians to reach senior command in the Red Army.[24] A noncommissioned officer in the tsar's army during World War I, Bagramian joined the Red Army in 1920 and helped solidify Bolshevik power in Armenia and Georgia during the Russian Civil War. A cavalry officer who commanded the cavalry regiment in the Armenian Rifle Division during the 1920s and 1930s, he graduated from the Frunze Academy in 1934 and the General Staff Academy in 1938, where he lectured for four years.[25] Eclipsed by famous members of Stalin's cavalry clique such as Zhukov and Eremenko, with Zhukov's assistance Bagramian was appointed chief of operations of 12th Army in the Kiev Special Military District in early 1940 and deputy chief of operations in the same military district three months later. Soon after war began, Bagramian became operations chief and deputy chief of staff of the Southwestern Front, where he served throughout the disastrous border battles and the retreat toward Kiev.

Bagramian earned notoriety in September 1941 when Timoshenko, newly appointed commander of the Southwestern Direction, sent him to the Southwestern Front with an order for the *front* (army group) to withdraw its forces from Kiev to avoid encirclement by the Germans. Although caught up in the ensuing Kiev encirclement, Bagramian managed to escape the cauldron with his staff. Retained by Timoshenko as chief of operations and appointed by the marshal as chief of staff in December 1941, Bagramian helped reestablish the main direction's defenses in the fall and planned its successful offensives at Rostov in November and December 1941 and at Barvenkovo-Lozovaia west of Izium during January 1942.[26] Based on his previous success, Timoshenko valued Bagramian's sage counsel as he planned his new offensives in spring 1942.

Because Timoshenko wore two hats as commander of the Southwestern Direction and its subordinate Southwestern Front, the planning meeting in early March also included the *front*'s chief of staff, Lieutenant General Pavel Ivanovich Bodin, the experienced former chief of staff of the *front*'s 9th Army. Like so many of his peers, the 42-year-old Bodin was a veteran of the Civil War and a graduate of both the Frunze and General Staff Academies. He had earned his spurs by planning the important role his army played in the successful defense during the summer and fall, for which Timoshenko appointed him chief of staff of the main direction and Southwestern Front in October 1941 (although he relinquished the former post to Bagramian in December). Bodin excelled in his new posts by planning the Rostov offensive in November and December 1941 and the Barvenkovo-Lozovaia offensive in January 1942.

Whether from genuine conviction or political expedience, these men all agreed with Timoshenko about the tempting prospects for an offensive in the Khar'kov region. Bagramian drew up a plan for the proposed operation and presented it on 20 March to a larger meeting of Timoshenko's *front* commanders.[27] At this meeting, Bagramian appeared confident of the outcome despite the lingering equipment and personnel shortages of Timoshenko's units. Khrushchev reportedly emphasized that Stalin himself had ordered the plan, and, therefore, it was guaranteed to succeed.[28] Ultimately, the assembled commanders agreed to the plan. The most charitable explanation for this acquiescence is that the commanders were convinced that the Khar'kov offensive must be part of a larger *Stavka* plan that, per Soviet tradition, was being kept secret from them.

The 20 March meeting resulted in a series of rosy reports from the Southwestern Direction to the *Stavka*. On 22 March, for example, Timoshenko, Khrushchev, and Bagramian forwarded their overall assessment for the spring-summer period. This report assumed that the desperate conditions of midwinter, in which German units had become dispersed and fragmented, would still exist later in the spring. At this stage in the war, Soviet military intelligence assessments were less than perfect about German orders of battle and capabilities, let alone future intentions. While noting that 3,500 German tank crewmen were assembled in the rear, at Poltava, to receive new vehicles, Timoshenko insisted there was no sign of reinforcement at the front line. The 22 March report therefore argued that, in order to forestall the expected German attack on Moscow, Southwestern Direction's forces should launch a series of minor adjustments, leading, after the spring thaw ended, to a major counteroffensive to push 240 kilometers westward to the middle Dnepr River. In retrospect, the poor state of readiness of the Soviet forces made this optimistic assessment seem even more surprising. Astonishingly, in the same report in which he recommended an offensive, Timoshenko indicated his rifle divisions averaged only 51.2 percent of authorized rifles and less than 24 percent of machine guns.[29]

Such estimates encouraged the Soviet dictator's aggressive tendencies. Summoned to Moscow, the three leaders of Southwestern Direction presented their plan to Stalin and Shaposhnikov on 27 March 1942. At this stage, Soviet preoccupation with defending the capital intervened; although Stalin wanted an offensive against Khar'kov, he was unwilling to reduce Moscow's defenses by providing the extensive reinforcements Timoshenko requested. Instead, the Military Council of the Southwest Direction went through several iterations of their plan, each more modest than the last, until they finally reached agreement with their chief.[30]

Meanwhile the other sectors of the Soviet defenses prepared for lesser offensives. On 9 April the *Stavka* ordered the Leningrad and Volkhov Fronts to prepare an attack to rescue 2nd Shock Army, which since January had been encircled south of Leningrad.[31] On 20 April Moscow instructed the Briansk Front to plan an offensive along the Kursk-L'gov axis to support Timoshenko's Khar'kov attack.[32] The next day another order required the Crimean Front to resume efforts to break out of the Kerch' Peninsula bridgehead and relieve Soviet forces besieged in Sevastopol'.[33] On 22 April Northwestern Front received instructions to make another attempt to reduce II Army Corps of German Army Group North's Sixteenth Army, encircled near Demiansk; Vasilevsky went in person to supervise preparations.[34] Finally, Karelian Front in the far north planned to push Finnish forces back to the 1940 border.[35]

All these operations were supposed to occur in late April or May, but the Khar'kov operation remained the crown jewel of the counteroffensive plan. Clearly, Stalin believed these widely dispersed attacks would place intolerable stress upon the overextended Germans. Instead, as the professional soldiers of the *Stavka* feared, the limited offensives of May 1942 merely dissipated Soviet assets that would have been better used to stop the coming German offensive.

THE KHAR'KOV PLAN

After repeated discussions and revisions, Timoshenko issued a scaled back yet still ambitious plan on 10 April.[36] Following a preparatory period of strategic deception and troop movements, Southwestern Front would launch two major attacks aimed to converge on Khar'kov. In the northeast, the massed infantry divisions of Major General V. N. Gordov's 21st Army and Lieutenant General D. I. Riabyshev's newly mobilized and redeployed 28th Army, supported by several tank brigades, would make a secondary attack out of the bridgehead on the west bank of the Northern Donets River at Staryi Saltov, northeast of Khar'kov. Farther south, Lieutenant General A. M. Gorodniansky's 6th Army and a specially tailored cavalry-rifle group (designated Group Bobkin after its commander, Major General L. V. Bobkin, Southwestern Front's assistant commander for cavalry forces) would mount the principal effort from the Barvenkovo bridgehead south of Khar'kov and west of Izium. Major General Aleksandr Alekseevich Noskov's 6th Cavalry Corps formed the nucleus of Group Bobkin. In light of the subsequent November Soviet offensive that penetrated Axis satellite armies to encircle Stalingrad, it is worth noting that, as early as May, the Soviet offensive at Staryi Saltov was carefully designed to punch through a sector defended by the poorly equipped 108th Hungarian Light Infantry Division.

Each infantry assault was intended to create a penetration that the new mobile forces of the Red Army could exploit. In the north, Major General V. D. Kriuchenkin's 3rd Guards Cavalry Corps, reinforced with a tank brigade, would race westward and then south toward Khar'kov. In the south, two of the new mechanized formations, Major General G. I. Kuz'min's 21st and Major General E. G. Pushkin's 23rd Tank Corps, were assigned to rush to and even beyond the city, cutting off German communications, while Group Bobkin's cavalry corps blocked German reinforcements from moving into the Khar'kov region from the west.

Timoshenko convinced Stalin to approve this plan despite the horrified reactions of Shaposhnikov and Vasilevsky. The minimum goal of this offensive was to shorten the front line and weaken the expected German offensive against Moscow, but obviously both Timoshenko and Stalin hoped for greater results. The aging marshal was not completely irrational, however. For example, Lieutenant General K. S. Moskalenko, commander of Southwestern Front's 38th Army, persuaded Timoshenko that the inexperienced, half-trained 28th Army could not make the northern attack without help; as a result, Timoshenko adjusted the plan to include Moskalenko's more experienced army as a flank guard for 28th Army.[37] Nevertheless, the Khar'kov offensive represented an unnecessary gamble, committing the newly formed formations of the Red Army before the German summer offensive developed and denying those formations several precious weeks of training time.

FORCE DISPOSITIONS

As Stalin and his main direction and *front* commanders planned their offensives, by dint of its strenuous mobilization efforts the NKO, from 1 December 1941 to 1 May 1942, had increased the Soviet Armed Forces' overall strength from roughly 9 million soldiers, organized into 314 divisions and 96 brigades of various types, to about 11 million soldiers, organized into 426 divisions and 148 brigades and supported by 9,325 tanks, 107,795 guns and mortars, 1,544 multiple rocket launchers, 14,967 combat aircraft (9,297 operational), 364,029 vehicles (269,993 trucks), and 1,275,323 horses (see Table 2).[38] By this time, the Red Army's personnel strength had reached about nine million soldiers—men and women—with about five million of these assigned to its field, or operating, army (*deistvuiushchaia armiia*) at the *front* and to the *Stavka* Reserve [*Reserv Verkhovnovo Komandovaniia*, RVGK].[39]

In Stalin's view, his large and powerful armed forces were already superior to the estimated force of 310 divisions, 6.5 million troops (5.8 million German), and 5,600 aircraft the Axis could employ along its Eastern Front.[40] Furthermore, along the important southern axis of the front, where most offensive operations would take place, the Red Army had increased its armored strength to just over 3,000 tanks, as opposed to the estimated 3,300 tanks and assault guns the *Wehrmacht* would be able to field.[41]

Despite its imposing strength on paper, the Red Army was victimized by extreme turbulence in personnel during the first ten months of fighting. For example, since 22 June 1941, when the Red Army fielded about 5.5 million soldiers, it had suffered just over six million casualties, with roughly 3.5 million killed, captured, or missing, and about 2.5 million wounded or fallen ill. Despite such an appalling toll, the NKO's mobilization measures had managed to increase the army's average monthly operating strength from three million soldiers in 1941 to about 4.2 million during the first quarter of 1942. The high turnover rate, however, not only had an adverse effect on personnel but also affected unit training, although most every soldier and commander who survived this bloodletting certainly emerged as a seasoned, experienced fighter.

By 1 May 1942, the Red Army's field forces, the Supreme High Command's (VGK) reserve, and the army's nonoperating forces were organized into *obedinenii* (large formations), including 12 *fronts*, 10 military districts, 4 fleets, 63 combined-arms armies, 1 *Protivovozdushnaia Oborona* (PVO, Russian air defense) army, 5 sapper (engineer) armies, 7 flotillas, and 2 operational groups.

Table 2. The Strength of the Soviet Armed Forces on 1 May 1942

Strength and Weaponry	Forces			
	Operating	VGK Reserve	Non-Operating	Total
Personnel	5,677,915	218,276	5,040,440	10,936,631
Weapons				
Guns and mortars	71,476	2,591	33,728	107,795
Rocket artillery	1,339	53	152	1,544
Tanks				
Heavy	660	47	237	944
Medium	1,291	88	577	1,956
Light	2,025	42	4,299	6,366
Specialized	44	—	15	59
Total	4,020	177	5,128	9,325
Aircraft				
Fighters (operational)	3,468	93	4,073	7,634
	(2,009)	(82)	(2,785)	(4,876)
Assault (operational)	331	95	127	553
	(218)	(87)	(69)	(374)
Bombers (operational)	1,170	59	3,590	4,819
	(696)	(56)	(2,257)	(3,009)
Reconnaissance	544	—	1,417	1,961
(operational)	(220)		(818)	(1,038)
Total	5,513	247	9,207	14,967
	(3,143)	(225)	(5,929)	(9,297)
Automobile Transport				
Vehicles (trucks)	239,227	3,765	121,037	364,029
	(179,971)	(3,072)	(86,950)	(269,993)
Tractors	22,250	214	17,443	39,907
Horses	751,399	49,261	474,663	1,275,323

Source: N. I. Nikoforov, ed., *Velikaia Otechestvennaia voina 1941–1945 gg.: Deistvuiushchaia armiia* [The Great Patriotic War, 1941–1945: The Operating Army] (Moscow: Animi Fortitudo, Kuchkovo pole, 2005), 541–542, 546–547.

Collectively, these large formations consisted of a dizzying array of smaller formations, units, and subunits representing all services (army, air force, navy) and force branches (infantry, tank and mechanized, artillery, air defense, engineers, etc.) (see Table 3).

From a strategic and operational standpoint, the most significant of these forces were those that made up the Red Army's field (operating) forces and VGK reserves (see Table 4).

The Red Army's field forces were subordinate to 10 *fronts*, 52 armies, and 2 operational groups deployed between the Arctic and Black Seas (see Table 5).

After committing most of its reserves to combat during the Red Army's winter offensive of 1941–1942, by spring the *Stavka* Reserve was relatively small. As of 1 May, the RVGK consisted of 1st Reserve and 58th Armies, with 2 and 5 rifle divisions, respectively, 2nd Guards Cavalry Corps' 4 cavalry divisions, 2nd Tank

Table 3. The Combat Composition of the Soviet Armed Forces on 1 May 1942

Types of Formations	Forces			Total
	Operating	VGK Reserve	Non-Operating	
Fronts	10	—	2	12
Military districts	—	—	10	10
Armies				
Combined-arms	52	2	9	63
PVO (Air defense)	1	—	—	1
Sapper	5	—	—	5
Operational groups	2	—	—	2
PVO zones	—	—	2	2
Fleets	3	—	1	4
Flotillas	3	—	4	7
Corps				
Rifle	6	—	5	11
Cavalry	9	1	4	14
Airborne	1	—	9	10
Tank	10	1	3	14
PVO	—	—	1	1
Aviation	2	—	1	3
PVO corps regions	2	—	—	2
Aviation groups	16	—	—	16
Squadrons	2	—	—	2
Divisions				
Rifle	313	10	103	426
Destroyer	—	—	1	1
Cavalry	32	4	24	60
Tank	—	—	2	2
Motorized rifle	4	—	2	6
PVO	2	—	—	2
Aviation	22	—	11	33
PVO division regions	11	—	2	13
Brigades				
Rifle	95	14	39	148
Destroyer	—	—	21	21
Ski	9	—	—	9
Airborne	5	—	31	36
Naval infantry	11	—	2	13
Tank	85	3	103	191
Motorized rifle	7	1	9	17
Artillery	1	—	1	2
Antitank	1	—	1	2
Engineer	1	—	—	1
Sapper	30	—	2	32
PVO	2	—	—	2
Aviation	5	3	4	12
Combat ships and cutters	11	—	9	20
PVO brigade regions	3	—	11	14
Fortified regions	17	—	35	52
Separate Regiments				
Rifle	6	—	6	12
Naval infantry	6	—	—	6

Table 3. Continued

Types of Formations	Forces			
	Operating	VGK Reserve	Non-Operating	Total
Cavalry	2	—	3	5
Motorized rifle	1	—	2	3
Motorcycle	3	—	4	7
Artillery	161	5	147	313
Antitank	91	5	33	129
Mortar	21	3	33	57
Rocket artillery	38	5	13	56
Antiaircraft artillery	57	—	22	79
Antiaircraft-machine gun	7	—	2	9
Engineer	1	—	—	1
Pontoon-bridge	—	—	2	2
Aviation	343	17	234	594
Separate Battalions (squadrons)				
Rifle	8	—	6	14
Ski	107	—	—	107
Naval infantry	15	—	7	22
Parachute-assault	1	—	1	2
Tank	49	—	21	70
Motorcycle	3	—	3	6
Machine gun	1	—	6	7
Machine gun-artillery	7	—	1	8
Artillery	37	—	34	71
Antitank	9	—	—	9
Mortar	12	—	3	15
Rocket artillery	44	—	6	50
Antiaircraft artillery	275	—	70	345
Antiaircraft-machine gun	4	—	—	4
Aerial sleigh (aerosanyi)	24	9	16	49
Armored car	1	—	—	1
Armored train	28	11	23	62
Engineer	143	—	20	163
Sapper	93	—	5	98
Pontoon-bridge	63	—	12	75
Aviation	22	—	34	56
Combat ships and cutters	108	—	63	109

Source: N. I. Nikoforov, ed., *Velikaia Otechestvennaia voina 1941–1945 gg.: Deistvuiushchaia armiia* [The Great Patriotic War, 1941–1945: The Operating Army] (Moscow: Animi Fortitudo, Kuchkovo pole, 2005), 544–545.
Note: VGK means Supreme High Command

Corps' 3 tank brigades and 1 motorized rifle brigade, as well as 3 rifle divisions and 14 brigades, 9 separate aero-sleigh battalions, 11 separate armored train battalions, 5 artillery regiments, 5 antitank artillery regiments, 3 mortar regiments, 5 guards-mortar regiments, 3 aviation brigades, and 33 aviation regiments.[42]

Because the *Stavka* anticipated conducting offensive operations in May and then confronting a major German offensive during the summer, its highest pri-

Table 4. The Composition of the Red Army's Field (Operating) Forces and Supreme High Command Reserve on 1 May 1942

RIFLE, AIRBORNE AND CAVALRY FORCES—6 rifle corps, 343 rifle divisions, 113 rifle brigades, 9 ski brigades, 5 airborne brigades, 11 naval infantry brigades, 6 separate rifle regiments, 6 separate naval infantry regiments, 17 fortified regions, 1 airborne corps, 5 airborne brigades, 10 cavalry corps, 36 cavalry divisions, 2 separate cavalry regiments, 8 separate rifle battalions, 107 separate ski battalions, 15 separate naval infantry battalions, and 1 separate machine gun battalion.

TANK AND MECHANIZED FORCES—11 tank corps, 88 tank brigades, 8 motorized rifle brigades, 1 motorized rifle regiment, 3 motorcycle regiments, 49 separate tank battalions, 3 separate motorcycle battalions, 1 separate armored car battalion, 33 aero-sleigh [*aerosanyi*] battalions, and 28 separate armored train battalions.

RVGK (*STAVKA* RESERVE), ARMY, AND CORPS ARTILLERY—2 corps PVO regions, 2 PVO divisions, 11 PVO division regions, 1 artillery brigade, 2 PVO artillery brigades, 166 artillery regiments, 96 antitank artillery regiments, 24 mortar regiments, 43 guards-mortar (*Katiusha* [multiple rocket launcher]) regiments, 57 antiaircraft artillery regiments, 7 antiaircraft machine gun regiments, 37 separate artillery battalions, 9 separate antitank artillery battalions, 12 separate mortar battalions, 44 separate guards-mortar battalions, 275 separate antiaircraft artillery battalions, and four separate antiaircraft machine gun battalions.

ENGINEER FORCES—1 engineer brigade, 30 sapper brigades, 1 engineer regiment, 143 separate engineer battalions, 93 separate sapper battalions, and 63 separate pontoon-bridge battalions.

AIR FORCES—2 aviation corps, 16 aviation groups, 22 aviation divisions, 8 aviation brigades, 360 aviation regiments designated either as fighter, bomber, or assault (ground support), and 22 separate aviation squadrons.

Sources: N. I. Nikoforov, ed., *Velikaia Otechestvennaia voina 1941–1945 gg.: Deistvuiushchaia armiia* [The Great Patriotic War 1941–1945: The Operating Army](Moscow: Animi Fortitudo, Kuchkovo pole, 2005), 544–545 and *Boevoi sostav Sovetskoi armii, Chast' 2 (ianvar'–dekabr' 1942 goda)* [Combat composition of the Soviet Army, Part 2 (January–December 1942)] (Moscow: Voenizdat, 1966), 60–73. Prepared by the Military-Scientific Directorate of the General Staff.

ority was to mobilize fresh forces to build up reserves. However, the buildup did not begin in earnest until May 1942.

RED ARMY LEADERSHIP

Over the course of four years of conflict, Hitler and Stalin gradually traded roles with regard to their military commanders. The German dictator, as described in Chapter 1, initially allowed his generals to use their professional judgment but gradually tightened control to the point where, by 1944–1945, each field commander was supposed to execute blindly any Führer order. By contrast, Stalin initially had zero trust and confidence in subordinates but over time came to recognize they could be allowed considerable flexibility and initiative in decision-making. The year 1942 was a crossroads in this respect. At the start of the summer campaign, Hitler was seeking total control but had not yet dismissed senior advisers and nominally independent commanders. For his part Stalin began the campaign by ignoring advice from men such as Shaposhnikov and

Table 5. Red Army Force Dispositions, 1 May 1942 (*fronts*, armies, and operational groups deployed from north to south)

KARELIAN FRONT (Lieutenant General V. A. Frolov)
    14th Army (Major General V. I. Shcherbakov)
    19th Army (Major General I. S. Morozov)
    26th Army (Major General N. N. Nikishin)
    32nd Army (Major General S. G. Trofimenko)

7TH SEPARATE ARMY (Lieutenant General F. D. Gorelenko)

LENINGRAD FRONT (Lieutenant General M. S. Khozin)
    Leningrad Group of Forces
        23rd Army (Major General A. I. Cherepanov)
        Coastal Operational Group
        42nd Army (Major General I. F. Nikolaev)
        55th Army (Major General of Artillery V. P. Sviridov)
        Neva Operational Group

    Volkhov Group of Forces
        8th Army (Major General F. I. Starikov)
        54th Army (Major General A. V. Sukhomlin)
        4th Army (Major General P. I. Liapin)
        59th Army (Major General I. T. Korovnikov)
        2nd Shock Army (Lieutenant General A. A. Vlasov)
        52nd Army (Lieutenant General V. F. Iakovlev)

NORTHWESTERN FRONT (Colonel General P. A. Kurochkin)
    11th Army (Lieutenant General V. I. Morozov)
    34th Army (Major General N. E. Berzarin)
    1st Shock Army (Lieutenant General V. I. Kuznetsov)
    53rd Army (Major General A. S. Ksenofontov)

KALININ FRONT (Colonel General I. S. Konev)
    3rd Shock Army (Lieutenant General M. A. Purkaev)
    4th Shock Army (Major General V. V. Kurasov)
    22nd Army (Major General V. A. Iushkevich)
    30th Army (Lieutenant General D. D. Leliushenko)
    39th Army (Lieutenant General I. I. Maslennikov)
    29th Army (Major General V. I. Shvetsov)
    31st Army (Major General V. S. Polenov)

WESTERN FRONT (Army General G. K. Zhukov)
    20th Army (Lieutenant General M. A. Reiter)
    5th Army (Major General I. I. Fediuninsky)
    33rd Army (Army General K. A. Meretskov)
    43rd Army (Major General K. D. Golubev)
    49th Army (Lieutenant General I. G. Zakharkin)
    50th Army (Lieutenant General I. V. Boldin)
    10th Army (Major General V. S. Popov)
    16th Army (Lieutenant General K. K. Rokossovsky)
    1st Sapper Army (Colonel V. V. Kosarev, Major General N. P. Baranov, 26 May–August 1942)

BRIANSK FRONT (Lieutenant General F. I. Golikov)
    61st Army (Lieutenant General M. M. Popov)
    3rd Army (Major General F. F. Zhmachenko)
    13th Army (Major General N. P. Pukhov)
    48th Army (Major General G. A. Khaliuzin)
    40th Army (Lieutenant General of Artillery M. A. Parsegov)
    6th Sapper Army (Colonel M. I. Chernykh, Colonel A. G. Andreev 17 May–14 June 1942)

(*continued*)

Table 5. Continued

SOUTHWESTERN FRONT (Marshal of the Soviet Union S. K. Timoshenko)
 21st Army (Major General V. N. Gordov)
 28th Army (Lieutenant General D. I. Riabyshev)
 38th Army (Major General of Artillery K. S. Moskalenko)
 6th Army (Lieutenant General A. M. Gorodniansky)
 7th Sapper Army (Colonel I. E. Pruss)

SOUTHERN FRONT (Lieutenant General R. Ia. Malinovsky)
 57th Army (Lieutenant General K. P. Podlas)
 9th Army (Major General F. M. Kharitonov)
 37th Army (Lieutenant General A. I. Lopatin)
 12th Army (Major General A. A. Grechko)
 18th Army (Major General F. V. Kamkov)
 56th Army (Major General V. V. Tsyganov)
 8th Sapper Army (Lieutenant General of Engineer Forces A. S. Gundorov)

CRIMEAN FRONT (Lieutenant General D. T. Kozlov)
 47th Army (Major General K. S. Kolganov)
 51st Army (Lieutenant General V. N. L'vov)
 44th Army (Lieutenant General S. I. Cherniak)

COASTAL ARMY (SEVASTOPOL') (Major General I. E. Petrov) (subordinate to the High Command of the North Caucasus Direction)

MOSCOW DEFENSE ZONE (Lieutenant General of NKVD Forces P. A. Artem'ev)
 3rd Sapper Army (Colonel I. N. Bryznov)

1ST *STAVKA* SHOCK AVIATION GROUP

2ND *STAVKA* SHOCK AVIATION GROUP

3RD *STAVKA* SHOCK AVIATION GROUP

4TH *STAVKA* SHOCK AVIATION GROUP

5TH *STAVKA* SHOCK AVIATION GROUP

6TH *STAVKA* SHOCK AVIATION GROUP

7TH *STAVKA* SHOCK AVIATION GROUP

8TH *STAVKA* SHOCK AVIATION GROUP

15TH *STAVKA* SHOCK AVIATION GROUP

16TH *STAVKA* SHOCK AVIATION GROUP

Sources: Boevoi sostav Sovetskoi armii, Chast' 2 (ianvar'–dekabr' 1942 goda) [Combat composition of the Soviet Army, Part 2 (January–December 1942)] (Moscow: Voenizdat, 1966), 60–73; *Velikaia Otechestvennaia. Komandarmy. Voennyi bibliographicheskii slovar'* [The Great Patriotic [War]. Army commanders. Military-bibliographical dictionary](Moscow: Institute of Military History, Russian Federation's Ministry of Defense, OOO "Kuchkovo pole," 2005); and David M. Glantz, *Red Army Command Cadre (1941–1945), Volume 1: Direction, Front, Army, Military District, Defense Zone, and Mobile Corps Commanders* (Carlisle, PA: Self-published, 2002).

Vasilevsky. Stalin, after seeing the results of his own self-confident, pugnacious attitude, by fall 1942 came to place greater faith in Soviet military leaders. In the disastrous battles of May through August, the Red Army paid the bitter cost necessary to gain Stalin's trust and change of heart.

Most senior-level generals who served Stalin have already appeared in this narrative—the efficient and intellectual Vasilevsky as Chief of Staff; the determined and belligerent troubleshooter Zhukov; the superannuated, politically motivated field commander Timoshenko. A combination of courage, competence, and political agility allowed Khrushchev, the future General Secretary of the Party, to survive the summer defeats and continue as the key political officer at Stalingrad. Other Soviet generals came and went, many of them relieved of command after a few weeks of desperate efforts to stem the German advance. But some rode out the storm to emerge more accomplished in fall 1942, and still others saw their star rise amid the summer's carnage.

In addition to Timoshenko, commander of the Southwestern Front, the generals most responsible for contending with advancing *Wehrmacht* forces during the spring and summer 1942 were Lieutenant Generals F. I. Golikov, R. Ia. Malinovsky, and D. T. Kozlov, the commanders of the Briansk, Southern, and Crimean Fronts, respectively. Filipp Ivanovich Golikov, 42 when he took command of the Briansk Front in April 1942, was a veteran of the Russian Civil War who served as a political officer and commissar at the division and military district levels during the 1920s before commanding a rifle regiment and division and mechanized brigade in the first half of the 1930s. Escaping the dragnets of the Great Purge of the military, the politically reliable Golikov commanded 45th Mechanized Corps in 1937, the Kiev Special Military District's Vinnitsa Army Group during the Czech crisis in 1938, and the Ukrainian Front's 6th Army during the Polish campaign in 1939. Elevated to lieutenant general in the famous Class of 4 June 1940, when stars fell on many survivors of the purges, Golikov became deputy chief of the Red Army General Staff and chief of the General Staff's Intelligence Directorate, posts he was occupying when war began in June 1941. Although it did no harm to his career, in April and May 1941 Golikov had warned Stalin of an impending German invasion—a warning that went unheeded.[43]

After the Barbarossa invasion began, Stalin dispatched Golikov as his personal emissary to Great Britain and the United States, where the general laid the delicate groundwork for future cooperation between the Soviet Union and its Western Allies. Returning from this successful venture in October, Golikov was assigned command of 10th Reserve Army, which he led with distinction in its defeat of Guderian's Second Panzer Army in the Tula region during the Red Army's Moscow counteroffensive. In reward for his contributions to the victory at Moscow, Golikov received command of 4th Shock Army, which he led during its dramatic advance toward Smolensk from February to April 1942. Stalin, hoping Golikov could replicate in summer 1942 his performance at Moscow in late 1941, assigned him command of Briansk Front in April 1942.[44]

Two years younger than Golikov, Rodion Iakovlevich Malinovsky rose to *front* commander in December 1941 when Stalin assigned the 43-year-old general to command the Red Army's Southern Front. Unlike Golikov, Malinovsky began his military career in 1914 at the outset of World War I, serving first as commander of a machine gun crew in the Russian Expeditionary Corps in France,

Josef Vissarionovich Stalin, Peoples' Commissar of Defense of the USSR and Supreme High Commander of the Armed Forces of the USSR

Army General Georgii Konstantinovich Zhukov, deputy Supreme High Commander of the Armed Forces of the USSR and commander of the Western Front

Marshal of the Soviet Union Boris Mikhailovich Shaposhnikov, chief of the Red Army General Staff

Colonel General Aleksandr Mikhailovich Vasilevsky, deputy chief of the Red Army General Staff

then later in a foreign regiment in the French Army's 1st Moroccan Division. Returning to Russia by way of the Far East in 1919, Malinovsky fought in the Russian Civil War and, after that fratricidal struggle ended, led at the platoon and battalion levels before commanding 3rd Cavalry Corps in the mid-1930s. Traveling abroad to serve as a volunteer on behalf of the Republicans in the Spanish Civil War, he received the Orders of Lenin and Red Banner. After Malinovsky served a brief stint teaching at the Frunze Academy, Stalin promoted him to major general in June 1940 and assigned him command of the Kiev Special Military District's 48th Rifle Corps in March 1941, a post he was occupying when Operation Barbarossa began. Because his corps fared well during the difficult fighting in Ukraine, Malinovsky's star rose precipitously thereafter, as he commanded 6th Army from August to December 1941 and Southern Front from December 1941 through the beginning of Operation Blau. During this period, his *front* successfully exploited its victory over Kleist's First Panzer Army at Rostov in November and then pressed German forces westward to the Mius River and Donbas region and across the Northern Donets River south of Khar'kov.[45]

The youngest of these three *front* commanders, Dmitri Timofeevich Kozlov was only 44 when he became commander of Trans-Caucasus Front in August 1941. A noncommissioned officer during World War I and the Civil War, Kozlov had commanded battalions and regiments, fought against Basmachi insurgents in Central Asia, and graduated from the *Vystrel'* Officers Improvement Course and Frunze Academy in the 1920s. After commanding a rifle regiment and 44th Rifle Division and teaching at the Frunze Academy in the 1930s, Kozlov ultimately led a rifle corps during the Soviet-Finnish War in 1939–1940. He was promoted to lieutenant general, also as part of the Class of 1940. Kozlov's future career pattern was firmly established in 1941 when he commanded the Trans-Caucasus Military District from January through June and, after Barbarossa began, Trans-Caucasus Front in August 1941 and its successor Crimean Front in January 1942. As a *front* commander, Kozlov secured the Soviet Union's southern borders with Turkey and Iran throughout the tense first six months of war and planned and skillfully conducted the Kerch-Feodosiia offensive, a large-scale amphibious operation that expelled German Eleventh Army's forces from the Kerch' Peninsula in eastern Crimea in December 1942.[46]

While Stalin held his *front* commanders personally responsible for stemming the *Wehrmacht* tide during the anticipated German offensive in summer 1942, the 15 generals who commanded the armies assigned to these *fronts* would feel the full fury of the German blow. These included Major General N. P. Pukhov and Lieutenant General of Artillery M. A. Parsegov, commanders of Briansk Front's 13th and 40th Armies; Major General V. N. Gordov, Major General of Artillery K. S. Moskalenko, and Lieutenant Generals D. I. Riabyshev and A. M. Gorodniansky, commanders of Southwestern Front's 21st, 38th, 28th, and 6th Armies; Lieutenant Generals K. P. Podlas and A. I. Lopatin and Major Generals F. M. Kharitonov, A. A. Grechko, F. V. Kamkov, and V. V. Tsyganov, commanders of Southern Front's 57th, 37th, 9th, 12th, 18th, and 56th Armies; and Major General K. S. Kolganov and Lieutenant Generals V. N. L'vov and S. I. Cherniak, commanders of Crimean Front's 47th, 51st, and 44th Armies.

All these generals except Grechko and Podlas, who were promoted in August and November 1941, respectively, were also members of the Class of 1940.[47] Although all had performed credibly as commanders prior to spring 1942, only six would command armies in the wake of Operation Blau. The other nine generals would experience varying degrees of misfortune during the spring and summer campaigns of 1942, including three who would perish in combat before Blau began, four whose poor performance during the operation prompted Stalin to relegate them to corps and division command throughout the remainder of the war, and two whom Stalin deemed unfit for subsequent field command.

Generals Pukhov and Parsegov, commanders of Briansk Front's 13th and 40th Armies, had little or no command experience before the war. Nikolai Pavlovich Pukhov, who was born in 1895, fought in World War I and the Civil War and joined the Red Army in 1918. A graduate of the *Vystrel'* Officers Improvement Course in 1926 and the Military Academy of Motorization and Mechanization in 1935, Pukhov commanded a rifle regiment in the 1920s and taught at *Vystrel'* in the 1920s. Transferring to the Red Army's fledgling mechanized forces, he became assistant chief of the Red Army's Auto-Armored Department in 1932, taught at the Red Army's Motorization and Mechanization Academy (RKKA Academy) in 1935, served as chief of the Khar'kov Armored School in 1938, and taught and was a department chief at the Red Army's Military-Management and Quartermaster Academies in the 1930s. Sent from the classroom to command 38th Army's 304th Rifle Division on 28 August 1941, the 46-year-old general was appointed to command Briansk Front's 13th Army in January 1942.[48]

Mikhail Artem'evich Parsegov, who was born 1899 and served as a common artilleryman in World War I and the Civil War, commanded an artillery battery, battalion, regiment, and division during the interwar years. He received his military education at the Tashkent Artillery School in 1921–1922, at the Frunze Academy in 1936, and at the Voroshilov Academy in 1948. Assigned chief of artillery in the Leningrad Military District in 1939 and in 7th Army during the Finnish War, Parsegov became a Hero of the Soviet Union and received the prestigious Order of Lenin for his role in planning and conducting the penetration of the Finns' formidable Mannerheim defensive line. As Southwestern Front's chief of artillery during Operation Barbarossa, Parsegov survived the harrowing border battles and ensuing struggles at Kiev and in the Donbas region. He then burnished his reputation as chief of the *front's* artillery during its victorious counteroffensive in the Elets region in December 1941 and as chief of the Southwestern Main Direction's artillery during the Barvenkovo-Lozovaia offensive in January 1942, when the Southwestern and Southern Fronts' armies seized the Barvenkovo bridgehead across the Northern Donets River south of Khar'kov.

As a reward for his accomplishments, the *Stavka* assigned 42-year-old Parsegov as commander of Briansk Front's 40th Army in March 1942.[49]

The four generals who commanded Southwestern Front's armies in spring 1942 had considerably more command experience than their counterparts in Briansk Front. Vasilii Nikolaevich Gordov, 44 when he was appointed to command 21st Army in October 1941, was also a veteran of World War I and the Civil War and had been an adviser with the Mongolian Peoples Army and assistant commander of a rifle regiment in the 1920s. After graduating from the Frunze Academy in 1932, Gordov served, in succession, as chief of staff of the Red Army's Training Directorate, the Moscow Infantry School, a rifle division (which he briefly commanded), and the Kalinin and Volga Military Districts. When the *Stavka* formed the new Central Front weeks after the German invasion began, it appointed Gordov as chief of staff of the *front's* 21st Army in July and as the army's commander in early August, only to replace him as commander when it transferred 21st Army to Briansk Front in late August. This enabled Gordov to avoid possible death or capture when 21st Army was encircled and largely destroyed during the battle for Kiev in September 1941. In the wake of this defeat, the *Stavka* appointed Gordov to command Southwestern Front's new 21st Army in October 1941, a post he retained throughout the 1941–1942 winter campaign.[50]

Dmitrii Ivanovich Riabyshev, 48 years old when he took command of the Briansk Front's 28th Army in February 1942, was an even more experienced commander than Gordov. Also a veteran of World War I and the Civil War, Riabyshev had served in the famed 1st Cavalry Army in the Civil War and commanded cavalry brigades in the North Caucasus and Turkestan Military Districts in the 1920s. He later graduated from the Frunze Academy and led 13th Don Cossack Cavalry Division and the equally famous 1st Cavalry Corps in the 1930s. Assigned to command the Kiev Special Military District's 8th Mechanized Corps in July 1940, in the wake of the Barbarossa invasion, his corps figured prominently in the Southwestern Front's counterstroke in the Brody and Dubno regions, arguably the largest tank battle in the war. In mid-July 1941, the *Stavka* reorganized the remnants of his mechanized corps, which had been decimated in the border battles, into a new 38th Army under Riabyshev's command and, in August, elevated him to command Southern Front. Thereafter, however, his fortune fluctuated wildly. When German Army Group South forced Riabyshev's *front* to abandon the "Great Bend" of the Don River in fall 1941, Stalin removed him from command, instead assigning him as commander of 57th Army in the *Stavka* Reserve. Because Riabyshev led this army effectively during the Red Army's 1941–1942 winter offensive, after he was hospitalized for an illness in February 1942 the *Stavka* appointed him to command 28th Army in March 1942.[51]

Kirill Semenovich Moskalenko was an experienced 39-year-old general when the *Stavka* assigned him commander of 38th Army in March 1942. He survived disaster after disaster to become one of the Red Army's most famous wartime army commanders. A cavalryman and artilleryman by trade, Moskalenko had joined the Red Army in 1920 and fought as an enlisted man during the Civil War. After attending the Artillery School, Moskalenko commanded at the battery and battalion levels in 1st Cavalry Army's 6th Chongar Cavalry Division in the 1920s. During the ensuing decade, he commanded 1st Special Cavalry Division in the Far East, an artillery regiment in a cavalry division, and a rifle regiment in the Kiev Special Military District's 2nd Mechanized Corps, one of the first four such corps formed in the Red Army. Moskalenko graduated from the prestigious Dzerzhinsky Political-Military Academy in June 1939 and thereafter served as chief of artillery in the famed 51st Perekop Rifle Division during the Finnish War in 1939–1940, chief of 35th Rifle Corps' artillery during the invasion of Romanian Bessarabia in spring 1940, and chief of artillery of Odessa Military District's 2nd Mechanized Corps in 1940 and 1941.

Because of Moskalenko's extensive experience in mechanized forces and artillery, in May 1941 the NKO assigned him to command the Kiev Special Military District's 1st Motorized Antitank Artillery Brigade, one of ten such brigades it formed to provide antitank support to its new mechanized corps. Although surprised by the German Barbarossa invasion and decimated in the ensuing fighting, Moskalenko's antitank brigade helped slow the German advance, reportedly destroying many German tanks during the first two months of war. Thereafter, Moskalenko commanded 5th Army's 15th Rifle Corps in September 1941 and, after surviving the Kiev encirclement and the destruction of his corps, led 13th Army's Cavalry-Mechanized Group in its successful counterstroke at Elets in December 1941. During the Red Army's ensuing winter 1941–1942 counteroffensive, Moskalenko commanded Southwestern Front's 6th Army during the partially successful Barvenkovo-Lozovaia offensive and 6th Cavalry Corps in February 1942 before being appointed to command 38th Army in March 1942.[52]

The last general in this quartet of Southwestern Front army commanders was Avksentii Mikhailovich Gorodniansky, who had been assigned command of the *front's* 6th Army in December 1941 at age 42. Gorodniansky fought as an infantry officer in World War I and the Civil War and graduated from Orel Infantry School in 1919 and the *Vystrel'* Officers Improvement Course in 1924. Thereafter, Gorodniansky commanded companies, battalions, and regiments in the 1920s and 1930s before being assigned commander of the 129th Rifle Division in Far Eastern Front's 2nd Red Banner Army in October 1940. After Gorodniansky's 129th Division was transferred west in fall 1941, it fought in Western Front's often chaotic battles around Vitebsk and Smolensk under 19th and 16th Army control and barely managed to escape encirclement and destruction at Smolensk. Elevated to command Briansk Front's 13th Army in late August, Gorodniansky led this army during its fierce but futile struggle against Guderian's Second Panzer Group (later Army) in August and September 1941. After escaping encirclement at the hands of Guderian's panzers at Briansk in October, he helped orchestrate Southwestern Front's successful counterstroke at Elets in December 1941. Assigned command of 6th Army in December, Gorodniansky led his army with distinction during Southwestern Front's Barvenkovo-Lozovaia offensive in January-February 1942, which left his army, together with three other armies from Southern Front, lodged in the Barvenkovo bridgehead, a large salient protruding westward across the Northern Donets River into German defensive lines south of Khar'kov in May 1942.[53]

The six generals who commanded Southern Front's armies on 1 May 1942 were, with the notable exception of General Tsyganov, just as experienced as their counterparts in Southwestern Front. Arguably the most experienced of these senior officers was Kuz'ma Petrovich Podlas, who at age 48 had been assigned command of 57th Army in February 1942. An enlisted man in World War I and junior officer in the Civil War, Podlas graduated from *Vystrel'* in 1925 and the Frunze Academy in 1930 and commanded a rifle regiment, division, and corps in the 1920s and 1930s. In 1938 he led Far Eastern Front's 1st Separate Red Banner Army in the battle against Japanese forces at Lake Khasan. Brought west as deputy commander of the Kiev Special Military District in late 1938, Podlas was caught up in Stalin's Great Purge and arrested by the *Narodnyi Kommissariat Vnutrennikh Del* (People's Commissariat of Internal Affairs—NKVD, or "secret police") in 1939. More fortunate than most others in a similar situation, Podlas was released in August 1940 and appointed inspector of infantry in the Kiev Special Military District. Two months into Operation Barbarossa, after German Army Group Center's advance faltered in the Smolensk region, prompting Hitler to order Guderian to wheel his Second Panzer Group southward toward Kiev, Stalin appointed Podlas to command Southwestern Front's new 40th Army, a scratch army formed to block Guderian's southward advance. Although he failed to fulfill this impossible task, Podlas remained in command of 40th Army throughout the remainder of the Barbarossa campaign, when his army helped halt the German offensive in the Kursk region in late 1941. As a reward, Podlas was appointed to command 57th Army in February 1942.[54]

Although far less experienced than Podlas, 43-year-old Fedor Mikhailovich Kharitonov had commanded 9th Army since September 1941. After joining the Red Army in 1919 and fighting as an enlisted man during the Civil War, Kharitonov graduated from *Vystrel'* in 1931 and served as chief of staff of 57th Rifle Corps' 17th Rifle Division and 57th Rifle Corps. He was later chief of combat training in the Moscow Military District and commanded a rifle regiment in 1931 and 2nd Airborne Corps on the eve of war. During the first few months of Operation Barbarossa, Kharitonov served as first deputy chief of staff and then chief of staff of the Southern Front and was assigned command of the *front*'s 9th Army in September. Despite his lack of command experience, his army escaped destruction at the hands of German First Panzer Army during the Melitopol' encirclement in October 1941 and, thereafter, played an instrumental role during Southern Front's victory at Rostov in November and December 1941 and during the Lozovaia-Barvenkovo offensive in January and February 1942, which propelled his army into the Barvenkovo bridgehead.[55]

Anton Ivanovich Lopatin, a former cavalryman who had been assigned command of 37th Army in October 1941 at age 45, was a veteran of World War I who had joined the Red Army in 1918. After fighting as a squadron commander in 1st Cavalry Army during the Civil War, Lopatin graduated from officers' courses at the Leningrad Cavalry School in 1925 and 1929 and rose to command a cavalry regimental school in the late 1920s, a cavalry regiment in November 1931, and the elite 6th Cavalry Division in 1937. Rising quickly in the wake of Stalin's military purges, Lopatin taught a cavalry tactics course in 1938, became the Trans-Baikal Front's inspector of cavalry in July 1939, deputy commander of Far Eastern Front's 15th Army in June 1940, and commander of the Kiev Special Military District's 31st Rifle Corps in November 1940, a post he was occupying when war began. After escaping destruction during the border battles because it was situated in the 5th Army's second echelon, Lopatin's corps helped slow Army Group South's advance in summer 1941 only to be encircled and destroyed at Kiev in September. More fortunate than his troops, Lopatin escaped encirclement and was appointed commander of 37th Army, which was then forming in the Southern Front's reserve, in October 1941. Lopatin's army spearheaded Southern Front's successful counteroffensive against Kleist's First Panzer Army in November and December 1941, which recaptured Rostov and forced Kleist to retreat to the Mius River line. Awarded the Order of Lenin for his performance at Rostov, Lopatin then led his army during its advance into the eastern Donbas region during the Red Army's winter offensive of 1941–1942.[56]

The youngest of Southwestern Front's army commanders in spring 1942 was Andrei Antonovich Grechko, who was 38 years old when he was appointed to command 12th Army in April 1942. Grechko had enlisted in the Red Army in 1919, served in 1st Cavalry Army's 11th Cavalry Division during the Civil War, and, after becoming an officer, had completed his military education at the Cavalry School in 1926, the Frunze Academy in 1936, and the General Staff Academy in 1941. Grechko commanded a cavalry platoon and squadron in the 1920s and the Moscow Military District's 1st Separate Cavalry Brigade in the 1930s before being appointed chief of staff of the Belorussian Special Military District's Separate Cavalry Division during the invasion of eastern Poland in 1939. A staff officer on the General Staff when Operation Barbarossa began, Grechko was assigned field command of Southern Front's 34th Cavalry Division in late July 1941 after the Red Army's senior officer cadre was decimated during the first few months of war. Grechko commanded the same cavalry division, often under control of General F. V. Kamkov's famous 5th Cavalry Corps, through March 1942 and, while doing so, participated in the defenses of Kremenchug in September 1941, Khar'kov in October 1941, and the northern Donbas region throughout fall 1941. Because he performed reliably during offensive operations in winter 1941–1942, Southern Front assigned Grechko command of a special operational group in March 1942 and 12th Army in April.[57]

The commander of Southern Front's 18th Army in spring 1942 was Fedor Vasil'evich Kamkov, who had been appointed to command the army in November 1941 at age 43 after performing brilliantly as commander of 5th Cavalry Corps during operations the previous summer and fall. A cavalryman through and through, Kamkov had enlisted in the tsar's army in World War I, joined the Red Army in 1918, and served as deputy commander of a cavalry regiment during the Civil War. After graduating from courses at the Leningrad Cavalry School in 1920 and 1924, Kamkov commanded 58th Cavalry Regiment in the 1920s, 6th Cavalry Division's 34th Cavalry Regiment in 1931, and the prestigious 3rd Cavalry Corps' 7th Cavalry Division in 1937. Transferring to the Red Army's new mechanized arm, Kamkov commanded 6th Mechanized Corps' 29th Motorized Division in June 1940, the Kiev Special Military District's 2nd Cavalry Corps in July 1940, and 5th Cavalry Corps from March 1941 through the outbreak of war in June 1941. When Barbarossa began, Kamkov's cavalry corps fought under 6th Army's control during the chaotic border battles and under 26th Army's control during the intense fighting south of Kiev, when it spearheaded counterstrokes that seriously disrupted German Army Group South's advance on Kiev. During and after the disastrous Kiev encirclement in September 1941, Kamkov's corps failed to contain Kleist's First Panzer Group in its bridgehead at Kremenchug in September. Thereafter, however, it performed gallantly in the defense of Khar'kov in October and played a major role in halting Army Group South's advance in October, for which Kamkov was awarded the Order of Lenin. In recognition of his well-deserved reputation as an audacious fighter, Kamkov became commander of Southern Front's 18th Army in November 1941 and led it in the successful Donbas and Rostov operations and the *front*'s ensuing winter 1941–1942 counteroffensive.[58]

The least experienced of Southern Front's army commanders in May 1942 was Viktor Viktorovich Tsyganov, who, despite being a cavalryman early in his career and a logistician thereafter, nevertheless rose to command the *front*'s 56th Army in November 1941 at age 45. A lieutenant of cavalry during World War I, Tsyganov had joined the Red Army in 1918 and ended his Civil War service as chief of staff of a shock (cavalry) brigade in Belorussia. During the interwar years, Tsyganov was a staff officer at the regimental, brigade, division, corps, and *front* levels in the Western and Belorussian Military Districts, punctuated by his graduation from the Frunze Academy in 1933 and teaching assignments at a variety of Red Army schools. After war broke out in June 1941, Tsyganov served as deputy chief of staff of the Southwestern Main Direction's Rear (Services) in August and September before commanding 38th Army during its unsuccessful defense of Khar'kov in late September and October 1941. However, after his army helped halt the German advance in November, in December the *Stavka* appointed Tsyganov to command Southern Front's 56th Army, which subsequently participated in the *front's* successful winter 1941–1942 offensives.[59]

With only one exception, the four generals who commanded Soviet armies in the Crimea on 1 May 1941 saw their military careers collapse even before Operation Blau began. In fairness to these officers, however, their failure as army commanders resulted as much from the interference of Stalin's notorious commissar henchman, Mekhlis, as it did from lack of command experience or poor performance as army commanders. The first of these ill-fated commanders was Konstantin Stepanovich Kolganov, who had been appointed to command the Crimean Front's 47th Army in February 1942 at age 46. A noncommissioned officer in World War I, Kolganov commanded a company and battalion during the Civil War. He rose through battalion and regimental commands to graduate from the Frunze Academy in 1933, command 75th Rifle Division in May 1938 and 17th Rifle Corps in January 1939, and become a department chief in the Red Army's Combat Training Directorate in 1940 and a section head in the General Staff's Intelligence Directorate in 1941. His association with General Golikov, the army's chief of intelligence, probably launched him on his subsequent rise to full army command. Months after Operation Barbarossa began, in October 1941 the *Stavka* appointed Kolganov deputy commander of Golikov's 10th Reserve Army. The army's subsequent victories during the Moscow counterstroke in December 1941 and the 1941–1942 winter offensive propelled Kolganov to command of 47th Army in February.[60]

Kolganov's colleague in Crimean Front, Vladimir Nikolaevich L'vov, who was appointed to command 51st Army in December 1941 at age 44, began his military career as a noncommissioned officer in the tsar's army during World War I before joining the Red Army in 1918. L'vov commanded a company and battalion during the Civil War, graduated from the RKKA Academy in 1924 and *Vystrel'* in 1931, and served as deputy commander of 32nd Rifle Division in 1924, an adviser to the Chinese Army in 1925, assistant commander of a rifle division in 1926, and commander of 3rd, 46th, and 37th Rifle Divisions in the 1930s. Thereafter, L'vov was chief of staff of the Trans-Caucasus Military District in 1937, an instructor at the Frunze Academy in 1930, deputy and assistant commander of the Baltic Special Military District from January to June 1940, and deputy commander of the Trans-Caucasus Military District from 19 July 1940 through the first two months of Operation Barbarossa. Shortly before German forces invaded the Crimea in September 1941, L'vov was assigned command of the Trans-Caucasus Military District's forces under Trans-Caucasus Front's control and led 51st Army in the Kerch-Feodosiia amphibious operation, which the same *front* conducted successfully in December 1941.[61]

The last of these generals, Stepan Ivanovich Cherniak, was appointed to command 44th Army in February 1942 at age 40. Already a lieutenant general and Hero of the Soviet Union in 1940, Cherniak had begun his military career during

World War I when he enlisted as a private in the tsar's army in January 1917. He then joined the Red Guards in November 1917, participated in the Russian Revolution, joined the Red Army in March 1918, and rose to command a platoon during the Civil War. Cherniak led a machine gun command in the Separate Bashkir Brigade's 2nd Rifle Regiment in 1921 and a platoon, company, and battalion in 37th Rifle Division's 111th Rifle Regiment late in the 1920s before graduating from *Vystrel'* in 1930. Thereafter, he commanded the Moscow Military District's 26th Separate Territorial Regiment in 1934 and the prestigious 1st Moscow Proletarian Rifle Division's 2nd Rifle Regiment in 1935 before volunteering in 1936 to become a military adviser to the Republican government during the Spanish Civil War. Returning to Moscow in late 1937, Cherniak was appointed assistant commander of 1st Moscow Motorized Rifle Division in September 1938 and led 136th Rifle Division in the Northwestern Front's 13th Army during the Finnish War in 1939–1940, when he earned the title Hero of the Soviet Union for his division's role in penetrating the Mannerheim defensive line. Cherniak was assigned command of the Trans-Caucasus Military District's 3rd Rifle Corps in April 1940 and, in the midst of that assignment, graduated from the Voroshilov General Staff Academy in 1941.

Cherniak resumed command of 3rd Rifle Corps shortly after Operation Barbarossa began, and when his corps was reorganized into a 46th Army in July 1941, the *Stavka* appointed him to command the new army. After Cherniak commanded this organization for five months, in December 1941 General Kozlov, commander of Trans-Caucasus Front, dispatched him to Sevastopol' to assume command of Separate Coastal Army, then under siege by Germany's Eleventh Army. However, when Admiral Oktiabr'sky, commander of the Sevastopol' Defensive Region, objected to this change in command, the *Stavka* relented, first assigning Cherniak deputy commander and then, on 8 February 1942, appointing him to command Crimean Front's 44th Army.[62]

Clearly more fortunate than his colleagues, Major General Ivan Efimovich Petrov, who was appointed command of Separate Coastal Army in October 1941 at age 45, somehow managed to escape the misfortunes experienced by the other army commanders in the Crimea—but only barely. A noncommissioned officer during World War I and a Red Army man since 1918, Petrov fought in the Civil War and commanded a cavalry squadron and regiment, a separate rifle brigade, and 1st Turkestan Mountain Rifle Division in the Central Asian Military District in the 1920s and 1930s, when his troops helped suppress the Basmachi insurgency. Petrov was educated at courses for the improvement of officers in 1926 and 1931. Promoted to major general in June 1940, Petrov had commanded the Central Asian Military District's 194th Rifle Division before being assigned command of 27th Mechanized Corps in the same military district in March 1941. After the *Stavka* moved his mechanized corps westward to the Voronezh and Smolensk regions in July 1941 and converted it into the separate 104th and 105th

Tank and 106th Motorized Divisions, it transferred Petrov to the Odessa region, where he commanded a separate cavalry division and the famous 25th Chapaev Rifle Division.

When advancing German and Romanian forces encircled and besieged Odessa in fall 1941, on 5 October 1941 the *Stavka* appointed Petrov to command Separate Coastal Army, with orders to defend the city at all cost. Skillfully orchestrating the city's defense, Petrov at one point even organized a counterstroke against besieging Romanian forces that enlarged the city's defensive perimeter. When the *Stavka* evacuated his army to the Crimea relatively intact in late October, Petrov organized the defenses of Sevastopol' in time to defeat attempts by Manstein's Eleventh Army to capture it by storm in November and December 1941. In spring 1942, like a thorn in their flesh, Petrov's army still held the Germans at bay. By this time, unlike many of his counterparts, Petrov had earned a well-deserved reputation as a superb organizer possessed with an iron will.[63]

If the *Wehrmacht's* prospects for success in the spring and summer of 1942 depended largely on the performance of its panzer corps and panzer and motorized divisions and the men who commanded them, the same could be said of the Red Army. With their gruesome battlefield education of 1941 behind them, Stalin, the members of his *Stavka*, and the generals who commanded the Red Army's *fronts* clearly understood that victory over the more experienced *Wehrmacht* in spring 1942, and if and when the Germans launched their anticipated summer offensive, would be largely determined by the combat effectiveness of the Red Army's fledgling armored forces. This meant, in particular, the combat performance of its three tank armies and 16 tank and mechanized corps, which would operate in southern Russia throughout the spring, summer, and fall of 1942. By extension, success depended on the leadership skills and tactical acumen of the three generals who would command tank armies and the 29 generals and colonels who would command tank and mechanized corps (see Appendix 1 for more complete biographies of these generals). Unless otherwise indicated, all of the corps commanders were generals of tank forces:

> *1st Tank Corps*—Major General Mikhail Efimovich Katukov; Colonel (Major General, 3 May 1942) Vasilii Vasil'evich Butkov on 19 September 1942.
>
> *2nd Tank Corps*—Colonel Semen Petrovich Mal'tsev; Major General Ivan Gavrilovich Lazarev on 10 June 1942; Major General Aleksandr Il'ich Liziukov on 15 July 1942; Colonel (Major General, 21 July 1942) Andrei Grigor'evich Kravchenko on 23 July 1942; and Major General Abram Matveevich Khasin on 14 September 1942.
>
> *4th Tank Corps*—Major General Vasilii Aleksandrovich Mishulin; and Major General Andrei Grigor'evich Kravchenko on 18 September 1942.
>
> *7th Tank Corps*—Colonel (Major General, 21 July 1942) Pavel Alekseevich Rotmistrov.

11th Tank Corps—Major General Aleksei Fedorovich Popov; and Major General Ivan Gavrilovich Lazarev on 22 July 1942.

13th Tank Corps—Major General Petr Evdokimovich Shurov; and Colonel Trofim Ivanovich Tanaschishin on 17 July 1942.

14th Tank Corps (reorganized as 6th Mechanized Corps, 30 September 1942)—Colonel (Major General, 13 May 1942) Nikolai Nikolaevich Radkevich; and Major General Semen Il'ich Bogdanov on 26 September 1942.

16th Tank Corps—Major General Mikhail Ivanovich Pavelkin; and Major General of Technical Forces Aleksei Gavrilovich Maslov on 15 September 1942.

17th Tank Corps—Major General Nikolai Vladimirovich Feklenko; Colonel (Major General, 3 May 1942) Ivan Petrovich Korchagin on 2 July 1942; Colonel Boris Sergeevich Bakharov on 21 July 1942; and Colonel (Major General, 10 November 1942) Pavel Petrovich Poluboiarov on 7 August 1942.

18th Tank Corps—Colonel (Major General, 3 May 1942) Ivan Danilovich Cherniakhovsky; Major General Ivan Petrovich Korchagin on 26 July 1942; and Colonel (Major General, 14 October 1942) Boris Sergeevich Bakharov on 11 September 1942.

21st Tank Corps—Major General Grigorii Ivanovich Kuz'min.

22nd Tank Corps (reorganized as 5th Mechanized Corps, 2 November 1942)—Colonel (Major General, 13 May 1942) Aleksandr Aleksandrovich Shamshin; and Major General Mikhail Vasil'evich Volkov on 2 November 1942.

23rd Tank Corps—Major General Efim Grigor'evich Pushkin; Colonel (Major General, 21 July 1942) Abram Matveevich Khasin on 5 June 1942; Major General Aleksei Fedorovich Popov on 30 August 1942; and Lieutenant Colonel Vasilii Vasil'evich Koshelev on 16 October 1942.

24th Tank Corps—Major General Vasilii Mikhailovich Badanov.

25th Tank Corps—Major General Petr Petrovich Pavlov.

28th Tank Corps (reorganized as 4th Mechanized Corps, 10 October 1942)—Colonel (Major General, 4 August 1942) Geórgii Semenovich Rodin; and Major General Vasilii Timofeevich Vol'sky on 11 October 1942.

1st Tank Army—Major General of Artillery Kirill Semenovich Moskalenko.

4th Tank Army—Major General Vasilii Dmitrievich Kriuchenkin.

5th Tank Army—Major General Aleksandr Il'ich Liziukov.

Because virtually all the officers in this group were eight to ten years younger than their counterparts in the *Wehrmacht*, to a man the German officers were far more experienced, particularly in the conduct of high-intensity combat operations. In fact, this experience gap represented the most formidable challenge Stalin and his commanders in the field had to overcome if they hoped to emerge victorious during spring and summer 1942. While this gap existed at all levels of command, it was most pronounced at the operational level, that is, at the level of panzer corps and, in the case of the Red Army, at the level of tank army, which the *Stavka* formed during the summer to contest the panzer corps. For example, on average the seven German generals who commanded panzer corps on 1 May 1942 were 13 years older than their three Soviet counterparts who commanded tank armies in 1942 and, on an individual basis, were as much as 18 years older than their counterparts. A function of their age but also Hitler's aggression, five of the seven commanded motorized corps throughout Operation Barbarossa in 1941, three led motorized or army corps during the western campaign in 1940, one commanded a corps during the Polish campaign in 1939, and the remaining two commanded panzer or motorized infantry divisions in the western campaign and Operation Barbarossa. Therefore, all seven fought extensively in Poland, France, and the Soviet Union.

In contrast, the three Red Army generals who were appointed to command tank armies in 1942—Generals Liziukov, Moskalenko, and Kriuchenkin—led tank and mechanized brigades or cavalry divisions prior to Operation Barbarossa, and only two had combat experience: Kriuchenkin, who commanded a cavalry division in the invasion of eastern Poland in September 1939, and Moskalenko, who was chief of a rifle division's artillery during the Finnish War in 1939–1940. All three generals received their real baptism of fire during the Barbarossa campaign, when Liziukov commanded a tank and motorized rifle division; Moskalenko an antitank brigade and rifle corps; and Kriuchenkin a cavalry division and corps. After defending or counterattacking in the most harrowing of circumstances during Operation Barbarossa, all three served as corps commanders during the ensuing 1941–1942 winter campaign before being appointed to command armies or tank armies in spring and summer 1942.

A similar mosaic of command and combat experience existed at the tactical level, that is, at the level of German panzer and motorized divisions and, in the case of the Red Army, at the level of tank and mechanized corps. Also five to ten years older than their Soviet counterparts, the 30 German generals who commanded Army Group South's panzer and motorized divisions on 1 May 1942 were experienced combat leaders who commanded panzer or motorized divisions or regiments successfully during the Polish and western campaigns in 1939 and 1940 and panzer or motorized divisions throughout Operation Barbarossa and the winter campaign of 1941–1942. On the other hand (see Table 6), the 29 Soviet generals or colonels who commanded Red Army tank corps on 1 May 1942 and would lead tank corps, mechanized corps, or tank armies in the summer and fall of 1942 were far less experienced, and those who held combat commands fought in far less advantageous circumstances than their German counterparts.

In terms of combat experience, Mishulin and Pavelkin commanded armored brigades in the struggle against Japanese forces at Lake Khasan or Khalkhin Gol

Table 6. The Previous Command and Staff Experience of the Commanders of Red Army Tank and Mechanized Corps and Tank Armies during Operation Blau

---

1 (Maslov)—Commanded only a mechanized corps before Operation Barbarossa and a mechanized corps during Operation Barbarossa;

1 (Pavelkin)—Commanded only a mechanized brigade and mechanized corps before and during Operation Barbarossa;

1 (Lazarev)—Commanded a tank brigade and mechanized corps before Operation Barbarossa and a mechanized corps and army during Operation Barbarossa;

1 (Feklenko)—Commanded a motorized-armored brigade, tank division, and mechanized corps before Operation Barbarossa and a mechanized corps and army during Operation Barbarossa;

1 (Butkov)—Chief of staff of a mechanized brigade and tank division before Operation Barbarossa and deputy commander of a mechanized corps during Operation Barbarossa;

1 (Kravchenko)—Chief of staff of a motorized rifle and tank division before Operation Barbarossa and chief of staff of a mechanized corps and commander of a tank brigade during Operation Barbarossa;

10 (Katukov, Mishulin, Korchagin, Bakharov, Badanov, Popov, Cherniakhovsky, Pavlov, Rodin, and Bogdanov)—Commanded tank divisions, tank or mechanized brigades, regiments, or battalions before Operation Barbarossa and tank divisions and tank brigades during Operation Barbarossa;

1 (Kuz'min)—Commanded a tank division before Operation Barbarossa and a tank division and tank brigade during Operation Barbarossa;

1 (Pushkin)—Commanded a tank division before and during Operation Barbarossa;

6 (Shurov, Tanaschishin, Radkevich, Khasin, Rotmistrov, and Vol'sky)—Commanded only tank or mechanized brigades, regiments, or battalions before and during Operation Barbarossa;

1 (Shamshin)—Chief of staff of a tank brigade and tank division before and during Operation Barbarossa; and

4 (Poluboiarov, Koshelev, Mal'tsev, and Volkov)—No command experience before commanding tank corps in 1942.

---

in 1938 and 1939; Feklenko commanded 57th Special Rifle Corps in the same fighting; Katukov and Kriuchenkin led troops in the invasion of Poland in September 1939; and Kravchenko and Rotmistrov participated in the Finnish War, the former as staff officer and the latter in command of a tank battalion. After the *Wehrmacht* savaged the Red Army's mechanized force structure in summer 1941, forcing the NKO to disband its mechanized corps, reorganize its tank divisions, and form new tank brigades, Maslov, Feklenko, and Lazarev headed armies (albeit briefly); Pushkin, Popov, Cherniakhovsky, and Volkov commanded tank or rifle divisions; Katukov, Mishulin, Kravchenko, Korchagin, Bakharov, Badanov, Tanaschishin, Radkevich, Kuz'min, Shamshin, Khasin, and Rodin led tank or motorized rifle brigades during fall 1941 and winter 1941–1942; and Bogdanov commanded the Mozhaisk Fortified Region. The remaining ten officers served either as chiefs of staff at various levels or in other command or staff positions in noncombat units until taking command of tank or mechanized corps in 1942.

Retrospectively, if experience was at a premium among these 32 Soviet tank commanders, Red Army military operations during 1942 would indeed provide a harsh but fruitful education for those who survived. While Generals Kuz'min, Liziukov, and Shurov perished early in these operations (Kuz'min in the battle for Khar'kov and Liziukov and Shurov during the initial stages of Operation

Table 7. The Fate of the Commanders of Red Army Tank and Mechanized Corps and Tank Armies during and after Operation Blau

---

2 (Rotmistrov and Moskalenko)—Deputy Ministers of Defense of the Soviet Union;
1 (Cherniakhovsky)—*Front* commander;
6 (Katukov, Rotmistrov, Bogdanov, Vol'sky, Kravchenko, and Badanov)—Tank army commanders;
2 (Moskalenko and Kriuchenkin)—Army commanders;
14 (Butkov, Mishulin, Pavelkin, Maslov, Bakharov, Poluboiarov, Tanaschishin, Radkevich,
    Shamshin, Pushkin, Popov, Pavlov, Lazarev, and Rodin)—Tank corps commanders;
3 (Korchagin, Khasin, and Volkov)—Mechanized corps commanders;
3 (Rotmistrov, Bogdanov, and Poluboiarov)—Marshals of Tank Forces;
1 (Moskalenko)—Marshal of the Soviet Union;
1 (Cherniakhovsky)—Army General;
4 (Katukov, Kravchenko, Vol'sky, and Butkov)—Colonel Generals of Tank Forces;
12 (Mishulin, Pavelkin, Feklenko, Korchagin, Badanov, Tanaschishin, Radkevich, Pushkin,
    Lazarev, Rodin, Kriuchenkin, and Volkov)—Lieutenant Generals of Tank Forces;
3 (Feklenko, Mal'tsev, and Koshelev)—No further commands;
3 (Kuz'min, Shurov, and Liziukov)—Killed in action before or during Operation Blau;
4 (Pushkin, Tanaschishin, Badanov, and Cherniakhovsky)—Killed-in-action 1943–1945; and
1 (Pavlov)—Prisoner-of-war 1943–1945.

Blau), many of the others emerged from the campaign with burnished reputations, higher rank, and far more important commands or duties (see Table 7).

The most notable Red Army generals during Operation Blau and the battle for Stalingrad did not appear on the scene until late summer, in particular just prior to and during the struggle for Stalingrad and during the height of the *Wehrmacht*'s advance deep into the Caucasus. Among these generals, most of whom commanded the new *fronts* (army groups), armies, and mobile corps that the *Stavka* raised and fielded to halt the German advance, the most important were Generals Eremenko, Chuikov, and Shumilov, the men most responsible for the defense of Stalingrad; and Generals Zhukov, Vatutin, and Rokossovsky, who, with Eremenko and Vasilevsky, became the chief architects of the Red Army's dramatic counteroffensive and ultimate victory. When all was said and done, however, whether they survived or perished during the spring and summer campaign of 1942, it was the generals and colonels who commanded the Red Army's fronts, armies, and tank corps in southern Russia during this campaign who paved the way for ultimate Red Army victory.

THE SOVIET SOLDIER

As the training level of the average German soldier declined, that of his Soviet counterpart rose. Thousands of Soviet soldiers still died needlessly in summer 1942, but these casualties gave both the surviving troops and their commanders a growing measure of experience and competence.[64]

The communist regime had indoctrinated its youth for at least a decade

Marshal of the Soviet Union Semen Konstantinovich Timoshenko, commander of the Southwestern Main Direction and Southwestern Front

Lieutenant General Filipp Ivanovich Golikov, commander of the Briansk Front

Lieutenant of General Roman Iakolevich Malinovsky, commander of the Southern Front

Marshal of the Soviet Union Semen Mikhailovich Budenny, commander of the North Caucus Main Direction and North Caucasus Front

Lieutenant General Vasilii Nikolaevich Gordov, commander of the Stalingrad Front

Lieutenant General Nikolai Fedorovich Vatutin, commander of the Voronzh Front

Colonel General Andrei Ivanovich Eremenko, commander of the Southeastern and Stalingrad Fronts

Lieutenant General Konstantin Konstantinovich Rokossovsky, commander of the Briansk and Don Fronts

Army General Ivan Vladimirovich Tiulenev, commander of the Trans-Caucasus Front

longer than had the Nazi state, and Soviet histories tend to glorify the socialist esprit of the Red Army soldier. Yet reading between the lines, the average Soviet soldier was apparently actuated by the more traditional motives of loyalty to comrades and patriotic defense of the nation—in addition to his fear of commissars and Stalin himself. Indeed, beginning in 1941 the Soviet state had consciously identified itself with Mother Russia in the struggle against the invaders, an identification that eventually gained a loyalty that Marxism alone had been unable to inspire. There were, of course, misunderstandings and friction between the officer corps (largely Great Russian) and various minority groups from all over the Soviet Union.[65] Indeed, some nationalities provided significant numbers of armed auxiliaries to support the Germans, or, like the Ukrainians, fought as guerrillas against both sides. In general, however, most of the peoples of the socialist state appeared united in their determination to eject the hated invader.

Moreover, the desperate struggle to defend the homeland meant that women as well as men bore the burdens of war. Female transport as well as combat pilots, air observers, antiaircraft gunners, switchboard, telephone, and radio operators, and doctors and nurses were prominent both in reality and in government propaganda; a few women were also scattered throughout the other military specialties, including snipers and even tank drivers.[66] Like their male counterparts, these women demonstrated the traditional Russian ability to endure unimaginable hardship while fighting with great ferocity.

CHAPTER 3

Preliminaries: April–June 1942

Before the main effort in summer 1942 both main forces, the *Wehrmacht* and the Red Army, conducted a series of operations designed to create favorable conditions for the pursuit of strategic aims. For Hitler, this meant jockeying his forces into ideal starting positions for Plan Blau; for fellow dictator Stalin, it meant conducting preemptive, if limited, offensive operations to disrupt and weaken the Germans' offensive preparations. Because the intense fighting during winter 1941–1942 did not subside until late April 1942, neither side was ready to attack on schedule, and both dictators found themselves approving delays that moved the start of operations deeper into May. The more experienced Germans won this race, getting in the first blows in the Crimea.

OPERATION BUSTARD HUNT (*TRAPPENJAGT*): THE BATTLE FOR KERCH'

For the Germans, clearing the Crimean Peninsula was a prerequisite to the summer offensive in order to secure their right flank and control the main base of the Red Navy's Black Sea Fleet. General von Manstein, the commander of Army Group South's Eleventh Army, had to clear the Red Army's 44th, 47th, and 51st Armies from the Kerch' Peninsula (the eastern tip of the Crimea) before he could defeat Separate Coastal Army and reduce its defenses in the fortress of Sevastopol'.

General Kozlov's Crimean Front, which defended the Kerch' Peninsula with General Cherniak's 44th, General Kolganov's 47th, and General L'vov's 51st Armies, had crammed 259,622 men, supported by 347 tanks, 3,577 guns and mortars, and 400 aircraft, into an area that measured only 18 kilometers across by 75 kilometers in depth (see Map 3).[1] In theory, this location was ideally suited for defense because the Germans would have to break through fortifications across the neck of the peninsula and then penetrate four successive defensive lines before reaching the port of Kerch' itself. Yet Kozlov's forces—with 23 rifle and 2 cavalry divisions, 6 rifle and 4 tank brigades, 1 separate rifle and 1 separate tank regiment, and 6 separate tank battalions, supported by 17 artillery regiments and 15 separate artillery battalions of various types—were densely packed while preparing to launch their own attack; this offensive orientation left them poorly deployed to defend themselves.[2] Moreover, all supplies for these units had to

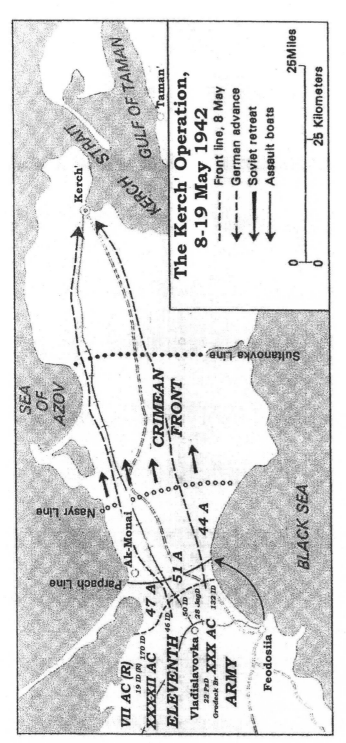

Map 3. The Kerch' operation, 8–19 May 1942

cross the Sea of Azov, a supply line that left them vulnerable to interdiction by German air and small naval units.

Kerch's importance was apparent to both sides, but the Soviets blundered in their response. Urged repeatedly by the *Stavka*, Kozlov, beginning in mid-January, submitted plan after plan for a full-scale offensive by his armies to rescue Separate Coastal Army, beleaguered in Sevastopol'. When the first of these offensives was aborted in late January after negligible gains, the Germans countered by defeating Kozlov's 44th Army and capturing Feodosiia, a port city just west of Kerch'. Angry and impatient, Stalin then intervened directly.

For much of the war, the dictator's normal practice was to send a so-called representative of the *Stavka* who was given complete authority to supervise operations at such a critical front. In late January, however, Moscow sent two such representatives to the Crimea, ostensibly to check on Kozlov's preparations for a decisive offensive to lift the German siege of Sevastopol'. In this case Stalin's lingering distrust of generals caused him to place a political hatchetman in charge rather than an experienced soldier. By 1942, Lev Zakharovich Mekhlis, chief of the Red Army's Main Political Directorate and deputy chief of the General Staff, already had a daunting reputation for purging the officer corps. During the German successes in 1941 he had sent numerous defeated commanders to die in front of impromptu firing squads. In the Crimea, Mekhlis openly bullied the men on the scene, disrupting working relationships by reshuffling senior officers. In particular, he replaced Kozlov's experienced chief of staff, Major General (and future Marshal of the Soviet Union) Fedor Ivanovich Tolbukhin, with the other visiting *Stavka* representative, Major General Pavel P. Vechnyi, Southwestern Main Direction's deputy chief of staff.[3]

The combination of a mediocre commander (Kozlov), a domineering and meddling commissar (Mekhlis), and an inexperienced staff proved fatal to Crimean Front. The resulting confusion, coupled with the crowded yet isolated position on the Kerch' Peninsula, had disastrous effects on troop readiness. With Mekhlis and Vechnyi interfering in every aspect of operational and tactical planning, Kolganov's 47th and L'vov's 51st Armies attacked on 27 February, only to see the offensive bog down and then totally collapse in less than a week. Another series of assaults in mid-April similarly ended in abject failure.[4] As the Soviet war correspondent, K. Simonov, later wrote:

> Everything was bogged down in the mud. Tanks did not go, guns were stuck somewhere behind, vehicles too; and shells were carried forward by hand. The people in the advance were senseless. Never before or since have I seen such a great number of people who were killed neither in battle nor in the attack but, rather, in systematic artillery strikes. Without fail, every 10 meters there was an individual subjected to that danger. The people were trampled and knew not what they were doing. There was neither a foxhole nor a slit trench around—nothing. Everything was taking place in these barren open

spaces and mud, and it was absolutely open on all sides of the field. Bodies were trampled down in the mud and died there, on that field, which, for some reason, seemed to be especially ghastly.[5]

As a result of this futile fighting, Crimean Front suffered 226,370 casualties from February through April 1942, with little more than frustration to show for its efforts.[6] Compounding the *front* commander's problems, Kozlov's distracted staff officers, even though they noted German preparations for an attack of their own, failed to penetrate Manstein's deception plans.

To attack Kozlov's densely packed but severely battle-worn force, Manstein's Eleventh Army could spare only two army corps, General of Artillery Maximilian von Fretter-Pico's XXX and Lieutenant General Franz Mattenklott's XXXXII, with one panzer and five infantry divisions, aided by the poorly trained and worse-led forces of three Romanian divisions (two infantry, one cavalry).[7] The remaining three German infantry divisions and two Romanian divisions were barely adequate to maintain the siege of Sevastopol'. Overall, the Soviet defenders at Kerch' outnumbered the attackers by a factor of two-to-one in personnel and artillery and even more in tanks, although in practice the deep, narrow shape of the peninsula meant that Kozlov was unable to bring all of his forces to bear at one location.[8]

Manstein did, however, have several advantages over his more numerous foes. First, regardless of the competence of frontline soldiers, at this stage in the war German staff personnel were still better prepared to plan and coordinate an offensive than were their Soviet counterparts. Second, Hitler recognized that his favorite general needed airpower to supplement his limited ground forces. Colonel General von Richthofen's VIII Air Corps, the premier tactical air unit in the *Luftwaffe*, provided more than 600 aircraft and up to 2,000 sorties per day to support the offensive. The vast distances of European Russia usually diluted the effectiveness of the *Luftwaffe*, but Richthofen's pilots achieved almost total air supremacy in the confined space of the Crimea while providing massive fire support to the ground advance.[9]

Third, Manstein's deception plans misled his opponents. During the winter battles, Crimean Front's 51st Army, which occupied the first line of defenses at Kerch' with 47th Army on its left, had pushed forward 5 or 6 kilometers on its right (northern) flank. This left a vulnerable bulge that seemed to invite a limited German attack to chop off the bulge and press the Soviets back against the seacoast. Using Mattenklott's weak XXXXII Army Corps, composed largely of Romanians, Manstein played on this weakness, convincing his opponents that the northern bulge was the main objective of his forthcoming attack. Instead, Manstein planned a much more daring main effort on his southern wing. Here, Fretter-Pico's XXX Army Corps, with one panzer and four infantry divisions plus an improvised motorized force consisting of German and Romanian troops and known as the Grodeck Motorized Brigade, was supposed to breach the initial Soviet defenses. Then, ignoring its open northern flank, the German force was

to thrust rapidly along the length of the peninsula, seizing the port of Kerch'
before the Soviets could organize an effective defense.

It was in this context that Operation Bustard Hunt began with the roar of German artillery at 0315 hours on 8 May 1942.[10] In addition to conventional field
artillery and close air support, Manstein had the services of the *Nebelwerfer* multiple rocket launchers, the *Luftwaffe's* 88mm antiaircraft guns, and some of the
heavy siege artillery assembled to reduce the defenses of Sevastopol'. After ten
minutes of shelling, the fires were redirected farther eastward, and German engineers and infantry began the hazardous task of clearing landmines and barbed
wire in order to penetrate the forward Soviet positions. Soviet counterfire
artillery and machine guns joined the din.

The noise covered up another clever—if risky—German maneuver. During
the previous night, four companies of 436th Infantry Regiment, floating in engineer assault boats, had paddled into the darkness of the Crimean Sea opposite
the southern end of the front line. Once the firing began, these troops of the
Bavarian 132nd Infantry Division started their outboard engines and motored
straight up an artificial waterway created by a broad Soviet antitank ditch. The
assault boats appeared unexpectedly in the midst of the Soviet defenders, dis-
rupting their defensive plans and attacking bunkers from an unexpected direction. By noon on 8 May, the German-Romanian Grodeck Motorized Brigade
began crossing a hastily erected bridge over the antitank ditch, and the first
Soviet defensive line was left behind in a mad dash to the east.

Late the next morning, 9 May, 22nd Panzer Division was able to penetrate
this same line at a point farther north. As the Germans pressed eastward, they
surprised a Soviet tank brigade in its assembly area, and the assault guns and
panzers shattered their opponents in a brief but vicious firefight.

Heavy rains on the night of 9–10 May turned the peninsula into a swamp,
bringing Manstein's advance to a near halt. This respite did not save the poorly
led defenders, however. Mekhlis appeared more concerned with escaping
responsibility than stopping the rout. As soon as the German offensive began,
the commissar telegraphed Stalin, demanding that Kozlov be replaced and claiming that Crimean Front had ignored his warnings until the last minute. Stalin
proved as implacable with his henchmen as he was with his generals, replying:

> You maintain the strange position of a mere onlooker who bears no responsibility
> for affairs on the Crimean Front. . . you are not a mere onlooker but the respon-
> sible representative of the [*Stavka*], who answers for all the successes and failures
> of the Front and is duty-bound to put right on the spot the mistakes made by
> the command. . . . If . . . you did not take every possible step to organize a
> repulse, but confined yourself to passive criticism, so much the worse for you.[11]

Mekhlis was demoted and never again served as a *Stavka* representative, Generals Cherniak and Kolganov of 44th and 47th Armies were relieved of command and

reduced to the rank of colonel, and General L'vov of 51st Army perished in the fighting. From the Soviet point of view, Mekhlis's disgrace was perhaps the only positive result of the debacle at Kerch'. In a single day (15 May), the German 170th Infantry Division's 213th Regiment covered more than 80 kilometers to reach the port itself, which fell the next day. Throughout 16 and 17 September, Manstein's howitzers and Richthofen's dive-bombers reduced the surrounded Soviet troops to a demoralized, formless mob. Only a few defenders escaped the trap, many by swimming across the half-frozen waters of the Kerch' Strait; according to German count, 170,000 became prisoners of war, versus 7,588 German casualties.[12] This lopsided victory, a painful replay of the previous year, confirmed German confidence in their own abilities and their contempt for the abilities of the Soviets.

PLANNING THE SECOND BATTLE OF KHAR'KOV

In fact, the only Soviet action that had any effect on Manstein's success in the Crimea was Timoshenko's own offensive at Khar'kov, an offensive that began four days after Bustard Hunt. This offensive so alarmed the Germans that Richthofen had to send part of his bombers north to aid in the defense. Ultimately, however, the Soviet offensive at Khar'kov proved as disastrous as the defense of Kerch'.

Initially, Timoshenko and his subordinates seriously underestimated the size and capability of their opponents. Soviet intelligence reports indicated that General Paulus's Sixth Army, the main force in the Khar'kov area, consisted of 12 understrength infantry divisions, with only 23rd Panzer Division in reserve near Khar'kov. That may have been an accurate assessment in March 1942, but by early May Sixth Army had been augmented both qualitatively and quantitatively. At the time of the Soviet offensive, Paulus had 15 capable infantry or rear-area security divisions, with another one en route from France, plus 3rd and 23rd Panzer Divisions and two smaller ad hoc battle groups.

Moreover, the Soviet assessment largely ignored First Panzer and Seventeenth Armies located south of the Barvenkovo bridgehead. Given the widely held belief that Hitler's summer offensive would again focus on Moscow, it is perhaps understandable that Soviet intelligence officers underestimated the strength of these two German armies, which were yoked under the command of Colonel General von Kleist. Kleist's command included 26 divisions and 5 smaller combat groups, including III Motorized Corps, 13th, 14th, and 16th Panzer Divisions, 60th Motorized Division, and the well-equipped SS motorized divisions *Leibstandarte* Adolf Hitler (LAH—Hitler's Body Guard) and *Wiking* ("Viking"). Although these units fell outside the planned area of Soviet operations, they were perfectly situated to counterattack northward into the flank of Timoshenko's advance. Every kilometer the Soviets advanced to the west would only increase this vulnerability. In effect, the Red Army was thrusting its head, eyes closed, into the lion's mouth.[13]

Timoshenko's operational directive, issued on 10 April and amended on 28 April, was complex to say the least, for he intended to encircle and destroy German Sixth Army in the Khar'kov region by enveloping it with two pincers. Advancing from the Staryi Saltov bridgehead on the western bank of the Northern Donets River northeast of Khar'kov, the first pincer consisted of Southwestern Front's 21st, 28th, and 38th Armies, supported by 3rd Guards Cavalry Corps. The second pincer, composed of Southwestern Front's 6th Army and Group Bobkin (an ad hoc headquarters equivalent to another field army), was supported by two new tank corps. The forces of this second pincer were to attack from the northern half of the Barvenkovo bridgehead, on the western bank of the Northern Donets River south of Khar'kov. All the while, Southern Front's 57th and 9th Armies were to defend the southern half of the Barvenkovo bridgehead.

North of Khar'kov, General Riabyshev's 28th Army was to lead Southwestern Front's main effort, using six rifle divisions, four tank brigades, and nine nondivisional artillery regiments to penetrate the prepared German defenses. Riabyshev's army was supported on the left by General Moskalenko's 38th Army and on the right by General Gordov's 21st Army. To break through rapidly, the Soviets allocated 59.2 guns and mortars per kilometer of front, with an average of 12 infantry support tanks per kilometer. By the third day, this penetration had to be sufficiently wide and deep to permit the mobile forces of Major General Vladimir Dmitrievich Kriuchenkin's 3rd Guards Cavalry Corps, consisting of three cavalry divisions and a motorized rifle brigade, to pass through at a point midway between Khar'kov and Belgorod.[14] With the cavalry leading, 28th Army would then wheel south, forming the northern arm of a pincer around Khar'kov.

Meanwhile, attacking from the Barvenkovo bridgehead, Southwestern Front's 6th Army, commanded by General Gorodniansky, would launch its own offensive from an area 75 kilometers south of Khar'kov. Eight rifle divisions, supported by 4 tank brigades and 14 additional artillery regiments, were ordered to push northwestward 30 kilometers in the first four days, seizing a line running southwestward from Zmiev. At this point, Generals Kuz'min's and Pushkin's brand new 21st and 23rd Tank Corps (each equivalent in size to a small German panzer division) would pass through the infantry units and push the attack to encircle Khar'kov. Major General Leonid Vasil'evich Bobkin, deputy commander of Southwestern Front's cavalry, headed Group Bobkin. This force, including two rifle divisions, one tank brigade, and Major General Aleksandr Alekseevich Noskov's 6th Cavalry Corps, would also press an attack, seeking to protect the left flank of 6th Army's penetration. Noskov had been assigned command of 6th Corps in February 1942 after leading 26th Cavalry Division throughout Operation Barbarossa and the ensuing winter campaign.[15]

In marked contrast to later Soviet offensives, most of the available forces were under the control of army-level headquarters, with very little held in reserve. As Southwestern Front commander, Timoshenko had only two rifle divisions, the three-division 2nd Cavalry Corps, and three separate tank battalions under his direct control. To some extent, the absence of reserves reflected the Soviets' continued preoccupation with Moscow, where most strategic reserve forces were concentrated. Still, the Southwestern Direction intended to employ an impressive force of 765,300 men and 923 tanks against Army Group South's force of 450 tanks, 392 of which were available for commitment in the battle for Khar'kov (see Table 8 at chapter's end).[16]

If the planning was complicated, the preparation for and execution of the offensive were disasters. Later in the war, the Red Army would master the complex problems of redeploying and supplying large formations, but in 1942 few Soviet staffs had significant experience with mounting such an offensive. Instead of following detailed, written schedules for redeployment, these staff officers attempted to resolve conflicts by issuing verbal instructions, which often confused more than they resolved. The need to conduct most movements at night, out of sight of German reconnaissance aircraft, only made matters more difficult. Throughout Southwestern Front, construction of new roads and airfields lagged far behind schedule, while German air strikes repeatedly demolished key bridges.

Moreover, many of the units assigned to the offensive had to move laterally behind the front lines, a crablike motion that brought them into conflict with the normal east-west supply lines of other formations. For example, the newly formed 28th Army, which was supposed to make the main effort in the north, had to control the movement of three rifle divisions from the *Stavka* Reserve and another three divisions being reassigned from other field armies. Before leaving their previous locations, these latter divisions had to participate in a reshuffling of units to free them from assigned defensive positions. Then, each division had to move men and supplies laterally and take up front-line positions, all the while dealing with higher and adjacent headquarters whose personalities and procedures were new and unknown to the division's staff.[17]

The original Soviet plan called for all headquarters to be in place by the start of April, leaving about two weeks to plan and practice for the offensive. In reality, many units did not arrive until the last minute. Stalin reluctantly approved a request to delay the offensive from 4 May to 12 May. Even then, however, the troops were far from ready. Of 32 nondivisional artillery regiments assigned to reinforce the attack of Southwestern Front, only 17 were actually in their firing positions by 11 May. On average, these artillery units had less than a two-day supply of ammunition on hand, even though they were scheduled to expend 5.5 days' worth of shells.[18]

DISASTER ON THE NORTHERN DONETS, 12–29 MAY

Despite these handicaps, the Soviet offensive caught the Germans unprepared and achieved considerable initial success (see Map 4). Beginning at 0630 on 12 May 1942, a one-hour artillery preparation followed by 15 minutes of air attacks pounded the defenses of German XVII Corps opposite the northern shock group

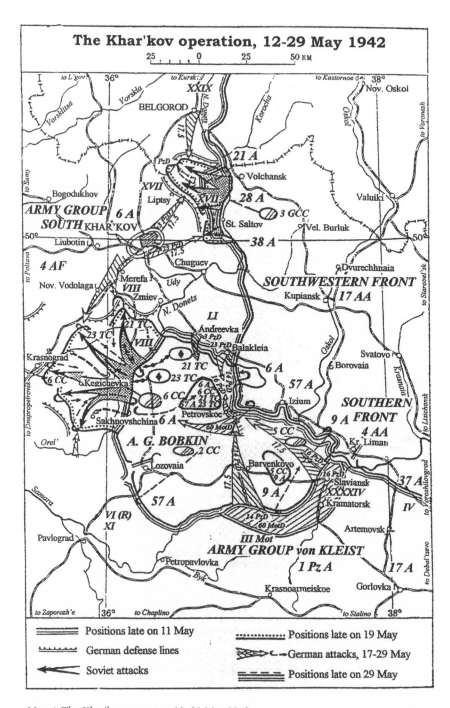

Map 4. The Khar'kov operation, 12–29 May 1942

of 28th Army, with 38th Army on its left flank and 21st on the right.[19] Although Riabyshev's 28th Army had the greatest concentration of resources, it encountered considerable difficulty in penetrating the prepared German defenses. The more experienced armies on Riabyshev's flanks actually advanced more on the first day than did the 28th. For example, a particularly skillful artillery preparation enabled 226th Rifle Division of Moskalenko's 38th Army to penetrate 10 kilometers on 12 May. Despite the slow movement in the middle, such success on the flanks facilitated the main attack and forced the Germans to commit reserve forces earlier than they wished.

Meanwhile in the south, Gorodniansky's veteran 6th Army, supported on the left by Group Bobkin, had even greater initial success. Gorodniansky's forces easily smashed through the lightly equipped Hungarian 108th Infantry Division and German 464th Security Division, both belonging to General of Artillery Walther Heitz's VIII Army Corps. 6th Cavalry Corps and the infantry-support tank brigades of Gorodniansky's army pushed forward, advancing as much as 15 kilometers by the end of the first day. Stalin was so pleased that he used Timoshenko's apparent success as an excuse to poke fun at the nay-sayers in the Red Army General Staff.[20]

General Paulus, in his first operation as commander of Sixth Army, was understandably cautious, even nervous, about the unexpected strength of the Soviet attacks. Paulus intended to conduct a purely defensive operation using bypassed strongpoints in Soviet villages as the postholes around which he would construct a fence. Yet Paulus's superior at Army Group South, Field Marshal von Bock, favored more aggressive measures. Within hours of the initial Soviet attack, Bock told Halder at OKH that Paulus's army was "fighting for its life."[21] Bock authorized Paulus to use 23rd Panzer, 71st Infantry, and 113th Infantry Divisions, all of which had been earmarked for the forthcoming German offensive. At least eight air groups from VIII Air Corps shifted northward from the Crimea to Khar'kov to help stem the Red tide, much to the frustration of Richthofen and Manstein. By noon on 13 May, the two panzer divisions, supported by infantry and dive-bombers, launched a major counterattack into 38th Army on the left (southern) flank of the northern penetration. Under this onslaught, 226th, 81st, and 124th Rifle Divisions of Moskalenko's army fell back to the Bol'shaia Babka River, where they set up defensive positions supported by three tank brigades. By the following day, Moskalenko had contained the German counterattack. In the process, however, 38th Army had been so mauled it abandoned its offensive role. Thereafter, the continued advance of Riabyshev's 28th Army exposed the left flank of the penetration to further counterattacks. Meanwhile, the Soviets' poor staff coordination delayed the commitment of the main exploitation force in the north, 3rd Guards Cavalry Corps.[22]

The southern penetration continued to have more success. By evening on 14 May, the third day of the offensive, Group Bobkin and Gorodniansky's 6th Army had penetrated the German defenses to a depth of up to 40 kilometers. Again, however, ineffective staff work delayed the forward movement of the two tank corps that were to exploit this breakthrough. 6th Army's staff assumed these units were moving forward, remaining close behind the spearheads, but in fact the two corps had not received instructions to leave their assembly areas. Given the growing German airpower over the battlefield, this meant the two tank corps could not enter the fray without several nights of concealed forward movement.

In the crisis, Bock again asked to use troops earmarked for Plan Blau, in this case to transfer units from Kleist's *Armeegruppe* (First Panzer and Seventeenth Armies) northward to defend Khar'kov. Hitler disapproved such a shift but permitted Kleist to conduct a much larger counteroffensive northward, into the rear of the Soviet advance. To this end, Hitler authorized the transfer of additional air units from the Crimea, to be followed eventually by 22nd Panzer Division. In effect, Kleist launched the southern half of Operation Fridericus, an existing German plan intended to pinch off the Soviet bulge west of the Donets River.[23]

This offensive kicked off on 17 May 1942, just as Timoshenko belatedly committed Kuz'min's 21st and Pushkin's 23rd Tank Corps to exploit northwest from 6th Army toward Khar'kov. Thus the entire Southern Front was off balance, focusing its attention and forces to the northwest at the same time the Germans attacked from the south. The leading edge of *Armeegruppe* Kleist was General of Panzer Troops Leo *Freiherr* Geyr von Schweppenburg's III Motorized Corps, consisting of 14th and 16th Panzer Divisions, 60th Motorized Division, 1st Mountain Division, 100th Jäger Division, 20th Romanian Infantry Division, and separate *Kampfgruppe* (combat group) Barbo, with a total of 170 tanks. On the first day of Fridericus, this corps punched northward 24 kilometers in the direction of Barvenkovo. In two days, 11 German divisions broke through the defenses of Southern Front's 9th and 57th Armies, which were supposed to protect the left flank of Southwestern Front in the Barvenkovo bridgehead, and advanced deep into the Soviet rear areas.[24] At the same time, Paulus shifted 23rd Panzer Division laterally around the northern bulge to launch another attack on the northern side of 28th Army's penetration. This forced Riabyshev to commit his main exploitation force, 3rd Guards Cavalry Corps, to contain this counterattack, thereby effectively negating the northern pincer of Timoshenko's offensive.

Senior Soviet leaders were remarkably slow to react to this new threat. Throughout 17 and 18 May, Timoshenko and his staff officers, including his commissar, Khrushchev, continued to focus on their own offensive and encouraged Stalin to believe that Southern Front's 9th and 57th Armies could contain the German counterattacks. Vasilevsky, acting as chief of the Red Army General Staff for the first time, failed to convince the dictator to recall the tank spearheads and redirect them against *Armeegruppe* Kleist. By the time Timoshenko acknowledged the danger on the evening of 19 May, only immediate flight could save any of the forces in the Khar'kov offensive. But Southwestern Front had no contingency plans for such a withdrawal; despite considerable supply stocks in the rear, forward troops ran short of fuel and ammunition. In this confused situation, the headquarters of Soviet armies, corps, and divisions lost communication with and control over subordinate units. By 23 May most elements of 6th, 57th, and 9th Armies, as well as Group Bobkin, were surrounded. A desperate break-out attempt failed on 25 May, although the Germans had to commit 1st Mountain Division to fill the gaps in the encirclement created by III Motorized Corps.

Three days later nothing remained of the Soviet offensive force except prisoners and dead bodies. 6th and 57th Armies were destroyed, as were large portions of the other armies involved in the offensive, including many armored formations. Officially, the Soviets suffered a gruesome toll in this battle: 266,927 casualties, of which 46,314 were evacuated to hospitals; 207,047 additional soldiers were killed, captured, or missing in action; and 652 tanks, 1,646 guns, and 3,278 mortars were lost. The Germans claimed they captured 239,036 prisoners and destroyed or captured 1,249 tanks, 2,026 guns and mortars, and 540 aircraft.[25] This toll included Lieutenant General Fedor Iakovlevich Kostenko, deputy commander of Southwestern Front; General Gorodniansky, 6th Army commander; General Podlas, 9th Army commander; General Bobkin; and virtually all division commanders from 6th and 9th Armies.

Despite their vast supplies of new weapons, the Soviet leaders proved as ineffective in 1942 as they had the previous summer. Poor staff work, lack of intelligence and reconnaissance, logistical problems, and hesitation about committing the new armored corps had sacrificed whatever chances the offensive originally enjoyed. By contrast, the German losses of 20,000 were less than one-tenth the number of Soviet prisoners they captured. General Paulus was lionized in the press and awarded the Knight's Cross for his successful defense. At the same time, thoughtful observers, including Paulus, were dismayed by the seemingly bottomless resources of the supposedly moribund Red Army.[26]

RIVAL ASSESSMENTS, JUNE 1942

The failed Khar'kov offensive did in fact put a serious dent in the Soviet reserves in the south. The loss of almost 300,000 troops, the outright destruction of 6th and 9th Armies and 21st and 23rd Tank Corps, and the heavy casualties suffered by 28th, 38th, and 57th Armies and 22nd Tank Corps significantly weakened the Southwestern Main Direction's defenses. More important, this weakness was at the very center of Army Group South's projected main attack axis for Operation Blau.

Stalin, recognizing the potentially catastrophic impact of the Crimean and Khar'kov failures on the Red Army's fortunes during the ensuing summer, even before the battle ended, in mid-May issued the first of many directives creating new armies within the RVGK (*Stavka* Reserve) to constitute a new strategic reserve (see Table 9 at the chapter's end). As a result, on 1 May this reserve included 2 armies (1st Reserve and 58th), 10 rifle divisions and 14 rifle brigades, 1 cavalry corps (2nd Guards) with 4 cavalry divisions, 1 tank corps (2nd) and 1 separate tank brigade, and a variety of specialized support units. By 1 June the reserve had grown to 1 tank and 7 reserve armies (3rd Tank and 1st–3rd and 5th–8th Reserve), 40 rifle divisions, 1 cavalry corps (2nd Guards) with 3 cavalry divisions, 3 tank corps (12th, 14th, and 15th), 2 separate tank brigades, and supporting units. Three more reserve armies and 4 more tank corps joined the roster by 1 July, increasing the strength of the *Stavka* Reserve to 2 tank and 10 reserve armies (1st–10th and 3rd and 5th Tank), 63 rifle divisions, 1 cavalry corps (2nd Guards) with 3 cavalry divisions, 7 tank corps (2nd, 7th, 11th, 12th, 15th, 18th, and 25th) and 5 separate tank brigades, and correspondingly increased numbers of supporting units. This provided Stalin with ample—if poorly trained—strategic reserves.[27] A flood of accompanying directives deployed these armies into deep reserve positions across the entire Soviet-German front but more heavily concentrated along the western (Moscow) and southwestern (Voronezh and Stalingrad) strategic axes.

Although Stalin's new strategic reserve was imposing on paper, many of the assigned formations and units were in the initial stages of organization and training and were hardly prepared for battle. More important, Stalin remained convinced the forthcoming German offensive would aim at Moscow, and as a result he was reluctant to divert large forces to meet Timoshenko's needs in the south. There the surviving, shaken Soviet units had less than a month to restore organization and morale. Meanwhile, Stalin demoted Bagramian, Southwestern Main Direction's hapless chief of staff, to command of Western Front's 16th Army; he bluntly criticized Timoshenko and Khrushchev for their command failures. (However, Stalin apparently recognized his own responsibility in the failure because he left Timoshenko in command of Southwestern Main Direction.) The dictator warned the main direction and front leaders, including (by implication) Nikita Khrushchev, that they would "answer with their heads" for the future defense of the Oskol and Northern Donets River lines east of Khar'kov.[28]

In the wake of the Khar'kov defeat, although Timoshenko and his Military Council were concerned about a new German offensive (which on 29 May they assessed could materialize "five to ten days" later), Stalin kept his attentions riveted on the Moscow axis, where he perceived the danger posed to the Soviet capital by German Army Group Center was genuine.[29] In addition to reinforcing this axis with four of his new reserve armies, Stalin also ordered Southwestern Front to "go over to the defense along the Volchansk and Balakleia line and southward along the eastern bank of the Northern Donets River with 21st, 28th, 38th and 9th Armies and prevent German forces from launching an offensive eastward from the Khar'kov region."[30] At the same time, Stalin cancelled the ambitious offensives he planned with the forces of Briansk Front (against Orel and Kursk in support of Southwestern Front's Khar'kov offensive) and instead ordered it to go over to the defense.[31]

By the end of the first week of June, Stalin reinforced Timoshenko's *front* with 7 rifle divisions, 4 separate tank brigades, and 4th, 13th, and 24th Tank Corps, thereby increasing the *front's* strength to 30 rifle divisions and 2 rifle brigades, 5 tank and 2 cavalry corps, and 8 separate tank brigades.[32] Apparently, the dictator felt this force was large enough to deal with any future German offensive in the region. He was mistaken.

The German picture after Kerch' and Khar'kov was mixed. Soviet opposition was obviously weaker, and the front line had been shortened prior to the main Blau offensive. Yet the cost had been considerable—the panzer units on which Paulus and Kleist depended for the main offensive experienced significant losses in men and matériel, while losing time needed to complete training and preparations. Meanwhile in the north, the Germans were straightening their defensive lines in front of Moscow and Leningrad, an effort that required additional resources and time. Across the board, the Germans found themselves revising schedules for forthcoming operations. On 28 May 1942, General Halder, chief of OKH, presented several revisions to Hitler. The Führer agreed in principle that Army Group South should continue its counteroffensive, pushing northeast of Khar'kov to take the Volchansk area. Only later would the Germans straighten their lines farther south, aiming at Izium and the nearby junction of the Oskol and Northern Donets Rivers.[33]

On 1 June 1942, Hitler flew from his headquarters in Rastenburg to Poltava, where he presided over a conference at Army Group South. Field Marshal von Bock and three of his army commanders—Kleist of First Panzer, Hoth of Fourth Panzer, and Paulus of Sixth—met with Hitler and Richthofen to finalize plans for the coming offensive. Hitler was preoccupied with two goals: destroying Soviet troop units, and seizing the Caucasus oil fields. Based on input from Halder and Bock, Hitler established a revised schedule for operations. On 7 June the Germans would attack simultaneously in the Volchansk area (Operation Wilhelm) and against the fortress of Sevastopol' (in Operation *Störfang* [Sturgeon Trap]). Five days later Kleist would attack to reduce the Izium salient (Operation Fridericus II). These preliminary operations would eliminate the Crimean threat and allow the Germans to build up supplies east of the Northern Donets River. On 20 June, after all these operations would supposedly be completed, the *Wehrmacht* would launch Operation Blau.[34]

SEVASTOPOL', 7–30 JUNE

For the Germans, completing these operations within three weeks was a tall order. Rains continued to delay Wilhelm until 10 June, but Manstein began his last attack in the Crimea on schedule (see Map 5).

The Soviet defenses at Sevastopol' were immensely strong, as indicated by Manstein's inability to reduce the fortress in late 1941. Mixed in with older, tsarist-era fortifications were modern concrete casemates with armored-gun cupolas and elaborate underground tunnels. These permanent defenses were

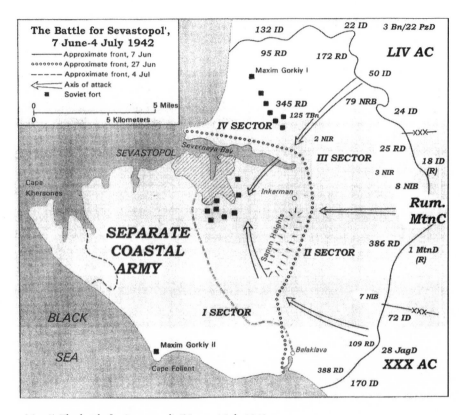

Map 5. The battle for Sevastopol', 7 June–4 July 1942

supplemented by 350 kilometers of trenches with minefields and wire barriers. The Soviet defenses were organized into two belts: an outer ring near Balaklava, 15–20 kilometers away from the port, and an inner ring approximately 5 kilometers from the center. The overall commander of Sevastopol' was Vice Admiral Filipp Sergeevich Oktiabr'sky, commander of the Black Sea Fleet. Most of the fortress's defenders, however, belonged to General Petrov's Coastal Army, which on 1 June consisted of seven rifle divisions (25th, 95th, 109th, 172nd, 345th, 386th, and 388th), one naval rifle brigade (79th), two naval infantry brigades (7th and 8th), two naval infantry regiments (2nd and 3rd), and two separate tank battalions (81st and 125th), supported by seven artillery regiments, two separate artillery battalions, and the "*Zhelezniakov*" [Iron-Stone] armored train.[35] In all, 106,600 troops, supported by 38 tanks, 606 guns and 1,061 mortars, 12 *Katiusha* multiple rocket launchers, and an armored train defended the fortress. These forces were augmented by another 23,500 men of 138th and 142nd Rifle Brigades, which the *Stavka* dispatched by sea to reinforce the fortress, the former on 12 June and the latter from 23 to 26 June.[36]

Petrov organized his defenses around Sevastopol' into four defensive sectors, arrayed from south to north, as follows:

- I Sector (Balaklava to the Chernaia River—7.5 kilometers)—109th and 388th Rifle Divisions;
- II Sector (Chernaia River to Mekenziia—12 kilometers)—386th Rifle Division and 7th and 8th Naval Infantry Brigades;
- III Sector (Mekenziia to the Bel'bek River—8.5 kilometers)—25th Rifle Division, 79th Naval Rifle Brigade, and 2nd and 3rd Naval Infantry Regiments;
- IV Sector (Bel'bek River to the Black Sea coast—6 kilometers)—95th and 172nd Rifle Divisions; and
- Reserve—345th Rifle Division, one regiment of 308th Rifle Division, and 81st and 125th Separate Tank Battalions.[37]

Under the circumstances, the typical German offensive—in which infantry assaults were preceded by a brief artillery preparation to force the defenders under cover—would have little effect. Instead, Manstein planned a five-day air and artillery bombardment to weaken the fixed defenses and smash most of the temporary field fortifications.[38]

In addition to as many as 600 aircraft under Richthofen, Manstein had about 167,000 soldiers, 80 tanks and assault guns, and 1,300 guns and mortars (2,045 by Soviet count) at Sevastopol', organized into seven German and two Romanian divisions. These forces included General of Cavalry Erik Hansen's LIV Army Corps, with 132nd, 22nd, 50th, and 24th Infantry Divisions; and General of Artillery Maximilian Fretter-Pico's XXX Army Corps, with Romanian Mountain Corps' 18th Infantry and 1st Mountain Divisions and German 72nd Infantry, 28th Jäger, and 170th Infantry Divisions. For armored support, Manstein's Eleventh Army had 3rd Battalion, 22nd Panzer Division (with about 30 Pz. III tanks), whose main body (Army Group South) had transferred to the Donbas region, and 190th, 197th, and 249th *Abteilungen* (Assault Gun Battalions), the latter with about 50 75mm assault guns. Finally, German XXXXII Army Corps' 46th Infantry Division and Romanian VII Army Corps' 10th and 19th Infantry Divisions and 8th Cavalry Brigade provided security for Manstein's rear area; Romanian 4th Mountain Division constituted his reserve.[39]

Manstein's guns were orchestrated by *Harko* 306 (*Höheres Artillerie Kommando* [Higher Artillery Command]), Eleventh Army's artillery headquarters. Pride of place went to Dora, an 800mm railroad cannon whose 7-ton shell could penetrate 24 feet of concrete. In addition, *Harko* 306 had three 533mm Karl siege mortars, each of which fired a shell weighing 1.5 tons, and six 420mm Gamma mortars with 1-ton shells. These massive weapons undoubtedly wrecked great destruction, but there were only a handful, and their rate of fire and accuracy were relatively low. For the German attack, therefore, smaller guns were almost equally important. In particular, the German air superiority over the

Crimea allowed Richthofen to divert most of his Flak (antiaircraft) division to ground support. By 1942, the *Luftwaffe's* 88mm antiaircraft gun was already legendary as a tank-killer. The high-velocity gun proved equally effective at penetrating armored strongpoints and smaller casemates at Sevastopol'. However, Richthofen's strong sense of *Luftwaffe* independence caused him to insist that these guns remain concentrated in large groups under air force commanders, rather than loaning them to *Harko* 306. This decision inevitably produced some tension and miscommunication during the battle.[40]

At 0350 hours on 7 June 1942, after a furious five-day aerial and artillery bombardment of the city's defenses and an intense one-hour artillery preparation, primarily against forts at Sevastopol', the infantry and engineer forces of Eleventh Army began the German assault.[41] The main effort was in the north, where Hansen's LIV Army Corps attacked 79th Naval Rifle Brigade and 172nd Rifle Division precisely at the junction of Defensive Sectors III and IV with four divisions and a reinforced infantry regiment. Romanian Mountain Corps was assigned a supporting role in the center (eastern) portion of the siege, with Fretter-Pico's XXX Army Corps in the south. Unfortunately, XXX Corps, controlling three German divisions, experienced delays in cleaning up the aftermath of the Kerch' battle. As a result, LIV Army Corps had to make the first attacks virtually alone. In the words of one of the German assault troops:

> This is the moment of the attack, and, in a raging tempo, it races down the slope, through the valley, and on the other side. . . . Companies, platoons, and groups one after the other move forward in the blue-gray powder smoke and thick dust. . . . The going is slow through the thick bushes. There is no chance for the groups and platoons to maintain contact here. The Bolsheviks hide in their numberless holes, and they let us pass and then fall on us from the rear. . . .
>
> An enemy machine gun nest suddenly appears in a small depression. Due to our fire, three men come out of it with their hands up. As we approach slowly, two others, who are still in the shelter, fire on us with the machine gun. Another takes his life. As we pass, another jumps up and fires at us from the rear. This is the Bolshevik method of combat. On the ground there is mine after mine. Next to me a company commander is flung into the air, he falls back, and almost lands, uninjured, on his feet. However, not everyone has such luck.[42]

These initial attacks on 7 June ended a bloody failure after three days of heavy fighting. Hitler, intent on rapid-maneuver victories in preparation for Operation Blau, suggested to Bock that Operation *Störfang* might have to be suspended. Within a few days Bock was inclined to agree, because the continued commitment of VIII Air Corps at Sevastopol' meant those aircraft would be late in redeploying to support the main offensive.[43]

Manstein's troops persisted, however, as XXX Army Corps joined the assault on 10 June. Thereafter, Sevastopol' became a precursor to Stalingrad, with small groups of soldiers fighting bitter hand-to-hand struggles for control of ruined buildings. The defenders used everything, including the corpses of comrades, to shore up positions. German flamethrowers, satchel charges, and hand grenades inflicted unspeakable carnage, yet the Red Army and Navy fought to the last breath. In 12 hours of fighting on 13 June, every officer in two battalions of German 16th Regiment, 22nd Infantry Division, was killed or wounded, leaving a replacement lieutenant to direct the assault on the ruined "Fort Stalin." By the time the battle was over, 16th Infantry was not the only colonel's command led by a lieutenant.[44]

The first break for the Germans came on 13 June 1942, when LIV Army Corps captured Maxim Gorki I (Battery No. 30), a massive fortification that anchored the northern end of the outer defensive belt. Large-caliber German guns had long since disabled the gun turrets of this fort, but the defenders fought on until only a handful of wounded Soviets remained alive. To make up for equally serious German losses, Army Group South gave Eleventh Army an additional infantry regiment and allowed it to swap two depleted regiments for stronger units from a division left at Kerch'. The struggle continued inch by bleeding inch. On 17 June, following ten days of struggle, the Germans finally swept six other forts on the northern end of the ring, pressing forward to Severnaia (Northern) Bay, a long, thin finger of water that divided Sevastopol' proper from the northern defenses. There, however, LIV Army Corps had to halt, waiting for the other two corps to make similar progress and come on line to the east and south.[45] The depleted German 22nd Infantry Division barely contained a brigade-sized Soviet counterattack on the morning of 18 June. Thereafter, the Germans slowly eliminated bypassed centers of resistance, while the Soviet defenders, resupplied only by submarine, gradually ran low on ammunition, food, and water.[46] Even so, the *Stavka* dispatched two rifle brigades to reinforce the garrison.

The final assault again demonstrated Manstein's ability to take a calculated risk. At 0100 hours on 29 June, troops from 22nd and 24th Infantry Divisions used engineer assault boats to cross Severnaia Bay in secret, seizing the city's power plant by surprise. An hour later, XXX Army Corps began the artillery preparation for its assault on Sapun Heights, the principal terrain obstacle southeast of Sevastopol'. The new offensive was so successful that on 30 June Admiral Oktiabr'sky persuaded the *Stavka* to authorize an evacuation. During the next four nights, key Soviet staff officers and commanders escaped by boat; the personnel remaining in the fortresses continued to defend themselves. In some instances, political officers committed suicide, blowing up their positions in an effort to take some attackers with them.[47]

According to German reports, Manstein's forces captured 97,000 prisoners, 631 guns, and 26 tanks.[48] Soviet records claim the Sevastopol' Defensive Region lost 200,000 soldiers from 31 October 1941 through 4 July 1942, including 156,880 killed, wounded, or missing, and in addition lost 95,000 prisoners, 622 guns, 758 mortars, and 26 tanks during the defense of the fortress city.[49] Although the defenders' actions were heroic, the only Soviet advantage gained was the temporary diversion of German dive-bombers and other scarce resources. In recognition of the ferocity of battle, the Soviet government awarded the entire city the Order of Lenin, and the Germans authorized all participants in the battle to wear the special Crimea Shield on their left sleeve. On 1 July 1942, Erich von Manstein was promoted to field marshal for his Crimean campaign.

WILHELM, 10–15 JUNE

By the time Sevastopol' fell, the focal point of German operations had already shifted to the north and east, specifically to the region east of Khar'kov, where Army Group South (now renamed Army Group B) was marching briskly eastward during the first phase of Operation Blau. However, before Bock's army group could begin its ambitious summer campaign, Sixth Army and First Panzer Army had to conduct two preliminary operations designed to seize favorable terrain they could use as jumping-off positions for Hitler's 1942 summer offensive. Therefore in June these two armies launched Operations Wilhelm and Fridericus II, even as Manstein's Eleventh Army was clubbing defenders at Sevastopol' into submission.

In Operation Wilhelm, Bock planned to employ Paulus's Sixth Army in dual fashion: first to liquidate the bridgehead occupied by the Southwestern Front's already shaken 21st and 28th Armies on the western bank of the Northern Donets River west of Volchansk and Staryi Saltov; and simultaneously to penetrate 38th Army's defenses opposite the German bridgehead on the eastern bank of the Northern Donets River southeast of Chuguev (see Map 6).[50] Once Sixth Army ejected the Soviets from the bridgehead, advancing in two pincers, its forces would seize Volchansk and crossings over the Northern Donets River south of the town and advance eastward to the Ol'khovatka region.

As commander of Sixth Army, Paulus intended Operation Wilhelm to be a double envelopment, with four infantry divisions (336th, 113th, 305th, and 79th) of Heitz's VIII Army Corps striking eastward through Volchansk to eliminate the Soviet bridgehead and then southeastward through Belyi Kolodez' to the Ol'khovatka region. Simultaneously, three infantry divisions (297th, 71st, and 44th) of General Walter von Seydlitz-Kurzbach's LI Army Corps, spearheaded by four mobile divisions (14th, 16th, and 22nd Panzer and 60th Motorized) of Geyr's III Motorized Corps (the latter transferred to Paulus for this occasion), would attack northeastward along the western bank of the Burluk River. Their mission was to link up with VIII Army Corps near Velikie Burluk, 20 kilometers south of Ol'khovatka. Although the operation involved a shallow advance of slightly more than 50 kilometers, if successful it would seriously damage Southwestern Front's 21st, 28th, and 38th Armies and thereby totally disrupt Timoshenko's defenses forward of the Oskol River.

Gordov's 21st, Riabyshev's 28th, and Moskalenko's 38th Armies were indeed enticing targets. Although their forces still clung to their own bridgehead at

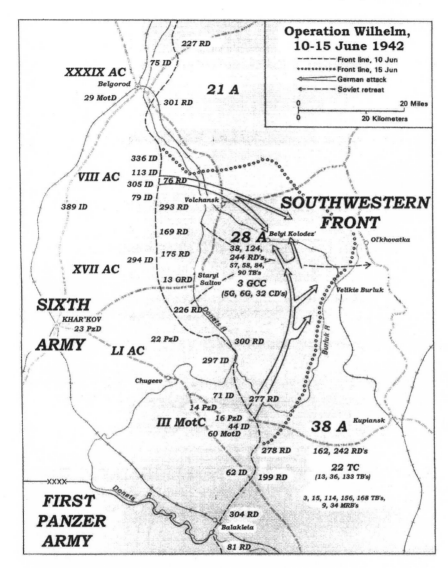

Map 6. Operation Wilhelm, 10–15 June 1942

Staryi Saltov and strained to contain the German bridgehead east of the Northern Donets River, all three armies had been shaken to the core by the failure of the Khar'kov offensive, and they had yet to receive requested replacements. As 38th Army's history indicated, "The failures of the Southwestern Front in May 1942 sharply worsened the situation in the country's south. They weakened our forces here at the very moment when the enemy was preparing his great

Major General Ivan Efimovich Petrov, the commander of the Coastal Army (center), observing the battle for Sevastopol with his chief of staff, General N. I. Krylov, and his chief of artillery, N. K. Ryzhi

Troops of the Crimean Front counterattacking in May 1942

Fighting in the vicinity of Kerch' in May 1942

German 600mm mortar "Karl" in a firing position of Sevastopol'

An unexploded 600mm German mortar shell in Sevastopol'

Black Sea Fleet ships laying a smokescreen in Sevastopol' harbor

Soviet naval infantry in combat at Sevastopol'

The Black Sea Fleet's cruiser *Tashkent* traveling to Sevastopol', 26 June 1942

summer offensive, which counted on a penetration to the Volga and into the Caucasus."[51]

On the eve of Operation Wilhelm, Timoshenko defended the Staryi Saltov bridgehead with two rifle divisions (76th and 293rd) from Gordov's 21st Army, flanked on the south by five rifle divisions (169th, 175th, 13th Guards, 226th, and 300th) in the first echelon of Riabyshev's 28th Army, which were supported by four weak tank brigades, three rifle divisions (38th, 124th, and 224th), and the three cavalry divisions of Kriuchenkin's 3rd Guards Cavalry Corps in Riabyshev's reserve. Complicating Soviet command and control, 28th Army had just taken over 38th Army's portion of the bridgehead, along with that army's 124th, 226th, and 300th Rifle Divisions.

This left Moskalenko's 38th Army the difficult task of defending the sector from the Northern Donets River east of Chuguev southward 60 kilometers to the west of Izium with five rifle divisions (277th, 278th, 199th, 304th, and 81st) in first echelon, supported by three tank brigades of 22nd Tank Corps (more than 100 tanks) and seven additional separate tank and motorized rifle brigades, and backed up by two rifle divisions (162nd and 242nd) in reserve. Appreciating the dangers he faced, Moskalenko concentrated all of his army's antitank units and artillery in the defensive sectors of 277th and 278th Rifle Divisions southeast of Chuguev and ordered the commander of 22nd Tank Corps, General Shamshin, to "dig his tanks into the ground up to their turrets" to protect the vital tank axis along the Khar'kov-Kupiansk railroad and road.[52] Moskalenko's fear was justified, for he was about to be struck by III Motorized Corps, whose 430 tanks in four mobile divisions significantly outnumbered his own tank force of roughly 250 tanks.[53]

Paulus's Sixth Army unleashed the two pincers early on 10 June, catching Gordov's, Riabyshev's, and Moskalenko's defenders by surprise.[54] Attacking at 0400 hours after a 45-minute artillery and air preparation, Heitz's VIII Army Corps took only two days to clear Gordov's and Riabyshev's forces from the Staryi Saltov bridgehead and capture Volchansk. By day's end on 11 June, just as VIII Corps' 113th, 305th, and 294th Infantry Divisions were reaching a point halfway between Volchansk and Velikie Burluk on the Burluk River, advancing in tandem, 22nd, 14th, and 16th Panzer Divisions of Geyr's III Motorized Corps (which took only 24 hours to demolish Moskalenko's defenses) were approaching Velikie Burluk from the south. Caught between twin pincers, Riabyshev's forces and those on Moskalenko's left (northern) wing desperately fought westward to escape the trap before it slammed shut.

The overstretched remnants of Southwestern Front could not match two concentrated attacks of this nature, and 28th Army began withdrawing almost as soon as the German attack was under way. However, rains returned on 11 June, slowing the mechanized spearheads of III Motorized Corps and giving Riabyshev time to withdraw the bulk of his forces from the trap and to organize a more effective defense farther to the rear. Tanks from 28th Army's 58th Tank Brigade took up defensive positions to prevent the Germans from completing their encirclement near Belyi Kolodez, and 22nd Tank Corps' 168th Tank Brigade launched a counterattack against III Motorized Corps' left flank, allowing most of the fugitives from 28th and 38th Armies west of Velikie Burluk to escape the intended encirclement.[55]

Despite the rainy weather, by nightfall on 15 June Paulus's two corps had closed to their designated objectives, which extended in an arc eastward around Volchansk southward just west of Ol'khovatka and farther southwest along the Burluk River to Balakleia on the Northern Donets River. By this time Paulus had withdrawn Geyr's III Motorized Corps into assembly areas southeast of Chuguev for a brief rest and refitting and replaced them at the front with the infantry divisions of Seydlitz's LI Army Corps. Reporting it had taken only 24,800 Soviet prisoners in Operation Wilhelm, the bulk of them from the shattered 28th Army, Paulus's army once again demonstrated the difficulties of encircling an elusive Soviet foe. Still, this operation served its intended purpose: securing Sixth Army's intended line of departure for the main offensive.[56] Worse for Timoshenko, it seriously weakened the very center of his Southwestern Front's defenses at a time when they needed to be the strongest.

The *Stavka* reacted forcefully in the wake of Operation Wilhelm. On 13 June, as the German offensive was developing, Timoshenko, Khrushchev, and Bagramian, the Southwestern Main Direction's (and Southwestern Front's) Military Council, discussed the situation with Stalin by secure Baudot radio-teletype (known as BODO). Timoshenko reported on the Germans' progress and informed Stalin that he was deploying 13th Tank Corps, commanded by General Shurov, to the Ol'khovatka region, where its roughly 180 tanks would be subordinated to Kriuchenkin's cavalry corps. In addition, Timoshenko told Stalin that he was forming a new defense line slightly rearward with Shamshin's 22nd Tank Corps and reinforcements being transferred from Southern Front's 57th Army, whose remnants had reverted to the *front*'s reserve after its encirclement and near destruction at the Barvenkovo bridgehead two weeks before. Responding to Stalin's urgent query about the fate of 28th Army, Timoshenko responded that he had little information about some of its rifle divisions; 169th, 75th, and 300th were "seriously battered"; 15th and 13th Guards were still "in good shape."[57] Stalin then promised Timoshenko two fresh tank brigades but denied him any additional rifle divisions, because "we do not have ready divisions."[58] Scolding Timoshenko for poor command and control of his forces, Stalin added, "You have more tanks than the enemy . . . the *Stavka* suggests you concentrate the operations of 22nd Tank Corps, 23rd Tank Corps, and 13th Tank Corps somewhere in one place, it seems in the Velikie Burluk region, and strike the enemy tank group in the flank."[59] Stalin concluded the discussion, noting, "Do not fear the Germans—the devil is not so black as he is painted."[60]

All the same, the dictator had seen the situation deteriorate catastrophically many times before. So on 15 June he ordered Briansk Front to dispatch its new 4th and 16th Tank Corps, commanded by Generals Mishulin and Pavelkin, respectively, and Major General A. I. Liziukov's new 5th Tank Army to the Novyi

Oskol, Kastornoe, and Efremov regions, respectively, in order to bolster South-western Front's sagging defenses.[61] The three formations were near full strength, with roughly 180 tanks in each separate tank corps and almost 400 in the tank army.[62] Two days later, Stalin directed Timoshenko:

> (a) Improve your defenses by all means possible, employing antitank and anti-personnel mines to a maximum, while also paying special attention to constructing as many types of obstacles as possible, first and foremost, anti-tank;
> (b) Prepare a counterstroke against the main enemy grouping. Conduct the counterstroke only on special order of the *Stavka* after you report your forces are ready.[63]

On 20 June Stalin transferred Mishulin's 4th Tank Corps and the fresh 91st and 159th Tank Brigades to Timoshenko's control and ordered the *front* com-mander to "hold 13th, 23rd, and 24th Tank Corps in full combat-readiness." Later the same day, Stalin directed his long-range aviation forces to conduct mas-sive air strikes at the junction of 21st and 28th Armies and along the Kursk axis.[64] Timoshenko, in further discussions with Stalin that day, revealed the startling news that his forces had captured Army Group South's plans from a downed Ger-man aircraft (see below), only to hear Stalin dismiss the captured order as "one corner" of the enemy's operational plan and direct him (Timoshenko) to continue the defensive and offensive preparations. Then—perhaps to punish Timoshenko for his previous defeat at Khar'kov as well as the current confused situation—on 21 June Stalin disbanded the Southwestern Main Direction Command, allocating all of its forces to the Southwestern and Southern Fronts and leaving Timo-shenko in command of only Southwestern Front. Hereafter, both *fronts* were to operate in direct subordination to the *Stavka*, with Vasilevsky coordinating their operations.[65]

FRIDERICUS, 22–25 JUNE

Before Timoshenko and his new *Stavka* coordinator could communicate with Stalin, Bock upped the ante by unleashing his second preparatory offensive: Operation Fridericus II.[66] Developing even more rapidly than Operation Wil-helm, Fridericus II's objective was to seize control of the transportation junction at Izium on the Northern Donets River and Kupiansk on the Oskol River. This would bring Kleist's First Panzer Army on line with Paulus's Sixth Army, ready to cross the Oskol River for the Blau summer offensive (see Map 7). Bock would have preferred to launch Operation Blau itself, or at least to rest and rebuild his units while waiting for Richthofen's dive-bombers to redeploy from the Crimea. Hitler, however, insisted on Fridericus II while waiting for Sevastopol' to fall.

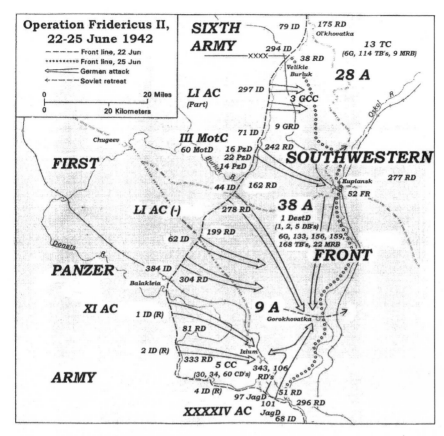

**Operation Fridericus II,
22-25 June 1942**

- – – – – – Front line, 22 Jun
- •••••••••• Front line, 25 Jun
- ⇐⇐⇐⇐ German attack
- ←– – – – Soviet retreat

| 0 | | 20 Miles |
| 0 | | 20 Kilometers |

SIXTH
ARMY

79 ID   175 RD
Ol'khovatka

294 ID
—XXXX—   38 RD
Velikie
Burluk

13 TC
(6G, 114 TB's, 9 MRB)

28 A

Chugeev

LI AC
(Part)

297 ID   3 GCC

9 GRD

III MotC
60 MotD   16 PzD
22 PzD
14 PzD

71 ID
242 RD

FIRST

SOUTHWESTERN

Kupiansk   277 RD

52 FR

44 ID   162 RD

LI AC (-)   278 RD

38 A
1 DestD
(1, 2, 5 DB's)
6G, 133, 156, 159,
168 TB's, 22 MRB

62 ID   199 RD

Donets

FRONT

PANZER   384 ID

304 RD

Balakleia

XI AC   1 ID (R)

9 A

Gorokhovatka

81 RD

2 ID (R)

Izium

333 RD   5 CC
(30, 34, 60 CD's)

343, 106
RD's

ARMY

4 ID (R)   97 JagD   51 RD
101   296 RD
XXXXIV AC   JagD
68 ID

Map 7. Operation Fridericus II, 22–25 June 1942

Moreover, Bock's plan for a straightforward advance to the new line of departure was not in accord with Hitler's insistence on encirclement battles to destroy the Red Army.[67] In short, the senior German commanders conducted the entire operation in a disgruntled mood with considerable internal friction.

In Fridericus II, which also involved twin pincers, the northern wing included four infantry divisions (297th, 71st, 44th, and 62nd) of First Panzer Army's LI Army Corps and was spearheaded by the four mobile divisions of Geyr's III Motorized Corps, which had just been transferred to Kleist's *Armeegruppe* from Sixth Army's control. This first pincer was to advance due eastward to capture Kupiansk on the Oskol River. Simultaneously, the second pincer, composed of three infantry divisions (97th and 101st Jäger and 68th) of First Panzer Army's XXXIV Army Corps, commanded by General of Artillery Maximilian de Angelis, was to advance northward across the Northern Donets River east of Izium, capture the city, and link up with III Motorized Corps' exploiting panzers south of Kupiansk. Together with four infantry divisions (German 384th and 1st Mountain and Romanian 1st and 2nd Mountain) from First Panzer Army's XI Army Corps, commanded by General of Infantry Karl Strecker, which were to attack eastward across the Northern Donets south of Balakleia, Paulus's and Kleist's combined forces were to encircle and destroy as many of Soviet 38th and 9th Armies' forces as possible west of the Oskol River. At this stage, Kleist retained his panzer and motorized divisions in reserve to preserve their strength for the main show to follow.[68]

Between Kleist's twin pincers stood Moskalenko's already worn-down 38th Army and the right wing of Major General Dmitri Nikitich Nikishov's 9th Army, which, though fresher, had not recovered from the wounds it suffered during its defeat at Khar'kov. Nikishov had previously served as chief of staff of the Leningrad Military District and Northern Front and deputy commander of 9th Army in 1941 and, as chief of Southwestern Front's Department for Fortified Regions during the first two quarters of 1942, had constructed many of the field fortifications his army defended. Subsequently, Nikishov replaced General Kharitonov as 9th Army commander after the Khar'kov disaster.[69] By this time, Moskalenko fielded a force of 6 rifle divisions (162nd, 242nd, 278th, 199th, 304th, and fresh 9th Guards) and 1 destroyer division (1st), supported by 6 tank brigades and 1 motorized rifle brigade, with about 200 tanks, and 15 RVGK (*Stavka* Reserve) artillery regiments. 1st Destroyer Division (with 1st, 2nd, and 5th Destroyer Brigades) fielded 48 76mm and 36 45mm antitank guns, 324 antitank rifles, and 12 37mm antiaircraft machine guns suitable for antitank work. To his army's rear was 52nd Fortified Region, manning fixed positions along the Oskol River line with six artillery–machine gun battalions, 7th Sapper Army's 21st Sapper Brigade, and 16th Special Designation RVGK Engineer Brigade, whose weaponry included tank-destroyer dogs (canines laden with explosives) in addition to its equipment for erecting obstacles.[70]

On 38th Army's left (southern) flank, Nikishov's 9th Army defended with its 81st and 333rd Rifle Divisions and 30th, 34th, and 60th Cavalry Divisions of Major General F. A. Parkhomenko's 5th Cavalry Corps deployed along the Northern Donets River west of Izium; its 343rd and 106th Rifle Divisions and 12th Tank Brigade defending the city itself; and its 51st and 296th Rifle Divisions and 78th Naval Rifle Brigade deployed along the northern bank of the Northern Donets east of the city.[71] Because of the heavy losses the Red Army had suffered during the Khar'kov encirclement in May, Nikishov had no choice but to employ 5th Cavalry Corps' divisions in its first echelon defenses. Parkhomenko, the corps' commander, was experienced and had led 20th Motorized Corps' 210th Motorized Division during Western Front's desperate struggle along the Dnepr River and at Smolensk in July 1941 and commanded cavalry corps since December 1941.[72] Weak in both infantry and tanks, Nikishov's forces in the Izium region were certainly no match for Kleist's attacking forces.

After repeated delays caused by June thunderstorms, the German offensive finally began at 0410 hours on 22 June 1942—the first anniversary of the Soviet-German war. On the southern flank of the bulge at Izium, XXXXIV Army Corps thrust northeastward toward Gorokhovatka. Geyr's III Motorized Corps—again leading the main attack—pressed eastward to Kupiansk on the Oskol River and then southward to meet with XXXXIV Army Corps by late afternoon on 24 June. Once again, however, many of Moskalenko's and Nikishov's soldiers managed to escape eastward, although First Panzer Army claimed it captured 22,800 prisoners from Southwestern Front's two armies.[73]

The German advance, though swift, was not always easy or successful. On 24 and 25 June, for example, the motorized infantry of III Motorized Corps' 16th Panzer Division, commanded by General Hube, met methodical, determined Soviet resistance when it closed in on the Moskovka and Oskol Rivers near Kupiansk:

> Slowly the men advanced, alternating between rushing forward and providing covering fire, into the accursed [*verhexten*—literally, bewitched] forest. They tried to move two kilometers eastward to the Moskovka, but machine gun fire threatened the flanks of the assault groups. The advance failed, and the battalion took cover. Wait for nightfall! Then the panzer grenadiers and tanks moved through the village. Suddenly the field exploded with the flash and crash of exploding fragments: Mines! Further advance was impossible; four tanks were lost. The 1st Battalion, 64th Panzer Grenadier Regiment, established a security line on a creek feeding into the Moskovka. Midnight passed. One hour of sleep, one hour on watch. At 0200 the 1st Battalion, 79th Panzer Grenadier Regiment, and the 1st Battalion, 64th Panzer Grenadier Regiment, began again and soon sensed that enemy resistance was weakening. The sun came up at 0555, illuminating the railroad bridge. Cautiously the troops prepared for the attack, bringing anti-tank and engineer elements to the front. But the bridge was shattered in multiple places. On the opposite bank, the enemy detected the Germans and swept the approach roads with heavy fire.[74]

Unknown to 16th Panzer Division's troopers, the strenuous Soviet defense at Kupiansk was mounted by Major General A. P. Beloborodov's 9th Guards Rifle Division, reinforced by 6th Guards Tank Brigade and 1st Destroyer Division. One of the most famous and distinguished divisions in the Red Army, 9th Guards had earned lasting fame during the battle for Moscow in October and November 1941, when, fighting as the 78th Rifle Division, it had arrived from the Far East and helped thwart Fourth Panzer Group's advance on the city. The division commander, Afanasii Pavlant'evich Beloborodov, would go on to command 2nd Guards Rifle Corps in 1942 and 1943 and 39th Army to war's end and during the Manchurian offensive in August–September 1945.[75]

While fighting continued at Kupiansk, the remnants of 38th Army's 162nd, 199th, 278th, and 304th Rifle Divisions made their way eastward out of encirclement and across the Oskol River to the safety of Moskalenko's new defensive line. However—and fortunately for the frustrated troopers of Hube's 16th Panzer Division—the neighboring 60th Motorized Division achieved a bridgehead over the Oskol River just north of Kupiansk, after which Geyr quickly withdrew his panzers into assembly areas to prepare for the main act of Operation Blau.

Fridericus II only compounded the damage inflicted on Timoshenko's defenses by Operation Wilhelm. In addition to savaging Moskalenko's 38th Army once again, the Germans cost Nikishov's 9th Army the better part of three rifle divisions in encirclement in and west of Izium, and Parkhomenko's 5th Cavalry Corps was so severely damaged that the *Stavka* had no choice but to disband it on 15 July. Despite the grievous damage done to Moskalenko's and Nikishov's armies and their supporting 22nd Tank and 5th Cavalry Corps, Timoshenko could take solace in the knowledge he still had several tank corps within reach, and the *Stavka* was concentrating its armor, particularly the new 5th Tank Army, on his *front*'s right (northern) flank.

THE REICHEL AFFAIR

Amid these prelude battles, a strange incident threatened the entire German plan for the 1942 summer offensive. To place this incident in perspective, however, one must recall its precursor, two years before.

In January 1940, a *Luftwaffe* liaison officer flying in a small aircraft from one part of western Germany to another had become lost and was forced to land in neutral Belgium. With him was a complete plan for the projected German offensive in the west, a plan that fell into Belgian (and eventually British and French) hands. Thereafter, Hitler adamantly insisted on tight security controls over all operational plans. Only major headquarters would receive copies, and under no circumstances were plans to be transported by air near the front lines. In fact, Führer Order No. 41 for Operation Blau specifically cited the security regulations that Hitler had instituted in the wake of the 1940 incident.[76]

Unfortunately, such precautions were directly contrary to the operating tradition of the German officer corps. Officers in general, and staff officers in particular, believed they needed to know the plans of higher and adjacent units in order to accomplish the commander's intent and execute their own plans intelligently. Indeed, this flow of information was a key to German flexibility and success in battle. Thus commanders routinely violated the spirit and sometimes the letter of Hitler's security order.

One such violation occurred in XXXX Motorized Corps. The corps commander, General Stumme, had written a one-page summary of Blau I, complete with initial objectives for XXXX Motorized Corps as well as Fourth Panzer Army. This summary was delivered by hand to Stumme's division commanders, who compounded the security problem by distributing it to their own staffs. The inevitable result was a breach of security. On the afternoon of 19 June 1942, the operations officer of 23rd Panzer Division, a general staff officer named Major Joachim Reichel, took off in a Storch liaison aircraft to reconnoiter the proposed route of march for his division to reach its attack positions. Reichel carried with him a copy of the memorandum together with his mapboard, on which the corps and army objectives were labeled. As in 1940, the aircraft went off course and crashed behind enemy lines. The pilot died in the ensuing fire, and Reichel was shot while attempting to escape.[77] A German combat patrol rushed to the area and located the wrecked aircraft and several graves but no documents. The Germans had to assume (correctly, as it happened) that the information about Plan Blau had fallen into Soviet hands.[78]

Stumme, his chief of staff, Lieutenant Colonel Franz, and Reichel's division commander, General von Boineburg-Lengsfeld, lost their jobs over this incident (the latter only temporarily). A court-martial convicted Stumme and Franz for security violations. Many officers, including Field Marshal von Bock, Reichsmarshall Göring, and OKW chief Keitel, intervened on their behalf, seeking to mitigate Hitler's justifiable anger. Ultimately, the general and his chief of staff were reassigned to North Africa, where Stumme died at the Battle of El Alamein.[79]

Whether this serious lapse in security would cause any damage depended on how each side reacted. Ultimately, the German commanders persuaded Hitler that it was too late to change, and the offensive began as scheduled. As for the Soviets, most senior commanders found the Reichel memorandum creditable, although Stalin dismissed it as one of many such possible plans. Yet even this incomplete indication of a forthcoming offensive in the south did not change the collective Soviet assumption that Moscow remained the main objective for the summer. As a result, the *fronts* opposite Army Group South received only limited reinforcements.[80]

On June 20, after Timoshenko had informed Stalin of the existence of the Reichel order, the dictator reacted by disbanding the Southwestern Main Direction Command the next day. However, he was then distracted by Fridericus II, the new German offensive. As First Panzer Army's forces were shattering the 38th and 9th Armies in the Izium region, Stalin reshuffled his field commanders, replacing Nikishov as 9th Army commander with the more experienced General A. I. Lopatin, then commander of 37th Army, and appointing Major General Petr Mikhailovich Kozlov, then deputy commander of Southern Front's 18th Army and a veteran of the *front*'s many battles since November 1941, to command 37th Army.[81] Perhaps as a precautionary measure should the captured order prove to be accurate, Stalin on 23 June reinforced the Briansk Front with 17th Tank Corps from the *Stavka* Reserve.[82] By this time Briansk Front, commanded by General Golikov, included five separate tank corps (1st, 3rd, 4th, 16th, and 17th) plus 2nd and 11th Tank Corps assigned to 5th Tank Army and 8th Cavalry Corps.

As Fridericus II progressed over the next three days, Stalin transferred 61st Army, with its supporting 3rd Tank Corps, from Briansk Front to Western Front and ordered North Caucasus Front to transfer the fresh 14th Tank Corps to Timoshenko's Southwestern Front, although two days later Stalin amended this order by reassigning the tank corps to Golikov's front.[83] Finally—within hours after the Germans began Operation Blau on 28 June—Stalin also released 24th Tank Corps to Golikov's control.[84] This increased the strength of Golikov's Briansk Front to seven tank corps, fielding in excess of 1,600 tanks, more than double the 733 tanks and assault guns that Fourth Panzer Army was assembling east of Kursk. By this time, Southwestern Front still fielded more than 640 tanks, opposing Sixth Army's 360 tanks. Although Stalin was still convinced the Germans would conduct their main offensive along the Moscow axis, ever prudent, he hedged his bets by forming a formidable tank concentration should a German offensive materialize in the south.

ON THE EVE

As Hitler intended, the *Wehrmacht's* victories in May and June did much to restore German confidence and morale. Given the uneven performance of Soviet forces, the Germans had every reason to expect a series of easy victories leading to their goal—the Caucasus oil fields. The danger lay not in defeat on the battlefield but in trying to advance too far, too quickly, with too little. If they attempted to seize everything at once, the Germans might allow everything to slip through their fingers, permitting the Red Army to escape and fight another day. But most German staff officers and commanders understood the limits under which they worked. Even in Army Group South, the German divisions had never recovered completely from the losses of the previous winter. Moreover, the vast distances and logistical problems involved in Operation Blau were almost as crippling as they had been in Operation Barbarossa the previous summer.

As Operations Wilhelm and Fridericus II demonstrated, the Germans could still seize territory and inflict tactical defeats—but they seemed unable to destroy their opponents completely. Like the British fighting the Continental Army during the American Revolution, the *Wehrmacht* might win every battle but could not win the war as long as its opponent remained in the field.

Soviet commanders might console themselves with such thoughts, but they were far from confident about the outcome of the coming German offensive. The fall of the Crimea, the failure of the Khar'kov offensive, and the easy German victories in subsequent operations only reinforced a nagging Soviet sense of inferiority. In addition to almost 450,000 soldiers lost in the twin disasters at Kerch' and Khar'kov, the limited-objective offensives Sixth Army and First Panzer Army conducted during June severely weakened Southwestern Front's 28th and 38th Armies at the very center of the southwestern axis and accorded Army Group South ideal jumping-off positions from which to launch an even grander offensive in the near future.

Moreover, the Soviets massed in the wrong places. Stalin and Vasilevsky continued to expect that the main summer offensive would be toward Moscow, an expectation indicated by the allocation of their best general, Zhukov, and 10 field armies to Western Front. This error in deployment was increased by the destruction of so many of Timoshenko's armies in the south during May and June, a destruction that forced the defenders to commit even less capable, less trained units—including the new tank armies—to premature battle. It was going to be a long, difficult summer for both sides.

By 27 June 1942, Hitler had assembled an imposing collection of Axis forces in the southern Soviet Union (see Tables 10, 11, and 12 for respective orders of battle and comparative force and tank strengths). It remained to be seen whether or not Stalin's prudent precautionary measures would prove adequate to forestall another summer of spectacular *Wehrmacht* victories.

Table 8. Comparative Tank Strengths in the Battle for Khar'kov, 11 May 1942

SOVIET		GERMAN	
Force	Tanks	Force	Tanks

NORTHERN SECTOR

21st ARMY   SIXTH ARMY

Force	Tanks	Force	Tanks
10th Tank Brigade	26 (6 KV, 4 T-34, 7 BT, 9 T-26)	3rd Panzer Division	45 (5 Pz. II, 34 Pz. III/50, 6 Pz. IV/75)
478th Tank Battalion	22 (1 BT, 9 T26, 12 T-37/38)		
Total	48 (6 KV, 4 T-34, 8 BT, 18 T-26, 12 T-37/38)		

28th ARMY

Force	Tanks	Force	Tanks
84th Tank Battalion	46 (10 KV, 20 T-34, 16 T-60)		
6th Guards Tank Brigade	43 (3 KV, 18 T-34, 7 BT, 1 T-26, 12 T-60, 2 trophy)		
6th Tank Brigade	46 (10 KV, 20 T-34, 16 T-60)		
90th Tank Brigade	46 (10 KV, 20 T-34, 16 T-60)	23rd Panzer Division	181 (34 Pz. II, 112 Pz. III/50, 32 Pz. IV, 3 Pz. Cmd)
Total	181 (33 KV, 78 T-34, 7 BT, 1 T-26, 60 T-60, 2 trophy)		

38th ARMY (22nd Tank Corps)

Force	Tanks	Force	Tanks
36th Tank Brigade	47 (17 T-60, 10 Mk-II, 20 Mk-III)		
13th Tank Brigade	44 (17 BT, 9 T-26, 18 Mk-II)		
133rd Tank Brigade	34 (22 T-34, 12 BT)	194th Assault Gun *Abteilung* (Battalion)	30 (Sturmgeschutz or StuG III)
Total	125 (22 T-34, 29 BT, 17 T-60, 9 T-26, 28 Mk-II, 20 Mk-III)		
Grand Total	354 (39 KV, 104 T-34, 44 BT, 28 T-26, 77 T-60, 12 T-37/38, 28 Mk-II, 20 Mk-III, 2 trophy)	Grand Total	256 (39 Pz. II, 146 Pz. III/50, 38 Pz. IV, 3 Pz. Cmd, 30 StuG-III)

SOUTHERN SECTOR

6th ARMY   ARMEEGRUPPE KLEIST

Force	Tanks	Force	Tanks
48th Tank Brigade	42 (10 KV, 16 T-34, 16 T-60)	14th Panzer Division	48 (est.)
5th Guards Tank Brigade	38 (1 KV, 18 T-34, 18 T-60, 1 Pz. III)		
38th Tank Brigade	44 (14 T-60, 30 Mk-II)		
37th Tank Brigade	42 (15 T-60, 27 Mk-II)		
21st Tank Corps	136 (20 KV, 38 T-34, 48 T-60, 10 Mk-II, 20 Mk-III)	16th Panzer Division	97 (29 Pz. II, 46 Pz. III, 23 Pz. IV)
64th Tank Brigade	46 (16 T-60, 10 Mk-II, 20 Mk-III)		

Table 8. Continued

SOVIET		GERMAN	
Force	Tanks	Force	Tanks
98th Tank Brigade	46 (10 KV, 20 T-34, 16 T-60)		
199th Tank Brigade	44 (10 KV, 18 T-34, 16 T-60)		
23rd Tank Corps	133 (58 T-34, 45 T-60, 30 Mk-III)	60th Motorized Division	21 (est.)
57th Tank Brigade	44 (18 T-34, 16 T-60, 10 Mk-III)		
130th Tank Brigade	43 (20 T-34, 13 T-60, 10 Mk-III)		
131st Tank Brigade	46 (20 T-34, 16 T-60, 10 Mk-III)		
Army Group Bobkin (7th Tank Brigade)	40 (7 KV, 5 T-34, 10 BT, 1 T-26, 17 T-60)	160th Panzer *Abteilung*	Unknown
Total	475 (38 KV, 135 T-34, 10 BT, 2 T-26, 173 T-60, 67 Mk-II, 50 Mk-III)	Total	166
Front reserve	94 (3 KV, 3 BT, 4 T-26, 52 T-60, 1 T-40, 1 T-37/38, 22 Mk-II, 11 Mk-III)		
71st Tank Battalion	27 (1 BT, 2 T-26, 20 T-60, 1 T-40, 1 T-37/38, 1 Mk-II, 1 Mk-III)		
132nd Tank Battalion	25 (2 BT, 2 T-26, 20 T-60, 1 Mk-II)		
92nd Tank Battalion	42 (3 KV, 12 T-60, 20 Mk-II, 10 Mk-III)		
Total	923 (80 KV, 239 T-34, 57 BT, 33 T-26, 302 T-60, 1 T-40, 13 T-37/38, 117 Mk-II, 81 Mk-III, 3 Pz. III)	Total	422

9th ARMY (Southern Front)			
12th Tank Brigade	10 (2 KV, 8 T-34)		
15th Tank Brigade	0		
121st Tank Brigade	32 (2 KV, 8 T-34, 20 T-60, 2 Pz. III)		
Total	42 (4 KV, 16 T-34, 20 T-60, 2 Pz. III)		
Grand Total	965 (84 KV, 255 T-34, 57 BT, 33 T-26, 322 T-60, 1 T-40, 13 T-37/38, 22 Mk-II, 11 Mk-III)		

Sources: Andrei Galushko and Maksim Kolomiets, *Boi za Khar'kov v mae 1942 god* [The battle for Khar'kov in May 1942], in *Frontovaia illiustratsiia* [Front illustrated] (Moscow: "Strategiia KM," 1999), 6-11; and Thomas Jentz, ed., *Panzertruppen: The Complete Guide to the Creation & Combat Employment of Germany's Tank Force, 1939-1942* (Atglen, PA: Schiffer Military History, 1996), 232.

Table 9. The *Stavka* Reserve (RVGK), 1 May–1 July 1942

Abbreviations	
Infantry, Airborne, and Cavalry	TDR—tank destroyer regiment
RC—rifle corps	GMR—guards-mortar regiments
CC—cavalry corps	MtrBn—mortar battalion
RD—rifle division	GMBn—guards-mortar battalion
GRD—guards rifle division	AABn—antiaircraft artillery battalion
CD—cavalry division	
RB—rifle brigade	*Tank and Mechanized Forces*
DB—destroyer brigade	TC—tank corps
FR—fortified region	MRB—motorized rifle brigade
	TB—tank brigade
Artillery	AeroSBn—aerosleigh battalion
AAR—army artillery regiment	MtcBn—motorcycle battalion
AR—artillery regiment	AtrBn—armored train battalion
GAR—gun artillery regiment	
HAR—howitzer artillery regiment	*Other*
LAR—light artillery regiment	G (prefix)—guards (with all other abbrevia-
MtrR—mortar regiment	tions)
ATR—antitank regiment	Op. Gp.—operational group

Army	Rifle, Airborne, and Cavalry	Artillery	Tank and Mechanized
		1 MAY 1942	
1st Reserve Army	29, 164 RDs	113, 114 MtrRs	
58th Army	9, 12, 15 GRDs; 154, 304 RDs		
Separate forces	196, 211, 309 RDs; 106, 109, 118, 119, 122, 126, 133, 134, 135, 148, 149, 150, 151, 153 RBs; 110 CDs; 2 GCCs (3, 4 GCDs, 20 CDs)	135, 399, 1,109 HARs; 151 GARs; 753 AARs; 438, 468, 507, 543, 612 ATRs; 33, 43, 44, 49, 50 GMRs; 151 MtrRs	2 TC (19, 26 TBs, 2 MRBs); 103 TBs; 21, 26, 31, 32, 34, 36, 42, 47, 48 AeroSBns; 11, 12, 27, 28, 32, 37, 39, 41, 42, 48, 51 AtrBns
TOTAL 2 armies	10 RDs, 14 RBs, 1 CC, 4 CDs	5 ARs, 5 ATRs, 3 MtrRs, 5 GMRs	1 TC, 3 TBs, 1 MRB, 9 AeroSBns, 11 AtrBns
1 JUNE 1942			
1st Reserve Army	29, 112, 131, 164, 193, 195, 214 RDs	114 MtrRs	
2nd Reserve Army	25 GRDs, 100, 111, 237, 303, 312 RDs		
3rd Reserve Army	107, 141, 159, 161, 167, 206, 219, 232 RDs		
5th Reserve Army	153, 197 RDs		
6th Reserve Army	174, 181, 184, 196 RDs		
7th Reserve Army	9, 15 GRDs, 147, 192 RDs		
8th Reserve Army	64, 120, 221, 231, 308, 315 RDs		

Table 9. Continued

Army	Rifle, Airborne, and Cavalry	Artillery	Tank and Mechanized
3rd Tank Army	154 RDs	1172 LARs; 62 GMRs	12 TCs (30, 86, 97 TBs); 15 TCs (96, 105, 113 TBs)
Separate forces	309, 340 RDs; 79 FRs; 2 GCCs (3, 4 GCDs, 20 CDs)	614, 1173, 1189, 1238, 1239, 1240, 1243 LARs; 151 MtrRs; 57, 61, 66 GMRs; 38 GMBns	14 TCs (138, 139 TBs); 34, 39, 55, 56 TBs; 28, 29, 47 AtrBns
TOTAL 7 reserve armies 2 tank armies	40 RDs, 1 FR, 1 CC, 3 CDs	8 LARs, 2 MtrRs, 5 GMRs, 1 GMBn	3 TCs, 2 TBs, 3 AtrBns

1 JULY 1942

Army	Rifle, Airborne, and Cavalry	Artillery	Tank and Mechanized
1st Reserve Army (64th Army)	18, 29, 112, 131, 164, 214, 229 RDs		
2nd Reserve Army	25 GRDs, 52, 100, 111, 237, 303 RDs		
3rd Reserve Army (60th Army)	107, 159, 161, 167, 193, 195 RDs		
4th Reserve Army	78, 88, 118, 139, 274, 312 RDs		
5th Reserve Army (63rd Army)	14 GRDs, 1, 127, 153, 197, 203 RDs		
6th Reserve Army (6th Army)	99, 141, 174, 206, 219, 232, 309 RDs		
7th Reserve Army (62nd Army)	33 GRDs, 147, 181, 184, 192, 196 RDs		
8th Reserve Army	64, 120, 221, 231, 308, 315 RDs		
9th Reserve Army	32, 93, 238, 279, 316 RDs		
10th Reserve Army	133, 180, 207, 292, 299, 306 RDs		
3rd Tank Army	154 RDs	1172 LARs; 62 GMRs; 470 AABns	12 TCs (30, 86, 97 TBs, 13 MRBs); 15 TCs (96, 105, 113 TBs, 17 MRBs); 2, 99, 166, 179 TBs
5th Tank Army	340 RDs	611 LARs; 66 GMRs	2 TCs (26, 27, 148 TBs, 2 MRBs); 11 TCs (53, 59, 160 TBs, 12 MRBs); 19 TBs
Separate forces	2 GCCs (3, 4 GCDs, 20 CDs); 6, 7, 8, 10 DBs	1180, 1246, 1247 LARs; 151 MRs; 72, 74 GMRs; 68, 69, 70 HGMRs; 314, 326 GMBns	7 TCs (3 GTBs, 62, 87 TBs, 7 MRBs); 18 TC (110, 180, 181 TBs, 18 MRBs); 25 TCs (111, 162, 175 TBs, 16 MRBs), 28 AtrBns
TOTAL 10 reserve armies 1 tank army	63 RDs, 4 DBs, 1 CC, 3 CDs	5 LARs, 1 MtrR, 7 GMRs, 2 GMBns, 1 AABn	7 TCs, 25 TBs, 7 MRBs, 1 AtrBn

Source: Boevoi sostav Sovetskoi armii, 2: 93, 113, 134.

Table 10. Axis and Red Army Force Dispositions in Operation Blau, 28 June 1942 (First and Seventeenth Armies as of 7 July) (from north to south, with army groups, separate armies, and tank forces in bold)

AXIS	SOVIET
The Army of Lapland (later Twentieth Mountain Army) (Colonel General Eduard Dietl)	**Karelian Front** (Lieutenant General V. A. Frolov) 14th, 19th, 26th, and 32nd Armies 7th Separate Army
Finnish Army	**Leningrad Front** (Colonel General L. A. Govorov)
Army Group North (Colonel General Georg von Küchler) Eighteenth Army Sixteenth Army Eleventh Army (in July)	23rd, 42nd, 55th, and 8th Armies and Coastal Operational Group
	Volkhov Front (Colonel General K. A. Meretskov) 54th, 4th, 59th Armies, 2nd Shock Army, and 52nd Army
	Northwestern Front (Colonel General P. A. Kurochkin) 11th, 34th, and 53rd Armies and 1st Shock Army
Army Group Center (Field Marshal Günther von Kluge) Ninth Army Third Panzer Army Fourth Army Second Panzer Army	**Kalinin Front** (Colonel General I. S. Konev) 3rd and 4th Shock Armies and 22nd, 30th, 39th, 29th, and 31st Armies
	Western Front (Colonel General G. K. Zhukov) 20th, 5th, 33rd, 43rd, 49th, 50th, 10th, 16th, and 61st Armies

Army Group South—Field Marshal Fedor von Bock

Armeegruppe von Weichs SECOND ARMY (Colonel General Maximilian *Freiherr* von Weichs an dem Glon) LV Army Corps (General of Infantry Erwin Vierow) 45th, 95th, 299th IDs and 1st SS IB	**Briansk Front** (Lieutenant General F. I. Golikov) 3rd Army (Lieutenant General P. P. Korzun) 60th, 137th, 240th, 269th, 283rd, and 287th RDs, 104th and 134th RBs, and **79th** and **150th TBs**
FOURTH PANZER ARMY (Colonel General Hermann Hoth) XIII Army Corps (General of Infantry Erich Straube) 82nd and 385th IDs and **11th PzD**	48th Army (Major General G. A. Khaliuzin) 6th Gds., 8th, 211th, and 280th RDs, 118th and 122nd RBs, 55th CD, and **80th** and **202nd TBs**
XXIV Panzer Corps (General of Panzer Troops Willibald *Freiherr* von Langermann und Erlenkamp) 377th ID, **9th PzD**, and **3rd MotD** (**11th PzD** on 4 July)	13th Army (Major General N. P. Pukhov) 15th, 132nd, 143rd, 148th, and 307th RDs, 109th RB, and **129th TB**
XXXXVIII Panzer Corps (General of Panzer Troops Werner Kempf) **24th PzD** and **"GD" MotD** (**16th MotD** on 4 July)	40th Army (Lieutenant General M. A. Parsegov) 6th, 45th, 62nd, 121st, 160th, and 212th RDs, 111th, 119th, and 141st RBs, and **14th** and **170th TBs**
HUNGARIAN SECOND ARMY (Colonel General Gusztav Jany) VII Army Corps (German) (General of Artillery Ernst-Eberhard Hell) 387th ID and Hungarian 6th LtD Hungarian III Army Corps Hungarian 7th and 9th LtDs and **16th MotD**	5th Tank Army (Major General A. I. Liziukov) 340th RD and **19th TB** **2nd Tank Corps** (Major General I. G. Lazarev) (**26th, 27th,** and **148th TBs** and 2nd MRB) **11th Tank Corps** (Major General N. N. Parkevich)(**53rd, 59th,** and **160th TBs** and 12th MRB)

Table 10. Continued

RESERVES
88th, 323rd, 34th, and 383rd IDs
VIII Air [*Flieger*] Corps (Fourth Air Fleet)
(General *der Flieger* Hans Seidemann)
Rear Area Command
Hungarian 105th Infantry Brigade
213th SecD

SIXTH ARMY (General of Panzer Troops
Friedrich Paulus)
XXIX Army Corps (General of Infantry
Hans von Obstfelder)
57th, 168th, and 75th IDs
VIII Army Corps (Lieutenant General
Walter Heitz)
389th, 305th, and 376th IDs
XXXX Panzer Corps (General of Panzer
Troops Georg Stumme)
100th JD, 336th ID, 3rd and **23rd PzDs**,
and **29th MotD**
XVII Army Corps (General of Infantry
Karl Hollidt)
113th, 79th, and 294th IDs
LI Army Corps (General of Artillery
Walter von Seydlitz-Kurzbach)
297th, 71st, 44th, 62nd, and 384th IDs
IV Air Corps (Fourth Air Fleet) (General
der Flieger Kurt Pfflugal)

2nd Air Army (Major General of Aviation
K. N. Smirnov)
205th, 207th, and 266th FADs, 208th
FBAD, 223rd BAD, and 225th, 227th,
and 267th AADs
6th Sapper Army (Lieutenant General
A. S. Gundorov)
17th, 18th, and 19th SBs
Front units
1st Gds. and 284th RDs, 2nd DD, and
118th, 157th, and **201st TBs**
1st Tank Corps (Major General
M. E. Katukov) (**1st Gds., 49th,** and
89th TBs and 1st MRB)
4th Tank Corps (Major General
V. A. Mishulin) (**45th, 47th,** and
102nd TBs and 4th MRB)
16th Tank Corps (Major General
M. I. Pavelkin) (**107th, 109th,** and
164th TBs and 15th MRB)
17th Tank Corps (Major General
N. V. Feklenko) (**66th, 67th,** and
174th TBs and 31st MRB)
24th Tank Corps (Major General
V. M. Badanov) (**4th Gds., 54th,** and
130th TBs and 24th MRB)
7th Cavalry Corps (Major General
I. M. Managarov) (11th, 17th, and
83rd CDs)
8th Cavalry Corps (Colonel I. F. Lunev)
(21st and 112th CDs)
Southwestern Front (Marshal of the Soviet
Union S. K. Timoshenko)
21st Army (Major General A. I. Danilov)
76th, 124th, 226th, 227th, 293rd, 297th,
301st, and 343rd RDs, 8th NKVD RD,
10th TB, and 1st MRB, 478th TBn
13th Tank Corps (Major General
P. E. Shurov) (**85th** and **167th TBs**
and 20th MRB)
28th Army (Lieutenant General
D. I. Riabyshev)
13th and 15th Gds., 38th, 169th, and
175th RDs and **65th, 90th,** and
91st TBs
23rd Tank Corps (Colonel
A. M. Khasin) (**6th Gds.** and **114th
TBs** and 9th MRB)
38th Army (Major General
K. S. Moskalenko)
162nd, 199th, 242nd, 277th, 278th, and
304th RDs, **133rd, 156th, 159th,** and
168th TBs, 22nd MRB, and **92nd TBn**
22nd Tank Corps (Major General
A. A. Shamshin) (**3rd, 13th,** and **36th
TBs**)

Table 10. Continued

AXIS	SOVIET
	9th Army (Lieutenant General A. I. Lopatin) 51st, 81st, 106th, 140th, 355th, 296th, 318th, and 333rd RDs, 18th and 19th DBs, **12th TB**, and **71st** and **132nd TBns**)
	5th Cavalry Corps (Major General F. A. Parkhomenko) (30th, 34th, and 60th CDs)
	57th Army (Major General D. N. Nikishov) no subordinate units
	8th Air Army (Major General of Aviation T. T. Khriukhin) 206th, 220th, 235th, 268th, and 269th FADs, 226th and 228th AADs, 221st and 270th BADs, and 271st and 272nd FBADs
	7th Sapper Army (Major General V. S. Kosenko) 12th, 14th, 15th, 20th, and 21st SBs
	Front units 9th Gds., 103rd, 244th, and 300th RDs, 1st DD, and 11th, 13th, 15th, and 17th DBs,
	57th, 58th, 84th, 88th, 158th, and **176th TBs**, 21st MRB, and composite **TBn**
	14th Tank Corps (Major General N. N. Radkevich) (**138th** and **139th TBs**)
	3rd Gds. Cavalry Corps (Major General V. D. Kriuchenkin) (5th and 6th Gds. and 32nd CDs)
	52nd, 53rd, 74th, 117th, and 118th FRs
FIRST PANZER ARMY (Colonel General Ewald von Kleist)	**Southern Front** (Lieutenant General R. Ia. Malinovsky)
XI Army Corps (Group Strecker) (General of Infantry Karl Strecker) (with Romanian VI Army Corps)	37th Army (Major General P. M. Kozlov) 102nd, 218th, 230th, 275th, and 295th RDs and **121st TB**
1st MtnD and Romanian 1st, 4th, 20th, and 2nd IDs	12th Army (Major General A. A. Grechko) 4th, 74th, 176th, 261st, and 349th RDs
III Panzer Corps (General of Panzer Troops Leo *Freiherr* Geyr von Schweppenburg)	18th Army (Major General F. N. Kamkov) 216th, 353rd, 383rd, and 395th RDs and **64th TB**
16th (temporarily in XIV PzC) and **22nd PzDs** and **SS "LAH" MotD** (temporarily in OKH reserve south)	56th Army (Major General. V. V. Tsyganov) 3rd GRC (2nd GRD and 68th, 76th, and 81st NRBs)
XIV Panzer Corps (General of Infantry Gustav von Wietersheim)	30th, 31st, and 339th RDs, 16th RB, 70th and 158th FRs, and **63rd TB**
14th PzD and **60th MotD**	24th Army (Lieutenant General I. K. Smirnov)
XXXXIV Army Corps (General of Artillery Maximilian de Angelis)	73rd, 228th, 335th, and 341st RDs
257th and 68th IDs and 97th and 101st JDs	4th Air Army (Major General of Aviation K. A. Vershinin)
IV Army Corps (General of Infantry Viktor von Schwedler)	216th and 217th FADs, 218th FBAD, 219th BAD, and 230th AAD

Table 10. Continued

295th, 76th, 94th, and 9th IDs
(to Eleventh Army by 7 July)
444th SecD
454th SecD

Seventeenth Army (Colonel General
Richard Ruoff)
LII Army Corps (General of Infantry
Eugen Ott)
111th and 370th IDs
Italian Expeditionary (Mobile) Corps
3rd Celere Mobile, 9th Pasubio, and 52nd
Torino Mobile IDs
XXXXIX Mountain Corps (General of
Mountain Troops Rudolf Konrad)
198th ID and 4th MtnD
LVII Panzer Corps (Group Wietersheim)
(General of Panzer Troops
Friedrich Kirchner)
**13th PzD, SS "Viking" MotD, Slovak
Mobile Div.**, and 125th, 73rd, and
298th IDs
Reserves
371st ID and **SS "LAH" MotD**
(temporarily from III Panzer Corps)

Note: As of 24 June, First Panzer and
Seventeenth Armies' panzer and motorized
forces were organized as follows:
III Panzer Corps (Group Mackensen),
with **14th** and **16th PzDs**, part of **22nd PzD**
and **60th MotD**
XIV Panzer Corps, with **13th PzD,
"LAH"** and **"Viking" MotDs**, Slovak Mobile
Division, and parts of 73rd and 125th IDs.
Army Group A reorganized its panzer and
motorized forces and activated **LVII Panzer
Corps** (Group Wietersheim) prior to the
beginning of Blau II.

Third Army (Romanian)
Army Group Reserve:
V Army Corps (General of Infantry
Wilhelm Wetzel) (HQ only)
HQ, Italian Eighth Army
Italian II Army Corps
Italian 2nd Sforcesca, 3rd Ravenna, and
5th Cosseria IDs
Hungarian IV Army Corps
Hungarian 10th, 12th, and 13th LtDs
HQ, Hungarian V Army Corps
Hungarian VII Army Corps
Hungarian 20th and 23rd LtDs

8th Sapper Army (Colonel D. I. Suslin)
10th, 11th, 23rd, 24th, 25th, 26th, 28th,
29th, and 30th SBs
Front units
347th RD, 89th and 73rd FRs, **5th Gds.,
15th,** and **140th TBs,** and **62nd** and
75th TBns

Table 10. Continued

AXIS	SOVIET
Eleventh Army (Colonel General Fritz-Erich von Manstein)	**North-Caucasus Front** (Marshal of the Soviet Union S. M. Budenny)
XXXXII Army Corps (General of Infantry Franz Mattenklott)	47th Army (Major General G. P. Kotov)
132nd ID	32nd Gds. and 77th RDs, 86th NRB, 103rd RB, and **126th TBn**
XXX Army Corps (General of Artillery Maximilian von Fretter-Pico)	51st Army (Colonel General A. M. Kuznetsov)
72nd and 170th IDs and 28th JD	91st, 138th, 156th, and 157th RDs, 110th and 115th CDs, 255th CR, and **40th TB**
LIV Army Corps (General of Cavalry Erik Hansen)	Coastal Army (Major General I. E. Petrov)
22nd, 24th, and 50th IDs, two regiments of 132nd ID, and 4th Romanian MtnD	25th, 95th, 109th, 172nd, 345th, 386th, and 388th RDs, 79th and 138th NRBs, 7th and 8th NIBs, and **81st** and **125th TBns**
Romanian Mtn. Corps (General Gheorghe Avramescu)	5th Air Army (Lieutenant General of Aviation S. K. Goriunov)
Romanian 1st MtnD and 18th ID	132nd BAD, 236th, 237th, and 265th FADs, and 238th AAD
	Front units
	1st RC (236th and 302nd RDs and 113th and 139th RBs)
	83rd, 142nd, and 154th NRB, **136th** and **137th TBs**, and **79th TBn**
	17th Cavalry Corps (Major General N. Ia. Kirichenko) (12th, 13th, 15th, and 116th CDs)
	Trans-Caucasus Front (Army General I. V. Tiulenev)
	44th Army (Major General A. A. Khriashchev)
	223rd, 414th, and 416th RDs and 9th and 10th RBs
	46th Army (Major General V. F. Sergatskov)
	3rd RC (9th and 20th MtnRDs)
	389th, 392nd, 394th, and 406th RDs, 155th RB, 63rd CD, and 51st FR
	Front units
	417th RD and **52nd TB**
	Stavka Reserve
	1st Reserve Army
	18th, 29th, 112th, 131st, 164th, 214th, and 229th RDs
	2nd Reserve Army
	25th Gds., 52nd, 100th, 111th, 237th, and 303rd RDs
	3rd Reserve Army
	107th, 159th, 161st, 167th, 193rd, and 195th RDs
	4th Reserve Army
	78th, 88th, 118th, 139th, 274th, and 312th RDs

Table 10. Continued

5th Reserve Army
  14th Gds., 1st, 127th, 153rd, 197th, and 203rd RDs
6th Reserve Army
  99th, 141st, 174th, 206th, 219th, 232nd, and 309th RDs
7th Reserve Army
  33rd Gds., 147th, 181st, 184th, 192nd, and 196th RDs
8th Reserve Army
  64th, 126th, 221st, 231st, 308th, and 315th RDs
9th Reserve Army
  32nd, 93rd, 238th, 279th, and 316th RDs
10th Reserve Army
  133rd, 180th, 207th, 292nd, 299th, and 306th RDs
3rd Tank Army
  154th RD and 2nd, **89th, 166th,** and **179th TBs**
  12th Tank Corps (Colonel S. I. Bogdanov) (**30th, 86th,** and **97th TBs** and 13th MRB)
  15th Tank Corps (Major General V. A. Koptsov) (**96th, 105th,** and **113th TBs** and 17th MRB)
  7th Tank Corps (Colonel P. A. Rotmistrov) (**3rd Gds., 62nd,** and **87th TBs** and 7th MRB)
  18th Tank Corps (Major General I. D. Cherniakhovsky) (**110th, 180th,** and **181st TBs** and 18th MRB)
  25th Tank Corps (Major General P. P. Pavlov) (**111th, 162nd,** and **175th TBs** and 16th MRB)
  2nd Gds. Cavalry Corps (Major General V. V. Kriukov) (3rd and 4th Gds. and 20th CDs)
  6th, 7th, 8th, and 10th DBs

Sources: AXIS FORCES: Horst Boog, Werner Rahn, Reinhard Stumpf, and Bernd Wegner, *Germany and the Second World War, Vol. VI, The Global War,* trans. Ewald Osers, John Brownjohn, Patricia Crampton, and Louise Willmot (Oxford: Clarendon Press, 2001), 965, for Army Group South's order of battle on 24 June 1942, as amended to the dates shown by "Lagenkarten, Anlage zum KTB Russland, 12 June–31 Dec 1942," *AOK II, Ia 29585/207,* in NAM T-312, Roll 1206; "Ia, Lagenkarten zum KTB 12, May–Jul 1942," *AOK 6, 22855/Ia,* in NAM T-312, Roll 1446; "Lagenkarten Pz. AOK 1, Ia (Armee-Gruppe v. Kleist), 1–29 Jun 1942," *PzAOK 1, 24906/12,* in NAM T-313, Roll 35; and "Lagenkarten, Anlage 9 zum Kreigstagebuch Nr. 3, AOK 17, Ia., 29 May–30 July 1942," *AOK 17, 24411/18,* in NAM T-312, Roll 696.
RED ARMY FORCES: *Boevoi sostav Sovetskoi armii, Chast' 2 (ianvar'–dekabr' 1942 goda)* [Combat composition of the Red Army, Part 2 (January–December 1942)](Moscow: Voenizdat, 1966), 124–128, 134–135. Prepared by the Military-Scientific Directorate of the General Staff.

Notes:
1. Soviet order of battle as of 1 July, *Armeegruppe* Weichs and Sixth Army as of 28 June, and First Panzer and Seventeenth Armies as of 7 July.
2. The OKW redesignated German motorized corps as panzer corps in late June.

Table 10. Continued

Table 11. The Strength of Axis and Soviet Armored Forces in Operation Blau, 28 June 1942

AXIS		SOVIET	
Force	Tanks	Force	Tanks
ARMEEGRUPPE VON WEICHS (FOURTH PANZER ARMY)		BRIANSK FRONT (13th, 40th A)	
9th PzD	144 (22 Pz. II, 99 Pz. III, 9 Pz. IV/short, 12 Pz. IV/long, 2 Pz. Cmd)	1st TC 1st GTB 49th TB 89th TB	170
11th PzD	155 (15 Pz. II, 124 Pz. III, 1 Pz. IV/short, 12 Pz. IV/long, 3 Pz. Cmd)	4th Tank Corp	145 (29 KV-1, 26 T-34, 30 T-70, 60 T-60)
		45th TB	59 (29 KV-1, 4 T-70, 26 T-60)
		47th TB	38 (8 T-34, 13 T-70, 17 T-60)
		102nd TB	48 (18 T-34, 13 T-70, 17 T-60)
24th PzD	181 (32 Pz. II, 110 Pz. III, 20 Pz. IV/short, 12 Pz. IV/long, 7 Pz. Cmd)	16th TC	181 (24 KV-1, 88 T-34, 69 T-60)
		107th TB	51 (24 KV-1, 27 T-34)
		109th TB	65 (44 T-34, 21 T-60)
		164th TB	65 (44 T-34, 21 T-60)
3rd MotD	54 (10 Pz. II, 35 Pz. III, 8 Pz. IV/long, 1 Pz. Cmd)	5th TA (as of 6–17 July)	641 (83 KV-1, 228 T-34, 88 Mk-II, 242 T-60)
		2nd TC	183 (26 KV-1, 88 T-34, 69 T-60)
		26th TB	65 (44 T-34, 21 T-60)
		27th TB	65 (44 T-34, 21 T-60)
		148th TB	53 (26 KV-1, 27 T-60)
		7th TC	212 (33 KV-1, 96 T-34, 83 T-60)
		3rd GTB	60 (33 KV-1, 27 T-60)
		62nd TB	65 (44 T-34, 21 T-60)
		87th TB	87 (52 T-34, 35 T-60)
		11th TC	181 (24 KV, 88 Mk-II, 69 T-60)
		53rd TB	61 (24 KV-1, 27 T-60)
		59th TB	65 (44 Mk-II, 21 T-60)
		160th TB	65 (44 Mk-II, 21 T-60)
		19th TB	65 (44 T-34, 21 T-60)
16th MotD	54 (10 Pz. II, 35 Pz. III, 8 Pz. IV/long, 1 Pz. Cmd)	17th TC	179 (23 KV-1, 88 T-34, 68 T-60)
		66th TB	49 (23 KV-1, 26 T-60)
		67th TB	65 (44 T-34, 21 T-60)
		174th TB	65 (44 T-34, 21 T-60)
"GD" MotD	45 (12 Pz. II, 2 Pz. III, 18 Pz. IV/short, 12 Pz. IV/long, 1 Pz. Cmd)	24th TC	141 (24 KV-1, 48 T-34, 52 T-60, 17 Mk-III)
		4th GTB	51 (24 KV-1, 27 T-60)
		54th TB	53 (28 T-34, 25 T-60)
		130th TB	37 (20 T-34, 17 Mk-III)
		Sep TBs:	200 (est.)
		129th TB, 13th A	
		14th TB, 40th A	
		170th TB, 40th A	
		115th TB, reserve	
		116th TB, reserve	

Table 11. Continued

AXIS		SOVIET	
Force	Tanks	Force	Tanks
Total	633 (101 Pz. II, 405 Pz. III, 48 Pz. IV/short, 64 Pz. IV/long, 15 Pz. Cmd)		1,657
SIXTH ARMY		SOUTHWESTERN FRONT (21st, 28th, 38th A)	
3rd PzD	162 (25 Pz. II, 104 Pz. III, 21 Pz. IV/short, 12 Pz. IV/long)	13th TC	163 (8 KV-1, 51 T-34, 30 Mk-III, 74 T-60)
		167th TB	50 (30 Mk-III, 20 -60)
		158th TB	48 (8 KV-1, 20 T-34, 20 T-60)
		85th TB	65 (31 T-34, 34 T-60)
23rd PzD	138 (27 Pz. II, 84 Pz. III, 17 Pz. IV/short, 8 Pz. IV/long)	23rd TC	128 (9 KV-1, 38 T-34, 3 M-3 med., 38 M-3 lt., 40 T-60)
		6th TB	38 (18 T-34, 20 T-26)
		91st TB	49 (9 KV-1, 20 T-34, 20 T-60)
		114th TB	41 (3 M-3 med., 38 M-3 lt.)
29th MotD	58 (12 Pz. II, 36 Pz. III, 8 Pz. IV/long, 2 Pz. Cmd)	22nd TC	55
		36th TB	29 (5 KV-1, 1 T-34, 1 Mk-II, 9 Mk-III, 13 T-60)
		3rd MTB	20
		13th TB	6
		14th TC	(Still forming and not committed)
		138th TB	
		139th TB	
		Sep. TBs	326
		10th TB, 21st A38	(3 KV-1, 12 T-34, 7 BT, 5 T-26, 11 T-60)
		478th TBn, 21st A	63 (2 BT-7, 2 BT-5, 14 T-26, 4 T-40, 41 T-37, T-38)
		6th GTB, 28th A	28 (5 KV-1, 7 T-34, 16 T-60)
		65th TB, 28th A	47 (24 KV-1, 23 T-60)
		90th TB, 28th A	40 (7 KV-1, 3 T-34, 15 M-3 lt., 15 T-60)
		133rd TB, 38th A	0
		156th TB, 38th A	8 (2 KV)
		159th TB, 38th A	48 (20 T-60, 28 Mk-III)
		92nd TBn, 38th A	23 (7 KV-1, 7 T-60)
		57th TB, *front*	
		58th TB, *front*	
		84th TB, *front*	
		88th TB, *front*	
		176th TB, *front*	
Total	358 (64 Pz. II, 224 Pz. III, 38 Pz. IV/short, 30 Pz. IV/long, 2 Pz. Cmd)		673

Table 11. Continued

AXIS		SOVIET	
Force	Tanks	Force	Tanks
FIRST PANZER ARMY		**SOUTHERN FRONT (9th, 37th A)**	
14th PzD	102 (14 Pz. II, 60 Pz. III, 20 Pz. IV/short, 4 Pz. IV/long, 4 Pz. Cmd)	12th TB, 9th A	2 (2 T-34)
16th PzD	100 (13 Pz. II, 57 Pz. III, 15 Pz. IV/short, 12 Pz. IV/long, 3 Pz. Cmd)		
22nd PzD	176 (28 Pz. II, 12 Pz. III, 11 Pz. IV/short, 11 Pz. IV/long, 114 Czech Pz. 38(t))	71st TBn, 9th A	51 (20 BT, T-26, 24 T-60, 2 Mk-II, 5 Mk-III)
60th MotD	57 (17 Pz. II, 35 Pz. III, 4 Pz. IV/long, 1 Pz. Cmd)	132nd TBn, 9th A	11 (3 T-34, 3 T-60, 1 Mk-II, 4 Mk-III)
		121st TB, 37th A	46 (8 KV, 18 T-34, 20 T-60)
Total	435 (72 Pz. II, 164 Pz. III, 50 Pz. IV/short, 27 Pz. IV/long, 114 Pz. 38 (t), 8 Pz. Cmd)	Total	110 (8 KV, 23 T-34, 20 BT, T-26, 47 T-60, 3 Mk-II, 9 Mk-III)
SEVENTEENTH ARMY		**SOUTHERN FRONT (12th, 24th, 18th, 56th A)**	
13th PzD	103 (15 Pz. II, 71 Pz. III, 12 Pz. IV/short, 5 Pz. Cmd)	64th TB, 18th A	8 (8 KV)
SS "Viking" MotD	53 (12 Pz. II, 36 Pz. III, 4 Pz. IV/short, 1 Pz. Cmd)	63rd TB, 56th A	55 (9 KV, 2 T-34, 14 T-26, 6 XT-26, 19 T-60, 5 T-37)
SS "LAH" MotD (reserve)	53 (12 Pz. II, 36 Pz. III, 4 Pz. IV/short (estimate)	140th TB, reserve	47 (9 KV, 20 T-34, 18 T-60)
		62nd TBn, reserve	36 (5 KV, 1 T-34, 18 BT, 12 T-26)
		75th TBn, reserve	16 (5 KV, 11 BT)
		2nd Res. TBn	6 (1 KV, 1 T-34, 1 Mk-II, 1 Mk-III, 2 T-60)
Total	209 (39 Pz. II, 143 Pz. III, 20 Pz. IV/short, 7 Pz. Cmd)	Total	168 (37 KV, 24 T-34, 29 BT, 26 T-26, 6 XT-26, 39 T-60, 5 T-37, 1 Mk-II, 1 Mk-III)
Grand Total	1,635 (276 Pz. II, 936 Pz. III, 156 Pz. IV/short, 121 Pz. IV/short, 114 Pz. 38 (t), 32 Pz. Cmd)	62 TBs	2,612
		***STAVKA* RESERVE**	
		18th TC	181 (24 KV-1, 88 T-34, 69 T-60)
		180th TB	51 (24 KV-1, 27 T-60)
		181st TB	65 (44 T-34, 21 T-60)
		110th TB	65 (44 T-34, 21 T-60)
		25th TC	166 (103 T-34, 63 T-60, T-70)
		111th TB	
		162nd TB	
		87th TB	

Table 11. Continued

	AXIS		SOVIET	
Force	Tanks		Force	Tanks
			Total	347 (24 KV-1, 191 T-34, 132 T-60, T-70)
			Grand Total	2,959

Sources: Maksim Kolomiets, Aleksandr Smirnov, *Boi v izluchine Dona, 28 iiunia–23 iiulia 1942 goda* [The battle of the bend of the Don, 28 June–23 July 1942] (Moscow: Strategiia KM, 2002); Thomas L. Jentz, ed., *Panzertruppen: The Complete Guide to the Creation & Combat Employment of Germany's Tank Force, 1933–1942* (Atglen, PA: Schiffer Military History, 1996); and V. A. Demin and R. M. Portugal'sky, *Tanki vkhodiat v proryv* [Tanks are entering the penetration] (Moscow: Voenizdat, 1988), 15.

Abbreviations

General	German	Soviet
A — army	Pz. II (SdKfz 121)—20mm gun	Mk-II—"Matilda" British
TC—tank corps	Pz. III (SdKfz 141)—50mm gun	Mk-III—"Valentine" British
PzD—panzer division	Pz. IV (SdKfz 161):	
MotD—motorized division	short—75mm L./24 gun	M-3 med.—M-3 "General Lee" American
TB—tank brigade	long—75mm L./4	M-3 lt.—M-3 "General Stuart" American
TBn—tank battalion	Pz. 38 (t)—Czech	
G (prefix) — guards		
Sep. — separate		

Table 12. Correlation of Opposing Forces in Operation Blau, 28 June 1942 (per Table 10)

Forces and Weapons	Axis	Soviet	Correlation
Divisions and brigades	68 German divisions (52 IDs, 9 PzDs, and 7 MotDs);	93 divisions (81 RDs, 12 CDs); 9 FRs; 90 brigades (62 TBs, 38 RBs)	1 : 1 (German/Soviet)
	21 allied divisions (8 Hungarian, 7 Romanian, and 6 Italian)		1.15 : 1 (Axis/Soviet)
Personnel	1.25 million (950,000 German, 300,000 allied)	1,715,000	1 : 1.8 (German/Soviet) 1 : 1.4 (Axis/Soviet)
Tanks	1,635 total	2,959 total	1 : 1.6
	1,327 combat (less Pz. II and Pz. Cmd)	2,300 combat	1 : 1.7
Guns/mortars	17,000	16,500	1 : 1
Aircraft	1,640	758	2.2 : 1

Notes:
1. German figures include Eleventh Army.
2. Soviet figures include the Briansk, Southwestern, and Southern Fronts.
3. Counts one German division as equivalent to two Soviet rifle or cavalry divisions and three rifle or tank brigades, and one Axis allied division as equivalent to one Soviet rifle division.
3. German infantry divisions include jäger and mountain versions but not security divisions.
4. German personnel strength does not include the *Luftwaffe*.
5. Combat tank strengths omit light models such as Pz. II and Pz. Cmd and T-60 tanks and do not count nonoperational tanks.

CHAPTER 4

Punch and Counterpunch: Blau I, 28 June–12 July 1942

The region in which Army Group B conducted Blau I formed a crude rectangle that simultaneously favored and disfavored the defending Soviets as well as the advancing German forces.

AREA OF OPERATIONS

Army Group B undertook the offensive known as Blau I in a rectangle that stretched from the Livny and Elets regions in the north roughly 300 kilometers southward to the Roven'ki region and from Kursk, Belgorod, and Kupiansk in the west about 230 kilometers eastward to Voronezh on the Voronezh River and Novaia Kalitva on the Don River (see Map 8). At the rectangle's four corners stood the cities and towns of Kursk (northwest), Elets (northeast), Kupiansk (southwest), and Novaia Kalitva (southeast). Two great river systems, the Northern Donets River with its tributaries and the Don River with its tributaries, marked the rectangle's western and eastern flanks. Between these two river systems was an expanse of gently rolling, relatively open steppe, typically a grass-covered surface pockmarked with occasional patches of light woods on the many low ridges and thickets of brush flanking the abundant rivers and streams traversing the region.[1]

Although the Northern Donets and the Don Rivers flowed roughly north to south, the many tributaries trended diagonally from the rectangle's middle into the rectangle's eastern and western flanks. From north to south on the western half, the Razumnaia, Koren', Korocha, Nezhegol, Volch'ia, and Oskol Rivers flowed southwestward into the Donets; and on the eastern half the Sosna, Potudan', Tikhaia Sosna, and Chernaia Kalitva moved southeastward, eastward, or northwestward into the Don. In the northwestern sector of the rectangle the Seim River flowed northwestward toward Kursk, and the northeastern sector was traversed by the Sosna River, which ran eastward to join the Don River east of Elets. The major tributaries of the Sosna (from west to east the Tim, Kshen', and Olym Rivers) flowed by and large northward into their parent river. In the same fashion, the Aidar River ran southward through the center of the southern sector of the rectangle, ultimately joining the Northern Donets River near Voroshilovgrad.

Although all of the rivers within this rectangle were easily crossed by bridge or by ford, their steep banks (usually higher on the western side) and the plentiful

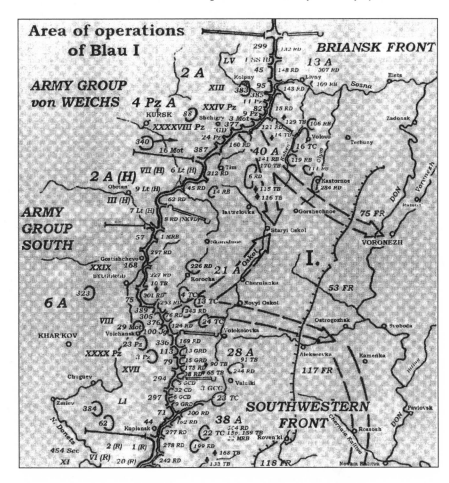

Map 8. Area of operations of Blau I

balkas (ravines) created by their many tributaries formed formidable military obstacles, especially when defended. This is especially true of the Oskol River, which rose southeast of the town of Tim and flowed southward through Staryi and Novyi Oskol to Valuiki and then wheeled southwestward through Kupiansk to join the Northern Donets River near Izium. Because of the restricted road and rail network that existed in 1942, the only major crossing sites over this river were (from north to south) at towns such as Staryi Oskol, Chernianka, Novyi Oskol, and Volokonovka. Even these routes—as was the case with all the roads and paths in the region—were difficult to negotiate in rainy weather.

The second major factor affecting military operations in Blau I was the rail and road network that existed in the region in 1942. As in other areas of the Soviet

Union, the government policy of constructing a limited number of roads to restrict population movement made railroad lines vital routes of communications, as well as important axes of advance by military forces, even in relatively traversable steppe terrain. Inside the rectangle, the rail net included three main north-south lines and one extending from west to east. From north to south, the first railroad line extended along the rectangle's western edge, from Orel southward through Kursk and Belgorod to the major city of Khar'kov. The second line ran from Elets southward via Kastornoe, Staryi and Novyi Oskol, and Volokonovka through the center of the region. The third, on the rectangle's eastern edge, extended from Griazi on the Voronezh River east of the Don southward through Voronezh, Rossosh', and Kantemirovka to the Millerovo region. Because the Germans already controlled the westernmost line, the second and third railroad lines and the major towns along them became key German military objectives.

As for lateral railroad lines extending from west to east, the only one of military significance traversing this region ran eastward from Kursk and, traversing the northern third of the rectangle, passed through Kastornoe, crossed the Don River, and terminated at Voronezh, which was situated on the Voronezh River about 10 kilometers east of the Don. This critical railroad, with its associated parallel roads, quite naturally became *Armeegruppe* Weichs's main axis of advance to the east. The only other railroad line traversing the rectangle from west to east entered the region at Kupiansk and then ran northeastward along the Oskol River to Valuiki before continuing northeastward across open country and then along the southern bank of the Tikhaia Sosna River to reach the Don River northeast of Ostrogozhsk. To exploit this railroad, any force advancing from the west would first have to negotiate a 50-kilometer stretch between the Volchansk region and the Oskol River at Volokonovka.

Before the Soviet Union built a more expansive system of highways after the war, the most trafficable roads in this region extending from west to east, which included the rights of way along the railroad, ran from the vicinities of Shchigry and Tim eastward through Kastornoe to Voronezh and, farther south, from the Volchansk region northeastward to Novyi Oskol on the Oskol River and then eastward through Nikolaevka (Alekseevka) and Ostrogozhsk to Svoboda on the Don River. Between these, relatively good roadways led from the valley of the Northern Donets River at Belgorod to Korocha and, farther south, from Kupiansk to Valuiki.

These terrain considerations had already figured into German military planning and would continue to do so in Operation Blau. For example, Sixth Army conducted Operation Wilhelm in mid-June for the purposes of eliminating Southwestern Front's bridgehead on the western bank of the Northern Donets River, capturing key crossing sites, and seizing an operational-scale bridgehead in the Volchansk and Kupiansk regions on the river's eastern bank to gain access to the road network east of the river. For the same reasons, *Armeegruppe* Weichs would conduct its main attack along the excellent communications routes from the region east of Kursk toward the Don River and Voronezh, and Sixth Army would make its main effort from the Volchansk region northeastward through Novyi Oskol toward the Don River near Ostrogozhsk.

Because German objectives in Blau II encompassed a region stretching south of where Blau I was to be conducted, terrain considerations affected the transition between the two operations. To pivot smoothly in this regard, the Germans realized that, once the forces *Armeegruppe* Weichs and Sixth Army reached the Don River and Voronezh and eliminated Soviet forces from the Blau I rectangle, they would have to defend the region they captured with part of their force and, simultaneously, wheel the remainder southward to link up with the forces of First Panzer Army advancing eastward north of Voroshilovgrad and then destroy the Soviet forces caught between the two pincers. Three major terrain factors, one natural and two man-made, would affect this transition. The natural feature was the regional river system, principally the Don River, which, after flowing southward from the area west of Voronezh, turned southeastward at Novaia Kalitva and then ran southeastward past Boguchar, Veshenskaia, and Kletskaia before turning southward and then westward (the Great Bend) that brought the river back to the Black Sea at Rostov. Because the left (eastern) bank of the Don River was vast, open country devoid of any reasonable military objectives, and because the objectives of Operation Blau were south of the Don, it seemed meaningless for the Germans to cross the river. Therefore, the Blau plan mandated that *Armeegruppe* Weichs seize and defend the Blau I rectangle with its Second and Fourth Panzer Armies and then release Fourth Panzer Army so that it could exploit southeastward in conjunction with Sixth Army, on its right. The first man-made terrain feature, the region's rail and road network, dictated the location where Fourth Panzer Army would make its turn and the ultimate axis of its subsequent advance.

The second man-made terrain feature, Voronezh, complicated German operations. Although its location on the Voronezh River, 10 kilometers east of the Don, was outside the likely boundaries of Blau I, because it was a major communications hub, and because its seizure would provide the Germans with a major foothold over the Don River, Hitler designated it as an important objective. Although the Germans captured the city with relative ease early in Operation Blau, Voronezh thereafter served as a magnet for German and Soviet forces alike. Understanding the city's strategic value, Stalin would orchestrate offensive after offensive to recapture the city, thereby confounding German plans to maximize the quantity of forces operating along their more vital strategic axes.

PENETRATION AND ENCIRCLEMENT, 28 JUNE–3 JULY

Armeegruppe Weichs, which was concentrated on the left wing of Bock's Army Group South, initiated Operation Blau I at dawn on 28 June with reconnaissance forces probing Soviet defensive positions across its front (see Map 9). Weichs's ersatz *Armeegruppe* consisted of infantry from his Second Army's LV, XIII, and VII Army Corps and panzers and motorized infantry (panzer grenadiers) from XXIV and XXXXVIII Panzer Corps of Hoth's Fourth Panzer Army, protected on their southern flank by the Hungarian Second Army. (Editor's note: After referring to their armored corps as "motorized" and their motorized infantry divisions as "motorized" during the first year of the war, the Germans, at about this time, instead referred to these corps as "panzer" and divisions as "panzer-grenadier," a convention to which this study will henceforth adhere.)

Hoth's and Weichs's artillery announced the beginning of Blau I with an intense 30-minute artillery preparation, while *Luftwaffe* supporting aircraft delivered concentrated air strikes against the Soviets' forward defenses and lines of communications. Stung by the devastating strikes, only limited Soviet counterfire responded to this barrage. Then, as German guns shifted aim to deeper targets, Hoth's armored spearheads rolled forward at 1000 hours, meeting minimal resistance. Preoccupied with the threat to Moscow and the local German offensives to the south during the two weeks previous, the Soviet defenders had not expected the Germans to attack due east from the Kursk region. Almost half of Bock's 68 German divisions, supported by a welter of satellite units, began the offensive with enormous success.

Weichs's massive armored thrust formed the northern pincer of a planned double envelopment, an operation aimed at encircling two Soviet armies, 40th Army on Briansk Front's left wing and 21st Army on Southwestern Front's right wing. Weichs's forces then planned to exploit rapidly eastward to the Don River and 6 kilometers beyond to Voronezh. By design, Weichs's armored spearheads, General von Langermann's XXIV Panzer Corps and General Kempf's XXXXVIII Panzer Corps, were to strike directly at the boundary between Briansk Front's 13th and 40th Armies and, once through the Soviets' defenses, fan out eastward toward the Don River and Voronezh and southeastward toward Staryi Oskol on the Oskol River to crush 40th Army and thereby turn Southwestern Front's right flank. To execute this sophisticated maneuver, XXIV Panzer Corps had 9th and 11th Panzer Divisions, which fielded 144 and 155 tanks, respectively, and another 54 tanks from 3rd Motorized Division, for an overall strength of roughly 350 armored vehicles. XXXXVIII Panzer Corps included 24th Panzer Division, with 181 tanks, and 16th and "GD" Motorized Divisions, with 100 and 45 tanks, respectively, for a rough total of 325 tanks.

Poised as they were opposite 40th Army on Briansk Front's left wing, Weichs's panzer spearheads posed a vital threat to Golikov's Briansk Front, as well as 21st Army, deployed on the right wing of Timoshenko's Southwestern Front. The 40th Army of Golikov's *front*, commanded by General Parsegov, defended the sector north and south of the town of Tim with five rifle divisions in its first echelon, 62nd, 45th, and 212th Rifle Divisions south of the town and 160th and 121st Rifle Divisions to its north, and one rifle division (6th) and three rifle brigades (111th, 119th, and 141st) in second echelon or reserve. Facing the 700-plus tanks

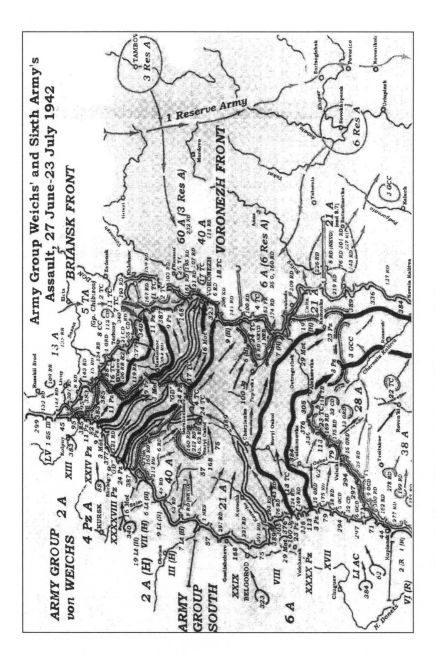

Map 9. Army Group Weichs's and Sixth Army's assault, 27 June–23 July 1942

in Weichs's panzer corps, Parsegov mustered 70-some tanks in his army's 14th and 170th Tank Brigades, backed up by General Pavelkin's 16th Tank Corps, with about 180 tanks, which was deployed behind the Kshen' River, northeast of Tim, in his army's right rear.

If Parsegov's 40th Army failed to parry Weichs's armored thrust, Briansk Front's entire center sector would be placed in jeopardy. There, astride the Sosna River west of Livny, General Pukhov's 13th Army defended with four rifle divisions in its first echelon, 15th and 143rd Rifle Divisions south of the Sosna and 148th and 132nd Rifle Divisions north of the river, and one rifle division (307th) and one rifle brigade (109th) in either second echelon or reserve. Pukhov's armor force included a single tank brigade (129th with about 40 tanks), backed up by General Katukov's 1st Tank Corps, with another 170 tanks, which was in *front* reserve northeast of Livny. Even farther to the north, on 13th Army's right, 48th Army, commanded by Major General Grigorii Alekseevich Khaliuzin, defended the region east of Orel on Briansk Front's right-center with a force of four rifle divisions, one cavalry division, and two rifle brigades, supported by two tank brigades.[2]

If Weichs's panzer forces were to make it through 40th Army's defenses, they also posed a deadly threat to the right wing of 21st Army, now commanded by Major General Aleksei Il'ich Danilov, the army's former chief of staff who had replaced Gordov only days before.[3] Because it was responsible for defending Southwestern Front's right wing, Danilov's army, with its nine rifle divisions and one tank and one motorized rifle brigade, was far stronger than its neighbors to the north. 21st Army defended the sector of the front west of Staryi and Novyi Oskol, opposite the bulk of Paulus's Sixth Army, with seven rifle divisions (124th, 76th, 293rd, 301st, 227th, 297th, and 8th NKVD) and one motorized rifle brigade (1st) deployed from left to right in its first echelon and with two rifle divisions (343rd and 226th) in second echelon. Lacking any tank brigades of its own, Danilov's army was supported by General Shurov's 13th Tank Corps with 163 tanks and, if necessary, could call upon other tank corps for assistance, principally, General Mishulin's 4th Tank Corps (145 tanks) and General Badanov's 24th Tank Corps (141 tanks), which were occupying assembly areas in the Novyi Oskol region along the Oskol River in Southwestern Front's reserve.

Paulus's Sixth Army formed the southern pincer. General Stumme's XXXX Panzer Corps led the attack, supported by infantry from the army's XXIX, VIII, and XVII Army Corps, striking eastward through Novyi Oskol toward Ostrogozhsk and northeastward toward Staryi Oskol. Stumme's panzer corps consisted of 3rd and 23rd Panzer Divisions, with 164 and 138 tanks, respectively, augmented by 58 tanks of 29th Motorized Division, for an overall strength of about 360 armored vehicles. Aimed at the junction between Southwestern Front's 28th and 21st Armies, this thrust sought to collapse 28th Army and force it southward, complete the encirclement and destruction of 40th and 21st Armies to the north, and facilitate the advance to the Don River and Voronezh. In turn, this attack would place Weichs's and Paulus's panzer corps in positions "hanging over"

Southwestern Front's right flank, from which they could initiate Blau II—the envelopment and destruction of the entire Southwestern Front.

In addition to threatening the left wing of Danilov's 21st Army, whose dispositions are described above, Paulus's armored spearheads also posed a deadly threat to Riabyshev's 28th Army. It defended the sector west of Oskol River from Volokonovka southward to Valuiki, with its five rifle divisions (38th, 175th, 15th, and 13th Guards, and 169th) arrayed from left to right in single echelon. These were backed up by the 65th, 90th, and 91st Tank Brigades, with roughly 90 tanks, and 244th Rifle Division in the region north of Valuiki assigned as Southwestern Front's reserve. In addition, Riabyshev could count on support from Colonel Khasin's 23rd Tank Corps, whose 128 tanks were in direct support of his army, and, possibly, from Mishulin's 4th and Badanov's 24th Tank Corps in the *front's* reserve. Finally, the Briansk Front held 17th Tank Corps, commanded by General Feklenko, with 179 tanks, in deep reserve in the Voronezh region.

While capitalizing on Stalin's preoccupation with the threat to Moscow, Bock's plan also recognized that Timoshenko's Southwestern Front was still reeling from its defeats in Operations Wilhelm and Fridericus II. However, Bock also realized that the *Stavka* had deployed (or was in the process of deploying) several new tank corps (as yet unidentified) to bolster the defenses on Briansk Front's left wing and at least three tank corps (4th, 13th, and 24th) to strengthen Southwestern Front.

Attacking in tandem along three chief axes, the two panzer corps of Weichs's *Armeegruppe* advanced rapidly eastward during the morning of 28 June, in the process tearing gaping holes in 40th and 21st Armies' forward defenses (see Map 10). Two divisions of Weichs's northernmost panzer corps, Langermann's XXIV, led the attack. General Balck's 11th Panzer Division crossed the Tim River and advanced 10 kilometers, crushing the defenses of 15th Rifle Division on the left wing of Briansk Front's 13th Army. Ten kilometers south, General Bässler's 9th Panzer Division of Langermann's corps lunged eastward toward the Tim River, collapsing the defenses of 121st Rifle Division on the right wing of Southwestern Front's 21st Army.

Simultaneous with Langermann's assault, Kempf's XXXXVIII Panzer Corps unleashed its attack 25–30 kilometers to the south. Major General *Ritter* von Hauenschild's 24th Panzer Division, with General Hörnlein's "GD" Panzer Grenadier Division echeloned to its left, raced southeastward from the Shchigry region toward the Tim River. This attack shattered the defenses of 40th Army's 160th and 212th Rifle Divisions and propelled Kempf's panzers to the western bank of the Tim River, 16 kilometers deep, where 24th Panzer Division's lead *kampfgruppen* seized an intact railroad bridge over the river. Although Soviet sappers tried to destroy the bridge, the attackers quickly tore the lit fuses and explosive charges out of the structure and rolled across with almost no pause.

Reporting that his army's divisions had suffered "significant losses" but "had not lost their combat capabilities," 40th Army's commander, Parsegov, turned to

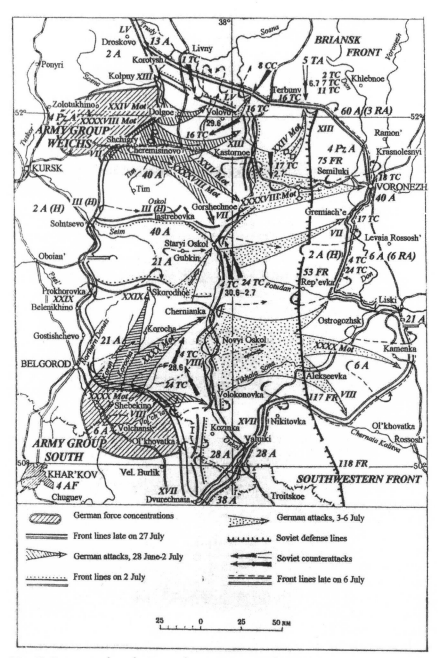

Map 10. Operations along the Voronezh axis, 28 June–6 July 1942

his *front* commander, Golikov, for assistance.[4] At Golikov's request, on the evening of 28–29 June the *Stavka* ordered Southwestern Front to transfer Mishulin's 4th and Badanov's 24th Tank Corps from the region west of Novyi Oskol, where they were supporting 21st Army's left wing, northward to the Staryi Oskol region, where they were to organize a counterstroke to restore 40th Army's shattered defenses.[5] At the same time, the *Stavka* ordered Golikov to shift Feklenko's 17th Tank Corps forward from Voronezh to Kastornoe to join the counterstroke and also reinforced Golikov's *front* with four fighter and three assault aviation regiments.[6] For his part, Golikov dispatched Pavelkin's 16th Tank Corps from his reserve to bolster the sagging defenses along the Kshen' River at the boundary between Pukhov's 13th and Parsegov's 40th Armies and 115th and 116th Tank Brigades, also from his reserve, to reinforce 40th Army.[7]

Despite these measures, as Soviet after-action reports concluded, Golikov's forces were suffering from a lamentable absence of effective command and control:

> 40th Army's commander and staff exhibited impermissible lack of concern in the army's sector for such an alarming and harrowing situation. The army command post was located in the Bykovo region, in 6th Rifle Division's defensive sector. Neither the army commander nor his deputies were in the right-wing divisions to organize the fighting personally or to refine the missions for the next day; instead, they continued to command by telegraph and telephone. The senior chiefs did not even assign missions to the two tank brigades that had joined the army; instead, this was done through staff officers.[8]

Frequent thunderstorms and intermittent heavy rains plagued Weichs's attacking forces during the first half of 29 June and forced Bock to postpone the advance of Paulus's Sixth Army for 24 hours. However, during the afternoon of 29 June, *Armeegruppe* Weichs's rapidly advancing panzers continued sowing chaos among the ranks of Golikov's Briansk Front. Preceded by another artillery preparation and protected by swarms of Stuka dive-bombers, Balck's 11th Panzer Division reached the Kshen' River west of Volovo, while the infantry accompanying it to the north pressed 13th Army's left flank and wing back northward toward Livny. Along the Kshen', Balck's panzers encountered Pavelkin's 16th Tank Corps, which had just reached the region with 40th Army's second-echelon 111th and 119th Rifle Brigades. Farther south, Bässler's 9th Panzer Division also reached the Kshen', where it encountered the defenses of 40th Army's 160th Rifle Division dug in along the eastern bank. By this time both panzer divisions were 25–30 kilometers deep into Briansk Front's defenses, leaving 121st Rifle Division in shambles.

Some 40 kilometers south, Hörnlein's "GD" Motorized Division and Hauenschild's 24th Panzer Division of Kempf's XXXXVIII Panzer Corps achieved spectacular feats on 29 June. Advancing another 30 kilometers, with "GD" echeloned to its left, Hauenschild's panzers forced their way across the Kshen' River west of Tim and continued their rapid eastward advance. In the process, the former cavalrymen of 24th Panzer encountered and dispersed 40th Army's 6th Rifle Division, and a forward *kampfgruppe* overran the army headquarters in the village of Bykovo. Although General Parsegov's staff escaped, they left their radios, maps, and equipment behind:

> On the evening of 29 June, a small group of enemy tanks, having penetrated the defenses of 40th Army's 6th Rifle Division, approached Bykovo, where this army's command post was located. The appearance of enemy tanks at the command post disorganized 40th Army's troop control. The army commander and headquarters were in the region southeast of Kastornoe [30 kilometers to the east], having left documents, including operational documents, in place. The army commander lost control of troop combat operations once and for all.[9]

Marring the day's spectacular progress, the *Luftwaffe* mistakenly bombed one of the spearheads of "GD" Division. Its pilots ignored aircraft recognition panels on the ground because they believed that no Germans could possibly have advanced so quickly.[10]

Although defeated on his *front*'s left wing, Golikov took consolation in the knowledge that Pukhov's 13th Army, now being reinforced by Katukov's powerful 1st Tank Corps, was offering a stubborn defense south of Livny, and the undamaged divisions on 40th Army's left wing were holding up Hungarian Second Army west of Tim. This was tempered, however, by the certainty that Weichs's panzers, if not halted, would surely achieve operational freedom and trap most of 40th Army's forces in the region south of Tim.

Faced with the massive breach in Briansk Front's defenses torn by Weichs's panzers (perhaps 40 kilometers wide and 35–40 kilometers deep), Stalin, the *Stavka*, and Golikov worked frantically to repair the damage. First, as Mishulin's 4th, Badanov's 24th, and Feklenko's 17th Tank Corps were completing their concentration in the Kastornoe and Staryi Saltov regions, Golikov ordered the fresh 284th Rifle and 1st Destroyer (Antitank) Divisions from his reserves to prepare an all-around defense at Kastornoe. In addition, he reinforced Pavelkin's 16th Tank Corps, which was facing Balck's 11th Panzer Division, with 106th Rifle Brigade, and he dispatched 8th Rifle Division and 80th Tank Brigade from 48th Army and 135th Rifle Brigade and 201st Tank Brigade from his own reserve to reinforce 13th Army's defenses south of Livny.[11] Finally, late in the evening, Golikov ordered Katukov's 1st and Pavelkin's 16th Tank Corps to launch a concerted counterstroke from the north and east, respectively, against Balck's 11th Panzer Division and its supporting infantry west of Volovo. However, as one Soviet critique noted, this counterstroke "was not smoothly controlled. . . . The attack axes were not refined on the ground, and an artillery preparation was not organized."[12]

Plagued by uncertainty and with his preparations going awry, Golikov discussed the situation with Stalin by secure Baudot radio-teletype early the next morning. After Golikov explained the precarious situation and Stalin reiterated the danger of 40th Army being encircled, the *front* commander informed his supreme commander about the measures he was taking, in particular the concentration of 4th, 24th, and 17th Tank Corps in the Staryi Oskol and Kastornoe regions. While 4th and 24th Corps were moving too slowly for his liking, Golikov was livid over the performance of Feklenko's 17th Tank Corps, which "as a result of the commander's lack of organizational talents . . . lost its combat service support elements on the march from Voronezh . . . and, therefore, was not supplied with fuel."[13]

Faced with the possible loss of 40th Army, Golikov requested Stalin's authorization to withdraw the army to a new defensive line halfway back to Voronezh. Objecting that a withdrawal to an unprepared position could inadvertently lead to a German rout, Stalin directed Golikov to organize a new counterstroke, this time concentrically toward Gorshechnoe (midway between Staryi Oskol and Kastornoe), with 4th and 24th Tank Corps from Staryi Oskol, 17th Tank Corps from Kastornoe, and 16th Tank Corps from the north. To ensure that this measure succeeded, Stalin sent General Fedorenko, the chief of the Red Army's Auto-Armored Directorate, to Briansk Front's command post to confirm that Golikov employed the available tank corps effectively. In Stalin's mind, it was a simple matter of numbers, as he added: "Remember well and truly—You now have more than 1,000 tanks, and the enemy does not have more than 500 tanks. That is first. And second, on an operational *front* of three enemy panzer divisions, you have assembled more than 500 tanks, and the enemy, 300–350 tanks at the most. Everything now depends on your skillful employment and precise command and control of these forces. Understand?"[14]

In practice, however, the various tank corps and, indeed, individual tank brigades would continue to fight as isolated, uncoordinated elements, much as the British Army fought Erwin Rommel in North Africa during 1941–1942. Most Soviet tank commanders at this stage of the war, inexperienced in commanding a force larger than a brigade, were unable to coordinate all combat elements in a synchronized attack, let alone ensure resupply of combat elements. The *Stavka's* response was an attempt to micromanage the fluid, complex battlefield by remote control. On 1 July General Vasilevsky telephoned Golikov to convey Stalin's orders in exhaustive detail. Fedorenko was to arrest Feklenko, commander of 17th Tank Corps, and Vasilevsky insisted that the other corps commanders maneuver their forces as armor rather than using slow, rigid infantry tactics.[15]

On 30 June, mere hours before Vasilevsky's conversation with Golikov, the situation along the southern wing of the Soviet-German front changed from mildly challenging to potentially catastrophic. This was because, after a delay of 24 hours caused by heavy rains, Paulus's Sixth Army unleashed its panzers early on 30 June. With a second pincer about to materialize from east of Khar'kov, the *Stavka* now confronted a serious threat to the entire Southwestern Front instead of a local defeat on Briansk Front's left wing.

Attacking at dawn on 30 June, Paulus spearheaded his advance with Stumme's XXXX Panzer Corps, flanked on the north with infantrymen from XXIX and VIII Army Corps and on the south from XVII Army Corps. In this instance, the infantry performed more spectacularly than Stumme's armor. By day's end, advancing northeastward from east of Belgorod and north of Shebekino, respectively, XXIX Corps' 168th Infantry Division and VIII Corps' 389th and 305th Infantry Divisions reached the western and eastern outskirts of Korocha, more than 20 kilometers deep into Soviet defenses. This assault not only tore a yawning gap at the junction of 21st and 28th Armies' defenses but also encircled several hapless rifle divisions (301st and 227th) and a tank brigade (10th) on 21st Army's left wing in a pocket southwest of Korocha.

Adding insult to injury, advancing from east of Volchansk in the vanguard of Stumme's panzer corps, Boineburg-Lengsfeld's 23rd Panzer Division and Breith's 3rd Panzer Division lunged eastward straight through the center of 28th Army's defenses toward Volokonovka, on the Oskol River in Southwestern Front's deep rear. However, resistance by 169th Rifle and 13th and 15th Guards Rifle Divisions, supported by Shurov's 13th Tank Corps, contained Stumme's advance to less than 10 kilometers on the first day of action. That evening, 28th Army's commander, Riabyshev, anxiously reported: "The forces of 28th Army have been fighting an intense holding action against enemy tank units (with up to 150–200 tanks) and infantry (up to an infantry division) attacking toward Volokonovka . . . since 0400 hours on 30 June 1942. Groups of 6–15 aircraft have been bombing our combat formations continuously all day."[16]

Riabyshev informed Timoshenko he was erecting new defenses along the Oskol River to his rear with his second echelon rifle forces and was moving Khasin's 23rd Tank Corps and 65th Tank Brigade, chopped off the *front*'s reserve to his army, to positions protecting the approaches to Volokonovka.

Nevertheless, with the left wing of Danilov's 21st Army now utterly shattered, Paulus's army corps were advancing northeastward almost unimpeded toward Novyi Oskol and a probable linkup with Weichs's forces advancing from the north. In fact, by day's end on 30 June, 24th Panzer Division of Kempf's XXXXVIII Panzer Corps, with "GD" Motorized Division in its wake, was closing on Gorshechnoe on the Oskol River north of Staryi Oskol. To the west a cordon of infantry from Weichs's VII Army Corps and Hungarian Second Army was advancing slowly but steadily southward, driving the remnants of 21st Army into a possible trap west of the Oskol River.

Nor had the situation improved farther to the north, where the two panzer corps of *Armeegruppe* Weichs were threatening to smash Soviet defenses along the Kshen' River (see Map 11). Although Pukhov's 13th Army was successfully containing the advance by the infantry divisions of Weichs's LV Army Corps along the approaches to Livny, 11th and 9th Panzer Divisions of Langermann's XXIV Panzer Corps, flanked by infantry divisions from XIII Army Corps, drove eastward across the Kshen' River west of Volovo and at Ditsevo. Langermann's

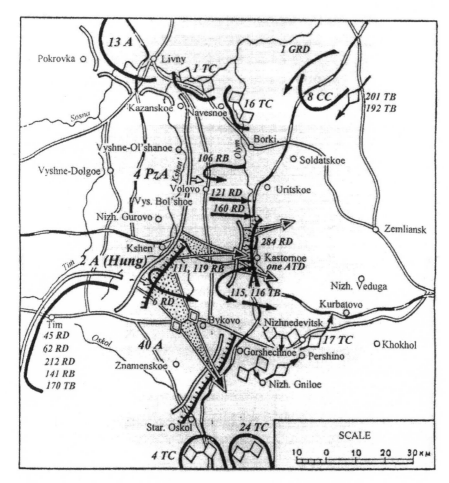

Map 11. Operations along the Voronezh axis, 30 June–2 July 1942

panzers pressed the now disorganized brigades of Pavelkin's 16th Tank Corps back toward Volovo, and the accompanying German infantry forced the remnants of 121st Rifle Division and 119th Tank and 111th Rifle Brigades back toward Kastornoe on the Olym River. By this time, after overrunning and dispersing 40th Army headquarters, Hauenschild's 24th Panzer Division of Kempf's XXXXVIII Panzer Corps reached Gorshechnoe, only 28 kilometers north of Staryi Oskol. There it battered elements of Golikov's reserve, including 115th and 116th Tank Brigades and elements of 40th Army's 6th and 160th Rifle Divisions. The only saving grace for Golikov on 30 June was that the fresh 284th Rifle Division, a Ukrainian division commanded by Colonel Nikolai Filippovich Batiuk, displayed "exceptional stubbornness" in defending Kastornoe.[17]

Nor did Golikov's planned counterstroke with his *front's* 1st, 16th, 17th, 4th, and 24th Tank Corps develop as anticipated. The assault by Katukov's 1st Tank Corps against LV Army Corps' advancing infantry divisions and 11th Panzer Division's left flank faltered due to poor command and control, and the armor of Pavelkin's 16th Tank Corps fared little better against Balck's forward elements along the Kshen' River. During his fight Pavelkin committed his corps' 107th and 164th Tank and 15th Motorized Rifle Brigades into combat on 29 June but held his 109th Tank Brigade in reserve. Thereafter, his corps lost roughly 15 percent of its armor during the day's heavy fighting along the Kshen' River, and when his corps resumed its attacks on 30 June, it lost another 14 KV tanks. The corps also suffered heavy losses in its battles with 11th Panzer Division on 1–2 July, forcing it to withdraw across the Olym River and, ultimately, to join forces with Katukov's depleted 1st Tank Corps. During the period from 28 June through 13 July, the armor strength of Pavelkin's tank corps fell from 181 to 45 tanks.[18]

Farther south, the concentric attacks by Briansk Front's tank corps against the "GD" and 24th Panzer Divisions at and east of Gorshechnoe also "developed indecisively." In particular, instead of attacking due west from Kastornoe, the hapless Feklenko maneuvered his 17th Tank Corps fruitlessly for two days, avoiding battle, and finally lost all control over his corps as his scattered tanks intermingled with those of 115th and 116th Tank Brigades after their defeat west of Kastornoe. Disorganized and uncoordinated, Feklenko's 17th Tank Corps lost 1,664 men and 141 of its 179 tanks during the fighting near Gorshechnoe.[19] This prompted his immediate relief by Vasilevsky. The remnants of Feklenko's tank corps finally withdrew across the Don River south of Voronezh after 3 July; it was immediately reinforced by 44 new T-34 tanks.

Meanwhile, Mishulin's 4th Tank Corps advanced northward with only two tank brigades and was defeated by 24th Panzer Division 10 kilometers south of Gorshechnoe. Badanov's 24th Tank Corps, delayed in concentrating its forces at Staryi Oskol, arrived south of Gorshechnoe too late to participate in the battle. Subsequently, from 2 July to 5 July, Mishulin's and Badanov's tank corps, together with the remnants of Feklenko's tank corps and other rifle divisions from Parsegov's 40th Army, conducted delaying actions back to the Don River south of Voronezh. Thus, largely because of poor command and control and the complete absence of communications between Golikov's tank corps, a force of about 600 Soviet tanks was unable to defeat—much less effectively engage—a force of three German divisions fielding less than 350 tanks.

Undeterred by Golikov's counterstroke, Weichs's and Paulus's forces continued their headlong advance on 1 July, straining to link their separate pincers near Staryi Oskol to encircle the rifle divisions of 40th and 21st Armies (isolated west of the Oskol River) and continue their eastward thrust toward the Don River and Voronezh. Spearheading Weichs's northern pincer, XXIV Panzer Corps' 11th and 9th Panzer Divisions pressed Pavelkin's 16th Tank Corps and supporting infantry of Parsegov's 40th Army toward the Olym River east of Volovo and west of Kastornoe, and XXXXVIII Panzer Corps' "GD" Motorized and 24th Panzer Divisions engaged and completed defeating Mishulin's 4th and Feklenko's 17th Tank Corps in detail east of Gorshechnoe. To the south, the infantry divisions of Paulus's XXIX and VIII Army Corps pushed northeastward to within 35 kilometers of Staryi Oskol and 10 kilometers from Novyi Oskol, while XXXX Panzer Corps' 23rd and 3rd Panzer Divisions pressed 28th Army eastward to the approaches to Volokonovka, albeit against far more determined resistance. After committing Khasin's 23rd Tank Corps into action on 1 July, Riabyshev, the army commander, reported, "Having encountered strong enemy resistance and counterattacks by up to 100–120 tanks, the attacks by 23rd Tank Corps were unsuccessful." More telling still, Riabyshev informed Timoshenko, "A gap has developed between Volokonovka and Ul'ianovka [13 kilometers to the south]" and that "the army has no forces to close the gap."[20] Therefore Riabyshev informed Golikov, his *front* commander, that he was attempting to withdraw his forces to new defenses along the Oskol River north and south of Volokonovka. However, at 1930 hours on 2 July, an obviously anxious Riabyshev described a situation that was far more perilous: "Beginning at 1400 hours, enemy tanks and infantry, with strong air support, enveloped both [of our] flanks and are pushing the units of the army toward the east. A critical situation exists, with the threat of being cut off from the crossings. I have decided to withdraw my units across the Oskol."[21]

By day's end on 1 July, the deteriorating situations in Golikov's Briansk Front and on the right wing of Timoshenko's Southwestern Front produced consternation within the *Stavka*. Pukhov's 13th Army, half of Parsegov's 40th Army, and the remnants of Briansk Front's five tank corps were still clinging—barely—to their defenses west of Livny southward along the Olym River past Kastornoe to Staryi Saltov. However, German panzers had breached this crude defensive line in the Gorshechnoe region, and 40th Army's entire left wing (45th and 62nd Rifle Divisions and the 141st Rifle and 170th Tank Brigades) was in danger of being encircled in the Tim region west of the Oskol River. If the Germans were able to close their two pincers at Staryi Saltov, all of Danilov's 21st Army and Shurov's supporting 13th Tank Corps would be caught in the same trap. Finally, since the defenses of Riabyshev's 28th Army and Khasin's 23rd Tank Corps were also nearing the point of collapse, part of his army was also threatened with encirclement west of Volokonovka.

Therefore, after discussing the situation with its two *front* commanders, the *Stavka* late on 1 July ordered Golikov and Timoshenko to withdraw their 40th, 21st, and 28th Armies and supporting tank corps to a new defensive line extending along the Olym and Oskol Rivers.[22] However, the withdrawal was chaotic at best, illustrated by the situation in Parsegov's 40th Army: During the night of 1–2 July the *front* headquarters organized the withdrawal of forces on 40th Army's left wing albeit "under conditions of the complete absence of control on the part of 40th Army's commander and staff, who by this time were already situated in Voronezh."[23] In fact, although Golikov and Timoshenko issued withdrawal orders to some divisions and brigades via radio, in most cases they could reach subordinate forces only by using special couriers who flew to the front lines in U-2s. Given German dominance of the air, this method was hazardous at best—and often fruitless.

Parsegov's and Danilov's forces began the retreat at dawn on 2 July, but they had to run a gauntlet of near constant German artillery fire and aerial strikes. The escape became even more harrowing and desperate the following day as the two German pincers closed in the Staryi Saltov region, blocking most of the planned escape routes. By nightfall on 3 July, the panzer grenadiers of General Henrici's 16th Motorized Division, which XXXXVIII Panzer Corps committed southward from its reserve to complete the encirclement, linked up with the forward infantry *kampfgruppen* of Paulus's XXIX and VIII Army Corps south of Staryi Oskol.[24] Compounding the difficulties that 40th and 21st Armies faced, farther south Paulus's main armored fist, 23rd and 3rd Panzer Divisions of Stumme's XXXX Panzer Corps, were pummeling Riabyshev's 28th Army and threatening to drive it back eastward across the Oskol River, further separating it from the armies encircled to the north.

Supported by the remnants of Khasin's 23rd Tank Corps, Riabyshev's 28th Army was able to withdraw most of its forces eastward to the Oskol River. However, given its previous losses—almost 50 percent of manpower and even more of tanks and heavy weapons—28th Army lacked the strength necessary to defend the river line successfully. As a result, Paulus's Sixth Army crossed the Oskol in two sectors early on 3 July: VIII Army Corps' 389th and 305th Infantry Divisions at Chernianka, and XXXX Panzer Corps' 23rd Panzer and 29th Motorized Divisions at Volokonovka. Wheeling northward, Paulus's panzers and infantry captured Novyi Oskol on the evening of 3 July.

His forces too threadbare to resist, Riabyshev withdrew his battered 28th Army steadily eastward toward the Tikhaia Sosna River, where Timoshenko ordered him to man a new defensive line extending from Valuiki on the Oskol River northeastward to Nikolaevka on the Tikhaia Sosna. To assist Riabyshev's army, Timoshenko ordered Moskalenko's 38th Army, still deployed on Riabyshev's left, to reinforce 28th Army with 22nd Tank Corps, 1st Destroyer Division, 13th and 156th Tank Brigades, and part of 52nd Fortified Region.[25] However, unless 40th and 21st Armies managed to extract enough of their forces from encirclement, Timoshenko lacked sufficient forces to plug the yawning gap in his defenses on Riabyshev's right flank, specifically the broad sector extending northeastward along the Tikhaia Sosna River from Nikolaevka and Ostrogozhsk to the Don River and then northward along the Don to Voronezh.

Meanwhile, the forces of Parsegov's 40th Army, which were encircled in the Tim region without their commander, made their way eastward in groups of various sizes, the most fortunate passing through gaps among the German divisions operating north of Staryi Oskol. Although supposedly retreating without particular pressure from pursuing Hungarian forces, the remnants of Parsegov's divisions and brigades finally joined the surviving tank forces of Mishulin's 4th, Badanov's 24th, and Feklenko's 17th Tank Corps southeast of Gorshechnoe. Together, but often in small groups, the surviving tankists and riflemen made their way painfully eastward and crossed the Don River to safety on 4 and 5 July. Although as many as half of Parsegov's men reached the Don, most divisions and brigades no longer existed as organized combat formations.

To the south, Danilov's 21st Army and Shurov's 13th Tank Corps suffered an even more tragic fate. Unable even to slow Sixth Army's furious advance northeastward, Danilov ordered his forces to begin their breakout westward toward the Oskol River early on 1 July. Danilov employed Shurov's tank corps, which had already lost more than half its 163 tanks, both as a battering ram to penetrate through Paulus's cordon of infantry, and as a shield to protect the army's escape. After a running two-day fight, during which Shurov was mortally wounded and two brigade commanders perished, the remnants of Danilov's army reached the Oskol River near Chernianka late on 2 July.[26] Once along the Oskol, Danilov's forces, also organized in small groups, tried to escape by exploiting the gap between Weichs's and Paulus's spearheads at Staryi and Novyi Oskol and between Paulus's advancing infantry divisions farther to the south. Like Parsegov's 40th Army—losing more than half its men and all equipment during its retreat to the Don and Tikhaia Sosna Rivers—Danilov's army was no longer a viable combat force.

With 40th and 21st Armies largely hors de combat, Riabyshev's 28th Army spread thin along the Tikhaia Sosna River, and an immense gap developing between Golikov's and Timoshenko's *fronts,* the two *front* commanders faced a problem: how to plug this gap before German armored columns were able to exploit it. Lacking fresh reserves, they had no choice but to ask Stalin for help.

While Golikov and Timoshenko struggled to extract their forces from multiple encirclements, Stalin was increasingly alarmed by a grim prospect: German panzer spearheads reaching Voronezh. If and when they did so, the dictator realized, they would sever key railroad links to the south, making strategic troop movements between Moscow and the southern Soviet Union far more difficult. Therefore, acting immediately to replace the armies that Bock's offensive was

Table 13. Stalin's Deployment of Reserve Armies, 2 July 1942

Reserve Army (Designation on 10 July)	Commander	Location
3rd Reserve Army (60th Army)	Lieutenant General M. A. Antoniuk	Don River north of Voronezh
6th Reserve Army (6th Army)	Major General F. M. Kharitonov	Don River south of Voronezh
5th Reserve Army (63rd Army)	Lieutenant General V. I. Kuznetsov	South of Novaia Kalitva
7th Reserve Army (62nd Army)	Major General V. Ia. Kolpakchi	The Stalingrad axis

Lieutenant General Dmitrii Ivanovich Riabyshev, commander of 28th Army

Lieutenant General Anton Ivanovich Lopatin, commander of 37th, 9th, and 62nd Armies

Lieutenant General Fedor Mikhailovich Kharinotov, commander of 9th Army

Lieutenant General Avksentii Mikhailovich Gorodniansky, commander of 6th Army

Lieutenant General Konstantin Appollonovich Koroteev, commander of 9th Army

Major General Kirill Semenovich Moskalenko, commander of 38th, 1st Tank and 1st Guards Armies

Lieutenant General Vasilii Ivanovich Chuikov, commander and deputy commander of 64th Army and commander of 62nd Army

Major General Vladimir Iakovlevich Kolpakchi, commander of 62nd Army

Major General Mikhail Stepanovich
Shumilov, commander of 64th Army

Major General Andrei Antonovich Grechko,
commander of 12th, 47th, and 18th Armies

Major General Vasilii Dmitrievich
Kriuchenkin, commander of 12th, 47th, and
18th Armies

erasing from his order of battle, early on 2 July, Stalin ordered four of his newly
formed reserve armies to bring their forces to full combat readiness and occupy
new defensive positions in the Briansk and Southwestern Fronts' rear area as
soon as possible (see Table 13).[27]

Stalin's directives assigned 3rd and 6th Reserve Armies to Golikov's Briansk
Front so it could restore his defenses north and south of Voronezh and, in a

remarkable exercise of insight, tasked 5th and 7th Reserve Armies with plugging the gap between the two forward *fronts* and thwarting any subsequent German drive eastward south of the Don River toward Stalingrad. In addition, Stalin ordered the Kalinin Front, situated near Moscow, to transfer 7th Tank Corps, commanded by Colonel Rotmistrov, southward to the Elets region, where it was to join 5th Tank Army and soon become part of another large counterattack force under Golikov's control.[28]

Meanwhile, Golikov took measures of his own to shore up the sagging defenses of his *front.* Just before moving his headquarters to Voronezh to organize the city's defenses, he transferred, on 2 July, 1st Guards and 340th Rifle Divisions, 201st and 192nd Tank Brigades, and 8th Cavalry Corps (the latter commanded by Colonel Ivan Fedorovich Lunev) from less active sectors of his *front* to reinforce 13th Army's defenses, which by now extended from the Livny region eastward more than 100 kilometers to the eastern approaches to Voronezh.[29] Lunev, a cavalryman who commanded a cavalry and motorized division before the war and a rifle division after war began, had led his cavalry corps since late May 1942.[30]

THE GERMAN ADVANCE TO VORONEZH, 4–6 JULY

Despite Stalin's and Golikov's firm decision-making, the job of restoring a coherent front was no mean feat (see Map 12). By day's end on 3 July, Parsegov's 40th and Danilov's 21st Armies were no longer viable combat entities, Golikov's five formidable tank corps were shadows of their former selves, and Riabyshev's 28th Army, defeated in three successive German offensives, was no longer capable of offering a credible defense to any German advance. Now Stalin's hope rested in the ability of his fragile reserve armies to contain the German advance along the Don River line and drive it back with the last powerful armor force at his disposal, the fledgling 5th Tank Army.

With the *Stavka's* defenses in southern Russia rent asunder, by early on 4 July the focal point of combat operations shifted to the Don River line, in particular the vital sector just west of Voronezh. The previous day, *Armeegruppe* Weichs had unleashed its armor forces in a concerted thrust eastward from the Oskol River toward the Don River and Voronezh. Advancing in columns of *kampfgruppen* arrayed from north to south, 11th and 9th Panzer Divisions of Langermann's XXIV Panzer Corps had completed demolishing 13th and 40th Armies' defenses along the Olym River at and north of Kastornoe; "GD" Motorized and 24th Panzer Divisions of Kempf's XXXXVIII Panzer Corps had done the same between Kastornoe and Staryi Oskol farther south.

By day's end on 3 July, the panzers of Balck's 11th Panzer Division, with XIII Army Corps' 88th, 385th, and 82nd Infantry Divisions echeloned to their left (west), were approaching the town of Zemliansk, almost halfway between the Oskol River and Voronezh. Although Bässler's 9th Panzer Division encountered

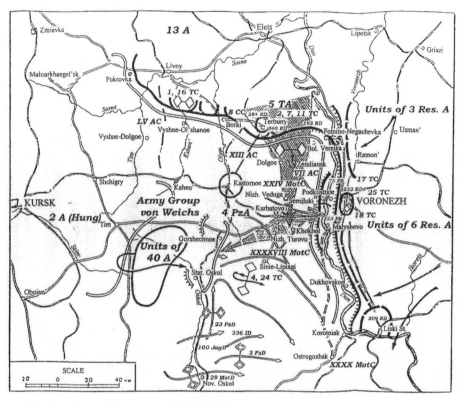

Map 12. Operations along the Voronezh axis, 4–15 July 1942

stouter resistance by 284th Rifle and 1st Destroyer Divisions at Kastornoe, the two mobile divisions, with the help of 3rd Motorized Division committed from Langermann's reserve, bypassed Kastornoe from the south. This forced Soviet defenders to withdraw northeastward to avoid encirclement. Farther south, but against far feebler resistance, Kempf's "GD" Motorized and 24th Panzer Divisions thrust eastward more than halfway from the Oskol to the Don River, brushing aside the remnants of 40th Army and its supporting 4th, 24th, and 17th Tank Corps, in full flight to the eastern bank of the Don (and presumed safety).

As the four armored spearheads continued their rapid advance eastward toward the Don and Voronezh, on 4 July Langermann wheeled his panzer corps' 11th and 9th Panzer Divisions sharply northeastward, where they began forming a cordon, with XIII Corps' infantry divisions, to protect the northern flank of the main axis of advance to Voronezh (see Map 13). At the same time, "GD" and 24th Panzer Divisions of Kempf's panzer corps, with 16th Motorized Division in their wake, pushed on toward the Don River and the western and southern outskirts of Voronezh proper, 6 kilometers beyond. By this time, the only forces

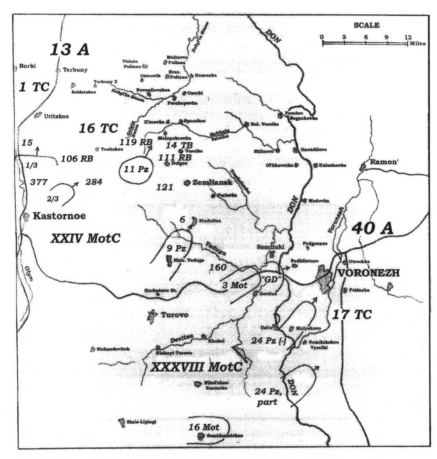

Map 13. The situation along the Voronezh axis on 4 July 1942

defending in the city's immediate vicinity were weak NKVD security forces, 3rd PVO (Air Defense) Division, and rear service elements of 40th Army (all within the city itself), and the immobile 75th and 53rd Fortified Regions (deployed west of the city proper). In the surrounding region, 3rd Reserve Army's 232nd Rifle Division occupied defenses along the Don River north of the city, and 6th Reserve Army's 309th Rifle Division, just arriving at Liski Station, manned defenses farther south along the eastern bank of the Don.[31] As these fragile forces prepared to their defense of Voronezh, early on 3 July Stalin relieved the hapless Parsegov as commander of 40th Army, assigning the daunting task to his replacement, Lieutenant General Markian Mikhailovich Popov, former commander of the Northern and Leningrad Fronts from 22 June to November 1941 and, thereafter, commander of the Western Front's 61st Army.[32] Voronezh was an easy target for the Germans.

At 1930 hours on 4 July, a single company of "GD" Motorized Division's 1st Motorized Infantry Regiment reached the town of Semiluki, on the Don River 9 kilometers west of Voronezh, where it found an unguarded bridge over the river:

[First Lieutenant] Blumenthal, commander of 7th Company, now gathered all of his men together and with these few . . . charged towards the bridge under covering fire from the heavy machine [gun] section, driving the enemy before them. Blumenthal's men pushed forward as far as the approach to the bridge. . . . For their part, the Bolsheviks kept up a lively fire from their bunkers on the other side of the river while individual groups attempted to recover the bridge site.

Time: roughly 20.00

The first action was to save the road bridge. Standing almost up to his neck in water, Corporal Hempel removed the demolition charges which were located on the bridge supports, and which were already burning, with his bare hands. In the same breath, Blumenthal and a few men raced across the bridge and reached the other side, unharmed, behind the fleeing Russians. Once there he immediately deployed his men to secure the approach to the bridge. In the meantime, using steel helmets and ammunition canisters, the soldiers extinguished the few small fires on the bridge. Still unaware of the situation, Russians repeatedly tried to cross the bridge. They were taken prisoner, and after an hour over 70 were in our hands.[33]

Early the next day, 5 July, XXXXVIII Panzer Corps' 24th Panzer Division also crossed the Don, and on 6 July Hauenschild's panzers and panzer grenadiers entered Voronezh virtually unopposed, as Popov withdrew his army's forces to the eastern bank of the Voronezh River just east of the city. Meanwhile, 23rd Panzer and 29th Motorized Divisions of Stumme's XXX Panzer Corps, leading Paulus's Sixth Army in its northeast thrust, had reached the Don River north of Ostrogozhsk, 75 kilometers south of Voronezh. Behind these spearheads, the infantry divisions of Sixth Army's XXIX, VIII, and XVII Army Corps attacked northwestward and eastward, seeking to encircle the remnants of 40th and 21st Armies west of the Don and, simultaneously, to drive 28th Army's forces from their weak defenses along the Tikhaia Sosna River. However, the inclement weather that had delayed Paulus's attack allowed many of these Soviet units to escape encirclement. Still, units that did escape lost all organization and cohesion and arrived at the Don with little fuel or ammunition.[34]

5TH TANK ARMY'S COUNTERSTROKE, 6–12 JULY

In an attempt to forestall total disaster, Stalin, shortly after midnight on 3 July, ordered Golikov to prepare another counterstroke, this time employing Major

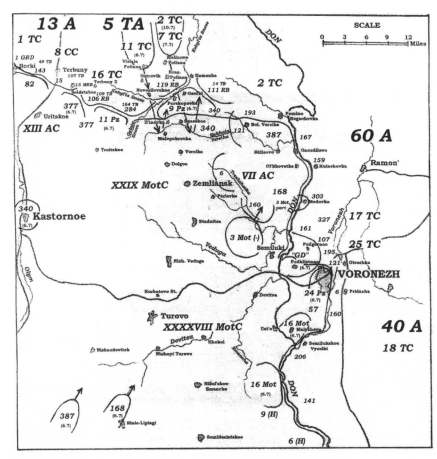

Map 14. The situation along the Voronezh axis from 6–14 July 1942

General A. I. Liziukov's fresh and reinforced 5th Tank Army (see Map 14). In the absence of any organized army headquarters operating northwest of Voronezh, Golikov was to employ Liziukov's army as an "operational group" in this region, "subordinating to him all of the tank corps operating along this axis."[35] Stalin entrusted this important task to 5th Tank Army not only because it was his most powerful armored force but also because he was impressed with Liziukov's record as a bold and effective commander. As described in the Prologue, Aleksandr Il'ich Liziukov had displayed skill and bravery while leading 1st Moscow (later 1st Guards) Motorized Rifle Division during the battle for Smolensk in August 1941, for which he was recognized as Hero of the Soviet Union. Thereafter, he displayed audacity and tenaciousness serving as deputy to Major General A. A. Vlasov, commander of 20th Army, which spearheaded Western Front's successful counterstroke northwest of Moscow in December 1941. Later Liziukov commanded the 2nd Guards Rifle Corps with equal success in the Red Army's offensive during winter 1941–1942.

As originally constituted in mid-June, Liziukov's 5th Tank Army had consisted of General Lazarev's 2nd and General Popov's 11th Tank Corps, plus the 340th Rifle Division, 19th Separate Tank Brigade, and several supporting elements for a total of 439 tanks. However, on 2 July Stalin had already subordinated Colonel Rotmistrov's 7th Tank Corps to Briansk Front, and while it was completing its regrouping to Elets, at 0200 hours on 5 July Stalin further assigned it to Liziukov's control, increasing 5th Tank Army's strength to 641 tanks.[36] Finally, Golikov also attached 1st Guards Cavalry Corps, commanded by Major General Viktor Kirillovich Baranov, to Liziukov's tank army. An experienced cavalry officer renowned for audacity, Baranov led 5th Cavalry Division during the treacherous fighting from March through November 1941 and its successor, 1st Guards Cavalry Division, during the battle for Moscow and the Red Army's winter offensive of 1941–1942. As a reward for his outstanding performance, the NKO appointed Baranov commander, 1st Guards Cavalry Corps, on 10 July 1942.[37] With this formidable force, the mission of Liziukov's army was: "To conduct an offensive toward Zemliansk [38 kilometers northwest of Voronezh] and Khokhol [56 kilometers southwest of Voronezh], sever the communications of the enemy's tank group penetrating to the Don River at Voronezh, and, by operating against his rear area, disrupt his crossing of the Don and assist the withdrawal of the units of 40th Army fighting in the Kastornoe region."[38]

While Liziukov's army was slowly assembling, on 4 July the *Stavka* placed the garrison in Voronezh under Golikov's control, assigned him 3rd, 5th, and 6th Reserve Armies (a total of 22 fresh but green rifle divisions and 1 rifle brigade), and released 18th and 25th Tank Corps from the *Stavka* Reserve to the Briansk Front.[39] It instructed Golikov to deploy General Pavlov's 25th and General Cherniakhovsky's 18th Tank Corps into assembly areas north and south of Voronezh, respectively, but to commit them to combat only with its express permission. Hedging his bets, Stalin also ordered 3rd Tank Army, which had formed less than a month before under the command of Lieutenant General Prokofii Logvinovich Romanenko, to deploy from the Tula region, south of Moscow, first to Elets and on 6 July to Efremov, 200 kilometers north of Voronezh. From there, 3rd Tank could either reinforce 5th Tank Army should its counterstroke succeed, or shore up Briansk Front's defenses north of Voronezh should it fail.[40] These reinforcements increased the strength of Golikov's *front* by 23 rifle divisions and 1 rifle, 5 motorized, and 16 tank brigades—more than 1,000 tanks.[41]

Stalin demanded that Golikov direct 5th Tank Army's counterstroke and defense of Voronezh personally from his forward command post in Voronezh; Golikov's deputy *front* commander, Lieutenant General N. E. Chibisov, and chief of staff, Major General M. I. Kazakov, would man the *front's* main command post farther to the rear. In practice, however, preparations for the counterstroke faltered immediately. Often out of radio contact, Golikov failed to control his forces effectively, and his command post had to scramble to a safer location east of the Voronezh River after German forces captured Voronezh on 5 July. In the absence of the *front* commander's orders, neither Chibisov nor Kazakov would take the initiative, prompting Stalin to send Vasilevsky, chief of the Red Army General Staff, to the region on 4 July to supervise and coordinate operations.

Even with Vasilevsky present, however, many subordinate formations in Liziukov's tank army were still en route to their designated assembly areas when the counterstroke began; thereafter they attacked piecemeal, brigade by brigade, as they arrived. Although a special aviation group commanded by Major General Grigorii Alekseevich Vorozheikin, 1st deputy commander of the Red Air Force, was supposed to provide air cover for Liziukov's counterstroke, German airpower prevailed, hindering all rail and road movements, particularly during daylight hours, further delaying the assembly of Liziukov's forces.[42] As a result, although Rotmistrov's 7th Tank Corps reached its assigned concentration area late on 5 July, 11th and 2nd Tank Corps did not close onto theirs until 0200 and 1000 hours on 7 July, respectively. Nonetheless, Liziukov issued Rotmistrov's corps its attack order at 0130 hours on 6 July, mandating that his forces jump off at 0600 hours sharp—only four and a half hours hence.

Deploying forward in unaccustomed haste, Rotmistrov's tank corps attacked with two tank brigades forward (67th and 87th Tank Brigades with about 120 tanks), which immediately surprised a *kampfgruppe* of roughly 50 tanks from Balck's 11th Panzer Division near the village of Krasnaia Poliana, 55 kilometers northwest of Voronezh, pushing the Germans back across the Kobyl'ia Snova River, 4 kilometers to the south (see Map 15).[43] Rotmistrov instructed his troops to "cling" to the retreating Germans, making it difficult for the *Luftwaffe* to intervene without inflicting casualties on their own. However, 7th Tank Corps was virtually unsupported during this attack—Popov's 11th Tank Corps began detraining that evening, and 2nd Tank Corps, now commanded by Colonel A. G. Kravchenko, who had replaced Lazarev only days before, was even farther behind in reaching its assembly areas. Thus, when he resumed the offensive early on 7 July, Rotmistrov, instead of being supported by two full tank corps, was assisted by only half of Popov's 11th Tank Corps—59th Tank Brigade and a battalion from 12th Motorized Rifle Brigade—with a total of about 50 tanks.[44]

During the day, the neighboring division of Langermann's XXIV Panzer Corps, Bässler's 9th Panzer, with about 120 "runners" (operational tanks), moved north from Zemliansk and joined the battle on Balck's right, engaging Rotmistrov's leading tank brigades. With these reinforcements, Langermann's panzers managed to hold the Kobyl'ia Snova River line, but only briefly. Once Popov committed the remainder of his tank corps on 8 July, the combined assault by Rotmistrov's and Popov's corps forced 11th and 9th Panzer Divisions' *kampfgruppen* to withdraw roughly 6 kilometers southward to new defensive positions along the Sukhaia Vereika River. There Liziukov's assaults petered out, in part

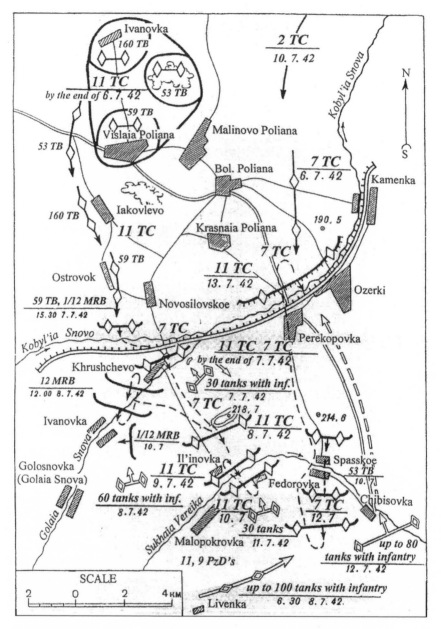

Map 15. The 5th Tank Army's counterstroke, 7–14 July 1942

because of intense German Stuka strikes and also because half the tanks in one tank battalion from Popov's corps got bogged down in a marsh. Dissatisfied by the slow progress, at 1830 hours Chibisov chided Liziukov: "Comrade Stalin orders you to seize Zemliansk today at all cost. In no circumstances bring 2nd Tank Corps forward, but instead keep it in second echelon. Penetrate farther with individual tanks and smash the enemy's rear and transport."[45] However, heavy German artillery fire, devastating air strikes, and swampy terrain along the banks of the Kobyl'ia Snova and Sukhaia Vereika Rivers, which inhibited tanks from maneuvering, prevented any further advance that day.

While the fight raged along the Sukhaia Vereika River, the *Stavka* recognized belatedly that, with Golikov's Briansk Front split in half by the advancing Germans and two additional reserve armies assigned to its control, there were too many formations in its sector for his inexperienced operational staff to control effectively. Accordingly, at 2100 hours on 7 July, Stalin ordered his sector be divided into two *fronts*. The new Briansk Front, now under the temporary command of Golikov's former deputy, 49-year-old General Nikandr Evlampievich Chibisov, was to defend the sector west of the Don River and Voronezh with 3rd, 48th, and 13th Armies, 5th Tank Army, 1st and 16th Tank and 8th Cavalry Corps, and Vorozheikin's aviation group. The new Voronezh Front, under Golikov's command, would defend the sector east of the Don River north and south of Voronezh with 40th Army, 3rd and 6th Reserve Armies, 4th, 17th, 18th, and 24th Tank Corps, and two aviation groups transferred from Briansk Front.[46] No stranger to heavy combat, Chibisov had fought in World War I, the Russian Civil War, and the Finnish War and commanded the Odessa Military District during the chaotic first few months of Operation Barbarossa before being appointed deputy commander of Briansk Front in September 1941.[47]

Stalin then ordered Chibisov's *front* (the new Briansk Front) "to sever the supply routes and rear area of the enemy tank group which has penetrated to the Don River at Voronezh by active operations toward the south along the western bank of the Don River toward Khokhol with 5th Tank Army, reinforced by 7th Tank Corps and one rifle division from 3rd Reserve Army," and Golikov's *front* (now the Voronezh Front) "to clear the enemy from the eastern bank of the Don River at all costs and firmly consolidate a defense along that bank within the limits of the *front*'s sector." The Voronezh Front's 3rd and 6th Reserve Armies were redesignated as 60th and 6th Armies, respectively. The former was commanded by Lieutenant General Maksim Antonovich Antoniuk, a veteran of the intense fighting in the Leningrad region, where he once commanded the ill-fated 48th Army. The latter was led by General Kharitonov, who had commanded 9th Army during the battle for Khar'kov but been replaced shortly thereafter by General Nikishov.[48]

In separate directives that underscored his belief that the battle was far from won, Stalin ordered a new 7th Reserve Army (with six rifle divisions) to assemble in the Usman' and Anna regions, 90 kilometers east of Voronezh, to back up

Golikov's forces and, the following day, directed Far Eastern Front to dispatch seven rifle divisions and three rifle brigades westward to join the *Stavka* Reserve.[49]

Meanwhile, Liziukov's 5th Tank Army continued its intense but disjointed fight along the Sukhaia Vereika River, attacking at 0400 hours on 9 July, with roughly 100 tanks from Rotmistrov's 7th Tank Corps on the left and 163 tanks of Popov's 11th Tank Corps on the right.[50] This was the first time Popov was able to deploy all four of his brigades on line for an attack. Although 19th Tank Brigade of Rotmistrov's corps managed to penetrate 9th Panzer Division's defenses along the Sukhaia Vereika River briefly, intense Stuka attacks drove his forces back, decimating two battalions of 7th Motorized Rifle Brigade. On Rotmistrov's right, Popov's 11th Tank Corps encountered an immediate counterattack by 11th Panzer Division near Khrushchevo, south of the Kobyl'ia Snova River, which caused one battalion of 12th Motorized Brigade to break and flee in "tank panic." Although its commander was relieved of command on the spot, the brigade, after being reinforced by five tanks, soon rejoined the fighting, but strong Stuka attacks and artillery fire prevented Popov's corps from crossing the Sukhaia Vereika.[51] Throughout this fight Liziukov dutifully retained Kravchenko's 2nd Tank Corps in his second echelon.

Although these two newly formed Soviet tank corps, each about the size of a German division, did not achieve their assigned missions, the mere fact that they could halt and push back XXIV Panzer Corps' 11th and 9th Panzer Divisions was remarkable, indicating the abilities of Rotmistrov and Popov (if not of Liziukov). Moreover, they achieved this advance despite the fact that the *Luftwaffe* held almost complete air superiority over the battlefield. However, the *Stavka* still believed Liziukov was facing only a single panzer division. Therefore, obviously conveying Stalin's impatience, during the fighting on 9 July, Vasilevsky bypassed the *front* headquarters, sending a direct order to 5th Tank Army directing Liziukov to avoid frontal assaults but instead to envelop the German spearhead by maneuvering southwest. The reality, however, was far different from Vasilevsky's perceptions. The 7th and 11th Tank Corps found themselves confronting massive counterattacks from both panzer divisions, supported by heavy Stuka strikes. Joined belatedly by Kravchenko's 2nd Tank Corps overnight on 9–10 July, all three corps suffered heavy casualties without achieving further advances.[52]

Resuming their assaults on 10 July against intensifying resistance, none of the tank corps registered any progress, though continuing to suffer heavy losses. After shifting laterally eastward in an attempt to bypass German defenses, the three tank corps attacked once again on 11 July, only to falter. By this time 11th Tank Corps fielded only 13 operational KV tanks and 6 British-built Matildas, while 7th Tank Corps had lost 12 more KVs and 2nd Tank Corps 12 KVs and T-34s and 4 T-60s, placing all three corps well below 50 percent strength.[53] By now it was clear the Germans were winning a battle of attrition.

However, while Liziukov's tank corps pounded XXIV Panzer Corps' defenses in vain, Langermann skillfully reorganized his defenses and assembled a strong counterattack force. He used the fresh 340th Infantry Division to relieve 11th Panzer Division on his corps' left (western) wing on 10 July. Then, after allowing 11th Panzer to rest and refit on 11 July, he launched a coordinated counterattack with both panzer divisions at dawn on 12 July. Striking the boundary between 7th and 11th Tank Corps, 11th Panzer Division drove 5 kilometers into Liziukov's rear and then swung eastward, outflanking 7th and 2nd Tank Corps and forcing them to withdraw in considerable disorder. Liziukov responded by reinforcing his sagging defenses with 193rd Rifle Division, just transferred from 60th (former 3rd Reserve) Army. However, while the fresh division was approaching the battlefield in dense column formation, it was pummeled by heavy Stuka strikes, which inflicted heavy casualties and left the division hors de combat. Liziukov attached its remnants to 11th Tank Corps and the cooperating 3rd Destroyer (Infantry Antitank) Brigade.[54]

On 13 July Liziukov finally managed to halt the German advance and stabilize his defenses by counterattacking with 26th Tank Brigade from the reserve of Kravchenko's 2nd Tank Corps. The brigade's 50 tanks purportedly struck a German *kampfgruppe* of 38 tanks and several battalions of motorized infantry by surprise at 1400 hours and, in a three-hour fight, killed 1,000 Germans and destroyed or damaged 15 German tanks at a cost of 5 men and 5 tanks of its own.[55] Despite this tactical feat, the more experienced Germans succeeded in mirroring what Stalin intended. By 15 July, when fighting subsided, 5th Tank Army had lost 7,929 men, including 1,535 killed, 3,853 wounded, and 2,541 missing, roughly half of its 641 tanks, 261 of them permanently, and 81 guns, 49 mortars, 300 machine guns, and 120 vehicles. Its forces had been pushed back across the Kobyl'ia Snova River, where they went over to the defense. Although the Red Army's claim that it inflicted 18,920 casualties on the Germans and destroyed 317 tanks and significant quantities of German weapons and equipment was no doubt inflated, the counterstroke exacted a heavy toll on 9th and 11th Panzer Divisions.[56] At the very least, the intense fighting northwest of Voronezh indicated that Hitler's new crusade east would be no cakewalk.

The flawed commitment of 5th Tank Army had also attracted the attention of Langermann's XXIV Panzer Corps and a large portion of the available *Luftwaffe* aircraft, leaving *Armeegruppe* Weichs's adjacent sectors devoid of reserves and air support. This should have facilitated two other more limited offensives the *Stavka* planned in support of Liziukov's main counterstroke: the first an assault by an armored and cavalry group against XIII Army Corps' defenses west of Liziukov's main attack axis, and the second an assault on Voronezh proper by 40th Army and 17th and 18th Tank Corps of Chibisov's Voronezh Front. However, to the *Stavka*'s consternation, neither supporting attack succeeded.

The first, which began on 8 July, was conducted by a mixed group consisting of Katukov's 1st and Pavelkin's 16th Tank Corps, Lunev's 8th Cavalry Corps, 1st

Guards Rifle Division, and two tank brigades—all under Katukov's command. Group Katukov, with a force of roughly 150 tanks, was to attack southward from the Borki and Terbuny regions, 70–80 kilometers northwest of Voronezh, to destroy German infantry defending between the Kshen' and Olym Rivers, then wheel east to envelop and help defeat XXIV Panzer Corps' divisions facing Liziukov's 5th Tank Army. However, despite encircling part of a German regiment, Katukov's attack failed when his forces faltered in the face of a skillful defense by 82nd Infantry Division. By 9 July the Germans had forced Katukov's forces back to their jumping-off positions.[57]

Golikov's second supporting offensive—which also began on 8 July shortly after German forces captured Voronezh—was conducted by the remnants of M. M. Popov's 40th Army, joined after 11 July by Antoniuk's 60th (former 3rd Reserve) Army, supported by the battle-weary remnants of 17th and 18th Tank Corps and Pavlov's fresh 25th Tank Corps. Now commanded by General Korchagin, Feklenko's successor, 17th Tank Corps had escaped eastward across the Don River a few days before with 65 of its original 179 tanks (but no KVs) and had been reinforced by 44 T-34s. Cherniakhovsky's 18th Tank Corps had fought in the streets of Voronezh from 5 to 7 July, in the process losing its 180th and 181st Tank Brigades and their entire complement of 116 tanks, when they were cut off by 24th Panzer Division during its advance into the city.

Driven on mercilessly by the *Stavka*, Golikov's forces repeatedly attacked Voronezh's suburbs from the north and east, attempting to cut off and destroy the spearhead of the German advance. Although Golikov advanced up to 8 kilometers despite heavy German artillery and antitank barrages, once again German air superiority smothered the offensive. In addition, inexperienced Soviet commanders were unable to respond to rapid changes in the battle, largely because they commanded from the rear, using written orders rather than radio communication. The obsessive Soviet desire for secrecy prompted them to avoid using radio for fear of having their signals intercepted by the Germans.

Antoniuk's 60th Army made its final effort on 11 and 12 July, first by committing more than 80 tanks from Korchagin's 17th Tank Corps and then, the next day, another 150 tanks from Pavlov's fresh 25th Tank Corps, together with seven understrength rifle divisions, committed in waves over the two days. During a three-day fight, German 3rd Motorized Division and, after it was relieved, XXIX Army Corps' 168th and 57th Infantry Divisions struggled with 60th Army's force on the flat, swampy lowlands north and west of Voronezh. Ultimately, however, the Soviets failed. Antoniuk, replaced by Cherniakhovsky because the latter was a "fighter," soon joined the rubbish heap of disgraced commanders.[58]

In the immediate wake of the intense fighting at and northwest of Voronezh, early on 15 July the outraged Stalin ordered 5th Tank Army dissolved and Liziukov demoted to command of 2nd Tank Corps.[59] Days before, Stalin had already shaken up his command structure in the Voronezh sector, in part because of Chibisov's and Liziukov's failed counterstroke, in part because Golikov had not acted decisively at Voronezh, and finally because the Germans had just expanded their offensive to encompass his Southern Front (see Chapter 5). On 13 July he reduced Chibisov to deputy commander of Briansk Front, with Lieutenant General K. K. Rokossovsky, the former commander of Western Front's 16th Army, as the new head of the *front*.[60] The next day, Stalin replaced Golikov, commander of Voronezh Front, with Lieutenant General N. F. Vatutin, deputy chief of the Red Army General Staff, and appointed Golikov as Vatutin's deputy.[61]

Both Rokossovsky and Vatutin had already earned the dictator's trust by displaying audacity and imagination in previous fighting. General Konstantin Konstantinovich Rokossovsky, 45 years old in July 1942, began the war as commander of Southwestern Front's 9th Mechanized Corps, which he led effectively in the *front*'s futile counteroffensive in the Dubno region during late June 1941. In command of Special Group Iartsevo in late July and August 1941, Rokossovsky's tenaciousness helped halt Army Group Center's advance during the battle for Smolensk, prompting Hitler to shift his focus from Moscow to Kiev during September. Although Rokossovsky's 16th Army was encircled and destroyed in the Viaz'ma region during early October 1941, following its resurrection late in the month he led the army with distinction during the defense of Moscow in November, the Moscow counteroffensive in December, and the Red Army's general offensive in winter 1941–1942. Respected by his superiors for an unusual frankness—if not the ability to resist bullying—and by his subordinates for an unwillingness to waste soldiers' lives unnecessarily, Rokossovsky was Stalin's choice for *front* command because he was a proven fighter who had demonstrated he could command large formations successfully.[62]

Known as the "boy wonder of the *Stavka*," Lieutenant General Nikolai Fedorovich Vatutin rose rapidly through key Red Army General Staff positions to command Southwestern Front at Stalingrad at a young 42. Because Vatutin had joined the Red Army in 1920, he saw only limited service in the Russian Civil War. After serving in staff, school, and infantry assignments during the 1920s, he graduated from the Frunze Academy, where he attracted the attention of Shaposhnikov, the academy director. Graduating from the General Staff Academy's partially purged class of 1937, Vatutin served in succession as chief of staff of the Kiev Special Military District, chief of the General Staff's Operations Directorate, and first deputy chief of the General Staff. During this period, the energetic general staff officer helped plan the invasion of eastern Poland in September 1939 and the incursion into Romanian Bessarabia in June 1940 and, under Zhukov's and Shaposhnikov's tutelage, shaped the Red Army's war and mobilization plans during the year preceding the outbreak of war. Despite his reputation as a consummate planner, Vatutin had long harbored a desire for field command.

After war broke out—despite Vatutin's requests to be given a combat command—Stalin began employing him as a personal representative in key operational sectors.[63] And soon after Stalin appointed him as Northwestern Front's chief of staff in late June 1941, Vatutin displayed an innate daring that earned him a reputation as the Red Army's most audacious fighting general. In that capacity, Vatutin orchestrated the Red Army's counterstrokes at Sol'tsy and Staraia Russa in July and August 1941; although they failed, the counterstrokes delayed the German advance on Leningrad and helped save that city. During the German advance on Moscow in October 1941, Vatutin formed and led a special operational group that halted the German advance at Kalinin and prevented German forces from severing the vital Moscow-Leningrad railroad line. Vatutin then coordinated Northwestern Front operations in the Demiansk region during January 1942, encircling a full German army corps. Returning to Moscow in May 1942 to become Vasilevsky's deputy in the General Staff, Vatutin in July requested field command and was assigned to command the new Voronezh Front.

With the heavy fighting in the Voronezh region at an end, albeit temporary, and a new group of experienced field commanders in charge along the Voronezh axis, Stalin turned his full attention to the south, where Bock's forces were expanding their offensive.

HITLER, BOCK, AND BLAU II
(OPERATION CLAUSEWITZ)

If Stalin underestimated the problems his field commanders faced in the Voronezh region, Hitler appeared unaware of the very existence of the Soviet effort. Instead, the German dictator became increasingly impatient with his generals, particularly Field Marshal von Bock, for allowing their forces to become tied down around Voronezh.

On 3 July Hitler, his OKH chief, Halder, and his OKW chief, Keitel, again boarded the Führer's four-engine Condor transport, flying to Army Group South headquarters at Poltava in an attempt to get the offensive back on schedule. Suffering under the heat of a Ukrainian summer but "in a receptive, friendly mood," Hitler was convinced that the Red Army, encouraged by the Reichel disclosures, would retreat to the Don River if not immediately engaged and encircled.[64] During a long, rambling conference he told Bock not to bother with a prolonged fight for Voronezh. Bock certainly understood the need to press the advance, asserting it would be folly to launch Blau II with infantry forces to avoid losing time—as someone at the conference suggested—as "this would make it impossible to encircle the enemy, who has gradually learned from past experience."[65]

However, like any other German field commander, Bock believed he had the latitude to use his forces as necessary—in this case securing a key transportation hub that was under persistent Soviet counterattack. Therefore, in the days following this conference, Bock temporarily retained all of Hoth's Fourth Panzer Army in the Voronezh region, all the while planning for its future turn south (see Map 16). Kempf's XXXXVIII Panzer Corps consolidated control over the vital

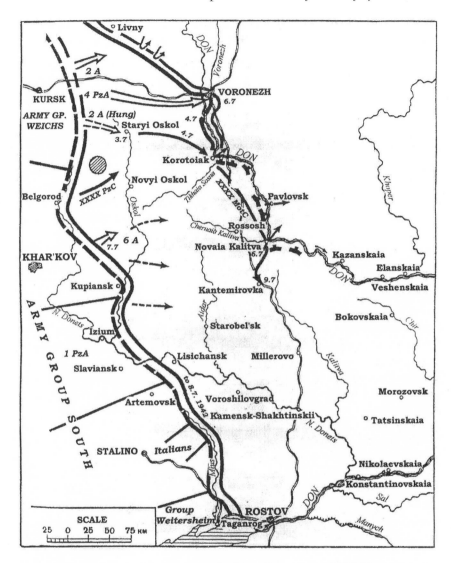

Map 16. The penetration of *Armeegruppe* Weichs's to Voronezh and XXXX Panzer Corps' turn to the south

Voronezh region, and Langermann's XXIV Panzer Corps protected *Armeegruppe* Weichs's vulnerable sector northwest of Voronezh.

Meanwhile, as Bock looked for the right time to move Hoth's panzers south, on the left wing of Paulus's Sixth Army 3rd and 23rd Panzer and 29th Motorized Divisions of Stumme's XXXX Panzer Corps struck northeastward from Staryi Oskol, reached Ostrogozhsk on the Tikhaia Sosna River and Korotoiak on the

Don River on 6 July, and then wheeled south toward Rossosh'. In the process, Stumme's panzers turned the right flank of Riabyshev's 28th Army, which was defending along the Tikhaia Sosna east and west of Nikolaevka (also called Alekseevka). This cut off Riabyshev's withdrawal routes eastward to the Don. Farther south, on XXXX Panzer Corps' right flank, the bulk of the infantry divisions of Sixth Army's VIII and XVII Army Corps pushed the main forces of Riabyshev's army from their shaky defenses, along the Tikhaia Sosna River near Nikolaevka, and forced them to withdraw southward toward Ol'khovatka and Rossosh' in increasing disorder. Meanwhile Paulus's remaining divisions and the follow-on forces of Hungarian Second Army continued bagging prisoners from the encircled and bypassed Soviet 40th and 21st Armies, whose remnants were still fleeing eastward across the Oskol River toward the Don.

In addition to the mild disagreement between Hitler and Bock at the 3 July conference in regard to the employment of Hoth's armor, Bock strenuously opposed Halder's proposal to transfer command of First Panzer Army from Bock's army group to Field Marshal Wilhelm List's new Army Group A. The original plan for Blau II, developed in April, had foreseen the need to divide Bock's forces, with Bock using his existing staff as Army Group B to continue the advance eastward toward the Volga River at Stalingrad, while a new Army Group A headquarters supervised the vital advance to the Caucasus. However, Bock argued that splitting his forces as Hitler wished was premature and would only confuse command and control, later confiding to his diary: "I stuck to my previous refusal because all planning, preparations, readying of forces, and so on was in my hands, and the participation of a second army group will only complicate command. Decisions are often required which must be made and put into action very quickly. I doubt if this would be possible with two army groups in command."[66]

Despite Hitler's decision to split Army Group South, Bock believed he still enjoyed the dictator's confidence. In fact, the field marshal's apparent "disobedience" on whether to fight for Voronezh, combined with his resistance to splitting his army group, irritated Hitler enormously.[67] Notwithstanding Bock's objections, the reorganization took effect on 7 July, with Army Group B retaining German Fourth Panzer, Second and Sixth Armies, and Hungarian Second Army; and Army Group A assuming command of First Panzer, Eleventh, and Seventeenth Armies in the lower Don region (see Table 14).

After beginning local pursuit operations in First Panzer Army's sector on 8 July, List launched the main forces of First Panzer and Seventeenth Armies on a concerted attack across the Northern Donets River and deep into the Donbas region on 9 July.

The German OKH regarded the Soviet counterattacks at Voronezh as insignificant. As Halder recorded in his diary on 5 July:

Von Bock calls me up to explain that these movements [at Voronezh] were conditioned by the threat to Hoth's southern flank (Fourth Panzer Army). . . .

Table 14. The General Organization of Army Groups B and A on 7 July 1942

ARMY GROUP B—Field Marshal Fedor von Bock
    Armeegruppe von Weichs—Colonel General Maximilian von Weichs
        Headquarters, Second Army
        LV Army Corps
        Fourth Panzer Army—Colonel General Hermann Hoth
            XIII, VII, and XXIX Army Corps; and
            XXIV, XXXXVIII Panzer Corps.
        Hungarian Second Army—Colonel General Gusztav Jany
            Hungarian III Army Corps
      Sixth Army—General Friedrich Paulus
          VIII, XVII, and LI Army Corps; and
          XXXX Panzer Corps.
    VIII Air Corps
    Reserve—Hungarian IV Army Corps
ARMY GROUP A—Field Marshal Friedrich List
    First Panzer Army—Colonel General Ewald von Kleist
        XI and XXXXIV Army Corps;
        III and XIV Panzer Corps; and
        Romanian VI Army Corps.
    Seventeenth Army (*Armeegruppe* Ruoff)—Colonel General Rudolf Ruoff
        IV and LII Army and XXXXIX Mountain Army Corps;
        LVII Panzer Corps; and
        Italian Expeditionary Corps.
    Reserve
        V Army Corps;
        Headquarters, Italian Eighth Army, with Italian II Army Corps; and
        Hungarian IV and VI Army Corps.

I [cannot] see any such threat. There are just some isolated armored units of the enemy which, in their desperation, attack in every direction but do not constitute any operational threat. . . . Von Bock has become completely dependent on Hoth's initiative and so has oriented the offensive towards Voronezh to a greater degree than he could [justify].[68]

On the other hand, far closer to the field of battle, Bock sensed the dangers and possible implications of the Soviets' actions near Voronezh, noting in his diary on 4 July, the day before Halder penned his impressions: "Weichs is worried because [Hoth's] panzer army has been attacked on its northern flank, and now major elements are pinned down there," adding, "On the panzer army's left wing the 11th Panzer Division is in heavy fighting with enemy forces attacking from the north."[69] The following day, Bock asserted, "Enemy resistance has stiffened at Voronezh . . . [and he is] moving in reinforcements from all sides," although adding, "A powerful Russian attack group at Uritskoe [the Sukhaia Vereika River] was attacked concentrically, including with tanks, and destroyed."[70]

For the moment, Hitler permitted Bock to continue with the occupation of Voronezh but tried to reinvigorate the overall offensive by reorienting its main

Chief of the Red Army's Main Armored Directorate, Colonel General Iakov Nikolaevich Fedorenko (center) meeting with Major General Aleksandr Il'ich Liziukov, the commander of the 5th Tank Army, and Major General Aleksei Fedorovich Popov, the commander of the 11th Tank Corps, in the Voronezh region in late June 1942

Antitank riflemen moving into firing positions on the Southwestern Front, June 1942

Red Army troops counterattacking near Krasnyi Luch, Southern Front, June 1942

Red Army troops fighting in the suburbs of Voronezh, July 1942

Destroyer German tanks in the vicinity of Voronezh, July 1942

Red Army antiaircraft units firing on German planes, Southern Front, July 1942

Soviet pontoon bridge across the Northern Donets River at Lisichansk, Southern Front, July 1942

effort from the north to the south. He ordered Paulus to send Stumme's XXXX Panzer Corps onward to the south, aiming to link up with First Panzer Army near Millerovo, 300 kilometers south of Voronezh. Hoth's Fourth Panzer Army, with Langermann's XXIV and Kempf's XXXXVIII Panzer Corps (less 9th and 11th Panzer Divisions from Langermann's corps), was supposed to leapfrog from behind Sixth Army's left rear, pushing southward as soon as it handed over the defense of Voronezh to Weichs's Second Army. When it reached Ostrogozhsk on the Chernaia Kalitva River and Novaia Kalitva on the Don River, it was to pick up Sixth Army's XXXX Panzer and VIII Army Corps, already en route to the region on Sixth Army's advancing left wing.

On 9 July, when List's newly activated Army Group A unleashed First Panzer and Seventeenth Armies on an offensive eastward and then southeastward parallel to the Northern Donets River toward Voroshilovgrad, a modified Blau II (code-named Operation Clausewitz) was under way. Confiding to his diary on 5 July that the battle will be "cut into two parts," Bock bitterly noted two days later: "The Army High Command is thus still hanging on to Blau II and would like to encircle a foe who is no longer there."[71]

CONCLUSIONS

From Hitler's and Bock's perspectives, Blau I was indeed a resounding success. Skillfully exploiting time-honored techniques of shock and maneuver, the classic characteristics of blitzkrieg, XXIV and XXXXVII Panzer Corps of *Armeegruppe* Weichs, together with XXXX Panzer Corps of Paulus's Sixth Army, conducted a near-perfect double-envelopment operation during their thrust to Voronezh. Advancing in twin pincers, the five panzer and four motorized divisions subordinate to these three panzer corps moved 170–200 kilometers eastward in the astonishingly brief period of 15 days; shattered Southwestern Main Direction's forward defenses at the boundary between its Briansk and Southwestern Fronts; encircled and destroyed the bulk of Briansk Front's 40th and Southwestern Front's 21st Armies, along with their supporting armor; and seized their assigned objectives in the Voronezh region and along the western bank of the Don River.

During the first six days of this advance, Weichs's and Paulus's panzers, panzer grenadiers, and infantry engaged the bulk of seven Soviet tank corps (1st, 16th, 4th, 24th, 13th, 23rd, and 17th) and many separate tank brigades, a force of almost 1,500 tanks. The Germans demolished four of these corps outright and severely damaged three more. Once in the Voronezh region, the two panzer divisions of Langermann's XXIV Panzer Corps defeated Soviet 5th Tank Army's hastily assembled force of more than 600 tanks with relative ease in nine days of near-constant heavy fighting. Simultaneously, the single panzer division and two motorized divisions of Kempf's XXXXVIII Panzer Corps fought two fresh Soviet tanks corps (25th and 18th), with another 300 tanks, to a standstill on the eastern approaches to the city.

Caught by surprise, neither Golikov's Briansk Front nor Timoshenko's Southwestern Front was capable of reacting quickly enough to stave off disaster. The speed of the German advance paralyzed all command and control in 40th and 21st Armies and severed the armies' communications with their parent fronts. Deprived of any knowledge about the real situation at the front, but nevertheless goaded on by an anxious *Stavka*, the two *front* commanders issued order after order that were utterly irrelevant to the situation. As a result, preplanned counterstrokes and counterattacks aborted even before they began, in a sordid process culminating in 5th Tank Army's clumsy and ill-fated counterstroke northwest of Voronezh. Therefore, neither *front* was able to stabilize the situation before the Germans seized their designated objectives.

From Stalin's vantage point in Moscow, the Germans' sudden, dramatic thrust toward Voronezh shook his confidence that the *Wehrmacht* main strategic focus was on the Moscow axis. Appreciating the deadly threat to the Red Army's strategic defenses should the Germans capture Voronezh, pierce the barrier of the Don River, or advance southeastward into the Donbas, Stalin reacted forcefully by ordering the immediate commitment of his new 5th Tank Army and the forward deployment of four fresh reserve armies from the *Stavka*'s strategic reserve.

However, since this process would take considerable time, and the *Stavka* and General Staff suffered from the same command and control and communications problems as his forward-deployed *fronts* and armies, at least in the short term many of the dictator's prudent precautionary measures proved futile to undo the damage already done.

Previous histories of Operation Blau have emphasized the overwhelming superiority of German forces advancing along the Voronezh axis, particularly in armor, and the rapidity and decisiveness of the German advance. They have also concluded that the fighting along this axis, though intense at times, was brief and relatively inconsequential and that Stalin, almost immediately, ordered his forces to "abandon the field" and withdraw to new defenses along the Don River. However, careful examination of what actually occurred during Blau I underscores that, even though *Armeegruppe* Weichs's and Sixth Army's advances were indeed rapid and decisive, the other generalizations are incorrect in three important respects.

First, from the outset and entirely throughout the German offensive, it is now clear that in addition to matching German strength in manpower, the armored strength of the Briansk and Southwestern Fronts' forces exceeded that of their foes, at least numerically. For example, Briansk Front fielded an initial force of about 1,000 tanks, against the 733 tanks in Hoth's Fourth Panzer Army, and one week after Blau I began was reinforced by 650 more tanks from 5th Tank Army. Likewise, Southwestern Front opposed Sixth Army's 360 tanks with a force of more than 650 tanks. However, although the Soviets enjoyed a better than twofold superiority in armor along both axes during Blau I, in the end the Soviets' lamentably poor logistical support system—particularly with regard to vital fuel and ammunition—and the inability of its tank force commanders to lead their armies, corps, and brigades effectively in combat largely negated this advantage.

Second, the fighting during Blau I was far more ferocious and consequential than previously described, especially in the vicinity of Voronezh. One can legitimately describe *Armeegruppe* Weichs's and Sixth Army's initial advances as mere cakewalks. Yet once the former captured Voronezh city, *Armeegruppe* Weichs and later Second Army would have to engage in a prolonged, month-long battle to hold its prize. During this struggle, a determined Stalin threw first a full tank army and later a reserve army and multiple tank corps into the fight in an attempt to not only recapture the Voronezh region but also to thwart the major German offensive developing to the south. These counterattacks did more than delay the redeployment of XXXXVIII Panzer Corps to the south, thereby weakening Army Group B's drive toward the Don River and Stalingrad. In addition, this fight inflicted heavy losses on German Second Army and tied down one or two German panzer divisions, which became stuck in the tar pit of fighting in the Voronezh region.

Third, Stalin, instead of hastily withdrawing his shaken armies to new, more defensible lines, underscored his firm belief that the Red Army could indeed halt and perhaps even defeat the German offensive by forcefully organizing and conducting large-scale counterstrokes and counteroffensives of its own. This was evidenced by the actions Stalin undertook to defeat German forces in and around Voronezh, if not to severely undermine German plans for Operation Blau in general. This would become even more apparent during Blau II, when Stalin—ordering his armies to stand firm in the face of the German onslaught—would throw four fresh armies, including two tank armies, into Bock's path to block the German advance toward the Great Bend of the Don River and Stalingrad on the Volga River beyond.

Despite *Armeegruppe* Weichs's spectacular success along the road to Voronezh, the stronger than anticipated Soviet resistance in the region created fresh dilemmas for Hitler. On the one hand, the Führer was anxious lest his armies fail to complete the anticipated encirclements called for in Blau I. On the other, he wanted Bock's Army Group South, now split into Army Groups A and B as planned, to commence Blau II on schedule. Impatient with what he perceived as Bock's unwarranted fixation on Voronezh, Hitler insisted Army Group B's new commander unfetter Hoth's Fourth Panzer Army from the "distractions" in the Voronezh region and instead employ it to spearhead his army groups' thrust southeastward into the Donbas (although he reluctantly permitted Bock to retain a portion of Fourth Panzer Army in the Voronezh region). At the same time, the dictator assigned Kleist's First Panzer Army to Army Group A so that it could spearhead the advance by List's new army group eastward into the Donbas region. Therefore, for the time being, Blau II would proceed as scheduled—but without the immediate participation of the entire Fourth Panzer Army. Only time would determine the wisdom of this decision.

CHAPTER 5

Blau II, 9–24 July 1942

By mid-July 1942 the first phase of Operation Blau had ended—to all appearances another German success. Yet the Red Army had demonstrated a disconcerting, if uneven, combat ability. This unexpected Soviet resistance, almost invisible to the German High Command, exacerbated Hitler's frustration with his field generals when he needed their professional abilities most. More serious, however, Soviet resistance around Voronezh had already begun to delay and weaken the German advance toward the Caucasus.

AREA OF OPERATIONS

As in Blau I, the region in which Army Group B's Sixth Army and Army Group A's First Panzer and Seventeenth Armies conducted Blau II formed a crude rectangle. Unlike the arena of Blau I, however, this rectangle oriented from west to east (see Map 17). This rectangle stretched from the Izium region on the Northern Donets River, Stalino, and Taganrog on the Mius River in the west roughly 400 kilometers eastward to Kletskaia on the Don River and Surovikino on the Chir River in the east and the towns of Svatovo, Kantemirovka, and Boguchar in the north 300 kilometers southward to Rostov and Tsimlianskaia on the Don River. Encompassing more than 100,000 square kilometers, the area of operations of Blau II was nearly twice that of Blau I (cf. Map 8 in Chapter 4). At or near the rectangle's four corners were the cities of Izium (northwest), the vast open region north of the Don River (northeast), the junction of the Don and Aksai Rivers (southeast), and the Gulf of Taganrog, the easternmost arm of the Sea of Azov (southwest).

Three great river systems, the Don, Northern Donets, and Mius, dominate this region and form most of its borders. These rivers affected the symmetry of German Army Group A's and B's offensive by funneling, or canalizing, their forces as they advanced eastward. The Don River, with its tributaries, formed the eastern half of the rectangle's northern border, while its western half conformed to the southern edge of the Blau I rectangle. The rectangle's eastern border was formed by the western base of the Great Bend of the Don River, a line that extended from Kletskaia on the Don southward to Nizhne Chirkskaia on the Don; its southern border followed the Don River from Nizhne Chirkskaia westward to Rostov and the Sea of Azov; and its eastern border extended north-

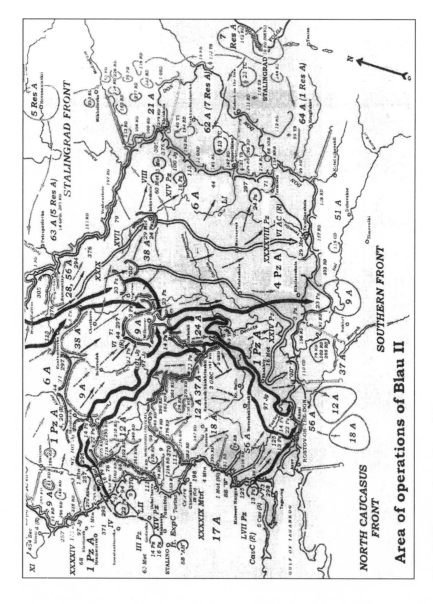

Map 17. The area of operations of Blau II

ward along the Mius River from the Sea of Azov across a narrow land bridge southwest of Voroshilovgrad to the Northern Donets River and farther northward along the Donets and Oskol Rivers to the Izium and Kupiansk regions. Beyond the eastern edge of this large rectangle lay the Great Bend of the Don River—the German Army's primary objective in Blau II. This bend is formed as the river flows eastward from Kletskaia, then flows southward and southwestward past Kalach to Tsimlianskaia, and finally returns westward to Rostov and the Sea of Azov. The Great Bend thus forms an immense watery arc; its apex points eastward, that is, toward Stalingrad on the Volga River.

The fighting in Blau II began along the northwestern and western flanks of the rectangle. In the northwest, Army Group B's Sixth Army and Fourth Panzer Army were clearing Soviet forces from the southern third of the Blau I rectangle and preparing to advance southeastward into the Blau II rectangle. In the west, Army Group A's First Panzer and Seventeenth Armies would begin their eastward advance in the broad sector extending from Izium on the Northern Donets River southward along the Northern Donets and Mius Rivers to Taganrog on the Sea of Azov. By this time, the lead elements of German Sixth Army had already reached the Don River, while the army's main forces deployed a line in a long arc stretching westward from the Don through Nikolaevka (Alekseevka) and Valuiki to Kupiansk on the Oskol River. From this starting position, Sixth Army was ready to push southward through the remainder of the Blau I rectangle and into the northern section of the Blau II rectangle. Therefore, the Soviet forces defending the western half of the Blau II area of operations—namely, the Southwestern Front's 28th, 38th, and 9th Armies—were deployed from the Izium region northward along the Northern Donets and Oskol Rivers to Nikolaevka (Alekseevka). Southern Front's 12th, 37th, 18th, and 56th Armies manned defenses along the Mius River northward to the northern Donets west of Voroshilovgrad. They faced the challenging task of having to defend themselves from two sides—against Sixth and Fourth Panzer Armies' forces from the north, as well as First Panzer and Seventeenth Armies' forces from the west.

The Don River, and its imposing Great Bend, was the most important terrain feature shaping the configuration of the German advance during Blau II. It posed a formidable size and depth and formed the northeastern and southern flanks of the rectangle. With nothing but empty expanses of steppe to its north and east as it flowed southeastward into the Great Bend, the upper Don River formed the left boundary of Army Group B's advance and also canalized advancing German forces, principally Sixth Army, southeastward into the Great Bend. In addition, because of the Don's extensive length, the German army group, even as it advanced, would have to leave forces behind to defend the river line. Similarly the lower Don, which formed the southern flank of the rectangle as it flowed westward past Rostov into the Sea of Azov, formed the right boundary of Army Group A's advance. And because the lower Don formed a topographical gateway into the Caucasus from the north—virtually a straight shot into the entire region—it became the army group's most vital immediate objective. The broad expanse between the upper and lower parts of the Don River was traversed by many tributaries, including the Boguchar and Tikhaia, which run northward into the upper Don; and the Kalitva, Glubokaia, Ol'khovaia, Bol'shaia, Nagol'naia, Berezovaia, Gnilaia, and Chir, which flowed southward into the Northern Donets River or into the lower Don itself.

The Northern Donets and Mius Rivers formed most of the rectangle's western flank and, therefore, became the extended jumping-off position for Army Group A's advance. However, Soviet defenses along the Mius River, which were formidable and extended eastward more than 60 kilometers to the fortified city of Rostov, and the geography of the Northern Donets River itself, affected how the German army group would have to conduct its offensive. First, the Soviets' Mius defenses deterred the Germans from striking eastward in this region. Second, the Northern Donets flowed southward and then southeastward along the northern half of the rectangle's western flank, turned eastward north of Voroshilovgrad, ran due east more than 100 kilometers, and then wheeled southward to join the Don River east of Rostov, forming a second large bend of its own. Although this second bend was roughly 120 kilometers east of the Mius River front, it added significant depth to the Soviet defenses along the Mius and protected the northern approaches to Rostov. Therefore, instead of confronting this dangerous defensive position directly, once Army Group A had raced eastward through open country north of the Great Bend of the Donets, it could envelop Rostov from the northeast and east. Army Group A therefore intended to conduct only a secondary attack eastward across the Mius with Seventeenth Army.

Tailoring their offensives to match the region's natural terrain, the German forces constituting Blau II's twin pincers were: first, Army Group B's Sixth and Fourth Panzer Armies attacking southeastward south of the Don; and second, Army Group A's First Panzer Army advancing eastward north of the Northern Donets. Both pincers exploited the rail and road systems in the region. Army Group B advanced along the main railroad line extending from the Voronezh region southward through Rossosh' and Kantemirovka to Millerovo and along the road network paralleling the southern bank of the upper Don and the railroad line to Millerovo. First Panzer Army would cross to the Northern Donets River's left (northern) bank northwest of Voroshilovgrad, lunge eastward across the open steppe south of Starobel'sk, and then swing southeastward along good roads south of Belovodsk and Millerovo to reach the Northern Donets at Kamensk-Shakhtinskii. Army Group A would then complete its drive by advancing southward along the main railroad line and roads passing through Shakhty to attack Rostov from the northeast.

In the context of Blau II, the local terrain offered little benefit to the Soviet defenses. Although Southern Front's 56th, 18th, and 37th Armies could defend the Mius River line with relative ease, the remainder of the region in the western half of the Blau II rectangle was essentially indefensible. This applied especially to the southern sector of the Blau I rectangle, where Southwestern Front's already shaken 38th and 28th Armies were in the process of withdrawing and, at best, manned only weak field defenses, as well as to the sector along and south of the Northern Donets from Izium southward to west of Voroshilovgrad, where Southwestern Front's 9th Army and Southern Front's 12th Army occupied tenuous defenses in the wake of Operation Fridericus II.

Realizing the fragility of these defenses, as well as the likelihood the Soviets could not contain a concerted German advance, the *Stavka*, after a cursory study of the terrain, demanded that Southwestern Front erect and man new defensive lines running north to south along the numerous rivers traversing the area between the upper Don and Northern Donets Rivers. These included, first, a new defensive line constructed hastily along the Aidar River, 56 kilometers east of the Oskol River and, ultimately, another defensive line extending from the upper Don southwestward to Kantemirovka and then southward along the Derkul' River through Belovodsk to the Northern Donets. In fact, however, none of these rivers was large enough to anchor a credible defense, and in any case the advancing German panzers, by exploiting the road networks, routinely overtook the proposed defensive positions before Red Army forces could even dig in. Thus, given the disadvantageous terrain, the armies of Southwestern and Southern Fronts were ripe for envelopment and destruction. It was just a question of how thorough that destruction would be.

BLAU II: THE BATTLE FOR THE DONBAS, 9–17 JULY

The Germans launched the second phase of the Blau campaign (Operation Blau II) on a shoestring (see Map 18). (Editor's note: The original Fall Blau [Case or Plan Blue] was revised, and its phases renamed, on a number of occasions. Thus, the second phase is sometimes referred to as "Clausewitz," while the third phase was labeled "Braunschweig." For simplicity, however, this text will refer to all variants of the original plan by the common name "Blau," followed, if appropriate, by a Roman numeral denoting the phase.) Rather than undertaking a major southern drive with Hoth's entire Fourth Panzer Army, instead the northern pincer consisted only of 3rd and 23rd Panzer and 29th Motorized Divisions, part of Stumme's XXXX Panzer Corps from Paulus's Sixth Army. Two of these divisions, Breith's 3rd Panzer and General Fremerey's 29th Motorized, had already begun their southward advance on 6 July while the forces of the Soviets' Voronezh Front were struggling to recapture their namesake city. The third division, Boineburg-Lengsfeld's 23rd Panzer, was still clearing escapees from Soviet 40th and 21st Armies along the western bank of the Don River north of Korotoiak. By nightfall on 6 July, 3rd Panzer Division had lunged southward from Ostrogozhsk on the Tikhaia Sosna River, advancing 25 kilometers, almost halfway to Rossosh'. On its left, 29th Motorized Division had cleared the southern bank of

Map 18. The Red Army's Donbas defensive operation, 7–24 July 1942

the Don River from Korotoiak eastward to a point opposite Liski (Sloboda) before wheeling south and drawing even with Breith's panzers.

Despite this spectacular advance, the two divisions soon ran short of fuel; reminiscent of the Barbarossa campaign the summer before, the German offensive had already exceeded its logistical capacity, and for two weeks in mid-July Army Group A had priority on gasoline.[1] With the limited fuel remaining to XXXX Panzer Corps, a *kampfgruppe* from Breith's 3rd Panzer Division, consisting of two tank companies and an artillery battery, moved forward on its own in an effort to preempt the Soviet defenses. At dawn on 7 July, this handful of Germans used surprise to seize the Kalitva River bridges at the transportation junction at Rossosh' and even captured part of Southwestern Front's headquarters.[2]

Meanwhile to the south, where Riabyshev's 28th Army was attempting to defend the Tikhaia Sosna River line, 305th and 376th Infantry Divisions of Sixth Army's VIII Army Corps thrust across the Tikhaia Sosna River at and south of Nikolaevka (Alekseevka). This unhinged Riabyshev's defenses and drove his army's right wing southward into the Chernaia Kalitva River valley northwest of Ol'kho-vatka. However, the defenses in the center and on the left wing of Riabyshev's army held firm, as did those of Moskalenko's 38th Army on Riabyshev's left, stretched southward along the Valui and Oskol Rivers past Valuiki and Kupiansk to Borovaia.[3]

As weak as it was, the limited effort by XXXX Panzer Corps was sufficient to unhinge Timoshenko's regional defenses. However, it remained to be seen whether it would occur in time to encircle and destroy Timoshenko's armies before they could escape eastward. Major General Vasilii Dmitrievich Kri-uchenkin, former commander of 3rd Guards Cavalry Corps and whom the *Stavka* had assigned to replace Riabyshev the night before, described the dete-riorating situation in a report to Timoshenko late on 6 July:[4]

1. Deeply enveloping the army's right flank with tank formations and infantry, the enemy captured Alekseevka [Nikolaevka] and, on the morning of 6 July, began advancing southeastward from the Alekseevka and Budenny line with forces of more than an infantry division with tanks (according to incomplete information, up to 80). The enemy reached the Gezev, Khlebishche, and Fil'ki line by 1000 hours. The enemy force of more than three infantry divisions and a tank division in the center and on the right flank has not displayed any activity since the morning of 6 July. . . .

3. Decision: The forces of 23rd Tank Corps, 32nd Cavalry Division, and 158th Tank Brigade will prevent the enemy advancing from the Alekseevka and Budenny line from reaching the right flank's rear. . . . There is a danger that the enemy can forestall us from occupying the fortified region along the Varvarovka, Kubraki, and Roven'ki line, just as he did in the Alekseevka [Nikolaevka] region. Therefore, in the event superior enemy forces appear on the army's right flank and the groups of the right flank are unstable, in order to preserve the fortified region, which has sufficient quantities of weapons, and preserve the army's forces, while holding the fortified region with our right flank, we intend to with-draw the army's forces gradually to the fortified region along the Aidar River in the Varvarovka and Roven'ki region, while creating cut-off positions facing north along the Kalitva River. I request you approve this decision.

Kriuchenkin, Shchitov [chief of staff][5]

Left with no other choice, Timoshenko approved Kriuchenkin's decision to prevent his army from being totally encircled and requested and received *Stavka* approval to withdraw Moskalenko's 38th Army from its exposed positions on 28th Army's left flank. According to Moskalenko:

On 6 July, two German corps—17th Army and 40th Tank—which were oper-ating north of our position, forced their way across the Tikhaia Sosna River. The forces of the *front* assigned to defend that river line did not succeed in reaching it. As for 28th Army, at this time it was already withdrawing behind the Chernaia Kalitva River.

Now the forces of 38th Army could easily circle around the enemy corps advancing from the north from the right. Evidently, therefore, on the night of 6–7 July, the *front* commander ordered we begin the withdrawal of the forces of our army to the rear defensive line along the Nagol'naia–Roven'ki–Kuriachevka–Belokurakino front, while leaving a covering force from each division along the Oskol River. The designated line was situated 35–40 kilometers east of the Oskol River and was occupied by battalions of 118th Fortified Region. The divisions of 38th Army anticipated reinforcing their defenses.

Twenty-four hours after receipt of the order concerning 38th Army's withdrawal, it was withdrawn to that line. However, by this time, the situation had once again changed, again for the worse.[6]

In fact, the *Stavka*'s 6 July withdrawal directive applied equally to all four Southwestern Front armies. Protecting their rear with covering detachments, the directives required Timoshenko to withdraw his armies as follows:

- *21st Army* to the eastern bank of the Don River from Chibisovka southward through Lozevo to Pavlovsk, where it was to prevent the Germans from crossing the river;
- *28th Army* to the Chuprin and Veidelevka line;
- *38th Army* to the Aidar and Roven'ki line by 8 July; and
- *9th Army* to the Belokurakino–Mostki–Kremennaia [*sic*] line.

In addition, the directive required 9th Army, which was defending the left flank of Moskalenko's army and the extreme left wing of Southwestern Front as a whole, to hold firmly to its new defensive line. This would permit the evacuation of vital industrial facilities in and around Lisichansk, situated on the northern bank of the Northern Donets River.[7] The 9th Army was now commanded by General Lopatin, former commander of 37th Army, who replaced Nikishov after 9th Army's defeat in Operation Fridericus II.

The "worsening" situation Moskalenko referred to on his northern flank was 3rd Panzer Division's seizure of the town of Rossosh', a vital road junction and crossing site on the Kalitva River, on 7 July (see Map 19). Compounding Moskalenko's and Kriuchenkin's growing dilemma, XXXX Panzer Corps the next day continued its rapid southward advance with 100 tanks. In the vanguard of Stumme's panzer corps, Fremerey's 29th Motorized Division raced halfway to Kantemirovka, and Breith's 3rd Panzer Division reached Ol'khovatka, both towns being located in 28th Army's deep right rear. This deep thrust threatened to envelop not only 28th and 38th Armies but also many of the rear service and combat support forces operating in Southwestern Front's rear area, including 31st and 9th Route (Roadway) and 39th Mechanized Battalions of Colonel A. N. Tkachev's 19th Separate Railroad Brigade, portions of 7th Sapper Army's 12th, 14th, 15th, 20th, and 24th Sapper Brigades, and many other road construction

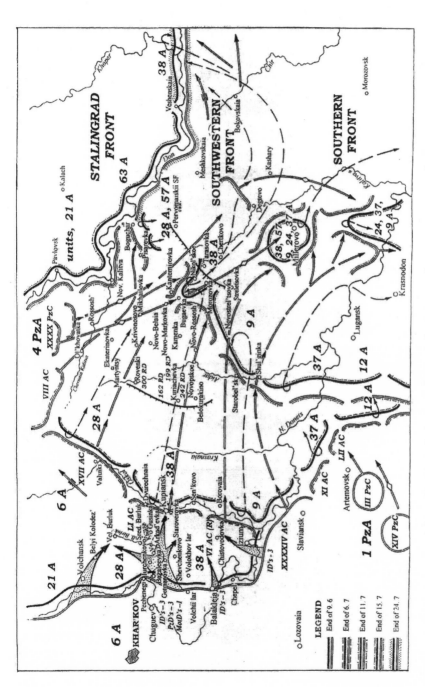

Map 19. Combat operations of the 28th, 38th, and 9th Armies between the Donets and Don Rivers, June–July 1942

and repair units, to say nothing of the *front*'s numerous logistical supply units and associated supply dumps and other installations. The presence of these forces along 28th and 38th Armies' lines of withdrawal caused utter confusion along all the roads leading to the rear.

Advancing headlong, Stumme's two armored divisions reached the crossings over the Kalitva River, preempting a special combat group that 28th Army had formed to defend those crossings. This group was commanded by General Pushkin, the *front*'s chief of Auto-Transport and former commander of 23rd Tank Corps during the May battle for Khar'kov. Pushkin's group consisted of the remnants of Shamshin's 22nd Tank Corps, 11th, 13th, and 15th Antitank Brigades, four machine-gun battalions from 52nd Fortified Region, and a mixed rifle regiment.[8] Although it mustered 40 serviceable tanks, all concentrated in the corps' 6th Guards Tank Brigade, the group lost most of these because they ran out of fuel and oil.[9] Pushkin then hastily withdrew his small forces to the southeast, creating an even larger gap between 28th and 38th Armies.

The next day, 8 July, XXXX Panzer Corps dispatched its 3rd and 23rd Panzer and 29th Motorized Divisions—which Moskalenko believed had a total of 300 tanks—southward into the gap toward Kantemirovka, even deeper in 28th and 38th Armies' rear. When Moskalenko requested permission to withdraw his forces farther east to the Aidar River, while a portion of his army formed a defensive screen between Roven'ki and Kantemirovka to assist 28th Army's eastward escape, Timoshenko demurred, approving the latter but insisting Moskalenko hold his new defensive positions farther west. Moskalenko claimed this decision only "complicated matters."[10] Moskalenko then formed a combat group consisting of 304th, 9th Guards, and 199th Rifle Divisions and 3rd Tank Brigade and dispatched it northeast to man his protective screen between Roven'ki and Kantemirovka. However, early on 9 July XXXX Panzer Corps' 23rd Panzer and 29th Motorized Divisions drove into Kantemirovka before Moskalenko's group could reach the town.

The day before, a second large German axe had begun to fall on Moskalenko's army and indeed on Timoshenko's entire front. At dawn on 8 July, Bock, recognizing that 38th and 9th Armies were beginning to withdraw, authorized the infantry forces on First Panzer Army's right wing and center to advance across the Oskol and Northern Donets Rivers in pursuit. Along the entire line from south of Kupiansk southward along the Oskol River and then eastward along the Northern Donets River to just west of Lisichansk, the infantry divisions of First Panzer Army's XI and XXXIV Army Corps crossed the two rivers and advanced 10–15 kilometers eastward. Crossing the Zherebet River, by nightfall they reached the approaches to the Krasnaia River, which by now was defended by 9th Army and the weaker half of Moskalenko's 38th Army. The same day, First Panzer Army's commander, Kleist, hastily shifted the panzer and motorized divisions of his III and XIV Panzer Corps forward into positions from which they could mount their main thrust against the left wing of Timoshenko's Southwestern Front and the right wing of Lieutenant General R. Ia. Malinovsky's Southern Front the next morning.

Poised to strike northeastward toward the Northern Donets River between Izium and Lisichansk, Kleist's panzer spearheads faced the defenses of Lopatin's 9th Army on the left wing of Timoshenko's Southwestern Front and the defenses of Kozlov's 37th Army and Grechko's 12th Army on the right wing of Malinovsky's Southern Front. Anchoring Timoshenko's right, Lopatin defended the sector from the boundary with 38th Army south of Kupiansk southward along the eastern banks of the Oskol and Northern Donets Rivers to Krasnyi Liman. Severely shaken by the losses it suffered in Operation Fridericus, Lopatin's army had five rifle divisions (318th, 296th, 51st, 140th, and 255th) deployed from left to right in first echelon, backed up by three rifle divisions (81st, 106th, and 303rd) and two destroyer brigades (18th and 19th) in second echelon or reserve. In addition, Lopatin's army included Parkhomenko's 5th Cavalry Corps, which had also been severely damaged in Fridericus, one tank brigade (12th), and two separate tank battalions (71st and 132nd), with roughly 65 tanks.

On the right wing of Malinovsky's Southern Front, 12th and 18th Armies manned defenses south of the Northern Donets River from east of Debal'tsevo northwestward to the river south of Krasnyi Liman, protecting the approaches to Voroshilovgrad and Lisichansk. Grechko's 12th Army defended the southern half of this sector with three rifle divisions (74th, 4th, and 261st) in first echelon, backed up by two more rifle divisions (176th and 349th) but no armor whatsoever. Kozlov's 37th Army, in the northern half of the sector, defended with four rifle divisions (218th, 230th, 295th, and 275th) in his first echelon and one rifle division (102nd) in second echelon, supported by 46 tanks in 121st Tank Brigade. Given the paucity of armor in 12th and 37th Armies, Malinovsky concentrated General Radkevich's 14th Tank Corps in the region east of the Northern Donets River. However, since Radkevich's corps was still in the process of forming, it had less than half of its 180 authorized tanks. Thus the forces arrayed opposite Kleist's intended penetration sector were no match for his two panzer corps.

Completing the dispositions of Southern Front on the eve of Kleist's assault, Malinovsky defended his *front*'s left wing and center with two armies deployed in defenses arrayed along the eastern bank of the Mius River from east of Taganrog on the Gulf of Taganrog northward to the Debal'tsevo region opposite Army Group A's Seventeenth Army. In the southern half of this sector, General Tsyganov's 56th Army defended with two rifle brigades (16th Rifle and 3rd Guards Rifle Corps' 68th Naval Rifle) and three rifle divisions (30th, 339th, and 31st) in first echelon, backed up by two more rifle brigades from 3rd Guards Rifle Corps (76th and 81st) and 63rd Tank Brigade with 55 tanks. To the rear, the army's 70th and 158th Fortified Regions manned fixed defenses in and around Rostov.

In the northern half of this sector, General Kamkov's 18th Army had three rifle divisions (395th, 383rd, and 353rd) in first echelon, backed up by one rifle division (216th) in second echelon (but again without armor). To compensate Kamkov's weakness, during the first week of July Malinovsky began forming yet another army, the 24th, to provide his *front* with a proper second echelon in depth. The 24th Army was commanded by Lieutenant General I'lia Kornilovich Smirnov, who had commanded 18th Army in February–April 1942 and then served on the Southwestern Main Direction Command's staff until mid-July. Later, Smirnov's successor was Major General Vladimir Nikolaevich Martsenkevich, who had led the *front's* 176th Rifle Division since July 1940.[11] By 9 July 24th Army consisted of just four rifle divisions (73rd, 228th, 335th, and 341st) distributed evenly in 12th and 18th Armies' rear area.

Kleist increased Moskalenko's and Timoshenko's misery by unleashing his panzers at dawn on 9 July. His infantry corps and their divisions continued their pursuit across his panzer army's entire front, advancing in two broad columns side by side. Meanwhile, 16th and 22nd Panzer Divisions of Geyr's III Panzer Corps and 14th Panzer and 16th Motorized Divisions of Wietersheim's XIV Panzer Corps crushed the bridgehead defended by Southern Front's 37th Army south of Lisichansk. They then captured the city and seized bridgeheads of their own on the northern bank of the Northern Donets on 10 July.

On Kleist's right (southern) flank, the infantry divisions of IV and LII Army Corps from General Ruoff's Seventeenth Army advanced eastward from the Artemovsk region toward Voroshilovgrad. The advance forced Southern Front's 12th Army to retreat toward the Northern Donets River. Step by step, but inexorably, the southern wing of Southwestern Front and the northern wing of Southern Front were engulfed in flames by day's end on 10 July.

Caught up in Sixth Army's rapid advance, Timoshenko on 6 July had been controlling the action from his auxiliary command post in Gorokhovka, near Rossosh', while the remainder of his staff was in the town of Kalach, 50 kilometers northeast of the Don at Boguchar (not to be confused with Kalach-on-the-Don, situated at the eastern apex of the Great Bend of the Don). Because these command posts could not communicate with each other, and both had only intermittent radio contact with armies and troops in the field, neither they nor the *Stavka* understood what was actually occurring. Timoshenko tried to take things in hand after 9 July when he finally reached his main command post at Kalach.

Meanwhile on 9 July, faced with mounting threats to both of his army's flanks, Moskalenko sent two urgent messages to Timoshenko and *Stavka* representative Vasilevsky, requesting they approve his further withdrawal. The response was:

1. You are not permitted slippage along the front to protect the threatened axis from the direction of 28th Army.
2. Establish a firm defense of your positions in accordance with orders.
3. Create a grouping of forces on your right wing and prevent an enemy penetration both on your right wing and at the junction with the forces of 28th Army.
4. There cannot be any sort of withdrawal.
5. Moskalenko will personally answer for defending the line in accordance with orders.[12]

Concerned that Moskalenko's message might be true, Vasilevsky consulted with members of the *front* staff, in particular Colonel I. N. Rukhle, the chief of operations, but they too were ignorant of the actual situation at the front line and mistakenly thought Kriuchenkin's 28th Army and Group Pushkin were successfully defending along the Chernaia Kalitva River. With the *front*'s main command post moved from the Rossosh' region eastward across the Don River to Kalach, neither Timoshenko and Vasilevsky nor any of the *front*'s staff realized what was actually occurring. At 1600 hours Moskalenko once again informed Timoshenko of 28th Army's and Group Pushkin's collapse and the Germans' rapid advance toward Roven'ki. This put the Germans deep in the rear of Timoshenko's supposedly fortified line south of Roven'ki. This time he asked permission to withdraw his army to the Kolesnikovka–Kantemirovka–Markovka line, well east of the Aidar River, lest his forces be cut off entirely.[13] When he received no reply because communications failed, at 2000 hours Moskalenko issued the withdrawal orders on his own authority. That night 38th Army's forces began their arduous attempt to escape eastward through Sixth Army's panzer cordon before it closed around them.

By the evening of 9 July, Paulus's armored pincer—the three mobile divisions of Stumme's XXXX Panzer Corps—formed a broad corridor through Timoshenko's defenses. This corridor extended eastward to the Don River near Boguchar southwestward through the Kantemirovka region to the Aidar River at Novo-Pskov. Fremerey's 29th Motorized Division, with Boineburg-Lengsfeld's 23rd Panzer Division in its wake, was concentrated east of Kantemirovka and poised to march on Chertkovo, only 35 kilometers south. Echeloned to the right of Stumme's main force were XVII Army Corps' 113th and 79th Infantry Divisions, with part of 23rd Panzer Division in support. These three forces closed in on the remnants of Kriuchenkin's 28th and Moskalenko's 38th Armies from the north. Farther west, 297th and 44th Infantry Divisions of Sixth Army's LI Army Corps pressed eastward across the Aidar River, driving before them the rear guards of Moskalenko's army.

Carefully cataloging the "bag" of Soviet forces in the pocket between the Aidar and Chertkovo Rivers, German intelligence organs correctly identified 22nd Tank Corps and 81st, 162nd, 199th, 242nd, 277th, 278th, and 304th Rifle Divisions of Moskalenko's 38th Army as well as 13th Cavalry Corps and 244th and 255th Rifle Divisions from Timoshenko's reserve and Lopatin's 9th Army. To the northwest and west, the remnants of Kriuchenkin's 28th Army were scattered across the landscape, either encircled by Sixth Army's follow-on infantry divisions (384th, 62nd, and 294th) south of the Tikhaia Snova River or northwest of Ol'khovatka or pursued by XVII and LII Army Corps' infantry divisions east and southeast of Roven'ki.

Kriuchenkin, whose headquarters had already been evacuated by light aircraft to the village of Baskovskaia on the southern bank of the Don River opposite Veshenskaia, reported his army's predicament to Timoshenko late on 10 July:

The headquarters of 28th Army arrived at Baskovskaia at 1600 hours on 10 July with the aim of assembling the army and putting its units in order. We have no communications with the units of the army, and the exact locations of its divisions are unknown. By day's end on 9 July . . . 13th Guards Rifle Division . . . was fighting in the Markovka region [10 kilometers west of Kantemirovka] . . . with 300 fighters [combat soldiers], 169th Rifle Division . . . was fighting in the Zhuravka region [7 kilometers northwest of Roven'ki] . . . with 100 fighters, 32nd Cavalry Division was fighting in the Krivonosovka region [40 kilometers east of Roven'ki], cut off from the crossing at Novo-Belaia [the Belaia River, 25 kilometers southeast of Roven'ki], with 50 sabers. 6th Guards Tank Brigade, combined with Khasin's [23rd Tank Corps] tanks, was fighting [south of Rossosh'] alongside 32nd Cavalry Division, with 6 tanks. . . . 15th Guards Rifle Division was fighting encircled in the Maliarov region [northeast of Roven'ki], 175th Rifle Division was fighting encircled in the Kopanka region [28 kilometers northwest of Roven'ki], but its subsequent route is unknown. After fighting in the Krivonosovka region, 1084th RGK Artillery Regiment is located in the Bol'shaia Napolovskii region (20 kilometers southwest of Baskovskaia) with 9 guns, and, after fighting in the Zhilin region, at 0100 hours 10 July, 594th Artillery Regiment was on the march at Chertkovo with 10 guns.

At the present time, the exact locations of the divisions are unknown; but it is most likely that the divisions no longer exist as organized formations and their encircled remnants are fighting their way eastward toward the Don River crossings. On 8, 9, and 10 July, the army's rear and the divisions have been moving in a continuous stream to the [Don River] crossings at Boguchar, Kazanskaia, and Veshenskaia.

Presently, several thousands of vehicles and a mass of transports of 28th, 38th, and 9th Armies, which expected to cross, have piled up in the Baskovskaia region since the bridge at Veshenskaia was destroyed on 9 July. Enveloping the army's right flank, the enemy reached its rear, forced its way into the combat formations of the units, cut off several units, and, by day's end on 9 July, reached the line of the Boguchar River with its leading tank and motorized units and occupied Anna Rebrikovskaia. The enemy is striving to cut off our units, which are withdrawing in disorder, from the Don River crossings. General Pushkin's group [22nd Tank Corps] did not protect the army's right flank. The enemy attacked from the line of the Chernaia Kalitva River against 28th Army's right flank and rear with up to two tank divisions and one motorized division. On the orders of its command, the units of the army withdrew successively to new positions, but the infantry, having carried on fighting daily for 40 kilometers, was not in any condition to withdraw to these lines and was subjected to tank attacks on the march, which led to the loss of command and control of the units, heavy losses, and the dispersal of the units. In fact, beginning on 3 July, the headquarters of the army lacked reliable communications with its divisions, telephone communication was absent, radio communication was poorly organized, with frequent interruptions and very slow transmissions. Communication by means of liaison officers was hindered by the great distances from the units, the vagueness of the situation, and the cutting of lines of communication by the enemy. Many liaison officers sent to the divisions did not return.

At present the divisions are no longer combat capable and are not in a condition to hold the enemy forward of the Don River. It is necessary to withdraw the units to the eastern bank of the Don River to assemble their personnel and equipment and put the units in order. The personnel are terribly worn out. There is no exact information about the combat and numerical composition of the units; these matters are being verified. Unable at present to control the divisions in combat, the military council and headquarters of the army will organize the effort of detaining and collecting the units and putting them in order. To prevent the enemy from spreading out farther to the southeast and south, I consider it necessary to move units forward from the depths [rear]. The 28th Army command has not received any combat orders or instructions on what to do from the headquarters of the Southwestern Front since 8 July.

Major General Kriuchenkin, Brigade Commissar Luchko[14]

Utterly ignorant of the situation at the front, Timoshenko ordered Kriuchenkin to concentrate his army to defend the region east of Kantemirovka and halt the German advance. Kriuchenkin, protesting vehemently, said, "The enemy had already reached the Kantemirovka, Titorevka, and Anna Rebrikovskaia line on 9 July," and continued complaining about the dilapidated state of his army but could do little more.[15] As Paulus's advancing infantry divisions mopped up the remnants of 28th Army's divisions encircled west of the Don, over the next three days the survivors of that army painfully made their way to the safety of the Don River, individually or in small groups. As they did, Kriuchenkin reported that elements of his army's 169th, 38th, and 175th Rifle, 13th and 15th Guards Rifle, and 32nd Cavalry Divisions, 23rd Tank Corps, and several artillery regiments made it back safely. However, by this time his divisions mustered only 40–400 fighters each, supported by no tanks and only a handful of guns and mortars. Kriuchenkin's army was a shell of its former self, consisting of headquarters and rear service elements but few combat troops. In this it resembled Danilov's 21st Army, whose remnants were still making their way across the Don River farther north after losing up to 80 percent of an original strength of more than 100,000 men. Within days, the *Stavka* would assign both armies and their few surviving troops to its newly formed Stalingrad Front.

As for Moskalenko, on 10 July he began concentrating his 38th Army's scattered divisions and maneuvering them eastward toward the railroad line between Kantemirovka and Chertkovo, all the while pressed from the rear by Sixth Army's 113th, 79th, and 297th Infantry Divisions. After 38th Army established radio contact with Southwestern Front headquarters later in the day, Timoshenko ordered Moskalenko to penetrate eastward to the north of Chertkovo. However, as the latter moved his forces eastward overnight on 10–11 July, XXXX Panzer Corps' 3rd and 23rd Panzer Divisions lunged south early on 11 July and captured Chertkovo, thereby blocking 38th Army's primary escape route. Moskalenko reacted quickly, shifting his route to the south toward Degtevo, south of Chertkovo, and Kashary. Stumme's XXXX Panzer Corps countered by speeding Breith's 3rd Panzer Division southward to Millerovo.

Meanwhile, XXXX Panzer Corps' rapid and deep advance, which overran many of Southwestern Front's airfields, forced both the *Stavka* and Timoshenko to react, although again belatedly and with little real effect. First, shortly after midnight on 10 July, in Stalin's name, Vasilevsky issued a directive authorizing a further withdrawal: "The *Stavka* sanctions an immediate organized withdrawal of the armies of the *front* to the Kazanskaia and Chertkovo front. The initial withdrawal line for the left wing of the *front*—Chertkovo, Belovodsk, and Shul'ginka [on the Aidar River]; and for the right wing of the Southern Front—Novo-Astrakhan', Trekhizbenka, and Cherkasskoe [west of Voroshilovgrad]."[16]

Hedging his bets further, Vasilevsky, in two new directives, also ordered Briansk and North Caucasus Fronts and the Red Army's Chief of Engineers to begin construction of a new defensive line in the Tambov region east of the Don River and to man a new defensive line along the southern bank of the lower Don River from the Sea of Azov eastward toward the Stalingrad region.[17] However, by this time, the advance by Sixth Army's XXXX Panzer Corps had rendered the first of these directives superfluous.

With most of his airfields falling into German hands, on 10 July Timoshenko ordered 8th Air Army to shift its aircraft to new bases farther to the rear, depriving 28th and 38th Armies of all air support. That same day, in the absence of air support and with no clear picture of the actual situation, Timoshenko took measures to shore up his defenses with 57th Army, a new headquarters with no assigned units commanded by General Nikishov, former commander of 9th Army. The marshal instructed Nikishov to assemble an ad hoc shock group formed from whatever forces the *front* could muster and regroup it northward to reinforce Moskalenko's 38th Army in the Kantemirovka region and help rescue 28th Army. At the same time, Vasilevsky ordered the Southern Front to assemble 73rd, 228th, 335th, and 341st Rifle Divisions of Smirnov's second-echelon 24th Army and dispatch them and a special tank group commanded by the *front's* chief of armor forces, Major General Vasilii Mikhailovich Alekseev, northeastward to block the panzer corps' advance in the Chertkovo region.[18]

Although 57th Army initially managed to assemble a small force consisting of 333rd and 278th Rifle Divisions (refugees from 9th and 38th Armies), and Radkevich's 14th Tank Corps (from the *front's* reserve), its path north was already blocked by XXXX Panzer Corps' deep advance toward Millerovo and points east. XXXX Panzer Corps' advance also forestalled any effective defense by 24th Army, prompting Malinovsky, Southern Front commander, to report the army was being driven back to the Millerovo–Rogalik–Vishniaki line "under great pressure."[19]

Despite the steady stream of German armor flowing eastward along the southern bank of the Don River and southward along the Kantemirovka-Millerovo road, Moskalenko had no choice but to organize the remnants of his army's forces into multiple columns and dispatch them eastward across the Kalitva River north and south of Degtevo. Dodging 23rd and 3rd Panzer Divisions' forces as best they could, the pitifully small remnants of these divisions that survived their dash through this German armored cordon reached the Kashary region late on 11 July. On 12 July, when Moskalenko's army finally reestablished radio contact with Southwestern Front headquarters, Timoshenko directed Moskalenko, together with 9th and 57th Armies, to withdraw his forces southward and join Southern Front's retreat to the Don. However, because he was unable to establish radio contact with Southern Front and soon lost contact with Southwestern Front as well, Moskalenko instead decided to take his chances by infiltrating to the east. Ultimately his forces passed through the new 62nd Army's forward defensive lines south of the Don River near Serafimovich on 15 and 16 July.[20]

The Red Army General Staff issued its last daily summary mentioning Timoshenko's encircled 28th and 38th Armies, as well as Nikishov's 57th Army, which was supposed to rescue them, at 0800 hours on 12 July. Although based on incomplete information, it bore mute testimony to the fate of Kriuchenkin's and Moskalenko's forces, as well as Danilov's, most of whose surviving troops had already crossed the Don to safety days before:

SOUTHWESTERN FRONT

21st Army is defending its previous positions along the eastern bank of the Don River with the forces of 3rd Cavalry Corps, 124th Rifle Division, 4th Antitank Brigade, and 51st Guards-Mortar Regiment. After pressing back its combat security, the enemy occupied the northwestern outskirts of Staraia Kalitva at 0530 hours on 11 July.

28th Army is withdrawing in disorder toward the southwest in fragmented groups. Its supply carts and auto-transport were crossing the Don River in the defensive sector of 63rd Army's 1st and 153rd Rifle Divisions on 10 July. The headquarters of 28th Army has lost control over its units and does not have information about the exact location of the army's units. The enemy has occupied the Bogomolov, Medova, Zhuravka, and Setrakovskii regions (28–65 kilometers southeast of Boguchar).

57th Army (2nd Tank Corps, 333rd Rifle Division, and 22nd Antitank Brigade) was fighting along the Monastryrshchina and Mikhailov line (28–40 kilometers southeast of Boguchar) on 11 July. On the night of 11–12 July, the army withdrew its units to the new Migulinskaia and Konovalov line (50–58 kilometers southeast of Boguchar).

38th Army was fighting with the enemy along the Kolesnikov and

Bugaevka (20 kilometers southeast and 5 kilometers southeast of Kantemirovka) and Veselyi and Brusovka line (18 kilometers southeast of Kantemirovka), while protecting the withdrawal of 28th Army. A radiogram from 38th Army reported that 199th Rifle Division was attacked by enemy tanks in the Chertkovo region at 1000 hours on 11 July.

9th Army's main forces were withdrawing to the Markovka (50 kilometers northeast of Starobel'sk), Evsug, and Novoaleksandrovka (30 kilometers southeast of Starobel'sk) line at 1700 hours on 11 July.

5th Cavalry Corps is on the march to the Belovodsk region.[21]

However, on 12 July Fourth Panzer and First Panzer Armies dashed any hopes the *Stavka* and Timoshenko harbored about erecting a coherent and viable defense line southward from the Don River through Kantemirovka, Belovodsk, and Trekhizbenka to Cherkasskoe. At dawn, the three armored divisions of Stumme's XXXX Panzer Corps and VIII Army Corps, now transferred from Paulus's Sixth to Hoth's Fourth Panzer Army, continued their dramatic southeastward advance deep into the flank and rear of the already shattered armies in the center of Timoshenko's Southwestern Front. Simultaneously, three more armored divisions of First Panzer Army's III and XIV Panzer Corps pressed eastward north of the Northern Donets River against the boundary between Timoshenko's Southwestern Front and Malinovsky's Southern Front.

In the most spectacular of these thrusts, Stumme's XXXX Panzer Corps fanned out to the southeast and south across a more than 100-kilometer-wide front, with *kampfgruppen* from Fremerey's 29th Motorized Division passing through Meshkovskaia on the Tikhaia River, 55 kilometers east of Chertkovo, and reaching Bokovskaia on the Chir River and Nizhne-Astakhov on the Bol'shaia River, 75 and 90 kilometers east-northeast of Millerovo, respectively. To the west, the main body of Breith's 3rd Panzer Division bypassed Millerovo, with its forward *kampfgruppe* marching southward west of the Kalitva River toward Kamensk-Shakhtinskii on the Northern Donets River, 75 kilometers east of Voroshilovgrad. Farther west, Boineburg-Lengsfeld's 23rd Panzer Division was advancing from Chertkovo southward toward Degtevo, in the process threatening to sever the withdrawal routes of Moskalenko's 38th Army to the east.

As for the remainder of Hoth's panzer army, the infantry of its VIII Army Corps, which had cleared the remnants of Soviet 40th and 21st Armies from the region west of the Don River while under Sixth Army's control, closed on the river from Pavlovsk southward to Boguchar, while the main body of Hungarian Second Army advanced to the Don River south of Voronezh on Fourth Panzer Army's left. Relieved from their tiring task of defending Voronezh against repeated Soviet assaults, by day's end on 12 July 24th Panzer and 16th and "GD" Motorized Divisions of Kempf's XXXXVIII Panzer Corps had closed up to the Tikhaia Sosna River at Nikolaevka (Alekseevka) and Ostrogozhsk. Although delayed for more than a day due to fuel shortages, they were prepared to move southward to Kantemirovka, where they were to join Fourth Panzer Army's advance to the Don River east of Rostov. Finally, farther to the rear, the infantry of Sixth Army's XVII and LI Army Corps were pushing the remnants of the defeated 28th Army and retreating 38th Army eastward across the Derkul' River on a line extending from Kantemirovka southward to Belovodsk.

Forming the southern pincer of Bock's grand drive to the east, 14th and 22nd Panzer Divisions of Geyr's III Panzer Corps, advancing in tandem in the vanguard of the First Panzer Army, pressed eastward across the Aidar River south of Starobel'sk, flanked on the left by Romanian VI Army Corps. At the same time, 16th Panzer and 16th Motorized Divisions of Wietersheim's XIV Panzer Corps crossed the river at Novyi Aidar. Both panzer corps pressed the rear guards of Moskalenko's 38th Army and Lopatin's 9th Army eastward toward Belovodsk. In the process, Kleist's panzers penetrated and then outflanked Southern Front's "final" defensive line between Novo-Astrakhan', Trekhizbenka on the Northern Donets River, and Cherkasskoe.

With the defenses of Timoshenko's Southwestern Front collapsing and Malinovsky's Southern Front incapable of providing any meaningful assistance, the *Stavka* suddenly recognized the gravity of the situation and drastically reorganized its forces—virtually writing off its 28th and 38th Armies.

THE FORMATION OF STALINGRAD FRONT

The rapid advance by Bock's armored spearheads exposed the severe limitations of the Soviets' faulty command and communications network. For example, dissatisfied with Southwestern Front's performance during the battle for Khar'kov and the Germans' subsequent attacks in Operations Wilhelm and Fridericus II, Stalin on 26 June had sent General Bodin, the chief of the General Staff's Operations Directorate, to replace Bagramian as Southwestern Front chief of staff. Realizing Stalin was unhappy with his performance as well, Marshal Timoshenko apparently regarded Bodin as a spy and largely ignored him. On 6 July, without warning, Timoshenko and his political officer, Khrushchev, left the *front's* main command post at Kalach to establish a new auxiliary or tactical headquarters at Gorokhovka, four and a half hours' drive away, leaving Bodin behind. Because Timoshenko neglected to take communications with him, an ominous period of several days ensued during which Moscow received no reports from the Southwestern Front commander. When Bodin eventually reestablished communications with both the forward command post and the General Staff in Moscow, he found himself caught between the two, answering for the failures of an organization over which he had no control. He tried to avoid criticizing his new chief, but eventually Vasilevsky had to order Timoshenko to return to the main command post at Kalach so he could coordinate the rapid retreat of his troops.[22]

Working with such problems, the Soviet commanders tried to maintain a continuous front, withdrawing rationally rather than retreating in disorder. In many instances they failed. As the Red Army moved eastward through that long, hot month, subjected to air strikes and sometimes cut off by German forward elements, many units lost their organization and communications.

Within two days after authorizing Timoshenko to withdraw his Southwestern Front armies to the Kazanskaia-Belovodsk defensive line on 10 July, Stalin realized this measure was futile. In addition to Hoth's panzers enveloping and defeating 28th and 38th Armies of Timoshenko's front, Kleist's panzers were now tearing an immense hole between Timoshenko and Malinovsky. This rendered all attempts to restore the situation with the reserve 57th and 24th Armies superfluous.

In response, early on 11 July the *Stavka* ordered Major General V. Ia. Kolpakchi's 62nd Army (former 7th Reserve Army), which consisted of six rifle divisions, "to immediately move the army's rifle divisions, which are occupying the defenses of Stalingrad and situated in the Stalingrad region, forward and occupy the Stalingrad line being prepared along the Karazhenskii (on the Don River, 18 kilometers southeast of Serafimovich), Evstratovskii, Kalmykov, Slepukhin, Surovikino Station, Farm No. 2 of State Farm 79, and Suvorovskii line."[23] Deploying by rail, the divisions were to begin moving no later than 11 July, man the new defenses with three divisions by the morning of 12 July, and complete forward deployment by 14 July. In addition, Stalin reinforced Kolpakchi's army with 18 artillery–machine gun battalions from 52nd and 115th Fortified Regions and assigned him three fresh rifle divisions (214th, 229th, and 29th Guards) to defend the line around Stalingrad proper. Once occupied, Kolpakchi's new main defensive line formed a gentle arc extending from north to south across the western base of the Great Bend, roughly halfway between the Chir River in the west and the Great Bend itself in the east, beyond which Stalingrad was only 50 kilometers to the east.

Early the next day, Stalin and Vasilevsky discussed the developing crisis with his Southern Front commander, Malinovsky, by Baudot teletype. Malinovsky began by informing Stalin that the Germans were continuing heavy attacks all along his front, that he had lost contact with 9th and 38th Armies, and that 37th, 12th, 18th, and 56th Armies were attempting to withdraw to a new defensive line; however, 24th Army's attacks to rescue 9th and 38th Armies were faltering. His worst fears confirmed, Stalin then had Vasilevsky read Malinovsky a directive the *Stavka* had prepared at 0215 hours:

The *Stavka* of the Supreme High Command orders:
1. For the sake of the convenience of controlling the forces of the Southwestern and Southern Fronts from a single center, transfer the Southwestern Front's 28th, 38th, 57th, and 9th Armies to the Southern Front, effective at 0600 hours on 12 July.
2. Rename the Southwestern Front the Stalingrad Front. After including 63rd Army (former 5th Reserve Army), 62nd Army (former 7th Reserve Army), 64th Army (former 1st Reserve Army), and 21st Army in the composition of

the Stalingrad Front, the Military Council of the Southwestern Front, with the *front*'s command and control, will immediately relocate to Stalingrad.

3. The mission of the Southern Front is to organize a decisive rebuff to the enemy advancing to the east between Millerovo and Migulinskaia, using reserves and part of the armies of the Southern Front.

4. The mission of the Stalingrad Front is to occupy the Stalingrad line west of the Don River firmly, with 62nd and 64th Armies, two naval rifle brigades, 18 artillery-machine gun battalions, and the students of eight military schools arriving from the North Caucasus, and under no circumstances permit an enemy penetration east of this line toward Stalingrad. Defend the eastern bank of the Don River with 63rd Army in the sector it occupies and prevent the enemy from forcing the Don River under any circumstances. Move 21st Army up to the Serafimovich region and to the east along the northern bank of the Don River, joining its right flank to 63rd Army's flank and its left flank to 62nd Army's flank, with the mission to prevent the enemy from forcing the Don River in this sector under any circumstance, and firmly protect the junction between 62nd and 63rd Armies.

I. Stalin, A. Vasilevsky[24]

About three hours later, the *Stavka* issued three directives implementing Stalin's decision to reorganize his forces in the Stalingrad region. These directives officially abolished Southwestern Front—renaming it Stalingrad Front—and appointed Timoshenko as its commander, with Khrushchev as commissar. The directives also transferred the *front* headquarters to Stalingrad and assigned Timoshenko's 63rd, 62nd, and 64th Armies.[25] The 63rd Army, commanded by Lieutenant General V. I. Kuznetsov, consisted of five rifle divisions (1st, 153rd, 197th, 203rd, and 14th Guards Rifle), Major General Kolpakchi's 62nd Army included six rifle divisions (192nd, 33rd Guards, 147th, 184th, 196th, and 181st), and 64th Army, commanded by Lieutenant General V. I. Chuikov, comprised six rifle divisions (131st, 229th, 29th, 18th, 214th, and 112th Rifle).

The new commander of 63rd Army, General Vasilii Ivanovich Kuznetsov, was an experienced officer who had commanded Central Front's 3rd and 21st Armies during the harrowing fighting south of Smolensk during the summer of 1941, 58th Army in November 1941, and 1st Shock Army during the battle for Moscow, where it had spearheaded Western Front's successful counterstroke northwest of Moscow.[26] Also a combat veteran, the commander of 62nd Army, General Vladimir Iakovlevich Kolpakchi, had served as chief of staff and deputy commander of Southern Front's 18th Army during its struggle with the advance by Kleist's First Panzer Group on Rostov in October and November 1941 and, later, as Briansk Front's chief of staff in late 1941 and early 1942.[27]

The commander of 64th Army—and the most famous of this threesome— was 41-year-old Lieutenant General Vasilii Ivanovich Chuikov, who later conducted the actual defense of Stalingrad throughout the remainder of the fall.[28]

The son of a peasant, Chuikov rose to command a regiment during the Russian Civil War. Thereafter, his career was divided almost equally between military schools, troop command, and repeated assignments as an adviser in Mongolia and China. Disgraced as commander of Northwestern Front's 9th Army during the ill-fated 1939–1940 war with Finland, Chuikov was exiled to be the Soviet military attaché to China. Even so, while serving as 9th Army commander, Chuikov ruthlessly executed senior officers in his army who Stalin deemed responsible for the embarrassing defeat.[29]

Although Chuikov wrangled his way back to European Russia after the German invasion, an automobile accident sidelined him for more than a year. Thus he did not meet the Germans in battle until summer 1942 when, as described below, he salvaged something from the repeated defeats of that summer.[30] His hard-headed perseverance and mixture of ruthlessness and competence led him to the perilous command of 62nd Army in September—just as the defense of Stalingrad began. Chuikov was an energetic rather than a brilliant soldier, but he had a knack for inspiring or intimidating subordinates. He was famous for an explosive temper that was quickly replaced by good humor. In the house-to-house struggle for the city, the earthy, practical Chuikov proved more effective than the high-strung, cerebral Paulus.

Still later on 12 July, the *Stavka* took further precautionary measures, ordering Marshal of the Soviet Union Semen Mikhailovich Budenny's North Caucasus Front to concentrate three rifle divisions (157th, 156th, and 91st) from his *front's* 51st Army, each supported by a guards-mortar regiment, to act as a covering force along the southern bank of the Don River east of Rostov. The *Stavka* also directed Malinovsky's Southern Front to dispatch its reserve tank brigade from Kamensk-Shakhtinskii to Stalingrad and to concentrate its air forces against the German armor columns moving toward Stalingrad.[31]

Finally, the *Stavka* delineated boundaries between Voronezh and Stalingrad Fronts and Stalingrad and North Caucasus Fronts, the former at Babka, on the Don River 15 kilometers northwest of Pavlovsk, and the latter at Verkhnekurmoiarskaia, on the Don River 150 kilometers southwest of Stalingrad. It also ordered Chuikov's 64th Army to deploy forward into the sector between Surovikino on the Chir River and Verkhnekurmoiarskaia on the Don River on Stalingrad Front's left wing.[32]

Despite Stalin's decisive measures, even this reorganization failed, largely because Kriuchenkin's 28th Army, Moskalenko's 38th Army, and Nikishov's 57th Army, which were supposed to join Malinovsky's Southern Front, were instead withdrawing from the eastern Donbas in disorder, out of communications with any headquarters and unlocatable for days. When Timoshenko was unable to provide the *Stavka* with any information about the fate of these three armies on 12 or 13 July, an impatient Stalin angrily rebuked the *front* commander early on 14 July:

The *Stavka* considers it intolerable and inadmissible that the Military Council of the *front* has not provided any information about the fate of 28th, 38th, and 57th Armies and 22nd Tank Corps for several days. From several sources, the *Stavka* knows that the headquarters of these armies have withdrawn across the Don, but neither these headquarters nor the Military Council of the *front* will report to the *Stavka* where the forces of these armies are, what is their fate, and whether or not they are continuing to fight or have been taken captive. It seems there are 14 divisions in these armies.

The *Stavka* wants to know where these divisions have gone.

The Military Council of the *front* is obliged to obtain all of the necessary information concerning the situation of these forces and work out measures to assist them if they have not already been taken captive. The *Stavka* considers it intolerable that the Military Council remains silent and displays no concern about the fate of these forces. The *Stavka* demands an immediate reply.[33]

The surviving skeletons of 28th, 38th, and 57th Armies finally reached Stalingrad Front's forward positions along the Don River beginning on 15 and 16 July. Early on 17 July the *Stavka* was left no choice but to transfer the depleted armies back to Timoshenko's tenuous control.[34] Because this decision weakened Southern Front, whose forces were retreating back toward the Don River at and east of Rostov, the *Stavka* then ordered Budenny's North Caucasus Front to reinforce its defenses along the Don River east of Rostov with 138th Rifle and 115th Cavalry Divisions from its 51st Army, restore order in Malinovsky's forces retreating across the Don, and extend 51st Army's defenses eastward along the Don to Verkhnekurmoiarskaia.[35] Up to this time, 51st Army had been manning a rear security line along the lower Don River west and east of Rostov to protect the northern approaches into the Caucasus region. The army's commander was 47-year-old Major General Trofim Kalinovich Kolomiets, who had commanded 32nd Rifle Corps during Western Front's struggle for Smolensk in summer 1941 and was appointed 51st Army commander in July 1942 after serving as its deputy commander since late July 1941.[36]

This directive, in turn, posed formidable new challenges to Budenny's North Caucasus Front, whose principal mission had been to defend western approaches to the North Caucasus against attack from the Crimea by manning defenses in the Taman' Peninsula and the eastern coast of the Sea of Azov with its 47th, 51st, and Coastal Armies, supported by 5th Air Army. By requiring Budenny to transfer part of Kolomiets's 51st Army to the Don River line east of Rostov, North Caucasus Front's defenses were stretched to its limits, especially because its Coastal Army had yet to recover from its July defeats in the Crimea. Nonetheless, with Southern Front's defenses collapsing, Budenny had no choice but to comply.

By this time, while 62nd and 64th Armies of Timoshenko's Stalingrad Front were struggling to erect coherent defenses astride the Great Bend of the Don east of the Chir River, 9th, 37th, 12th, 18th, and 56th Armies of Malinovsky's Southern Front were withdrawing hastily southward, frantically attempting to escape Fourth and First Panzer Armies' advancing pincers, which were closing on the Don from the north. From the *Stavka*'s perspective, the most important unanswered question was exactly where the Germans would direct their main attack. Would they continue their rapid advance toward Stalingrad, thereby threatening Timoshenko's two fresh armies behind the Chir? Would they shift the center of gravity of operations toward Rostov on the Don to complete the rout of Malinovsky's armies and perhaps cross the Don River and penetrate deeply into the Caucasus region? Or would they attempt to do both simultaneously? Only Hitler could answer these questions.

HITLER ALTERS COURSE

Hitler, convinced that Soviet forces were fleeing from the eastern Donbas region in disorder, believed that Bock had lost a great opportunity to destroy the Red Army in the field. He was determined not to lose another in the future. Ignoring the desperate battles around Voronezh and the growing problems of providing fuel to fast-moving units, he fumed about Bock's continued delays, perhaps also reflecting on Bock's inability to capture Moscow six months before. By 12 July Hitler and the OKH believed the Soviets were intent on defending the Millerovo–Kamensk-Shakhtinskii–Rostov line, and, therefore, it was essential for Hoth's Fourth Panzer Army to overcome this line as soon as possible. As Halder recorded in his diary:

> The Führer expressed his utmost displeasure over the delay in the move to the front of 23rd Panzer Division (pinned down by an attack from the west [by Moskalenko's 38th Army]), 24th Panzer Division, and *Grossdeutschland*, as well as of the two other motorized divisions of Fourth Panzer Army. He blames the failure on the fact that 24th Panzer Division and *Grossdeutschland*, against the Führer's order, were sent into Voronezh, causing a delay that could have been avoided.[37]

Bock was vehement in disagreement, as these bitter thoughts in his diary demonstrated that same evening:

> During the night a directive arrived from the Army High Command for a continuation of operations:
>
> "Army Group B [Bock] is to proceed in the general direction of the north of the [Northern] Donets, sending all available forces [Hoth's Fourth Panzer Army] ahead in the direction of Kamensk [Kamensk-Shakhtinskii], with the

objective of engaging the enemy north of the Don and destroying him by attacking his rear. The remaining forces [Paulus's Sixth Army] are to cover this movement to the east and create conditions for the advance in the direction of Stalingrad."

Apart from being unclear, this directive scatters my weak armored units to the four winds.

Sending all available forces ahead in the direction of Kamensk is impossible on account of the road conditions. Each motorized unit now needs its own road.[38]

Bock then recorded his own intentions, as well as the OKH's vexing response:

Six tributaries run from north and northeast to the south into the Donets in front of the 4th Panzer Army's front. It will be impossible to send the leading element, the XXXX Panzer Corps, forward along two land ridges between these rivers toward the Donets between Kamensk and Forschtadt. The following XXXXVIII Panzer Corps will be sent forward toward the commanding plateau which extends south from Bokovskaya through Morozovskaya. If the area of Morozovskaya is reached, the corps can be sent to the right and straight across the Don toward the Donets or left toward the enemy forces threatening the entire operation from the east. I brought up these thoughts with *Oberst* von Grolman of the Army High Command yesterday when the Army High Command was considering deploying my panzer forces in the country cut by rivers south of Millerovo. They were probably not understood, for during the night a telegram came from the Chief of the General Staff [Halder] to Sodenstern [Bock's chief of staff] with the request to "oppose any unnecessary broadening of the deployment of the mobile forces to the east. The army's next mission lies to the south. Turning of the units to the south against the rear of the enemy holding north of Rostov must be possible at any time. Deployment of mobile forces in a southeasterly or easterly direction is justifiable only as required to provide the necessary flanking cover."[39]

Objecting strongly, Bock advised the OKH early on 13 July:

The enemy opposite the 4th Panzer Army and the northern wing of Army Group A is withdrawing, with elements to the east and southeast and strong elements to the south. I believe the destruction of significant enemy forces will not be achieved in an operation which is strong in the center and weak on the wings and whose main direction of advance leads through Millerovo into the midst of the enemy. Instead, the main thrust by the 4th Panzer Army should be directed through the Morozovskaya area into the area of the mouth of the Donets and east while guarding its rear and eastern flank.[40]

This was too much for Hitler. After noon on 13 July, he decided to relieve Bock as commander of Army Group B, replacing him with Weichs, commander of Second Army. A chagrined Bock described his relief:

> In the afternoon, *Feldmarschall* Keitel informed me by telephone that by order of the *Führer*, the 4th Panzer Army was to join Army Group A, as had been envisioned by the supreme command. Further he took me completely by surprise by passing on to me an order that *Generaloberst* von Weichs was to take over my command of Army Group B, and that I was being placed at the disposal of the *Führer!*"[41]

From his vantage point in the OKH, Halder noted dryly:

> The Führer accordingly ruled to relieve commander of AGp. B, and he also wanted to relieve the chief of staff [Sodenstern]. Only the reminder to the Führer that commander South exclusively was responsible for the ill-conceived proposal for the frontal attack instead of the prepared rear attack on Izyum, and that the former plan had been opposed by his chief of staff, averted a simultaneous change of commander and chief of staff, with all its consequences.[42]

Bock left his command two days later without the usual exit interview with Hitler and never again occupied a senior command position.[43]

On that same day, Hitler discarded much of the preexisting plan for Blau III (now code-named Operation Braunschweig). Without mentioning Blau III's original objective of Stalingrad, OKH, late on the evening of 13–14 July, sent teletype orders to the two army groups, reorienting the entire offensive southward and southwestward, ostensibly in an attempt to encircle the two Soviet *fronts* and prevent them from withdrawing eastward (see Maps 20 and 21). The new operation stripped Army Group B of Fourth Panzer Army and almost half of Sixth Army, leaving Weichs's army group to perform the role of a flank or rear guard to protect Army Group A's main attack to the south. This left German Second Army, now commanded by Colonel General Hans von Salmuth, who had commanded XXX Army Corps of Manstein's Eleventh Army in the Crimea during the 1941 campaign and the first half of 1942, to defend the sector at and west of Voronezh. To do this, Second Army deployed its LV, XIII, and VII Army Corps and 9th and 11th Panzer Divisions, as well as Jany's Hungarian Second Army, defending the Don River sector from Ust'e, 5 kilometers southwest of Voronezh, southward to Pavlovsk.[44] Paulus's Sixth Army had to protect the Don River front from Pavlovsk south to Meshkovskaia with XVII, XXIX, and VIII Army Corps—but no armor whatsoever.

The main effort now shifted to List's Army Group A, which assumed control of the three panzer corps (XXIV, XXXXVIII, and XXXX) of Hoth's Fourth Panzer

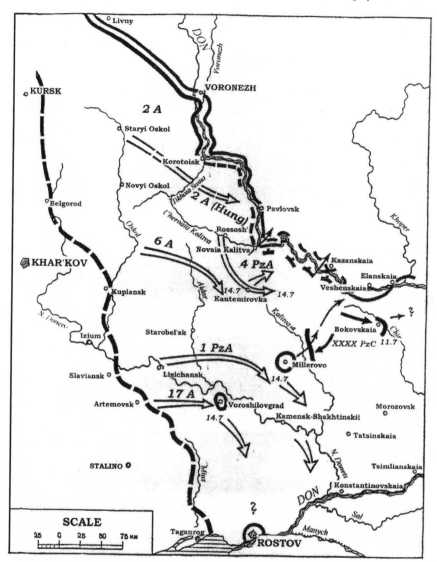

Map 20. The situation on the receipt of Hitler's 13 July order

Army, with the infantry of Sixth Army's VIII and LI Army Corps attached. Although still short on fuel, Hoth's army received orders to thrust southeastward to the lower Don River from Konstantinovskaia, 120 kilometers east of Rostov, and eastward through Nikolaevskaia to Tsimlianskaia, 210 kilometers east of Rostov. Kempf's XXXXVIII and Stumme's XXXX Panzer Corps would advance abreast from left to right (east to west), protected on the left by Langermann's XXIV

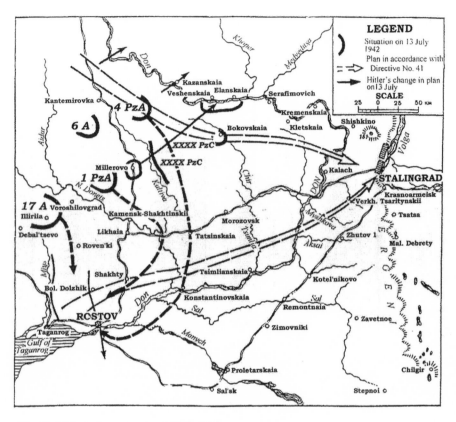

Map 21. Hitler's change in plan, 13 July 1942

Panzer Corps (which would be transferred back to Sixth Army on 22 July) and VIII and LI Army Corps. When XXXXVIII Panzer Corps (16th, 29th, and "GD" Motorized and 24th Panzer Divisions) wheeled southward along the west bank of the Chir River from the Bokovskaia region, VIII and LI Army Corps, supported later by XXIV Panzer Corps' 3rd Motorized Division, were to consolidate their positions south of the Don River at Serafimovich and along the Chir River. In the process, Hoth was to extend his left wing, pivoting slightly toward the south.

Simultaneously, III and XIV Panzer Corps of Kleist's First Panzer Army were to advance eastward north of the Northern Donets River and Voroshilovgrad toward Millerovo. This would encircle 9th Army (Southwestern Front's left wing) and 37th and 24th Armies (Southern Front's right wing) between its advancing armor and that of XXXX Panzer Corps' 3rd and 23rd Panzer Divisions on Fourth Panzer Army's right wing. Thereafter, leaving XXXIV Army Corps to mop up encircled Soviet forces, Kleist was to wheel his two panzer corps southward toward Kamensk-Shakhtinskii, parallel with XXXX Panzer Corps, to reach the

Don River between Konstantinovskii and Novocherkassk, 40–120 kilometers east of Rostov. Once along the Don, Kleist's panzers were to turn back westward, toward the great rail and river junction of Rostov.

In the meantime, the other half of List's army group, Ruoff's Seventeenth Army (with VI and LI Army Corps, Italian Expeditionary Corps, and XXXXIX Mountain and LVII Panzer Corps), would press Southern Front's 12th, 18th, and 56th Armies eastward from the Voroshilovgrad region and across the Mius River to the south. Eventually these forces would wheel southward to drive the Soviet forces back toward Rostov and into the teeth of Kleist's panzer divisions advancing on that city from the northeast and east. Thus, Hitler and the OKH envisioned the two panzer armies splitting the two Soviet *fronts* in the region and then encircling and destroying large portions of both *fronts*, first in the Millerovo region, and then north of Rostov. By erasing as many as six armies from the Red Army order of battle, Hitler anticipated a far easier advance toward Stalingrad and an equally successful exploitation across the Don River into the Caucasus.[45]

Three days later, on 16 July, Hitler moved Führer headquarters from East Prussia to Vinnitsa permanently. This new headquarters, code-named *Wehrwolf* (Werewolf), included Halder but only the operations staffs of OKW and OKH, leaving many professional staff officers behind. From there the German dictator attempted—like his counterpart in the Kremlin—to supervise the conduct of battle in immense detail. The move was a clear signal of Hitler's declining trust in the German officer corps.

THE ADVANCE TO THE DON: THE MILLEROVO ENCIRCLEMENT AND THE BATTLE FOR ROSTOV, 17–24 JULY

Even before he moved his headquarters, Hitler had begun redirecting his scarce reserves in a manner that further stretched German resources. Although he had begun the eastern campaign convinced that Great Britain posed little threat to Western Europe, by early July he worried that Churchill might launch a desperate attack into the soft underbelly of Europe to take pressure off the Soviets and to respond to political criticism about the fall of Tobruk in North Africa. As a result, on 6 July Hitler placed restrictions on any use of the elite 1st SS Motorized Division *Leibstandarte* Adolf Hitler (LAH, Hitler's bodyguard), which should have led First Panzer Army's advance. Three days later, the German leader ordered that this division, the newly formed 2nd SS Motorized Division *Das Reich* ("R"), and several other new units be sent to France rather than committed in the east.[46]

On 11 July, Führer Directive No. 43 specified that Manstein's Eleventh Army, fresh from its victory at Sevastopol' and previously earmarked to assist in the seizure of Rostov, would now use part of its forces in an advance across the Kerch' Strait to secure the vital Soviet naval bases at Anapa and Novorossiisk and facilitate a further advance toward Maikop deep into the Caucasus. Given the

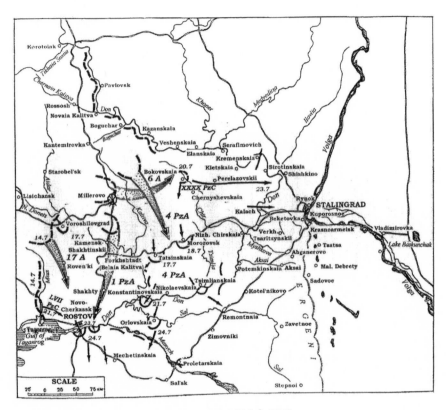

Map 22. German operations to seize Rostov, 14–24 July 1942

shortage of transportation vessels, such an amphibious movement was risky at best. This operation, code-named Blücher, originally had an execution date of mid-August, although on 13 July Manstein received a change, ordering him to be prepared by the beginning of the month.[47]

The explanation for these enormous plans is self-evident: From the Führer down to the infantry private, the Germans understandably—if mistakenly—believed that the Red Army was nearing the end of its strength. Although Hitler was accurate in his fear that the enemy was escaping, the *Wehrmacht* continued to plunge ahead virtually unopposed. By mid-July Timoshenko's new Stalingrad Front was in tatters, its forward armies (21st, 28th, and 38th) withdrawn or withdrawing across the Don River with only a fraction of their original strength. Although Stalingrad Front's 63rd Army manned defenses along the northern bank of the Don River from Babka to Veshenskaia, it was defending a 90-kilometer-wide sector with only five rifle divisions. The 62nd and 64th Armies, with six divisions each, were still hastily deploying forward to occupy defenses along an equally wide front traversing the Great Bend of the Don east of the Chir

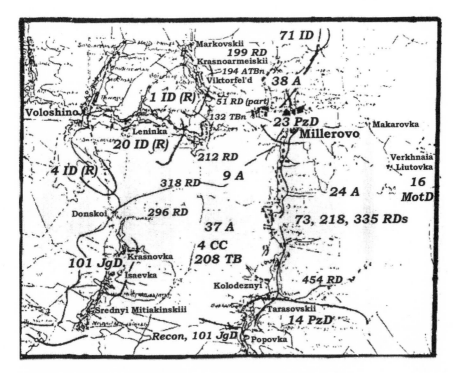

Map 23. The Millerovo encirclement, 17 July 1942 (the German perspective)

River. Confirming Bock's judgment, Stalingrad Front's forward defenses were ripe for preemption and subject to defeat in detail on the approaches to Stalingrad—but only if an adequate armored force was available to do so. At the same time, the enormous hole that Paulus's army had torn at the boundary between Stalingrad and Southern Fronts also validated Hitler's and OKH's judgment—that Malinovsky's Southern Front was also ripe for destruction—but only if Hoth's and Kleist's panzer armies moved quickly enough.

Despite persistent problems with fuel, which delayed the advance of 24th Panzer and "GD" Motorized Divisions, and the terrain difficulties described by Bock, Hoth's and Kleist's panzer divisions performed brilliantly during the earliest days of Hitler's new gambit (see Map 22). Advancing southward from the Bokovskaia region at dawn on 14 July, 29th Motorized Division of Kempf's XXXXVIII Panzer Corps had marched more than 25 kilometers by nightfall, reaching halfway to Morozovsk. To the west, in the vanguard of Stumme's XXXX Panzer Corps, Breith's 3rd Panzer Division lunged southward from just east of Millerovo, reaching halfway to Kamensk-Shakhtinskii and blocking the withdrawal routes of Moskalenko's 38th, Nikishov's 57th, and Lopatin's 9th Armies to the east. By this time, Boineburg-Lengsfeld's 23rd Panzer Division had already occupied Millerovo and was fending off repeated attacks by Moskalenko's army, which was now scattered west and south of that town.

Even farther west, Kleist's First Panzer Army continued its drive east, with General Heim's 14th Panzer Division from Wietersheim's XIV Panzer Corps crossing the Glubokaia River at Tarasovsky, 20 kilometers south of Millerovo, while Romanian VI and German XXXXIV Army Corps closed in on that town from the west. At the same time, Kleist assembled 16th Panzer and 60th Motorized Divisions of Geyr's III Panzer Corps south of Starobel'sk for a brief rest.

At dawn on 15 July, 3rd Panzer Division from Fourth Panzer Army linked up with Heim's 14th Panzer Division from First Panzer Army 40 kilometers south of Millerovo, catching the remnants of 38th, 57th, 9th, 24th, and 37th Armies in a trap west and southwest of the town (see Map 23). At this point, List had every reason to believe that another great battle of encirclement was at hand.[48] However, the encirclement never really closed. Although 23rd, 3rd, and 14th Panzer Divisions managed to establish a crude cordon of armor north, east, and south of the pocket, the cordon was porous at best. Hoth's and Kleist's follow-on infantry were still west of the town, unable to keep up with the armor and fill the gaps between the panzer divisions' scattered *kampfgruppen*.

Making matters worse, XXXXVIII Panzer Corps' "GD" Motorized and 24th Panzer Divisions, which were supposed to cut off the Soviets' escape routes farther east, were delayed by fuel shortages and could not begin their southward advance from Verkhniaia Makeevka and Nizhne-Astakhov until 15 July. By day's end their columns were too overextended to trap Soviet forces escaping eastward in small groups. Even though they were thoroughly fragmented and no longer combat capable, the forces of Moskalenko's 38th Army, with some remnants of 57th, 24th, and 9th Armies in their train, made eastward—and out of the trap. The bulk of the riflemen in Kozlov's 37th Army retreated southward west of the Glubokaia River.[49] The OKW's morning operational summary for 16 July describes the scene:

Weather. Suffocating heat, with occasional thunderstorms and rain.

Along the Gusev-Millerovo line, large enemy forces supported by numerous tanks are trying to penetrate to the southeast across the Glubokaia River. All of the attacks have been beaten off, and we have captured a wealth of material. In XXXX Panzer Corps' sector, one panzer division captured a bridgehead in the Kovalev region and reached Krasnovka [5 kilometers north of Kamensk-Shakhtinskii].

According to information from air reconnaissance, the bridge in Kamensk is not damaged. On 14th Panzer Division's front, the Reds' strong tank attacks from the northwest toward Verkhne-Tarasovka have misfired, and the enemy has suffered heavy personnel losses. Twenty-five tanks were destroyed. Units of the army group lined up with the Fourth Panzer Army in the Vodianskaia region [south of Kazanskaia].[50]

As a result of the failed encirclement at Millerovo, the two panzer armies had become neighbors. Although this concentrated the mechanized units for a powerful thrust, as Bock predicted it also meant that Hoth and Kleist were in direct competition for use of the limited number of supply routes that could sustain their advance. It also made future encirclements more difficult because the two panzer armies were so close together.

Field Marshal List, commander of Army Group A, was aware that the campaign depended upon troop units and logistics that were already overtaxed. His German units were rapidly consuming spare parts and supplies, and he had serious mental reservations about the Axis (i.e., non-German) units under his control. Italian Eighth Army, for example, had not yet had enough combat experience to coalesce as an effective organization. Overall, German officers considered few Axis units to be more than marginally capable. Nevertheless, List had no choice but to continue the offensive with the Axis units in tow.

On 16 July, List presented his simple yet ambitious plans to his assembled army commanders and chiefs of staff at Gorlovka. Employing 14th and 22nd Panzer Divisions of Geyr's III Panzer Corps as its spearhead, First Panzer Army would advance southeastward, cross the Northern Donets east of Kamensk-Shakhtinskii, and wheel Geyr's panzers westward to outflank the Soviets' defenses at Kamensk-Shakhtinskii from the east. XXXXIV Army Corps would assist in reducing the Millerovo pocket and then attack southward along the Glubokaia River to capture Kamensk. Geyr's divisions would then lunge southward through Shakhty and Novocherkassk to capture Rostov by assaulting from the east, thereby encircling and destroying Southern Front's 12th, 18th, and 56th Armies before they could withdraw south across the Don River at Rostov. Meanwhile Ruoff's Seventeenth Army would press the retreating Soviets from the north.

Kleist's neighbor to the east, Hoth's Fourth Panzer Army, would push onward to the Don River with Kempf's XXXXVIII and Stumme's XXXX Panzer Corps and then pivot westward or southwestward, as circumstances suggested. On the left wing of Hoth's main attack, Kempf's panzer corps would advance southward from the Morozovsk and Skosyrskaia regions toward the Don River at and west of Tsimlianskaia with its 29th Motorized, 24th Panzer, and 16th Motorized Divisions and, later, "GD" Motorized Division; on Kempf's left, after clearing the eastern portion of the Millerovo pocket, XXXX Panzer Corps' 3rd and 23rd Panzer Divisions would advance to the Don River east and west of Konstantinovskaia. As XXXX Panzer Corps neared the river, it would revert to reserve with its 23rd Panzer Division; 3rd Panzer, now joined by 16th and "GD" Motorized Divisions from XXXXVIII Panzer Corps, would continue operations under the control of Langermann's XXIV Panzer Corps headquarters.

Finally, beginning on 18 July, Ruoff's Seventeenth Army, with Italian Eighth Army in support, would attack southeastward through Voroshilovgrad and from the Kuibyshevo region across the Mius River, seeking to tie down the defenders, while the two panzer armies converged on the rail-river-road hub at Rostov. The infantry units, so often left behind by the advancing armored spearheads, would have to march hard to protect the northern flank of this advance.[51]

List's spearheads plunged forward against little or no opposition: Between 15 and 18 July, XXXXVIII and XXXX Panzer Corps' widely dispersed divisions covered almost 200 kilometers to reach the lower Don. Dust and heat seemed greater obstacles than anything the Red Army offered. Everywhere they went in mid-July, the Germans encountered long columns of Soviet troops scurrying eastward, seeking to escape encirclement. Captured Soviet soldiers seemed confused and demoralized. In a few instances, Soviet units surrendered en masse, but most of the defenders, however disheartened, continued the struggle.

One symptom of this was the small number of Soviet prisoners who fell into German hands. For example, First Panzer Army came up empty-handed when it attempted to encircle the remnants of Southern Front's 9th, 37th, and 12th Armies near Kamensk-Shakhtinskii during 17–19 July. Under steady German pressure from the north and west, but skillfully employing strong rear guards, Malinovsky managed to withdraw well more than half the troops of his 12th, 18th, and 56th Armies southward toward Rostov. By day's end on 21 July, III Panzer Corps' 22nd and 14th Panzer Divisions were just reaching the Novocherkassk region, 40 kilometers east of Rostov, and XXIV Panzer Corps' "GD" Motorized Division of Hoth's Fourth Panzer Army was still 30 kilometers north and east of Novocherkassk. In fact, during the first three weeks of Operation Blau overall, Army Group A captured only 54,000 Soviet soldiers, a far cry from the huge encirclements of 1941.[52] The chief reason for this "empty bag" was that, because there were too few infantry divisions to close the sack, tens of thousands of Soviet soldiers, individually or in small groups, managed to escape eastward or southward, some forming partisan bands, but many others ultimately rejoining the ranks of the Red Army.

As demonstrated by Fourth Panzer Army, however, one thing the Germans could do was gain ground. For example, Fremerey's 29th Motorized Division of Kempf's XXXXVIII Panzer Corps, on the panzer army's extreme left (eastern) wing, had crossed the Don River near Tsimlianskaia by 21 July. On its right (western) flank, the same corps' 24th Panzer Division was east of Nikolaevskaia and just north of the Don. Farther west, XXIV Panzer Corps' 23rd and 3rd Panzer Divisions were at and east of Nikolaevskaia, all forming an intermittent curtain of armor along the northern bank of the Don.

On the left (northern) flank of Hoth's main attack, Sixth Army also resumed active operations. On 17 July Hitler had ordered Paulus's army to expand its operations to the east to prevent the Soviets from forming a stronger defense in the Great Bend of the Don. At the same time, the Führer returned control of VIII and LI Army Corps from Hoth to Paulus and reinforced them with 16th Panzer and 60th Motorized Divisions of Wietersheim's XIV Panzer Corps, which had just redeployed northeastward to the Bokovskaia region from the battlefield around Millerovo. After heavy rains near the Great Bend brought operations to

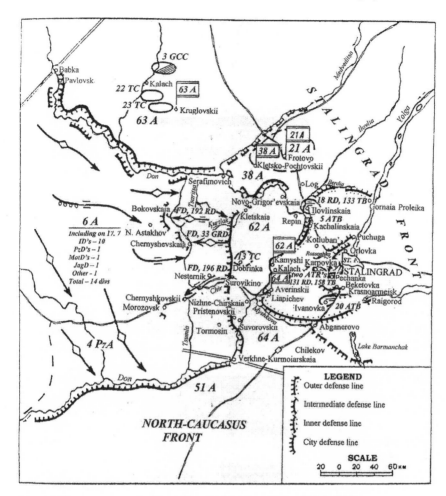

Map 24. The situation in the "Great Bend" of the Don River, 22 July 1942

a virtual halt from 18 through 20 July, on 21 July the infantry divisions of Paulus's VIII and LI Army Corps, supported by XIV Panzer Corps' 3rd and 60th Motorized and 16th Panzer Divisions, pushed slowly eastward toward Serafimovich on the Don and toward the Chir, crossing the latter river in three places by nightfall. The next day, 22 July, 3rd Motorized Division bypassed Serafimovich to the south and approached the western outskirts of Kletskaia; to the south, 16th Panzer Division advanced a third of the way between the Chir River and Kalach-on-the-Don River (see Map 24).

This advance brought the leading elements of Paulus's Sixth Army into direct contact with the forward detachments of Kolpakchi's 62nd Army defending east of the Chir (see Chapter 6). In turn, this encounter precipitated an entirely new phase of Blau, the first act in a prolonged play that would ultimately see Paulus's Sixth Army defeat the forces of Stalingrad Front in the Great Bend of the Don, cross the river, and, within weeks, begin the fight for Stalingrad proper.[53] Meanwhile, almost anticlimactically but in accordance with Hitler's intent, List's Army Group A lumbered toward Rostov in search of illusive quarry.

Clearly, although the *Stavka* proved unable to coordinate its defenses along the Voronezh, Stalingrad, and Rostov axes, it continued to resist fiercely wherever German forces advanced. Far northwest of Voroshilovgrad, IV and LII Army Corps of Ruoff's Seventeenth Army had resumed their advance toward the city on 15 July, exploiting the successful advance by Kleist's panzers north of the Northern Donets River.

With *Stavka* authorization, Malinovsky on 16 July ordered all the armies of Southern Front to begin an orderly, five-stage withdrawal to the Don River south of Rostov, at the rate of 20 kilometers per night over five nights, being protected by strong forward detachments.[54] The same day, Grechko's 12th Army abandoned Voroshilovgrad and began a fighting withdrawal southward. Advancing slowly in its wake, IV Army Corps' 94th and 371st Infantry Divisions occupied the city on 17 July. However, when Kleist's panzers began threatening his right flank and deep rear, Malinovsky on 18 July ordered his armies to accelerate their withdrawal to create separation between his forces and their pursuers. As a result, as German Seventeenth Army's IV and LII Army Corps drove Soviet 12th Army's rear guards southward from Voroshilovgrad, on the right flank the three infantry divisions of the Italian Expeditionary Corps captured Krasnyi Luch from Kamkov's withdrawing 18th Army on 19 July. To the east, remnants of 37th, 24th, and 9th Armies, which, under the protection of 12th Army's rear guards, were fighting southward along the Glubokaia River to escape the pocket south of Millerovo, streamed southward across the Northern Donets east and west of Kamensk toward Rostov, the Don River, and safety.

After learning that III Panzer Corps' 14th Panzer Division had passed through Shakhty late on 20 July and was en route to Novocherkassk, General Kirchner's LVII Panzer Corps joined Seventeenth Army's pursuit by advancing southeastward across the Mius, driving the rear guards of Tsyganov's 56th Army back toward Rostov. The next day Heim's 14th Panzer Division captured Novocherkassk, and on 22 July LVII Panzer Corps encircled Rostov's outer defenses with 13th Panzer Division from the west and 22nd and 14th Panzer Divisions, converging from the north and east. By this time, 18th and 56th Armies of Malinovsky's Southern Front had withdrawn most of their forces from the city and across the Don River, protected by 70th and 158th Fortified Regions and NKVD security forces that were defending the city and protecting Southern Front's retreat.[55] Although Malinovsky twice ordered 56th and 18th Armies to defend the city, too many of 18th Army's forces had already withdrawn across the Don to do so effectively. By this time, 56th Army still had several divisions in Rostov proper, but 18th Army had only two regiments in the city.[56]

Therefore, Tsyganov organized the Rostov defenses primarily with forces from his 56th Army, establishing two concentric inner and outer defensive belts around the city. 2nd Guards Rifle Corps' 2nd Guards Rifle Division and 68th, 76th, and 81st Naval Rifle Brigades defended both belts on the western approaches; 30th, 339th, and 31st Rifle Divisions and 16th Rifle Brigade manned defenses on the northern and eastern sectors of the belts; and the two fortified regions and NKVD security forces erected and manned fortified positions within the city's streets, squares, and buildings.[57]

Winning the race to the city, 13th and 22nd Panzer Divisions, supported by 5th SS Motorized Division "Viking," thrust southward rapidly through the city streets, bypassing opposition and reaching the main bridge across the Don, in the very heart of Rostov, on 23 July. However, Tsyganov's forces destroyed the bridge just as the advance guard of 13th Panzer Division reached the river. In any case, these German armored elements were poorly equipped to secure the city. For months, Rostov's civilian laborers had worked to build field fortifications, street obstacles, minefields, and reinforced bunkers. NKVD security troops defended every city block, inflicting considerable casualties on the attackers. 125th Infantry Division drew the onerous assignment of clearing Rostov, a struggle that lasted from 24 to 27 July. This hand-to-hand infantry competition for Rostov foretold the Stalingrad struggle. Meanwhile several teams of Brandenburgers—the elite special operations troops of the German Army—tried to seize the Don River bridges south of Rostov, on the road to Bataisk. After surprising the Soviet bridge guards on the night of 25–26 July, the Brandenburgers had to hold the bridges for 24 hours before the first panzers arrived to secure the objective. First Panzer Army then began preparing for its advance southward, toward the Caucasus.[58]

Despite capturing Rostov and securing the Don River line along a distance of more than 150 kilometers east of the city, to the chagrin of both List and Hitler, the ambitious German pincer operation had bagged only 83,000 prisoners by First Panzer Army's count. Fourth Panzer and Seventeenth Armies had captured far fewer. By directing Army Group A's three armies to converge on the Rostov region, Hitler had also fulfilled Bock's predictions. Terrain and logistical problems—to say nothing of heavy Soviet resistance—slowed the German advance and prevented it from encircling the bulk of Malinovsky's forces. And when the operation finally ended, 20 of List's divisions were situated within 50 kilometers of the city, most lacking direction as to what to do next.

Worse still, by committing more than half of the *Wehrmacht's* strength in southern Russia to the advance on Rostov, Hitler and the OKH had starved Paulus's Sixth Army of the forces it needed to press its advance east and, at the same time, permitted Stalingrad Front's forward armies to solidify their defenses west of the Great Bend. Furthermore, the Rostov "diversion" provided the *Stavka* time to hatch new plans for major coordinated counterstrokes to thwart Army Group B's advance eastward toward the Don River and Stalingrad.

On the positive side for the Germans, with Rostov now in List's hands the gateway to the Caucasus lay wide open. In addition, by the beginning of the final week of July, the entire Southwestern Front and about a quarter of Southern Front had been destroyed as combat-effective formations; the new Stalingrad and Voronezh Fronts consisted of hastily assembled and poorly equipped reserve armies manned by green and poorly trained troops; and the remnants of Southern Front that escaped outright encirclement and destruction were now shaken and scarcely able to defend the Don River line. Although estimates conflict, the armies subordinate to Army Groups A and B reported capturing about 70,000 Soviet prisoners in Blau I and another 88,000 in Blau II, a total of more than 150,000 men.[59]

However, the latest Russian accounts of the Red Army's casualties during Blau I and Blau II assert that Briansk, Voronezh, Southwestern, and Southern Fronts and the Azov Flotilla suffered a total of 568,347 casualties from 28 June through 24 July 1942, including 370,522 killed or captured and 197,825 wounded or sick, out of 1,310,800 soldiers who participated in these operations (see Appendices). The same sources admit the four *fronts* lost 2,436 tanks, 13,716 guns and mortars, and 783 combat aircraft.[60] These recent sources, it should be noted, include many soldiers who went missing in action and did not return to the Red Army's ranks until many days and even weeks later.

Although Soviet and Russian sources claim that 88,689 Red Army soldiers were captured during Blau I and Blau II (based largely on partial German counts), it is more likely the actual figure was closer to 150,000. For example, in addition to a higher figure from a more accurate German count, German records state that the number of Red Army prisoners in German POW camps or working as slave laborers in German industry rose from 1,153,520 on 1 July 1942 to 1,303,709 on 1 August 1942, roughly an increase of 160,000 men, most of whom were captured in southern Russia. It must also be noted that these POW counts include Red Army prisoners held in camps within the Soviet Union itself; this might add as many as 50,000 POWs to the tally.[61] Similarly, because it is likely that official Soviet and Russian sources have routinely underestimated Red Army casualty figures throughout the war by as much as 30 percent, the Red Army's irreplaceable losses (killed, captured, deserted, or missing in action) during this period were probably closer to 500,000 soldiers of the 1.3 million who participated in these operations.[62]

Regardless, whichever estimates are correct they do not tell the full story of the damage that Army Groups A and B inflicted on the Red Army's Southwestern and Southern Fronts during the first two phases of Operation Blau. The harsh reality was that Southwestern Front, which on 28 June had five field armies (9th, 21st, 28th, 38th, and 57th) and an overall strength of more than 610,000 men, was replaced by 24 July with Stalingrad Front, which consisted of eight armies (new 62nd, 63rd, and 64th, the 51st from the North Caucasus Front, and the remnants of 21st, 28th [soon 4th Tank], 38th [soon 1st Tank], and 57th Armies) and an overall strength of 540,000 men. Considering the strength of Stalingrad Front's four new armies, which fielded about 30 rifle division equivalents and a total of roughly 200,000 men (including 68,462 in 62nd Army, 34,464 in 64th Army, and roughly 50,000 each in 63rd and 51st Armies), this meant that roughly 340,000 of Stalingrad Front's soldiers were survivors of the 610,000 men who Southwestern Front had fielded almost a month before.[63]

HITLER'S DIRECTIVE NO. 45

Despite Hitler's frustration with Bock, by the beginning of the third week of July Army Group B's victory in Blau I and Army Group A's spectacular progress in Blau II convinced the dictator that his summer offensive was an unqualified success. Halder attempted to convince the Führer that the Soviets were conducting a planned withdrawal, but Hitler—believing that the Soviet troops were indeed fleeing for their lives—would have none of it. Once the Germans seized the key communications hub of Rostov, Hitler concluded that his opponents would be incapable of mounting a credible defense west of the Volga River. Therefore, in his mind, the gateway was clear for his cherished advance into the Caucasus. Führer Directive No. 45, which Hitler issued on 23 July to provide guidance on the continuation of Blau III (Operation Braunschweig), reached major headquarters over the next two days. It began with the confident assertion:

> In a campaign of a little more than three weeks, the deep objectives I set for the southern flank of the Eastern Front have, in substance, been reached. Only weak forces from Timoshenko's Army Group have succeeded in avoiding encirclement and reaching the southern bank of the Don. However, we must expect the retreating forces will be reinforced at the expense of forces in the Caucasus. Besides, a concentration of enemy force groupings has been detected in the Stalingrad region, which he apparently intends to defend stubbornly.[64]

Based on this optimistic assessment, Hitler attempted to do too much, too quickly, over too large an area. In essence, he decided to complete rather than continue Blau III by capturing Stalingrad, the primary objective in Blau II, and advance to seize the Caucasus and Caspian oil fields—the ultimate objectives of Blau IV. As outlined in Directive No. 45, Hitler planned to complete Blau III by projecting Army Groups A and B forward along two parallel but sharply divergent axes (see Map 25).

During the first stage of a three-stage operation code-named Edelweiss (Blau IV renamed), List's Army Group A was to attack southward to "encircle and destroy the enemy forces withdrawing across the Don in the region south and southeast of Rostov."[65] The eastern arm of List's pincers, Kleist's First and Hoth's Fourth Panzer Armies, would advance "southwestward towards Tikhoretsk [150 kilometers south of Rostov] from bridgeheads in the Konstantinovskaia and Tsimlianskaia regions," while, as previously ordered, "strong forward elements" from Fourth Panzer Army would "sever the railroad line between Stalingrad and

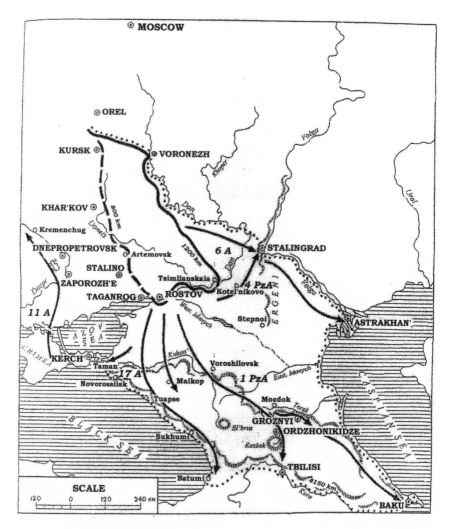

Map 25. Hitler's new plans of 23 and 30 July 1942

Tikhoretsk."[66] Simultaneously, List's second pincer (light infantry and mountain divisions from Ruoff's Seventeenth Army and Romanian Third Army, reinforced by Romanian Mountain Corps), would attack southward across the Don from the Rostov region toward Tikhoretsk. As the first stage ended, List was to transfer two panzer formations (including 24th Panzer Division) from his army group to Army Group B to "continue the latter's offensive operation toward the south-east," and "GD" Motorized Division was to "move no farther than the Manych River line and, if necessary, prepare for transfer to the West."[67]

After destroying enemy forces south of the Don, during the second stage of Edelweiss, List's army group was to "capture the eastern coast of the Black Sea to paralyze the enemy's Black Sea Fleet and its Black Sea ports."[68] Supporting this operation, Romanian Mountain Corps would cross Kerch' Strait as soon as Army Group A's forward progress permitted and join Army Group A's main forces in an attack southeastward along roads paralleling the Black Sea coast. Meanwhile, the force of mountain infantry and light infantry divisions attacking southward from Rostov would "force the Kuban' River and seize the high ground in the Maikop and Armavir regions" deeper into the Caucasus. During the third stage of Edelweiss, another force consisting chiefly of panzer and motorized formations was to "seize the Grozny region [in Chechnia]" and "cut the Ossetian and Georgian military highways with part of its forces, if possible in the [Caucasus Mountain] passes," while also conducting "an attack along the coast of the Caspian Sea to capture the Baku region" in oil-rich Azerbaijan.[69]

Yet Army Group A was significantly weaker during this exploitation phase, because Hitler allocated five divisions of Manstein's Eleventh Army, plus the army's heavy siege artillery that had pounded Sevastopol', to assist in a planned future offensive to capture Leningrad later that summer. In addition, as previously noted, Hitler's continuing concerns about an invasion of France had already prompted him to reassign 1st SS Motorized Division "LAH" to the West, where it was to reequip as a panzer division, and to earmark "GD" Motorized Division for possible deployment to the West as well.

Most significant of all, Führer Directive No. 45 transferred XXIV Panzer Corps, with two panzer divisions, from Army Group A to Army Group B and, for the first time, assigned Weichs's army group the primary mission of capturing, rather than simply neutralizing, Stalingrad:

As was ordered previously, the task of Army Group B is . . . to develop the Don defenses [i.e., protect the strategic flank] and, by a thrust forward to Stalingrad, to smash the enemy forces concentrated there, to seize the city, as well as cutting off the neck of land between the Don and the Volga.

Thereafter, panzer and motorized forces must strike out along the Volga to reach Astrakhan and also paralyze all movement along the main channel of the Volga in that region.

These operations by Army Group B are code-named *Fischreiher* [Heron].[70]

Hitler instructed the *Luftwaffe* to support these operations, both by close air support and by deeper raids to destroy railroads and pipelines, to drop mines in the Volga River, and otherwise to disrupt Soviet lines of communication. However, because the Germans hoped to seize the Caucasus oil fields intact, the 23 July order forbade air strikes against those facilities.

The final paragraph of Directive No. 45 underscored the unbound ambitiousness of Hitler's aims in the East during the summer campaign of 1942:

The operations now being prepared in the sectors of Army Groups Center and North must be conducted rapidly, one after the other. To a significant degree, these will secure the utter defeat of enemy forces and the degradation in the morale of his troops and commanders.

Army Group North will be prepared to seize Leningrad by the beginning of September. This operation will be code-named *Feuerzauber* [Fire Magic].

To this end, five divisions will be transferred from Eleventh Army, together with heavy artillery, as well as reserve units from the High Command.

Two German and two Romanian divisions will remain temporarily in the Crimea, and, as previously designated, 22nd [Panzer] Division will be subordinated to the commander of forces in the southeast (Balkans).[71]

In addition to assigning its two army groups new, more ambitious missions, Directive No. 45 also mandated a significant regrouping of forces between the army groups and, in some cases, between their subordinate armies. In Army Group B, for example, German Second Army, which was deployed on the army group's left wing, still consisted of LV, XIII, and VII Army Corps, supported by 9th Panzer Division and a small reserve. In the army group's center-left, Hungarian Second Army continued to control Hungarian III and VII Army Corps, reinforced by one German infantry division. On the army group's long right wing, Sixth Army controlled XXIX, XVII, VIII, and LI Army and XIV Panzer Corps (with 16th Panzer and 3rd and 60th Motorized Divisions), augmented on 22 July by XXIV Panzer Corps' headquarters and 24th Panzer Division from Fourth Panzer Army.

On Army Group A's left wing, Fourth Panzer Army was the big loser. After transferring VIII and LII Army Corps (Hoth's entire left wing) to Sixth Army on 17 July Hitler, five days later transferred XXIV Panzer Corps headquarters and XXXXVIII Panzer Corps' 24th Panzer Division from Hoth to Paulus. Hitler's directive also regrouped XXXXVIII Panzer Corps' 16th and "GD" Motorized Divisions to First Panzer Army's III Panzer Corps. This left Hoth's panzer army with XXXXVIII Panzer Corps, truncated to just 29th Motorized Division and one Romanian infantry division, and XXXX Panzer Corps, with 3rd and 23rd Panzer Divisions.

Hoth's loss was Kleist's gain. Operating in Army Group A's center, Kleist's First Panzer Army now consisted of III Panzer Corps, with 14th Panzer and 16th and "GD" Motorized Divisions, and XXXXIV Army Corps. Once the traffic jam had ended around Rostov, Kleist's army also picked up LVII Panzer Corps, with 13th Panzer and SS "Viking" Motorized Divisions, and LII Army Corps. On Army Group A's right wing, after List's forces captured Rostov and were untangled, the bulk of Ruoff's Seventeenth Army became Group Ruoff, which consisted of German IV, V, and XXXXIX Mountain Corps and Romanian Third Army's Cavalry Corps, with the headquarters of Romanian I Army Corps in reserve. Finally, after capturing Rostov, Seventeenth Army's XI Army Corps reverted to OKH reserve.[72]

Given the ambitious nature of Führer Directive No. 45, the extensive troop movements it involved, and the resulting balance of forces along each designated axis of advance, it is small wonder that many observers have identified it as the fatal point at which the struggle in Stalingrad city became inevitable. Repeating the strategic mistakes he had made during summer 1941, when he had asked the *Wehrmacht's* three army groups to accomplish too much with too few forces across too large an area, Hitler compounded this strategic error not once but twice in July 1942. First, in early July he had split Army Group South, ordering Army Group B to operate along two strategic axes (Voronezh and Stalingrad) and Army Group A to operate along one (Rostov). This seriously weakened the *Wehrmacht's* main thrust across southern Russia and produced confusion as to what, in reality, was the most critical strategic objective.

Second, by issuing Directive No. 45 Hitler directed Army Groups A and B to conduct major offensives along two distinct and completely divergent strategic axes, toward Stalingrad and into the Caucasus, while still requiring Army Group B to continue to defend the Voronezh axis. In addition to diluting the strength of both army groups' offensives, this left Army Group B's defenses near Voronezh and along the Don River front vulnerable to Soviet counterstrokes, strained German logistics to the breaking point, and prevented either army group from supporting the other as the campaign developed. As a result, by the time Operation Blau III (Braunschweig) reached its culminating point in early fall 1942, the *Stavka* was prepared to exploit its inherent vulnerabilities.

The vulnerabilities created by Directive No. 45 become apparent from a careful examination of the resulting balance of opposing forces along each of the designated axes of advance (see Table 15).

Weichs's Army Group B, with 3 armies, 11 corps (2 panzer), 37 divisions (3 panzer and 2 motorized), and 386 tanks deployed in the sector from northwest of Livny southward and southeastward past Voronezh and along the Don and Chir Rivers to the Tormosin region, south of Surovikino, faced a Soviet force of 9 armies, 99 division equivalents (18 tank), and roughly 1,939 tanks.[73] Because German divisions were almost twice as strong as their Soviet counterparts and many Red divisions were woefully understrength, Weichs's forces may have achieved rough parity with their foes in terms of infantry, but they were clearly inferior in armor by a factor of perhaps five-to-one.

Because the bulk of Army Group B's combat strength lay in its Sixth Army, Soviet superiority was most pronounced in the sectors of the German and Hungarian Second Armies. For example, Salmuth's German Second Army, with 14 divisions (1 panzer) and 96 tanks deployed in the sector from northwest of Livny to south of Voronezh on the army group's left wing, faced 2 Soviet armies, parts of 2 other armies, and 1 operational group, with 42 division equivalents (10 tank) and more than 500 tanks.[74] In the army group's center, Hungarian Second Army, with 6 infantry divisions (1 German) but no armor defending along the Don River from south of Voronezh to just north of Pavlograd, faced 1 Soviet army and part of a second, with roughly 10 division equivalents (2 tank) and about 200 tanks.[75]

Table 15. The Correlation of Opposing German and Soviet Forces along the Voronezh, Stalingrad, and Caucasus Axes on 25 July 1942

GERMAN	SOVIET

ARMY GROUP B (frontage—725 kilometers)

VORONEZH AXIS

Second Army (250 kilometers) (LV, XIII, and VII Army Corps), with 13 infantry divisions, 1 panzer division, 1 infantry brigade, and 96 tanks.

Briansk Front (part, 48th, 13th, and 60th Armies and Group Chibisov) and *Voronezh Front* (part, 40th Army), with 24 rifle divisions, 12 rifle brigades, 8 tank corps, 2 cavalry corps, 7 tank brigades, and over 500 tanks.

Hungarian Second Army (130 kilometers) (III and VII Army Corps), with 6 infantry divisions and no tanks.

Voronezh Front (part, 40th and 6th Armies), with 7 rifle divisions, 1 rifle brigade, 2 tank corps, 1 tank brigade, and 200 tanks.

STALINGRAD AXIS

Sixth Army (345 kilometers) (XXIX, VIII, XVII, and LI Army Corps and XIV and XXIV Panzer Corps), with 13 infantry divisions, 2 panzer divisions, 2 motorized divisions, and 290 tanks.

Stalingrad Front (63rd, 21st, 57th, 62nd, and 64th Armies and 1st and 4th Tank Armies), with 40 rifle divisions, 2 rifle brigades, 4 tank corps, 1 cavalry corps, 11 tank brigades, 10 separate tank battalions, and 1,239 tanks.

TOTAL: 32 infantry divisions, 3 panzer divisions, 2 motorized divisions, 1 infantry brigade, and 386 tanks.

TOTAL: 71 rifle divisions, 15 rifle brigades, 14 tank corps, 3 cavalry corps, 19 tank brigades, 10 separate tank battalions, and 1,939 tanks.

ARMY GROUP A (frontage—325 kilometers)

CAUCASUS AXIS

Fourth Panzer Army (170 kilometers) (XXXXVIII and XXXX Panzer Corps), with 1 infantry division, 3 panzer divisions, 1 motorized division, and 200 tanks.

Stalingrad Front (51st Army), with 4 rifle divisions, 2 cavalry divisions, 2 tank brigades, and 60 tanks.

First Panzer and Seventeenth Armies (155 kilometers) (IV, V, XI, XXXXIV, and LII Army Corps, XXXXIX Mountain Corps, and III and LVII Panzer Corps), with 20 infantry divisions, 3 panzer divisions, 4 motorized divisions, and 235 tanks.

North Caucasus Front (9th, 12th, 18th, and 56th Armies), with 21 rifle divisions, 1 cavalry division, 4 rifle brigades, 1 tank corps, 5 tank brigades, 1 motorized rifle brigade, 2 separate tank battalions, and 193 tanks.

TOTAL: 21 infantry divisions, 6 panzer divisions, 5 motorized divisions, and 435 tanks.

TOTAL: 25 rifle divisions, 3 cavalry divisions, 4 rifle brigades, 1 tank corps, 7 tank brigades, 1 motorized rifle brigade, 2 separate tank battalions, and 253 tanks.

Sources: Boevoi sostav Sovetskoi armii, 2: 146–150; Maksim Kolomiets and Il'ia Moshchansky, "Oborona Kavkaza (iiul'-dekabr' 1942 goda)" [The defense of the Caucasus (July–December 1942)], in *Frontovaia illiustratsiia*, 2–2000 [Front illustrated, 2: 2000] (Moscow: "Strategiia KM," 2000), 5; "Lagenkarten, 8 July–5 October 1942," *AOK II, Ia, 2585/207a*, in NAM T-312, Roll 1207; "Ia, Lagenkarten Nr. 1 zum KTB Nr. 13, Jul–Oct 1942," *AOK 6, 23948/1a*, in NAM T-312, Roll 1446; "Feindlagekarten, PzAOK 1, Ic, 29 Jun–31 Jul 1942," *PzAOK 1, 24906/24*, in NAM T-313, Roll 38; and "Anlage 3 zum Tatigkeitsbericht, OAK 17, Ic, 20 Jul–25 Jul 1942," *AOK 17, 24411/33*, in NAM T–312, Roll 679.

Despite its supposed power and vital mission, Paulus's Sixth Army was also not markedly superior to its foe. With 17 divisions (2 panzer and 2 motorized) and roughly 290 tanks deployed in the sector from Pavlovsk on the Don River to Surovikino on the Chir, Sixth Army faced 7 Soviet armies (2 tank), with about 52 division equivalents (5 tank) and 1,239 tanks.[76] Although more than half the Soviet divisions were severely understrength and refitting after their previous escapes from encirclement, after Timoshenko committed his 1st and 4th Tank Armies into combat, his tank force outnumbered Paulus's by a factor of better than four-to-one.[77]

List's Army Group A, with 3 armies, 10 corps (3 panzer), 32 divisions (6 panzer and 5 motorized), and 435 tanks operating in the sector from Tsimlianskaia on the Don River westward to Rostov and the Gulf of Taganrog, faced a Soviet force of 5 armies, about 34 division equivalents (3 tank), and 253 tanks. Given the dilapidated state of most of North Caucasus Front's divisions, List's forces, operating along a front half as wide as that of Army Group A under Weichs, were clearly superior in both infantry and armor. German superiority was most pronounced on Army Group A's left wing, where Hoth's Fourth Panzer Army, with 5 divisions (3 panzer) and 200 tanks in the sector along the Don from Tsimlianskaia westward to Konstantinovskaia faced 1 Soviet army with roughly 7 division equivalents (1 tank) and 60 tanks.[78] Kleist's First Panzer and Ruoff's Seventeenth Armies, with 27 divisions (3 panzer and 4 motorized) and 235 tanks deployed in the sector from Konstantinovskaia westward to Rostov along and south of the Don River in Army Group A's center and on its right wing, faced 4 Soviet armies, about 28 division equivalents, and 193 tanks.[79] However, since many, if not most, of the defending Soviet rifle divisions and brigades were at severely reduced strength, the 5 armies opposing Army Group A fielded only 112,000 men, with weak artillery support.[80] Thus, List's army group was numerically superior to its foes in both infantry and armor.

Mitigating against this superiority, the five infantry divisions subordinate to the Italian Eighth Army by this time had already been transferred from Army Group A's to Army Group B's control, and III Panzer Corps' 22nd Panzer Division would soon be transferred to Army Group B. In addition, Kleist's First Panzer Army, which had been designated to perform only a supporting role in Operation Blau, was never at full strength and had experienced unexpected if modest losses of men and material during the Khar'kov battles of May. As a result, the army's panzer and motorized divisions began the summer offensive with an average strength of 40 percent, which declined to 30 percent by 16 July. Therefore, by 25 July the seven German and Slovak mobile divisions assigned to Kleist's and Ruoff's armies fielded a total of 235 serviceable tanks, ranging from a high of 94 tanks in 13th Panzer Division to a low of 24 in 22nd Panzer Division.[81]

Even a cursory study of the correlations of opposing forces along the Voronezh, Stalingrad, and Caucasus axes make the vulnerabilities of Hitler's 23 July plan vividly clear. It was true that his plan allocated Army Group A more than enough forces to carry out the initial advance into the Caucasus region successfully, that is, Fourth and First Panzer and Seventeenth Armies with about 435 tanks against five Soviet armies with roughly 250 tanks. However, it failed to provide Army Group B with sufficient forces to advance by itself on Stalingrad. Specifically, while Paulus's army would begin its offensive with slightly fewer than 300 operational tanks and could be reinforced with another 50–80 tanks en route to the city, it would be opposed initially by five Soviet armies, ultimately supported by more than 1,200 tanks, and probably by additional Soviet reinforcements as it neared Stalingrad. Compounding the difficulty of Paulus's task, during its offensive his army would have to cross the expansive Don River and then breach formidable defenses around Stalingrad before occupying the city and, thereafter, fight for each city block if the Soviets decided to defend it—which they ultimately did.

These problems notwithstanding, the most serious deficiency in Hitler's plan was its neglect of the Voronezh axis and adjacent Don River front. In combination, Salmuth's German Second Army and Jany's Romanian Second Army, as well as the two army corps on the left wing of Paulus's Sixth Army, were vulnerable to concerted Soviet counterattacks and counterstrokes. These Axis forces mustered a paltry total of some 100 tanks to oppose the Soviet force of roughly 700 tanks operating around or west of Voronezh. Hitler may not have known that such a formidable tank force existed or, if he did, simply dismissed it as inconsequential. Still, if the Soviets ever learned to employ their tanks effectively, they could have devastating consequences for the *Wehrmacht*. Convinced his generals would learn, Stalin proved quick in his attempts to exploit German vulnerabilities.

In addition, given the rapid advance of the two German army groups and the even greater advances projected by Directive No. 45, fuel became ever more important as a factor that inhibited German maneuver of critical mobile divisions. As the Germans moved farther and farther from their railheads, they experienced growing shortages of gasoline. In a few instances, the *Luftwaffe* delivered barrels of gasoline to improvised forward airfields, but this mere trickle could not sustain the advance of the large units. In fact, during the capture of Rostov Sixth Army had temporarily halted due to fuel shortages, allowing Soviet defenders time to reorganize their defenses. Just as in 1941, German optimism exceeded the realities of time, space, and logistics.

Recognizing the *Wehrmacht*'s vulnerabilities, Stalin did everything in his power to thwart the German advance. First and foremost, he began to organize virtually simultaneous attacks in the Voronezh sector and against the nose of Sixth Army as it advanced eastward across the Chir River into the Great Bend of the Don and toward Stalingrad. As early as 17 July, he directed Briansk Front to form a strong offensive west of Voronezh in support of offensive operations already being conducted by Voronezh Front's 60th Army against German defenses around Voronezh and ordered Voronezh Front to commit its 40th and 6th Armies in support of this offensive.[82] This offensive was to begin on or about

21 July. The next day, Stalin reinforced Briansk Front with 2nd and 4th Reserve Armies from the *Stavka* Reserve, which would later form a new 38th Army and join Briansk Front's main effort.[83]

Turning his attention to shoring up the Don River front between Rostov and Stalingrad, Stalin on 21 July subordinated Malinovsky's Southern Front directly to the *Stavka* and assigned it responsibility for defending the Don from Bataisk (west of Rostov) eastward to its junction with the San River, while Budenny's North Caucasus Front protected the river line from the San eastward to Verkhne-Kurmoiarskaia.[84] After talking with Malinovsky on 22 July, Stalin once again adjusted his defenses along and south of the Don and also relieved Timoshenko as commander of Stalingrad Front, replacing him with General Gordov, former commander of 21st Army.[85]

More important, late on 22 July, Stalin ordered 1st and 4th Tank Armies be formed within Stalingrad Front around the nucleus of the headquarters of the destroyed 38th and 28th Armies, respectively.[86] Left unsaid was Stalin's intention to employ these armies in a concerted counterstroke. 4th Tank Army would consist of General Shamshin's 22nd and General Khasin's 23rd Tank Corps and 1st Tank Army of Colonel Tanaschishin's 13th and Colonel Rodin's 28th Tank Corps. In addition to these refurbished corps, each tank army would include three rifle divisions transferred from Far Eastern Front and two antitank and antiaircraft artillery regiments. Stalin assigned General Kriuchenkin, former commander of 28th Army, to command 4th Tank Army, with Major General of Tank Forces Vasilii Vasil'evich Novikov as his deputy. Novikov had commanded 28th Mechanized Corps and its successor, 47th Army, during Operation Barbarossa and the same military district's 45th Army in Iran since December 1941.[87] General Moskalenko, former commander of 38th Army, became 1st Tank Army commander, with General Pushkin, former commander of 23rd Tank Corps, as his deputy. The next day Stalin ordered Southern, North Caucasus, and Stalingrad Fronts to do all in their power to prevent the Germans from constructing pontoon bridges across the Don.[88]

While Stalin and the *Stavka* adjusted their defenses along the Stalingrad and Caucasus axes, the forward elements of Paulus's Sixth Army on 17 July began advancing eastward across the Chir River into the Great Bend. While crossing the Chir, Sixth Army's advancing armor encountered the detachments thrown forward by Kolpakchi's 62nd Army, precipitating a weeklong battle that intensified steadily as the Germans advanced. As fighting continued between the Chir and the Don, Stalin without hesitation ordered his forces along the Voronezh axis to join the battle against Paulus's Sixth Army. Within days, Paulus's army found itself decisively engaged along two major axes, and within ten days Stalin's actions would once again force Hitler to alter his plan.

CONCLUSIONS

The *Wehrmacht* demonstrated rapidity and depth of advance, and it performed as impressively during Blau II as it had during Blau I. In less than one week, the twin pincers of Army Groups B and A, advancing eastward and southeastward in tandem, severely damaged Southwestern Front's 21st, 28th, and 38th Armies and Southern Front's 9th Army and positioned themselves to envelop and destroy virtually all Soviet forces in the Donbas region. With its forces caught wrong-footed once again, the *Stavka* initially ordered its two *fronts* to man a new defensive line to the rear rather than abandon the Donbas region, and to re-inforce their new defenses with 57th and 24th Armies from their reserves. Beginning on 12 July, however, the three panzer divisions of XXXX Panzer Corps, now spearheading the Germans' northern pincer under the control of Army Group B's Fourth Panzer Army, bypassed Millerovo to the east, cutting off 28th and 38th Armies' routes of withdrawal to the east. Simultaneously, spearheading the Germans' southern pincer, the four armored divisions of First Panzer Army's III and XIV Panzer Corps struck along Army Group A's left wing, penetrated Southern Front's defenses north of Voroshilovgrad with ease, and forced the *front's* 9th and 37th Armies to withdraw eastward in disorder toward the region south of Millerovo.

As the two German pincers closed around Southwestern Front's armies and those on Southern Front's left wing, the *Stavka* frantically attempted to form a new strategic defensive front along the Don River and southward across the eastern Donbas region to Rostov. On 12 July, virtually writing off its armies encircled at and south of Millerovo, the *Stavka* assigned the remnants of these armies to Malinovsky's Southern Front and ordered him to rescue the forces encircled in the Millerovo region and to man new defenses from Millerovo southward across the Northern Donets River to Rostov. At the same time, the *Stavka* formed a new Stalingrad Front, ostensibly a renamed Southwestern Front but in reality an entirely new entity under Timoshenko's command, and ordered it to erect defenses along the Don and Chir Rivers, particularly in the Great Bend of the Don, to protect the approaches to Stalingrad. Timoshenko's new *front* consisted of the new 60-series armies, including 62nd, 63rd, and 64th Armies formed from 7th, 5th, and 1st Reserve Armies, respectively. However, the Germans' continued rapid advance rendered many of these measures irrelevant. Encircled in the Millerovo region and unable to join Southern Front, the remnants of 28th, 38th, and 57th Armies fled eastward across the Don, leaving Southern Front's shattered 9th, 24th, and 37th Armies to defend its open right wing south of Millerovo and its 12th, 18th, and 56th Armies, now backed up by North Caucasus Front's 51st Army, to defend the Mius River line and the approaches to Rostov.

At this juncture, Hitler fundamentally altered his plans for the next stage of Operation Blau. Elated over his forces' past successes but concerned lest Soviet forces escape intact from the eastern Donbas region, the Führer on 12 July decided to shift the axis of his main attack away from Stalingrad—the objective of Blau III—and instead turn the bulk of his panzer forces southeastward toward the lower Don River and Rostov to ensure the destruction of Soviet forces in the region. When Bock objected, Hitler replaced him with Weichs on 13 July. Implementing his new plan, Hitler left Sixth Army to protect the Don River front with its infantry and also concentrated XXIV, XXXXVIII, and XXXX Panzer Corps in Hoth's Fourth Panzer Army. The dictator assigned Hoth to Army Group A's control and ordered List to wheel this armor southward through the eastern Donbas to the lower Don. There, in cooperation with First Panzer Army advancing from the northwest, it was to destroy all Soviet forces in the eastern Donbas and Rostov regions. This maneuver, conducted between 17 and 24 July, succeeded in outflanking and defeating Southern Front's armies defending the Mius River line and the approaches to Rostov, captured Rostov, and propelled Army Group A's forces to the lower Don. Facing this new German juggernaut, the armies of the Southern Front abandoned Rostov and withdrew in disorder to new defenses along the lower Don.

Despite encircling and destroying a sizeable portion of Malinovsky's forces in the region south of Millerovo and along the approaches to Rostov, Hitler's gambit failed to trap even half the Soviet forces defending the eastern Donbas and Rostov regions. While the Germans' maneuver indeed decimated Southern Front's 9th, 37th, and 24th Armies and about half its 12th Army in the Kamensk-Shakhtinskii region, the *front*'s 18th and 56th Armies and roughly half its 12th Army succeeded in escaping southward through Rostov, albeit in considerable disorder. From a strategic standpoint, although Hitler's decision to wheel reinforced Army Group A southward toward Rostov and the lower Don succeeded, the Rostov "diversion" shifted the center of gravity of Operation Blau away from Stalingrad, thereby undermining the intent of Blau III. This posed Hitler with a strategic dilemma, namely, whether to continue his advance into the Caucasus, resume his march toward Stalingrad, or conduct both operations simultaneously. Characteristically audacious, the Führer chose the latter.

Hitler was elated by what he considered to be relatively easy victories in the Donbas region and at Rostov, and Führer Directive No. 45 ordered Army Group B to thrust eastward across the Don and capture Stalingrad and Army Group A to exploit southward into the Caucasus to seize its rich oil fields at Maikop and Baku. List's army group, led by Fourth Panzer Army's XXXX and XXXXVIII Panzer Corps and First Panzer Army's LVII Panzer Corps, was to clear Soviet forces from the Caucasus in a three-phase operation. Bock's army group, spearheaded by Sixth Army's XIV and XXIV Panzer Corps, was to conduct the decisive drive through the Great Bend of the Don to Stalingrad and the Volga beyond, while the armies on its left wing defended its ever-extending front along and west of the Don River.

In essence, therefore, Directive No. 45 required Army Groups B and A to operate along three distinct strategic axes, namely, in the Voronezh region, toward Stalingrad, and into the Caucasus. Because this violated the precept that one army group should be responsible for each strategic axis, Hitler's strategy was risky indeed. However, because the Soviets' strategic defenses were in such a dilapidated state, only time would tell whether or not the *Stavka* would be capable of exploiting the vulnerabilities inherent in Hitler's new plan.

Previous histories of Operation Blau have argued that Army Group B's dramatic advance to the Chir and Army Group A's equally significant thrust to the lower Don at and east of Rostov were virtual "cakewalks" because Stalin and his *Stavka* simply ordered the forces of Southwestern and Southern Fronts to withdraw out of harm's way rather than defend the region. As a result, they describe the fighting during Blau II as desultory. As a corollary, they fault the German army groups for permitting the Soviets to withdraw and thus avoid the immense losses they had suffered during encirclements in Operation Barbarossa the year before. These judgments are only partially correct.

Although the German advance was indeed dramatic, closer examination of events during Blau II indicates that the operation also involved intense, if episodic, fighting, particularly in the Millerovo region, because, as the directives he issued indicate, Stalin insisted his two *fronts* conduct a determined defense rather than a general withdrawal. To the credit of German commanders who orchestrated the offensive, this Soviet defense clearly failed—however, not because the Red Army chose to withdraw rather than fight. Moreover, Germans' failure to reap the fruits of victory by taking tens if not hundreds of thousands of Red Army prisoners as they had in 1941 did not mean that the Soviet forces in the region escaped unscathed, ready to fight another day. In fact, most of the armies of Southwestern and Southern Fronts that became wholly or partially encircled in the eastern Donbas and Rostov regions, including 28th, 38th, 9th, 12th, 37th, 18th, 56th, 24th, and 57th, were either virtually destroyed or survived as mere shadows of their former selves. Rather than reconstituting these armies, the *Stavka* had no choice but to disband them and form new ones in their stead. As for the tens of thousands of Red Army troops who were not bagged by the Germans, some formed or joined partisan forces, many others eventually rejoined the Red Army days, weeks, or even months later, and others simply went incognito.

Thus, as was the case in Blau I, Blau II was indeed a magnificent victory for the *Wehrmacht*. However, it was also an empty victory of sorts that in no way justified the unfettered optimism and new ambitiousness demonstrated by the German Führer.

CHAPTER 6

The German Advance into the Great Bend of the Don, 23–31 July 1942

At the beginning of the fourth week of July 1942, Germany's Army Group A was firmly established at Rostov, with its forward elements across the Don River on a broad front south and east of the city. To the north, Army Group B was stretched from the Livny region eastward to the Don River near Voronezh, southeastward along the Don to Kletskaia, and then southward across the Chir River to the Tormosin region. While its German and Hungarian Second Armies clung to their defenses on the army group's left wing at and west of Voronezh, the divisions on the left wing of Paulus's Sixth Army were advancing slowly eastward, filing into a cordon of defensive positions stretching along the southern bank of the Don River from Voronezh to Kletskaia. Beginning on 17 July, one week before List's forces captured Rostov, the bulk of Sixth Army began concentrating on the army's right wing, feeling out Soviet defenses to the east and posturing for an advance eastward into the Great Bend of the Don and beyond to Stalingrad on the Volga. Dazzled by these valuable twin targets—the city of Stalingrad and the oil-rich Caucasus region—Adolf Hitler was intent upon capturing both objectives simultaneously.

On the opposite side of the front, Josef Stalin was equally determined to hold the Volga, a major north-south supply route that was also the last major water obstacle in European Russia, and a region near the Great Bend of the Don, which protected the approaches to the Volga. He demanded that Stalingrad Front hold firmly to its defenses along the Don and forward of the Great Bend while Briansk and Voronezh Fronts unleashed their armies in a concerted assault against Army Group B's long right wing. With Hitler's attentions divided between the enticing twin targets, a major clash at Stalingrad had become virtually inevitable.

AREA OF OPERATIONS

As in Blau I and II, the unique configuration of the topography and river systems near the Great Bend of the Don, and of the lands near Stalingrad itself, largely determined the location, form, and nature of the impending struggle between Bock's Army Group B and Gordov's Stalingrad Front—if not the ultimate outcome as well. The most critical terrain aspect was the river system that traversed and dominated the region, in particular the mighty Volga and Don Rivers. By a quirk of geography, although both rivers coursed from north to south roughly parallel to each other, they converged as they approached Stalingrad, the Don River in a large bend sweeping eastward directly opposite a mirror-image (but somewhat shallower) westward-projecting bend in the Volga. Before much of the Don River valley was flooded by dams associated with the Volga-Don Canal, which the Soviet Union built after war's end, the Don itself, with a width ranging from less than 100 meters to several hundred meters, was a formidable obstacle in either direction. This made the few bridges across the Don, such as those at Trekhostrovskaia and Kalach, key terrain features.

West of the Don, within the Great Bend, the relatively flat and open terrain sloped gently from north to south, from elevations reaching up to 250 meters in the north to even flatter ground reaching to roughly 150 meters in the south. A series of lesser rivers, including (from west to east), the Chir and its northern extensions, the Tsutskan and the Kurtlak, the Berezovaia, the Dobraia, the Liska, and several smaller streams, traversed the steppe from north to south north of where the Chir River turned to the east; south of where the Chir turned to the east, the Tsimla River did the same. The steep banks of these rivers, together with numerous *balkas* (ravines) formed by their tributaries, offered natural obstacles to rapid movement across what would otherwise be considered as good tank country. Finally, as was the case with all major rivers in the southern Soviet Union, the rivers' right (western) banks were steep, often rising more than 100 meters above the riverbed, with small or nonexistent adjacent low ground; the eastern banks were characterized by extensive lowlands, marshes, and swamps. While this terrain configuration favored defense against attacks from the east, it disfavored effective defense against attacks from the west.

East of the Don, a narrow land bridge of 50–70 kilometers separated the Don from the Volga River and Stalingrad. The land bridge itself was lower-lying open steppe rising 30–80 meters in the west to about 150 meters on the high ground overlooking the Volga and Stalingrad. Like the terrain within the Great Bend, the land bridge was also traversed by numerous *balkas* and both wet and dry riverbeds running from east to west into the Don, such as the Karpovka, which flowed into the Don south of Kalach, and several small rivers, including the Tsaritsa, Orlovka, and Mokraia Mechetka, along with its tributary, the Mechetka, and several smaller and normally dry streams, which flowed from the heights above Stalingrad into the Volga. The southern extremity of the Don-Volga land bridge widened appreciably to about 100 kilometers, ultimately joining the steppe stretching from the region south of the Don eastward to the Volga south of Stalingrad. This region, which contained the main railroad line running from Stalingrad southwestward to Krasnodar, was traversed by numerous rivers such as the Sal, Aksai, Myshkova, and Donskaia Tsaritsa, which flowed into the Don River from southeast to northwest, and was pockmarked with their associated *balkas.*

The road network within the Great Bend and the land bridge to the east was underdeveloped, consisting of a few main roads paralleling the Don and Volga Rivers, as well as lesser roads and tracks crisscrossing the steppe. As elsewhere in the southern Soviet Union, ground communications relied primarily on rail rather than roads. The main railroad line traversed the region eastward from the Donbas through Morozovsk and Surovikino north of the Chir River into Stalingrad from the west. Another main railroad line extended from Moscow southward into Stalingrad and then on to Astrakhan', near where the Volga flows into the Caspian Sea. Together with the Volga River, all important north-south and east-west roads and railroads converged on Stalingrad, making it the most important transportation hub in the region.

Thus, Stalingrad and its suburbs formed a man-made island in the midst of vast, almost treeless steppe, beginning at the Don River and continuing eastward beyond the Volga. The barren, almost flat terrain and hot weather had a mesmerizing effect on both sides during the war. And there was no way the Germans could avoid battle in the city. The configuration of the Don, with the Great Bend pointing directly toward Stalingrad, naturally funneled, or canalized, advancing German forces to the eastern end of the bend, where the only bridges across the river were located. Once German forces crossed the Don, even if they also advanced eastward from the steppe south of the Great Bend (as they ultimately did), the configuration of the land bridge and the rivers it contained, combined with the necessity for protecting their overextended northern and southern flanks along the Don and Sal Rivers, would lead them inexorably to Stalingrad and the Volga.

Compounding the Germans' problems with the terrain, the Soviets hampered the advancing forces by destroying water wells and evacuating villages as they retreated (a policy known to world history as scorched earth). Mitigating against this policy, however, many of the Don Cossacks who occupied this region seemed more willing to aid the German invaders than the Great Russian oppressors. Cossacks often welcomed the Germans and, in some instances, enlisted as auxiliary troops. Thus the approaches to Stalingrad were not as inhospitable to the Germans as Moscow might have wished.

SIXTH ARMY'S ADVANCE TO THE DON, 17–25 JULY

In accordance with Hitler's 17 July order, unaltered by the 23 July directive, Sixth Army was supposed to resume active operations toward the east as soon as possible. To do this, Hitler reinforced Paulus with VIII and LI Army Corps from Hoth's Fourth Panzer Army and XIV Panzer Corps' headquarters and 16th Panzer and 60th Motorized Divisions from Kleist's First Panzer Army. Wietersheim's XIV Panzer Corps then took control of 3rd Motorized Division. Wietersheim's corps, with Seydlitz's LI Army Corps advancing in its wake, had just participated in the encirclement battle in the Millerovo region, while the forward elements of Heitz's VIII Army Corps were spearheading the German advance into the Bokovskaia region on the upper Chir River. Thereafter, both corps moved their forces into assembly areas east of Kantemirovka to spearhead Paulus's advance into the Great Bend of the Don River. Their initial target, the eastern extremity of the Great Bend west of Stalingrad, lay 150 kilometers to their front; Stalin's namesake city lay only 200 kilometers away.

Although Paulus intended to advance eastward with XIV Panzer Corps in his vanguard, heavy rains delayed the forward deployment of reinforcements.[1] As Wietersheim's panzers and Seydlitz's infantry slogged forward through the endless mud, on 19 and 20 July LI Army Corps' two lead infantry divisions, 113th Infantry and 100th Jäger, pushed eastward through the village of Pronin on the Tsutskan River, where they engaged and defeated the forward elements of the Soviet 62nd Army. By day's end on 20 July, Heitz's infantry neared the Kurtlak River both north and south of Perelazovskii.[2] To the south, 71st Infantry Division of Seydlitz's LI Army Corps was marching steadily eastward toward the Chir River north of Chernyshkovskii, behind which other forward detachments of Kolpakchi's 62nd Army were digging in.

By nightfall the next day, Paulus had concentrated enough of his army forward to be able to resume the advance toward the key Don River crossings early the next morning (see Map 26). Sixth Army's forces at the western base of the Great Bend at this time included VIII Army Corps, with its 79th Infantry, 100th Jäger, and 113th Infantry Divisions deployed from the Don River southward to just west of Perelazovskii on the Kurtlak River, and its 305th Infantry Division in reserve. On VIII Corps' left, XVII Army Corps' 376th and 384th Infantry Divisions were in the region south of Kazanskaia on the Don, and on VIII Corps' right LI Army Corps' 297th and 71st Infantry Divisions had already reached the western bank of the Chir across a broad front, with 44th Infantry Division approaching from the corps' reserve. Paulus's armored spearheads, XIV Panzer Corps' 3rd and 60th Motorized and 16th Panzer Divisions, were completing their concentration north as well as south of Bokovskaia, ready to lead the eastward assault. Thus configured, Paulus's attacking force consisted of five infantry, one panzer, and two motorized divisions, totaling roughly 120,000 men and 150 tanks and assault guns.[3]

Opposite Paulus's main shock group, Stalingrad Front, commanded by Timoshenko until 22 July and thereafter by Gordov, defended the sector from Kletskaia on the Don southward across the Chir to Verkhne-Kurmoiarskaia on the Don, with all of Kolpakchi's 62nd Army deployed north of the Chir and Chuikov's 64th Army still deploying forward south of the Chir (see Map 24). In 62nd Army's rear area, the surviving remnants of Moskalenko's 38th and Kriuchenkin's 28th Armies were defending north and east of the Don, while their other shattered divisions were refitting and refilling with personnel in the Stalingrad region. More important for any future successful defense, Stalingrad Front was

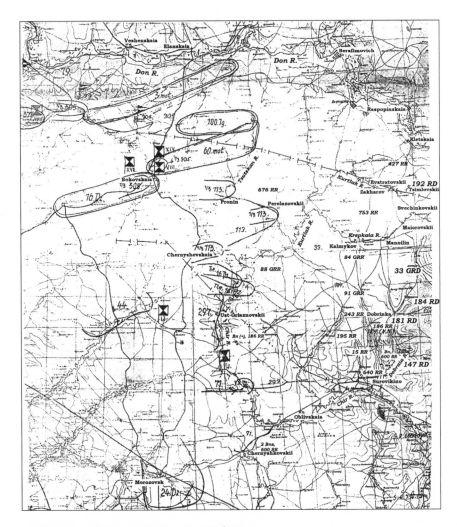

Map 26. The Sixth Army's situation, 21–22 July 1942

frantically resting and refitting the few tank and cavalry formations that had been fortunate enough to escape the devastation and bloodletting in the Donbas region. These included 22nd and 23rd Tank and 3rd Guards Cavalry Corps, situated in 63rd Army's rear north of the upper Don, and 13th Tank Corps, located in 62nd Army's rear near Surovikino on the northern bank of the Chir. Pursuant to Stalin's 22 July order, the headquarters of 28th and 38th Armies were hastily forming the new 1st and 4th Tank Armies from those surviving tank corps.

By late on 21 July, Kolpakchi's 62nd Army consisted of six rifle divisions, five of which (196th, 147th, 181st, 33rd Guards, and 192nd) were deployed uniformly

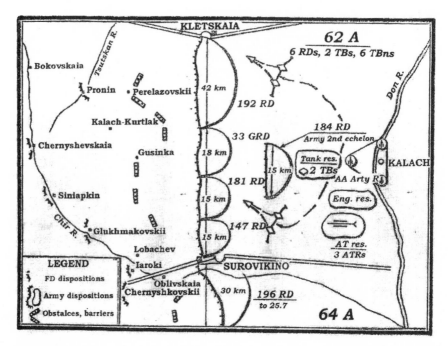

Map 27. The 62nd Army's defensive plan and operations of its forward detachments, 17–22 July 1942

from left to right across the Great Bend from Surovikino on the Chir northward to Kletskaia on the Don. The 184th Rifle Division and 40th Tank Brigade were in reserve (see Map 27). Each rifle division had already dispatched a forward detachment consisting of a rifle regiment, reinforced by tanks and artillery, to occupy security and intermediate positions up to 20 kilometers forward of their main defensive belts. In addition, Kolpakchi's army included six separate tank battalions (644th, 645th and 648th–651st), some supporting its forward detachments but most in reserve, and, for artillery support, three gun artillery regiments, nine antitank artillery regiments, one mortar regiment, four guards-mortar (*Katiusha*) regiments and one guards-mortar battalion, and one antiaircraft artillery regiment. Thus, 62nd Army fielded 383 guns, 1,138 mortars, and 277 tanks.[4]

South of the Chir, Chuikov's 64th Army consisted of six rifle divisions, two naval rifle brigades, two tank brigades, and three student rifle regiments made up of student officers from the Zhitomir and Ordzhonikidze Infantry Schools and the Krasnograd Machine Gun–Artillery School. Chuikov positioned 29th, 214th, and 229th Rifle Divisions, 154th Naval Rifle Brigade, and part of 121st Tank Brigade west of the Don River; 112th Rifle Division along the Chir at the junction of 62nd and 64th Armies; and 204th and 208th Rifle Divisions, 66th

Naval Rifle Brigade, and 137th Tank Brigade along or east of the Don River.[5] Actually, because no German forces appeared in his sector prior to 22 July, Chuikov's forward detachments did not begin to man forward positions along the Tsimla River until late that day. By this time, Chuikov's army fielded 226 guns, 622 mortars, and 55 tanks, bringing the total armor strength of the force facing Sixth Army's shock group to 332 tanks as opposed to Paulus's 150 (see Table 16 at chapter's end).[6]

Paulus's plan called for his forces to penetrate the Soviet defenses protecting the Great Bend by advancing with "wedges" of tanks, break through to the Don River as quickly as possible, roll up the enemy's forces on the river's western bank from the flanks, cut off their withdrawal back across the river, and destroy them in *Kesseln* (cauldrons) west of the river (see Map 28). Spearheading this advance, XIV Panzer Corps' three divisions were to:

> Break through toward the east by crossing the Liska [River] toward the Don, wheel to the right and advance south in the stretch between the Liska and the Don, and link up with 24th Panzer and 297th Infantry Divisions, advancing from the Don bridgehead at Rychkovskii. The two combat wedges will meet in the area west of Kalach. The 100th Jäger Division, 376th and 305th Infantry Divisions, and 113th and 44th Infantry Divisions, confronting the mass of Russians from the west, will contain the enemy and force him to the east.[7]

On 22 July, without delay after their assembly, XIV Panzer Corps' 3rd and 60th Motorized and 16th Panzer Divisions, supported by VIII and LI Army Corps' four infantry divisions, pushed eastward, engaging the forward detachments of Kolpakchi's 62nd Army. Passing south of Veshenskaia on the Don, Lieutenant General Helmuth Schlömer's 3rd and Major General Otto Kohlermann's 60th Motorized Divisions, flanked by 100th Jäger and 113th Infantry Divisions, advanced halfway from Bokovskaia to Kletskaia by nightfall. To the south, Hube's 16th Panzer Division, with 297th and 71st Infantry Divisions on its right flank, thrust eastward across the Chir River. That evening, Kolpakchi reported the forward detachments of his army's 192nd, 33rd Guards, 181st, 147th, and 196th Rifle Divisions were engaging enemy infantry and tanks across his entire front, and 192nd Division's forward detachment had been forced to withdraw to Perelazovskii. At the same time, Chuikov reported that the forward elements of 29th and 214th Rifle Divisions were in place and engaging German forces along the Tsimla River.[8]

Paulus's three armored divisions continued their rapid advance on 23 July, tearing through Kolpakchi's forward security belt and advancing 25–40 kilometers eastward of the Kurtlak and Chir Rivers, about halfway between Bokovskaia and the vital crossing points over the Don River at Trekhostrovskaia and Kalach. By nightfall, 3rd and 60th Motorized Divisions' panzer grenadiers reached the

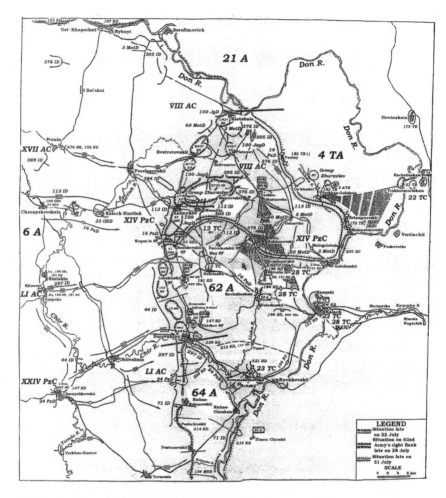

Map 28. Operations in the Great Bend of the Don River, 23–31 July 1942

Kletskaia region, and 16th Panzer Division's tanks pushed to within 10 kilometers of Kolpakchi's main defenses along the Dobraia River north of Surovikino.

Characteristic of this advance, Hube's panzer division organized its forces for the advance to the Don River into four *kampfgruppen* (combat groups) built around 2nd Panzer and 64th and 79th Panzer Grenadier Regiments and the engineer (pioneer) battalion. The strongest of these was *Kampfgruppe* Lattmann, which consisted of Panzer Detachment (*Abteilung*) von Strachwitz (from the division's panzer regiment), Panzer Grenadier Battalion Mues, Artillery Detachment Zientsch, and the division's 16th Motorcycle Battalion (K-16). *Kampfgruppen* von Witzleben and Reinisch were made up of panzer grenadier battalions, reinforced by artillery and engineers, and the fourth *kampfgruppe, Kampfgruppe* Strehlke, was to protect the division's eastern flank with the division's engineer (pioneer) battalion.[9]

Acknowledging that Sixth Army required even greater armor support if it was to reach Stalingrad quickly, that same day Hitler assigned 24th Panzer Division and the headquarters of Langermann's XXIV Panzer Corps to Paulus's army. With the promise of additional armor support, Paulus then revised his plans to capture Stalingrad by an armor coup de main. Relying on speed to overcome remaining Soviet defenses in his path, Paulus formulated a plan to envelop the Soviet 62nd and 64th Armies west of the Don River and to seize the key crossing sites over the Don River north and south of Kalach preliminary to a general advance by all of his available armor and infantry eastward to capture the prize city. Spearheading his northern pincer, 3rd and 60th Motorized and 16th Panzer Divisions of Wietersheim's XIV Panzer Corps, accompanied and supported by VIII Army Corps' four infantry divisions, were to attack toward the Don River at Trekhostrovskaia and Kalach to encircle the Soviet 62nd Army west of the Don and then force the river and advance on Stalingrad's northern suburbs via the railroad from the northwest.

Simultaneously, a southern pincer spearheaded by 24th Panzer Division of Langermann's XXIV Panzer Corps and accompanied by LI Army Corps' three infantry divisions was to pierce the Soviet 64th Army south of the Chir River, cross the river, and advance to Kalach to encircle and destroy Chuikov's army. Thereafter, Langermann's forces were to force the Don River south of Kalach and advance on Stalingrad's southern suburbs from the west. Once the two panzer corps reached the Volga River north and south of Stalingrad, they were to seize the city by concentric attacks from north and south. However, the two corps combined controlled only two panzer (16th and 24th) and two motorized (3rd and 60th) divisions, with a force of about 200 tanks against the 1,289 tanks ultimately fielded by Stalingrad Front.[10]

In addition to Sixth Army's relative paucity in armor, Paulus's plan was also hamstrung by persistent supply shortages. Army Group A had already received priority on all supplies for its pursuit into the Caucasus, and Army Group B was further hampered by a staff error. At the OKH, supply planners did not make allowance for the shift of the two panzer corps to Sixth Army. At the end of July, Hitler personally ordered the redirection of 750 tons of transport capacity from First Panzer Army to Sixth Army, but by the time this change could take effect, Paulus's forces had been shortchanged for more than two weeks. Moreover, as the Germans moved farther away from their supply base, the advance was increasingly dependent on stopgap logistical measures. JU-52 transport aircraft, diverted from other missions, brought limited amounts of fuel and ammunition forward to sustain the spearheads, but transporting highly flammable materials in this manner was extremely risky.[11]

On the same day Paulus submitted his plan for the final advance on Stalingrad, his subordinate headquarters began reporting intensifying resistance from 62nd and 64th Armies' forces defending the Great Bend of the Don. Clearly, the fuel shortages that slowed Paulus's advance had allowed the Red Army to form a new line of resistance, even if tenuous (at best). Yet, given XIV Panzer Corps' rapid forward progress on 23 July, with its flanks "hanging in the air" in both the Kletskaia and Surovikino regions, Kolpakchi's 62nd Army seemed perfectly positioned to fall into the trap formed by Paulus's double envelopment. To the south, because it had deployed fewer than half of its forces forward, Chuikov's 64th Army was even less prepared to resist effectively. Recently reassigned from the *Stavka* Reserve, this army's green divisions had become fragmented and intermingled as they arrived by railroad and moved by foot across the Don River. Because the bridges in its sector would support only light tanks, most of its tank brigades were delayed east of the river, unable to cross.

Making matters worse, during this critical period 64th Army may also have been afflicted by severe command turbulence. Although not substantiated by any other Russian sources, which uniformly maintain that Chuikov commanded 64th Army from 10 July until 4 August, in his memoirs Chuikov asserts that Timoshenko or the *Stavka* assigned Gordov to replace him on 19 July, although he remained as Gordov's deputy until resuming command on 22 July, when Gordov became commander of Stalingrad Front. According to Chuikov, Gordov's solution to the bridge problem was to locate his reserve divisions and much of his artillery east of the Don River, leaving the forward units in the bend without a defense in depth. Under a clear sky dominated by the *Luftwaffe*, remnants of shattered Soviet units roamed the steppe, confused and disheartened.[12]

These problems within 64th Army were only exacerbated by equal turbulence at the *front* level, when on 21 July Stalin finally concluded that Timoshenko was unequal to the challenge of command. After summoning Gordov to Moscow, he appointed him commander of Stalingrad Front, effective 23 July, with Khrushchev remaining as his member of the Military Council and General Bodin as his chief of staff. By this time, Gordov's *front* controlled eight armies (63rd, 62nd, 64th, 51st, 57th, 21st, 28th, and 38th) as well as 8th Air Army and the Volga River Flotilla. On paper, at least, the defense of Stalingrad seemed well in hand.[13]

However, Gordov was hamstrung, on the one hand by his lack of accurate information from the front, and on the other by continued micromanagement from Moscow. For example, on the evening of 23 July, as Paulus was completing his plan to create the encirclement west of the Don, Gordov reported to Stalin that the enemy had smashed 62nd Army's forward defenses east of the Chir River with a force of 150 tanks and, despite losing 35 tanks, was headed toward the Don bridges and Stalingrad—thereby implying he would have trouble defending the crossings. Stalin, however, insisted that Gordov retain control of the so-called Don bulge on a line from Kletskaia southward to Nizhnaia Kalinovka and directed nine-tenths of all air support be concentrated against XIV

Panzer Corps on 62nd Army's northern flank.[14] Vasilevsky and other key officers commuted between Moscow and Gordov's headquarters to guarantee the defense of the Don bulge, carrying harsh orders from Stalin.

Despite Stalin's increasingly strident entreaties, Paulus's two pincers recorded spectacular advances on 24 July (see Map 29). Attacking from the Kletskaia region, one behind the other, 3rd and 60th Motorized Divisions of Wietersheim's XIV Panzer Corps sliced through 192nd Rifle Division's defenses on 62nd Army's left wing and advanced more than 50 kilometers southeast. By nightfall, Schlömer's panzer grenadiers were less than 10 kilometers from Kalach on the Don. Together with Kohlermann's panzer grenadiers, which were advancing in their wake, Schlömer's men had established a long but loose cordon of armor stretching from just south of Kletskaia southeastward to the Don, containing the remnants of the two shattered rifle divisions on 62nd Army's left wing in a bridgehead south of Kremenskaia and Sirotinskaia on the Don River.

To the south, but advancing at a far slower pace because of 24th Panzer Division's late arrival, LI Army Corps' 297th and 71st Infantry Divisions, supported later in the day by 24th Panzer Division of Langermann's XXIV Panzer Corps, attacked eastward along both banks of the Chir, driving 64th Army's forces back to the Surovikino-Tormosin line.[15] In between the two pincers, the three *kampf-gruppen* from Hube's 16th Panzer Division and VIII Army Corps' 113th Infantry Division tore holes through 62nd Army's center, captured Perelazovskii, and pressed Kolpakchi's forces back another 15 kilometers toward the Don.

Paulus's twin attacks penetrated 62nd Army's defenses with relative ease. Late on 23 July, Kolpakchi reported that the forces on his army's right wing were fighting a "fierce defensive battle with enemy tanks (150–200) and infantry [3rd and 60th Motorized Divisions], supported by aircraft," 33rd Guards Rifle Division was struggling with another force of 150 enemy tanks (16th Panzer Division), and 147th Rifle Division was engaging enemy motorcycle units (297th Infantry Division) along the Chir. Later in the evening, Kolpakchi admitted that his 192nd Rifle Division was withdrawing under intense pressure, but 40th Tank Brigade was counterattacking successfully.[16]

However, by day's end on 24 June, 62nd Army's situation worsened considerably as Kolpakchi radioed that his 192nd and 184th Rifle Divisions had withdrawn northeast under pressure from up to 100 enemy tanks and were defending a large bridgehead south of the Don River east of Kletskaia. More ominously still, although 181st and 147th Rifle Divisions appeared to be holding firm in the army's center, and Colonel Tanaschishin's 13th Tank Corps was successfully engaging a large enemy tank force on the army's right-center, Kolpakchi conceded that "information about the location of the army's formations by nightfall was not available due to an absence of communications."[17]

By day's end on 24 July, the three divisions of Wietersheim's XIV Panzer Corps' armor and the supporting 113th Infantry Division had loosely encircled a third of Kolpakchi's army on the high ground in the Maiorovskii region,

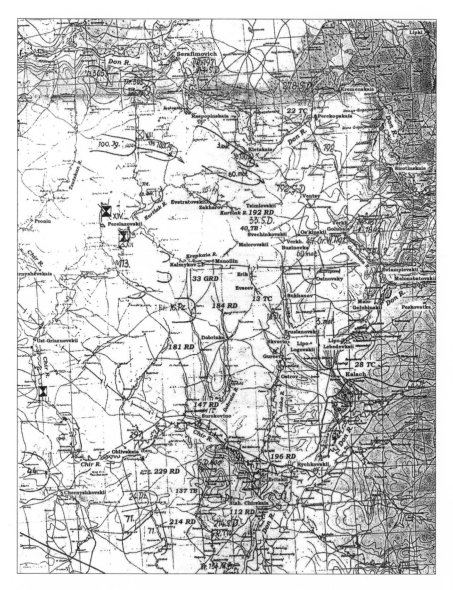

Map 29. The Sixth Army's situation, 23–24 July 1942

between the Kurtlak and Krepkaia Rivers north of Manoilin. However, at this critical moment, Wietersheim had to slow his advance and consolidate by early evening because of acute shortages of fuel and stiff enemy resistance north of Kalach.[18] The encircled forces included 33rd Guards Rifle Division, portions of 192nd and 184th Rifle Divisions, 40th Tank Brigade, and 644th Tank Battalion, all under the command of Colonel Konstantin Andreevich Zhuravlev, chief of 62nd Army's Operations Department, who had flown into the encirclement in a U-2 aircraft.[19] If XXIV Panzer Corps' 24th Panzer Division could breach 64th Army's defenses along the lower Chir and reach Kalach, the remainder of Kolpakchi's army could also be encircled and destroyed. From his perspective in the OKH, an optimistic Franz Halder recorded, "Sixth Army is in continuous advance toward the Don, west of Stalingrad. The enemy, still putting up stiff opposition in some places, is being enveloped."[20]

With 62nd Army threatened with encirclement, Stalin reacted with characteristic forcefulness by ordering Gordov to accelerate the formation of the new 1st and 4th Tank Armies and then throw them into the breach to rescue Kolpakchi's army. However, by this time Tanaschishin's 13th Tank Corps, which had been designated to become a part of Moskalenko's new 1st Tank Army, had already joined the battle against 16th Panzer Division north of Manoilin. But only its 166th and 169th Tank Brigades were engaged; 163rd Brigade was still in 62nd Army's reserve far to the rear. At the time, General Rodin's 28th Tank Corps, also earmarked to join 1st Tank Army, was still on the eastern bank of the Don near Kalach, in the same general area as Khazin's 23rd Tank Corps. Finally, Shamshin's 22nd Tank Corps, which was supposed to join the new 4th Tank Army, was still assembling in 63rd Army's sector north of the Don. Therefore, Kolpakchi's army had to begin its counterattacks with only Tanaschishin's truncated tank corps, whose mission was to break through 16th Panzer Division's defenses and rescue Zhuravlev's group. However, since Zhuravlev had no communications with Kolpakchi, the former ordered his encircled group to break out northward toward Kletskaia.[21]

Early on 25 July, Kolpakchi organized yet another counterattack to support Tanaschishin's 13th Tank Corps and halt and drive back Sixth Army's northern pincer before it reached Kalach. After turning its sector on the army's left wing over to 64th Army's 229th Rifle Division, 196th Rifle Division and 649th Tank Battalion were to attack northward along the Liska River toward Skvorin, 25 kilometers northwest of Kalach, to cut off the advancing enemy panzers and to help Tanaschishin's tanks rescue Group Zhuravlev. Early the next day, Gordov ordered Rodin's 28th Tank Corps to join the counterstroke by crossing the Don and attacking northward from Kalach with as much of his corps as possible. However, all of these counterattacks were too disjointed to evolve into a genuine counterstroke with any prospects of real success.[22]

In rude defiance of Kolpakchi's and Gordov's countermeasures, the two pincers of Paulus's Sixth Army fought hard to complete their envelopment of Kolpakchi's 62nd Army on 25 and 26 July against sharply intensifying Soviet resistance. Although still plagued by fuel shortages, in two days of heavy fighting, arrayed from left to right (east to west), 3rd and 60th Motorized and 16th Panzer Divisions of Wietersheim's XIV Panzer Corps managed to form a semicoherent front of tanks and panzer grenadiers stretching from the Don River north of

Kalach westward to Skvorin in the Liska River valley. In Wietersheim's rear area, however, VIII Army Corps' 100th Jäger and 113th Infantry Divisions, supported by most of 16th Panzer Division's tanks, had to perform the arduous triple tasks of containing 62nd Army's two divisions that had withdrawn into the Kremenskaia and Sirotinskaia bridgehead south of the Don, defeating and destroying the encircled Group Zhuravlev, and, simultaneously, contending with Soviet forces attempting to relieve Group Zhuravlev. From afar Halder described Wietersheim's dilemma: "Our troops, with tremendous punch, but badly disrupted into groups, battered through a bitterly resisting enemy as far as the Don. It remains to be seen whether we shall yet succeed in capturing the Kalach bridge." Halder added what by now was a usual lament: "Lack of fuel caused sizeable elements of the armored and motorized divisions to lag behind."[23]

Paulus's problems mounted because, beginning on 25 July, Tanaschishin's 13th Tank Corps and 196th Rifle Division, reinforced early on 26 July by 55th and 56th Tank Brigades of Rodin's 28th Tank Corps, which went into action north of Kalach, continued to press their attacks northward along the entire front from Manoilin eastward to the Don. The Red Army General Staff's daily operational summary captured the ferocity of the fighting:

> *62nd Army's* 192nd and 184th RDs [rifle divisions] and 40th TB [tank brigade], together with units of 1st Tank Army, continued intense defensive fighting along the Zakharov (17 kilometers southwest of Kletskaia), Tsimlovskii, and Maiorovskii (13–27 kilometers south of Kletskaia) line. The remaining units of the army continued holding their previous positions.
>
> *1st Tank Army.* After overcoming enemy resistance in the "10th Year of October" [*X let Oktiabria*] [State Farm] region (12 kilometers northeast of Kalach on the Don), 28th TC [tank corps] was advancing slowly to the north. The units of 13th TC counterattacked toward Manoilin and captured this point by 1800 hours. The forces of 62nd and 1st Tank Armies have destroyed 120 enemy tanks and up to 2,000 enemy soldiers and officers during the period from 22 through 25 July.[24]

These counterattacks abruptly halted XIV Panzer Corps' forward progress toward Kalach. The 16th Panzer Division reported that a force of 60 Soviet tanks, apparently from Tanaschishin's 13th Tank Corps, succeeded in penetrating into their rear area, and 3rd and 60th Motorized Divisions asserted that they were under assault by 200 Russian tanks north of Kalach.[25] By day's end on 26 July, Kolpakchi's army clung tenaciously to a bridgehead 65 kilometers wide and 32 kilometers deep on the western bank of the Don from north of Kalach southward to Nizhne-Chirskaia.

Adding to Paulus's problems, stiffening resistance by Chuikov's 64th Army south of the Chir prevented his army's southern pincer from crossing the river near Nizhne-Chirskaia and reaching Kalach from the south. In two days of heavy fighting, XXIV Panzer Corps' 24th Panzer Division and LI Army Corps' 297th and 71st Infantry Divisions, attacking south of the Chir, and 44th Infantry Division, now attacking eastward along the river's northern bank, pressed 64th Army's 229th and 214th Rifle Divisions and 137th Tank Brigade eastward to the western outskirts of Surovikino and the lower Chir near Nizhne-Chirskaia. The advancing forces even managed to capture a small bridgehead across the lower reaches of the river. However, because Chuikov's forces stymied any further advance, a gap 35 kilometers wide remained between the points of Paulus's two pincers.[26]

As early as 26 July, therefore, it was abundantly clear that Sixth Army would have difficulty completing its encirclement of 62nd Army unless it received significant reinforcements. Yet even as Paulus's chief of staff was reporting to his army group counterpart that "for the moment a certain crisis has developed," it was Kolpakchi who was about to receive those needed reinforcements—in the form of 1st and 4th Tank Armies.[27] Chiming in from the OKH, an increasingly pessimistic Halder wrote, "Hard battles west of Stalingrad. The enemy, split into four groups, is fighting doggedly and throwing in new forces, including much armor, across the Don. There must still be a strong force in Stalingrad. Lack of fuel and ammunition!"[28]

STALINGRAD FRONT'S COUNTERSTROKE, 26–31 JULY

Stalin persistently demanded that Stalingrad Front exploit the more than 600 tanks in its still forming 1st and 4th Tank Armies. Therefore, at 2000 hours on 26 July, Gordov ordered the two tank armies, as well as infantry from 21st, 62nd, and 64th Armies and aircraft from 8th Air Army, to mount a concerted counterstroke against Paulus's northern pincer (see Map 28):

- *1st Tank Army's* [Moskalenko] 13th and 28th Tank Corps, 158th Tank Brigade, and 131st Rifle Division will attack from the march from the Kalach region toward Verkhne-Buzinovka to destroy the opposing enemy and capture the Verkhne-Buzinovka region by day's end on 27 July. Subsequently, the army will attack toward Kletskaia. Begin the attack at 0300 hours 27 July.
- *4th Tank Army's* [Kriuchenkin] 22nd Tank Corps and 133rd Tank Brigade will cross to the western bank of the Don on the night of 27–28 July and attack westward from the Trekhostrovskaia and Peskovatka line in the morning to reach the Verkhne-Golubaia region by day's end. Cooperating with 1st Tank Army, destroy the opposing enemy in successive attacks toward Verkhne-Buzinovka and restore the situation on 62nd Army's right wing.
- *21st Army* [Danilov] will attack toward Kletskaia and Evstratovskii with

three–four rifle divisions to destroy the opposing enemy and cut his communications routes to the rear. Subsequently, prevent the penetrating enemy from withdrawing to the west.

- *62nd Army* [Kolpakchi] will hold its present positions and prevent the enemy from broadening the penetration front on its right wing.
- *64th Army* [Chuikov] will destroy the enemy grouping on the left bank of the Chir River and prevent his forces from crossing to the river's right bank. To do so it is necessary to withdraw 212th Rifle Division and 137th Tank Brigade from the Surovikino and Eritskii line and deploy them along the left bank of the Chir River; it must move 66th Naval Rifle Brigade and the army's three student regiments to the Rychkovskii region and employ them as an army reserve.[29]

Powerful and menacing on paper, Gordov's planned counterstroke involved three tank corps and two tank brigades, equipped with more than 450 tanks, two-thirds of which were new heavy or medium models, five rifle divisions, and all of 8th Air Army's aircraft, which were to fly in support of 1st Tank Army. However, the tank armies were suffering from serious teething problems, not surprising because, according to Stalin's order forming them, 1st Tank Army was to have been combat-ready by 28 July and the 4th Tank by 1 August; now both were to go into action on 26 July. Largely because of their hasty formation and premature commitment:

> The tank armies were not ready for coordinated combat operations. They had just completed forming and were not sufficiently combat cohesive. During the four days when they were bringing their tank corps up to strength, the armies' commanders and staffs did not have the opportunity to become familiar with their forces. Communications were inadequate in the tank corps and especially in the armies. Only six and one half hours, moreover during the nighttime, were allocated to prepare the counterstroke. In these circumstances it was not only impossible to organize coordination and command and control but also to assign the forces their combat missions on the ground.[30]

Complicating matters, Tanaschishin's 13th Tank Corps had already suffered heavy losses in its fight against 16th Panzer Division and probably fielded no more than 80 operational tanks. Moreover, the two full tank brigades of Rodin's 28th Tank Corps were already engaged and bloodied north of Kalach, and the logistical support for both armies was either weak or nonexistent.[31]

Beset by these problems, only Moskalenko's 1st Tank Army, most of which was already in action anyway, renewed its assaults at the designated time, 0300 hours on 27 July. The bulk of Kriuchenkin's 4th Tank Army failed to go into action until two days later, and even then it did so in fragmented and uncoordinated fashion. As of 1700 hours on 27 July, for example, Shamshin's 22nd Tank

Corps had lost many of its 180 tanks to mechanical problems, and only 17 had crossed the Don and reached their designated jumping-off positions.

Dutifully resuming its assaults before dawn on 27 July, 1st Tank Army attacked northward across the roughly 45-kilometer-wide front from the Manoilin region eastward to the Don River north of Kalach, with Tanaschishin's 13th Tank Corps, by now reinforced by its third tank brigade (163rd), on its left, 196th Rifle Division in its center, and Rodin's fully concentrated 28th Tank Corps on its right. As the *Luftwaffe* pounded Moskalenko's advancing troops unmercifully, conducting more than 1,000 aircraft sorties on 27 July, both Gordov and Vasilevsky, Stalin's personal observer from the *Stavka*, observed the action from his forward command post on the western bank of the Don northwest of Kalach.[32] Hindered by the incessant air attacks, Moskalenko's forces made only limited gains by nightfall:

> *62nd Army:* 192nd and 184th RDs and 40th TB withdrew to a line from the northern outskirts of Svechinikovskii (23 kilometers south of Kletskaia) to Polovoi Stan (22 kilometers southwest of Kletskaia) under heavy enemy pressure.
>
> 33rd GRD [guards rifle division], with a regiment of 181st RD and the Krasnodar [Infantry] School, continued to fight bitterly to restore the positions they lost in the Kalmykov region on the division's right wing. Fighting was going on for possession of Kalmykov (35 kilometers southwest of Kletskaia [and 10 kilometers west of Manoilin]).
>
> 181st and 147th RDs defended their previous positions.
>
> 196th RD reached the line Marker 146.0, Marker 111.6, and Skvorin [25 kilometers northwest of Kalach].
>
> *1st Tank Army*, as a result of offensive fighting, reached the [following] positions:
>
> 28th TC, with a regiment of 131st RD—Lipo-Lebedevskii—Lipo-Logovskii [20–23 kilometers north of Kalach and 5 kilometers east of Skvorin];
>
> 13th TC, with one TB, was situated in the Evseev region (40 kilometers south of Kletskaia), a second TB—east and southeast of Manoilin, and its third TB was approaching Hill 189.9 (46 kilometers southwest of Kletskaia).[33]

Tellingly, this General Staff summary made no mention of 4th Tank Army, since it had yet to cross the Don River. Nevertheless, by nightfall the tanks of Tanaschishin's 13th Tank Corps had driven a deep wedge through the forward defenses of Hube's 16th Panzer Division, forcing part of the division to dig in along the Dobraia River at Manoilin and another group to withdraw westward and join forward elements of 113th Infantry Division. To the east, 196th Rifle Division and Rodin's 28th Tank Corps forced 3rd and 60th Motorized Divisions to withdraw 5 kilometers to new defensive positions. Tanaschishin's assaults on 16th Panzer Division on 27 July were particularly ferocious and damaging:

Numerous Russian tanks were attacking the German positions in front of their bridgehead from the south and southwest and made it impossible for them to unite with 24th Panzer Division coming in from the south. They threw T-34s in continuous succession at Kalach on the Don toward the west and in the north at Kletskaia over the Don toward the south, cut off the return route and supply for the advancing XIV Panzer Corps, and tried to lock the corps in the "Don sack" and destroy it.

KG [*Kampfgruppe*] Reinisch, which was sent northward to Roshka to secure the flanks, was facing heavy fighting at the Russians' main blocking line between Kalmykov and Manoilin. In Manoilin alone the Russians were attacking on 27 July with an armada of 200 tanks. The Germans managed to destroy 77 combat vehicles in the heavy fighting. North of Kalmykov, KG Krumpen wanted to break through the Russians' blocking line at Bol'shoi Osinovskii. The Russians were attacking from the north with superior forces and managed to encircle it in a "*Kessel*" [cauldron]. All available forces were moving to this danger point. The division was split into three parts, all of which were involved in heavy fighting and were cut off from any supply. A truly testing time! KG Lattmann and Witzleben were supplied with fuel from the air by He-111 bombers. Encircled by 45 tanks, KG Witzleben had to retreat from Ostrov to Gureev and finally to Eruslanovskii. Driven away by German infantry divisions, now the enemy was even attacking from the west.[34]

With the strength of Wietersheim's XIV Panzer Corps reduced by attrition to about 100 tanks, the onslaught of well over 200 Soviet tanks made it virtually impossible for the panzers to continue their advance despite the devastating work of supporting Stuka dive-bombers. From the OKH, Halder described the problem: "The battle of Sixth Army west of the Don is still raging with unabated fury. Apparently the central part of the enemy line, heavily supported by armor, is holding while our wings are advancing."[35]

Nor did the situation improve on 28 July, when, according to the Red Army General Staff's daily report (see Map 30):

62nd Army, cooperating with the units of *1st Tank Army*, continued to fight bitterly with penetrating enemy tanks and motorized infantry.

13th TC, attacking along the Manoilin and Maiorovskii axis beginning on the morning of 28 July, linked up with 40th TB and units of 192nd and 184th RDs by 1500 hours. The corps was fighting on the approaches to the western outskirts of Verkhne-Buzinovka, Erik (40 kilometers south of Kletskaia), and Evseev, after advancing 15–18 kilometers. Enemy tanks and motorized infantry are in front of the corps.

28th TC and 131st and 196th RDs repulsed two counterattacks by the enemy on 28 July, knocking out and destroying up to 40 of his tanks.

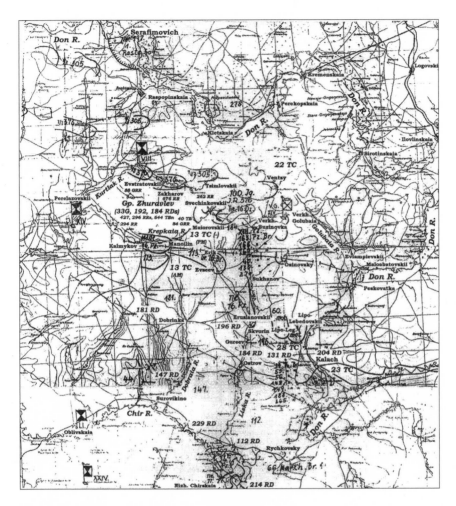

Map 30. The Sixth Army's situation, 27–28 July 1942

23rd TC crossed to the western bank of the Don River in the vicinity of Kalach-on-the-Don.

204th Rifle Division concentrated in the Kalach-on-the-Don region, with one regiment on the western bank of the Don. . . .

4th Tank Army continued crossing the Don River with its units. The units of the army were moving toward the Verkhne-Buzinovka region and were situated along the Khmelevskaia (52 kilometers southeast of Kletskaia)-Verkhne-Golubaia-Evlampievskii-Malonabatovskii (60 kilometers southeast of Kletskaia) line by the morning of 28 July.

The forward units of 22nd Tank Corps captured the Ventsy (15 kilometers northeast of Verkhne-Buzinovka)-Os'kinskii (13 kilometers east of Verkhne-Buzinovka) regions by 1500 hours on 28 July.

176th TB was on the march in the Vertiachii region.[36]

Once again, 16th Panzer Division felt the brunt of Moskalenko's and Tanaschishin's onslaught:

In the north, artillery fire began. Here KG Krumpen was fighting at Verkhne-Buzinovka. On 27 July the *kampfgruppe* that was isolated in Bol'shoi Osinovskii managed to free itself and, the next morning, moved southeast via Rybinskii and Zymkov in order to join KG Lattmann's troops in Sukhanov. At the bridge at the southwestern entrance of Verkhne-Buzinovka, it came to a standstill. A Russian regiment with 11 tanks managed to catch them by surprise, enter the village from the west, and, in the course of it, attacked 100th Light Division's 50th Infantry Regiment, which was holding the fort there and destroyed it. Now it was facing the approaching [Russian] combat group. They managed to fend off the initial attack. Krumpen ordered the formation of a defense. As the light was fading, the hoarse sound of the Russians' [tank] sirens could be heard again; the attack broke down under the combined fire. Around 2230 hours the Russians sneaked toward the firing positions of 5th Battery, 16th Artillery Regiment.[37]

As 62nd Army's daily report indicated, by nightfall on 28 July Tanaschishin's 13th Tank Corps, now being personally supervised by General Pushkin, Gordov's chief of armored forces, succeeded in propelling most of its remaining tanks and motorized riflemen far enough forward to link up with and rescue the encircled Group Zhuravlev. However, because Tanaschishin lacked air and artillery support, the cost was extreme: 13th Tank Corps lost all but 40 of its tanks by day's end on 27 July and, despite adding 40th Tank Brigade's tanks to its arsenal, even more tanks the following night.[38] Meanwhile, to the southeast, although its rate of advance slowed, Rodin's 28th Tank Corps pressed 3rd and 60th Motorized Divisions back another 2–3 kilometers northward from Kalach.

In desperation, Paulus reinforced VIII Army Corps with 376th Infantry Division and ordered the corps' forward divisions, 100th Jäger and 305th Infantry, to wheel southward toward Verkhne-Buzinovka, reinforce the beleaguered 16th Panzer Division, and block any attempt by Group Zhuravlev and 13th Tank Corps to withdraw eastward. However, this meant that VIII Army Corps had to leave merely a light screening force, reinforced by 16th Panzer Division's *Kampfgruppe* Strehlke, to defend against any Soviet attack southward out of their bridgehead at Kremenskaia and Sirotinskaia—the precise point where Shamshin's 22nd Tank Corps was supposed to be attacking.

The 16th Panzer Division experienced the brunt of this swirling battle between XIV Panzer Corps and 1st and 4th Tank Armies during the last few days of July:

> On the morning of 29 July, the Russians were feeling their way toward the *kampfgruppe's* flanks and began to attack incessantly. Radio signal: Division order—Rapidly assemble all units in the vicinity of Sukhanov! The following information came rushing in—24 enemy tanks are approaching Verkhne-Buzinovka from the east and northeast. An escape was now impossible. The *kampfgruppe* found itself under heavy tank fire. Although KG Reinisch managed to get through as far as Sukhanov and Osinovskii, it was impossible to unite all of the division's parts.
>
> Heavy tank forces were facing each other on both sides of the front. They surrounded each other and were trying to encase each other. The size of the field of operations was 100 × 100 kilometers. There was no front. Like destroyer and cruiser forces at sea, the tanks were fighting on the sandy seas of the steppe, struggling for favorable gun positions, driving the opposition into the corner, holding the fort for hours on end or locations for days, breaking free, and turning around and chasing again after the enemy. And while the tanks were clawing at each other in the overgrown steppe, the air fleets were fighting in the cloud-free sky of the Don, fighting their opponents in the hiding holes of the *balkas,* blowing ammunition supplies into the air, and setting fuel supply columns on fire.
>
> In the case of 16th Panzer Division, the enemy seemed to be the winner. Never before had the position of the division been so critical. The linkup seemed impossible. On the evening before 30 July, 2nd Battalion, 64th Panzer Grenadier Regiment, under Captain Mund (later Batsche) dared to escape. The main *Rollbahn* [road] was reported to be clear of enemy. Suddenly Russian tanks were advancing out of gullies, firing at close range at the marching detachment, and blowing it up. Senior Lieutenant Kleinholz, a company commander in 16th Panzer Jäger Battalion, lost his life. Part of the convoy reassembled but was attacked by the Russians once again. The remainder managed to escape and join KG Lattmann in Sukhanov.
>
> Now Colonel Krumpen received an order to form a defensive line to the west and northwest and await the arrival of support.
>
> Even in the Sukhanov area, the situation was becoming serious. In the south Eruslanovskii had been vacated. On 30 July the enemy was attacking 16th Motorcycle Battalion under Captain Dörnemann. In the north Russian tanks were positioned at Nizhne-Buzinovka. Panzer Detachment von Strachwitz and 2nd Company, 16th Panzer Grenadier Battalion, managed to destroy 15 tanks, put 28 guns out of action, and take 600 prisoners in the course of a counterattack.
>
> Further east of Sukhanov, parts of KG Reinisch managed to form a hedgehog [defense] near Osinovskii. The enemy was attacking continuously

between Hills 187.7 and 225.1. On the eastern edge of the hedgehog, Lieutenant Grimberg, of 1st Company, 16th Pioneer Battalion, managed to advance with his entire battalion. Seven Russian tanks fell victim to the Flak attack.

On 1 August, when the engineers of independent KG Strehlke, which had erected a security positions facing east, managed to detect Russian columns in front of their positions, the Panzer Pioneer Squadron under Lieutenant Günter Schmitz succeeded in advancing against the surprised enemy and forced them to flee. Two Pak guns and four vehicles were destroyed.

KG Krumpen had successfully accomplished its mission the day before. Part of 60th Infantry Division (mot) had set off from the southwest to attack Verkhne-Buzinovka; however, they had to stay put 2 km outside of the town since they had been unable to cross the river. The enemy was distracted. Forty of their own tanks had gone under cover. Now KG Krumpen started to advance toward the town. The 9th Company, 2nd Panzer Regiment, under Senior Lieutenant Blücher, was facing a heavy tank and infantry defense. The enemy was using low-flying aircraft. Verkhne-Buzinovka was captured in the evening; although the enemy was not yet giving up. The Siberians, brought in from the Far East, had to be pried out of their gun holes one by one in close combat. Their toughness was nevertheless not able anymore to forestall the linkup of 16th Panzer Division. The enemy had to retreat. Protected by rearguards made up of tanks, the three-division-strong column withdrew toward the northeast and across the Don.[39]

Nor did Paulus receive any good news from his southern pincer by day's end on 28 July. Although XXIV Panzer and LI Army Corps managed to expand their bridgehead across the lower Chir River to a depth of about 3 kilometers, they were not able to overcome the fierce resistance by Chuikov's 64th Army and advance northward to Kalach. In addition, unknown to Paulus, Stalingrad Front was moving Khazin's 23rd Tank Corps from its reserve into forward assembly areas near Kalach. If this tank corps, together with Shamshin's 22nd Tank Corps, with a combined force of well more than 200 tanks, could move quickly enough, Paulus's northern pincer indeed faced a potential disaster. However, given the previous performance of Soviet tank forces, this remained a large and problematic what-if. From the OKH, Halder put a happier, though far less accurate, face on the situation: "Due to a lack of fuel and ammunition, Sixth Army was unable to attack," adding wishfully, "After suffering a defeat in his violent attacks (nine new armored brigades), the enemy appears to be retreating behind the Don."[40]

Despite Paulus's discomfiture, neither the *Stavka* nor Gordov was satisfied with the results of their supposedly coordinated counterstroke:

In spite of the huge force of tanks participating in the counterstroke, in essence, a sharp improvement in the situation in 62nd Army's sector did not occur on 27

July. First of all, mistakes were permitted in the organization of the counter-stroke. The extremely high level of enemy air activity created major problems for the forces' combat operations. The forces were insufficiently organized and controlled. Enemy aircraft continuously disrupted wire communications between the formations and their headquarters, and the headquarters employed their radios unskillfully. As a result, even within the formations, there was no sound communications. Fearing the enemy would intercept their messages, often commanders and their staffs did not use their radios at all to the detriment of command and control of forces during the battle.[41]

Although Kolpakchi's 62nd Army and more than half of Moskalenko's 1st Tank Army successfully fended off Paulus's northern pincer and held firm to their bridgehead on the western bank of the Don River through the end of July, Group Zhuravlev and the remnants of Tanaschishin's 13th Tank Corps continued their unequal struggle against encirclement in the region between Verkhne-Buzi-novka and Manoilin (see Map 31). Hemmed in between elements of VIII Army Corps' 100th Jäger and 305th Infantry Divisions attacking from the north and east and 113th Infantry and 16th Panzer Divisions from the west and south, Zhu-ravlev had no choice but to order his forces to break out to the east. Burdened by more than 500 wounded Red Army soldiers and running out of both fuel and ammunition, Zhuravlev on 29 July ordered his tattered group to attack north-eastward through Verkhne-Buzinovka to link up with Shamshin's 22nd Tank Corps, supposedly already advancing to rescue the encircled force.

With the remnants of Tanaschishin's tanks in his van, Zhuravlev's forces fought a two-day running battle with elements of 100th Jäger, 16th Panzer, and 113th Infantry Divisions before they finally reached 4th Tank Army's lines near Os'kin-skii and Verkhne-Golubaia late on 31 July. By this time, Zhuravlev's force had shrunken to a mere 5,000 men, with 66 tanks and two artillery regiments.[42] After the Red Army General Staff noted "13th TC captured Verkhne-Buzinovka at 1400 hours on 29 July" in its daily summary for 29 July (yet failing to mention the fate of Zhuravlev's force on 30 July), on 31 July the daily summary cryptically reported, "192nd and 184th RDs withdrew to the Golubaia, Verkhne-Golubaia regions, where they are putting themselves in order."[43]

Partially explaining why a portion of Group Zhuravlev was able to escape, the OKW's operational summary for 30 July noted, "North of that region [northwest of Kalach], about 40 Russian tanks penetrated from the west and destroyed XIV Panzer Corps CP [command post]. Organized efforts are being made to destroy this enemy force."[44] The perspective of 16th Panzer Division provides an even more vivid portrayal of this desperate but confused struggle:

The Russians attacked with 40 tanks on the morning of 31 July. Everywhere the attack came to a halt, and 8 tanks were destroyed. At 0725 hours, armored Henschel fighters and Ju-88's struck toward Maiorovskii and Eruslanovskii.

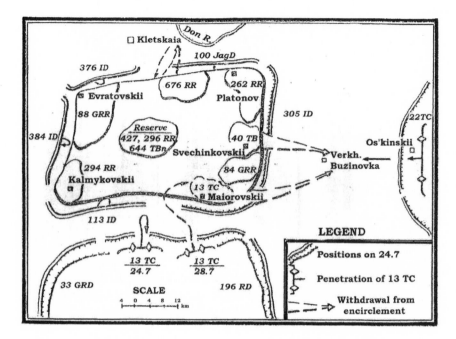

Map 31. The encirclement and breakout of Group Zhuravlev, 24–31 July 1942

The enemy suffered losses and was destroyed. A Focke-Wulf close-reconnais-sance plane was throwing boxes of chocolates with the writing "Collected for you by your close-reconnaissance companions," over their own front lines. The 16th Panzer Division was able to witness the destruction of seven Russian bombers that day.

The enemy attempted a renewed advance about midday. Panzer Company Mueller managed to destroy another 8 tanks. In cold-blooded fashion, the motorcyclists' gunners let the T-34s roll over them in their ditches and man-aged to fend off an infantry attack. Stukas threw themselves at Maiorovskii. A hail of grenades and artillery accompanied the rumble of the flights of heavy bombers. The enemy was retreating everywhere. When his tank concentration at Skvorin was struck by a German Stuka attack in the evening, the enemy lost any will to resume his attacks.[45]

The next day the Germans reported destroying 66 Soviet tanks in this region and capturing 2,000 enemy prisoners.[46] Describing the tenuous situation that Paulus's northern pincer faced, Franz Halder, in a more pessimistic tone, recorded, "A wild battle is raging in Sixth Army sector inside the Don bend west of Stalingrad; we do not have yet an accurate picture of its development. Sixth Army's striking power is paralyzed by ammunition and fuel supply difficulties."[47]

Hitler meeting with Army Group South's staff

German tanks advancing into the Great Bend of the Don, July 1942

German motorcycle troops in the Great Bend of the Don, July 1942

German troops overlooking the Don River

Red Army 76mm field gun in its firing position in the Great Bend of the Don, July 1942

Red Army troops defending the Great Bend of the Don, July 1942

The failure of most of Zhuravlev's group to escape was a direct result of the ineffectiveness of Kriuchenkin's 4th Tank Army and, in particular, of Shamshin's 22nd Tank Corps. With an initial strength of 180 tanks, Shamshin's corps, if properly employed, should have played a decisive role in the defeat of Paulus's northern pincer. However, when the corps finally went into action on 29 July, its 182nd and 173rd Tank Brigades managed to employ only 96 operational tanks because their remaining 36 tanks had already broken down. In addition, Shamshin retained 176th Tank Brigade, with 29 operational tanks, in his reserve and 133rd Heavy Tank Brigade, with its formidable force of KV tanks and the reinforcing 22nd Motorized Rifle Brigade, in the forests west of Trekhostrovskaia on the Don, on his extreme right wing.[48]

Shamshin committed his tanks into action without conducting a proper reconnaissance and without infantry support. As a result, the first two attempts by 182nd and 173rd Tank Brigades to capture Ventsy and nearby Mukovninskii (6 kilometers northeast of Verkhne-Buzinovka) from 100th Jäger and 113th Infantry Division and a supporting *kampfgruppe* from 16th Panzer Division failed miserably and cost the two brigades 13 destroyed tanks (11 T-34s and 2 T-70s). Resuming their assaults on 30 July, this time with 176th Tank Brigade attacking toward Osinovskii on the corps' left wing but with 133rd Tank and 22nd Motorized Rifle Brigades both still motionless on the Don's eastern bank, the three tank brigades lost another 41 tanks (25 T-34s, 11 T-70s, and 5 T-60s) and the commander of 176th Tank Brigade. During this fighting, the remnants of Tanaschishin's 13th Tank Corps finally linked up with Shamshin's dwindling forces, with 13th Tank Corps' remaining 66 tanks forming a new 169th Tank Brigade in 22nd Tank Corps.[49] Thereafter, Shamshin's tank corps, together with 184th and 192nd Rifle Divisions, continued daily attacks against VIII Army Corps' defenses south of the Kremenskaia and Sirotinskaia bridgehead but with distinctly diminishing effect.

As the heavy fighting continued to pound Paulus's northern pincer, intense fighting also took place along the Chir and Don River fronts to the south, where Chuikov's 64th Army was parrying Paulus's southern pincer. By 28 July, seizing and expanding a bridgehead across the Chir at Nizhne-Chirskaia, XXIV Panzer Corps' 24th Panzer Division and LI Army Corps' 297th and 71st Infantry Divisions now posed twin threats: first to the adjoining flanks of 62nd and 64th Armies; and second to Stalingrad itself, because the bridgehead and associated railroad line were situated on the most direct route to the city. In reaction to these threats, at 1645 hours on 28 July, the *Stavka* gave the following order to Stalingrad Front:

> While continuing operations to destroy the enemy in the Verkhne-Buzinovka region completely, the *front*'s main mission over the next few days is, at all cost, to defeat the enemy who have reached the western bank of the Don River south of Nizhne-Chirskaia by no later than 30 July by means of active

operations by the forces of 64th Army and the employment of 204th and 321st Rifle Divisions and 23rd Tank Corps, which have reached the Kalach region, and restore fully the defenses here along the Stalingrad line, while subsequently driving the enemy back across the Tsimla River.[50]

The same order required Gordov to strengthen the southwestern sector of Stalingrad's defenses and instructed him how best to employ nine fresh rifle divisions it had sent to his reserve. Earlier the same day, the *Stavka* had already taken measures to protect Stalingrad Front's left flank and also, by extension, the southwestern axis of advance into Stalingrad city by combining Southern Front and North Caucasus Front into a single entity—a new North Caucasus Front commanded by Budenny, with Malinovsky and Cherevichenko as his deputies.[51] With its headquarters in Armavir, Budenny's expanded *front* was not only to halt the Germans' advance from the Rostov region southward from the Don River but also to drive German forces from Bataisk and back across the Don.[52]

Anticipating the *Stavka's* order, Gordov had already ordered 204th and 321st Rifle Divisions from his own reserve, 1st Tank Army's 163rd Tank Brigade and, later, its full 23rd Tank Corps and 204th Rifle Division, 62nd Army's 229th and 214th Rifle Divisions, and the *front's* 8th Air Army to conduct such a counterattack.[53] Once again, however, the planned assault faltered with very little to show for the effort, largely because not enough time was available to coordinate and control it properly. Amid this intense but confused struggle, Gordov on 30 July replaced Chuikov as commander of 64th Army with 46-year-old Lieutenant General M. S. Shumilov and appointed Chuikov as his deputy. Mikhail Stepanovich Shumilov was a combat-experienced general who had commanded a rifle corps during the invasion of eastern Poland in September 1939 and the Finnish War in 1939–1940 and Northwestern Front's 8th Army during Operation Barbarossa. He later served as deputy commander of 55th Army during the battle for Leningrad in fall 1941 and 21st Army in the May 1942 battle for Khar'kov.[54]

Thus, by late on 30 July, to the *Stavka's* chagrin, Stalingrad Front's planned counterstrokes with its 1st and 4th Tank Armies had been aborted with heavy losses. The intense fighting throughout the last eight days of July cost 62nd and 64th Armies and 1st and 4th Tank Armies well more than half of their 1,239 tanks, the majority due to mechanical breakdown. XIV Panzer Corps alone reported destroying 482 Soviet tanks (with Sixth Army as a whole reporting more than 600).[55] The fate of 1st and 4th Panzer Armies' four tank corps underscored this extreme loss. For example, Tanaschishin's 13th Tank Corps lost 86 of its 152 tanks and Rodin's 28th Tank Corps well more than two-thirds of its 178 tanks. Although they continued to fight during the first week of August, Shamshin's 22nd Tank Corps saw about 80 percent of its 180 tanks put out of action by 6 August, and Khazin's 23rd Tank Corps squandered more than two-thirds of its 178 tanks during the same period. Also reflecting the accuracy of German claims, Kolpakchi's 62nd Army lost most of the 320 tanks assigned to its two tank brigades and six separate tank battalions during late July and the remainder in early August.

Stalin himself acknowledged this appalling toll by citing 1st and 4th Tank Armies' disastrous losses as evidence of either incompetence or outright sabotage on the part of the Red Army's commanders and soldiers:

> Our tank units and formations often suffer greater losses through mechanical breakdowns than they do in battle. For example, in the Stalingrad Front, when we had a significant superiority in tanks, artillery, and aircraft over the enemy, during six days of battle, twelve tank brigades lost 326 out of 400 tanks, of which about 200 were lost to mechanical problems. Many of the tanks were abandoned on the battlefield. Similar instances can be observed in other *fronts*.
>
> Since such a high incidence of mechanical defects is implausible, the Supreme High Command sees in it covert sabotage and wrecking on the part of certain tank crews who try to exploit small mechanical problems to leave their tanks on the battlefield and avoid battle.[56]

Despite the staggering tank losses that Stalingrad Front suffered during its defense of the Great Bend of the Don, it still remained a dangerous fighting force on 1 August. The *front* retained roughly 500 tanks in its weapons inventory—still more than double the number of tanks in Paulus's two panzer corps—even while Soviet industry was sending a steady flow of new tanks to the area. For example, by 8 August, although decimated in the July counterstroke, Tanaschishin's 13th Tank Corps, now made up of new tank brigades, fielded 136 tanks (120 T-34s and 16 T-70s), and 133rd Tank Brigade had 40 KV tanks.[57]

Thus, operating under the most arduous circumstances, with their forces often thoroughly intermixed, Sixth Army's VIII Army and XIV Panzer Corps had indeed broken the back of 1st and 4th Tank Armies' counterstroke. While fending off incessant assaults by forces far superior in numbers to their own, and despite many problems, they also managed to erect more resilient and continuous defense lines to confine 4th Tank Army and its supporting rifle forces in their bridgehead south of Kremenskaia and Sirotinskaia on the Don and to restrict Kolpakchi's 62nd and Moskalenko's 1st Tank Armies to their bridgehead on the western bank of the Don.[58] However, Paulus's northern pincer paid a high price for these modest successes. In addition to losing more than half of their 150 operational tanks, albeit many only temporarily, XIV Panzer Corps' three armor divisions failed to reach Kalach from the north.[59] Underscoring Paulus's frustration, by the time Gordov's counterstroke faltered on 30 July, Sixth Army's southern pincer, XXIV Panzer and LI Army Corps, was still confined to a small bridgehead over the Chir near Nizhne-Chirskaia and had also failed to reach Kalach from the south.

By month's end Paulus's attempt to encircle all Soviet forces west of the Don

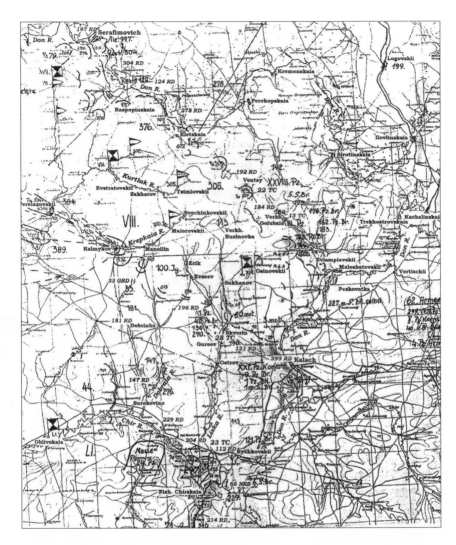

Map 32. The Sixth Army's situation, 31 July 1942

had failed; with that, Hitler's ambitious hopes to seize Stalingrad by a coup de main from the march were also dashed (see Map 32). In effect, although at tremendous cost, Gordov's four armies defending along and west of the Don had fought Paulus's spearheads to a standstill. Moreover, the stalemate that had ensued was likely to persist unless Paulus's army received significant reinforcements.

Whether or not Hitler appreciated this situation, others in the OKW and OKH did. For example, in a situation conference at the OKW on 28 July, operations chief Jodl announced, "pompously," according to Halder, "The fate of the Caucasus will be decided at Stalingrad, and, in view of the importance of the battle, it would be necessary to divert forces from AGp.A to AGp.B."[60] Describing Jodl's remarks as a "dressed-up version of my own proposal," whose significance the "illustrious company of the OKW" were "finally able to grasp," Halder, too, strongly supported the idea of diverting forces to assist a beleaguered Paulus.[61] Hitler's decision to act on this proposal within a matter of days was mute acknowledgement that the Führer had seriously underestimated the Red Army's strength along the Stalingrad axis.

At least in part, Halder and others in the OKW and OKH had a more accurate appreciation of strategic realities than did Hitler. This is because they understood that the Red Army, in addition to its determined resistance along the Stalingrad axis, was operating far more aggressively than normal in many other sectors of the front. In this sense, they understood Stalin better than they did their own Führer—for this was Stalin's strategic intent.

THE OREL AND VORONEZH AXES, 20–26 JULY

As early as the first week of July 1942, Stalin was determined to halt and then defeat the German advance east across southern Russia by employing the same strategic formula he had applied against Hitler's forces conducting Operation Barbarossa the summer before. Specifically, Stalin decided to rely on resolute defensive operations, if necessary including timely local withdrawals, to slow or halt the Germans. At the same time, he insisted on multiple counterattacks and counterstrokes in virtually every front sector to produce maximum attrition among Axis forces and to prevent them from reinforcing the vital Stalingrad axis and, at the proper time and place, on a massive counteroffensive to defeat Hitler's thrust and drive his forces back to their starting positions. Because the Red Army was in a far better state in 1942 compared to 1941, he anticipated accomplishing this task in a far briefer period than the previous year.

While Bock's and List's Army Groups B and A were pummeling Southwestern and Southern Fronts' armies in the intense heat of July, to the north the *Stavka* orchestrated a series of counterstrokes to delay or at least weaken the German advance toward Stalingrad. Hastily planned and conducted, the first of these counterstrokes was designed to support the offensive by Briansk Front's 5th Tank and 40th Armies at and west of Voronezh. In its 2 July directive, the *Stavka* ordered Zhukov's Western Front to attack the forward defenses of Army Group Center's Second Panzer Army, 85–120 kilometers north and northeast of Orel, and "encircle and destroy the enemy's Bolkhov grouping."[62]

Zhukov's plan called for Lieutenant General K. K. Rokossovsky's 16th Army and Lieutenant General P. A. Belov's 61st Army, supported by the full-strength

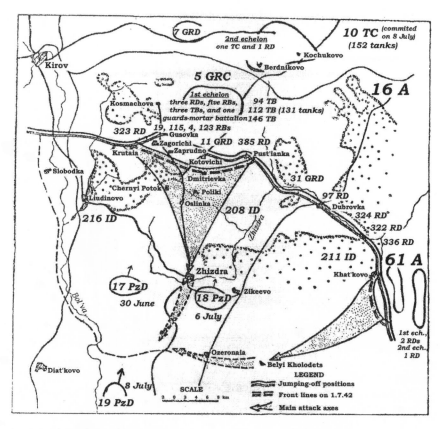

Map 33. The 16th Army's operations along the Zhizdra River, 6–14 July 1942

10th and 3rd Tank Corps, commanded by Major Generals V. G. Burkov and D. K. Mostovenko, respectively, to begin their assault at dawn on 5 July, the 16th Army along the Zhizdra River north of Orel and the 61st Army due north of Bolkhov (see Maps 33 and 34). The attacking forces, with a total of almost 600 tanks, significantly outgunned the opposing German forces, which included four German infantry divisions and about 100 tanks and assault guns.[63] However, during this fight the Germans were able to reinforce their defenses with elements of 17th and 18th Panzer Divisions on 7 July and 19th Panzer Division on 8 July, increasing their armored strength by an additional 200 tanks.

Konstantin Konstantinovich Rokossovsky, who played a minor role as commander of an army located in the wings of the main stage to the south, would soon make a reappearance as commander of Voronezh Front and, in September, as commander of Don Front, a successor to the original Stalingrad Front, which would support 62nd Army's desperate defense of Stalingrad. Rokossovsky had

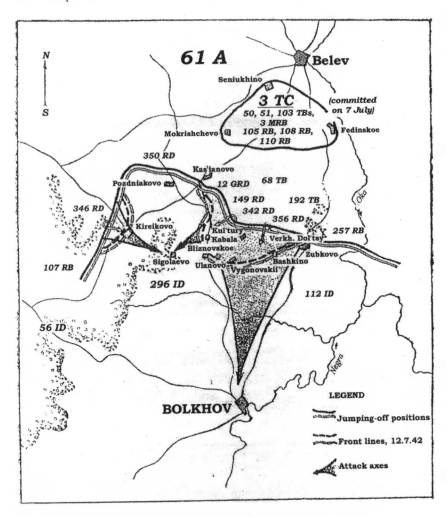

Map 34. The 61st Army's operations along the Bolkhov axis, 5–12 July 1942

previously commanded Southwestern Front's 9th Mechanized Corps in its dramatic but failed counterstroke against First Panzer Army in the Dubno region in late June 1941 and Group Iartsevo in its tenacious defense against Army Group Center east of Smolensk in August. He was assigned command of 16th Army in July 1941 at age 45 and led the army during its successful defense and counterstroke at Moscow in November and December 1941. Known as a determined and skilled fighter, Rokossovsky used his army to spearhead efforts by Zhukov's Western Front to divert German forces from Operation Blau in summer 1942 and would soon begin to contribute significantly to victory in the operation by receiving command of Briansk Front in July 1942.[64]

The commander of 61st Army, Pavel Alekseevich Belov, was the Red Army's most famous cavalry general after Budenny. Belov had led the 2nd (later 1st Guards) Cavalry Corps during the summer and fall campaign of 1942, earning lasting renown for the significant role his corps played in defeating Guderian's Second Panzer Army during the Red Army's Moscow counterstroke in December 1941 and for the raid his corps conducted deep into German Army Group Center's rear during the ensuing winter campaign. For these exploits, the *Stavka* appointed Belov, then 45 years old, to command 61st Army in June 1942.[65] And the heads of 16th Army's 10th Tank Corps and 61st Army's 3rd Tank Corps were no less experienced. The former, Vasilii Gerasimovich Burkov, had led a tank division during Operation Barbarossa, and the latter, Dmitri Karpovich Mostovenko, had commanded Western Front's 11th Mechanized Corps during the struggle in the Grodno region of Belorussia in late June and July 1941 and survived the ensuing Minsk encirclement to head a department within the General Staff throughout the remainder of 1941 and early 1942.[66]

Attacking as Zhukov ordered, Rokossovsky's and Belov's armies almost broke through the German infantry divisions' defenses. Just as at Voronezh, however, the Red Army's attacking forces displayed their inexperience, with coordination problems arising between Western Front headquarters and its subordinate elements. Once again, despite a superiority in armor of better than three-to-one over the Germans, the two Soviet tank corps encountered many of the same teething problems as their counterparts to the south. Unable to coordinate tanks and supporting infantry, artillery, and engineers effectively, both suffered heavy losses, 10th Tank Corps nearly all of its 152 tanks and 3rd Tank Corps a significant proportion of its armor. To the *Stavka's* consternation, Zhukov's costly failure had no visible effect on the German advance in the south.[67]

Undeterred by its failed counterstrokes in early July, throughout the remainder of the month the *Stavka* repeatedly ordered Briansk and Voronezh Fronts to continue hammering the northern flank of the German offensive. Such attacks were based on a mistaken belief that Axis forces in the Voronezh region were as vulnerable in late July as when they first reached the area two weeks before. In fact, by mid-July General Salmuth's German Second Army had organized a conventional infantry defense of great strength, backed by a small number of counterattack reserve forces. The core of this reserve was 9th Panzer Division, whose 94 tanks and panzer grenadiers were concentrated in assembly areas in the Vishne Veduga and Turovo regions, 25–30 kilometers west of Voronezh.[68] Along the Don River south of Voronezh, Hungarian Second Army presented a more likely avenue for penetration, but for months the centralized nature of Soviet planning failed to exploit this weakness.

The initial fighting for Voronezh, coupled with the winding course of the Don River, had produced a convoluted front line that invited each side to pinch off

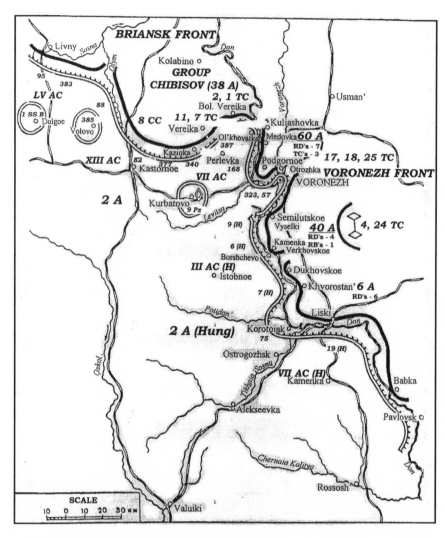

Map 35. The situation in the Voronezh region, 20 July 1942

salients defended by the other (see Map 35). Just west of Voronezh, Briansk Front's newly formed 60th Army held a bulge around the town of Podgornoe on the western bank of the Don. This salient was, in turn, flanked by two reciprocal German bulges, the Zemliansk and Ol'khovatka salient, west of Podgornoe, which was defended by German VII Army Corps' 377th, 340th, and 387th Infantry Divisions and one regiment of 323rd Infantry Division, and Voronezh itself, which after the departure of XXXXVIII Panzer Corps' mobile divisions

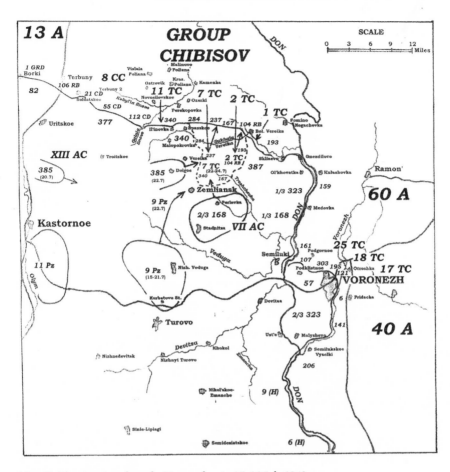

Map 36. The situation along the Voronezh axis, 15–26 July 1942

was defended by VII Corps' 168th and 57th Infantry Divisions, with the remainder of 323rd Infantry Division in reserve.

On 17 July, seeking to exploit this twisted front line, the *Stavka* ordered Briansk Front to punch southward west of Voronezh and Voronezh Front to attack westward through Voronezh to envelop, encircle, and destroy German forces in the Ol'khovatka-Zemliansk salient and the Voronezh region (see Map 36). Briansk Front's 38th Army was to attack southward from west of Ol'khovatka, capture Zemliansk and Nizhne-Veduga, cross the Veduga River, and then wheel eastward to attack from the rear German forces defending Voronezh. Simultaneously, the Voronezh Front's 60th and 40th Armies, commanded by Generals Antoniuk and M. M. Popov, were to attack German forces in Voronezh from the Podgornoe salient in the west and from the east to capture the city and link up with Briansk Front's forces west of the city. The attack would begin on 18 July and end on 21 July. As was his custom, Stalin assigned field commanders explicit, detailed instructions, specifying both the forces that were to conduct the attack and their daily objectives.[69]

Rokossovsky, the newly appointed commander of Briansk Front, assigned his deputy, General Chibisov, the task of personally controlling 38th Army's shock group for the offensive, an operational group named for its commander. This was a common practice at the time, and Chibisov was a reasonably efficient officer. Ultimately, Operational Group Chibisov included five rifle divisions (284th, 340th, 237th, 167th, and 193rd), a separate rifle brigade (104th), Liziukov's 2nd, Rotmistrov's 7th, and A. F. Popov's 11th Tank Corps, which had formerly composed 5th Tank Army, plus two separate tank brigades and supporting artillery.[70] Although the three tank corps had suffered heavy losses in the first half of July, replacements from the NKO's Auto-Armored Directorate increased the tank strength of the three corps to more than 100 tanks each by 17 July. To further increase the combat power of this attack, Rokossovsky allocated General Katukov's 1st Tank Corps, with almost 100 tanks, to serve as an armored reserve and possible exploitation force deployed behind the eastern flank of Chibisov's assault. With these reinforcements, Group Chibisov fielded as many as 500 tanks; however, many of his infantry formations were so newly formed and inexperienced they were virtually incapable of major offensive action.[71] Group Chibisov was opposed by German VII Army Corps' 340th and 387th Infantry Divisions, which, in addition to their own assault and antitank guns, were supported by slightly more than 90 tanks fielded by 9th Panzer Division, in reserve south of Zemliansk.[72]

While Chibisov was to launch Briansk Front's main attack from the north, General Vatutin's neighboring Voronezh Front was to conduct two supporting attacks from the east. Here, Antoniuk's 60th Army, with seven rifle divisions supported by Korchagin's 17th, Cherniakhovsky's 18th, and Pavlov's 25th Tank Corps, had the mission of breaking out of the Podgornoe salient and cutting the key road west of Voronezh. At the same time, Popov's 40th Army, with four rifle divisions supported by two tank brigades, was to penetrate German defenses south of Voronezh, seeking to link up with the other two forces and assist in the encirclement and destruction of all German forces in the Voronezh region.[73] Vatutin's two armies mustered a force of about 300 tanks, 166 of them in Pavlov's 25th Tank Corps. The 60th and 40th Armies faced German VII Army Corps' 168th Infantry Division northwest of Voronezh and 57th Infantry Division in and south of the city. Although the two German divisions fielded only antitank and a handful of assault guns, their defenses were anchored on the Voronezh River and urban terrain, and 9th Panzer Division also served as their reserve.

Inevitably, such an elaborate plan took more preparation time than expected. Yet on 21 July 1942 Briansk and Voronezh Fronts, with heavy air support, launched a coordinated offensive against German defenses west and east of

Voronezh. Attacking southward between the villages of Spasskoe and Malaia Vereika, 18 kilometers north of Zemliansk, Group Chibisov's 340th Rifle Division and A. F. Popov's 11th Tank Corps slammed against the defenses of the German 340th Infantry Division north of Spasskoe, but the assault faltered without appreciable gains. Farther east, 62nd and 87th Tank Brigades of Rotmistrov's 7th Tank Corps, supported by Batiuk's veteran 284th Rifle Division, fared somewhat better, pushing up to 4 kilometers deep along the boundary between German 340th and 387th Infantry Divisions. On Rotmistrov's left, the two lead tank brigades of 2nd Tank Corps, now commanded by the disgraced Liziukov, with 237th and 167th Rifle Divisions in their van, matched Rotmistrov's advance, thrusting up to 5 kilometers southward from Bol'shaia Vereika. In the process, they surrounded several battalions of the German 387th Infantry Division's 542nd Regiment in the village of Kalver'ia and pushed the remainder southward to Sukharevka.[74]

By day's end on 22 July, Rotmistrov's and Liziukov's lead brigades and supporting infantry thrust southward another 2 kilometers, reaching within 2 kilometers of the key road junction at Zemliansk. In the process, they surrounded 387th Infantry Division's entire 542nd Regiment. Although 11th Tank Corps, now commanded by General Lazarev, still remained stalled to the west, Rotmistrov's 7th and Liziukov's 2nd Tank Corps, with extensive air, artillery, and infantry support, had torn a gap 20 kilometers wide by 10 kilometers deep in the German VII Army Corps' defenses.[75]

Reacting quickly, Salmuth's Second Army moved decisively to hold the Voronezh salient while containing and halting Chibisov's penetration. First, beginning on the night of 21–22 July, Salmuth shifted two of 168th Infantry Division's regiments, which had previously been defending Voronezh's northwestern suburbs, to new assembly areas southeast of Zemliansk, from which they were to establish blocking positions south of Sukharevka to forestall any further Soviet advance and prepare to strike the nose of Chibisov's penetration. These regiments arrived just in time to slow and eventually halt the advance of 26th and 148th Tank Brigades of Liziukov's 2nd Tank Corps late on 22 July. Then, overnight on 22–23 July, Salmuth ordered Bässler's 9th Panzer Division to move into position southwest of Zemliansk, where, together with 385th Infantry Division (regrouped from the west), it was to conduct an assault against the western flank of Chibisov's penetration (see Map 37). Suspecting such a move, Chibisov, overnight on 22–23 July, reinforced Liziukov's tank corps with 193rd Rifle Division, to no avail. By this time, the designated German counterattack forces were converging quickly on their jumping-off positions north of Zemliansk.

Meanwhile, at Voronezh proper, attacking more than a day late on 22 July, Antoniuk's 60th Army launched heavy assaults against German defenses northwest of Voronezh city. Because this attack took place only hours after 57th Infantry Division had relieved 168th Infantry Division in its defenses south of Podgornoe, Antoniuk was able to push his 161st Rifle Division forward to the

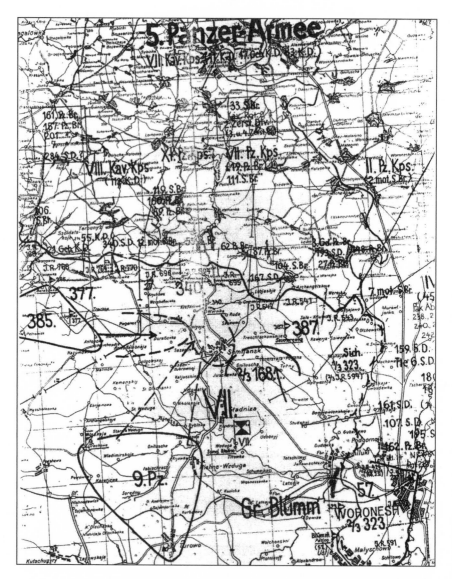

Map 37. The Second Army's situation, 0000 hours 23 July 1942

Don River opposite Semiluki (10 kilometers northwest of Voronezh) and his 107th Rifle Division and part of Pavlov's 25th Tank Corps across the Semiluki-Voronezh road, briefly cutting the main German communication route 8 kilometers west of the city. However, Antoniuk's assault soon faltered under withering antitank and artillery fire, which forced the Soviets back and away from the Voronezh-Semiluki road. Farther east, the remainder of Pavlov's tank corps, together with 60th Army's 303rd and 195th Rifle Divisions and the tank brigades of Cherniakhovsky's 18th Tank Corps, fought their way into Voronezh's north-western suburbs, and the army's 121st Rifle Division, supported by 17th Tank Corps, struck German defenses on the eastern side of the city.[76]

Voronezh's suburbs saw intense fighting for several days more. However, despite their best efforts, the attacking Soviet forces were unable to sustain the offensive. Although Vatutin's forces managed to retain a small wedge in German defenses east of the Don River at Semiluki, heavy German air strikes and coun-terattacks repulsed or halted any subsequent attacks.

With the situation in Voronezh stabilized, on 23 July Second Army completed assembling its forces for a counterattack planned to commence early the next day against Chibisov's penetration north of Zemliansk. Salmuth's plan called for converging assaults against the Soviet penetration by Bässler's 9th Panzer Divi-sion from the west, with 385th Infantry Division in support, and by 168th and 387th Infantry Divisions from the south and east.[77] Meanwhile, on 23 July Ger-man artillery pounded Soviet penetration forces, which by this time included 62nd and 87th Tank Brigades of Rotmistrov's 7th Tank Corps and elements of 340th, 284th, 193rd, 237th, and 167th Rifle Divisions, supported by Group Chibisov's 201st and 118th Tank Brigades. By now 2nd Tank Corps' 26th and 148th Tank Brigades were themselves half-encircled north of Sukharevka by the advancing 168th Infantry Division.

Overnight on 22–23 July, after receiving no news about the fate of 2nd Tank Corps' two lead brigades, Chibisov castigated Liziukov for committing his corps piecemeal and ordered him personally to determine the whereabouts of his brigades, support them with the remainder of his corps, and fulfill his mission at all cost. Already distraught over being relieved as commander of 5th Tank Army, Liziukov reacted decisively, and somewhat rashly. After ordering his sec-ond echelon 27th Tank and 2nd Motorized Rifle Brigades to attack southward to locate and link up with his isolated forward brigades, Liziukov, at 0900 hours on 23 July, accompanied by Regimental Commissar Assopov and a driver, left his headquarters at Bol'shaia Vereika in a single KV tank, determined to fulfill Chibisov's demands (see Map 38). Maneuvering his tank about 3 kilometers southwestward along the valley of the Sukhaia Vereika River and then another kilometer southward through the woods east of the village of Lebiazh'e, Liziu-kov's tank, now separated from his second-echelon brigades, came under Ger-man antitank fire near Hill 188.5. In a brief encounter the tank was destroyed and its occupants perished. Thereafter, the circumstances of his death remained a mystery for more than 60 years.[78]

With the Soviet defenses softened up and Chibisov's thrust at a standstill, Salmuth unleashed his counterattack at dawn on 24 July (see Map 39). By night-fall, 9th Panzer Division's tanks had carved a 10-kilometer-deep corridor north-ward, splitting 11th and 7th Tank Corps and threatening to cut the Soviet lines of

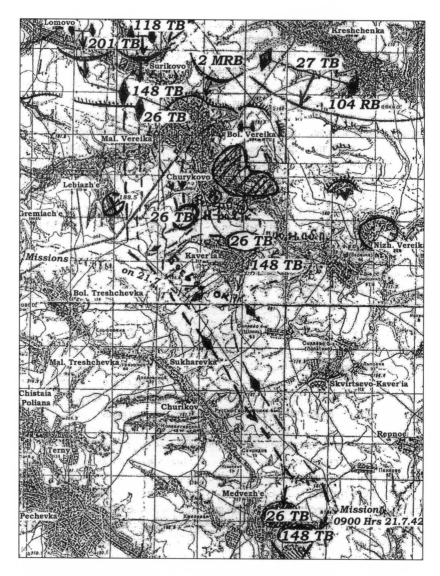

Map 38. The 2nd Tank Corps' situation, 23 July 1942

communication into the penetration from the north. The next day, 9th Panzer and 385th Infantry Divisions wheeled sharply eastward, advancing 5 kilometers and isolating part of 7th Tank Corps and most of 2nd Tank Corps and their supporting 237th, 193rd, and 167th Rifle Divisions in an elongated pocket northeast of Zemliansk (see Map 40).[79] Salmuth's forces closed their trap around this pocket on 26 July, catching half of Rotmistrov's 7th Tank Corps, all of Liziukov's

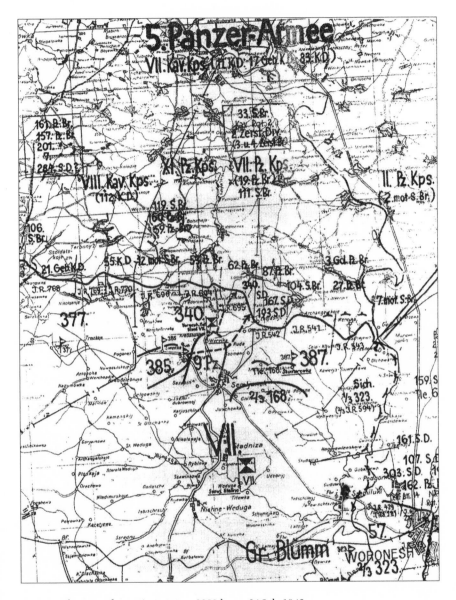

Map 39. The Second Army's situation, 0000 hours 24 July 1942

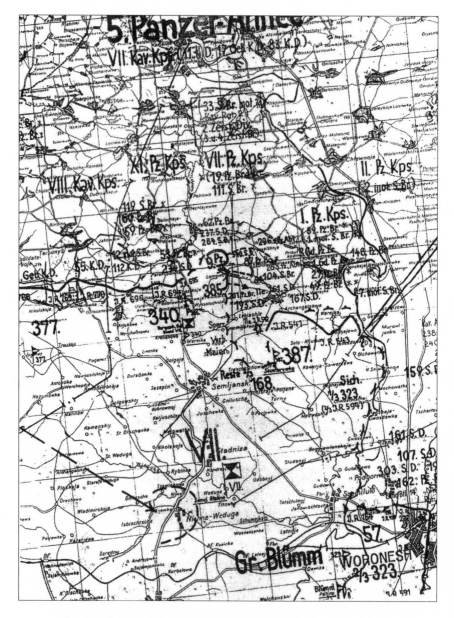

Map 40. The Second Army's situation, 0000 hours 25 July 1942

2nd Tank Corps, and their supporting rifle forces in a partial encirclement west and southwest of Bol'shaia Vereika. At this juncture, Chibisov threw Katukov's relatively fresh 1st Tank Corps into the struggle to rescue the beleaguered units.

Supported by its accompanying infantry, 9th Panzer Division mopped up most of the surrounded Soviet units by 27 July and restored German Second Army's original front northwest of Voronezh (see Map 41). Although Chibisov's counterstroke was undoubtedly better organized and more effective than previous efforts, it ultimately failed in its primary task of cutting off Voronezh and forcing the Germans to reallocate forces away from their main offensive thrusts to the south. Nevertheless, Rokossovsky's and Vatutin's forces hammered the German shoulder and flank through the remaining summer. Although these efforts seemed to have little effect on either Hitler or the subsequent course of Operation Blau, the constant pressure on Salmuth's German Second Army tied down its forces at and west of Voronezh at a time when Paulus's Sixth Army was starved for forces along the Don River front and along the approaches to Stalingrad. From the OKH's perspective, the constant threat at Voronezh forced it to retain 9th Panzer Division in the Voronezh region until 10 August and, when it departed for Army Group Center, move 27th Panzer Division into the region by 1 September and 11th Panzer Division back to the region by mid-September.[80] While denying Blau's main thrust on Stalingrad the strength of one or two panzer divisions, the Soviet threat at Voronezh ultimately also forced Hitler to reach his fateful decision to commit Italian and Romanian armies to defend the overextended flanks of Paulus's Sixth Army along the Don River northwest of Stalingrad and the Volga River south of Stalin's namesake city.

NOT A STEP BACK!

As the drama unfolded across southern Russia and the crises he faced multiplied day after day, Stalin became even more insistent on the need for the Red Army to stand and fight—if necessary to the death. Frustrated by repeated collapses of Soviet forces in the region, the dictator decided to reemphasize the draconian defensive measures he had employed the previous year. The result was an order that proved critical to the continued Soviet defense, dated 28 July 1942, drafted by Vasilevsky, and extensively rewritten by Stalin. Although its official title was People's Commissariat of Defense Order No. 227, the decree became infamous by its title—*Ni Shagu Nazad!* or "Not a Step Back!"

Citing the Soviet Union's catastrophic economic and manpower losses of the previous year against the backdrop of an apparent breakdown in military discipline, Stalin explained why further retreat had become impossible, stating, "The enemy is throwing new forces forward to the front and, despite increasing losses, is thrusting forward, bursting into the depths of the Soviet Union, capturing new regions, devastating and smashing our cities and villages, and raping, robbing,

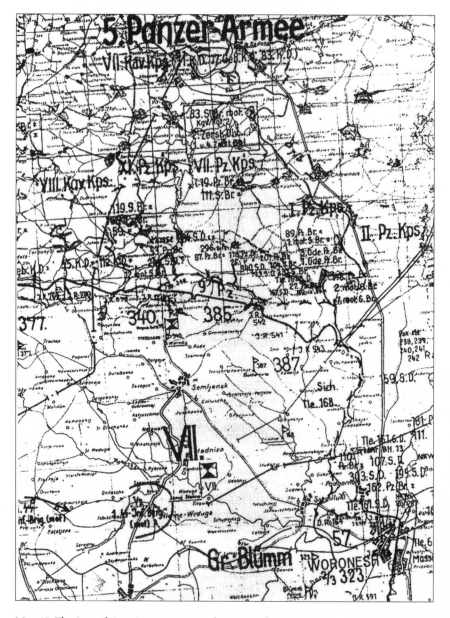

Map 41. The Second Army's situation, 0000 hours 27 July 1942

and murdering our population." [81] Convinced that "some foolish people at the front are consoling themselves with discussions that we can retreat farther to the east since we have great territories, much land, and a large population, and that we will always have an abundance of bread [grain]," Stalin accused these soldiers of wishing "to justify their shameful behavior at the front," concluding that "such talk is spurious and false through and through, and it is advantageous only for our enemy." [82]

Therefore, he declared, "We must radically nip in the bud the talk that we have an opportunity to retreat without end and that our great territory, our great and rich country, and our large population and bread will always be in abundance," because "such talk is false and harmful, and it weakens us and strengthens the enemy because, if the retreat does not cease, we will be left without bread, without oil, without metal, without raw materials, without mills and factories, and without railroads." Concluding the time had come "to end the retreat," Stalin announced the slogan: "Not a step back!" He declared forcefully, "We must stubbornly defend every position and every meter of Soviet territory to the last drop of our blood and cling to every shred of Soviet land and fight for it to the utmost." [83]

Striking at the very heart of the problem, Stalin asked "What are we short of?" and answered his own question rhetorically: "We are short of order and discipline in our companies, battalions, regiments, and divisions, in our tank units, and in our aviation squadrons. This is now our main shortcoming. We must institute the strictest of order and iron discipline in our army if we wish to save the situation and defend our Homeland." Therefore, he continued, because "we can no longer tolerate commanders, commissars, and political workers whose units and formations willfully abandon their positions," and because "we can no longer tolerate it when commanders, commissars, and political workers permit a few panic-mongers to determine the situation on the field of battle so that they entice other soldiers to retreat and open up the front to the enemy," these "panic-mongers and cowards must be exterminated on the spot." [84]

Proclaiming that "company, battalion, regimental, and division commanders, and associated commissars and political workers, who retreat from their combat positions without orders from higher commands must be treated as 'enemies of the Homeland,'" Stalin demanded that all commanders and commissars implement a series of stringent measures designed to restore "iron discipline" within the Red Army's ranks "to defend our land, to save the Motherland, and to exterminate and conquer the hated enemy." [85]

Specifically, Stalin ordered all *front*, army, corps, and division commanders to "unconditionally liquidate the mood of retreat in the forces and halt the propaganda that we must and can supposedly retreat farther to the east and that such a retreat will supposedly not be harmful," and "relieve from their posts army [corps, division, regiment, and battalion] commanders and their commissars who permit unauthorized retreats by their forces from occupied positions without an order from [their senior commanders] and send them to the *Stavka* [or to the *fronts*] for trial by military court."[86]

In addition, Stalin ordered the creation of new generations of penal battalions and so-called blocking detachments within each of the Red Army's operating *fronts* and armies. Criminal soldiers relegated to penal battalions were "to redeem themselves with their blood for their crimes against the Homeland," and the blocking detachments were "to shoot panic-mongers and cowards on the spot in the event of panic and unauthorized retreat" (see below). Specifically, depending on the situation, Stalin ordered *fronts* to form "one to three penal battalions (of 800 men each), assign all junior and senior commanders and corresponding political workers from all types of forces who have been guilty of violating discipline by their cowardice or unsteadiness to them, and place them in the most dangerous sectors of the front"; and armies to form "from 5 to 10 penal companies (of from 150–200 men each), assign common soldiers and noncommissioned officers who have been guilty of violating discipline by cowardice and unsteadiness to them, and place them in dangerous army sectors."[87]

Carrying out Stalin's decree with customary ruthlessness, Zhukov reportedly assigned tanks to reinforce the blocking detachments' grisly work in some armies. A. S. Shcherbakov, a senior official of the Communist Party, had replaced the dreaded Lev Mekhlis as head of the army's Main Political Administration, but informers and NKVD security troops continued to enforce loyalty and punish failure on the battlefield. Anyone suspected of cowardice was assigned to a penal unit, which in its turn received a series of suicidal combat missions. Even inside the *Stavka* any appearance of defeatism was dealt with harshly. For example, when the acting chief of operations, Major General Piotr Georgievich Tikhomirov, submitted a report on the reasons for the defeat at Khar'kov, Stalin disagreed violently with Tikhomirov's critique of command decisions.[88] The unfortunate general found himself reassigned as deputy commander of 42nd Army outside Leningrad. Order No. 227 became the ultimate expression of fear as a motivational tool.[89]

This draconian measure reinforced and reemphasized the already desperate actions to shore up defenses at Stalingrad. Suffering in the seemingly interminable heat of July and August 1942, hundreds of thousands of local residents labored to construct four lines of defensive fortifications around the city, including huge antitank ditches reinforced by mines and other obstacles. Missing, however, were Red Army troops to occupy those defenses.

No amount of intimidation and effort could offset the inexperience and tactical disadvantages under which the Red Army labored that summer. On 25 July, for example, German 24th Panzer and 71st Infantry Divisions, with strong *Luftwaffe* support, attacked the right flank of Chuikov's 64th Army south of the Chir. The defending 229th Rifle Division had been able to bring five of its nine infantry battalions into line, but the supporting 137th Tank Brigade could muster only 35 tanks, the majority of them light T-60s, with limited fuel supplies. By the afternoon of 26 July, the Germans had penetrated 229th Rifle Division's defenses, but Chuikov managed to patch together a new defensive line using elements of 112th Rifle Division and 66th Naval Rifle Brigade.[90]

That evening, the psychological effects of blitzkrieg—the constant fear of being cut off by German armor—produced an unreasoning panic among rear area units. While Chuikov was absent from his command post, his chief of staff ordered several units to withdraw east of the Don even though a German air attack had destroyed the floating bridge at Nizhne-Chirskaia. Chuikov countermanded the order but lost several of his best staff officers to air attacks while those men rallied the mass of troops at river crossings. Finally, 64th Army was able to reestablish its lines, but it was out of touch with 62nd Army, and Gordov continued to bully both armies with unrealistic orders to counterattack. Under these circumstances, it was astonishing that the Soviets in the Great Bend of the Don were able to put up a defense that 24th Panzer Division's history described as "tough" and "grimly obstinate."[91]

CONCLUSIONS

By 31 July Paulus's Sixth Army had recorded some notable successes. XIV Panzer Corps—its northern pincer—had succeeded in penetrating the main defensive belt on 62nd Army's right wing and had advanced more than 50 kilometers to reach the Don River northwest of Kalach. On Sixth Army's left wing south of the Chir River, XXIV Panzer Corps—its southern pincer—had pressed 64th Army eastward to the Don and had also captured a small foothold across the lower Chir. The Soviets credited these failures to "the overall weakness of our antitank and antiaircraft defenses and the unprepared nature of our defenses in an engineering sense," particularly on 62nd Army's right wing.[92]

The most serious problem was the failure of Soviet *front,* army, and division commanders to concentrate their antitank guns, antitank rifles, and artillery (both indirect and direct fire) in coherent antitank strongpoints or regions to engage German panzer forces more effectively. The same problems with the employment of antiaircraft guns and machine guns made it impossible to counter the effects of *Luftwaffe* air strikes, particularly deadly against Soviet armor concentrations, artillery positions, and supply lines. Finally, severe mistakes emasculated the impact of 1st and 4th Tank Armies' counterstrokes. First, 62nd and 63rd Armies squandered the offensive potential of the more than 300 tanks in their eight separate tank battalions by employing them in so-called penny-parcel packets in support of infantry, when it would have been more useful to employ these battalions to increase the shock power of the tank armies' tank corps.

Most, if not all, Soviet counterstrokes and counterattacks were so hastily planned that headquarters controlling the operations failed to arrange for routine coordination and mutual support among attacking forces and their supporting arms. As a result, when the forces went over to the attack in staggered fashion—some prematurely and others late, and frequently without necessary armor, artillery, and air support or protection—the Germans were able to engage and defeat them piecemeal.

However, Soviet studies qualify the criticism of their forces, noting, "In spite of the difficulties the inexperienced Soviet forces encountered, the enemy failed to penetrate to Stalingrad. Moreover, the resistance to the enemy grew steadily."[93] Reliving its glorious exploits at the gates of Moscow the previous fall, the *Stavka*—after three weeks of fighting in summer heat, after losing the bulk of six field armies and almost an entire *front*—by the end of July 1942 had raised four new field and two tank armies and employed them to erect a new strategic front capable of mounting a credible defense along the Don River line. More than any other single factor, the appearance and combat performance of these reserves convinced Paulus that he could not complete his mission unless reinforced.

Seconding Paulus's judgment, Soviet critiques noted:

The ever-increasing resistance by Soviet forces compelled the German-Fascist command to commit 12 of Sixth Army's 15 divisions into battle by 30 July. This exposed Sixth Army's left wing, which was stretched along the Don River for 400 kilometers and turned out completely unprotected, even more. Therefore, at the end of July, the German-Fascist command was forced to narrow the offensive sector of Sixth Army to 170 kilometers by moving Italian Eighth Army up to the Don between Hungarian Second and German Sixth Armies and assigning to it [Italian Eighth Army] 29th [XXIX] Army Corps (62nd, 294th, and 336th Infantry Divisions), with its defensive sector, from Sixth Army, as well as two security divisions (213th and 403rd).[94]

The combination of tenacious defense against German forces at the Great Bend, incessant (though usually unsuccessful) Soviet counterattacks and counterstrokes there and elsewhere along the front, and German Sixth Army's continuing and increasingly vexing supply problems—particularly in regard to fuel and ammunition—brought Paulus's army to an abrupt halt by 28 July. The ferocity of Kolpakchi's 62nd Army within the Great Bend, stiffened by the determined if uncoordinated assaults by Moskalenko's 1st and Kriuchenkin's 4th Tank Armies, thwarted Paulus's northern pincer well short of Kalach. South of the Chir and shaky at times, the fighting defense by Chuikov's 64th Army also contained Paulus's southern pincer short of Kalach. Although 24th Panzer Division captured a small foothold over the lower Chir, Chuikov's men prevented the pincer from reaching across the Don River.

Frustrated by the heavier than anticipated Soviet resistance within the Great Bend, Paulus's Sixth Army had to eliminate the Soviet 62nd Army's bridgehead in the eastern extremity of the bend before it could begin accomplishing its priority task: crossing the Don River and penetrating eastward to the gates of Stalingrad. Clearly, unless significantly reinforced, it lacked the capability. Moreover, reinforcements would come only if and when Hitler revised his overall campaign plan.

Thus the swirling mass of pitched struggles near the Great Bend of the Don River was far more intense, prolonged, and significant than described in previous accounts in three important respects. First, in terms of scope, the counterstroke by 1st and 4th Tank Armies at the Great Bend, in conjunction with the action along the Voronezh axis later in July, was in reality an attempt on Stalin's part to organize a genuine counteroffensive. The goal of that counteroffensive was to halt Army Group B's offensive in its tracks. Second, 62nd Army's resistance inside the Great Bend's eastern embrace, as well as 64th Army's defense to the south, was far fiercer than Paulus anticipated or subsequent histories have described. As a result, Sixth Army's projected rapid advance to Kalach on the Don and to Stalingrad on the Volga beyond faltered miserably and was revived only after Hitler fundamentally revised his offensive plans. Third and most telling of all, the combat attrition experienced by Sixth Army's infantry, panzer, and motorized divisions in this heavy fighting, particularly in infantrymen and panzer grenadiers, would haunt the army when it finally reached and began struggling to capture its ultimate target: the city of Stalingrad.

Table 16. The Correlation of Armor Forces at the Beginning of the Battle in the Don Bend, 22 July 1942

AXIS		SOVIET	
Force	Tanks	Force	Tanks
SIXTH ARMY		STALINGRAD FRONT	
		63rd Army	**68** (estimated)
		36th Tank Brigade	
		134th Tank Brigade	
		193rd Tank Brigade	
		546th Separate Tank Battalion	
		647th Separate Tank Battalion	
3rd Motorized Division	**40**	4th Tank Army (26.7)	**200**
60th Motorized Division	**40**	22nd Tank Corps	**180** (96 T-34s, 58 T-70s, and 26 T-60s)
16th Panzer Division	**70**		
		173rd Tank Brigade	66 (32 T-34s, 21 T-70s, and 13 T-60s)
		176th Tank Brigade	48 (32 T-34s and 16 T-70)
		182nd Tank Brigade	66 (32 T-34s, 21 T-70s, and 13 T-60s)
		133rd Heavy Tank Brigade	**20**
		62nd Army	**320** (180 KVs, T-34s, and Mk-3s)
		40th Tank Brigade	46
		121st Tank Brigade	45
		644th Separate Tank Battalion	30–40
		645th Separate Tank Battalion	30–40
		648th Separate Tank Battalion	30–40
		649th Separate Tank Battalion	30–40
		650th Separate Tank Battalion	30–40
		651st Separate Tank Battalion	30–40
		1st Tank Army (26.7)	**350**
		13th Tank Corps	**152** on 22 July, **123** (74 T-34s and 49 T-70s) on 26 July
		163rd Tank Brigade	
		166th Tank Brigade	
		169th Tank Brigade	
		28th Tank Corps	**178** (88 T-34s, 60 T-70s, and 30 T-60s)
		39th Tank Brigade	
		55th Tank Brigade	
		56th Tank Brigade	
		158th Heavy Tank Brigade	**20**
24th Panzer Division	**140**	64th Army	**55**
		137th Tank Brigade	
Total	**290**		**993**

Table 16, *Continued*

AXIS		SOVIET	
Force	Tanks	Force	Tanks
		Front	**68**
		6th Guards Tank Brigade	
		6th Tank Brigade	
		65th Tank Brigade	
		156th Tank Brigade	
		254th Tank Brigade	
		652nd Separate Tank Battalion	
		23rd Tank Corps	**178** (88 T-34s, 60 T-70s, and 30 T-60s)
		99th Tank Brigade	
		189th Tank Brigade	
		158th Heavy Tank Brigade	
GRAND TOTAL	**290**	GRAND TOTAL	**1,239**

Sources: Iu. P. Babich, *Podgotovka oborony 62nd Armiei vne soprikosnovaniia s protivnikom i vedenie oboronitel'noi operatsii v usloviiakh prevoskhodstva protivnika v manevrennosti (po opytu Stalingradskoi bitvy)* [The preparation of the 62nd Army's defense in close proximity to the enemy and the conduct of the defensive operation in circumstances of enemy superiority in maneuver (based on the experience of the battle of Stalingrad)] (Moscow: Frunze Academy, 1991), 13; and *Stalingrad: Zabytoe srazhenie* [Stalingrad: The forgotten battles] (Moscow: ACT, 2005), 90.
Note: Numbers in bold indicate the strengths included in the grand total. Those not in bold are the strength of subordinate units.

CHAPTER 7

Endgame in the Great Bend of the Don, 1–19 August 1942

The temporary setbacks that Sixth Army encountered in the Great Bend of the Don River would highlight and drive home the grave faults of Führer Order No. 45, which demanded that German forces do everything simultaneously—too much, too few, too far.

HITLER ALTERS COURSE

Hitler, like Stalin, was increasingly frustrated by the course of events on the battlefield and took out his frustrations on staff officers. The dictator, for example, on 23 July tongue-lashed Halder for what he perceived as criticisms of his decisions:

> In consequence of the concentration of army ordered by the Fuehrer on 17 July over my opposition and the diversion of 24th Armored [Panzer] Division to Sixth Army, directed by him on 21 July, it is becoming obvious even to the layman that the Rostov region is crammed with armor which has nothing to do, while the critical outer wing at Tsimlyanskaia is starving for it. I warned emphatically against both these developments.
>
> Now that the result is so palpable, he explodes in a fit of insane rage and hurls the gravest reproaches against the General Staff.[1]

Halder then confided to his diary bitter sentiments that might well have been written by a Soviet officer at the same time:

> This chronic tendency to underrate enemy capabilities is gradually assuming grotesque proportions and develops into a positive danger. The situation is getting more and more intolerable. There is no room for any serious work. This so-called leadership is characterized by a pathological reaction to the impressions of the moment and a total lack of any understanding of the command machinery and its possibilities.[2]

Despite, or perhaps because of Halder's warning, Hitler, in an effort to revitalize Sixth Army's advance, decided to return Fourth Panzer Army headquarters and two of its corps (XXXXVIII Panzer and IV Army Corps) from Army Group A to Army Group B. On 30 July, while the action swirled in the Great Bend of the Don River, General Jodl emerged from a conference with the dictator to announce, "The fate of the Caucasus would be decided at Stalingrad, and, in view of the importance of the battle, it would be necessary to divert forces from AGp. A to AGp. B, if possible, south of the Don."[3]

For the first time, Hitler had explicitly made Stalingrad a priority but still insisted that "First Panzer Army must at once wheel south and southwest to cut off the enemy now being pushed back step by step from the Don by Seventeenth Army, before he reaches the Caucasus."[4] Halder considered this decision the "rankest nonsense," because "this enemy is running for dear life and will be in the northern foothills of the Caucasus a good piece ahead of our armor, and then we are going to have another unhealthy congestion of forces before the enemy front."[5]

Nevertheless, that night Halder telephoned the commanders of the two army groups to warn of the change. Informed he would have to continue the advance with Seventeenth Army and only the understrength panzer divisions of First Panzer Army, Field Marshal List accepted the necessity of abandoning the projected Tikhoretsk encirclement but opposed giving up forces to Sixth Army, arguing it would be a "great gamble" to send a "relatively weak force" deep into the Caucasus.[6] Adding insult to injury, when List asked Halder to ensure that "GD" Motorized Division remained to cover his left flank, Halder replied that transportation shortages would keep this division in the region until 12 August, but after that it would begin rail movement to Western Europe. In sarcasm the OKH chief assured List that the diversion of troops from his army group would at least ease his supply problems.[7] Despite the visible shortage of assets in the East, Hitler remained concerned about the probability of an Allied attack in the West.[8]

The next day, OKH translated Hitler's new offensive concept into a formal order to the two army groups. The order noted that, on 29 July, German advance guards had severed the last rail connection from the Caucasus to central Russia, thereby isolating the Caucasus. Thus, while the Soviets would undoubtedly try to defend the Caucasus, "no reinforcements worth mentioning" could be sent there from the interior; however, the Russians would throw "every bit of available strength" into the Stalingrad region to keep its "vital artery"—the Volga River—open.[9] To counter the Soviet intent, Hoth's Fourth Panzer Army, now consisting of four German and four Romanian divisions under German XXXXVIII Panzer and IV Army Corps and Romanian VI Army Corps, was to turn northeast and attack toward Stalingrad, converging with Sixth Army (see Table 17). Despite this reinforcement, which amounted to about 150 tanks, the mission of Army Group B remained unchanged.

Hitler's 31 July order did flesh out the concept of operations for Army Group A; First Panzer Army was to drive toward Maikop, seeking to intercept and surround its retreating Soviet adversaries. Only a screen of motorized units would protect the eastern flank of this long thrust. Once at Maikop, the mountain divisions would seize the Caucasus passes en route to Baku.[10]

Table 17. The Organization of Fourth Panzer Army, 1–15 August 1942

FOURTH PANZER ARMY—Colonel General Hermann Hoth
    XXXXVIII Panzer Corps—General of Panzer Troops Werner Kempf
        14th Panzer Division—Major General Ferdinand Heim
        29th Motorized Division—Major General Max Fremerey
    IV Army Corps—General of Infantry Viktor von Schwedler
        94th Infantry Division
        371st Infantry Division
        297th Infantry Division (from army reserve in mid-August)
    Romanian VI Army Corps—Lieutenant General Corneliu Draglina
        Romanian 1st Infantry Division
        Romanian 2nd Infantry Division
        Romanian 4th Infantry Division
        Romanian 20th Infantry Division
    Reserve — (from Sixth Army on 14 August)
        24th Panzer Division (to XXXXVIII Panzer Corps in mid-August)
        297th Infantry Division (to IV Army Corps in mid-August)

Source: Hoorst Boog, Werner Rahn, Reinhard Stumpf, and Bernd Wegner, *Germany and the Second World War, Volume 4: The Global War* (Oxford: Clarendon Press, 2001), 964.

As for Paulus's Sixth Army, in addition to offering assistance from a truncated Fourth Panzer Army, OKH allocated to Army Group B Italian Eighth Army, which, though attached to Seventeenth Army during its advance on Rostov, had not been needed. Now OKH decided to redeploy the rested army's six infantry divisions northeastward through Millerovo to the Don River front, where in stages they were to relieve Sixth Army's divisions so the latter could join Paulus's main shock group in the Great Bend of the Don. The first of these Italian divisions was 3rd Celere (Mobile), reflecting an unusual Italian concept that combined motorized and *Bersigliere* elite troops that supposedly moved more rapidly than conventional infantry. On 30 July 3rd Celere Division began relieving XVII Army Corps' 384th and 389th Infantry Divisions, which were in reserve opposite the Soviet bridgehead on the southern bank of the Don at Serafimovich. This permitted Paulus to shift those two divisions eastward, with 384th joining VIII Army Corps (then deployed opposite the Soviet 4th Tank Army's bridgehead south of Kremenskaia) and 389th joining Paulus's reserve. This left XVII Army Corps the task of defending opposite the Soviet's Serafimovich bridgehead.[11]

Thereafter, OKH kept Sixth Army's XXIX Army Corps, with 336th, 294th, and 62nd Infantry Divisions, and its XVII Army Corps, with 3rd Celere and 79th Infantry Divisions, along the southern bank of the Don until Italian Eighth Army's remaining divisions slowly moved into positions along the more than 200-kilometer-wide sector extending along the southern bank of the Don from Pavlovsk eastward to the mouth of the Khoper River, 30 kilometers west of Serafimovich. The Italian army began occupying its new defenses on 11 August and completed the process on 15 August. Finally, on 1 August the OKH also released XI Army Corps' headquarters and 76th and 295th Infantry Divisions from its reserve to Paulus's Sixth Army to assist its efforts to clear Soviet forces from the Great Bend.

Thus, in addition to committing Hoth's Fourth Panzer Army to the struggle for the Don River and Stalingrad, by 1 August the OKH had reinforced Sixth Army with three infantry divisions, two German and one Italian. These reinforcements permitted Paulus to shift four fresh German infantry divisions eastward into the critical battle for the Great Bend (see Table 18). Hitler was convinced these re-inforcements were more than sufficient to ensure safe passage of the Don and the quick conquest of Stalingrad.

While Hitler and the OKH reorganized their forces to completely crush So-viet forces in the Great Bend of the Don and renew their advance on Stalingrad, Stalin also took measures to increase the viability of his defenses along the ap-proaches to Stalingrad. On 28 July, exercising foresight, he had ordered Briansk Front to preserve 5th Tank Army headquarters intact so he could assign fresh forces to it in the future and employ it in counterstrokes along the Stalingrad axis.[12] The next day he ordered Stalingrad Front to withdraw six rifle divisions from the former 21st, 28th, and 38th Armies and turn them over to the *Stavka* Reserve so the NKO could refit them for future operations.[13] Then, to shore up the defenses on Stalingrad Front's right flank south of the Don, Stalin on 30 July transferred control of 51st Army from the North Caucasus to Stalingrad Front and the next day adjusted the boundary between the two *fronts* accordingly.[14]

Late on 31 July, to restore discipline in his forces defending the Great Bend (in reaction to a perceived unwillingness of 62nd Army's 192nd and 184th Rifle Divisions to follow his orders to the letter), Stalin directed 62nd and 64th Armies to implement Order No. 227 by forming blocking detachments to prevent unau-thorized troop withdrawals:

> Within a two day period, form blocking detachments numbering up to 200 men each made up of personnel from the Far Eastern divisions that have reached the front, which you will place in the immediate rear, primarily be-hind 62nd and 64th Armies' divisions. Subordinate the blocking detachments to the military council of the armies through their special departments [*Os-obye otdeli*—OOs]. Assign special department officers with the greatest mil-itary experience to head these blocking detachments.[15]

Finally on 2 August, but only after German Fourth Panzer Army began its eastward advance south of the Don on 31 July, Stalin ordered the Red Army's Main Directorate for the Formation and Manning of Forces to redesignate its elite airborne division as guards rifle divisions and begin moving these forces to the Stalingrad region from the *Stavka* Reserve.[16] The first two of these divisions, 35th and 36th Guards Airborne (Rifle) Divisions, began redeploying on 5 August, with an anticipated arrival date in the Stalingrad region of 12 August.

Despite these measures, the heavy fighting in and south of the Great Bend

Table 18. The Organization of Sixth Army and Cooperating Forces of Army Group B, 1–15 August 1942

SIXTH ARMY—General of Panzer Troops Friedrich Paulus
    XVII Army Corps—General of Infantry Karl Hollidt
        79th Infantry Division
        113th Infantry Division (in mid-August)
        Italian 3rd Celere [Mobile] Division
        22nd Panzer Division—Lieutenant General Wilhelm von Apell (from AGp. B's
            reserves on 8 August and to XI Army Corps on 15 August)
    VIII Army Corps—Lieutenant General Walter Heitz
        376th Infantry Division
        305th Infantry Division
        113th Infantry Division (to XVII Army Corps in mid-August)
        100th Jäger Division (to XI Army Corps in early August)
        384th Infantry Division
        389th Infantry Division (from XI Army Corps in mid-August)
    XIV Panzer Corps—General of Infantry Gustav von Wietersheim
        16th Panzer Division—Major General Hans-Valentin Hube
        60th Motorized Division—Major General Otto Kohlermann
        3rd Motorized Division—Lieutenant General Helmuth Schlömer
    LI Army Corps—General of Artillery Walter von Seydlitz-Kurzbach
        44th Infantry Division
        71st Infantry Division (to XXIV Panzer Corps in mid-August)
        24th Panzer Division (to XXIV Panzer Corps in early August)
        297th Infantry Division (to XXIV Panzer Corps in early August)
        295th Infantry Division (from XI Army Corps in early August and to XXIV Panzer
            Corps in mid-August)
    XI Army Corps—General of Infantry Karl Strecker
        Croat 369th Infantry Regiment
        76th Infantry Division (to XXIV Panzer Corps in early August)
        295th Infantry Division (to LI Army Corps in early August)
        100th Jäger Division (from VIII Army Corps in early August)
        389th Infantry Division (from Sixth Army reserve in early August and to VIII Army
            Corps in mid-August)
        22nd Panzer Division (from XVII Army Corps in mid-August)

RESERVE:
    XXIV Panzer Corps (headquarters only [activated early August])—General of Panzer
        Troops Willibald *Freiherr* von Langermann und Erlenkamp
        24th Panzer Division—General of Panzer Troops Bruno *Ritter* von Hauenschild
            (from LI Army Corps in early August and in Fourth Panzer Army's reserve in
            mid-August)
        71st Infantry Division (from LI Army Corps in mid-August and in LI Army Corps
            in mid-August)
        76th Infantry Division (from XI Army Corps in early August)
        297th Infantry Division (from LI Army Corps in early August and in Fourth Panzer
            Army's reserve in mid-August)
        398th Infantry Division (to XI Army Corps in early August)

ARMY GROUP B's control:
    XXIX Army Corps—(to Italian Eighth Army on 11 August)
        336th Infantry Division
        294th Infantry Division
        62nd Infantry Division
        Italian 3rd Infantry Division Ravenna (on 11 August)
        Italian 52nd Motorized Infantry Division Torino (on 11 August)

Table 18. Continued

ITALIAN EIGHTH ARMY—General Italo Garibaldi
    II Army Corps (headquarters only after 11 August)
        Italian 5th Infantry Division Cosseria (to Eighth Army's reserve in early
            August and to II Army Corps on 15 August)
        Italian 3rd Infantry Division Ravenna (to XXIX Army Corps on 11 August)
        Italian 2nd Infantry Division Sforzesca (to XXXV Army Corps in
            mid-August)
    XXXV Army Corps
        Italian 9th Infantry Division Pasubio
        Italian 52nd Infantry Division Torino (to XXIX Army Corps on 11 August)
        Italian 2nd Infantry Division Sforzesca (from II Army Corps in mid-August)
    Reserve:
        Italian 5th Infantry Division Cosseria (from II Army Corps in early August
            and to II Army Corps on 15 August)
RESERVE:
    1st SS Brigade (mid-August)
    22nd Panzer Division (to Sixth Army's reserve in early August, to XVII Army Corps on
        8 August and to XI Army Corps on 15 August)

Source: Hoorst Boog, Werner Rahn, Reinhard Stumpf, and Bernd Wegner, *Germany and the Second World War, Volume 4: The Global War* (Oxford: Clarendon Press, 2001), 964.

had severely weakened 62nd and 64th Armies and their supporting 1st and 4th Tank Armies. In particular, the heavy attrition in tanks experienced by the two tank armies left Gordov's forces in an increasingly threadbare state. If and when Sixth Army received reinforcements, Gordov, as well as the *Stavka*, realized it would be increasingly difficult for Kolpakchi's and Chuikov's forces to hold their forward defenses (see Table 19).[17]

    Coupled with the general weakening of most of his *front*'s rifle divisions, many of which were well under 50 percent strength, the tank strength of Gordov's Stalingrad Front also fell precipitously during the last ten days of July. Although the *front*'s precise tank losses remain obscure, according to Stalin's statements and other fragmentary reports, by 1 August the *front* had lost well more than half the 1,239-plus tanks it had fielded on 22 July. It would lose at least 100 more during the German operations to reduce the Soviet bridgehead on the western bank of the Don during the first two weeks of August. Stalingrad Front's tank strength ebbed to about 250 tanks by mid-August, and the new Southern Front fielded another 200 tanks. Coupled to the more than 250 tanks Sixth Army fielded at month's end, Hitler's decision to wheel Fourth Panzer Army, with its 150 tanks, toward Stalingrad increased the armor strength of the German advance on Stalingrad to well more than 400 tanks—creating rough parity in armor between the two sides. If Stalingrad Front, with its superiority in armor of better than five-to-one, was unable to prevail over Paulus's army in July, there were scant prospects it could do so successfully in August, when it achieved little better than parity in tanks.

Table 19. The Organization of Stalingrad Front on 1 August 1942

STALINGRAD FRONT—Lieutenant General V. N. Gordov
    63rd Army—Lieutenant General V. I. Kuznetsov
        14th Guards, 1st, 127th, 153rd, 197th, and 203rd Rifle Divisions
        36th, 134th, and 193rd Tank Brigades, 546th and 647th Separate Tank Battalions
    21st Army—Major General A. I. Danilov
        9th Guards, 63rd, 76th, 124th, 226th, 277th, 278th, 293rd, 300th, 304th, 321st, and 343rd Rifle Divisions and 33rd Motorized Rifle Brigade
    4th Tank Army—Major General V. D. Kriuchenkin
        18th and 205th Rifle Divisions and 5th Separate Destroyer Brigade
        22nd Tank Corps (133rd, 173rd, 176th, 182nd Tank and 22nd Motorized Rifle Brigades)
    62nd Army—Major General V. Ia. Kolpakchi
        33rd Guards, 147th, 181st, 184th, 192nd, and 196th Rifle Divisions, student rifle regiment, and 2nd Ordzhonikidze Infantry School
        40th Tank Brigade and 644th, 645th, 648th, 649th, 650th, and 651st Separate Tank Battalions
    64th Army—Lieutenant General M. S. Shumilov (replaced Lieutenant General V. I. Chuikov on 30 July)
        29th, 112th, 204th, 214th, and 229th Rifle Divisions, 66th and 154th Naval Rifle Brigades, and 3 student rifle regiments from the Zhitomir, 1st Ordzhonikidze, and Krasnodar Machine Gun–Mortar Schools
        121st and 137th Tank Brigades
    1st Tank Army—Major General K. S. Moskalenko
        131st and 399th Rifle Divisions
        13th Tank Corps (163rd, 166th, 169th Tank and 20th Motorized Rifle Brigades); 23rd Tank Corps (99th and 189th Tank and 9th Motorized Rifle Brigades); 28th Tank Corps (39th, 55th, 56th Tank and 32nd Motorized Rifle Brigades); and 158th Tank Brigade
    57th Army—Major General F. I. Tolbukhin
        15th Guards and 38th Rifle Divisions and 13th Separate Destroyer Brigade
    51st Army—Major General T. K. Kolomiets
        91st, 138th, 157th, and 302nd Rifle and 110th and 115th Cavalry Divisions
        135th and 155th Tank Brigades and 125th Separate Tank Battalion
    7th Sapper Army—Major General of Technical Forces V. S. Kosenko
        12th, 14th, 15th, 20th, and 21st Sapper Brigades
    8th Air Army—Major General of Aviation T. T. Khriukhin
        206th, 226th, and 228th Assault Aviation Divisions
        220th, 235th, 268th, and 269th Fighter Aviation Divisions
        270th and 271st Bomber Aviation Divisions
        272nd Fighter-Bomber Aviation Division
        13th Guards Bomber Aviation, 8th Reconnaissance Aviation, and 23rd, 282nd, 633rd, and 655th Mixed Aviation Regiments
    Front Forces:
        3rd Guards Cavalry Corps (5th and 6th Guards and 32nd Cavalry Divisions)
        87th, 126th, 244th, and 422nd Rifle Divisions
        15th, 20th, 22nd, and 24th Separate Destroyer Brigades
        Three student rifle regiments, Vinnitsa, Groznyi, and 3rd Ordzhonikidze Infantry Schools
        54th, 115th, and 118th Fortified Regions
        6th Guards, 6th, 65th, 156th, and 254th Tank Brigades and 652nd Separate Tank Battalion

Source: Boevoi sostav Sovetskoi armii, Chast 2 (ianvar'–dekabr' 1942 goda) [Combat composition of the Soviet Army, Part 2 (January-December 1942)] (Moscow: Voenizdat, 1966), 148–149.

FOURTH PANZER ARMY'S ADVANCE TO
ABGANEROVO, 31 JULY–14 AUGUST

The mechanized troops of Hoth's Fourth Panzer Army, which were expecting to participate in the heady pursuit of shattered Soviet forces deep into the Caucasus, were dismayed to hear they now had to perform the far more onerous task of fighting their way into Stalingrad. Hoth's plan called for Kempf's XXXXVIII Panzer Corps to advance rapidly and secure a lodgment in the southern portion of the city by a surprise attack. Yet the corps' veteran panzers and panzer grenadiers were skeptical, remembering the bloody street fighting in Smolensk the previous year.[18] Nevertheless, after regrouping into their bridgehead across the Don River at Tsimlianskaia on 31 July, Hoth's forces, supported by IV Army Corps, lunged out of the bridgehead at dawn the next day and wheeled eastward across the open steppe (see Map 42). North of the Chir River, Sixth Army remained motionless across a front of more than 100 kilometers, still short of the Don River at Kalach, with the bulk of Kolpakchi's 62nd Army on its front because Paulus's forces were still waiting to replenish their fuel and ammunition.

Deployed in the vanguard of Hoth's panzer army, XXXXVIII Panzer Corps spearheaded its advance with Heim's 14th Panzer Division, followed closely by Fremerey's 29th Motorized Division. As Kempf's panzers and panzer grenadiers sped northeastward from south of the Don River, Romanian VI Army Corps, crossing to the southern bank east of Tsimlianskaia, protected the panzer corps' left flank. Kempf's assault caught General Kolomiets's 51st Army by surprise, striking precisely at the boundary between the army's defending 91st and 157th Rifle Divisions and literally splitting the army in two. As Kempf's panzers tore their defenses apart, 157th and 138th Rifle Divisions, defending the army's right wing, withdrew in considerable disorder eastward toward Kotel'nikovo. There they expected to link up with a relief force dispatched by General Shumilov's 64th Army to protect its threatened left flank. To the west, the divisions on 51st Army's left wing fell victim to First Panzer Army's XXXX Panzer Corps, whose advancing divisions drove the three defending Soviet divisions southward in disorder toward the Sal River. As candidly noted in the 51st Army history:

> The forces of 51st Army suffered heavy casualties during the defensive battles, and all of its divisions were very short of personnel. The army withdrew without any of its weapons and equipment. Its units and formations ended up cut off from their rear services, which were based along the Tikhoretsk-Sal'sk railroad. From this moment a very dramatic stage in the combat operations of the army began, during which it fought as small, uncoordinated, and exhausted detachments, with a gap of more than 90 kilometers with 64th Army and an even larger gap on its left flank with 28th Army. Command and control was destroyed. Major General T. K. Kolomiets gave the order, "Operate independently, depending on the situation."[19]

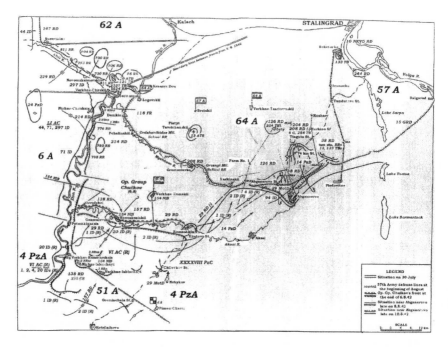

Map 42. Operations on the southwestern approaches to Stalingrad, 30 July–10 August 1942

By nightfall on 1 August, General Heim's 14th Panzer Division had thrust eastward more than 40 kilometers toward the western approaches to Kotel'nikovo, prompting the Red Army General Staff to report:

> As a result of an enemy penetration of its front in the Nizhne-Zhirov region (30 kilometers west of Dubovskoe), the left wing of 157th Rifle Division withdrew behind the Sal River. . . . According to information requiring confirmation, enemy tanks and infantry reached the vicinity of Gashun Station (15 kilometers northeast of Zimovniki).[20]

Faced with this crisis, the *Stavka* tapped its reserves in the Stalingrad region, dispatching Siberian 208th Rifle Division, 6th Guards Tank Brigade (the remnants of the former 23rd Tank Corps with 44 new T-34 tanks), and a tank destroyer artillery regiment by rail to Kotel'nikovo and the Aksai River line. It also sent 126th Rifle Division to the Abganerovo region, just south of the Aksai River and only 70 kilometers southwest of Stalingrad. At the same time, Shumilov, 64th Army's new commander, sent 154th Naval Rifle Brigade southward to the Nizhne-Iablochnyi region (25 kilometers north of Kotel'nikovo) to block the enemy advance and moved his army headquarters to the Verkhne-Tsaritsynskii region, 50 kilometers north of Abganerovo and the same distance southwest of Stalingrad, from which he could better control his forces.

Finally, by day's end Gordov ordered the woefully small 57th Army, now commanded by Major General F. I. Tolbukhin and assigned to Stalingrad Front's reserve, to move its 15th Guards and 38th Rifle Divisions from Stalingrad proper to new defensive positions extending from Raigorod on the Volga River, 40 kilometers southeast of Stalingrad, westward to Krasnyi Don, on the eastern bank of the Don River 30 kilometers south of Kalach. 57th Army was to back up 64th Army and protect the approaches to the Volga River south of the city.[21] Its commander, Fedor Ivanovich Tolbukhin, had served as chief of staff of Trans-Caucasus, Caucasus, and Crimean Fronts in 1941–1942 and survived the disaster at Kerch' before becoming deputy commander of the Stalingrad Military District in May 1942.[22]

As XXXXVIII Panzer Corps continued its rapid advance, Fremerey's 29th Motorized Division, reportedly with a force of 40 tanks, reached Kotel'nikovo, midway between the Sal and Aksai Rivers, at 1100 hours on 2 August, where its advanced guard caught the lead elements of 208th Rifle Division as they were detraining, routing the Soviet troops and capturing several railroad trains.[23] After clearing 208th Rifle Division from the town by 1500 hours, the motorized division dispatched patrols northeastward toward the Aksai River, a scant 100 kilometers southwest of Stalingrad. By this time, led by its 64th Motorcycle Battalion, Heim's 14th Panzer Division, which had bypassed Kotel'nikovo to the east, lunged northeastward more than 25 kilometers virtually unopposed, capturing the town of Darganov, about 35 kilometers from the town of Aksai on the Aksai River.[24] Kolomiets's 51st Army was in such disorder that the General Staff could only record, "On 2 August the forces of 51st Army fought stubbornly with enemy tanks and infantry on the left [southern] bank of the Don River. Precise information about the positions of the army's forces has not been received. Their situation is being determined."[25]

With the situation swirling out of control, Shumilov, late on 2 August, indeed created the relief force 51st Army had expected, a special operational group commanded by his deputy, General Chuikov. Chuikov's so-called Southern Operational Group consisted of 29th Rifle Division, shifted southward from the Don River front, and 154th Naval Rifle Brigade, dispatched to the region the previous day, both controlled by a special headquarters detached from 64th Army headquarters. To ease Shumilov's task, Gordov also transferred the three rifle divisions on his army's right wing (229th, 204th, and 112th), together with their defensive sector between Surovikino on the Chir and Nizhne-Chirskaia on the Don, to Kolpakchi's 62nd Army.[26] In essence, Gordov castled Shumilov's entire army to the right so that it could better protect the Aksai River line. However, by this time it was too late.

On 3 August the panzers of Heim's 14th Panzer Division advanced another 30 kilometers, capturing the village of Zhutovo, 18 kilometers south of Aksai, and sending patrols northward to the outskirts of Aksai. With Chuikov's defense line seriously threatened, Gordov reinforced his deputy's operational group with 6th Guards Tank Brigade (44 tanks) and two regiments of *Katiusha* multiple rocket launchers. By this time Shumilov had also ordered 51st Army's 138th and 157th Rifle Divisions, which had just completed their retreat northward into 64th Army's lines, to reinforce Chuikov's Southern Group.[27] However, despite all of these promised reinforcements, most of the reinforcing units were still en route late on 3 August, leaving Chuikov with four rifle battalions and five artillery batteries to defend the Aksai River against a full German panzer division. And even these forces were running short of ammunition.

Facing such weak opposition, while attacking abreast 29th Motorized and 14th Panzer Divisions swept northward across the Aksai River with a force of roughly 150 tanks, capturing Aksai and pressing the left wing of Chuikov's operational group 5–10 kilometers north of the river line. Echeloned to XXXXVIII Panzer Corps' left, Romanian VI Army Corps' 1st and 2nd Infantry Divisions pressed the remainder of Chuikov's group northward from Kotel'nikovo, forcing 208th Rifle Division's remnants to withdraw to Chilekovo Station, more than halfway to the Aksai River. The fighting on 4 August proved extraordinarily fierce and difficult for Chuikov's Southern Operational Group because ammunition was running out and *Luftwaffe* aircraft pounded their positions unmercifully.

By nightfall on 4 August, Chuikov's group, which consisted by now of 29th, 138th, 157th, and 208th Rifle Divisions, 154th Naval Rifle Brigade, 6th Guards Tank Brigade, and two regiments of *Katiushas* (at least on paper), proved incapable of maintaining a coherent defense. Its forces were strung out across a 60-kilometer front from the Don River eastward to Aksai; 29th Rifle Division, at full strength with 11,000 men, was still en route to the Aksai from the Don front; its other divisions numbered from 1,500 to 4,500 men; its tank support had dropped to about 40 tanks; and its supporting artillery numbered only 100 guns and about 200 mortars. Worse still, the remainder of Kolomiets's 51st Army (two rifle divisions, one cavalry brigade, and two tank brigades) were still retreating toward Elista, some 85 kilometers southwest of the Aksai River.[28] With his defenses so fragile, Chuikov realized it was only a matter of time before the Germans crushed them. Chuikov was not alone in these concerns. Ever since the front south of the Don River had collapsed on 1 August, both Gordov at Stalingrad Front headquarters and Stalin and his *Stavka* in Moscow realized they faced grave peril. Unless something was done, German forces could advance on Stalingrad virtually unimpeded.

Stalin recognized that Stalingrad Front was simply unable to coordinate operations across almost 800 kilometers of front. Therefore, on the night of 1 August, Stalin summoned Colonel General Andrei Ivanovich Eremenko from sick leave, where he was recovering from a leg wound he had received in the spring, to attend a State Defense Committee (GKO) meeting in his Kremlin office.

Eremenko was an experienced 49-year-old general who had most typified the

Stavka's unrealistic expectations regarding the performance of its senior commanders during the early stage of the war. Eremenko had joined the tsar's army in 1913 and the Red Army in 1918, serving as the chief of staff of a cavalry brigade and deputy commander of a cavalry regiment in Budenny's 1st Cavalry Army during the Civil War. After war's end, Eremenko graduated from the Higher-Cavalry School in 1923, the Command Cadre Course in 1925, and the Frunze Academy in 1935. In between his schooling, he commanded a cavalry regiment in December 1929, a cavalry division in August 1937, and 6th Cavalry Corps in 1938, which he led during the occupation of eastern Poland in September 1939. In June 1940 the NKO assigned Eremenko to command the Red Army's new 3rd Mechanized Corps and, in December 1940, to command the prestigious 1st Red Banner Far Eastern Army, where he was serving when the war began. Promoted to the rank of lieutenant general in June 1941, Eremenko was known as the "Russian Guderian" because of his prewar experience as a mechanized corps commander.[29]

In early July 1941, shortly after war began, the *Stavka* recalled Eremenko from the Far East and appointed him deputy commander of Western Front, where he served during the initial stages of the battle for Smolensk. When the *Stavka* decided to mount a counteroffensive to halt the German advance on Moscow in late August 1941, it named Eremenko commander of the new Briansk Front and assigned him the utterly unrealistic task of striking and defeating the southern flank of Army Group Center, Guderian's famed Second Panzer Group. Thoroughly outmanned, outgunned, and outfought by Guderian's forces, Eremenko's *front* was shattered in heavy fighting in September. Thereafter, during the initial stages of Army Group Center's final advance on Moscow (Operation Typhoon), Eremenko's forces were encircled and largely destroyed in the Briansk region in October 1941.

In December, after Eremenko recuperated from wounds he suffered during the fighting around Briansk, Stalin assigned him as commander of newly formed 4th Shock Army, one of three such armies destined to spearhead the Red Army's counteroffensive in the Moscow region. Spearheading the ensuing counteroffensive in January 1942, Eremenko's new army conducted a spectacular advance toward Smolensk, deep into Army Group Center's rear area. Now, as a reward for the feats Eremenko had achieved during the battle for Moscow, Stalin appointed him to command Stalingrad Front. In just over a month's time, Eremenko would begin the grisly task of feeding units into Stalingrad, a meat grinder of urban warfare, to provide the Soviet defenders just enough men and munitions to wear down the Germans while husbanding most of his strength for later counterattacks. Under these circumstances, it is understandable that Eremenko and his commissar, Khrushchev, remained east of the Volga, aloof from the tactical battle. Had they become involved personally in the day-to-day struggle, they would have been unable to retain their objectivity about the larger issues of the campaign.

Therefore, in his Kremlin office, Stalin informed Eremenko that he had decided to split Stalingrad Front in two and assign him one of the new *front* commands. After Eremenko and Vasilevsky studied the situation in detail at the General Staff on 2 August, they gathered that evening in Stalin's office, where they discussed the situation with Major General V. D. Ivanov of the General Staff and General Golikov, former commander of the Voronezh Front who was now about to become commander of 1st Guards Army, a fresh army of primarily airborne forces.

Disturbed to learn that the dividing line between the two *fronts* was to extend from Kalach along the Tsaritsa River through Stalingrad to the Volga River, Eremenko tried to persuade Stalin and Vasilevsky to maintain unity of command in the Stalingrad region by assigning the entire city to one of the *fronts*. Stalin reacted angrily, insisting to Vasilevsky, "Everything stays as we proposed. The Stalingrad Front is split into two *fronts;* the boundary line between the two *fronts* will run along the line of the Tsaritsa River and then on to Kalach."[30] After further discussion, Stalin agreed to create a new and truncated Stalingrad Front with Gordov still in command and a new Southeastern Front commanded by Eremenko.[31]

With a decision reached, the *Stavka* issued the directive implementing Stalin's decision at 0530 hours on 4 August and specific instructions to its new *front* commanders early the next day:

For the sake of improving command and control, the *Stavka* of the Supreme High Command orders:

1. Divide the Stalingrad Front into two *fronts*—the Stalingrad and Southeastern.

2. These *fronts* will consist of:

Stalingrad Front—63rd, 21st, 62nd Armies, 4th Tank Army, and 28th Tank Corps;

Southeastern Front—64th Army (29th, 204th, and 131st Rifle and 38th and 15th Guards Rifle Divisions and 6th Guards Tank Brigade), 51st Army (138th, 157th, 91st, 302nd, and 208th Rifle Divisions, 115th Cavalry Division, and 135th and 155th Tank Brigades), 1st Guards Army (37th, 38th, 39th, 40th, and 41st Guards Rifle Divisions), 57th Army (35th and 36th Guards Rifle Divisions and 126th, 244th, and 422nd Rifle Divisions), and 13th Tank Corps.

Simultaneously, provide the Southeastern Front's 64th and 51st Armies with all of the special service units in these armies, as well as all forces (schools, artillery units, and units of 118th Fortified Region) situated along the southern face of the Stalingrad external defense line.

Transfer half of all of the Stalingrad Front's aircraft to the Southeastern Front. Together, Comrades Vorozheikin and Stepanov will report fulfillment.

3. Leave the Stalingrad Front's command and Military Council as presently configured.

4. Colonel General Comrade Eremenko, A. I., is appointed as the commander of the Southeastern Front, Major General Comrade Zakharov, G.

F.—as the chief of staff of the *front*, effective when he is freed of his duties as the deputy chief of staff of the North Caucasus Front.

5. The headquarters of the Stalingrad and Southeastern Fronts will be in Stalingrad.

6. Within five days, the chief of the General Staff will create a *front* command for the Southeastern Front in Stalingrad by employing individual personnel and installations of the former Southern Front and command and service units of 1st Tank Army.

7. The boundary line between the Stalingrad and Southeastern Fronts is established from Morozovsk through Verkhne-Chirskaia to Stalingrad (all, besides Stalingrad, inclusive for the Stalingrad Front).

The Stalingrad-Surovikino railroad is for the general use of the Stalingrad and Southeastern Fronts.

8. The Stalingrad Front's immediate mission is to defeat the enemy penetrating at the junction of 21st and 62nd Armies of the Stalingrad defensive line and, after restoring the defense along that line, firmly protect Stalingrad from the northwest and west.

Subsequently, have in mind conducting an offensive toward Morozovsk.

The Southeastern Front's immediate mission is to halt further movement of the enemy toward the southern face of the Stalingrad external defense line from the south at all cost and in no circumstances permit him to penetrating that defense line, as well as preventing the enemy from reaching the Volga south of Stalingrad.

Subsequently, occupy Zhutovo and Kotel'nikovo and throw the enemy back behind the Sal River.

9. The Southeastern Front will begin controlling its forces separately beginning on 7 August 1942. Before that time the responsibility for the defense of Stalingrad rests fully with the commander of the Stalingrad Front.

Report fulfillment.

I. Stalin, A. Vasilevsky[32]

These directives disbanded Moskalenko's already shattered 1st Tank Army, assigning its remnants to 62nd Army and employing its headquarters as the nucleus for the headquarters of the new Southeastern Front, with Moskalenko temporarily serving as Eremenko's deputy.[33] In compensation for his loss of 1st Tank Army, the *Stavka* assigned Gordov's *front* Golikov's new 1st Guards Army, which the *Stavka* formed in another directive it issued the same day. Golikov's army was created around the nucleus of the headquarters of former 2nd Reserve Army and was to consist of five elite guards airborne divisions recently converted to guards rifle divisions (37th through 41st). It was to become operational but directly subordinate to the *Stavka* by 6 August.[34] A final directive late on 5 August sent Golikov's divisions and their supporting artillery to Stalingrad by rail at the highest possible speed.[35]

In addition to these changes, the *Stavka* on 3 August also shook up its army command cadre in the Stalingrad region, replacing Kolpakchi as commander of 62nd Army with General Lopatin, former commander of 9th Army. Kolpakchi became Golikov's deputy in 1st Guards Army. Once Stalingrad Front's air assets were subdivided, 16th Air Army supported Stalingrad Front, and 8th Air Army supported Southeastern Front.

In retrospect, Soviet critiques considered Stalin's decision to split Stalingrad Front into two parts to have been ill-advised:

At least in principle, the *Stavka*'s decision about dividing the Stalingrad Front into two separate *fronts* was correct and expedient in the operational situation that existed along the Stalingrad axis on 5 August. However, the determination of the *fronts*' defensive sectors in this decision was unfortunate. The city of Stalingrad, toward which the enemy was delivering his main attack, turned out to be at the junction of the two *fronts*. 62nd Army, which remained in the Stalingrad Front, carried out the immediate defense of the city from the west, but it happened to operate in the sector of its neighbor, the Southeastern Front. Subsequently, all of this complicated the organization of the city's defense, cooperation between the *fronts*, and the command and control of all forces and weapons. The decision the *Stavka* made concerning the division of the Stalingrad Front's aviation between the two *fronts* led to the dispersal of its forces, hindered the centralized employment of aircraft in the interests of the ground forces on the most threatened Stalingrad axes, and weakened protection of the city from the air.

Thus, the mistakes permitted by the *Stavka* in subdividing the Stalingrad Front subsequently hindered command and control of the forces and had a negative effect on the results of the defensive battle.[36]

Four days later, when Stalin finally began to realize his 5 August decision was indeed ill-advised, he compounded his error by issuing a new directive on 9 August subordinating Stalingrad Front's forces in the Stalingrad region to Eremenko's Southeastern Front:

The *Stavka* of the Supreme High Command orders:

1. Subordinate the Stalingrad Front to Colonel General Eremenko, the commander of the Southeastern Front, effective at 0600 hours on 10 August, leaving Comrade Eremenko in command of the Southeastern Front as well.

2. Appoint Lieutenant General Comrade Golikov as deputy to Comrade Eremenko in the Southeastern Front, relieving him of his duties as commander of 1st Guards Army.

3. Appoint Major General Comrade Moskalenko as commander of 1st Guards Army.

4. Appoint Colonel Saraev, the commander of 10th NKVD Division, as the chief of Stalingrad's garrison.

5. Both Comrade Eremenko and Comrade Gordov must bear in mind that the defense of Stalingrad and the defeat of the enemy advancing on Stalingrad from the west and south has decisive importance for our entire Soviet front.

The Supreme High Command obligates both Colonel General Eremenko and Lieutenant General Gordov not to spare their forces and to stop at no kind of sacrifice to save Stalingrad and smash the enemy.

I. Stalin, A. Vasilevsky[37]

While Stalin was adjusting his forces and command relationships in the Stalingrad region, for the moment neither Gordov nor Eremenko had sufficient forces to halt or even slow the advance of Fourth Panzer Army. Because Lopatin's 62nd Army, in its bridgehead west of Kalach, was still decisively engaged against Sixth Army, the task of defending the southern approach to Stalingrad fell to Shumilov's 64th Army, in particular Chuikov's operational group.[38]

Resuming its advance on 5 August with 36th Panzer Regiment in the lead, 14th Panzer Division thrust 30–40 kilometers northward from Aksai, bypassing Group Chuikov's weak left flank along the Aksai River and reaching Abganerovo Station on the Kotel'nikovo-Stalingrad railroad line, 70 kilometers southwest of Stalingrad, and Plodovitoe, 10 kilometers to the east.[39] With his left flank turned, Chuikov faced a chaotic situation. Traveling from place to place along the Aksai River, Chuikov issued orders directly to his battalion commanders, many of whom had lost contact with their divisions. Because all available Red Army aircraft were still supporting 62nd Army farther north, the *Luftwaffe* roamed over the battlefield unopposed, bombed newly arrived troops as they detrained, and, at one point, knocked Chuikov's command radio out of operation.

The Red Army General Staff summed up Chuikov's desperate situation:

64th Army continued to occupy its previous positions and conducted a partial regrouping of its forces with the aim of reinforcing the Zhutovo-Abganerovo axis.

The enemy continued the movement of its tank units (48th Panzer Corps) to the southern face of the external defense line of the Stalingrad Fortified Region.

Group Chuikov has occupied a defense along the northern bank of the Aksai River on [the following] front: 138th RD—Gorodskii (17 kilometers north of Verkhne-Kurmoiarskaia) and Novoaksaiskii; 157th RD—Novoaksaiskii and Chikov; and 29th RD—Chikov and Klykov (40 kilometers northeast of Verkhne-Kurmoiarskaia).

126th RD was fighting with an enemy force of up to a company of submachine gunners with 10 tanks, which had wedged into our defenses in the Abganerovo region (70 kilometers southwest of Stalingrad), on 5 August.[40]

Despite the perilous position that his operational group occupied, Chuikov's group somehow managed to halt Fourth Panzer Army's left wing along the Aksai River for 12 days. This forced Hoth to divide his forces and fight two separate battles, the first in the Abganerovo region against the bulk of 64th Army, and the second along the Aksai River against Chuikov's Southern Group. As a result, Chuikov's stout defense prevented Hoth from concentrating his forces for a decisive advance on Stalingrad's southern suburbs. Thereafter, from 5 through 17 August, the left wing of the panzer army, consisting of Romanian VI Army Corps' 1st, 20th, 2nd, and 4th Infantry Divisions, supported by IV Army Corps' 294th Infantry Division, conducted a near-constant series of assaults against Chuikov's defenses.[41] Although these forces achieved a small infantry bridgehead over the Aksai River on 5 August at the junction between 138th and 157th Rifle Divisions, the Soviets pushed them back with a dawn counterattack the next day. Two days later, Romanian 1st Infantry Division penetrated Chuikov's defenses west of Zalivskii, midway between Aksai and the Don River. However, the defending 157th Rifle Division, reinforced by a regiment from 29th Rifle Division, counterattacked both flanks, again driving the attackers back, reportedly "destroying up to two battalions of enemy infantry and, by 0600 hours, digging in along the Novoaksaiskii and Chikov line."[42] Otherwise, the situation along Chuikov's front stabilized with only minor local withdrawals until 13 August, when 64th Army, worried about a possible encirclement of Chuikov's forces, ordered Chuikov's group to conduct a phased withdrawal under the protection of strong rear guards, northward to the Myshkova River.[43]

During this stalemate, Chuikov closely observed German tactics and began to develop the innovative responses he later applied in the defense of the city. Because the German and non-German Axis commanders were anxious to minimize casualties, they prepared each attack carefully, timed to coincide with the few opportunities for *Luftwaffe* air support. Seeing this, Chuikov attempted to disrupt the German preparations, launching surprise artillery raids just before the impending German attack or withdrawing his troops a short distance to avoid the artillery and air strikes aimed at his positions. The results were as frustrating for the Germans as they were encouraging for the disheartened Soviet soldiers.[44] For much of this battle, Chuikov's communications were so poor that he received no direct information from the *front* headquarters.

Eremenko, the new *front* commander, apparently never received Chuikov's proposals for stronger counterattacks; however, his *front* did not remain idle. While Chuikov's Southern Group was stubbornly defending along the lower Aksai River, Southeastern Front created a second line of defense along the Myshkova River, 25–40 kilometers to the north, manning this line with rifle regiments from officer training schools, which did little more than hold key river-crossing sites. Shumilov then withdrew the remainder of 64th Army along the Don, redeploying them eastward to the Abganerovo region on the most direct axis to Stalingrad. For once, Soviet commanders had anticipated the next German objective correctly.

Leaving the Romanians behind to fight Chuikov's group, Kempf's XXXXVIII Panzer Corps on 6 August consolidated its hold on the Abganerovo region, sending *kampfgruppen* from 14th Panzer and 29th Motorized Divisions northward to Tinguta Station and Tinguta, 10 kilometers closer to Stalingrad. In their wake, IV Army Corps' 94th Infantry and 4th Romanian Infantry Divisions secured the Aksai region, applying pressure to the left flank of Chuikov's Southern Group. As pressure increased on Shumilov's forces in the Abganerovo sector, essentially 126th and 38th Rifle Divisions with minimal artillery support, Shumilov obtained Gordov's approval to organize a counterattack against XXXXVIII Panzer Corps' spearhead on 9 August. Lacking any understanding of the real conditions on the ground, the *Stavka* on 6 August had expressed "indignation" that Gordov's *front* had "permitted a penetration by enemy tanks through the southern face of Stalingrad's defense line without offering necessary resistance." It had "demanded categorically" that Gordov "personally restore the situation along the Stalingrad defense line at all costs in the immediate future" and "destroy the penetrating enemy tanks or drive them to the south."[45]

Despite the *Stavka*'s unrealistic demands and threats, Shumilov spent three days reinforcing 64th and 57th Armies' front, dispatching 204th, 208th, and 422nd Rifle Divisions and 13th Tank Corps to the Zety and Tundutovo regions, 10–15 kilometers north of Tinguta Station and Tinguta, and scraping together a credible counterattack force. Shumilov managed to concentrate his counterattack force in the region north of XXXXVIII Panzer Corps' forward outposts by day's end on 8 August. By this time, it consisted of 38th, 157th, and 204th Rifle Divisions, the reorganized 13th Tank Corps, two student regiments, two artillery regiments, one regiment of *Katiusha* multiple rocket launchers (76th), one heavy artillery battalion, and one armored train. The 13th Tank Corps, still under Colonel Tanaschishin's command but now consisting of 6th Guards, 13th, and 254th Tank Brigades, fielded 34 operational tanks (30 T-34s and 4 T-70s) on 8 August and another 51 tanks (44 T-34s and 7 T-70s) in various stages of repair.[46] On 9 August, after the counterattack began, Shumilov reinforced his counterattack force with 133rd Tank Brigade, which was equipped with 40 KV heavy tanks. In addition, between 7 and 30 August, Shumilov's *front* sent Tanaschishin's tank corps another 97 tanks, distributed as follows: 6th Guards Tank Brigade—35 T-34s and 16 T-70s; 254th Tank Brigade—21 T-34s and 17 T-70s; and 13th Tank Brigade—8 T-70s.[47]

Thus, when it began its counterattack on 9 August, Tanaschishin's tank corps fielded 68 tanks, and Shumilov's counterattack force was supported by 396 guns and mortars. During the day, 133rd Tank Brigade added its 40 heavy tanks to the battle. Given the dwindling strength of 14th Panzer and 29th Motorized Divisions, on 9 August Shumilov's counterattack force enjoyed a better than three-to-one superiority over the two German divisions in manpower, two-to-one in artillery, and virtual parity in armor.[48]

The counterattack force struck at dawn on 9 August, commencing a fierce two-day battle along and east of the Tikhoretsk-Stalingrad railroad line. The counterattack struck Fremerey's panzer grenadiers and Heim's panzers virtually simultaneously from three sides. Advancing southeastward from the Zety region, 126th Rifle Division and part of 254th Tank Brigade (14 T-34 tanks) attacked the forward elements of 29th Motorized Division, which were dug in along the railroad line at 74 km Station (on the railroad line the same distance south of Stalingrad's center), 10 kilometers south of Tinguta Station, from the west. At the same time, 204th and 208th Rifle Divisions and 13th Tank Corps' main force (6th Guards and part of 254th Tank Brigade), advancing southward along the railroad from Tinguta Station, attacked 29th Motorized Division's defenses along the railroad line from the north. Farther east, 38th Rifle Division, supported by 13th Tank Brigade and, later in the day, 133rd Tank Brigade, assaulted 14th Panzer Division's defenses south of Tinguta from the vicinities of State Farms Nos. 2 and 3, that is, from the north and east.[49]

The coordinated Soviet counterassault caught 29th Motorized Division by surprise, inflicting considerable casualties on Fremerey's panzer grenadiers and forcing him to withdraw his forward forces southward almost 10 kilometers to new defenses north of Abganerovo Station by late on 10 August.[50] During this fight, heavy volley fire from three regiments of *Katiushas* helped pry the panzer grenadiers from their defenses at 74 km Station. During this fight, the Romanian forces along the Aksai River attempted to penetrate 157th Rifle Division's defenses near Zalivskii to lessen the pressure on XXXXVIII Panzer Corps. However, these assaults also failed with heavy losses.[51] To the east, similarly heavy assaults on 14th Panzer Division's defenses south of Tinguta by Shumilov's 38th Rifle Division and 13th and 133rd Tank Brigades forced Heim to withdraw his forces about 5 kilometers and occupy all-around defensive positions protecting the town of Plodovitoe.[52]

During this fighting, the OKW daily summary noted, "Counterattacks by large enemy forces were repelled in intense fighting in the region between the Don and the Volga southwest of Stalingrad."[53] The Red Army General Staff's daily reports for 9 and 10 August provided greater detail, while its subsequent report on 11 August reported that 64th Army had accomplished its mission:

[9 August]
    64th Army conducted a counterattack against the enemy grouping in the vicinity of 74 km Station-Abganerovo-Plodovitoe with part of its forces at 0600 hours on 9 August.
    157th RD [Rifle Division] was fighting to destroy the enemy in the vicinity of Hill 78.9 and Popova *Balka* [ravine]. Seven guns, 5 heavy and 9 light ma-

chine guns and about 350 rifles were seized, and up to 120 enemy soldiers were destroyed [killed] in the fighting.

126th RD reached the northwestern outskirts of Abganerovo Station with its left wing by 1800 hours on 9 August.

38th RD was engaged in intense fighting for the 74 km Station-Kosh (3 kilometers southeast of 74 km Station) line, having driving the enemy back 2–3 kilometers from this region.

The units of 204th RD were fighting in the vicinity of 74 km Station.

[10 August]

64th Army occupied its former positions on its right wing, and, in its center and on its left wing, it fought offensively with the enemy with part of its forces and occupied [the following] positions:

[214th, 138th, 157th, and 29th RDs and 118th FR (Fortified Region) were defending the lower Aksai River line from the Don River to west of Aksai];

126th RD was defending the line Hill 124.0-Svinnaia *Balka*-Hill 127.3-Kudomiasov *Balka;*

204th RD was attacking and reached the line north of Abganerovo—6 kilometers southeast of 74 km Station-State Farm No. 3 (8 kilometers southeast of Tinguta Station) by 1400 hours on 10 August;

The units of 13th Tank Corps were operating together with the rifle forces on the left wing of the army.

[11 August]

64th Army was occupying its previous positions on its left wing, and, on its right wing, 126th RD was fighting fiercely with the enemy along the Kapkinskii (25 kilometers west of Abganerovo)-Hill 124.0 line. The division liquidated the enemy group penetrating in the vicinity of Katrusheva *Balka* and Zdaniaia Myshkova *Balka* regions by 1900 hours on 11 August. The remnants of the enemy have been thrown back from the forward edge of our units' defenses. . . .

204th and 38th RDs and part of the forces of 208th RD liquidated the penetration in the vicinity of 74 km Station as a result of two days of heavy fighting and reached the Motor Tractor Factory (7 kilometers southeast of Abganerovo)-Hill 115.3 (10 kilometers northeast of Abganerovo)-State Farm (13 kilometers northeast of Abganerovo) line by 2000 hours on 10 August.[54]

The OKW confirmed these reports on 12 August, noting, "The enemy attacks south of Stalingrad were repelled. Defending strongly fortified field positions along and south of the Myshkova River, the enemy is offering stubborn resistance."[55]

The fact was that, by 11 August, Hoth's Fourth Panzer Army was broken.

Once again a carefully planned advance by inadequate force had fallen well short of achieving its objectives (i.e., reaching Stalingrad's southern outskirts). Just as with Paulus's plan to envelop and destroy the Soviet 62nd Army west of the Don River, Hoth's panzer army proved unequal to the task Hitler had assigned it. Shumilov's deputy, Chuikov, stoutly defended along the lower Aksai River, thereby tying down more than half of Fourth Panzer Army's forces. At the same time, by carefully marshaling his threadbare reserves, Shumilov was able to assemble and commit a counterattack force of sufficient size and strength to checkmate Hoth's armored spearheads in the Abganerovo region. Although the strength of Tanaschishin's 13th Tank Corps fell from 68 tanks on 8 August to 26 tanks on 12 August, the total of 64 tanks remaining in Shumilov's force on that day was more than adequate to check 29th Motorized and 14th Panzer Divisions.[56]

Thereafter, the front in the Abganerovo region stabilized on 12 August and remained quiet until the night of 17–18 August, when renewed German pressure prompted Shumilov to withdraw Chuikov's Southern Group from its exposed positions forward of the Myshkova River.

Thus, by 12 August it was clear that Hoth's panzer army indeed needed reinforcement if it was to continue its advance toward Stalingrad. The OKH struggled to provide those reinforcements, this time in the form of XXIV Panzer Corps' 24th Panzer Division (with 82 more tanks), which was still resting and refitting in assembly areas south of the Chir River. Meanwhile, Hitler and the OKH turned their attention to the Don River front in the vicinity of Kalach, where Paulus's Sixth Army was at last completing its time-consuming task of eliminating 62nd Army's bridgehead on the western bank of the Don River.

SIXTH ARMY'S ADVANCE TO KALACH,
1–11 AUGUST

While Shumilov's 64th Army and Chuikov's Southern Operational Group were thwarting Fourth Panzer Army's advance south of the Don, Paulus's Sixth Army belatedly moved to consolidate its control over the Don River (see Map 43). As his army stood motionless from 1 to 6 August, with his XIV and XXIV Panzer Corps immobilized due to a lack of fuel, Paulus reorganized his forces and incorporated new forces assigned to his army by the OKH. Within Sixth Army, Paulus assigned VIII Army Corps' 305th, 113th, and 384th Infantry Divisions the task of containing 4th Tank Army in its bridgehead south of Kremenskaia and Sirotinskaia on the Don. Meanwhile, XIV and XXIV Panzer Corps, operating as northern and southern pincers as before, were to advance concentrically toward Kalach-on-the-Don. Cooperating with 16th Panzer and 60th and 3rd Motorized Divisions of Wietersheim's northern pincer, XI Army Corps' 384th and 389th Infantry and 100th Jäger Divisions were to protect XIV Panzer Corps' right flank

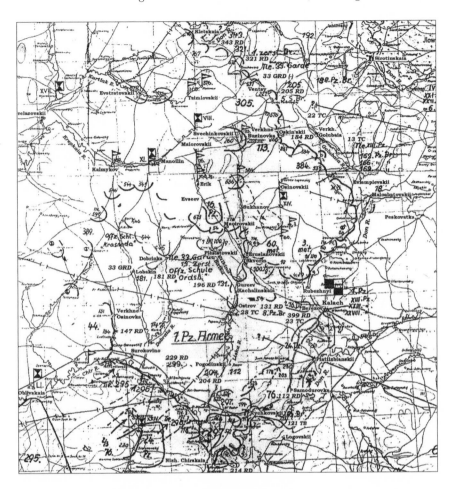

Map 43. The Sixth Army's situation, 6–7 August 1942

and press 62nd Army back toward Kalach from the northwest. To the south, co-operating with 24th Panzer and 71st, 76th, and 297th Infantry Divisions of Langermann's southern pincer, LI Army Corps' 44th and 295th Infantry Divisions were to crush 62nd Army's defenses along the Chir River by advancing from the west and southwest.[57]

Thus, the reinforcements Paulus received from the OKH (XI Army Corps) and from the commitment of Italian divisions farther north along the Don allowed him to free up his armored divisions for their decisive thrust toward Kalach and finally provided them with enough infantry support to accomplish their missions. More important still, the respite permitted Paulus to increase his armor force to a total of about 330 tanks at a time when the armor strength of the opposing Soviet 62nd Army and 4th Tank Army had fallen to well less than 300 tanks.[58] In addition, Sixth Army's supply situation improved sufficiently in early August to offer good prospects for success before fuel shortages interfered. Originally, Paulus planned to launch the new offensive on 8 August; however, Hitler's groundless fear that the Soviets were about to withdraw and escape the pocket forced Sixth Army to begin its offensive prematurely on 7 August.

Although the *Luftwaffe* was increasingly overcommitted by the diverging offensives of Army Groups A and B, Lieutenant General Martin Fiebig's VIII Air Corps was able to provide the close air support necessary to launch another blitzkrieg attack. While Khriukhin's 8th Air Army attempted to disrupt the German assembly and subsequent advance, the Red Air Force, like the Red Army, was still struggling to reinforce its efforts in the Stalingrad area. The Soviet fliers were no match for the *Luftwaffe* in terms of aircraft quality, training, and numbers.[59]

On the eve of Paulus's new Cannae-style assault, Lopatin's 62nd Army had just incorporated the forces of the defunct 1st Tank Army and the portion of 64th Army west of the Don River (229th and 212th Rifle Divisions, part of 204th Rifle Division, and 121st and 137th Tank Brigades) into its forces. 62nd Army was therefore defending its shrinking bridgehead west of Kalach with eight full rifle divisions (33rd Guards and 147th, 181st, 196th, 131st, 229th, 112th, and 399th), Khasin's 23rd and Rodin's 28th Tank Corps, student rifle regiments from the Krasnodar and Ordzhonikidze Officers Schools, four tank brigades (137th, 121st, 158th, and 40th), and the remnants of six separate tank battalions. Lopatin assigned the bulk of former 1st Tank Army's forces, including 23rd and 28th Tank Corps, to defend the northern half of his bridgehead. The divisions of his 62nd Army protected the western portion of the bridgehead, and forces transferred from 64th Army held the southern portion along the Chir River. In all, his bridgehead was defended by roughly 100,000 men supported by fewer than 150 tanks. By this time, north of Lopatin's army, Kriuchenkin's 4th Tank Army defended the bridgehead south of the Don near Kremenskaia and Sirotinskaia with Shamshin's 22nd Tank Corps, remnants of Tanaschishin's 13th Tank Corps, and 184th, 205th, 192nd, and 18th Rifle Divisions.[60]

Attacking southward at dawn on 7 August from the Maiorovskii region, 30 kilometers northwest of Kalach, multiple *kampfgruppen* from Hube's 16th Panzer Division smashed through the defenses of 33rd Guards and 131st Rifle Divisions and reached the northern outskirts of Kalach by nightfall (see Map 44):[61]

> Kalach and the Russian bridgehead had not yet fallen. After successfully fending off the enemy's counterattacks, 16th Panzer Division was replaced by an infantry division and assembled for a renewed advance toward the inner Don bend.
>
> At the point was KG [*Kampfgruppe*] Sieckenius, with 120 combat vehicles

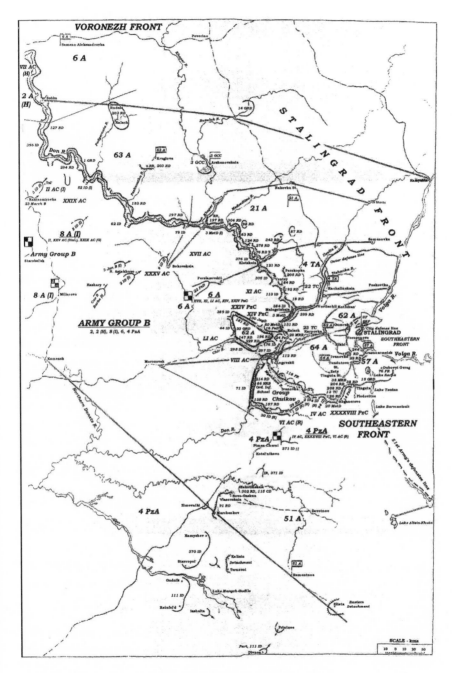

Map 44. The situation along the Stalingrad axis, 8–10 August 1942

of the Panzer Regiment, followed by KG Lattmann (Mues' 16th Panzer Grenadier Battalion, 1st Battalion, 79th Panzer Grenadier Regiment, 1st Company, 16th Panzer Jagt Battalion, and 1st Battery, 16th Artillery Regiment). The division moved south on 7 August at 5:00 hours in the morning, rolling over the attacking infantry of the 100th Light [Jäger] Division and Croatian gunners. . . . At 0815 hours Panzer Detachment von Strachwitz seized the bridge over the Liska [River] at Ostrov. The companies of Mues' Battalion under Mutius, Bruno, and Lenz were clearing the defensive positions rolled over by the panzers. KG Reinisch (79th Panzer Grenadier Regiment) took over providing protection toward the west in the evening.

KG Krumpen was still involved in the inexorable fighting at Eruslanovskii. It, together with 1st Battalion, 64th Panzer Grenadier Regiment, 16th Motorcycle Battalion, and 9th Company, 2nd Panzer Regiment, began to attack the village two hours after its right neighbor (100th Jäger Division) advanced at 0600 hours.

Fondermann's battalion managed to advance as close as 800 meters to the edge of the village; but the combined fire from all types of weapons pinned the men down. As support, 2nd Company, 16th Motorcycle Battalion, moved into the village from the right. 1st Battalion, 64th Panzer Grenadier Regiment, followed, but the enemy engaged it with fire from the flank; the commander was wounded and the commander of 2nd Company, 64th Panzer Grenadier Regiment, Senior Lieutenant Blömecke, took over the battalion.

In the meantime, the right flank unit had reached Skvorin. The division ordered—Halt the attack, capture the enemy! KG Krumpen was subordinated to 100th Jäger Division. At 1600 hours an order arrived—Capture the village without regard to losses! At 1730 hours the *kampfgruppe* resumed its attacks and engaged in heavy fighting. The tank combat wedge turned left and moved eastward toward Kalach. The panzer grenadiers were emptying the ditches of enemy who were still resisting stoutly on both sides of the march-route. The attackers were greeted by heavy artillery and Stalin organ [*Katiushas*] fire; the Russians' positions were saturated with 7.65 Pak [76mm field guns]. But fighter-bombers and Stukas were constantly hindering the enemy's resistance.

Soon after, the enemy began to feel pressure from 3rd Infantry Division (mot.), which was advancing from the north. 24th Panzer Division was advancing from the south. The counterattacks by Christie tanks failed, and Berezov [2 kilometers west of Kalach] in front of the Don fell at 1700 hours.[62]

Advancing in the panzers' wake, XI Army Corps' 100th Jäger and 389th Infantry Divisions lunged southward up to 10 kilometers. They reached the Dobrinka region, 40 kilometers west of Kalach and 25 kilometers north of Surovikino, compressing the Soviet pocket from the north. Far to the south, Hauenschild's 24th Panzer Division burst out of its bridgehead near Nizhne-

Chirskaia on the northern bank of the lower Chir River, smashed 112th Rifle Division's defenses, and advanced 35 kilometers across the steppe to the southern outskirts of Kalach.[63] Marching rapidly in the panzers' wake, XXIV Panzer Corps' 76th and 297th Infantry Divisions carved a corridor along the western bank of the Don, isolating many of 62nd Army's forces to the west. Shortly after darkness fell, the lead elements of 16th and 24th Panzer Divisions linked up near Kalach, completing the cordon around Lopatin's 62nd Army.

The Red Army General Staff's daily operational summary captured the disastrous course of events:

> 62nd Army, beginning on the morning of 7 August, was fighting fiercely with enemy forces of up to an infantry division and 100 tanks, with strong air support, in the Plesistovskii, Silkina *Balka*, and Novomaksimovskii regions [8–10 kilometers south of Maiorovskii]. The enemy penetrated the defensive front of our units by 1300 hours on 7 August, and a group of up to 70 tanks captured the Ostrov and Volodinskii region [20 kilometers west of Kalach] by 1500 hours, and a second group of 70–80 tanks reached the vicinity of Hill 118.2 [15 kilometers north of Nizhne-Chirskaia].
>
> 196th RD is fighting in encirclement in the Plesistovskii and Silkina *Balka* region.
>
> 112th RD, under pressure of a numerically superior enemy attacking toward Chir Station, was fighting intensely and withdrawing to the Pogodinskii-Hill 133.1-Motor Tractor Factory [15 kilometers north of Chir Station] line with its right wing units. The left wing units of the division were holding on to the Rychkovskii region [10 kilometers east of Chir Station].
>
> 33rd Gds. RD, having taken over the defensive sector from units of 181st RD, occupied a defense along the line Hill 189.9 (13 kilometers north of Lobakin Farm)–Hill 191.3–Berezovyi (18 kilometers north of Lobakin Farm) [50–60 kilometers west of Kalach].
>
> 147th RD, having relieved the left wing units of 181st RD, was defending along the line Hill 146.5-Verkhne Osinovka-Surovikino.
>
> 181st RD concentrated in the Dobrinka region on the morning of 7 August.
>
> 399th RD withdrew to the line Hill 185.4-Motor Tractor Factory No. 2, as a result of an enemy tank penetration from the north.[64]

At dawn on 8 August, 16th and 24th Panzer Divisions wheeled their panzers 90 degrees and began pressing the eastern face of Lopatin's encircled army back toward the west (see Map 45). From 16th Panzer Division's perspective:

> On the morning of 8 August, Russian artillery and Stalin organs served as a morning greeting. German Stukas and fighter-bombers pounded the enemy. The enemy was still holding two bridges over the Don.

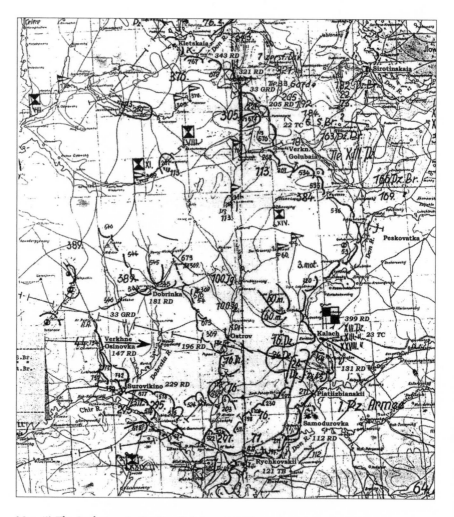

Map 45. The Sixth Army's situation, 8–9 August 1942

At Hill 150.7 20 enemy tanks stood ready to fight in the light of the morning sun. 16th Panzer Division accepted the challenge. The "Iron Knights [*Eisenritter*]" fought bitterly; the panzer shock troops destroyed several T-34s in close combat. The Russians were defeated; nevertheless, the 16th Panzer Division also suffered losses.

At midday KG Reinisch began to attack the northern bridgehead. Lenz's panzer grenadier company rolled past the tanks into Berezov and down into the Don valley. The men spied the Don, which flows at a width of 200 meters past steep banks toward the south. Part of the bridge caught fire and later blew up. The second bridge also caught fire.

In despair over their lack of success, the Russians began furious air strikes against the western bank. Fuel and ammunition vehicles blew up, and there were considerable losses among their crews. The Russians set the steppe on fire with phosphorus bombs. The wind carried the glowing heat and biting smoke clouds toward the Germans' positions.

At the same time, the Russians employed their forces west of the Liska [River] to fall onto the backs of the Germans along the Don. Their tanks managed to break through at Gureev and were causing confusion.

Parts of 16th Panzer Division wheeled around, rolled back to the Liska sector, and formed a bridgehead with its front facing toward the west. With the help of 60 combat vehicles [tanks and armored personnel carriers], they formed a strong hedgehog defense. There were still six Russian divisions operating in the Germans' rear along the Don. Resistance was increasing everywhere. The fight for the "Great Bend in the Don [Grossen Donbogen]" and the bridgehead at Kalach was complete.[65]

At the same time, advancing side by side, XI Army Corps' 389th Infantry and 100th Jäger Divisions descended on Lopatin's shrinking perimeter from the north, and LI Army and XXIV Panzer Corps' 44th, 295th, 297th, and 76th Infantry Divisions did likewise from the west, south, and southeast. Caught between the two closing pincers, the surviving soldiers of Lopatin's army had no choice but to fight their way out through German lines, surrender, or simply die in place. Once again, the Red Army General Staff's operational summary summed up Lopatin's dilemma: "*62nd Army* was fighting fierce defensive battles with tank units of the enemy penetrating into its rear west of Kalach on the Don on 8 August. . . . The enemy reached the crossing over the Don in the Kalach-Piatiizbianskii-Samodurovka regions [10–20 kilometers south of Kalach] with his forward units."[66]

The summary went on to note that 131st Rifle Division and 28th Tank Corps (without tanks) were withdrawing to the Rubezhnyi region, 10 kilometers north of Kalach, under heavy pressure; 229th Rifle Division was still defending Surovikino; 112th Rifle Division was clinging to its positions at Rychkovskii; and elements of 399th and 196th Rifle Divisions had made their way to safety east of the Don. However, the location of 147th and 33rd Guards Rifle Divisions was unknown.[67]

Paulus's army took another three days (9–11 August) to totally eradicate the Kalach pocket. As it did so, and as the perimeter of Sixth Army's encirclement ring shrank, Paulus began peeling off freed-up infantry divisions and regrouping them to the north, where he already anticipated the necessity for eliminating the pesky bridgehead still defended by Soviet 4th Tank Army south of Kremenskaia. Once again, the Red Army General Staff watched closely as Sixth Army snuffed the life out of Lopatin's 62nd Army:

[9 August]

62nd Army fought in encirclement with penetrating enemy tanks with part of its forces, simultaneously, withdrawing units to the eastern bank of the Don.

Northern Group (181st RD and 33rd Gds. RDs), which were located in the Plesistovskii-Dobrinka region at 1100 hours on 9 August, have been ordered to fight their way to the crossings over the Don at Kalach.

Southern Group (147th and 229th RDs), which were situated in the Bol. Osinovka-Buratskaia *Balka*-Vodianaia *Balka* region on the morning of 9 August, have been ordered to withdraw to the railroad bridge at Logovskii [28 kilometers south of Kalach].

23rd TC (20 tanks) and 157th Artillery-Machine Gun Battalion were defending bridgehead fortifications in the Kalach-on-the-Don region.

112th RD and 121st TB (27 tanks) captured the Rychkovskii and Samodurovka regions, where they are defending the bridgehead fortifications in the vicinity of Rychkovskii. . . .

[10 August]

62nd Army continued to fight in encirclement with its units on the western bank of the Don River and the units, which have withdrawn to the left bank of the river, were defending the Il'menskii-Kustovskii-Cherkasov-Logovskii line [from 20 kilometers north to 30 kilometers south of Kalach].

33rd Gds. RD and 181st RD were fighting in encirclement in the region west of Gureev-Kachalinskaia (22–25 kilometers northwest of Kalach) at 0400 hours on 10 August.

131st RD occupied a defense along the Il'menskii-Kustovskii line.

175th Arty–MG Bn [Artillery–Machine Gun Battalion], reinforced by the senior lieutenants course, occupied the Kustovskii-Cherkasov defensive line.

112th RD, with 158th and 160th Arty–MG Bns, was defending the Cherkasov-(incl.) Logovskii defense line.

Information has not been received about the remaining units of the army.

[11 August]

62nd Army was defending its previous positions along the eastern bank of the Don River with part of its forces. We did not succeed in establishing communications with the forces of the encircled 181st RD, 33rd Gds. RD, and 229th and 147th RDs on 11 August.[68]

After trying in vain to encircle and destroy 62nd Army for more than three weeks, Paulus's Sixth Army finally announced it had completed this task on 12

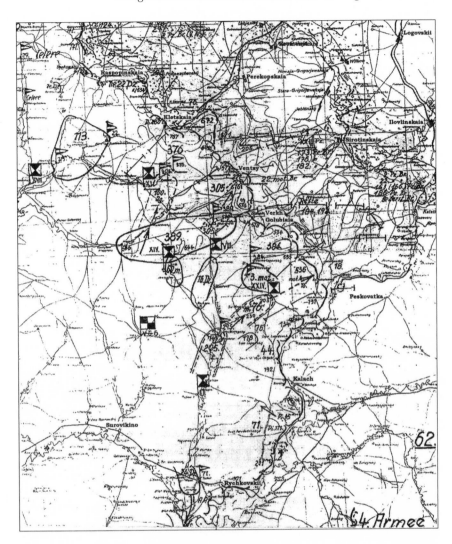

Map 46. The Sixth Army's situation, 12–13 August 1942

August (see Map 46). By its own count, Sixth Army encircled and eliminated eight Soviet rifle divisions (33rd Guards, 131st, 147th, 181st, 196th, 204th, 229th, and 399th), two officers' detachments from Red Army military schools (Krasnodar and Ordzhonikidze), ten tank (39th, 56th, 99th, 121st, 129th, 137th, 149th, 166th, 169th, and 298th) and two motorized rifle brigades (3rd and 20th), and one destroyer brigade (13th). In the process, Paulus claimed to have destroyed 270 tanks and 560 guns and captured more than 35,000 soldiers from the 62nd

Red Army tanks in ambush positions in the Great Bend of the Don, August 1942

Sappers constructing a bridge across the Don River, August 1942

Infantry of the Stalingrad Front counterattack near Kalach-on-the-Don, August 1942

Stalingrad Front counterattack near Kalach-on-the-Don, August 1942

Army and 1st Tank Army.[69] For its part, 16th Panzer Division recorded, "The history of the war later included these battles among the classic tank battles. 16th Panzer Division captured 8,300 prisoners and destroyed 275 tanks and 298 guns. Since 22 June 1941, 1,000 tanks had fallen victim to the division."[70]

Soviet documents, however, indicate that even though 62nd Army indeed lost much of 33rd Guards, and 181st, 147th, and 229th Rifle Divisions, most of 112th, 131st, and 196th Rifle Divisions' surviving soldiers escaped across the Don, as did most of 23rd and 28th Tank Corps' troops, although without their tanks. Thus, roughly half of Lopatin's 62nd Army probably escaped eastward to fight another day.

For the first time in Operation Blau, as indicated by an information bulletin the OKW issued on 12 August, many of the Germans thought they had achieved the kind of spectacular victory that had been so common in 1941:

> In the Great Bend of the Don River west of Kalach, the ground forces under the command of General of Panzer Troops Paulus, with the active support of antiaircraft artillery and aircraft under the command of Colonel General Baron von Richthofen, destroyed the main forces of the Soviets' 62nd Army and a significant portion of 1st Tank Army. In this decisive battle, 75,000 men were captured, and more than 1,000 tanks and 750 artillery pieces of all types were captured. The enemy suffered significant personnel losses.[71]

However, a more sober analysis of Army Group B's operations during this period indicates that Paulus's advance to Kalach as well as Hoth's advance to Abganerovo were essentially episodic in nature, improvised, and far less decisive than initially judged. At the time they conducted these operations, neither force possessed the requisite strength to accomplish its assigned mission in one bound. Thus, Sixth Army's initial attempt to encircle 62nd Army west of the Don faltered short of its objective during the last week of July because of stout Soviet resistance and fierce counterstrokes. Thereafter, Paulus was able to reinvigorate his advance only after resting his forces for more than a week, receiving reinforcements, regrouping his forces, and replenishing their fuel and ammunition. Although Hoth's advance from Tsimlianskaia eased Paulus's task and managed to unhinge 64th Army's defenses south of the Don, it also faltered in the Abganerovo region after about a week of fighting due to heavy Soviet resistance and counterattacks.

Even after Paulus's Sixth Army finally eliminated the Soviet 62nd Army at Kalach on 11 and 12 August, its work was far from done. Before Paulus could mount the decisive stroke to Stalingrad, he still had to deal with more Soviet forces west of the Don; this time it was Kriuchenkin's 4th Tank Army, whose forces still clung to their bridgehead across the Don south of Kremenskaia and Sirotinskaia. Making matters more difficult for Paulus, the tank strength of his armored divisions, 16th and 24th Panzer and 3rd and 60th Motorized Divisions, decreased by roughly 20 percent during the operation to destroy 62nd Army. For example, 24th Panzer Division began the operation with 116 tanks and ended it with 82 tanks.[72]

The reality facing Hitler and the OKH on 12 August was such that, with Hoth's panzer army stalled at Abganerovo, Paulus's Sixth Army had to clear Soviet forces from the entire west bank of the Don River before it and Hoth's Fourth Panzer Army could hope to conduct their decisive drive to the Volga River and Stalingrad.

ORGANIZING STALINGRAD'S DEFENSES

To place the forthcoming battle in strategic context: The fall of Kalach convinced the Soviet leadership that a climactic battle in the Stalingrad region was imminent. Somewhat belatedly, therefore, on 9 August Stalin conceded to General Eremenko's concerns about unity of command in the region, but the dictator's solution was Byzantine, to say the least. While Eremenko officially became the overall commander of the Stalingrad defense, he now had to operate through the two separate *front* headquarters—Stalingrad and Southeastern. Gordov remained commander of Stalingrad Front, but since it was operationally subordinated to Eremenko's Southeastern Front, he was, in essence, Eremenko's deputy. In turn, Southeastern Front received a new deputy commander in the person of Golikov, although Eremenko sent Golikov out to the *front* as a troubleshooter rather than keep him at headquarters. In turn, Moskalenko replaced Golikov as commander of 1st Guards Army, whose lead divisions were then detraining in the Frolovo region, 28 kilometers north of the Don, in 4th Tank Army's rear area.

On 12 August, Stalin superimposed yet another layer of supervision over Eremenko, sending a troika of senior officials to Stalingrad with the dubious mission of guiding Eremenko in the defense of Stalingrad. This included Vasilevsky as the *Stavka*'s representative; Georgii Maksimianovich Malenkov, one of Stalin's closest political henchmen, as representative of the Communist Party Central Committee; and Lieutenant General Aleksandr Aleksandrovich Novikov, the Red Air Force chief.[73] The next day the *Stavka* formally reduced Gordov to the post of Eremenko's deputy—but still in charge of the Stalingrad Front.[74]

Within the constraints of this bizarre command arrangement, the *Stavka* and Eremenko attempted to strengthen their defenses before the inevitable German blow landed. For example, on 11 August the *Stavka* gave priority in all rail movements to 1st Guards Army so that it could reinforce Stalingrad Front's right wing. 1st Guards was destined for the Ilovlia region, 20 kilometers east of the Don at Sirotinskaia, where it was to establish a second defensive belt with two divisions by 14 August to back up 4th Tank Army. After releasing three more rifle divisions and 77th Fortified Region from its reserve to create a new defensive belt behind 64th and 57th Armies south of Stalingrad, the *Stavka* formed a new 16th Air

Army, under the command of Major General of Aviation Sergei Ignat'evich Rudenko, to support Southeastern Front, and reinforced 8th Air Army with 447 aircraft from 21 aviation regiments.[75] Finally, to protect the immense gap formed between the Southeastern and North Caucasus Fronts in the Elista region and to protect Astrakhan' on the Volga River, the *Stavka* on 12 August dispatched 34th Guards Rifle Division to defend Astrakhan', and the People's Commissariat of Communications Routes sent its 47th Separate Railroad Brigade to defend the 350-kilometer-long railroad line between Astrakhan' and Kizliar in the North Caucasus.

With these decisions reached, Vasilevsky and Eremenko met together during 9–12 August to plan the forthcoming defense. Assuming that the Germans had satisfied the prerequisites for a general advance on Stalingrad by reaching the Don River at Kalach, they therefore concluded the enemy would try to eliminate 4th Tank Army's bridgehead and then proceed toward Stalingrad with two shock groups, the first from the vicinity of Kalach-on-the-Don, with 10–11 divisions, and the second from the Plodovitoe region, with 5–7 divisions. Therefore, the two generals decided to organize Stalingrad Front's defenses in the sector along the eastern bank of the Don from Babka southward through Kletskaia to Kalach. Their priority was to create a defense in depth in 4th Tank Army's sector from Kletskaia to Bol'shenabatovskii and 62nd Army's sector from Bol'shenabatovskii southward to Kalach. Eremenko and his deputy Gordov assigned the *front's* armies the following missions:

- *63rd Army* [V. I. Kuznetsov] (1st and 14th Guards Rifle Divisions and 127th, 153rd, 197th, and 203rd Rifle Divisions) will firmly defend the left bank of the Don in the 200-kilometer-wide sector from Babka to the mouth of the Khoper River, paying special attention to protecting the Borisoglebsk axis from the south;
- *21st Army* [Danilov] (63rd, 76th, 124th, 278th, 304th, 343rd, and 96th Rifle Divisions, reinforced by the disbanded 28th and 38th Armies' artillery) will defend the 140-kilometer-wide sector from the mouth of the Khoper River to Melo-Kletskii and retain two rifle divisions in army reserve;
- *4th Tank Army* [Kriuchenkin] (321st, 18th, 205th, 192nd, and 184th Rifle Divisions, 5th Antitank Artillery Brigade, 22nd Tank Corps, and 54th Fortified Region) will hold the 50-kilometer-wide bridgehead on the right bank of the Don River from Melo-Kletskii to Malonabatovskii [35 kilometers north of Kalach], while protecting the approaches to Stalingrad from the northwest and the railroad sector from Povorino to Stalingrad. Retain 22nd Tank Corps in army reserve in the Rodionov region [15 kilometers behind the front lines];
- *1st Guards Army* [Moskalenko] (37th, 38th, 39th, 40th, 4th, and 41st Guards Rifle Divisions), after deploying forward to Ilovlinskaia Station

[near Ilovlia], must concentrate 39th Guards Rifle Division in the Trekhostrovskaia region by the morning of 14 August and, by day's end, each of three rifle divisions in the Khokhlachev, Perekopskaia and Perekopka, and Novo-Grigor'evskaia regions [15–20 kilometers behind 4th Tank Army's front lines]; and

- *62nd Army* [Lopatin] (399th, 112th, and 131st Rifle Divisions, 20th Motorized Brigade, 28th Tank Corps, and 115th Fortified Region), after withdrawing behind the Don River, will occupy and firmly defend the 90-kilometer-wide sector from Lake Peschanoe to the mouth of the Donskaia Tsaritsa River, protecting the most direct route to Stalingrad from the west and rescue the army's forces encircled west of the river [33rd Guards and 196th, 399th, 147th, 181st, and 229th Rifle Divisions]. Create a dense tactical defense with 98th Rifle Division in the Peskovatka, Sokarevka, and Illarionovskii sector [32–15 kilometers north of Kalach] and with 87th Rifle Division in the Illarionovskii, Sovetskii, and Sredne-Tsaritsynskii sector [15 kilometers north to 20 kilometers south of Kalach], both divisions in the *front*'s reserve. Prepare a rear defensive belt in the Kotluban', Rossoshka River, and Karpovka sector [20–25 kilometers east of the Don River], organizing the first defense line in the Novo-Alekseevskii and Karpovka sector [30–35 kilometers east of Kalach] employing separate chemical companies, 4th Guards-Mortar Battalion (M-30), and 5 T-34 tanks. 28th Tank Corps, refitting in the Illarionovskii region, will be in army reserve. The army will be allocated 5,000 antitank and anti-personnel mines to strengthen the defense.[76]

As sound as Stalingrad Front's defense plan appeared on paper, in practice it was fatally flawed. First, time and distance constraints prevented Moskalenko's 1st Guards Army from moving into the region and occupying its assigned defensive positions by the designated time. When its divisions finally began arriving a day or two late, they lacked supporting artillery, specialized support units, horse and vehicular transport, ammunition, supplies, and basic heavy weapons.[77] The divisions then received what they could of this matériel as they deployed forward, usually under incessant German air attacks. Second, Eremenko's assumption that 62nd Army's encircled forces would make it safely back across the Don was also mistaken.[78] Too weak to mount any sort of credible relief effort, 62nd Army had to make do with scattered survivors of many of its divisions. Third, the Germans denied Eremenko time to provide any of his armies with their promised reinforcements, support, or supplies.

As for Southeastern Front, Eremenko and Vasilevsky planned a stubborn defense along the Myshkova River, Abganerovo, State Farm "Privolzhskii" (Volga), and Raigorod line to prevent the Germans from reaching Stalingrad from the south. To shorten the front, strengthen this defensive line, and generate reserves, the two generals decided to withdraw the *front*'s right wing (Group Chuikov) back from the Aksai River. Finally, to protect the *front's* long and weak left wing, they decided to withdraw Kolomiets's 51st Army eastward to defenses between Lakes Tsatsa and Sarpa (west of the Volga and 50–64 kilometers due south of Stalingrad). Eremenko's plan assigned the *front's* armies the following missions:[79]

- *64th Army* [Shumilov] (29th, 38th, 126th, 138th, 157th, 204th, and 208th Rifle Divisions, 13th Tank Corps [13th, 254th, and 133rd Tank Brigades, 6th Guards Tank Brigade, and 38th Motorized Rifle Brigade], 66th and 154th Naval Rifle Brigade, 118th Fortified Region, and the Zhitomir and Groznyi Officers Schools) will withdraw Group Chuikov to the external defensive belt by 12 August and occupy a defense in the 120-kilometer-wide sector from Logovskii [on the Don River 10 kilometers north of the Myshkova River] to Tinguta Station [50 kilometers south of Stalingrad], protecting the shortest route to the city from the southwest. Concentrate the army's main forces along the Tebektenerovo (12 kilometers east of Kapkinskii), Abganerovo Station, and Tinguta line.[80]
- *57th Army* [Tolbukhin] (15th, 35th, and 36th Guards Rifle Divisions and 244th and 422nd Rifle Divisions and 6th Tank Brigade [19 tanks], the Vinnitsa Infantry School Regiment, 255th Cavalry Regiment, and 76th Fortified Region) will firmly defend the 70-kilometer-wide sector from State Farm No. 4 (4 kilometers east of Tinguta) and State Farm "Privolzhskii" to Raigorod and prevent the enemy from penetrating to Stalingrad from the south;[81]
- *51st Army* [Kolomiets] (91st and 302nd Rifle Divisions, 115th Cavalry Division, and 125th, 135th, and 155th Tank Brigades, without tanks) will withdraw northeastward toward Zavetnoe [95 kilometers south of Aksai] and Obil'noe [55 kilometers south of Malyi Derbety], fighting a delaying action across a 150-kilometer-wide front, and must occupy a defense along the Malyi Derbety and Lake Sarpa line south of Stalingrad by 16 August to hold firmly to the defile between the lakes and prevent the enemy from reaching the Volga;
- *8th Air Army* [Lieutenant General of Aviation V. N. Zhdanov] (268th, 220th, 235th, and 269th Fighter Aviation Divisions, 270th and 271st Bomber Aviation Divisions, 272nd Night Bomber Aviation Division, 206th, 226th, and 228th Assault Aviation Divisions, and 23rd, 655th, 282nd, and 633rd Mixed Aviation Regiments) will assist 62nd Army's forces in destroying the enemy blocking the withdrawal routes of the army's formations retreating from the right bank of the Don River and support their crossing to the left bank and also reliably protect the regrouping of forces and the concentrating of reserves in both *fronts;*[82]
- *Volga Military Flotilla* (1st and 2nd Brigades of River Ships, and the separate brigade of trawlers), in cooperation with 57th Army, will prevent the enemy from approaching the forward edge of the external defensive line

in the Raigorod region and also the detached enemy group from reaching the Volga in the sector from Raigorod [south] to Kalganovki with its main force;[83]

- *Stalingrad Military District* [Lieutenant General V. F. Gerasimenko] (34th Guards Rifle Division, two mixed regiments of the Astrakhan Military School, and 78th and 116th Fortified Regions), subordinate to the Southeastern Front, effective 15 August, will defend the Astrakhan' Fortified Region and the approaches to Astrakhan' and the Volga from the west and northwest, while protecting the Elista axis especially firmly. At the same time, dispatch strong mobile reconnaissance detachments to the State Farm No. 10, Sarpa, Altsynkhuta, Chilgir, and Iashkul' line to block enemy movement from the Elista region.

In addition to constructing multiple defensive lines in depth, Eremenko ordered both *fronts* to plant minefields and create security belts forward of each of their defensive lines and to form mobile reserves, each reinforced by one *Katiusha* multiple rocket launcher regiment and one antitank artillery regiment, to operate along key axes.

The *Stavka's* 9 August directive subordinating Stalingrad Front to Eremenko's control, and the decision to colocate its headquarters with that of Southeastern Front in Stalingrad, seriously undermined Gordov's ability to control his forces effectively because it was so distant from its subordinate armies. In addition, the decision to establish Stalingrad Front's auxiliary command post in the Bol'shaia Rossoshka region, on the Rossoshka River 30 kilometers west of Stalingrad, and Southeastern Front's at Beketovka, on the Volga 20 kilometers south of Stalingrad—both 20–30 kilometers behind their respective front lines—placed undue strain on already weak communications systems.[84] The general shortage of radios, the limited range and poor technical reliability of existing radios, and similar shortages of wire communications equipment hindered the ability of both the *fronts* and their armies to command and control forces effectively. Thus, the armies were forced to rely on liaison officers dispatched to subordinate divisions and brigades by aircraft, vehicle, and, sometimes, tanks. The paucity of experienced staff officers in most headquarters compounded the problem.[85]

In addition, overextended supply lines, and the cannibalizing of Stalingrad Front's supply organs and facilities to create a logistical structure in Southeastern Front, hindered effective logistical support of both *fronts*. Loss of the critical Stalingrad-Tikhoretsk and Stalingrad-Likhaia railroad lines west of Stalingrad forced both *fronts* to rely on the Povorino-Stalingrad railroad, which ran into Stalingrad from the north, and, to a lesser extent, the Stalingrad-Astrakhan' railroad line. However, the Germans subjected the main line north of Stalingrad to near constant bombing and interdiction and, beginning in late August, even to artillery fire from the right bank of the Volga. As a result, the *fronts* and armies suffered constant shortages of supplies, in particular ammunition, foodstuffs, and weaponry of all types. For example, on 15 August Stalingrad Front's armies had 1.6–1.9 combat loads of rifle ammunition, 5.8–9.9 combat loads of artillery ammunition, and 2.1–3.2 refills of fuel in its armies' warehouses; as a result of its heavy fighting, the 62nd Army had only 0.28 loads of rifle ammunition, 2.0 loads of artillery ammunition, and 1.4 refills of fuel.[86] The stocks in Southeastern Front's armies were lower still, with only 1.2–1.5 loads of rifle ammunition, 1.0–1.5 loads of artillery ammunition, and 1.0–2.5 refills of fuel.

In addition, the *fronts* also lacked adequate transport to move these supplies. For example, as of 15 August Stalingrad Front was supported by three auto-transport battalions with a total 265 vehicles, while each division in 4th Tank and 62nd Armies had 40–60 trucks.[87] Therefore, from the very beginning of the Stalingrad defense, Soviet forces had to operate on a logistical shoestring, carefully preserving on-hand stocks and improvising at every stage.

Even before Eremenko and Vasilevsky could implement their carefully developed defensive plan in the face of these mounting problems, Paulus's Sixth Army threw a monkey wrench into their efforts by suddenly striking at 4th Tank Army's defenses in the northeast corner of the Great Bend (i.e., to the south of the Don).

SIXTH ARMY'S ADVANCE INTO THE NORTHEAST CORNER OF THE GREAT BEND, 15–19 AUGUST

While Paulus's victory at Kalach cheered the Germans, it fell far short of restoring the momentum of Army Group B's advance. Although Kalach-on-the-Don was indeed the shortest axis of advance for Sixth Army to reach Stalingrad, the terrain immediately east of Kalach was frequently broken up by deep *balkas* that would be much easier for the Soviets to defend than they would be for German mechanized units to traverse. Moreover, an advance due east from Kalach would soon bring Sixth Army into close proximity with Fourth Panzer Army, complicating supply routes and eliminating any opportunity for another large-scale encirclement. A march on Stalingrad from Kalach would also leave Paulus's left (northern) flank highly vulnerable to counterattacks by the only large tank force still available to the Soviets (4th Tank Army's 22nd Tank Corps), plus 21st Army and whatever other forces the *Stavka* might be able to deploy forward from its reserves.

Based on these considerations, and for the third time in three weeks, Paulus on 10 August once again decided to regroup his forces and conduct another carefully orchestrated offensive—this time to clean out the northeast corner of the Great Bend, the bridgehead south of Kremenskaia and Sirotinskaia on the Don, which was defended by Stalingrad Front's 4th Tank Army. Even before his Sixth Army completed the liquidation of Soviet 62nd Army forces encircled west of Kalach, Paulus began shifting forces from the encirclement ring northward to reinforce his army's VIII Army Corps, which was containing the Soviet forces in the smaller bridgehead. He began transferring XIV Panzer Corps' 16th Panzer and 60th and 3rd Motorized Divisions northward on 10 August; as they completed their movement, XI Army Corps' 389th Infantry and 100th Jäger Divisions and LI Army Corps' 76th and 295th Infantry Divisions followed on 11 and 12 August.[88]

Paulus's attack plan concentrated eleven divisions (one panzer, two motorized, and eight infantry) from XIV and XXIV Panzer and XI, VIII, and LI Army Corps in the 55-kilometer-wide sector between Kletskaia on the Don and Bol'shenaba-tovskii on the Don (see Map 46). This force was to attack northeastward to destroy 4th Tank Army's forces defending the northeast corner of the Great Bend and then capture bridgeheads over the Don River to facilitate Sixth Army's subsequent drive to the Volga River and Stalingrad. Spearheading the assault, XIV Panzer Corps' 60th and 3rd Motorized Divisions would smash through the center of 4th Tank Army's defenses on 15 August and capture the southern bank of the Don River south of Sirotinskaia, while 16th Panzer Division would wheel eastward to reach the Don River at Trekhostrovskaia. Wietersheim's panzer corps was to spearhead its main attack with 16th Panzer Division's *Kampfgruppe* Sieckenius (2nd Panzer Regiment), Panzer Detachment (*Abteilung*) Strachwitz, and assault guns from 384th Infantry Division.[89]

To divert 4th Tank Army's attention and draw its reserves away from Paulus's main attack sector, XI Army Corps' 376th Infantry and 100th Jäger Divisions were to commence their assault on 13 August against 4th Tank Army's right wing south of Kletskaia. As XIV Panzer Corps' mechanized divisions began their main attack on 15 August, VIII Army Corps' 305th, 389th, and 384th Infantry Divisions and XXIV Panzer Corps' 76th and 295th Infantry Divisions were to support their attack, advance in their wake, and secure the southern bank of the Don River from Trekhostrovskaia southward to Vertiachii and Peskovatka, wherever possible seizing crossings over the river and capturing bridgeheads on the eastern bank.[90] Farther south, LI Army Corps' 44th and 71st Infantry Division would attack to secure the western bank of the Don from Kalach northward to Peskovatka.

The timing of Sixth Army's offensive was critical to Army Group B's subsequent advance on the Volga River and Stalingrad. Specifically, Paulus's army had to clear the bridgehead quickly enough to be able to coordinate closely with Hoth's Fourth Panzer Army when it resumed its advance on Stalingrad from the southeast, tentatively planned to begin on or about 18 August. In the meantime Paulus, to give Hoth sufficient strength to resume his advance, on 12 August released 24th Panzer and 297th Infantry Divisions for their movement eastward to join Hoth's army. They completed their redeployment on 18 August. In addition, while his forces were clearing Soviet troops from their last foothold west of the Don, Paulus frantically rebuilt his stocks of critical supplies, especially the fuel and ammunition necessary to sustain the final drive to the Volga.

General Kriuchenkin's 4th Tank Army had been defending the 50-kilometer-wide bridgehead on the southern bank of the Don from Melo-Kletskii to Malonabatovskii since early August, when its attempted counterstroke had ended in defeat. A tank army in name only on 1 August, Kriuchenkin's forces consisted of 18th, 184th, 192nd, and 205th Rifle Divisions, arrayed from left to right along the front from Malonabatovskii on the Don northwestward to Melo-Kletskii on the Don. The 54th Fortified Region, whose artillery–machine gun battalions were defending the northern bank of the river, was backed up by 5th Destroyer Brigade and the remnants of Shamshin's 22nd and Tanaschishin's 13th Tank Corps, each fielding scarcely more than 20 tanks. During the first week of August, Stalingrad Front reinforced 4th Tank Army with 321st Rifle Division, which Kriuchenkin inserted on his army's right flank and, on the night of 12–13 August, with the remainder of 21st Army's 343rd Rifle Division, which already had moved part of its forces into positions on 4th Tank Army's right flank in the bridgehead.[91]

On 4th Tank Army's right, General Danilov's 21st Army defended the 40-kilometer sector along the northern bank of the Don from the Melo-Kletskii region westward to the mouth of the Khoper River, 30 kilometers west of Serafimovich, with its 76th, 278th, 124th, 96th, and 304th Rifle Divisions arrayed from left to right. Danilov retained 63rd Rifle Division in his army's reserve and 343rd Rifle Division in the western extremity of 4th Tank Army's bridgehead. Because 1st Guards Army, which was supposed to man a second defensive belt in Kriuchenkin's bridgehead, was still en route to the region, and 4th Tank Army fielded only about 45 tanks, Kriuchenkin's army was indeed ripe for rapid defeat.[92]

True to his plan, Paulus on 13 August unleashed XI Army Corps' 376th Infantry and 100th Jäger Divisions in a diversionary assault against 4th Tank Army's right wing in the Sredne and Perekopka regions. As reported by the Red Army General Staff:

> *4th Tank Army* conducted stubborn fighting against attacking enemy infantry supported by 50–60 tanks and bombers with its right wing units beginning on the morning of 13 August and was continuing to defend its previous positions on its left wing.
>
> 321st RD conducted fierce fighting with an enemy force of up to a regiment of infantry with 50–60 tanks beginning at 0630 hours on 13 August, and, under pressure, the units of the division withdrew [10–15 kilometers] to the Malyi Iarki-Mokryi Log *Balka*-Hill 134.4 line at 1430 hours. Fighting is raging along this line. . . .
>
> [In *21st Army's* sector,] 343rd RD, having crossed the Don River in the Kremenskaia-Perekopskaia region, was fighting in the Melo-Kletskii region with part of its forces.[93]

After Sixth Army's diversionary attack forced 321st and 343rd Rifle Divisions to withdraw, as Paulus expected, Kriuchenkin reinforced the threatened sector on the night of 13–14 August with 5th Destroyer Brigade and an antitank artillery regiment from his army's center. Alarmed by the attack, Gordov also rushed reinforcements to Kriuchenkin's army, beginning with 193rd Tank Brigade (about 25 tanks) from 62nd Army, two tank battalions and three artillery regiments from 21st Army, and 22nd Antitank Artillery Brigade from his *front's* reserve on the night of 13–14 August. Later, he added four antitank artillery regiments from 57th Army on the night of 14–15 August. As Gordov did so, he instructed Kriuchenkin to employ the fresh antitank regiments to defend the vital crossing sites over the Don River at Vertiachii and Peskovatka.[94]

Paulus unleashed his main attack against 4th Tank Army at 0630 hours on 15 August after pummeling Kriuchenkin's defenses with a two-hour artillery preparation (see Map 47). Protected by a swarm of Stuka dive-bombers, 16th Panzer and 60th and 3rd Motorized Divisions of Wietersheim's XIV Panzer Corps, supported by VIII Army Corps' 305th, 389th, and 384th Infantry Divisions, demolished the defenses of 192nd, 184th, and 205th Rifle Divisions in the center of Kriuchenkin's army and pushed rapidly eastward. From 16th Panzer Division's vantage point:

> Meanwhile, the enemy was assembling in the inner Don bend and was blocking with three divisions between Podgorskii and Golubinskii. The division was moving north via Sukhanov and Mukovkin and from there to the east.
>
> At 0200 hours in the morning on 15 August, fighters, Stukas, and fighter-bombers opened the attack. The division had orders to move forward in the inner Don bend toward the river, drive around the bend, and form a sack only open toward the west. Sixth Army's infantry divisions, which were already alerted, would operate there [west of the sack].
>
> KG Sieckenius rolled through the [advancing] infantry and cut through the Russians' fortified positions south of Blizhniaia-Perekopka. The Russians defended fiercely and bitterly, and some elements held out in the steep *balkas*. After the tanks broke through, they renewed their attacks, destroyed the *Werfer* [six-tube mortar] batteries, and fired at vehicles transporting the wounded. Mues' battalion had to turn back in order to mop up the area. An intense battle began. Numerous antitank rifles were captured.
>
> Panzer Detachment von Strachwitz managed to move forward to the Don at Trekhostrovskaia. The bridges there had already been destroyed. Dörmann's battalion secured the river to the east.[95]

With Kriuchenkin's defenses under devastating assault, the Red Army General Staff recorded:

> *4th Tank Army* was continuing to conduct fierce defensive fighting with enemy forces of up to 4–5 infantry divisions, one motorized division, and one panzer division on 15 August. The enemy managed to penetrate our defensive

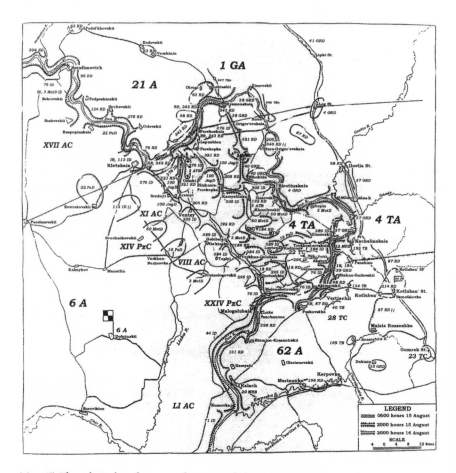

Map 47. The 4th Tank and 1st Guards Armies' defense, 15–16 August 1942

front on the army's left wing and reach the Kamyshinka–Bol'shaia Kubantseva *Balka*–Rytnyi burial mound line (37–62 kilometers southeast of Kletskaia) by 1500 hours.

321st RD was fighting along the Malyi Iarki–Osinki–Hill 184.1 line.

205th and 192nd RDs, enveloped by the enemy from the flanks, were fighting in encirclement in the Os'kinskii region.

182nd TB was fighting with 30 enemy tanks in the vicinity of the Motor Tractor Station (10 kilometers south of Kamyshinka) at 1400 hours 15 August.

184th RD was fighting in the region 12 kilometers southeast of Kamyshinka.

39th Gds. RD reached the Hill 185.0–Kalachkin line.

A regiment of 40th Gds. RD crossed to the western bank of the Don River and concentrated in the Sirotinskaia region.

98th and 198th TBs received the mission to cross the Don River in the Vertiachii region for joint operations with the units of 39th Gds. RD.

The situation in 343rd RD and 647th and 697th Sep. TBns is being verified.[96]

Thus, while all of 4th Tank Army's divisions were either encircled or withdrawing under heavy pressure, parts of 1st Guards Army's 39th and 40th Guards Rifle Divisions were en route to the Sirotinskaia and Trekhostrovskaia regions, respectively, to support Kriuchenkin's beleaguered forces.

By nightfall, Kohlermann's 60th Motorized Division had traversed more than 20 kilometers, reaching the southern bank of the Don River south of Sirotinskaia. On Kohlermann's right, after wheeling sharply to the east, Strachwitz's *kampfgruppe* from Hube's 16th Panzer Division pushed on to the western bank of the Don River at Trekhostrovskaia. During its advance, the panzers of Hube's division overran Kriuchenkin's headquarters at 1200 hours, destroying his ability to command and control his forces effectively. To the south, Paulus's secondary attack force, XXIV Panzer Corps' 76th and 295th Infantry Divisions, obliterated the defenses of 18th Rifle Division on Kriuchenkin's left wing, advancing more than 15 kilometers to capture Akimovskii, on the western bank of the Don opposite the key crossing at Vertiachii.[97]

In addition to depriving Kriuchenkin of his ability to control his forces, Paulus's decisive assault split 4th Tank Army into two parts, forcing its 205th and 321st Rifle Divisions, as well as 21st Army's 343rd Rifle Division, to withdraw northward toward Kremenskaia and its 18th, 184th, and 192nd Rifle Divisions and 22nd Tank Corps' single tank brigade to withdraw eastward toward the Don River north and south of Akimovskii.[98]

After evaluating the rapidly deteriorating situation, and pressured by the *Stavka* and Eremenko, Gordov, late on 15 August, ordered Moskalenko to commit the remainder of his 1st Guards Army's 40th, 37th, and 39th Guards Rifle Divisions, which had finally completed detraining at Ilovlia Station, into the bridgehead to reinforce Kriuchenkin's shattered forces and conduct a counterstroke of their own at dawn on 17 August. Gordov's counterstroke, which the *Stavka* ordered Eremenko's deputy to "personally supervise," required 321st, 205th, and 343rd Rifle, and 40th Guards Rifle Divisions to counterattack from behind 4th Tank Army's right wing north of Sirotinskaia and 37th and 39th Guards and 18th Rifle Divisions and 22nd Tank Corps' 182nd Tank Brigade to do so from behind the tank army's left wing northwest of Vertiachii.

At the same time, 62nd Army's fresh 98th Rifle Division, reinforced by 193rd Tank Brigade and 5th Guards-Mortar Regiment and, later, by 214th Rifle Division, was to cross the Don at Vertiachii overnight on 15–16 August and attack westward toward Rodionov. Meanwhile, 21st Army's 63rd Rifle Division was to

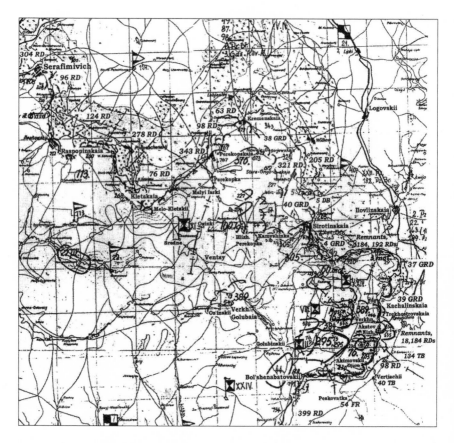

Map 48. The Sixth Army's situation, 16–17 August 1942

conduct a simultaneous attack against the left wing of Paulus's forces along the Don at and north of Melo-Kletskii.[99] Finally, Gordov ordered 8th Air Army to support the counterstroke and protect 1st Guards Army's forces as they deployed forward with all available aircraft.

Despite Gordov's elaborate planning, his counterstroke faltered from the start. Paulus's forces continued their advance on 16 August, pressing Kriuchenkin's forces and the reinforcements from Moskalenko's 1st Guards Army inexorably northward into their shrinking bridgeheads south of the Don (see Map 48). From 16th Panzer Division's vantage point:

> On 16 August KG Sieckenius and Panzer Detachment von Strachwitz moved [southward] toward Verkhne-Akatov; the assault guns of 384th Infantry Division were combing through the wooded areas in the direction of the Don and

were doing their job well. 16th Panzer Division seized Hill 132.4 and Nizhne-Akatov on the Don. The infantry managed to fight their way across the river. That evening Panzer Detachment von Strachwitz managed a surprise attack. In two stages it assaulted Trekhostrovskaia from the direction of the Don high road and, after heavy fighting, reached the bank of the Don here too. At the last moment, several Russians succeeded in setting the bridge on fire in the middle. Protected by fire from Lieutenant Gerke's panzer column, the MTW [armored personnel carrier] column of Lieutenant Kleinjohann (3rd Company, 16th Pioneer Battalion) drove onto the bridge, removed the parts that were burning, and saved the western part of the crossing.

Overnight on 17 August, the lead vehicles of the infantry advancing from the southwest arrived. The sack was closed at the Don. 16th Panzer Division took 800 prisoners and destroyed 14 tanks and 78 guns.[100]

Omitting any reference to Gordov's counterstroke, the Red Army General Staff reported, "*4th Tank Army* continued stubborn defensive fight with enemy tanks and infantry units advancing to the Don River along the Trekhostrovskaia and Malonabatovskii front (30 kilometers northeast of Kalach)."[101] The daily summary asserted that 343rd Rifle Division's strength had eroded to only "230 bayonets and 6 guns," the "remnants of 184th Rifle Division" had finally escaped to the Don near Nizhnyi Akatov, and 1st Guards Army's 40th, 37th, and 39th Guards Rifle Divisions had joined battle but were all fighting defensively under heavy enemy pressure.[102]

On the left wing of Paulus's attacking forces, XI Army Corps' 376th Infantry Division captured Kremenskaia during the day and, together with 100th Jäger Division, pushed 343rd and 321st Rifle Divisions back into a narrow 5–10-kilometer-deep strip of territory stretching from Kremenskaia southward to Sirotinskaia on the southern bank of the Don. Only the timely arrival of 1st Guards Army's 38th and 40th Guards Rifle Divisions late in the day prevented XI Army Corps from utterly destroying the battered Soviet divisions and liquidating the bridgehead entirely.[103]

Farther south, 60th and 3rd Motorized Divisions pressed the remnants of 192nd and part of 184th Rifle Divisions back toward the Don before 1st Guards Army's 37th and 39th Guards Rifle Divisions could push all of their forces across the river.[104] In heavy fighting late on 16 August, the two motorized divisions inflicted "heavy losses" on the two guards divisions, ultimately seizing the river's entire southern bank within the Great Bend west of Ilovlia. To the south, VIII Army Corps' 389th and 384th Infantry Divisions and XXIV Panzer Corps' 76th and 295th Infantry Divisions closed up to the Don from Trekhostrovskaia southward to Vertiachii, seizing footholds over the river near Nizhnyi Akatov and thereby preempting any Soviet assault from the river's eastern bank. Late in the day, Paulus ordered Hube's 16th Panzer Division withdrawn so it could rest and refit.[105]

While pondering its own achievements, 16th Panzer Division's history provided an assessment of XIV Panzer Corps' and Sixth Army's achievements, as well as an epitaph for the defeated Soviet 4th Tank Army:

> The battle in the Don steppe was finished. The losses within their own ranks were high. Mues' [panzer-grenadier] battalion alone had suffered 300 losses. All told, 1,000 tanks were destroyed and 750 guns were captured, but only 88,700 prisoners were taken. Together with the Kharkov *Kessel* [cauldron], this meant 240,000 prisoners. Although the Russians managed great advances from the secure areas on the other side of the Don, they nevertheless managed to avoid being captured en masse in the cauldron. Although the Germans succeeded in conquering the industrial region and 500 km of steppe with losses amongst their own ranks, it had not been possible to destroy significant portions of the Red Army. The Russians had employed a new technique. At the beginning of the advance, locals were already reporting to the men of 16th Panzer Division that officers and commissars had mentioned the Volga as the objective of the retreat and informed them that, if they would join them, they would be able to find work and bread. 16th Panzer Division interpreted the retreat as a sign of weakness, and the K.T.B. [war diary] of 64th Panzer Grenadier Regiment recorded on 13 July 1942, "The Russian soldier on the southern front is tired of fighting and without energy due to the repeated retreats."

> Hitler, too, thought of having inflicted a great blow to the Russians in the Great Bend of the Don. This made him focus again on the dangerous double target: the Caucasus and Stalingrad.[106]

Because of the heavy losses it had suffered in two days of fighting, 4th Tank Army was essentially "no longer combat capable" by day's end on 17 August. By this time its 18th, 184th, 205th, 321st, and 343rd Rifle Divisions were decimated, 22nd Tank Corps' 182nd Tank Brigade fielded only 7 tanks, 22nd Motorized Rifle Brigade had only 200 men, and, except for 4th and 40th Guards Rifle Divisions (the former was still detraining at Ilovlia), all of 4th Tank and 1st Guards Armies' rifle divisions had run out of ammunition. In desperation that evening, Gordov ordered Moskalenko's 1st Guards Army to take control of 4th Tank Army's 321st, 343rd, and 205th Rifle Divisions, "hold on to [the] bridgehead in the small bend of the Don, reinforce its defenses, disrupt any enemy crossing to the left bank of the Don, and occupy defenses along the Kremenskaia, Shokhin, and Sirotinskaia front and further along the left bank of the Don to the mouth of the Ilovlia River."[107] To ensure Moskalenko's army could do so, Gordov reinforced it with most of 4th Tank Army's surviving artillery and 23rd Rifle Division from his own reserve. Gordov also ordered Danilov's 21st Army to defend the sector of the Don on 1st Guards Army's right flank and the rump forces of Kriuchenkin's 4th Tank Army to dig in and hold their pitifully small bridgehead on the Don's southern bank, a task that Kriuchenkin's forces were unable to accomplish.

With the virtual ruin of 4th Tank Army, the weakest sector of Stalingrad Front's defenses was now the region at the junction of 1st Guards and 62nd Armies' defenses, specifically the stretch along the eastern bank of the Don from the mouth of the Ilovlia River southward to Lake Peschanoe. The only forces available to defend this sector were 4th Tank Army's weakened 18th Rifle, 39th Guards, and 184th Rifle Divisions, which had withdrawn eastward across the Don. To remedy this weakness, Gordov ordered Lopatin's 62nd Army to shift its 98th Rifle Division and one regiment from 87th Rifle Division northwest to the Vertiachii and Peskovatka regions. At the same time, the deputy *front* commander concentrated 214th and the remainder of 87th Rifle Divisions in the Kotluban' and Samofalovka regions, 20 kilometers east of Vertiachii on the Don, to serve as his *front's* new reserve.[108]

Despite Gordov's attempts to salvage at least a portion of his *front's* bridgehead south of the Don, Paulus concluded by the end of 17 August that his offensive to clear Soviet forces from the northeast corner of the Great Bend was a complete success. As his forces mopped up previously bypassed Soviet soldiers in the southern two-thirds of the bridgehead throughout the day, Paulus ordered XI Army Corps to withdraw from the Kremenskaia region and establish a firm defensive line just south of the town and reinforced XI Corps' defenses with a *kampfgruppe* from General von Apell's 22nd Panzer Division, whose main body was supporting XVII Army Corps farther to the west. On 17 and 18 August Paulus withdrew XIV Panzer Corps' 3rd and 60th Motorized Divisions into assembly areas to the rear, where they rested and refitted with 16th Panzer Division. The infantry divisions of XI, VIII, and LI Army Corps then assumed responsibility for defending the southern bank of the Don. On 18 and 19 August, VIII Army Corps' 389th and 384th Infantry Divisions and LI Army Corps' 76th and 295th Infantry Divisions worked hard to seize and expand their bridgeheads across the Don north and south of Vertiachii.[109]

On 18 and 19 August, with Sixth Army's forces finally lodged firmly on the western bank of the Don, Paulus could plan for the next stage of his advance—the decisive final drive to the Volga and Stalingrad.

CONCLUSIONS

If Paulus was pleased with his army's successful offensive to clear Soviet forces from the remainder of the Great Bend, the *Stavka* was not. Instead, it credited the defeat to "the untimely reinforcement of 4th Tank Army with forces and weapons," which, despite its directives, "led to undesirable consequences."[110] In retrospect, the *Stavka* believed Gordov had ample reinforcements available on 10 August with which to reinforce 4th Tank Army's defenses before they collapsed, including 98th and 87th Rifle Divisions in the *front*'s reserve behind 62nd Army, 63rd and 343rd Rifle Divisions in 63rd Army's reserve, and 214th and 196th Rifle and 33rd Guards Rifle Divisions, refitting in Southeastern Front's reserve. Rather than tapping these forces, Gordov attempted to reinforce 4th Tank Army with forces from 1st Guards Army, an unrealistic decision because Moskalenko's army did not arrive in the region in time to provide effective help to Kriuchenkin's forces. The *Stavka*'s criticism, however, was not entirely justified because several of these reinforcing divisions, in particular 196th and 33rd Guards, were far too weak to take part in the counterstroke.

From Paulus's perspective, the destruction of 4th Tank Army was an absolute prerequisite for any subsequent advance on Stalingrad. Even though his Sixth Army had satisfied this prerequisite, there were several cogent reasons for continued concern. First, it had taken longer than a month—from 17 July, when it unleashed its forces for its eastward drive into the Great Bend, to 19 August, when it seized most of the Great Bend's northeast corner—for Sixth Army to accomplish the initial mission assigned to it by Hitler.

Second, rather than accomplishing this task in a "single bound," as implied in Hitler's order, Paulus ultimately had to do so by organizing and conducting four distinct and separate offensives, the first on 17 July and, subsequently, on 23 July, 8 August, and 15 August. Although this stop-and-start method of conducting offensive operations was at least in part a result of recurring fuel and ammunition shortages, it was also a product of the overall weakness of Paulus's army relative to the opposition.

Because Sixth Army proved incapable of sustaining any sort of offensive into the Great Bend prior to 17 July without mechanized support, Hitler reinforced Paulus with XIV Panzer Corps' three divisions by 22 July and, after its advance slowed once again on 25 July, with XXIV Panzer Corps' 24th Panzer Division. When Paulus's advance faltered short of its objective (Kalach) on 28 July, Hitler attempted to revitalize the advance on Stalingrad on 31 July by committing XXXXVIII Panzer Corps of Hoth's Fourth Panzer Army in an advance on the city from the southwest. During 8–11 August, while Hoth's army was conducting its advance on Abganerovo, Paulus finally completed clearing 62nd Army from its bridgehead west of the Don and captured Kalach. However, by this time Hoth's drive had bogged down at Abganerovo, forcing Hitler to order Paulus to conduct yet another offensive against the northeast corner of the Great Bend to complete preparations for the final drive on Stalingrad. Even after Paulus accomplished this task, Fourth Panzer Army would require reinforcements before it could join Sixth Army's drive to the city, this time in the form of 24th Panzer Division.

Third, during Paulus's advance, the opposing Soviet forces proved stronger and far more resilient than Hitler, OKH, or Army Group B anticipated. Although Sixth Army destroyed all or a significant part of three Soviet armies (21st, 28th, and 38th) during its drive eastward in early and mid-July, by month's end it faced five more Soviet armies (63rd, 21st, 4th Tank, 62nd, and 1st Tank). After destroying or seriously damaging three of these armies (62nd and 1st and 4th Tank) during the first half of August, at midmonth it still faced five Soviet armies (63rd, 21st, 1st Guards, 4th Tank, and 62nd). Faced with Red Armies reappearing, seemingly from Soviet graveyards, Paulus's forces managed to advance eastward 55–70 kilometers between 17 and 31 July, at a rate of advance of roughly 4–5 kilometers per day, and another 30–35 kilometers from 1 through 19 August, at a rate of advance of only about 1.5–1.75 kilometers per day. With the *Stavka* rushing all available forces to the Stalingrad region, there were no grounds for Hitler, OKH, Army Group B, or Paulus to believe Sixth Army's advance across the remaining 60–70 kilometers to the Volga River and Stalingrad would be any easier than before.

Fourth, although Sixth Army succeeded in destroying well more than half of Stalingrad Front's 62nd and 1st Tank Armies and a significant portion of 4th Tank Army during its advance into the Great Bend, it failed to match the *Wehrmacht's* decisive victories in Operation Barbarossa the year before or during the initial stages of Operation Blau. Given the immense numbers of Red Army soldiers who escaped the slowing German juggernaut, the *Stavka's* proven track record for fielding fresh reserve armies had to be disconcerting to every German from Hitler down to the lowliest *landser* (infantry private) in Sixth Army's ranks.

Fifth, while Paulus's Sixth Army was indeed inflicting severe damage on Red Army forces, attrition was also draining his forces, as well as those of Hoth's Fourth Panzer Army. In short, Sixth and Fourth Panzer Armies' "offensive cutting edges" were dulling perceptively, a situation exacerbated by persistent vexing fuel and ammunition shortages. For example, partly because of wear and tear and partly because of enemy resistance, by the end of July Sixth and Fourth Panzer Armies' panzer and motorized divisions were reduced in strength by well more than 50 percent. Although XIV Panzer Corps' 16th Panzer and 3rd and 60th Motorized Divisions managed to keep some 60–70 and 30–40 of their tanks operable, respectively, 24th Panzer Division's tank strength fell from 141 tanks on 18 July, to 116 on 10 August, to 82 on 15 August.[111] 14th Panzer Division, which fielded 102 tanks on 28 June, was able to muster only 24 tanks on 12 August after the intense fighting in the Abganerovo region.[112] All the while, Sixth and Fourth Panzer Armies' divisions suffered personnel casualties ranging from several hundred to more than 1,500 in some of the more heavily engaged divisions. This, combined with the rigors of a summer campaign, further sapped the armies' strength and staying power.

Although neglected in many earlier histories of Operation Blau, in part because Soviet historians either obscured or utterly ignored the subject for many years, the long struggle in the Great Bend of the Don River (lasting more than three weeks) was not only far more intense and costly to both sides than previously thought but also was far more significant. In reality, when considered together, 62nd and 64th Armies' determined defense of the Great Bend, 1st and

4th Tank Armies' counterstrokes in the Great Bend, and Briansk and Voronezh Fronts' counterstrokes at and west of Voronezh represented a genuine effort by Stalin and the *Stavka* to orchestrate a strategic counteroffensive designed to halt German Army Group B's forces in their tracks. Although the ensuing fighting decimated 62nd Army, it also seriously weakened Sixth Army, explaining at least in part why Paulus's army would experience major difficulties when it tried to rid Stalingrad of its stubborn defenders six weeks later. Nonetheless, within days after it cleared Soviet forces from the western bank of the Don, Sixth Army and Hoth's Fourth Panzer Army would begin what they believed would be a triumphal final advance on Stalin's namesake city.

CHAPTER 8

The German Advance to the Volga River, 20 August–2 September 1942

The Volga River and the city of Stalingrad were squarely in German sights, the gateway to victory open to their advancing forces.

ARMY GROUP B'S OFFENSIVE PLAN

On 19 August 1942, Paulus issued his order for the attack on Stalingrad. The first paragraph of this order reflected his concerns about Soviet capabilities and intentions:

Top Secret

A.O.K. 6 [Sixth Army Command]   Army Hqs., 19 August 1942
Ia [Operations Department] Nr. 3044/42. ts   1845 hours
        11 copies
        Copy Nr. 9

Army Order
for the Attack on Stalingrad
(Map: 1:100,000)

1. The Russian forces will defend the Stalingrad region stubbornly. They occupy the high ground on the eastern bank of the Don, west of Stalingrad, and have built defensive positions there in great depth.

It must be assumed that it is possible they have assembled forces, including armored brigades, ready to counterattack, both in the Stalingrad area and in the area north of the isthmus between the Don and Volga.

Therefore, in the advance across the Don toward Stalingrad, the army must reckon with enemy resistance in front and with heavy counterattacks against the northern flank of our advance.

It is possible the annihilating blows struck during the past few weeks will have destroyed the enemy's means for fighting determined defensive actions.[1]

Given this confusion, Paulus's concept of the operation was characteristically conservative and even defensive in tone—simply for Sixth Army to "occupy the isthmus between the Don and Volga north of the railway line Kalach-Stalingrad" and "protect its own northern and eastern flank."[2] Sixth Army would conduct its main attack in the 23-kilometer-wide sector along the Don between Ostrovskii

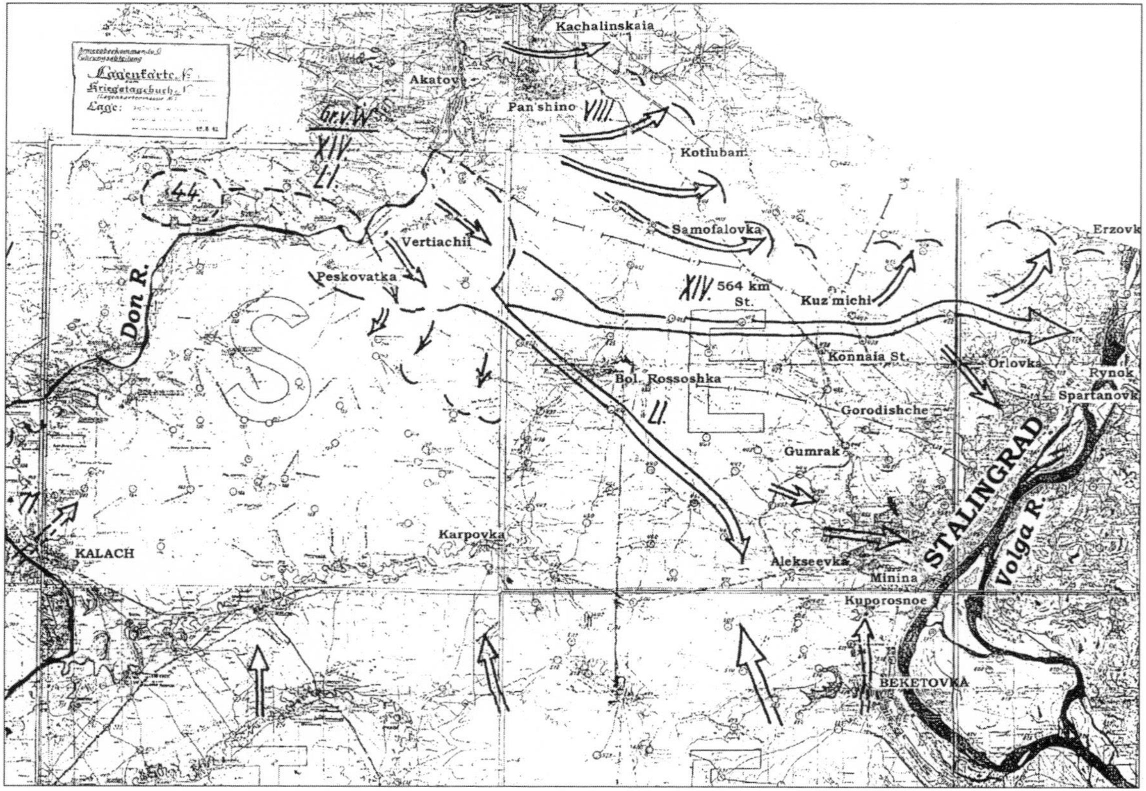

Map 49. The Sixth Army's offensive plan, 19 August 1942

(Trekhostrovskaia) and Peskovatka, with its main effort near Vertiachii in the southern half of the sector (see Map 49). With infantry protecting the flanks, panzer and motorized forces would thrust eastward along the high ground north of the Rossoshka River into the region due north of Stalingrad and then to the western bank of the Volga. Infantry divisions advancing in the panzers' wake would wheel southward and fight their way into and occupy Stalingrad city from the northwest, while other infantry divisions conducted a secondary advance southeastward toward the Rossoshka River to link up with the panzer forces of Hoth's Fourth Panzer Army advancing from the south. Only after Paulus's and Hoth's forces had linked up would the infantry of the two armies begin mopping up Soviet forces bypassed south of the Rossoshka and Karpovka Rivers from the northeast. The forces Paulus retained on the Don's western bank would either reinforce his main advance or assist in the mopping-up operation in the steppe southwest of Stalingrad.[3]

Paulus then assigned his forces specific missions:

3. Objectives:

XXIV Panzer Corps will hold the west bank of the Don from the army's right boundary to Luchinskoe [18 kilometers south of Kalach] and, with 71st Infantry Division, will prepare to leave a minimum security force to hold the Don while establishing a bridgehead on either side of Kalach, from which 71st Infantry Division will advance eastward.

The release of this corps headquarters for further employment elsewhere is to be prepared for.

LI Army Corps [76th and 295th Infantry Divisions] will seize a further bridgehead across the Don on either side of Vertiachii. For this purpose the following units at present under XXIV Panzer Corps will be temporarily placed under its command, viz.: artillery, engineer, traffic control, antitank and necessary signals units.

As soon as XIV Panzer Corps shall have advanced eastward from the bridgehead, LI Army Corps will become responsible for covering the right flank of the advance.

With this intention, LI Army Corps will attack across the Rossoshka [River] between Nizhnyi-Alekseevskii [35 kilometers west of Stalingrad] and Bol. Rossoshka [25 kilometers west of Stalingrad], occupy the high ground west of Stalingrad, and will temporarily establish southwesterly contact with the advancing mobile forces of neighboring [Fourth Panzer] army to our right.

The corps will then capture and occupy the central and southern parts of Stalingrad. Meanwhile weak forces will form a covering line between Pesko-vatka [30 kilometers northeast of Kalach] and Nizhnyi-Alekseevskii [35 kilo-meters west of Stalingrad]. A special Army order will decide when the time has come to annihilate the Russian troops located south of this line and north of the Karpovka River.

XIV Panzer Corps [16th Panzer and 3rd and 60th Motorized Divisions], after the capture of the bridgehead by LI Army Corps, will push forward through the bridgehead, advancing eastward over the high ground north of Malaia Rossoshka [28 kilometers west of Stalingrad] and Konnaia Station [18 kilometers northwest of Stalingrad] to the Volga north of Stalingrad. It will prevent all river traffic and cut all rail communications immediately to the north of the city.

Elements of this corps will attack Stalingrad from the northwest and occupy the northern parts of the city. In the north, a covering line will be established running along the high ground southwest of Erzovka and south of the Gratshevaia stream. While so doing, closest contact will be maintained with VIII Army Corps advancing from the west.

VIII Army Corps [305th, 389th, and 384th Infantry Divisions] will cover the northern flank of XIV Panzer Corps. It will launch a sharp attack in a southeasterly direction from the bridgehead captured between Nizhnyi Gerasimov [10 kilometers south of Trekhostrovskaia] and Ostrovskii [Trekhostrovskaia] and, then, swinging steadily north, will form a line, which must so far as possible be proof against attack by armored forces, between Kuz'michi [20 kilometers northwest of Stalingrad] and Kachalinskaia [7 kilometers east of Trekhostrovskaia]. Close contact will be maintained with XIV Panzer Corps;

XI Army Corps [100th Jäger Division, 376th and 44th Infantry Divisions, and 22nd Panzer Division] and *XVII Army Corps* [79th and 113th Infantry Division, and Italian Celere Motorized Division] will cover the northern flank of the Army.

XI Army Corps will hold the line of the Don from Melo-Kletskii to the left Army boundary.

XI Army Corps will release 22nd Panzer Division, as soon as possible, to Army reserve. This division will be assembled ready for action in the Dalyi-Perekopskaia-Orekhov-Selivanov region [10–15 kilometers south of the Don at Kletskaia].

4. D-Day and H-Hour will be announced in a special order.

5. Boundaries as given on map attached.

6. *VIII Air Corps* will give air support to the Army's attack, with points of main effort initially in LI Army Corps' sector, later switching to the line of advance of XIV Panzer Corps.

7. Army H.Q. as of dawn, 21 August: Osinovskii [35 kilometers north of Kalach].

8. Contents of the order may only be communicated to subordinate commands, and only such parts as are relevant to the future operations by the subordinate command in question may be communicated.

This order is not to be carried by plane. Attention will be drawn to the secret nature of such parts of this order as are communicated to subordinate commands.

The Commander-in-Chief

[signed] Paulus[4]

It is one of the sad ironies of this war that early on 16 August, only two days before Paulus published his attack order, 534th and 535th Regiments of VIII Army Corps' 384th Infantry Division had stormed across the Don at Akatov and seized a bridgehead on the eastern bank. Described by a German war correspondent as "one of the most senseless actions of the entire war," for eight days 384th Division, reinforced on 17–18 August by 389th Infantry Division, fought a vicious battle in the region against 4th Tank Army's 39th Guards and 214th Rifle Divisions and 62nd Army's 98th Rifle Division, supported by 193rd Tank and 22nd Motorized Rifle Brigades and 468th Antitank Regiment. By the time the fighting ended, the two German divisions suffered 300 dead—only to see Paulus abandon part of the bridgehead and conduct his main attack further south.[5] Although the strong Soviet resistance at Akatov undoubtedly contributed to Paulus's decision to shift the point of his main attack southward, so also did the marshy terrain east of the Don River at Akatov, which was clearly unsuited to high-speed armor operations, as did the appearance of the fresh 1st Guards Army, which Sixth Army would have to engage head-on if it attacked eastward from the Akatov region.

Regardless of Paulus's motives, he ultimately decided to launch his main attack through a new bridgehead at Vertiachii, 13 kilometers south of Akatov, which LI Army Corps' 76th and 295th Infantry Divisions were to capture in an assault crossing early on 21 July. Once this bridgehead was secure, 16th Panzer and 3rd and 60th Motorized Divisions of Wietersheim's XIV Panzer Corps would begin a dash toward the Volga, with VIII and LI Army Corps' infantry divisions advancing in their wake to protect the panzer corps' northern and southern flanks. Simultaneously, Hoth's Fourth Panzer Army would resume active operations toward Stalingrad from the southwest. Paulus's confidence that XIV Panzer Corps could reach the Volga River was bolstered when "aerial reconnaissance detected only weak opposition between the Don and Volga."[6]

All this time, Army Group B would have to keep a sharp eye on Soviet forces arrayed opposite its ever-lengthening left wing along the southern bank of the Don River. As early as 6 August, for example, a local attack by Voronezh Front's 6th Army had seized a small bridgehead on the Don's western bank at Storozhevoe and Korotoiak, 45 kilometers south of Voronezh.[7] Although this attack forced the thinly stretched light infantry divisions of Hungarian Second Army to retreat only a few kilometers, it provided the Soviets a foothold on the southern bank of the Don. Farther north, Briansk and Voronezh Fronts had renewed their offensive against the Voronezh bulge on 12 August (see Chapter

Six). While these offensives distracted the Germans at the time, they neither recaptured Voronezh nor attracted German reserves from elsewhere in the theater.[8] However, Sixth Army's easterly advance into the Great Bend forced Paulus to leave significant forces far to his rear along the Don, first to stiffen the defenses of Hungarian Second Army and, later, to reinforce Italian Eighth Army, whose divisions moved forward to the Don between 11 and 15 August. By 19 August these forces included XXIX Army Corps' 336th, 294th, and 62nd Infantry Divisions, temporarily attached to Italian Eighth Army.

Underscoring the inherent risks of his planned assault on Stalingrad, Paulus planned to conduct his offensive between Kachalinskaia and Kalach with XIV Panzer Corps' 16th Panzer and 3rd and 60th Motorized Divisions and VIII and LI Army Corps and XXIV Panzer Corps' 305th, 389th, 384th, 79th, 295th, and 71st Infantry Divisions—a total of three armored and six infantry divisions. This force was roughly equivalent in size and strength to the four armored divisions and six infantry divisions his army had employed to destroy 62nd and 1st Tank Armies in the Great Bend during the period from 23 July through 11 August. Now his force of a similar size would face the remnants of 4th Tank and 62nd Armies, at the least, plus whatever portion of 1st Guards Army the Soviets could bring to bear against Paulus's left flank. Meanwhile, Paulus's remaining forces— one panzer and five infantry divisions subordinate to XVII and XI Army Corps— would have to defend his long left wing along the Don River against 21st Army, roughly half of 1st Guards Army, and whatever other forces the Soviets could commit to this region. Therefore, the success of Paulus's plan depended directly on how quickly his shock group could reach the Volga and capture Stalingrad before its offensive momentum ebbed, as well as on the effectiveness of the advance by Hoth's small Fourth Panzer Army on Stalingrad from the southwest. As evidenced by his army's previous operations, this would be no mean task, particularly in light of the Soviets' proven capabilities for fielding new reserve armies, corps, and divisions.

STALINGRAD FRONT'S PLANS

Sixth Army's rapid seizure of the northeast corner of the Great Bend and the damage done to 4th Tank Army placed Stalingrad Front in a precarious situation. In the brief period of 16–20 August, Paulus's army crushed 4th Tank Army's defenses and pushed its remnants and the reinforcements it received from 1st Guards Army out of the southern two-thirds of the Kremenskaia bridgehead. By nightfall on 20 August, rump forces of 4th Tank and 1st Guards Armies clung to a narrow defensive bridgehead from Kremenskaia southeastward to Sirotinskaia in the western half of the bridgehead. In the eastern half, however, the German assault drove the two armies' 39th Guards, 18th and 184th Rifle Divisions, and 22nd Motorized Brigade pell-mell across the Don River north of Akatov. Hard on their heels, VIII Army Corps' 384th and 389th Infantry Divisions captured Akatov and seized a bridgehead on the Don's eastern bank.

Pounded by nonstop Stuka attacks but lacking adequate air support of their own and running short or out of fuel and ammunition, 4th Tank and 62nd Armies' understrength divisions were not able to destroy the German foothold on the Don's eastern bank. As fighting continued east of Akatov, on 20 August Paulus ordered LI Army Corps' 76th and 295th Infantry Divisions to prepare for an assault across the river near Vertiachii, 12 kilometers south of Akatov, while Wietersheim concentrated his three mobile divisions on the Don's western bank so that they could advance into the bridgehead and begin the drive to the Volga.

Although preoccupied with the Germans' rapid advance into the Caucasus, the *Stavka* and Eremenko scrambled to shore up Soviet defenses west of Stalingrad. From 1 August through 20 August, the *Stavka* reinforced Stalingrad Front and Southeastern Front with 15 fresh rifle divisions and 3 tank corps. Five of the rifle divisions reinforced Stalingrad Front's defenses at Kalach, and the three tank corps were due to reach Stalingrad by 23–24 August. At the same time, the *Stavka* ordered Kriuchenkin's 4th Tank Army not only to hold its bridgehead at Kremenskaia but also to expand it south of Sirotinskaia by moving its forces forward to "the Perekopskaia, Blizhniaia Perekopka, Golubaia, and Golubaia River line on the right bank of the Don." After being reinforced by three or four divisions, Kriuchenkin's army was to "attack southwestward into the flank of enemy forces penetrating into the small bend of the Don" and, with additional reinforcements, "employ the expanded bridgehead for an attack toward the southwest" into Sixth Army's rear.[9]

Believing the Germans would launch their attack on Stalingrad from the Trekhostrovskaia region, 5 kilometers north of Akatov, Eremenko concluded he could forestall such an attack only by establishing strong defenses along the Don River in that sector and by organizing strong multiple counterattacks against Sixth Army's flanks by Stalingrad Front's center and right wing. Initially, he ordered Lopatin's 62nd Army to man an intermediate defensive line roughly 20 kilometers east of the Don from Trekhostrovskaia southward to Kalach with 35th Guards, 87th, and 196th Rifle Divisions, forces from the Ordzhonikidze Military School, and two of 115th Fortified Region's separate artillery–machine gun battalions.[10] To further strengthen Stalingrad Front's right wing, he also ordered Lopatin to regroup Rodin's 28th Tank Corps (now consolidated into 182nd Tank Brigade) to the Vertiachii region. However, these forces were in various stages of reconstruction and were too understrength to be of practical use. In addition, Lopatin concentrated all of his army's artillery in gun and antitank artillery groups and dispatched these groups to his army's right wing.[11]

To repel any German forces attempting to force the Don River in the Akatov region, Eremenko ordered Lopatin to form two shock groups and employ them in a joint counterattack along two axes converging on the river at Akatov. The first shock group, consisting of 35th Guards Rifle Division, 169th Tank Brigade, and two antitank regiments, was to concentrate in and attack from the Fastov, Pan'shino, and Kotluban' State Farm regions, 3–15 kilometers east of Akatov. The second, made up of 214th Rifle Division, 32nd Motorized Rifle Brigade, and 40th and 134th Tank Brigades, was to conduct its attack from the Gerasimovka *Balka* and Kotluban' regions, 5–20 kilometers southeast of Akatov. To forestall any German penetration east of the river, Eremenko, during the evening on 18 August, ordered 23rd and 84th Rifle, 27th Guards Rifle, and 298th Rifle Divisions, which the *Stavka* had just released to him from its reserves, to occupy reserve concentration areas from Sirotinskaia southward to Kotluban' State Farm, 20–30 kilometers behind the front lines, by day's end on 22 August.[12] However, despite Eremenko's best efforts, by nightfall on 19 August Sixth Army's main shock group of nine divisions faced only five weak rifle divisions from 4th Tank and 62nd Armies along the Don front from Akatov southward to Peskovatka.

In addition to these strictly defensive measures, Eremenko also formulated an ambitious plan for multiple counterstrokes to engage as many of Sixth Army's forces as possible and tie them down to forestall any Sixth Army offensive along the Don. Therefore, on the night of 18–19 August, he issued fresh orders to all of Stalingrad Front's armies to be prepared to mount coordinated counterattacks on 19 and 20 August:

- *1st Guards Army* [38th, 41st, 40th, and 4th Guards Rifle and 321st and 23rd Rifle Divisions] must stubbornly defend the sector from Starodonskoi to the mouth of the Ilovlia River [a 20-kilometer sector east of Sirotinskaia] with part of its forces [4th Guards and 321st and 23rd Rifle Divisions] and attack with three divisions [41st, 38th, and 40th Guards Rifle] from the Kremenskaia and Shokhin line [in the northern half of the small bridgehead] toward Blizhniaia Perekopka, Os'kinskii, and Verkhne-Golubaia;
- *62nd Army* [98th, 399th, 112th, 214th, and 131st Rifle Divisions, 20th and 32nd Motorized Rifle Brigades, 40th and 134th Tank Brigades, and 28th Tank Corps] will force the Don in the Vertiachii and Peskovatka sectors on the night of 19–20 August with two rifle divisions, reinforced by tank brigades [214th and 98th Rifle Divisions and 40th and 134th Tank Brigades], and reach the Golubaia River in the Hill 197 and Malonabatovskii sector [west of the Don] by attacking toward the north and northwest, where it will dig in;
- *4th Tank Army* [192nd, 184th, and 18th Rifle and 37th and 39th Guards Rifle Divisions and 22nd Tank Corps] will defend in place along the left bank of the Don and prevent the enemy from crossing the Don. If 1st Guards and 62nd Armies attacks are successful, be prepared to join the attack;[13]
- *63rd Army* [1st and 14th Guards Rifle and 127th, 153rd, 197th, and 203rd Rifle Divisions], continuing to defend its positions stubbornly, will attack from the Elanskaia and Zimovskii [the 15-kilometer sector west of the

Khoper River] line [southward] toward Chebotarevskii, Klinovoi, and Perelazovskii with two rifle divisions [197th Rifle and 14th Guards Rifle], in
cooperation with 21st Army, and will reach the Kotovskii, Bol'shoi, and
Kalmykovskii regions [15–20 kilometers south of the Don] by the end of
the second day. Subsequently, attack toward Perelazovskii [58 kilometers
south of the Don];

- *21st Army* [304th, 96th, 124th, 278th, 76th, 343rd, and 63rd Rifle Divi-
sions] will attack from the Zimovskii and Kuznechikov line [the 15-kilome-
ter sector east of the Khoper River] toward Verkhne-Fomikhinskii with
two divisions [96th and 304th Rifle] and reach the Verkhne-Fomikhinskii
and Karanchev regions [20–25 kilometers south of the Don] with its forward units by the end of the second day. In the event of success, within
one–two days, begin an attack with all of your forces toward Bazkovskii,
Evstratovskii, and Manoilin [20–30 kilometers south of the Don]; and

- *8th Air Army*, after 1st Guards and 62nd Armies have begun their attack,
will employ all of its aircraft in direct support of the ground forces, primarily to attack enemy tank and mechanized forces.[14]

By launching these converging assaults along Sixth Army's entire front, Eremenko hoped to satisfy the *Stavka* demands he display *aktivnost* (activeness) by
applying enough pressure to forestall any German offensive eastward toward the
Volga. However, given the weakness of his forces and the short time they had to
prepare their attacks, these counterattacks were predestined to failure. While
he seriously underestimated the strength of Paulus's Sixth Army, Eremenko overestimated the strength of his own and complicated matters by assigning unreal-
istically deep missions to his armies and failing to provide them with necessary
artillery, armor, and air support. (For example, his order required 1st Guards
Army to attack a German force almost twice its size.) Moreover, by the time the
counterattack was to commence, Sixth Army had already defeated 4th Tank and
62nd Armies and had seized bridgeheads across the Don, leaving 1st Guards
Army to fight in the Kremenskaia and Sirotinskaia bridgeheads in virtual isolation. Although the counterattacks by Moskalenko's 1st Guards Army forced
Paulus to relinquish some territory south of the Don, it did nothing to forestall
his main attack toward Stalingrad. Therefore, instead of joining a general counterattack, Lopatin's 62nd Army, at dawn on 21 August, suddenly found its forces
under a general assault by German forces in the Vertiachii region.

SIXTH ARMY'S ASSAULT AND ADVANCE
TO THE VOLGA, 21–23 AUGUST

Overnight on 20–21 August, Paulus's designated assault forces (76th Infantry
Division's 178th and 203rd Regiments and 295th Infantry Division's 516th and

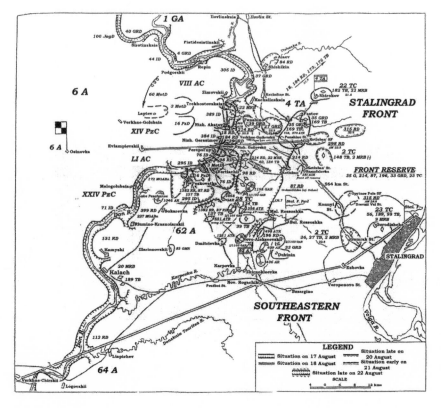

Map 50. The 4th Tank and 62nd Armies' defense, 17–22 August 1942

517th Regiments, all from LI Army Corps) occupied their jumping-off positions along the western bank of the Don River opposite Vertiachii (see Map 50). A German war correspondent described the scene during the initial hours of the assault:

> The night before the attack was clear and starry, the wind blew from the south-east, and a light mist lay over the Don. For reasons of visibility and to facilitate the clearing of the enemy's minefields, zero hour had been fixed for 0310 hours. Without any preliminary barrage, Sixth Army's assault troops moved across the river in one hundred and twelve assault craft and one hundred kapok rafts of 912th Assault Boat Commando. One hour and fifty minutes later, all the combat troops of 516th Infantry Regiment were in position on the eastern bank; 517th Infantry Regiment met with strong enemy resistance and needed four hours and twenty minutes to get across.

Matters did not go so smoothly with 76th Infantry Division; 178th Infantry Regiment did indeed establish its allotted bridgehead at Akimovskii relatively quickly, but 203rd Regiment met desperate resistance. At 1630 hours the pontoon bridge at Lutchenskii was in position, and a bridge was built at Akimovskii by 0730 hours on the 22nd of August.

The twenty-ton pontoon bridges were subjected to heavy bombing during the night of the 23rd of August, no fewer than seventy-six separate attacks being made on them. The bridges remained unscathed.

The northerly crossing of the Don was made by Sixth Army at the cost of seventy-four dead and three hundred fifty-one wounded. Nineteen assault craft and twenty-six kapok rafts were shot to pieces.[15]

On the other side of the hill, the Red Army General Staff's daily report at 0800 hours on 22 and 23 August captured the days' disturbing events:

[22 August]

4th Tank Army fought a fierce defensive battle with an enemy force of up to two infantry regiments, which crossed to the left [eastern] bank of the Don River in the vicinity of Hill 110.1 [4 kilometers north of Trekhostrovskaia]-Trekhostrovskaia-Lake Gromok (8 kilometers south of Trekhostrovskaia), all day on 21 August.

37th Gds. RD was fighting along the Hill 110.1 [4 kilometers north of Trekhostrovskaia]-Pan'shinka River line [2 kilometers north of Trekhostrovskaia] with its left wing units.

214th RD and 193rd TB fought a fierce battle with the enemy along a line from the Pan'shinka River to the western outskirts of Verkhne-Gnilovskii [5 kilometers south of Trekhostrovskaia and due east of Akatov] all day on 21 August. A battalion of enemy infantry with 8 tanks captured Verkhne-Gnilovskii and was advancing toward Pan'shino.

27th Gds. RD was concentrating in the Bol. Shirokaia-Bol. Potainaia-Kalachino region.

62nd Army was fighting against enemy forces of up to an infantry division, which crossed to the left bank of the Don River in the Verkhne-Gnilovskii-Peskovatka [22 kilometer south of Trekhostrovskaia] sector with its right wing units.

98th RD was fighting along the Verkhne-Gnilovskii-Vertiachii line [5–16 kilometers south of Trekhostrovskaia].

One regiment of 98th RD and 228th and 229th Antitank Battalions were fighting in encirclement in the Vertiachii region.

87th RD was fighting on the western and northern outskirts of Peskovatka.

The enemy began crossing the Don River with tanks, motorized infantry, and motorcycles at 1500 hours on 21 August.[16]

[23 August]

4th Tank Army was fighting stubbornly against the enemy on the left bank of the Don River with part of its forces [on 22 August].

37th Gds. RD destroyed up to two battalions of enemy infantry [from 384th Infantry Division], which were crossing to the left bank of the Don River, by a counterattack and occupied the Lake Il'men'-Pan'shinka River line [2–3 kilometers north of Trekhostrovskaia].

214th RD and 193rd TB were defending the Lake Krivoe-northern outskirts of Verkhne-Gnilovskii [1–2 kilometers north of Trekhostrovskaia] line.

39th Gds. RD was concentrating in Pan'shino [3 kilometers east of Akatov].

298th RD was moving forward from the Shishkin region to a new concentration area at 1900 hours on 22 August.

The situation of the remaining units of the army is unchanged.

62nd Army was fighting a stubborn battle with the enemy in the Verkhne-Gnilovskii-Peskovatka sector on the left bank of the Don with part of its forces.

98th RD and 40th TB were fighting with an enemy force of up to an infantry regiment in the region north of Vertiachii.

A rifle regiment of 87th RD and 137th TB withdrew to the Marker 47.1-Marker 67.9 line [southeast of Vertiachii] under pressure from an enemy force of up to an infantry regiment with tanks.

35th Gds. RD reached the Kotluban'-Sredniaia *Balka* defense line [20 kilometers east of Akatov] at 1100 hours on 22 August.

87th RD (less one rifle regiment), the Ordzhonikidze Infantry School, and 86th Antitank Battalion were organizing a defense along the Kotluban-*Balka*-Mal. Rossoshka line [22 kilometers east of Vertiachii].

196th RD was preparing a defense along the Mal. Rossoshka-Novo-Alekseevka line [22–25 kilometers southeast of Vertiachii].[17]

By day's end on 22 August, Paulus's main shock group was firmly lodged in bridgeheads east of the Don River (see Map 51). VIII Army Corps' 389th and 384th Infantry Divisions defended the 2–4 kilometer-deep northern portion of the bridgehead east of Akatov against nonstop Soviet counterattacks. LI Army Corps' 76th and 295th Infantry Divisions controlled a larger bridgehead, by now 5–8 kilometers deep, on both sides of Vertiachii. Throughout the day and into the night, the panzers and panzer grenadiers of Hube's 16th Panzer and Schlömer's 3rd Motorized Divisions moved forward into the bridgehead, occupying their assigned jumping-off positions before dawn. Overnight, Soviet guns, howitzers, *Katiusha* rockets, and night-bombers did their best to destroy the two floating bridges, each 140 meters long, that German engineers had constructed across the waters. Although the bridges survived, the Germans lost 76 killed and 351 wounded to Soviet fire in the bridgehead.[18]

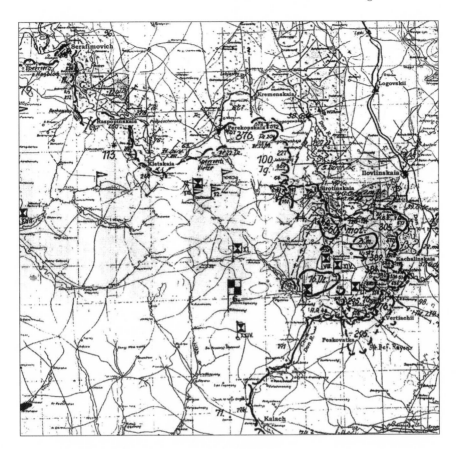

Map 51. The Sixth Army's situation, 20–21 August 1942

At dawn the following day, the floodgates opened wide on Eremenko's defenses. As reported by the Red General Staff:

> In the *Stalingrad Front*, fierce defensive fighting was going on all day on 23 August with tank and motorized units of the enemy, which have penetrated the defensive front of our forces in the Pan'shino-Vertiachii-Peskovatka sector. The enemy, exploiting his offensive with tanks and motorized infantry, was approaching directly to the northern outskirts of Stalingrad city. . . .
>   [While *4th Tank Army* continued its attacks against the German bridgehead at Akatov,] *62nd Army* continued fierce defensive fighting with enemy forces, which forced the Don River in the Vertiachii and Peskovatka region on its right flank. The enemy penetrated to the northern outskirts of the city of Stalingrad with the forces of a tank and a motorized division.

196th RD, with the Ordzhonikidze Infantry School, went over to the offensive beginning on the morning of 24 August from the Boburkin-Novoaleksandrovskii line with the mission to capture the Peskovatka region.

The positions of the army's remaining formations are being verified.[19]

Indeed, with utter disregard for their flanks, 16th Panzer and 3rd Motorized Divisions burst from the confines of the Vertiachii bridgehead at 0430 hours on 23 August:

> At the head of XIV Panzer Corps, 16th Panzer Division crossed the 140-meter-long pontoon bridge over the Don on the night of Sunday 23 August. At 4.30 hours the tanks of KG Sieckenius broke out of the bridgehead in a broad wedge-formation as if on a drill field, followed closely by KG Krumpen and v. Arensdorff. To the left, 3rd and to the right 60th Infantry Divisions (mot.) rolled to the east.
>
> Supported by armored Henschel-129 fighter-bombers, the divisions pushed through the strong and deep fortified positions the enemy built in typical fashion.
>
> In accordance with time-honored panzer tactics, they chose an advance route over the high ground. Ignoring the enemy along the banks of the streams and the gullies on their flanks, 16th Panzer Division rolled toward the east. In close formations, the Stukas carried their bombs to Stalingrad and, with their spirits high, sounded their sirens close to the turrets of the advancing tanks on their return journey. After a tough fight, 16th Panzer Division overcame the Tartar Ditch and crossed the Frolov-Stalingrad railroad south of Kotluban. Trains were set on fire. The enemy seemed to be totally taken by surprise. They made good headway in their advance.[20]

Led by 16th Reconnaissance Battalion, 16th Panzer Pioneer Battalion, and 2nd Panzer Regiment, Hube's panzer division advanced in two columns; 79th Panzer Grenadier Regiment on the left and 64th Panzer Grenadier Regiment on the right were both reinforced by companies from the Panzer Pioneer Battalion (see Map 52). The division's 16th Panzer Artillery Regiment and 16th Panzer Antitank Battalion accompanied 2nd Panzer Regiment. As Hube's powerful armored column moved rapidly eastward across the steppe, Schlömer's 3rd Motorized Division, also in columns of *kampfgruppen*, followed closely.

Emerging from the bridgehead, Hube's panzers brushed aside 62nd Army's defending divisions, leaving the defenders no choice but to recoil southward. Encountering virtually no resistance, Hube's columns thrust almost due east along a high ridge south of Kotluban', relying on speed to preempt any Soviet defenses. As the two armored divisions' 120 tanks and more than 200 armored personnel carriers stirred up clouds of dust on the arid grasslands of the steppe, aircraft from VIII Air Corps conducted 1,600 sorties that day, many of the Stukas

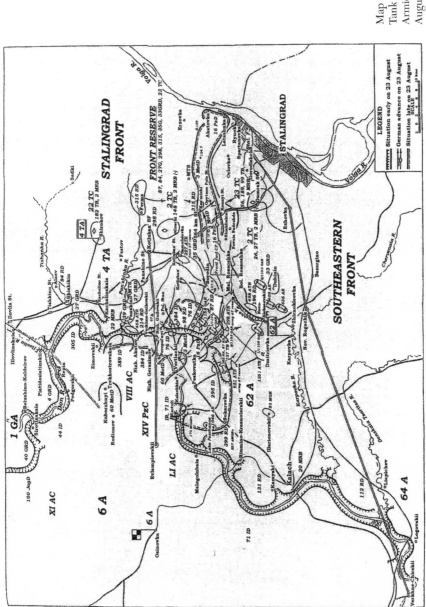

Map 52. The 4th Tank and 62nd Armies' defense, 23 August 1942

in direct support of XIV Panzer Corps, but mostly against Stalingrad itself.[21] The advancing panzers passed the ancient Tartar trench, a natural antitank ditch, before the defenders could react, and soon they crossed a railroad line northwest of Stalingrad near 564 km Station (named for the distance to Moscow), where they shot up several locomotives but did not pause to assess the damage. They did, however, stop briefly when they came in sight of their objective: "In the early afternoon, the commanders of the tanks saw on the horizon the imposing silhouette of Stalingrad toward the right on the horizon, spreading out for 40 kilometers along the Volga. Pit-head frames, chimneys, tower blocks, and chimneys were visible against the smoke clouds rising from fires. Far in the north, out of the formless distance, the vast outline of a cathedral-like [factory] was visible."[22]

At about 1500 hours, the advancing *kampfgruppen* of von Strachwitz's Panzer Detachment from 2nd Panzer Regiment and 2nd Battalion, 64th Panzer Grenadier Regiment, approached Stalingrad's northern suburbs of Latashanka, Rynok, and Spartanovka (named Spartakovka on period maps but Spartanovka after the war) and the Stalingrad Tractor Factory south of the Mokraia Mechetka River. There they encountered gunfire from heavy antiaircraft guns and antitank guns operated by women, as well as infantry hurling grenades. However, virtually every one of these first rounds fired in the battle for Stalingrad missed Strachwitz's tanks. The Germans were more accurate in response, smashing 37 different antiaircraft gun positions. When the Germans later examined these positions, the reason for the Soviet inaccuracy became obvious—the gun crews were composed entirely of civilian women, apparently factory workers and members of Stalingrad's antiaircraft defense (MPVO). Essentially these defenders were locals who had received only rudimentary instruction.[23]

In the wake of Strachwitz's *kampfgruppe*, whose parent panzer regiment had orders to reach the western bank of the Volga and block the main road north of Rynok, 4 kilometers north of the Mokraia Mechetka River and the northern edge of Stalingrad's factory district, 79th Grenadier Regiment struck out toward the town of Rynok, 1.5–2 kilometers north of the river. Meanwhile 64th Grenadier Regiment advanced toward the village of Spartanovka, on the northern bank of the Mokraia Mechetka River:

And then the first tanks stood at the high western bank of the Volga. The wide, dark river was flowing still and majestic, carrying barges in tow down river, and on the other side the Asian steppe spread out into infinity. Pride, happiness, and astonishment glowed on the faces of the men. Toward nightfall the division occupied all-round hedgehog defenses on the northern edge of the town close to the river. Feverishly, the *kampfgruppen* prepared for battle the next day. Already the Russians were bombarding them with tank and Flak [antiaircraft] fire. Like sheet lightning, the bright light of the shots flickered across the starlit skies.[24]

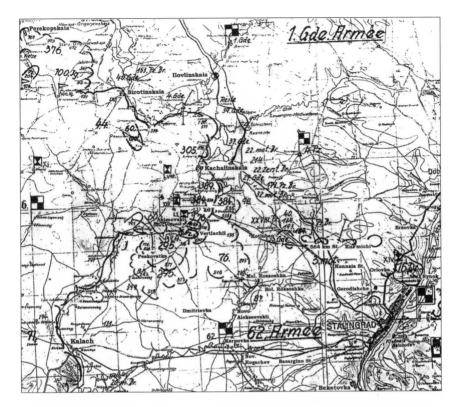

Map 53. The Sixth Army's situation, 22–23 August 1942

By evening, 16th Panzer Division, along with XIV Panzer Corps headquarters, had reached the high bank overlooking the Volga River from Akatovka southward to Rynok, where they set up an all-around hedgehog-type defense (see Map 53):[25]

At the division's command post in the heart of the hedgehog, the radio operators were sitting in their vehicles in front of the green-illuminated scales of the humming radios and were signaling the information about having reached the Volga by Morse code into the night. Motorcycle messengers arrived with new orders. The General and his Ia [operations officer] were putting their heads together over a map. Spartanovka and Rynok in the south had not yet been captured. These suburbs rose out of the defense ring like thorns in their flesh. The fortified position of the Volga was therefore particularly endangered; the enemy would try to cut the Germans off from the Volga again by advancing from south to north along the bank via Latashanka, Vinnovka, and Akatovka. And how was the situation in the division's rear? The 3rd and 60th Infantry Divisions (mot.) had not yet arrived. But even then could the narrow corridor between the Don and the Volga be held?[26]

Strung out far to the rear along the route taken by 16th Panzer Division, the remainder of Hube's division and 3rd and 60th Motorized Divisions, which were following in its wake, also laagered for the night.[27] Typically, Paulus's mobile forces had far outrun supporting infantry divisions, and Wietersheim's panzer corps had no communications with the follow-on VIII Army Corps. At 2310 hours Hube's headquarters reported on its progress by telephone to Wietersheim's headquarters, "*Kampfgruppe,* 79th Panzer Grenadier Regiment, first German troops to reach Volga 1835 hours. One company, 2nd Panzer Regiment, occupied Spartanovka. Enemy resistance initially weak, but strengthening. Strong attacks from the north expected. Outstanding support was given by VIII Air Corps."[28] Thirty minutes later, Hitler radioed Hube's division: "16th Panzer Division will hold its positions in all circumstances."[29]

Surprised by the rapid German dash to the Volga, Stalingrad's Defense Committee worked feverishly to defend the city's northern outskirts. At this time, the only forces at its disposal were Colonel A. A. Saraev's 10th NKVD Rifle Division, destroyer battalions manned by factory workers, detachments of volunteer Peoples' Militia, and local MPVO antiaircraft units. Initially 800–1,000 militiamen took up positions along the southern bank of the Mokraia Mechetka River, just north of the Tractor Factory. These troops were soon reinforced by about 30 tanks recently repaired in the Tractor Factory and manned by the very workers who had repaired them, as well as by several antitank guns produced by the nearby Barrikady Factory. Overnight on 23–24 August, the Defense Committee dispatched 10th NKVD Division's 282nd Rifle Regiment to the Mokraia Mechetka River and ordered other reserves to join the defense.[30]

Meanwhile, far to the west, Eremenko and Lopatin tried to repair the damage done by the German thrust to the Volga and, if possible, cut off and destroy their penetrating forces. On 21 August Eremenko had ordered Lopatin's 62nd Army to organize yet another counterattack against the Germans' bridgehead at Vertiachii, this time with four divisions and a tank brigade.[31] However, Wietersheim's dash had preempted such an attack. Although 8th Air Army conducted about 500 air sorties to halt the German advance during 20–22 August, by day's end on 22 August VIII and LI Army Corps had expanded their bridgehead to a width of more than 45 kilometers and depths ranging from 5 kilometers in the north to more than 10 kilometers in the south. Compounding Eremenko's dilemma, 29th Motorized and 14th Panzer Divisions of Hoth's Fourth Panzer Army, now reinforced by 24th Panzer and 297th Infantry Divisions, on 21 August pressed northward from the Plodovitoe region south of Stalingrad. This attack wedged 15 kilometers into the defenses at the boundary of 64th and 57th Armies. It forced Eremenko to reinforce 57th Army's defenses with four antitank artillery and four guards-mortar regiments from 62nd and 4th Tank Armies, as well as 23rd Tank Corps' 56th Tank Brigade from Southeastern Front's reserves.[32]

The only saving grace for Eremenko were the counterattacks conducted by 63rd and 21st Armies along the Don River west of Serafimovich and by 1st Guards Army in its bridgehead south of Kremenskaia, which tied down Sixth Army's forces in those sectors and won for Eremenko a vital bridgehead across the Don at Serafimovich (see below). However, pressed by Sixth Army's main advance, Lopatin's 62nd Army could not take part in those attacks. Instead it struggled to erect cohesive and durable defenses along its extended front from north of Kalach eastward to the northwestern approaches to Stalingrad. Its 399th and 131st Rifle Divisions and 20th Motorized Rifle Brigade defended from the Don south of Peskovatka eastward to the Rossoshka River, and its 196th Rifle and 33rd Guards Rifle Divisions manned defenses farther east of the Rossoshka River.

While Lopatin's forces clung desperately to the southern flank of XIV Panzer Corps' corridor to the Volga River, Eremenko tried to hold the western portion of the corridor's northern face with 4th Tank Army's 214th Rifle Division and the remnants of its 39th Guards Rifle Division and 62nd Army's already shattered 98th Rifle Division. Farther east, 4th Tank Army's 87th Rifle and 35th Guards Rifle Divisions, reinforced by part of 214th Rifle Division, established defenses between Kotluban' and Bol'shaia Rossoshka. Finally, late on 23 August, Eremenko reinforced 4th Tank Army's defenses with 315th Rifle Division from his reserves, which occupied defenses on 35th Guards Division's left.[33] With these threadbare defenses in place, and hounded by the *Stavka*, Eremenko and his army commanders desperately sought a way to liquidate the narrow corridor held by Wietersheim's XIV Panzer Corps, which pointed like a dagger toward Stalingrad.

THE STRUGGLE FOR THE VOLGA CORRIDOR: THE SOVIET COUNTERSTROKES AT KOTLUBAN' AND ORLOVKA, 23–29 AUGUST

By nightfall on 23 August, the thrust by Sixth Army's XIV Panzer Corps to the Volga River north of Stalingrad placed the *Stavka's* defenses in the entire southern sector of the Soviet-German front in peril. In addition to threatening the city itself, the panzer advance had also driven a deep wedge between Eremenko's Stalingrad Front and Southeastern Front, severing most communications between Moscow and the Caucasus. Compounding this threat, southwest of the city the spearhead of Hoth's Fourth Panzer Army had reached Tinguta Station, only 35 kilometers southwest of Stalingrad's southern suburbs, in position to cut off the withdrawal routes of Lopatin's 64th Army back through the city.

Faced with this crisis but lacking adequate forces, Eremenko improvised as best he could. To defend the northwestern approaches to the city, the *front* commander ordered the Defense Committee to move a battalion of naval infantry from the Volga River Flotilla and two battalions of student officers from the Stalingrad Political-Military School into defenses along the Sukhaia Mechetka River. Tank destroyer battalions and People's Militia Detachments made up of workers from the Tractor, Red October (Krasnyi Oktiabr'), and Barrikady Factories manned defenses around the Tractor Factory. The Defense Committee then reinforced these troops with 60 tanks (manned by factory workers), 45 tractors, more than 150 machine guns, and 40 guns repaired by these factories. Assisted by naval gunfire from the Volga Flotilla, these forces contained 16th Panzer Division's thin line of panzer grenadiers north of the Mokraia Mechetka River.[34]

While these forces were solidifying the defenses north of the city, Eremenko began concentrating forces that could crush Sixth Army's corridor to the Volga River and end the threat to Stalingrad from the north. First, late on 22 August, 2nd Tank Corps began assembling in the Gorodishche region, 8 kilometers northwest of Stalingrad. Commanded by A. G. Kravchenko, who been promoted to major general one month before, the tank corps had been split apart by the German advance to the Volga. Although its main body (headquarters, 26th and 27th Tank Brigades, and half of its 2nd Motorized Rifle Brigade) was at Gorodishche, its 148th Tank Brigade and the other half of its motorized rifle brigade were north of the corridor. To prevent the Germans from reinforcing their own forces within the corridor and then attacking into Stalingrad, Eremenko on the evening of 23 August ordered the main body of Kravchenko's tank corps and the remnants of 23rd Tank Corps, still commanded by General Khasin, to "occupy a defense along the line of Height Markers 135.4, 147, 6, and 143.6, Novaia Nadezhda, and Shishiliankin [20–25 kilometers northwest of Stalingrad] and prepare a counterstroke toward Orlovka and Erzovka" against 16th Panzer Division's rear.[35]

At the same time, Eremenko ordered General Feklenko, the disgraced former commander of 17th Tank Corps who now commanded the Stalingrad Tank Center, to organize an inner defensive line around Stalingrad's northern and western periphery extending from Rynok on the Volga westward to Orlovka and then southward through Gorodishche and Verkhniaia El'shanka to Kuporosnoe, Stalingrad's southernmost suburb (see Map 54). Feklenko received command of Colonel Saraev's 10th NKVD Rifle Division, reinforced by 99th Tank Brigade and 21st and 28th Separate Tank Battalions for this purpose. The *front* commander then reinforced this line with an antitank artillery regiment from 57th Army and an operational group of naval gun ships from the Volga Naval Flotilla. Feklenko's special "combat sector," consisting of 50 T-34 tanks, was responsible for defending the key Tractor Factory.[36]

To further bolster Stalingrad's defenses, Eremenko ordered the Stalingrad Training Center to form three antitank artillery regiments and one gun artillery battalion and to deploy them into firing positions on the northern outskirts by

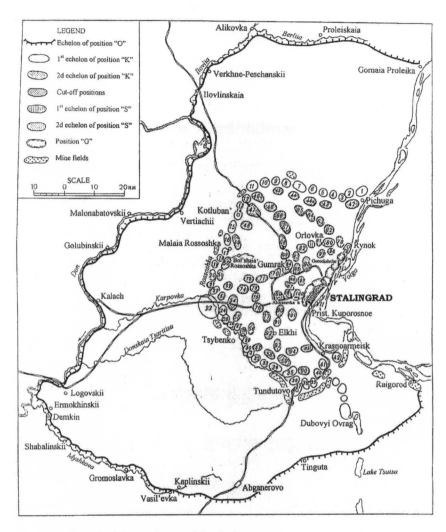

Map 54. Stalingrad's defensive lines and fortified positions

the morning of 24 August. This would increase the number of guns south of the Sukhaia Mechetka River to 156 tubes.[37] Meanwhile, the *front* commander designated the fresh 124th, 115th, and 149th Rifle Brigades, which were due to reach Stalingrad by 27 August, to act as the city's reserves and to man Stalingrad's inner defensive line. In an attempt to counter the Germans' heavy aerial bombardment of the city, Eremenko concentrated all 560 available antiaircraft guns inside Stalingrad. However, the city sprawled some 45 kilometers from north to south, which undermined the effectiveness of this measure.

To stiffen Eremenko's backbone—as if it needed further stiffening— Stalin early on 24 August telephoned him with a new direct order:

Comrades Vasilevsky, Eremenko, and Malenkov

I advise you: First, resolutely and without fail, close the gap through which the enemy's forces have penetrated to Stalingrad with our forces and encircle the enemy forces that have penetrated and destroy them. You have all of the forces for this, and you can and must do it.

Second, hold on to your positions along the front west and south of Stalingrad unconditionally, do not withdraw units from the front to liquidate the penetrating enemy, and unconditionally continue the counterattacks and offensives by our forces to throw the enemy back beyond the limits of the Stalingrad external defensive line.[38]

Due to Eremenko's vigorous defensive measures, but also because of their own weakness, neither Hube's 16th Panzer nor Schlömer's 3rd Motorized Divisions proved able to penetrate Stalingrad's northern defenses in the intense fighting that took place between 24 and 26 August. As early as the morning of 24 August, 16th Panzer Division's 16th Panzer Pioneer Battalion, with attached antitank and artillery batteries, managed to seize the landing site for a large rail ferry, just north of the Tractor Factory and the mouth of the Mokraia Mechetka River, cutting all rail communications between Kazakhstan and Stalingrad. However, with their supporting infantry divisions still lagging far to the west and with more than half of their forces preoccupied with holding the Volga River line and the northern face of their narrow corridor, 3rd Motorized and 16th Panzer Divisions were far less successful in their assaults on the city. By this time, 16th Panzer Division's hedgehog was indeed in a precarious position:

When the first Focke-Wulf reconnaissance aircraft arrived in the dawn of 24 August and gave the signal for new flight missions, 16th Panzer Division began reporting for duty.

At 0440 hours KG Krumpen (consisting of the headquarters, 64th Panzer Grenadier Regiment, 3rd Battalion, 2nd Panzer Regiment, 1st Battalion, 64th Panzer Grenadiers, 1st Battalion, 79th Panzer Grenadiers, 1st Company, 16th Panzer Pioneer Battalion, 2nd Battalion [+], 16th Artillery Regiment [Geisser], and 3rd Battery, 51st *Werfer* Artillery Regiment [Brendel]), attacked southeastward toward Spartanovka and its higher fortified positions, with the "Big Mushroom" [*Grossen Pilz*] in its southern part. The Russians, however, were already firing on the advancing grenadiers to the north; they had positioned themselves in the stream beds southwest of the town in battalion strength with 10 tanks and were constantly reinforcing [these positions].

The attack was not able to move forward. The enemy held Spartanovka. Farther west, at Orlovka, he took the initiative and advanced toward 1st Battalion, 64th Panzer Grenadiers (Captain Dörmann), south of the railroad. The on-call Stukas dropped their bombs from high altitude due to the heavy air defenses and managed to strike only occasional targets among the continuously reinforcing Russian formations. The 4th Battery, 16th Artillery Regiment, fired as if there were no tomorrow. Panzer Detachment Bassewitz arrived in relief; nevertheless, the T-34s succeeded in breaking through to the regiment's command post. The break through was mopped up by evening, and a continuous southern front was established over the hills and gullies. It extended from Hills 135.4 and 144.2 to 147.6 north-northwest of Orlovka.

In the north, KG von Arensdorff (consisting of the headquarters, 79th Panzer Grenadier Regiment, 1st Battalion, 2nd Panzer Regiment, 2nd Battalion, 64th Panzer Grenadiers, 16th Motorcycle Battalion, 2nd Battalion, 79th Panzer Grenadiers, Artillery Detachments Zinkel and Naskolb, and 2nd Company, 16th Panzer Jagt [Hunter] Battalion) had succeeded in capturing several prominent hills with ease and dug themselves in. Feverishly, they dug foxholes and machine gun and grenade throwing positions; the artillery and tanks were into position, camouflaging themselves to avoid detection by aircraft. Pioneers erected obstacles, laid mine fields, and reconnoitered supply routes, and prepared roads.

The Russians were regrouping troops from the Voronezh region and throwing them against the northern front between the Don and the Volga. As early as the afternoon, they arrived at Erzovka and pressed against 16th Panzer Division's positions.

The eastern front of the hedgehog extended along the Volga from Akatovka in the north through Vinnovka and Latashanka in the south; from there it turned inland from the bank toward Rynok and Spartanovka. KG Strehlke (16th Panzer Pioneer Battalion, 12th Company, 64th Panzer Grenadiers, and 12th Battery, 16th Artillery Regiment) seized Flak Hill 0.6 and occupied the vital railroad ferry station—capturing considerable enemy material. It then received orders to halt the ship traffic, defend against any enemy attempt to land, and hold the endangered corner position outside of Rynok (with 1st and 2nd Companies, 16th Panzer Pioneers). Numerous boats and monitors fell victim to their grenades during their [the enemies'] first attempt to break through to the south on the first day. Only on the other side, in the very visible airfield on the eastern bank, were Russian planes able to land despite the artillery fire. The men were hiding in the vineyards in the small suburbs of Datschi and Latashanka. After fighting for weeks on end in the treeless steppe, they were now hoping for a few days break in this fertile "magic garden" of walnut trees, oak trees, and sweet chestnut, potatoes, tomatoes, and wine.

The 16th Panzer Grenadier Battalion (Mues) and 2nd Battalion, 2nd Panzer Regiment, were in reserve at the command post in the dairy farm in the heart of the hedgehog. Thus, on 24 August 16th Panzer Division formed a hedgehog with three fronts along the Volga.

Still, the thorns of Spartanovka and Rynok pierced the hedgehog's flesh, the connection to the west was still missing, and the Russians were still reinforcing their forces.[39]

Fighting intensely, and supported by his own armor and unpainted T-34s fresh off the factory's assembly lines, Feklenko's combat sector staved off all German attempts to capture Rynok and Spartanovka, cross the Mokraia Mechetka River, and reach and seize the Tractor Factory. At one point, Feklenko's tanks overran the headquarters of 64th Panzer Grenadier Regiment, forcing Hube's forces to withdraw from Spartanovka to new defensive positions just south of Rynok. By this time, all three of XIV Panzer Corps' divisions were almost out of fuel and resorting to a series of hedgehog defenses to protect themselves. On the night of 24–25 August, the *Luftwaffe* attempted to airdrop supplies to 16th Panzer Division, but most of the parachutes fell outside German lines. Hube, a one-armed veteran of World War I, was almost frantic in his messages to higher headquarters, although he outwardly displayed his legendary calm, insisting on getting his customary sleep even while surrounded. In a meeting at his headquarters, he informed his staff and subordinates:

> The shortage of ammo and fuel is such that our only chance is to break through to the west. I absolutely refuse to fight a pointless battle that must end in the annihilation of my troops, and I therefore order a break-out to the west. I shall personally take responsibility for this order and will know how to justify it in the proper quarters. I absolve you, gentlemen, from your oath of loyalty, and I leave you the choice of either leading your men in this action or handing over your command to other officers who are prepared to do it. It is impossible to hold our positions without ammunition. I am acting contrary to the Führer's orders.[40]

His confidence was restored almost immediately when a combat group of 3rd Motorized Division fought its way forward, bringing 10 tanks and a column of 250 trucks carrying ammunition, fuel, and food. Increased Soviet pressure, however, continued to jeopardize Hube's defenses, preventing his division from making any progress against Stalingrad's northern defenses:

> By surprise, on 25 August the Russians broke into the southern front from the western edge of Spartanovka. Panzer Detachment Warmbold and the Panzer Grenadiers threw them out again. The Volga front reported Russian preparations for a landing; the northern front signaled, "Russian troops in the strength of one army are advancing! Still no connection with LI Corps." Then, the follow-on infantry divisions passing by the tank wedge were not able to cope with the Russian strong points and could not link up. All supply for XIV Panzer Corps on the Volga stopped. The bulk of the rear services [baggage

trains] were held back because the terrain between the Don and the Volga and west of the Don did not provide necessary cover and [the routes of] Rear Service Train II had been established to Potemkinskaia, west of the Chir. Now they [the rear services] were waiting with loaded trucks for the signal to march. The route, however, was blocked by the Russians. He-111 bombers supplied XIV Panzer Corps with ammunition and fuel by air.

The situation for the division was particularly critical, and their lives hung by a thread. However, a personal order from Hitler had told them to hold their positions at all cost. He had his eye on the Orient Front [*Vordere Orient*], where Rommel had advanced from El Alamein against Alexandria and intended to link up with 1st Panzer Army in Persia.[41]

Despite the arrival of vital supplies, on the afternoon of 26 August Wietersheim, Hube's corps commander, radioed Paulus, "It is not possible with our present forces to stay on the Volga and hold open the communications to the rear. . . . Will have to pull back tonight. Report decision." Paulus's response was terse: "Do not retreat."[42] As the fighting intensified during the remaining few days of August, with his division suffering up to 500 casualties per day and chronically short of ammunition, Hube was left with no choice but to abandon Rynok on 31 August and withdraw to a new defensive line 2 kilometers north of the town. Thus ended the first and, as it turned out, the best opportunity for German forces to capture Stalingrad.[43] Cryptically the Red Army General Staff's daily summary for 26 August read, "By day's end on 26 August, Group Feklenko fought its way to the Latashanka and Pereval'nyi regions [4 kilometers north of the Mokraia Mechetka River]."[44]

From the German point of view, worse would follow. Although news that Germans were in the northern suburbs of his namesake city reportedly evoked a stream of curses from Stalin, the *Stavka* had sufficient reserve forces to respond effectively to Hube's bold advance. To an even greater extent than Feklenko's determined defense of the Tractor Factory, Eremenko's vigorous employment of these reserves created the predicament in which Sixth Army's XIV Panzer Corps found itself during the last week of August.

When it learned of Hube's penetration to the Volga River late on 23 August, the *Stavka* the next day demanded Eremenko restore the situation and later dispatched vital reinforcements to the beleaguered *front* commander from its carefully marshaled reserves. These included Pavelkin's 16th and Mishulin's 4th Tank Corps and the 64th Rifle Division dispatched to the Bol'shaia Ivanovka, Zavarykin, and Malaia Ivanovka regions in Stalingrad Front's deep rear. At the same time, it ordered 173rd, 221st, 116th, 24th, and 308th Rifle Divisions to move to the Stalingrad region by rail. Finally, late on 24 August the *Stavka* took further measures to back up Stalingrad Front by ordering the Volga Military District to deploy yet another army. Thus 66th Army, commanded by Lieutenant General Stepan Andrianovich Kalinin, formed around the nucleus of the district's

8th Reserve Army, in the Kamyshin region, on the eastern bank of the Volga River 150 kilometers north of Stalingrad:

1. Form 66th Army, consisting of 231st, 120th, 99th, 49th, 299th, 316th, 207th, and 292nd RDs.
2. Transfer the command of 8th Reserve Army to form the command of 66th Army, renaming it 66th Army. Situate the army's headquarters in the town of Kamyshin [150 kilometers north of Stalingrad].
3. Appoint Lieutenant General S. A. Kalinin as the commander of 66th Army, relieving him of his duties as commander of the Volga Military District. Appoint Major General M. I. Kozlov as deputy commander of 66th Army.[45]

In addition to eight rifle divisions, Kalinin's 66th Army was to include three tank brigades, two *Katiusha* regiments, and a mixed aviation corps, with one assault-bomber aviation division (three regiments of IL-2 aircraft and two regiments of Pe-2) and one fighter mixed aviation division—consisting of two regiments of Yak-1 airframes, one regiment of LaGG-3s, and one regiment of P-40 Kittyhawks—all provided by the Red Army's appropriate main directorate. Should Eremenko's defenses falter, reasoned the *Stavka*, this new army would be able to prevent the Germans from advancing northward from the Stalingrad region. Kalinin, 66th Army commander, had led Western Front's 24th Army during the battle for Smolensk in July 1941 and served as deputy commander of the same *front* to November 1941.[46]

Understanding it would take days for these reserves to reach their designated assembly areas, Eremenko late on 23 August created a shock group in the Samo-falovka region, north of the western base of XIV Panzer Corps' corridor, and ordered it to counterattack southward to sever the corridor and isolate the German forces operating farther east (see Map 55). Commanded by Major General Kirill Alekseevich Kovalenko, who had led 242nd Rifle Division throughout Operation Barbarossa and, after its formation in summer 1942, became Stalingrad Front's deputy commander, this group consisted initially of 35th and 27th Guards and 298th Rifle Divisions, Rodin's 28th Tank Corps, and 169th Tank Brigade. Its mission was to:

Deploy into the Panshino and Kotluban' sector [from the eastern bank of the Don River 18 kilometers to the southeast], attack toward the southwest, and, in conjunction with the forces of 62nd Army, crush the formations of the enemy's XIV Panzer Corps, which have penetrated to the Volga, close the penetration in the Kotluban' Station and Bol'shaia Rossoshka sector, and restore the situation on 62nd Army's right flank by reaching the Don River line.[47]

Simultaneously, Lopatin's 62nd Army was to "attack northward from the Malaia Rossoshka region with 87th Rifle Division and, in cooperation with Group

Map 55. The Stalingrad Front's counterstrokes, 23–29 August 1942

Kovalenko, destroy the enemy group which has penetrated."[48] In addition, to prevent the forces of LI Army Corps concentrating along the southern face of the corridor's western base (295th Infantry Division and part of 71st Infantry Division) from advancing southward toward Kalach and Stalingrad, Lopatin's army was to establish a defensive line in the sector from Novo-Alekseevskii on the Rossoshka River westward to the Don River and man it with 33rd Guards Rifle Division and 157th Separate Artillery–Machine Gun Battalion.

At the same time, in order to encircle and destroy XIV Panzer Corps' forces in the eastern end of the corridor (3rd Motorized and 16th Panzer Divisions), a special operational group consisting of Kravchenko's 2nd and Popov's 23rd Tank Corps, under the command of Lieutenant General Andrei Dmitrievich Shtevnev, who had commanded 7th Mechanized Corps' 14th Tank Division in 1940 and 1941 and was now chief of Stalingrad Front's Armored and Mechanized Forces, was to "attack from the Orlovka region [8 kilometers northwest of Stalingrad] toward Erzovka [15 kilometers north of Stalingrad] on the morning of 24 August."[49]

Eremenko hoped the counterattacks by Groups Kovalenko and Shtevnev would be strong enough to collapse XIV Panzer Corps' defenses and force Wietersheim to withdraw his panzers back to the Don. Still, the attack preparations were too hasty, and both attacking forces suffered from poor command and control and coordination. Group Kovalenko attacked at 1800 hours on 23 August, that is, only five hours after receiving its attack order. Attacking on Kovalenko's right wing, 27th Guards and 298th Rifle Divisions were not able to even dent the defenses of VIII Army Corps' 384th Infantry Division. However, farther east Kovalenko's 35th Guards Rifle Division and 169th Tank Brigade, which attacked southward from the Samofalovka region, smashed through 60th Motorized Division's hedgehog defenses and linked up with 62nd Army's 196th Rifle Division near Bol'shaia Rossoshka by 0200 hours on 24 August. However, after running out of ammunition, Kovalenko's forces were unable to maintain their grip on the corridor and were forced to withdraw northward.

According to the OKW's operational summary for 24 August:

On XIV Panzer Corps' front, two Russian regiments attacked our forces from the northwest, attacking eastward through Point 137 (32 kilometers northwest of Stalingrad), and the enemy concentrated a large group with tanks (up to 30–40 tanks) northwest of Rossoshka and in Orlovka (northwest of Stalingrad). The enemy attacked unsuccessfully at Konnyi Station, northwest of Gorodishche, and at Orlovka, where he lost 16 tanks and, along the Volga, the enemy is still holding on to Mechetka. South of the railroad station at Kotluban' and the village of Kotluban', after several tank attacks during which he lost 24 tanks, the enemy has dug in, also digging in many of his tanks.

On VIII Army Corps' front, enemy attacks supported by tanks were repulsed east of Kislov (9 kilometers southwest of Pan'shino).[50]

After observing Group Kovalenko's operations on 23 August, Eremenko overnight ordered 27th Guards and 298th Rifle Divisions to continue their attacks toward Vertiachii and 35th Guards Rifle Division toward Peskovatka to converge on the Don River and close the gap at the western base of the Germans' corridor. Stalin demanded Eremenko and the representative of the *Stavka*, Vasilevsky, close the corridor and destroy the German forces that had penetrated to the Volga.

On 24 August, while German aircraft pounded Lopatin's and Kovalenko's forces, Paulus restored the situation in the western end of the corridor by moving the remainder of 60th Motorized Division forward to support its beleaguered

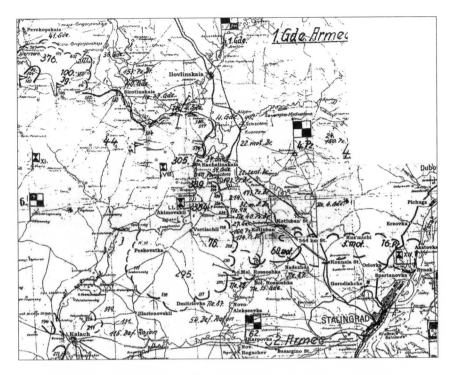

Map 56. The Sixth Army's situation, 24–25 August 1942

forward elements (see Map 56). Throughout the day, 63rd, 21st, and 1st Guards Armies continued their nonstop assaults on the left wing of Paulus's army along the Don River; 4th Tank Army defended on its right wing and, with 27th Guards and 298th Rifle Divisions on its left, tried in vain to dislodge 384th Infantry Division from its defenses northeast of Vertiachii. Meanwhile to the south, Lopatin's 62nd Army struggled to hold its positions on the southern face of the corridor, and Group Kovalenko's 35th Guards Rifle Division and 169th Tank Brigade once again captured Malaia Rossoshka, linking up with 62nd Army's 87th Rifle Division. To the east, Group Shtevnev managed to advance 6 kilometers, pressing 16th Panzer Division's forces back to the heights 1.5–2 kilometers northeast of Orlovka. During this action, a battalion from 87th Rifle Division's 101st Regiment captured the village of Vlasovka, near Malaia Rossoshka, and held it for several hours against strong German counterattacks before relinquishing it the next morning. The survivors of this battalion—all 33 of them—later received awards for their bravery.[51]

Despite such examples of individual and group bravery, conditions for Stalingrad Front deteriorated by the hour. Stalingrad itself was set aflame by German bombs, and Eremenko's counterattacks had achieved very little of lasting value. In addition, Eremenko's air support fell precipitously, largely due to the high attrition rate in aircraft, pilots, and crews but also due to the necessity for rebasing 8th Air Army's aircraft at airfields out of harm's way. Making matters worse, after failing to break through 57th Army's defenses at Tinguta Station, Hoth soon began moving his forces west of the railroad line preparatory to launching a new attack on Stalingrad from the southwest (see below).

Faced with this deteriorating situation, Eremenko on 24 August decided to shift the focus of his counterattacks to Stalingrad Front's left wing by employing tank and rifle reinforcements provided by the *Stavka* to destroy XIV Panzer Corps' forces in the eastern half of their corridor, in particular at and west of Erzovka. To that end, he issued new orders to Stalingrad Front:

- *4th Tank Army* must attack [southward] toward Vertiachii with its left wing (27th Guards and 298th Rifle Divisions) on the morning of 25 August to destroy the enemy who have penetrated and reach the left bank of the Don in the Nizhne-Gnilovskii and Vertiachii sector;
- *62nd Army* must firmly hold on to its defensive lines along the left bank of the Don on its left wing and, with its right wing, which will include 35th Guards Rifle Division and 169th Tank Brigade, attack [northward] toward Peskovatka and capture the Vertiachii and Peskovatka line by day's end;
- *Group Kovalenko*, consisting of 16th and 4th Tank Corps and 84th, 24th, and 315th Rifle Divisions, will attack [southward] toward Sukhaia Mechetka *Balka* and Marker 147.0 [5–10 kilometers north of Stalingrad] on the morning of 25 August and destroy the opposing enemy, while covering the Karpovskaia *Balka* and Kuz'michi front from the west;
- *Group Shtevnev*, consisting of 2nd and 23rd Tank Corps, will protect the Kuz'michi and Konnaia Station line and, in cooperation with 16th and 4th Tank Corps, will attack toward Orlovka and Marker 147.0 [5–10 kilometers north of Stalingrad] on the morning of 25 August to encircle and destroy the enemy grouping that has penetrated into the region north of Stalingrad.
- *64th Rifle Division* [just arrived from the *Stavka* Reserve] must occupy a defense along the Spartak and Pichuga line to prevent the Germans from penetrating [northward along the Volga] toward Kamyshin;
- *63rd and 21st Armies and 1st Guards Army* will continue their offensives in accordance with their previous missions.[52]

Eremenko's plan thus called for Groups Kovalenko and Shtevnev to launch converging attacks against the defenses of XIV Panzer Corps' 3rd Motorized and 16th Panzer Divisions north and northwest of Stalingrad with a force of about 350 tanks, while also protecting the deployment of the fresh 66th Army into the Kamyshin region. To increase the strength of Group Kovalenko, Eremenko reinforced it with Mishulin's 4th and Pavelkin's partially refitted 4th and 16th Tank Corps. To improve command, control, and coordination of his attacking forces, Eremenko on 26 August organized an auxiliary command post for Stalingrad Front in the village of Malaia Ivanovka, 42 kilometers northwest of the Don River and 65 kilometers north of Stalingrad, and directed the *front's* deputy commander, Kovalenko, and its chief of staff, Major General D. N. Nikishov, who had commanded Southern Front's 9th Army during the July fighting, to control the action from this site. Although Eremenko's signal forces managed to establish direct wire communications between this auxiliary command post and all of the *front's* subordinate armies except the 62nd, German bombing raids frequently disrupted these communications, forcing units to rely on radio transmissions and liaison officers.[53]

Still, Eremenko's new series of counterattacks were no more successful than previous efforts (see Map 57). By nightfall on 24 August, 60th Motorized Division had established an elaborate hedgehog defense, protected by a dense network of interlocking artillery and machine-gun fire and numerous antitank strongpoints. In addition, on the 60th's left and right flanks, 384th and 295th Infantry Divisions organized ambushes, prearranged artillery concentrations, and local counterattack forces made up of infantry and tanks to strike the attacking Soviets wherever they threatened to penetrate. As Eremenko's shock groups concentrated for the attacks, German Stukas unmercifully pounded his troops throughout the entire duration of these attacks, disrupting their combat formations and hindering their timely reaction to altered situations. As a result the assaults, when they occurred, were late, disorganized, and poorly coordinated.

Attacking 24 hours late—at dawn on 26 August—with a force of about 350 tanks, Groups Kovalenko and Shtevnev encountered strong and effective resistance by XIV Panzer Corps' 3rd and 60th Motorized and 16th Panzer Divisions. By assaulting 3rd Motorized Division's defenses before his group's 16th and 4th Tank Corps were able to concentrate all of their 250 tanks, Kovalenko's offensive front was simply too wide for him to employ tanks effectively. As a result, his counterattack faltered within hours with heavy losses. To the south, Shtevnev committed the 100 tanks of 2nd and 23rd Tank Corps to piecemeal assaults against 16th Panzer Division's defenses north of the Mokraia Mechetka River instead of concentrating them for a drive on Orlovka and Erzovka. Pounded by German Stukas, these attacks also ended in failure.[54] They did, however, produce many anxious moments for 16th Panzer Division:

> On 26 August the Russians attacked from Spartanovka and Rynok toward the endangered southeastern flank of the hedgehog with furious anger. The enemy assembled anew at Orlovka. During the night Red tanks broke through the northern defenses. It was bright moonlight. While the bulk [of the tanks] fell victim to their own artillery, a T-60 broke through to the main road. Here it was met by a German motorcycle and side-car with Senior Lieutenant

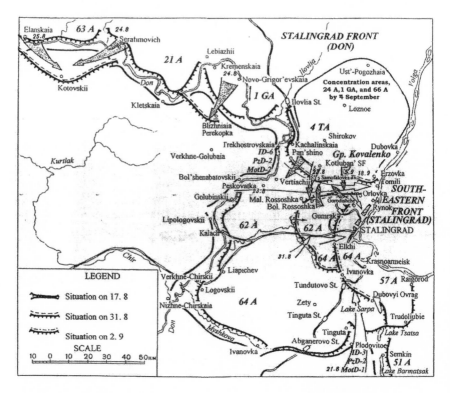

Map 57. Soviet counterattacks and counterstrokes, August–September 1942

Radue (1st Company, 64th Panzer Grenadier Regiment). Thinking it was a German tank, the side-car driver halted it. The tank stopped and a man opened the hatch. Knowing he had made a mistake, the German pulled out his gun and began shooting at the tank driver in the turret. The Russian disappeared and moved off in haste. The hatch in the turret remained open. The motorcycle followed and pulled up next to the tank, and the Senior Lieutenant jumped onto the bar of the side-car and threw a hand grenade into the open hatch. Flames began coming out of the tank and it stopped and burned.[55]

Meanwhile to the west, attacking concentrically from north and south, the shock groups on 4th Tank Army's left wing and 62nd Army's right ran into a meat grinder courtesy of 384th and 295th Infantry Divisions' defenses east of Vertiachii. The two pincers managed to compress the width of the corridor to only 4 kilometers, forcing Paulus to resupply his forces in the eastern extremity of the corridor by airdrop. Nonetheless, 4th Tank and 62nd Armies' forces simply could not link up and totally encircle XIV Panzer Corps' partly isolated mobile divisions.

As Eremenko's forces launched attack after attack against the dangerous German corridor to the Volga, the *Stavka* offered the *front* commander and its representative, Vasilevsky, both advice and practical assistance. For example, early on 26 August, Stalin questioned the wisdom of Eremenko's piecemeal counterstrokes, instead suggesting he employ multiple shock groups of army size.

> There is a misunderstanding regarding 24th [Rifle] Division. I request you not commit it to combat, since we are thinking of forming an army of five divisions, including 24th RD, and deploying it north of Kachalinskaia. Another army—the Saratov, consisting of eight divisions—will stand beside this new army. Both armies will occupy a front facing south in the Dubovka region from the Don River north of Kachalinskaia to the Volga and, after advancing to the south, will link up with the Stalingrad Front. One army will be commanded by Kozlov, and the other, by Kalinin. I request you confirm receipt immediately.[56]

This message referred to the new 24th Army, which the *Stavka* formed the next day in an order signed by Stalin and Vasilevsky:

1. Form 24th Army in the Kudanovskii, Rakovka, Abramov, Frolovo, and Evstratovskii regions [30–50 kilometers north of the Don River].
2. Appoint Major General Kozlov, D. T., as commander of 24th Army, freeing him of his duties as commander of 9th Reserve Army, and appoint Major General Korneev, N. V., as the chief of staff of 24th Army, relieving him as chief of staff of 9th Reserve Army.
3. Include in 24th Army: 173rd, 221st, 308th, 292nd, and 207th Rifle Divisions; two tank brigades from the chief of the GABTU [Main Auto-Armored Directorate], and 217th Tank Brigade from 66th Army; the command of 9th Reserve Army with supporting units and facilities, having renamed the command of 9th Reserve Army the command of 24th Army; and organizations forming in the Volga Military District for 65th Army.[57]

Although Eremenko's counterstrokes failed to achieve their optimum result, and the *Stavka's* preventative measures would take days, if not weeks, to realize the destruction of Wietersheim's panzer corps, Paulus was not able to restore routine communications in the corridor until 30 August. In the meantime, Hube's panzer and Schlömer's panzer grenadiers endured three harrowing days in near-total isolation, prompting a German general to later note: "As a result of these counterattacks, the enemy succeeded in cutting off the panzer corps, which, for several days, was forced to repel attacks and receive its supplies by air and from small groups which made their way through to them at night and protected by tanks."[58] In turn, this situation prompted Wietersheim's request to Paulus to withdraw his panzer corps and Paulus's denial of his request.

As Groups Kovalenko and Shtevnev struggled in vain to crush XIV Panzer Corps' forces in the corridor, Kriuchenkin's 4th Tank and Lopatin's 62nd Armies did likewise against VIII and LI Army Corps' 384th, 76th, and 295th Infantry Divisions, defending the corridor's western base. Although these forces, as well as Groups Kovalenko and Shtevnev, continued assaults for several more days, they were unable to register significant gains. In fact, they had to give ground in several sectors by early on 29 August.[59] Reflecting its heavy tank losses, the tank strength of Group Kovalenko's 4th Tank Corps eroded to just 23 tanks by day's end on 28 August, and 16th Tank Corps shrank to similar levels.[60]

However, during this period Group Shtevnev captured Orlovka and the hills to the northeast, and General Feklenko's 99th Tank Brigade was able to capture Spartanka village, north of Stalingrad, and reach the southern edge of Rynok, ultimately compelling Hube's forces to withdraw farther north.[61] Group Feklenko's assaults dented, but failed to break, 16th Panzer Division's defenses:

> In the early morning hours of 27 August, the enemy broke through the southeastern front and managed to enter the center of the hedgehog. The alarm was sounded. Drivers, rear service troops, and cooks all reached for their machine pistols and grenades and began attacking the Russians. With coarse shouts of "Urrah," however, a workers battalion stormed the positions of 12th Company of 64th Panzer Grenadier Regiment, but the Pak [antitank gun] and motorcycle sections held as firm as a rock and the *Nebelwerfers* [multibarreled rocket launchers] aimed their shells at the enemy rushing out of Rynok.
>
> At about 1000 hours, they managed a renewed advance. The Russians wanted to push through to the north along the bank [of the Volga] and push the Germans away from the Volga. They managed to find the weakest part of the hedgehog. By using continuously loaded assault guns, AT-mines, and detonators, the pioneers were able to put 16 tanks out of action and hold their positions.
>
> At 1415 hours the Germans began their counterattack. Its objective was Rynok. Stukas assaulted the town. The 16th Motorcycle Battalion under Captain Dörmann and 2nd Company, 16th Panzer Pioneers, attacked from the west, and 1st Company, 16th Panzer Pioneers, and subordinate groups attacked from the north. At about 1700 hours, they were repulsed by heavy fire. At twilight 16th Motorcycle Battalion reported once again and managed to enter the northern part of Rynok in intense fighting. By the time twilight faded in the east, all but the southern outskirts of Rynok was in their hands.

The "pest boil" [*Pestbeule*] in the hedgehog was captured. The 1st Company, 16th Panzer Pioneers, occupied the new positions. They were digging graves for many fallen soldiers at the southern outskirts of Latashanka.[62]

To the west, although the assaults by Group Shtevnev caused anxious moments for the entire XIV Panzer Corps, they too faltered before achieving their objectives:

As the battles were raging along the southeastern front, the Russians also attacked the southeastern front at Orlovka against the seam [boundary] with 3rd Infantry Division (mot.). On the night of 27 August, outposts in ditches at the front heard the rattling of the tracks of T-34s. At the first glow of gunfire, massed enemy infantry prepared to assault Hill 147.6. The division's reserve was alerted. Stukas dropped their bombs and Battalion Mues [16th Panzer Grenadiers] its shells into the masses. Unstoppable, however, the Russians pushed their way across Hill 147.6 and brought assault guns, antitank rifles, and machine guns into position. His artillery observers helped the Russian infantry to advance by maneuvering its fires from favorable positions. There was one Russian regiment for each German company.

The railroad embankment, the backbone of the position, was lost. Now the situation had become extremely critical. The brave Senior Sergeant Altemöller (64th Regiment) received a round in his head. Staff Sergeant Gröteke replaced him. In another location, rear service troops were manning the foxholes. The counterattack began at 9.30 hours. After a preparation by the artillery, Müller's panzer company and von Mutius' MTW [armored personnel carrier] company advanced from the left toward Hill 144.2. They surprised the Russians, who were convinced of their success, and threw them out of their new positions, capturing rich booty. The enemy quickly assembled for a counterattack. Müller's panzer company barged right in, and Lenz's MTW company jumped off and attacked Hill 147.6 frontally. The men cleared the strong field positions on close combat. Lieutenant Philippi and ten men from 64th Regiment perished. The railroad embankment and prominent Hills 144.2 and 147.6, however, were back in their hands again.[63]

Although Soviet critiques credit the failure of Eremenko's counterstrokes at Kotluban' and Orlovka to the overall weakness of his forces and a multitude of other already familiar reasons, the 350 tanks fielded by Kovalenko's and Shtevnev's groups, if employed properly, should have been able to accomplish more. However, as on numerous previous occasions, 16th Panzer and 3rd Motorized Divisions employed their 50–60 operational tanks and hundreds of armored personnel carriers far more skillfully and in closer coordination with supporting artillery, antitank guns, and infantry. Coupled with the deadly curtain of *Luft-*

Colonel General Andrei Ivanovich Eremenko, commander of the Southeastern Front, with his chief of artillery, V. N. Matveev, and his commissar, Nikita Sergeevich Khrushchev (left to right)

A reserve rifle regiment moving into defensive positions at Stalingrad

Civilians preparing defensive trenches on the outskirts of Stalingrad

Red Army riflemen counterattack in Stalingrad's suburbs

A workers' battalion in defensive positions in Stalingrad

waffe air support, Wietersheim's forces were able to overcome Soviet armor superiority and hold firmly to their corridor. But as described by 16th Panzer Division's history, Hube's victory was indeed costly:

> The 27th of August was a hot day for 16th Panzer Division as the tank crews lay in ditches and fought a positioned struggle on all sides—in the midst of the enemy together with 60th Infantry Division (mot.) and 3rd Infantry Division (mot.). Every available man was on duty with his weapon, nevertheless, the Russians far outnumbered them. There was no peace under sweet chestnut trees in the vineyards. After just a few days, all that was left north of Stalingrad was rubble and inexorable fighting. In those days, 1st Battalion, 64th Panzer Grenadier Regiment, alone suffered 154 losses. Ammunition and supplies were short; the men from the ammunition convoys were on the move day and night in order to supply their comrades at the front. During this quarter of a year, 16th Panzer Division's ammunition battalion under Captain Grosse alone transported 6,000 tons to Stalingrad. During 1941 and 1942, this 500-man-strong battalion suffered 40 dead and 70 wounded. But, during these last days of August, even convoys under tank protection were not able to pass through the corridor because of the Russians' barrages.[64]

In fact, the "narrowness" of Hube's victory was indicative of more serious problems to come, particularly if the *Stavka* continued its impressive flow of fresh tanks in great quantities to its forces and if Eremenko's troops finally learned how to employ those tanks effectively.

As it was, given the poor employment of its armored forces, poor command and control and coordination, a near absence of routine communications, weak artillery and air support, and, at best, tenuous logistical support, Eremenko's counterstrokes were condemned to failure. Although his forces had indeed given Paulus, Wietersheim, and Hube a fright, the *front* commander by day's end on 28 August had squandered most of his imposing armored forces, and his fresh reserve divisions were a shambles. In the wake of this failure, Eremenko and the *Stavka* had two urgent questions to answer: First, with its outer defenses penetrated, what was the best means to defend Stalingrad? Second, if a withdrawal to the city was necessary, what was the best means to rescue 62nd and 64th Armies, which were increasingly isolated west of the city?

62ND ARMY'S STRUGGLE, 23–29 AUGUST

As heavy fighting continued along the northern and southern flanks of XIV Panzer Corps' narrow corridor to the Volga River, Lopatin's 62nd Army had the task of defending the northern, northwestern, and western approaches to the city along an extended front arcing from the Volga River south of Rynok westward past Orlovka along the southern flank of the corridor to the Don River south of Peskovatka and southward along the Don to the Kalach region. With Groups Feklenko and Shtevnev anchoring the army's right flank north and northwest of the city, the main forces of Lopatin's 62nd Army struggled to maintain cohesive defenses along the western half of the corridor's southern flank and the western bank of the Don. At dawn on 24 August, with Wietersheim's panzers on the Volga's western bank, 76th and 295th Infantry Division of Seydlitz's LI Army Corps, which had been reinforced the night before by 71st Infantry Division's 191st Regiment, began pressing Lopatin's forces southeastward and southward from the Peskovatka region. By 1400 hours on 24 August, the advancing infantry of 295th Infantry Division pushed forward to the village of Sokarevka, 10 kilometers south of Peskovatka, threatening to outflank and encircle 62nd Army's 399th Rifle Division, which was still defending the western bank of the Don River south of Peskovatka. LI Corps' advance was also threatening the remaining forces on 62nd Army's left wing and both 62nd and the 64th Armies' rear areas.[65]

Thus, Lopatin's army faced a dilemma. On its right wing, south of the eastern half of the corridor, Groups Feklenko and Shtevnev were pounding XIV Panzer Corps' forces in the corridor. On its right-center, 37th Guards Rifle and 87th Rifle Divisions were struggling with XIV Panzer Corps' 60th Motorized Division and supporting 76th Infantry Division north of the Rossoshka River from Bol'shaia Rossoshka to Novo-Alekseevskii. On its left-center, 196th Rifle and 33rd Guards Rifle Divisions and 115th Fortified Region's 50th, 52nd, 157th, and

160th Artillery–Machine Gun Battalions defended the sector from Novo-Alekseevskii westward to Dmitrievka. On its left wing, 399th, 131st, and 112th Rifle Divisions and 20th Motorized Rifle Brigade faced 71st Infantry Division westward to the Don River and along the Don north and south of Kalach.[66] Compounding Lopatin's problems, the rifle divisions defending along the Don River, weakened in previous battles, numbered less than 2,000–3,000 men each, and he had few tanks in support.

The 62nd Army's commander had shared his growing concerns with the chief of the Red Army General Staff and Eremenko in messages he sent to both at 1400 hours and 2300 hours on 23 August, in which he asked for permission to withdraw his forces along the Don River eastward to the so-called middle (i.e., intermediate) defensive line along the Rossoshka River. Despite these entreaties, Lopatin at 2400 hours bowed to Eremenko's previous orders and reported he was ready to attack toward Vertiachii with his 87th Rifle and 35th Guards Rifle Divisions, in cooperation with 4th Tank Army's attack on Vertiachii from the north. After receiving Lopatin's conflicting transmissions regarding his reluctance to attack, followed shortly by his new attack plan, at 0515 hours on 24 August, a confused and obviously angry Stalin sent a caustic message to Eremenko criticizing his and also Vasilevsky's conduct of the defense. Pointing to Briansk Front's defense in the Orel region the year before, Stalin faulted Eremenko for failing to establish a deeply echeloned defense and for squandering his forces in fruitless counterattacks along various axes, while permitting the Germans to create the corridor and maneuver their forces freely within it, adding: "In my opinion, you ought to withdraw Lopatin and also 64th Army to the next defensive line, east of the Don. You must construct the defensive line secretly and in full form so that it does not turn into a rout. You must organize rear guards, capable of fighting to the death in order to let the armies' forces withdraw."[67]

Reassured by Lopatin's later message agreeing to attack and Eremenko's continued optimism, Stalin at 1500 hours on 25 August dispatched a new message to the *front* commander:

> We received a new report from Lopatin on 25 August in which he informs us about his decision to cut off the enemy that have penetrated to the Don, and, if Lopatin is really able to fulfill his decision, then I propose to help him fulfill that decision. In this regard our morning directive concerning the withdrawal of 62nd and 64th Armies cannot be considered obligatory.

After 62nd and 4th Tank Armies' joint counterstroke toward Vertiachii failed, overnight on 24–25 August, the remaining two regiments of LI Army Corps' 71st Infantry Division assaulted across the Don River north of Kalach. This attack forced 62nd Army's 399th and 131st Rifle Divisions to withdraw five to eight kilometers to the east. Alarmed by the new threat, late on 25 August, Lopatin once again sought Eremenko's permission to withdraw the forces on his army's

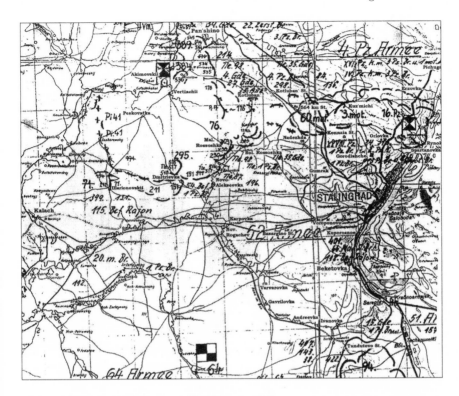

Map 58. The Sixth Army's situation, 26–27 August 1942

left wing back to the Rossoshka River. However, Eremenko was now preoccupied with the counterstrokes by Groups Kovalenko and Shtevnev, which were to take place the following day. He, therefore, again denied Lopatin's request.[68]

Confirming Lopatin's fears, at dawn on 26 August Seydlitz's LI Corps began a general assault against 62nd Army's center and left wing (see Map 58). Supported by waves of Stukas, 76th and 295th Infantry Divisions attacked southeastward from their expanded bridgehead in the Vertiachii and Peskovatka regions, driving back 196th Rifle and 35th Guards Rifle Divisions and 169th Tank Brigade toward the Rossoshka River line. To the west, opposite 62nd Army's left wing, 71st Infantry Division advanced eastward from Kalach, turning 399th Rifle Division's left flank and pressing the neighboring 131st Rifle Division and 20th Motorized Rifle Brigade eastward toward Illarionovskii, midway between the Don and Rossoshka Rivers. Continuing their steady advance on 27 August, 295th and 71st Infantry Divisions nearly encircled 399th Rifle Division northeast of Kalach by nightfall. At the same time, the forward elements of 295th Infantry Division approached within mortar range of the main Kalach-Stalingrad railroad

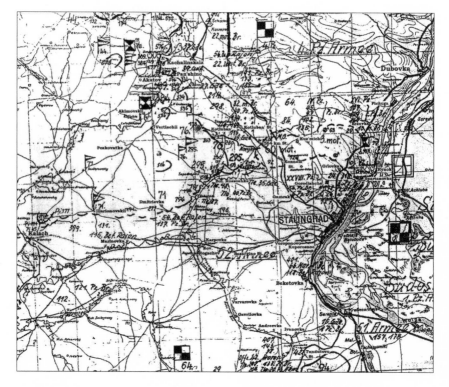

Map 59. The Sixth Army's situation, 28–29 August 1942

line, east of Illarionovskii, threatening to cut off the withdrawal routes of all of the forces on 62nd Army's left wing eastward toward Stalingrad.[69]

However, at this point on the night of 27–28 August, LI Corps suddenly ceased its assaults southward toward the Rossoshka River and the Kalach-Stalingrad railroad line and began shifting its 295th and 76th Infantry Division toward the northeast, leaving 71st Infantry Division to deal with Lopatin's left wing (see Map 59). Seydlitz did so because Paulus needed LI Corps' two infantry divisions to help defeat the counterattack by Group Shtevnev against the southern face of XIV Panzer Corps' beleaguered corridor and, thereafter, to spearhead his planned advance on Stalingrad from the northwest. This permitted the forces on Lopatin's left wing, including the survivors of 399th Rifle Division, as well as 131st and 112th Rifle Divisions and 20th Motorized Rifle Brigade, to maintain a coherent defensive front north of the Kalach-Stalingrad railroad line. Over the next few days, they began withdrawing their forces back to 62nd Army's main defense line along the Rossoshka River. This maneuver accorded with Paulus's original plan, that is, it assigned the task of encircling and liquidating Soviet forces west of Stalingrad to weaker follow-on infantry forces. However, because Sixth Army had left only 71st Infantry Division in this sector, Hoth's Fourth Panzer Army would have to effect the encirclement—if it was to occur at all.

By 29 August 71st Infantry Division reached the Rossoshka River north and south of Malaia Rossoshka southward to Novo-Alekseevka and still threatened the Kalach-Stalingrad railroad to the west. From Lopatin's and Eremenko's perspectives, these attacks were driving the forces on 62nd Army's left wing literally into 64th Army's rear area. Therefore, to improve command and control, at 2400 hours on 29 August, with the *Stavka's* approval, Eremenko transferred 62nd Army to Southeastern Front's control.[70] By this time, after resuming their advance on 18 August, the forces of Hoth's Fourth Panzer Army reached Southeastern Front's intermediate defensive line in the sector from Tundutovo Station eastward to Solianka, 50 kilometers south of Stalingrad, on the evening of 25 August (see below). There Hoth halted his advance from 26 to 28 August to regroup the divisions of his XXXXVIII Panzer Corps westward to a more favorable attack axis.

Because the counterstrokes Eremenko conducted toward Vertiachii on 25 August had failed, and neither 62nd nor the 64th Army had as yet withdrawn to Stalingrad's intermediate defensive line, on 26 August, for a second time, the *Stavka* queried Eremenko about the wisdom of withdrawing 62nd Army's left wing and the entire 64th Army to this line. Once again Eremenko demurred, indicating his reluctance to do so in another message to the *Stavka* on 27 August. However, after the counterstrokes by 62nd Army and 4th Tank Army and Groups Kovalenko and Shtevnev failed, the question became moot because Seydlitz's corps had already reached the intermediate defensive line, and Eremenko had no reserves capable of driving its forces back toward Kalach.

Had Eremenko decided to withdraw 64th Army in timely fashion, such a decision would have created a more coherent defensive line west of Stalingrad and would have permitted Eremenko to create vital reserves by significantly shortening his defensive front. However, the *front* commander did not do so throughout this critical period because he remained reluctant to abandon any territory to the Germans and was convinced his counterstrokes and counterattacks would succeed in pushing Paulus's forces back to the Don River. Almost inevitably, Eremenko's misplaced confidence placed Shumilov's 64th Army in a most vulnerable position.

As Eremenko's forces were locked in a death struggle with Paulus's Sixth Army, Stalin dispatched General Zhukov to the Stalingrad region in the hope that he could repeat his stellar performance defending Leningrad and Moscow the previous year. Appointed by Stalin as deputy supreme commander on 26 August, the same day Zhukov relinquished command of Western Front to Konev and, after consulting with Stalin in Moscow, flew to the Stalingrad region on 29 August. After landing at Kamyshin, where 66th Army was assembling, he took stock of the situation and, four hours later, drove to Stalingrad Front headquarters at Malaia Ivanovka. Typically, his first order of business was offensive in nature, supervising a counterstroke by 1st Guards Army as a prelude to an even larger combined counterstroke by the new 66th and 24th Armies (see Chapter 10).[71]

FOURTH PANZER ARMY'S ADVANCE, 17 AUGUST–2 SEPTEMBER

In addition to playing a decisive role in Army Group B's offensive toward Stalingrad, at least indirectly the renewed advance of Hoth's Fourth Panzer Army saved Paulus's XIV Panzer Corps by making it impossible for the Red Army to hold out west of the city. As described above, Army Group B's offensive plan called for Hoth's army to advance northward from the Abganerovo and Plodovitoe regions and push its XXXXVIII Panzer Corps toward and into Stalingrad's southern suburbs, while its cooperating infantry (IV Army Corps and Romanian VI Army Corps) linked up with Paulus's infantry west of Stalingrad and encircled and destroyed Soviet forces isolated west and southwest of the city. Weichs's plan called for Hoth to initiate his attack on 17 August, several days before Paulus began his advance across the Don to the Volga River north of Stalingrad, so as to keep the defending Soviets off balance.

Hoth's final plan called for Kempf's XXXXVIII Panzer Corps, now consisting of 14th and 24th Panzer Divisions (the latter transferred from Sixth Army's XXIV Panzer Corps) and 29th Motorized Division, to attack northward in the sector from Plodovitoe eastward to Lake Tsatsa, pass west of Krasnoarmeisk (on the Volga 20 kilometers south of Stalingrad), and penetrate into Stalingrad's southern suburb of Beketovka. 24th Panzer Division's principal mission was to protect the shock group's right flank by clearing Soviet forces from Tundutovo and the lake region south of Stalingrad and then advance on Beketovka from the south.[72] On Kempf's left, IV Army Corps, with 371st and 297th Infantry Divisions (the latter also newly arrived from Sixth Army's XXIV Panzer Corps), was to advance due north along the Kotel'nikovo-Stalingrad railroad line from Abganerovo through Tundutovo and the region west of Stalingrad to effect the linkup with Sixth Army's LI Army Corps advancing from the northwest.

Farther west, in the 70-kilometer-wide sector from the eastern bank of the Don River northeastward to just west of Abganerovo, Romanian VI Army Corps' 20th, 1st, 2nd, and 4th Infantry Divisions were to protect Hoth's long left flank and help contain and ultimately destroy Soviet 64th Army in partial isolation between the Don and Stalingrad. By 17 August Hoth's army fielded 180–200 tanks, including 82 tanks in 24th Panzer Division, slightly fewer in 14th Panzer Division, and the remainder in 29th Motorized Division.[73]

Facing Hoth, Eremenko's Southeastern Front defended with Shumilov's 64th Army deployed across the 120-kilometer front from the Tinguta region to Logovskii on the Don; Tolbukhin's 57th Army defended the 70-kilometer sector from the Tinguta region eastward to Raigorod on the Volga River. Shumilov's army consisted of 29th, 38th, 126th, 138th, 157th, 204th, and 208th Rifle Divisions, Tanaschishin's 13th Tank Corps, 66th and 154th Naval Rifle and 6th Tank Brigades, 118th Fortified Region, and forces from the Zhitomir and Groznyi Officers Schools. Shumilov's armored force amounted to about 100 tanks, with about 70 in 13th Tank Corps and the remainder in 6th and 56th Tank Brigades (the latter having arrived on 21 August).[74] Shumilov defended the sector from Tinguta westward to Vasil'evka on the Myshkova River with his 38th, 204th, and 126th Rifle Divisions, backed up by 29th and 138th Rifle Divisions and 154th Naval Rifle Brigade in second echelon, and 13th Tank Corps, which was concentrated southeast of Tinguta Station. His army's 157th Rifle Division, 118th Fortified Region, 66th Naval Rifle Brigade, and two school regiments defended the extended front along the Myshkova River from Vasil'evka to the Don River, and 208th Rifle Division was in army reserve.[75] Tolbukhin's 57th Army, which included 15th, 35th, and 36th Guards Rifle and 244th and 422nd Rifle Divisions, forces from the Vinnitsa Infantry School, 255th Cavalry Regiment, and 76th Fortified Region, was deployed in two-echelon formation across its defensive front, with 15th and 36th Guards Rifle Divisions in first echelon.[76]

On Southeastern Front's virtually wide-open left flank, Kolomiets's 51st Army, which consisted of 91st and 302nd Rifle and 115th Cavalry Divisions and the tankless 125th, 135th, and 155th Tank Brigades, was still withdrawing northeastward to man its assigned defensive line, extending from Malyi Derbety southward to Lake Sarpa and designed to protect the approaches to the Volga far south of Stalingrad.

Hoth's challenge of mounting a credible offensive effort toward Stalingrad from the south was no mean task. The manpower strength of his panzer army was likely less than that of Shumilov's and Tolbukhin's armies, about one-third of his force was Romanian, and, although his panzer force outnumbered the tank force of Southeastern Front by better than two-to-one, given likely attrition it would be difficult to sustain his advance with a meager force of no more than 200 tanks. By the time Hoth's forces attacked on 20 August, for example, 24th Panzer Division fielded a total of 94 tanks, including 5 Panzer II command tanks.[77] In addition, the ration strength of his divisions belied their actual combat strength. For example, although 24th Panzer Division's ration strength stood at 15,590 men, its actual combat strength was only 9,862 men.[78]

After delaying his assault for several days because of fuel and lubricant shortages, Hoth unleashed his assault against Shumilov's defenses at and east of Abganerovo at 0700 hours on 20 August (see Map 60). A strong artillery preparation and air strikes preceded the assaults. Attacking northward on the left wing of Hoth's shock group, 94th and 371st Infantry Divisions, supported by a *kampfgruppe* from 29th Motorized Division, advanced 4–5 kilometers to the north, forcing 64th Army's 204th and 126th Rifle Divisions to abandon their defenses

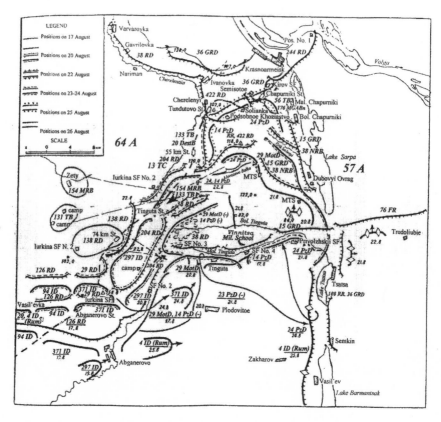

Map 60. The 64th and 57th Armies' defense, 17–26 August 1942

at Abganerovo Station. Shumilov then reinforced his two retreating rifle divisions with 29th Rifle Division and 13th Tank Corps' 13th and 133rd Tank Brigades. Together, these forces established new defenses protecting Iurkino Station, 2 kilometers north of Abganerovo Station. Simultaneously, a *kampfgruppe* from 14th Panzer Division, also reinforced by part of 29th Motorized Division, pressed northward 4 kilometers, capturing Tinguta and forcing the defending 38th Rifle Division to take up new defenses along the northern bank of the Malaia Tinguta River.[79] As fighting continued, by 20 August Shumilov withdrew 138th Rifle Division and 154th Naval Infantry Brigade into reserve defensive positions at 74 km Station and Zety, 5 kilometers to the rear of his forward defenses.[80] On Hoth's right wing, 24th Panzer Division's attack faltered, first due to the difficult sandy terrain, thereafter because of intense Soviet air attacks and stout resistance on the ground.[81]

When the advance by Hoth's forces north of Abganerovo Station faltered late on 20 August because of heavy Soviet resistance, Fourth Panzer Army's commander shifted the focus of his attention to his army's left wing. There, on 21 August, Heim's 14th Panzer Division crossed the Malaia Tinguta River and pushed about 4 kilometers north, driving a wedge between 64th Army's 38th Rifle Division and 57th Army's 15th Guards Rifle Division. At the same time, Hauenschild's 24th Panzer Division struck the center of 15th Guards' defenses, capturing Volga (Privolzhskii) State Farm and crossing the Malaia Tinguta River farther east. Hard-pressed on its right wing and center, 15th Guards Rifle Division and a cooperating rifle regiment from the Vinnitsa Infantry School withdrew northward 10 kilometers to man new defenses stretching westward along the Dubovyi *Ovrag* (ravine) and Morozov *Balka* from the northwestern bank of Lake Sarpa to 74 km Station, situated on the railroad line an equal distance south of Stalingrad. Hauenschild then wheeled 24th Panzer Division (with 30–40 tanks) toward the west in an attempt to capture Tundutovo Station. Tolbukhin reacted quickly, reinforcing 15th Guards Division with the fresh 422nd Rifle Division from the *front*'s reserve. Together the two divisions fought Hauenschild's panzers and panzer grenadiers to a standstill short of the station. According to the Red Army General Staff's daily operational summary:

> *57th Army* fought a fierce defensive battle with enemy tanks advancing from Lake Tsatsa toward Hill 86.0 (5 kilometers southwest of Dubovyi *Ovrag*) beginning on the morning of 21 August.
>
> In the defensive sector of 15th GRD, a group of enemy tanks, numbering up to 80 vehicles, reached the region 6–8 kilometers southeast of Tundutovo Station (14 kilometers southwest of Krasnoarmeisk) at 1600 hours.
>
> Up to 60 enemy tanks have been destroyed by the units of the army in the fighting on 21 August.
>
> 108th RR [Rifle Regiment], defending the region between Lakes Tsatsa and Barmantsak, withdrew to the main defensive line southeast of Lake Sarpa under enemy pressure.[82]

Despite 15th Guards Division's stout defense east of Tundutovo Station, by the evening of 21 August Kempf's XXXXVIII Panzer Corps had carved a wedge 15 kilometers wide and 20 kilometers deep between the defenses of 64th and 57th Armies. Unless this wedge was blunted, a further German advance would threaten to encircle Shumilov's army from the east. Therefore, to strengthen its defenses in this sector, Southeastern Front on 21 and 22 August dispatched six antitank artillery regiments to the Solianka and Ivanovka regions from its own and Stalingrad Front's reserves. Shumilov assigned five of the regiments to 57th Army and one to 64th Army, with instructions that they allocate one regiment to support each of their forward rifle divisions.[83]

Having failed to break through 57th Army's defenses south of Tundutovo Station, Hoth on 22 August began redeploying XXXXVIII Panzer Corps' divisions west to attack 64th Army's left wing in the Tinguta Station region.[84] In heavy fighting throughout the day, a *kampfgruppe* from 14th Panzer Division, attacking from the east, together with the newly arrived 297th Infantry Division, advancing from the south, reached the southern and eastern approaches to the station, forcing 138th and 204th Rifle Divisions to establish all-around defenses to protect the station. That evening 64th Army reported it was engaged in "fierce defensive fighting with enemy tank and motorized forces" and that 38th Rifle Division, with subunits from the Vinnitsa Infantry School, "was fighting an intense battle with enemy tanks and motorized infantry and was withdrawing to a new defensive line north of the Tinguta forested area."[85]

Late on 22 August, realizing the Germans had altered the direction of their main attack, Shumilov established a new defensive line along the railroad line north of Tinguta Station and astride the railroad line south of the station. He manned the part of the line north of Tinguta Station with 154th Naval Rifle, 20th Destroyer, and 133rd Tank Brigades and 186th and 665th Antitank Artillery Regiments from his *front*'s reserve, and he reinforced 138th and 204th Rifle Divisions' defenses east and south of the station with a mortar regiment and guards-mortar battalion, 56th Tank Brigade, and an artillery–machine gun battalion from 118th Fortified Region.

Despite these measures, Hoth's forces resumed their assault early on 23 August, attacking Soviet defenses at Tinguta Station with 29th Motorized and 297th Infantry Divisions. According to the OKW's daily summary, "Advancing on Stalingrad from the south, Fourth Panzer Army repelled an enemy attack on its right wing and, together with units attacking toward the northwest, reached the railroad line on both sides of Tinguta Station." The Red Army General Staff also described the ensuing two-day battle:

[24 August]

64th Army—157th RD drove the enemy from the region west of Vasil'evka.

127th RD, repelling attacks by small groups of enemy, occupied a defense along the line Hill 97.3–Kosh–Tebektenerovo–the railroad hut 5 kilometers southwest of 74 km Station by day's end on 23 August.

138th RD occupied a defense along the line of the railroad hut 5 kilometers southwest of 74 km Station-"K" (4 kilometers northeast of 74 km Station).

204th and 29th RDs, the Vinnitsa Infantry School, and subunits of 15th Gds. RD were fighting half encirclement in the vicinity of Tinguta forest.

The positions of the army's remaining units are unchanged.

[25 August]

64th Army withdrew the units of 38th and 204th RDs to the line 1 kilometer north of 74 km Station–Kosh (7 kilometers west of Tinguta Station)–Farm No. 2-Hills 116.6–120.2 on the night of 23–24 August.

The positions of the remaining armies of the *front* remain unchanged. The enemy did not conduct offensive operations on 24 August.[86]

While Shumilov's forces were fighting 29th Motorized and 297th Infantry Divisions to a virtual standstill in and around Tinguta Station, in 57th Army's sector to the east XXXXVIII Panzer Corps' 14th and 24th Panzer Divisions pressed northward, advancing 4–6 kilometers from Dubovyi *Ovrag* from 21 to 24 August. During this fighting, Colonel Gustav Adolf Riebel, commander of 24th Panzer Division's 24th Panzer Regiment, was killed by a Soviet shell burst.[87] By this time, the armor strength of Hauenschild's panzer division had fallen by more than a third, to 54 tanks.[88] Although these nonstop attacks ultimately forced 57th Army's 15th Guards and 38th Rifle Divisions to give ground, Tolbukhin's antitank reinforcements took a heavy toll on Kempf's tanks, reportedly destroying or damaging as many as 60 armored vehicles. Facing possible stalemate along this axis as well, overnight on 23–24 August Hoth concentrated all three of Kempf's mobile divisions in the region north of Dubovyi *Ovrag*.

Early on 25 August, Hoth's combined force of about 160 tanks (250 according to Soviet count) lunged northward toward Solianka and Ivanovka on the Chervlennaia River, 15 kilometers south of Beketovka and 30 kilometers from the center of Stalingrad.[89] The assault penetrated 57th Army's defenses at the boundary between its 422nd and 244th Rifle Divisions and advanced 8 kilometers, capturing Solianka and part of the Chervlennaia River's southern bank.[90] However, once Kempf's panzers reached the river line, artillery and mortar fire from the defending 422nd, 244th, and 15th Guards Rifle Divisions, the latter joining the fray from second echelon, separated 14th and 24th Panzer Divisions' tanks from supporting infantry. Concentrated antitank artillery fire and counterattacks by 6th Tank Brigade then destroyed or damaged many of 14th Panzer's tanks, and although 24th Panzer subsequently managed to carve a 100- to 150-meter gap in the Soviets' defenses, both panzer divisions had no choice but to return to their jumping-off positions by day's end on 26 August.

During this fighting at 0805 hours, 14th Panzer Division reported to its parent corps, "Heavy combat with enemy tanks at [Hills] 107.4–115.8. All Panzer IV long knocked out, all panzers except 5 are knocked out. 24th Panzer-Division staying to cover the flank to the west. Advisable for 24th Panzer Division to continue further to the north."[91] By evening 24th Panzer Division reported, "This combat is extremely bitter and costly and will continue the entire day. Panzer Regiment still has 13 panzers. One Russian tank was hit 10 times without success, 3 were shot up, and 2 others withdrew on fire."[92]

On 26 and 27 August, thwarted in his attempt to push Kempf's XXXXVIII Panzer Corps into Stalingrad's southern suburbs, Hoth placed his forces on the defensive and redeployed 14th and 24th Panzer Divisions of Kempf's panzer

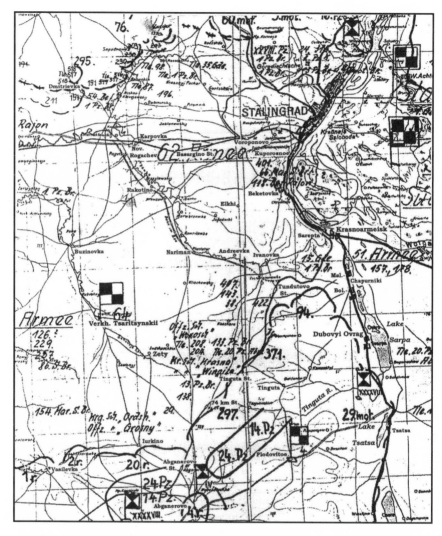

Map 61. The Fourth Panzer Army's situation, 26–27 August 1942

corps back to the Abganerovo Station region (see Map 61). He replaced them with IV Army Corps' 297th, 371st, and 94th Rifle Divisions, which occupied defensive positions stretching from Abganerovo Station northeastward east of the railroad line to Solianka and then eastward to Dubovyi *Ovrag* and Lake Sarpa. On Hoth's extended right wing, one regiment of 29th Motorized Division was then assigned responsibility for protecting the gaps between Lakes Sarpa, Tsatsa, and Barmantsak.[93]

Thus, as always, the controlling issue for Hoth was to get enough infantry forces, both German and Romanian, to hold the flanks of his penetration. His failure to do so, combined with Tolbukhin's effective defense south of the Chervlennaia River, forced him to search for yet another "path of least resistance." Despite the necessity for "wasting" part of 29th Motorized Division on the tiresome mission of flank protection, Hoth was determined to employ his remaining armor to good effect. By this time 24th Panzer Division reported it had 57 tanks in working order, but 14th Panzer had far fewer.[94] Even more disconcerting for Hoth was the high attrition rate among personnel. For example, by 26 August the combat strength of 24th Panzer Division's 21st and 26th Grenadier Regiments had decreased by almost 30 percent and that of its 24th Panzer Regiment by almost 10 percent.[95] Also marring what would turn out to be a successful redeployment, on 26 August 24th Panzer Division lost yet another regimental commander, this time Colonel Wilhelm von Lengerke, commander of 21st Grenadier Regiment, who perished from a Soviet shellburst while sitting in his headquarters wagon.[96]

Urged on by his army group commander, Weichs, Hoth renewed his offensive at the end of August after he located a weak spot in the Soviets' defenses. This weak spot, the 20-kilometer sector from Vasil'evka on the Myshkova River eastward to Abganerovo Station, was defended by 64th Army's 126th Rifle Division, since by this time XXXXVIII Panzer Corps' advance to the Chervlennaia River had forced Shumilov to shift most of his army's forces to the northeast to deal with the twin threats to Tinguta Station and the Solianka region. Worse, 126th Rifle Division lacked 80 percent of its required artillery.[97]

Exploiting the obvious Soviet weakness, Hoth concentrated XXXXVIII Panzer Corps' 24th and 14th Panzer Divisions, supported by the bulk of 29th Motorized Division and flanked on the left by Romanian VI Army Corps' 2nd Infantry Division, in the 15-kilometer sector from east of Vasil'evka to just north of Abganerovo Station. With an advantage of better than four-to-one in infantry and absolute superiority in artillery and armor, Hoth finally achieved his decisive breakthrough (see Maps 62 and 63). Attacking by surprise at dawn on 29 August with a force of about 100 tanks (49 from 24th Panzer Division), Kempf's armor and supporting infantry overwhelmed 126th Rifle Division and advanced almost 20 kilometers north by day's end, capturing Zety on the Tsaritsa River and forcing 29th and 138th Rifle Divisions to abandon their defenses at Iurkino and Tinguta Station.[98]

Late on 29 August, the OKW reported triumphantly:

Fourth Panzer Army: XXXXVIII Panzer Corps' offensive caught the Russians unawares; at first they offered weak resistance, which later strengthened. Individual groups of encircled enemy fought to the death. In front of the corps' right wing in the region 10 kilometers north of Abganerovo railroad station, the enemy withdrew to the north; in front of the corps' left wing they were

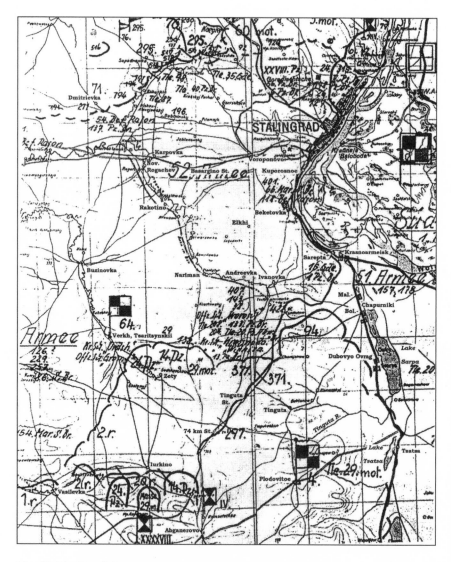

Map 62. The Fourth Panzer Army's situation, 28–29 August 1942

thrown back from Zety (40 kilometers west of Dubovyi Ravine) and from Marker 150 (6 kilometers northeast of Zety). Only individual enemy tanks appeared; several tanks located on the western flank did not take part in the fighting.

On IV Corps' left wing, the enemy made an effort with separate groups, which, as a result of XXXXVIII Panzer Corps' offensive, withdrew to the

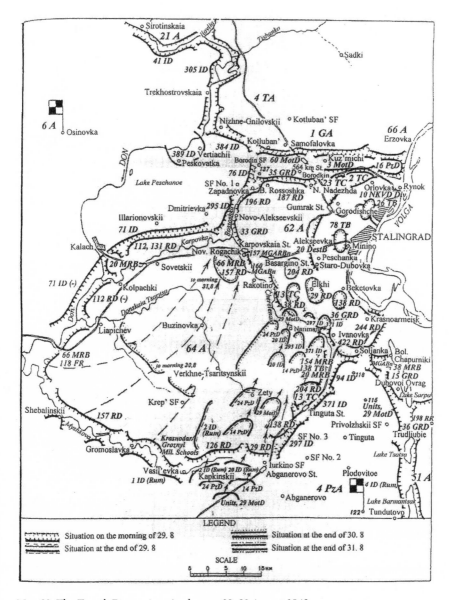

Map 63. The Fourth Panzer Army's advance, 29–31 August 1942

northeast. The enemy was thrown back to the north from the area 4 kilometers north of Tinguta Station.[99]

That evening Shumilov confirmed Kempf's victory to the Red Army General Staff:

The units of *64th Army* fought stubborn defensive battles with enemy forces of up to two infantry divisions and 78 tanks in the Vasil'evka-Tebektenerovo sector all day on 29 August.

Twenty-two enemy tanks approached the Zety region (17 kilometers northwest of Tebektenerovo) at 1400 hours where they dispersed and began operating separately. The enemy infantry were cut off from the tanks in front of the forward edge of our defenses.

Another group of tanks, numbering up to 40, reached the Kosh region (9 kilometers northwest of Tebektenerovo).

172nd Artillery Machine Gun Battalion was fighting with enemy tanks in the Zety region.

The Krasnodar Infantry School was on the march from the Tinguta region to the Zety region. The school was subjected to bombing while on the march.

Changes did not occur in the positions of the army's units.[100]

The collapse of 126th Rifle Division's defenses also unhinged 64th Army's defenses along the railroad line, forcing 29th and 138th Rifle Divisions to withdraw northward and posing a threat to both 64th and the 62nd Armies' rear areas. Because Shumilov had already committed all of his second echelon and reserves to combat along the Chervlennaia River, he lacked any reserves to restore his defenses along the Tsaritsa River farther north. Therefore, as Kempf's forces continued their northward advance on 30 August, in the afternoon Eremenko had no choice but to order Lopatin and Shumilov to withdraw their forces to new defensive lines well to the rear. His orders required Lopatin's 62nd Army to occupy new defenses from Zapadnovka on the Rossoshka River southward to Novyi Rogachik, where the railroad crossed the Chervlennaia River 30 kilometers due west of downtown Stalingrad. He also directed Shumilov's 64th Army to man defenses from Novyi Rogachik southeastward along the Chervlennaia River to Ivanovka, 25 kilometers southwest of Stalingrad. As before, Tolbukhin's 57th Army was to defend the sector from Ivanovka eastward to Dubovyi *Ovrag* at the northern end of Lake Sarpa.[101]

To ensure the integrity of Stalingrad's inner defenses, Eremenko bolstered them by deploying 2nd Tank Corps' 26th Tank Brigade and 397th and 398th Antitank Artillery Regiments in the forest west of Barrikady Factory and 78th Tank Brigade and 498th and 1251st Antitank Artillery Regiments in Stalingrad's hilly suburb of Minina, due west of the city's center. Slightly to the south, he deployed 20th Destroyer Brigade in the suburbs of Nikolaevka and Peschanka.

Eremenko also ordered Tolbukhin to withdraw 57th Army's right wing to a new defense line from Ivanovka southeast along the Chervlennaia River to Lake Sarpa and Raigorod and Kolomiets's 51st Army to continue defending the gaps between the lakes due south of Stalingrad.

Meanwhile, Eremenko directed Lieutenant General Vasilii Filippovich Gerasimenko, the commander of the Stalingrad Military District who had headed Northern Front's 23rd Army during Operation Barbarossa, to hold firmly to his defensive lines protecting Astrakhan' and to block any German advance to the Volga in that region. Finally, on 31 August the *Stavka* ordered Gerasimenko to reorganize this district's headquarters into the new 28th Army, effective 5 September, with headquarters in Astrakhan'.[102] Stalin's decision to form a new army in the Astrakhan' region forced Hoth to commit 16th Motorized Division from his army's reserve to protect the front along his panzer army's extended right flank from Elista to Astrakhan', thereby further diminishing the forces he could concentrate near Stalingrad.

Hoth immediately exploited Eremenko's decision to withdraw 64th Army to new defenses far to the rear. Hoth hoped to cut off that portion of Shumilov's army still defending the large bulge extending southwestward to the Don River. To that end, on 31 August Kempf's panzer corps drove northward across the Chervlennaia River (see Map 64). In its vanguard, 24th Panzer Division's *kampf-gruppe* seized a sector of the Kalach-Stalingrad railroad line just east of Basargino Station, only 20 kilometers due west of Stalingrad's center. By this time, Hauenschild's tank force had fallen to 41 operational tanks.[103] Shumilov's forces struggled to contain the advance both to permit his forces operating to the west to escape eastward toward Stalingrad and to gain time necessary for other forces to strengthen Stalingrad's inner defensive line. However, the speed of Kempf's advance and heavy German air support prevented his forces from halting the German advance short of the railroad line. In addition to splitting Shumilov's 64th Army in half and threatening to cut off and destroy the half still located between Basargino Station and the Don River, 24th Panzer Division's northward thrust also placed the portion of Lopatin's 62nd Army still defending the sector north of the Kalach-Stalingrad railroad line (against 71st Infantry Division of Sixth Army's LI Corps) in jeopardy.

However, on 1 September, instead of thrusting northward to link up with Sixth Army's forces, thus encircling the portions of 64th and 62nd Armies still operating to the west, Hauenschild wheeled a portion of his 24th Panzer Division eastward in an attempt to drive into Stalingrad from the west (see Map 65). Fortunately for Shumilov, 20th Destroyer Brigade halted this raid late in the day along the western outskirts of Stalingrad's Peschanka suburb. Hauenschild's panzer division then withdrew to occupy all-around defenses astride the railroad east and southeast of Basargino Station, with 29th Motorized Division laagered to the south. Although 24th Panzer Division's armor strength had fallen to as few as 31 tanks days before, it managed to muster 56 tanks on 1 September. How-

Map 64. The Fourth Panzer Army's situation, 30–31 August 1942

ever, the actual combat strength of its principal regiments continued to erode to 1,266 men in its panzer regiment and 1,274 and 1,575 men, respectively, in its 21st and 26th Grenadier Regiments.[104] Kempf and Hoth were disconcerted, however, with the large gap that had formed between 14th and 24th Panzer Divisions, the inability of the former to defeat and destroy the enemy to its front, and 24th Panzer Division's failure to link up with Sixth Army's forces to the north.

Map 65. The Fourth Panzer Army's situation, 1–2 September 1942

This promised to make it far more difficult to liquidate Soviet forces still operating along the Don as well as those occupying the bulge between southern Stalingrad and Beketovka.

Nevertheless, the Red Army General Staff recorded Hoth's dangerous progress toward Stalingrad's western defenses:

[31 August]
64th Army, in accordance with an order from the command, withdrew its units to new defensive lines on the night of 30 August.

66th NRB [Naval Rifle Brigade] and 157th RD withdrew and occupied a defense in the Novo-Petrovskii-Krep' [Timbering] State Farm sector along the Erik River.

204th and 138th RDs are being withdrawn into the army's reserve.

Information about the arrival of 126th, 208th, and 29th RDs in their new defense line has not been received. The remaining units of the army continued to stay in their previous positions.

Units of 13th TC and 179th and 176th Arty MG Bns [Artillery–Machine Gun Battalions] fought defensive battles with enemy forces of up to two battalions of infantry and tanks which approached the Chervlennaia River in the Nariman-Andreevka sector.

[1 September]

64th Army, while fighting fierce battles with enemy tanks (90) and infantry which had penetrated to the Tsybinko region (28 kilometers southwest of Stalingrad), continued the withdrawal of its units to the main defensive line on the Bereslavskii (36 kilometers southwest of Stalingrad)–Gavrilovka–Ivanovka (26 kilometers south of Stalingrad) front along the Chervlennaia River.

66th NRB reached the Bereslavskii–(incl.) Tsybinko line.

157th RD, fighting with enemy tanks, withdrew to the Tsybinko–Gavrilovka line.

204th RD was fighting with enemy tanks along the Gavrilovka–Marker 92.0 (5.5 kilometers southeast of Gavrilovka) line all day on 31 August. Enemy tanks reached the Iagodnyi–Hill 128.0 (25 kilometers southwest of Stalingrad) line by day's end on 31 August.

138th, 126th, 29th, and 38th RDs and 154th NRB, which number 500–1,000 men in each division (without equipment), are concentrating in the region 10–20 kilometers southwest of Stalingrad.

[2 September]

64th Army was fighting fierce defensive battles against enemy tanks and infantry which have penetrated into the depth of the army's defensive belt. The enemy succeeded in penetrating defensive line "K" in the Staryi Rogachik–Varvarovka sector and reached the internal defensive line in the region west of Voroponovo Station [1 kilometer west of Peschanka] with small groups of tanks.

66th NB, 157th RD, and the two schools were fighting in encirclement in the Staryi Rogachik-Skliarov-Rakotino-Kravtsov regions.

138th RD is situated in second echelon defenses along the Peschanka *Balka* line.

20th TDB [Tank Destroyer Brigade] repelled attacks by enemy tanks along the Alekseevka–Peschanka line.

39th TB was defending the Staro-Dubrovka-Hill 134.4 line.
154th NRB was located in the Elkhi region.
38th RD occupied the defense line Hill 152.5-Krutaia *Balka.*
29th and 126th RDs assembled in the Beketovka-Staraia Otrada region.[105]

In addition to unhinging the right wing of Shumilov's 64th Army, 24th Panzer Division's penetration to Basargino Station also facilitated a further advance by Sixth Army's LI Corps, which by day's end on 31 August had already penetrated 62nd Army's defenses along the Rossoshka River and was about to reach the Kalach-Stalingrad railroad line near Novyi Rogachik. If it did so, it would likely cut off and destroy all of 62nd and 64th Armies' forces already half-encircled west of the Rossoshka and Chervlennaia Rivers. This included 62nd Army's 131st and 112th Rifle Divisions and 64th Army's 157th Rifle Division, 20th Motorized Rifle and 66th Naval Rifle Brigades, and two school regiments. If these forces were destroyed, and if LI Corps continued its eastward march, it was likely the corps would have sufficient forces to penetrate into Stalingrad from the west.

At this juncture, however, decisive action by Shumilov and a faulty decision by Paulus combined to forestall further Soviet disaster. First, to save the half-encircled forces, Eremenko at 2000 hours on 1 September ordered 62nd and 64th Armies' partly isolated forces to withdraw to the "Novaia Nadezhda, Peschanka, and Ivanovka line as rapidly as possible."[106] At the same time, because of heavy fighting in the Kotluban' region to the north, a cautious Paulus was reluctant to commit any forces from Wietersheim's XIV Panzer Corps in a risky advance toward the south to reinforce LI Corps and cut off withdrawing Soviet forces. Despite repeated messages from his army group commander, Weichs, Sixth Army's commander did not authorize an attack southward until 2 September, by which time Lopatin and Shumilov had already withdrawn their half-encircled forces into the city's defenses. Making matters worse, Paulus redeployed part of LI Corps' 71st Infantry Division northeastward to reinforce the advance by the army corps' main forces across the Rossoshka River instead of dispatching the entire 71st Division southward to cut the railroad line and the Soviet withdrawal routes to Stalingrad (see Map 63).[107]

In the meantime, with Hoth's approval, Kempf late on 1 September issued fresh orders to 24th Panzer Division: "At 0900 hours, 24th Panzer Division will set out over the railway line and thrust forward via Hill 147.3 up to the *Schafzucht* [sheep pen] area—BW [unknown abbreviation] 5 kilometers east of Pitomnik, there to reach the forces of 6th Army pushing down from the northeast (20th Romanian Division will set out at the same time to cover 24th Panzer-Division's west flank)."[108]As was the case in its late August offensive, Hauenschild organized his 24th Panzer Division for combat into two *kampfgruppen,* with a small reserve (see Table 20).[109]

When they began their advance early on the morning of 2 September, how-

Table 20. The Combat Organization of 24th Panzer Division, 2 September 1942

Kampfgruppe Broich, led by Colonel Fritz *Freiherr* von Broich, the commander of 24th Infantry
    Brigade, with:
        21st Panzer Grenadier Regiment;
        89th Panzer Artillery Regiment (less its 2nd Battalion);
        Detachment, 53rd *Werfer* Regiment;
        3rd Battalion, 24th Panzer Regiment, with attached pioneer and flak sections;
        Armored elements, 1st Battalion, 26th Panzer Grenadier Regiment;
        670th Panzer Jägt [Hunter] Detachment;
        Staff and 10th, 11th, and 12th Batteries, 89th Panzer Artillery Regiment;
        One heavy and one light battery, 1st Battalion, 5th Flak Battalion;
        3rd Company, 602nd Flak Battalion;
        800th Special Designation [z.b.V.] Company; and
        One pioneer company.
Kampfgruppe Edelsheim, led by Colonel Maximilian *Reichsfreiherr* von Edelsheim, the
    commander of 26th Panzer Grenadier Regiment, with:
        40th Panzer Jäger Detachment, with flak section;
        2nd Battalion, 89th Panzer Artillery Regiment;
        2nd Battalion, 26th Panzer Grenadier Regiment;
        602nd Flak Battalion (less 3rd Company);
        One pioneer company; and
        Two heavy batteries, 1st Company, 5th Flak Battalion.
Reserve, with
        86th Panzer Reconnaissance Battalion;
        4th Motorcycle Detachment; and
        40th Panzer Pioneer Battalion (less two companies).

ever, the reconnaissance elements of 24th Panzer Division found no enemy forces to their front. By this time, the forces of Lopatin's 62nd Army had completed occupying their new defenses from Rynok through Orlovka and Gumrak to Peschanka, around Stalingrad's northern and western outskirts, and the forces of Shumilov's 64th Army had successfully occupied their assigned defensive positions from Staro-Dubrovka through Elkhi to Ivanovka, to protect the western and southwestern outskirts of the city.

However, the hastily organized withdrawal, particularly in the western and southern sectors of the city, adversely affected the future durability of the defense in these sectors by preventing the construction of defenses in depth and proper fortifications. On the positive side, even after suffering heavy losses in the previous week of intense fighting, Eremenko's Southeastern Front on 31 August still fielded 101 tanks with another 114 in various stages of repair, as compared with only 88 functional tanks on 23 August.[110] Henceforth, the Germans had no choice but to contemplate a major struggle to capture the city of Stalingrad. In this respect, if no other, the counterstrokes by Eremenko's Stalingrad Front against XIV Panzer Corps' corridor in the Kotluban' region ultimately reaped major benefits.

In the wake of 62nd and 64th Armies' withdrawal, 71st Infantry Division of Sixth Army's LI Corps and Romanian 20th Infantry Division of Fourth Panzer Army's Romanian VI Corps linked up northwest of the railroad station at Voroponovo late on 2 September, establishing the boundary line between the two armies along the Tsaritsa River (see Map 65). Initially, 24th Panzer Division's *Kampfgruppe* Edelsheim was to protect the division's eastern and western flanks, while *Kampfgruppe* Broich was to advance north to Hill 147.3 to link up with Sixth Army's forces. However, when reconnaissance determined enemy resistance along the railroad line was weak if not nonexistent, shortly after noon XXXXVIII Panzer Corps ordered Hauenschild's panzer division to advance eastward and northeastward "with its left wing on the railroad line and reach the mouth of the Tsaritsa River and the area south of there in the city of Stalingrad." Because Heim's 14th Panzer Division would not be ready to join the attack until the next morning, 24th Panzer Division then received orders to reconnoiter up the Tsaritsa Gulley and attack eastward on 3 September, with its left wing north of the railroad, while, the same day, 14th Panzer Division advanced toward Peschanka and 29th Motorized Division protected the corps' right (eastern) flank.[111] Within days, 71st Infantry Division of Seydlitz's LI Corps, whose advance had been stymied by Soviet defenses for several days, captured Gumrak Station, 22 kilometers from the city center. Paulus then ordered the corps to continue its drive into Stalingrad proper.[112]

THE SITUATION IN STALINGRAD

As Lopatin's and Shumilov's 62nd and 64th Armies were struggling to defend the approaches to the city and managing to save the remnants of their forces to fight another day, Eremenko and Stalingrad's civilian Defense Committee worked feverishly to shore up defenses. As early as 23 August, for example, the Defense Committee ordered all the major factories and smaller industrial facilities to form workers' battalions to protect their enterprises, reinforce the inner defenses, and maintain order on the streets. At the same time, local MPVO antiaircraft units, medical platoons, and fire brigades worked independently to provide a modicum of air-raid warnings, medical support, and firefighting within the city's designated "quarters." By this time Stalingrad was packed with refugees from the fighting in the Great Bend of the Don River as well as the normal population of factory workers, children, and other noncombatants.[113] Colonel N. V. Reznikov, chief of a team of General Staff officers responsible for assisting Southeastern Front, described the situation in a report on 20 August:

> The city is overcrowded. People are living in the open, in parks and on the bank of the Volga, in boats, and so on. The evacuation of the city is being held up by lack of transport and by the inefficient work of the evacuation authorities. People waiting for transport at the evacuation depots have to live there for five or six days. . . . All schools and recreation centers are packed with wounded. The hospitals continue to remain in the city. Black-out measures are bad.

When Reznikov recommended that Eremenko declare a state of siege in the city and evacuate its population, Stalin refused because he wanted to avoid panic. Instead, Soviet security organizations redoubled their efforts to maintain order and turn civilians into militias. On 24 August the Defense Committee once again chimed in by directing the evacuation of all women, children, and wounded to the eastern bank of the Volga River. The city's port authorities and the Volga Military Flotilla were responsible for carrying out this task. However, by the time this evacuation finally began it was too late, and a large portion of the citizens of Stalingrad were trapped in the city throughout the approaching battle.

On 29 August the military councils of the two *fronts* mobilized 1,000 Communist Youth (Komsomol) and Communist Party members to fill out military units defending along the Tsaritsa River and the next day assembled 2,500 People's Militiamen and workers and dispatched them to the front. The Defense Committee also ordered the city's able-bodied population to erect barricades, obstacles, and fortifications around and within every industrial factory and facility to convert them into fortresses.[114]

Complicating matters, the NKVD, the paramilitary organization responsible for the actual defense of the city proper, reinforced its principal defense force, Saraev's 10th NKVD Division, with additional units transferred from various locations east of the Ural Mountains. When Eremenko assumed control of an amalgam of NKVD and militia units in Stalingrad, the traditional antagonism between the NKVD and the Red Army added yet another burden. Nonetheless, Eremenko employed the NKVD troops, Feklenko's special operational group north of the city, and other forces mustered from Stalingrad Front and Southern Front reserves to form a sketchy defensive line around the city to back up Lopatin's and Shumilov's forces.

Meanwhile, German aircraft continued bombarding Stalingrad. As Paulus's and Hoth's forces fought toward Stalingrad, Richthofen's aircraft had launched a murderous bombardment of the city, beginning the most concentrated aerial bombardment of the German-Soviet conflict. On Sunday, 23 August, for example, VIII Air Corps flew the first of a series of raids apparently intended to demoralize the city's defenders and population. After numerous false alarms, the inhabitants at first ignored the air-raid sirens. In any event, the city had far too few bomb shelters for its population. Although some of the bombers attacked factories, rail yards, and the telephone exchange, most of the destruction fell on residential areas. The wooden houses on the southern end of the city were incinerated by firebombs. The petroleum storage tanks near the Volga River caught fire, igniting flames and smoke that continued for the next several days. Streets began to fill with rubble, complicating the task of both defenders and attackers. On 25 August and numerous subsequent days, the *Luftwaffe* returned in a round-the-clock series of air raids.[115]

The Red Air Force was ill-prepared to counter this threat. Like its German counterpart, it was overextended to support the Stalingrad, Southeastern, and

North Caucasus Fronts. Moreover, the Soviets had deliberately curtailed air operations in the late summer in order to train and build up new formations for future operations. This, plus the technical and tactical inferiority of many Red air units, produced a one-sided air battle that allowed Richthofen to attack almost at will. Only later in the campaign would the Red Air Force pose a serious threat to the *Luftwaffe*.[116] After the initial series of raids beginning on 23 August, a subsequent series in late August and early September concentrated on the Krasnyi Oktiabr' (Red October) and Barrikady (called Red Barricade by the Germans) Factories and the city's center, leaving large sections of the city in flames.[117]

THE SIDESHOWS AT SERAFIMOVICH AND KLETSKAIA, 21–28 AUGUST

While 62nd Army and 4th Tank Army were struggling to forestall Sixth Army's drive toward Stalingrad and demolish XIV Panzer Corps' corridor to the Volga River, on Stalingrad Front's right wing, along the Don River, General Kuznetsov's 63rd and General Danilov's 21st Armies conducted a joint offensive against Italian and German forces defending along the river's southern bank west of Serafimovich. Originally, this attack was part of Eremenko's grand scheme to pressure Sixth Army's left wing. This pressure would supposedly force Paulus to abandon his advance to the Volga. In addition, at the *Stavka's* direction, Eremenko also sought to capture a bridgehead on the Don's southern bank for use in future offensive operations. At the time, 21st Army occupied defenses along the Don from the Kletskaia region westward to the Khoper River with a force of six rifle divisions, and 63rd Army from the Khoper River westward to Pavlovka with seven rifle divisions.

Eremenko issued his attack order on 19 August (see above and Maps 57 and 66). It required the two armies to attack southward across the Don with a force of four rifle divisions, two on 63rd Army's left wing and two on 21st Army's right wing, in the 30-kilometer sector west of Serafimovich. The combined force was to capture a 20- to 25-kilometer-deep bridgehead on the river's southern bank and, if possible, exploit the offensive into Sixth Army's left rear in the Perelazovskii and Manoilin regions, 30–50 kilometers south of the Don. Kuznetsov planned to conduct his river crossing with 14th Guards and 197th Rifle Divisions deployed from left to right (east to west) in the 15-kilometer sector west of the Khoper River. Danilov's plan called for 96th and 304th Rifle Divisions to attack across the river in the 15-kilometer sector from Serafimovich westward to the Khoper. Once across the river, the two army commanders were to expand their bridgeheads using their second-echelon rifle divisions; if the attacks were successful, Major General I. A. Pliev's 3rd Guards Cavalry Corps, the *front's* mobile group, was to exploit southward with its 5th and 6th Guards and 32nd Cavalry Divisions.[118] Issa Aleksandrovich Pliev, like his counterpart, Belov, one of the

Red Army's most audacious cavalry generals, had commanded the elite 3rd Guards Cavalry Division during Operation Barbarossa and took command of a cavalry corps in late 1941 at age 38.[119]

On the southern bank of the Don, Italian Eighth Army's XXXV Corps defended the line opposite 63rd Army's attack sector with 2nd Infantry Division Sforzesca. The Italians had taken over responsibility for defending this sector on 15 August, only four days before. On the Italian right, Sixth Army's XVII Corps defended the river on both sides of Serafimovich, opposite 21st Army's intended attack. This sector belonged to German 79th Infantry Division, but the bulk of the division's forces were concentrated at and south of Serafimovich, leaving only its reconnaissance battalion and a blocking detachment (*Sperrverband*) to defend the 15-kilometer sector west of town.[120] This defensive configuration meant that about one and a third Axis divisions, roughly 15,000 men, of which only half defended the river line, would face four Soviet divisions totaling roughly 30,000 men. Because of the river obstacle, neither Soviet assault force would be able to employ armor in its initial assault.

Attacking at dawn on 20 August, 63rd Army's shock group achieved immediate success. The Soviets crossed the river, overcame Sforzesca Division's defenses, and seized a bridgehead 2–3 kilometers deep on the southern bank. To the east, however, although 21st Army's 304th Rifle Division temporarily seized a small foothold on the southern bank from 79th Infantry Division's reconnaissance battalion, 96th Rifle Division's assault immediately faltered in front of 79th Division's defenses at Serafimovich. As the attacking armies reported to the Red Army General Staff late on 21 August:

> *63rd Army* conducted offensive fighting on the right bank of the Don River with part of its forces. . . .
>
> 197th RD was fighting along the line 3 kilometers south of Rubezhinskii-Pleshakovskii-Verkhnyi Matveevskii [on the river's southern bank] with its forward units at 1100 hours on 20 August. The main forces of the division were continuing to cross the Don River.
>
> 14th Gds. RD was fighting along the line Tiukovnovskii-Zatonskii-Zimovskii [also on the Don's southern bank] with its forward units at 1100 hours on 20 August and crossing the Don River with its main forces. Captured: 63 enemy prisoners, 6 guns, 15 mortars, 23 machine guns, 125,000 rounds of ammunition, and one radio. . . .
>
> *21st Army* was continuing offensive fighting on the right bank of the Don River with its left wing units but, having encountered strong enemy fire resistance, had no success and remained in its previously occupied positions.[121]

Continuing their advance over the next two days, 63rd Army's two attacking divisions were soon reinforced by 203rd Rifle Division and 21st Army's 304th Rifle Division, which finally managed to push across the river. They then

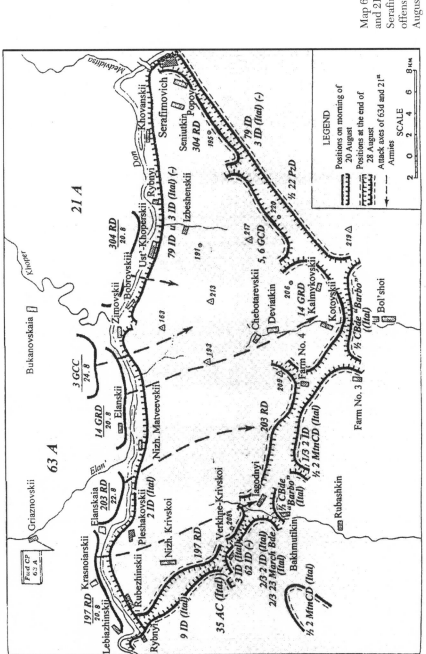

Map 66. The 63rd and 21st Armies' Serafimovich offensive, 20–28 August 1942

LEGEND

Positions on morning of 20 August

Positions at the end of 28 August

Attack axes of 63d and 21st Armies

SCALE

2 0 2 4 6 8 км

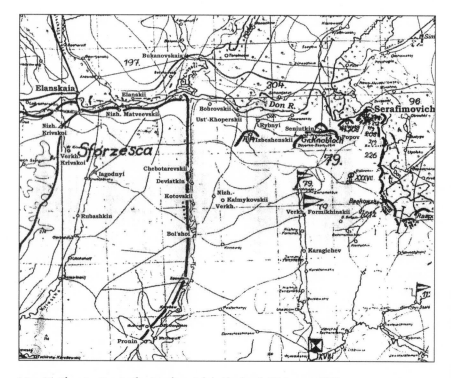

Map 67. The situation in the Serafimovich bridgehead, 19 August 1942

expanded their bridgehead to a depth of 2–10 kilometers, although they made virtually no progress in the vicinity of Serafimovich proper (see Map 67). As the two armies reported to the General Staff late on 22 August:

> *63rd Army* continued to conduct offensive fighting on the right bank of the Don River with its left wing units. . . .
>
> 197th RD was continuing to develop its attack and captured Rubezhinskii, Hill 208.0, and Hill 204.0 [5 kilometers south of the river].
>
> 14th Gds. RD captured the line Hill 236.0–Chebotarevskii line [10 kilometers south of the river].
>
> 203rd RD reached the vicinity of Hill 224.0 with one regiment and was crossing the Don River with its remaining forces.
>
> *21st Army,* while continuing its offensive, was fighting along the line Hill 213.0–the northern outskirts of Izbushenskii [2 kilometers south of the Don]–Popov–the northern outskirts of Serafimovich to (incl.) Beliavskii [0.5 kilometers south of the Don] with units of 304th and 96th RDs at 1300 hours on 22 August.[122]

Given the limited progress of the Soviet attack and continuing effective *Luft-waffe* air support, Army Group B did not send any reserves to the affected region, instead relying on Sforzesca and 79th Infantry Divisions to deal with the situation by using local reserves. By this time, the attacking units lacked sufficient forces to expand the bridgehead farther and were experiencing ammunition shortages due to the difficulty of transporting supplies across the Don. Making matters worse, although it was supposed to cross the Don on the night of 21–22 August, 203rd Rifle Division was delayed because of the shortage of boats and the intense German air activity. The division ultimately did not make it across until late on 24 August. Therefore, Stalingrad Front ordered General Pliev to move 3rd Guards Cavalry Corps into the bridgehead overnight on 22–23 August. In cooperation with 63rd and 21st Army formations, his mission was to "attack toward Hills 213, 217, and 220, reach the region in the vicinity Hill 217 by day's end on 23 August," and, subsequently, "attack toward Verkhne-Fomikhinskii."[123] However, a shortage of river-crossing equipment once again delayed Pliev's crossing until late on 24 August.

As fighting continued, the Germans detected the presence of Pliev's cavalrymen in the bridgehead late on 24 August, reporting, "On XVII Army Corps' front . . . enemy cavalry (presumably units of 3rd Guards Cavalry Corps) appeared south of Bobrovskii [on the southern bank of the Don near the mouth of the Khoper River]. . . . [On] Italian Eighth Army's [front], the enemy is continuing strong pressure against the army's right wing."[124]

After finally completing its arduous concentration on the river's southern bank, Pliev's cavalry, together with reinforcing 203rd Rifle Division, began its assault by midday on 25 August. Striking hard at the boundary between the Italian Sforzesca and German 79th Infantry Divisions, 14th Guards and 203rd Rifle Divisions, flanked on the left by Pliev's 5th and 6th Guards Cavalry Divisions, drove southward up to 10 kilometers, threatening to split the defending divisions apart. As the Red Army General Staff recorded late on 25 August:

63rd Army was continuing to defend its previous positions on its right wing and in its center and was conducting offensive fighting and repelling occasional counterattacks by the enemy with its left wing units. The enemy, offering strong resistance, withdrew toward the south.

197th and 203rd RDs were fighting in their previous positions.

14th Gds. RD, having overcome enemy resistance in the Chebotarevskii region, captured the Hills 236.0 and 209.0 (5 kilometers southwest of Chebotarevskii) and Deviatkin [12 kilometers south of the Don] regions by 0930 hours on 25 August.

5th Gds. CD reached the bend in the road 10 kilometers southeast of Chebotarevskii [20 kilometers south of the Don] with two regiments at 0300 hours on 25 August without encountering enemy resistance. 26 Italian prisoners were captured.

6th Gds. CD was situated in the vicinity of Hill 193, 10 kilometers west of Bobrovskii [15 kilometers south of the Don]. . . .

21st Army was fighting offensive battles in its previous positions with separate detachments on its right wing on 25 August.[125]

The heavy Soviet assaults forced Sforzesca Division to withdraw the forces on its right wing to new defenses farther to the rear. To the east, 79th Infantry Division regrouped its 212th Regiment from its right wing along the Don to reinforce and extend its left wing so as to protect the approaches to the villages of Kalmykovskii and Bol'shoi on its left flank. Simultaneously, overnight on 25–26 August, Italian Eighth Army began reinforcing Sforzesca Division's defenses, first, with its Celere (Mobile) Division and, later, with its Cavalry Brigade Barbo. This force finally managed to contain Pliev's and 63rd Army's advance on 28 August (see Map 68). However, as reflected by its daily report to the Red Army General Staff, Stalingrad Front's 63rd and 21st Armies and Pliev's cavalry corps had already achieved their principal initial objectives:

63rd Army was continuing to conduct offensive fighting with its left wing units on 27 August and was occupying its previous positions on its right wing and in its center. Information has not been received about the combat actions and positions of the units.

The units of 203rd RD captured the Iagodnyi, Bakhmutkino, and Rubashkino regions (50 kilometers southwest of Serafimovich) at 1900 hours on 26 August, after a stubborn battle. [Although unreported, 3rd Gds. CC's 5th and 6th Gds. CDs were still deployed on the division's left flank].

21st Army. 304th RD was digging in along the line southeast of Kalmykovskii–Izbushenskii–Hill 195.0 (7 kilometers south of Khovanskii).

1st and 21st Destroyer Battalions were fighting in the Seniutkin-Popov regions.

96th RD captured the town of Serafimovich and reached the line the road junction 2 kilometers southwest of Zatonskii–the slopes of Hill 197.0 (2 kilometers south of Serafimovich)–Veliaevskii on the night of 26–27 August, after stubborn fighting.

178th RD crossed to the left bank of the Don River in the Podpeshinskii- (incl.) Lastushinskii sector.

76th RD occupied a defense in the Lastushinskii-Druzhilinskii sector along the eastern bank of the Don River.

63rd RD was fighting for possession of the Mal. Iarki–Logovskii region with part of its forces.

124th RD concentrated in the vicinity of the woods southwest of Novoaleksandrovka, with the mission to relieve the units of 96th RD on the night of 28 August.[126]

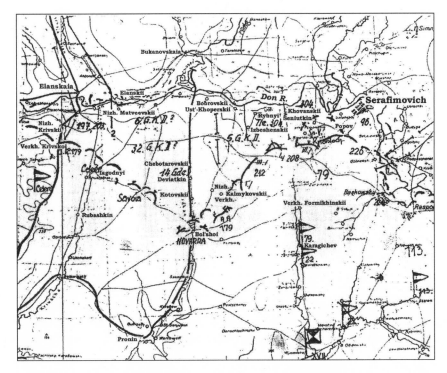

Map 68. The situation in the Serafimovich bridgehead, 29 August 1942

By this time, the combined Soviet assault force had carved a bridgehead 50 kilometers wide and up to 25 kilometers deep on the southern bank of the Don west of Serafimovich. During the battle, Stalingrad Front reported capturing 1,200 prisoners of war, mostly Italian troops, 30 guns, 65 mortars, 265 machine guns, 1,250 rifles, and 30 trucks, together with tons of ammunition and other supplies.[127] Once in the bridgehead, Kuznetsov, Danilov, and Pliev established a deeply echeloned defense, with Pliev's 6th Guards Cavalry Division and 96th Rifle Division (replaced by 21st Army's 124th Rifle Division) in the two armies' reserves.

The Soviets later criticized the inability of the two armies to advance farther and credited these failures to hasty planning, excessively broad attack sectors, a shortage of river-crossing equipment, and logistical problems. Nonetheless, the short and violent bridgehead battles had momentous implications: In addition to underscoring the weakness of the overstretched Axis defenses along the Don, the *Stavka* did not fail to note the poor performance and vulnerability of the Italian forces. From the German perspective, they were fixated on what they considered was the decisive struggle along the Stalingrad axis. Thus—and to their ultimate regret—the Germans tended to dismiss the struggle at Serafimovich as a minor incident in an unimportant and inconsequential sector of the front. For example, after Halder noted in his diary on 25 August, "A deep penetration in the Italian sector," on 27 August he concluded, "The penetration in the Italian sector turned out to be not so serious."[128] Ominously, however, on 29 August the chief of the OKH recorded, "In the Italian sector, the situation has not been aggravated, but it has not been set right either."[129] Less than three months later, the Germans would come to rue this neglect.

Developments to the east compounded the ill (and overlooked) future consequences of the Axis defeat at Serafimovich. In the equally neglected Soviet bridgehead in the northeast corner of the Great Bend, Moskalenko's 1st Guards Army matched 63rd and 21st Armies' feats. In accordance with Eremenko's 19 August order, the guards army of six rifle divisions was supposed to "attack with three divisions from the Kremenskaia and Shokhin line [in the northern half of the small bridgehead] toward Blizhniaia Perekopka, Os'kinskii, and Verkhne-Golubaia" to expand the Soviet bridgehead to encompass the entire river bend east of Kletskaia.[130] Moskalenko planned to do so at dawn on 22 August with a shock group consisting of 41st, 38th, and 40th Guards Rifle Divisions, with the army's 23rd Rifle Division in second echelon and a handful of supporting tanks from the remnants of 4th Tank Army's tank brigades.

Opposite Moskalenko's main attack sector, Sixth Army's XI Corps defended with its 376th Infantry and 100 Jäger Divisions and two regiments of 44th Infantry Division stretched across the bridgehead from Perekopskaia, 10 kilometers south of Kremenskaia on the Don, and eastward to Sirotinskaia on the Don. General Apell's 22nd Panzer Division (with about 60 tanks), which had been operating against 21st Army's 63rd Rifle Division east of Kletskaia, constituted XI Corps' reserve.[131]

Attacking on 22 August, in the ensuing five days of heavy fighting, Moskalenko's three guards divisions, reinforced by 23rd Rifle and 4th Guards Rifle Divisions, forced XI Corps' troops to withdraw 8–10 kilometers south of their original defenses (see Maps 69 and 70). On 24 August, to help repel the Soviet assaults, Sixth Army and XI Corps committed 204th and 129th Panzer Detachments to the fight, as well as 22nd Panzer Division, although the latter soon shifted westward to help contain the Soviet attacks at Serafimovich on 27 August.[132] As was the case at Serafimovich, German reports underplayed the importance of the fighting in the Kletskaia bridgehead, simply noting on 24 August:

The enemy undertook an unsuccessful attack in front of XI Army Corps west of Sirotinskaia. At present the enemy is attacking west of Iablonskii with 20 tanks. The offensive, which the enemy conducted with two regiments on a broad front east of Perekopskaia, was halted south of Perekopskaia after some

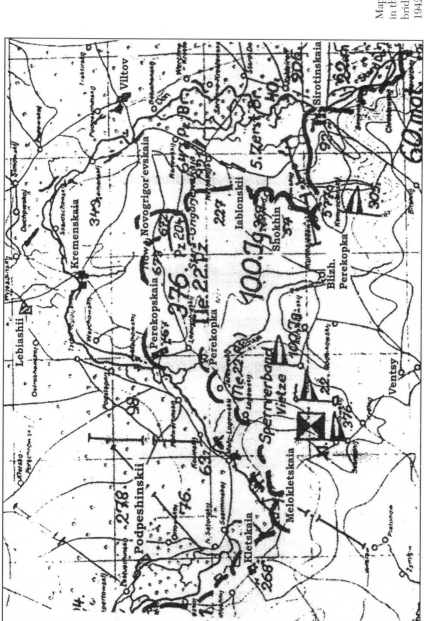

Map 69. The situation in the Kletskaia bridgehead, 19 August 1942

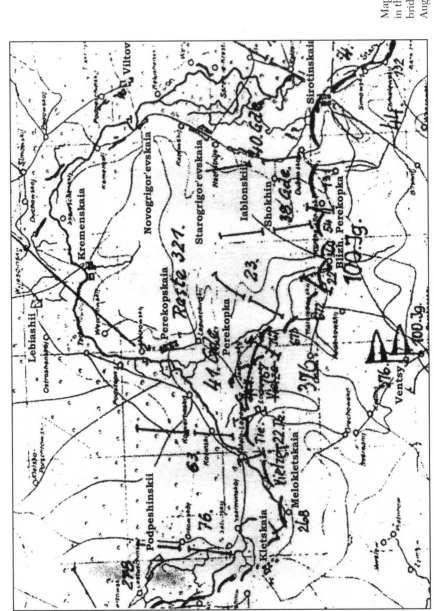

Map 70. The situation in the Kletskaia bridgehead, 29 August 1942

initial success. On the corps' left wing, we can liquidate the small local enemy penetrations.[133]

Once the fighting ended, XI Corps' defenses stretched 35 kilometers from the Don River 10 kilometers northeast of Kletskaia eastward to the Don at Sirotinskaia, leaving Moskalenko's army with a 35-kilometer-wide and 30-kilometer-deep bridgehead on the southern bank of the Don. However, the *Stavka* and Eremenko had bigger plans for his army. Two days after fighting ended, on the night of 31 August, Moskalenko turned his sector in the bridgehead, together with his 38th, 40th, and 41st Guards Rifle Divisions, over to Danilov's 21st Army. He then moved his 1st Guards Army headquarters to the Sadki region east of the Don. On 1 September his army, now consisting of the newly assigned 4th and 37th Guards and 23rd and 116th Rifle Divisions, reinforced by Rotmistrov's fresh and refitted 7th Tank Corps, prepared to join a new round of offensives in the Kotluban' region during early September.

Together with 63rd and 21st Armies' attacks at Serafimovich, 1st Guards Army's offensive near Kletskaia tied down vital German reserves, particularly 22nd Panzer Division and two panzer detachments, preventing them from reinforcing Paulus's main advance on the Volga. More important, the twin offensives secured for Stalingrad Front two operational-scale bridgeheads on the Don River's southern bank, which the *Stavka* would put to good use within three months' time. For the moment, however, Weichs's army group and Paulus's Sixth Army considered them to be mere nuisances.

CONCLUSIONS

The fighting during the last ten days of August was significant in several respects, and its course and outcome had major implications for how the subsequent battle for Stalingrad would be fought. Certainly, Hitler and every German could justifiably conclude that this stage of Operation Blau had been successful simply because Paulus's and Hoth's armies had indeed linked up west of the city. This junction stranded 62nd and 64th Armies on a narrow belt of land stretching southward along the western bank of the Volga River. In so doing the two German armies had destroyed one Soviet army outright (1st Tank) and had severely damaged three more (4th Tank, 62nd, and 64th) and had killed, wounded, or captured tens of thousands of Red Army troops and destroyed as many as 400 Soviet tanks. This brought the gruesome toll of Red Army losses since mid-July to a staggering total of well more than 300,000 soldiers and 1,000 tanks. Now all that had to be done was to eliminate the remnants of 62nd and 64th Armies and seize Stalingrad itself or, in light of Hitler's decision to bomb the city into rubble, to capture its ruins.

However, thoughtful reflection on Sixth Army's and Fourth Panzer Army's performances during the second half of August leads to a somewhat more sober appraisal of what had actually occurred—an appraisal that sharply contradicts previous accounts of the fight in several important respects. For example, the triumphal dash by Wietersheim's XIV Panzer Corps from the Don to the Volga in the astonishingly brief period of just three days indeed erased all memories of its embarrassing failure to reach Kalach-on-the-Don in a single bound during the second half of July. Once Wietersheim's panzers reached the Volga, however, his corps proved too weak to penetrate into and hold the northern portion of Stalingrad. In fact, instead of seizing the northern half of the city as ordered, his forces had to fight hard for their very survival. At one point Wietersheim and Hube had to request permission to retreat.

The hard reality was that, as on many occasions before, a force of well under 200 tanks was too weak and too slender a reed to perform the ambitious mission assigned to it. As a result, unless and until Fourth Panzer Army brought its weight to bear on Soviet forces south of the city, Paulus's forces to the north remained in a situation resembling little better than a stalemate. All the while, losing up to 500 men per day, Wietersheim's XIV Panzer Corps was in danger of slowly bleeding to death.[134] Fighting south of Stalingrad, Hoth's Fourth Panzer Army, a panzer army in name only with only one panzer corps, was also too weak to carry out its assigned mission in one bound. Although it ultimately succeeded in collapsing Southeastern Front's defenses, it did so only in a series of offensive "spurts" and after multiple regroupings, even after the OKH reinforced Hoth's army with 24th Panzer and 297th Infantry Divisions.

Although the combined forces of Paulus's and Hoth's armies managed to eliminate 1st Tank Army from the Red Army's order of battle and severely damage 4th Tank, 62nd, and 64th Armies, defiantly the *Stavka* raised two new armies (24th and 66th) to replace them, as well as a third (28th) to defend the Astrakhan' axis. Within days after Paulus and Hoth closed the gates on Stalingrad from the west, Zhukov would employ 24th and 66th Armies, together with 1st Guards Army, to remind Weichs and Paulus that capturing Stalingrad would require a major battle outside as well as inside the city.

Finally, as all Germans from Hitler down to the lowliest *Wehrmacht* private focused their attentions on the climactic advance on Stalingrad, the Hungarian, Italian, and German forces on Army Group B's and Sixth Army's overextended left wing had to endure multiple assaults by Stalingrad Front's 63rd, 21st, and 1st Guards Armies against their defenses along the southern bank of the Don River. Although they did so successfully, they also committed the cardinal error of leaving sizeable Red Army bridgeheads on the Don's southern bank. If the names of strange and remote places like Serafimovich and Kletskaia meant little to Hitler, OKH, or Army Group B in August and September 1942, by year's end they would become rallying cries to every Soviet and curses to every German. Furthermore, the Axis loss of these bridgeheads and the German failure to retake them underscored another truth lost on Hitler and the OKH: The reality was that Army Group B was stretched too thin—as early as August and September 1942—to liquidate these bridgeheads. Given Hitler's resolve to capture Stalingrad at all costs, this reality would become even grimmer still by November and ultimately prove fatal to Army Group B.

In short, as already indicated by its combat performance during the month of July and the first half of August, Sixth Army's advance in late August still showed that Paulus's army lacked sufficient strength to accomplish all of the missions assigned to it. While it was able to compensate for this shortcoming in the late summer by sheer willpower and persistence, the most important unanswered question was whether the army's will would continue to prevail in the fall. The battle inside Stalingrad would answer this question.

CHAPTER 9

The Struggle on the Flanks, 25 July–11 September 1942

The unspeakable agonies of Stalingrad are so fascinating that sometimes participants and historians tend to focus narrowly on the struggle for this great city. Yet the true nature of the battle becomes apparent only when viewed in the context of the wider war. For the German invaders, the demands of other fronts not only delayed their advance to Stalingrad but also diverted scarce resources that might have made victory possible. For the Soviet defenders, the battle was always a balancing act—the Soviet regime had to commit sufficient men, weapons, and ammunition to deny the city to the Germans while at the same time husbanding as many resources as possible for use elsewhere. Thus, before turning to the urban struggle itself, we must first consider the simultaneous challenges of the German advance into the Caucasus, which formed an integral part of Operation Blau, and the Soviet offensives launched elsewhere during late July, August, and September 1942.

OPERATION EDELWEISS: ARMY GROUP A'S ADVANCE INTO THE CAUCASUS

Opposing Forces

As he looked southward from Rostov in late July, Field Marshal Wilhelm List, commander of Army Group A, faced a daunting task. After capturing Rostov on 24 July, he was already operating at the extreme end of a tenuous supply chain, and he now had to contemplate going even farther, over increasingly hostile terrain (see Maps 71 and 72). The straight-line distance from Rostov to the Maikop oil fields was 290 kilometers, while the distance to the Chechen oil refinery complex at Groznyi was close to 650 kilometers. To capture Baku—the holy grail of petroleum on the Caspian Sea—List's troops would have to cover more than 1,100 kilometers, greater than the entire distance the Germans had already traveled to reach Rostov from their 1941 invasion points. Moreover, the German objectives were so widely dispersed laterally that German forces had to advance along a front of more than 300 kilometers wide.[1]

Simply stating these vast distances does not begin to suggest the challenges posed by the terrain. Although the area immediately south of Rostov, traversed from east to west by the mighty Kuban' River, was one of rich collective farms, the

Map 71. The Caucasus region (West)

cultivated region rapidly tapered off to the east into a high plateau, virtually a salt desert. Here, both sides would need not only food, ammunition, and gasoline but also water, an essential to keep both men and draft animals alive. In turn, this hostile, boiling wasteland gave rise to the Caucasus Mountain range, 1,100 kilometers long and 100–200 kilometers deep, whose peaks rose to heights of more than 5,600 meters and where supply routes became even rarer and more valuable.

In Führer Directive No. 45, dated 23 July, Hitler had ordered Army Group A to attack southward across the Don River, with two powerful pincers converging on Tikhoretsk, 150 kilometers south of Rostov, and "encircle and destroy the enemy forces withdrawing across the Don in the region south and southeast of Rostov."[2] List's eastern pincer, consisting of Hoth's Fourth and Kleist's First Panzer Armies, a force of roughly 435 tanks, would conduct the army group's

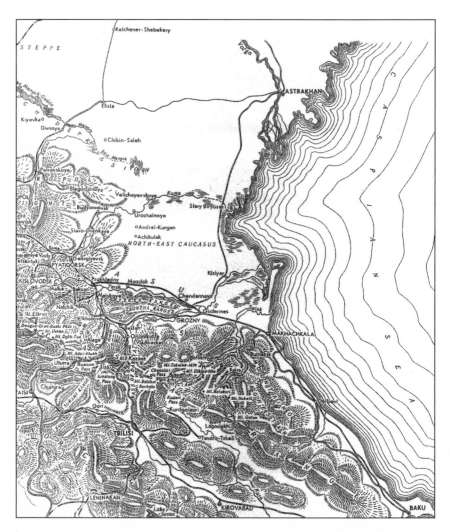

Map 72. The Caucasus region (East)

main attack southward from its bridgeheads across the Don east of Rostov and strike at Tikhoretsk from the north and northeast. The army group's western pincer, *Armeegruppe* Ruoff, consisted of Seventeenth Army and Romanian Third Army, later reinforced by Eleventh Army's Romanian Mountain Corps. This force was to attack eastward across the Kerch' Strait from the Crimea into the Taman' Peninsula, then advance on Tikhoretsk from the north and west. After completing the Tikhoretsk encirclement, the bulk of the two panzer armies would march southward to seize the Caucasus oil fields, while a portion of the two armies protected the army group's left flank, and Ruoff's infantry cleared Soviet forces from the Taman' region, captured the eastern coast of the Black Sea, and protected Army Group A's western flank.

List ordered his eastern pincer, initially Fourth Panzer Army's XXXXVIII and XXXX and First Panzer Army's III Panzer Corps, to commence its advance on 24 July, seize or expand bridgeheads across the Don River, press southward across the Sal and Manych Rivers to capture Sal'sk, and prepare for the decisive thrust toward Tikhoretsk. On the pincer's left wing, Kempf's XXXXVIII Panzer Corps was to consolidate the hold on its bridgehead at Tsimlianskaia with Fremerey's 29th Motorized Division. In the center, Geyr's XXXX Panzer Corps, with Breith's 3rd and Major General Erwin Mack's 23rd Panzer Divisions, was to attack southward toward the Sal and Manych Rivers from their bridgehead at Nikolaevskaia. Geyr, former commander of III Panzer Corps, had just replaced Stumme as commander of XXXX Corps as a consequence of the Reichel Affair. General Mack had replaced Boineburg-Lengsfeld for the same reason. On the right, III Panzer Corps, now commanded by Geyr's successor, General Mackensen, was to seize and expand bridgeheads west of Konstantinovskaia and overcome Soviet defenses along the western reaches of the Manych River with General Sigfrid Henrici's 16th and General Walter Hörnlein's "GD" Motorized Divisions. While the advance by his eastern pincer developed, Kleist's First Panzer Army hastily shifted the headquarters of Kirchner's LVII Panzer Corps, Major General Traugott Herr's 13th Panzer and SS Lieutenant General Felix Steiner's SS "Viking" Motorized Divisions, as well as XXXXIV Army Corps' 97th and 101st Jäger Divisions, eastward from the Rostov region to reinforce the eastern pincer's advance.

As List's panzers jockeyed into position for the decisive advance on Tikhoretsk, his western pincer, the infantry of Ruoff's Seventeenth Army, initially supported by First Panzer Army's LVII Panzer Corps, was to clear Soviet forces from Rostov and capture a bridgehead south of the Don at Bataisk. This would serve as a launching pad for the subsequent advance on Tikhoretsk. Ruoff's forces completely cleared Soviet forces from Rostov on 26 July and captured their bridgehead at Bataisk on 27 July. Therefore, 13th Panzer and SS "Viking" Motorized Divisions were not able to join the eastern pincer's advance until 29 July, by which time its panzers had already crossed the Sal and reached the Manych.

Faced with List's onslaught, the defending Soviet commanders confronted geographic challenges almost equal to those facing the Germans. As the Red Army retreated, it would be moving closer to the petroleum supplies at Groznyi and to the growing flow of American Lend-Lease aid coming through Iran. Yet this withdrawal would carry the defenders steadily farther and farther away from the centers of Soviet power—the sources of troops and ammunition. The railroad line from Rostov southeast toward Baku was jammed with trains carrying refugees and the components of factories being evacuated. As a result, this key line was as useless to the Soviets as it was to the Germans.[3] Moreover, the forces available for this defense were as inadequate as those of their opponents. Only the four field armies of Rodion Iakovlevich Malinovsky's Southern Front had survived the disaster in the eastern Donbas relatively intact. These included Grechko's 12th, Kamkov's 18th, Kozlov's 37th, and Ryzhov's 56th Armies, totaling only 112,000 combat soldiers, 169 guns, and 17 operable tanks, supported by 130 combat aircraft.[4] Intermingled with the divisions and brigades of these armies, most of which were mere shells of their former selves, were scattered groups of soldiers from the *front's* already shattered 9th and 24th Armies, which the *front* command had ordered to withdraw southward to reassemble and refit in the Sal'sk region far to the south.

Thus, what few forces Malinovsky could muster to restore coherent defenses along and south of the Don River were themselves weak, barely organized in a military sense, and lacking even the most basic armor, artillery, and air support. As a result of tremendous exertions under chaotic circumstances, Malinovsky by late on 25 July was able to cobble together a semicoherent defensive line stretching from the Kagal'nik region, south of the Don River's delta, eastward along the southern bank of the Don for 370 kilometers to the Tsimlianskaia and Verkhne-Kurmoiarskaia regions with his threadbare 18th, 12th, 37th, and 51st Armies. As he did so, he tried to withdraw the largely intact 56th Army into reserve positions south of the Eia River and the remnants of the already decimated 9th and 24th Armies to assembly areas near Sal'sk still farther to the rear. Malinovsky also received small but critical reinforcements from the *Stavka* in the form of Major General N. Ia. Kirichenko's fresh 17th Cavalry Corps from Budenny's North Caucasus Front (see Table 21). Nikolai Iakovlevich Kirichenko, who had commanded Western Front's 26th Mechanized Corps during the battle for Smolensk in July 1941 and 38th Separate Cavalry Division from July 1941 through January 1942, had received command of 17th Cavalry Corps on 10 June 1942 at age 47.[5]

The Initial Advance, 25–31 July

While List's army group built up supplies for its main thrust into the Caucasus and its right wing liquidated the Soviet forces defending Rostov, two of the three panzer corps constituting his eastern pincer pushed southward from the Don River at 0800 hours on 25 July (see Map 73).[6] XXXXVIII Panzer Corps' 29th Motorized Division remained riveted to its defensive positions around its bridgehead at Tsimlianskaia, fending off strong counterattacks by 51st Army. Meanwhile, Breith's 3rd Panzer Division of Geyr's XXXX Panzer Corps, reinforced by a *kampfgruppe* from Mack's 23rd Panzer Division, pushed southward from the Don River at Nikolaevskaia, brushed aside 51st Army's defending 302nd Rifle and 110th Cavalry Divisions, and advanced southward 15 kilometers. Breith captured a bridgehead across the Sal River at the village of Kalininskii (near Orlovka) by nightfall.[7]

Stiffening Soviet resistance, however, and fresh reinforcements from 51st

Table 21. The Southern and North Caucasus Fronts' Defensive Dispositions on 25 July 1942 (from east to west)

SOUTHERN FRONT (Colonel General R. Ia. Malinovsky)

  18th Army (Major General F. V. Kamkov), with 383rd, 395th, and 216th Rifle Divisions, 68th Naval Rifle Brigade, and remnants of 236th Rifle Division and 16th Rifle Brigade, defending the 50-kilometer sector from Kagal'nik at the mouth of the Don River eastward to Kiziterinka (20 kilometers southeast of Rostov), opposite Seventeenth Army;

  12th Army (Major General A. A. Grechko), with 4th, 261st, and 353rd Rifle Divisions and remnants of 176th, 341st, and 349th Rifle Divisions, defending the 40-kilometer sector from Kiziterinka (20 kilometers southeast of Rostov) eastward to Belianin (50 kilometers east of Rostov), opposite First Panzer Army's III Panzer Corps;

  37th Army (Major General P. M. Kozlov), with 74th, 230th, and 295th Rifle Divisions and remnants of 102nd, 218th, and 275th Rifle Divisions, defending the 65-kilometer sector from Bogaevskaia (Ashinov), 50 kilometers east of Rostov, eastward to Konstantinovskaia, 115 kilometers east of Rostov, opposite Fourth Panzer Army's XXXX Panzer Corps;

  51st Army (Major General Kolomiets), with 156th, 302nd, 91st, 157th, and 138th Rifle and 110th and 115th Cavalry Divisions and 135th and 155th Tank Brigades, defending the 171-kilometer sector from Konstantinovskaia eastward to Verkhne-Kurmoiarskaia, 281 kilometers east of Rostov, opposite Fourth Panzer Army's XXXXVIII Panzer Corps;

  56th Army (Major General A. I. Ryzhov), with five rifle divisions and three rifle brigades in the *front's* second echelon south of the Eia River; and

  24th Army (Major General V. N. Martsenkevich) and *9th Army* (Major General F. A. Parkhomenko) reorganizing south of the Egorlik River and Sal'sk.

NORTH CAUCASUS FRONT (Marshal of the Soviet Union S. M. Budenny)

  17th Cavalry Corps (Major General N. Ia. Kirichenko), with 12th, 13th, 15th, and 116th Cavalry Divisions, reinforced by 56th Army's 30th and 385th Rifle Divisions, supplementing the Southern Front's 18th Army;

  47th Army (Major General G. P. Kotov), with 32nd Guards and 77th Rifle Divisions, 103rd Rifle Brigade, and 126th Separate Tank Battalion, defending the eastern coast of the Sea of Azov; and

  1st Separate Rifle Corps (Colonel M. M. Shapovalov), with 83rd Naval and 139th Rifle Brigades, soon reassigned to reinforce the Southern Front.

Source: Boevoi sostav Sovetskoi armii, Chast 2 (ianvar'–dekabr' 1942 goda) [Combat composition of the Soviet Army, Part 2 (January–December 1942)] (Moscow: Voenizdat, 1966), 150–151. For 1st Separate Rifle Corps, A. A. Grechko, *Bitva za Kavkaz* [The battle for the Caucasus](Moscow: Voenizdat, 1973), 55; and *"Stavka VGK: Dokumenty i materialy 1942"* [The Stavka VGK: Documents and materials, 1942]. In *Russkii arkhiv: Velikaia Otechestvennaia [voina]* [The Russian archives: The Great Patriotic (War), vol. 16 (5–2)] (Moscow: "TERRA," 1996), 530.

Army's 91st Rifle Division forced Geyr to suspend his advance for three days until the remainder of Mack's panzer division deployed forward to support its advance. On XXXX Panzer Corps' right (to the west) at dawn on 25 July, Henrici's 16th Motorized Division, en route to join Mackensen's III Panzer Corps the next day, forced its way across the Don at Susatskii, just south of the junction with the Sal River, capturing a bridgehead from surprised and already demoralized defenders of Kozlov's 37th Army. By nightfall, the lead elements of Hörnlein's "GD" Motorized Division also entered the bridgehead, and together the two mobile divisions began preparations to bust out southward and southeastward from the bridgehead at dawn the next day.

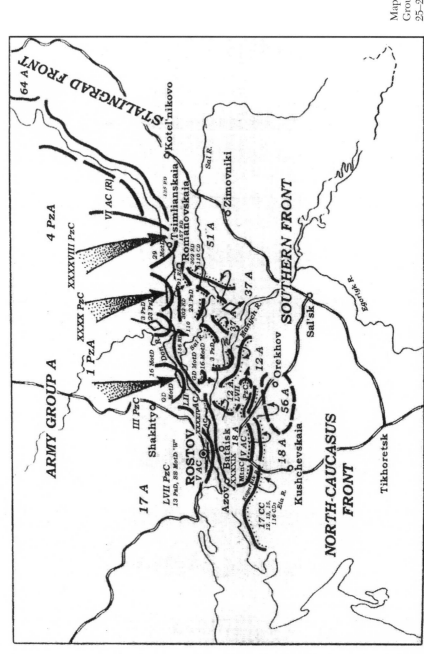

Map 73. Army Group A's advance, 25–28 July 1942

In addition to driving a sizeable dent into the defenses of Kolomiets's 51st Army, XXXX and III Panzer Corps' attack tore a 20-kilometer hole through the defenses of Kozlov's 37th Army. This separated the 37th from Kolomiets on its right, turned the right flank of Grechko's 12th Army, and threatened to unhinge Southern Front's entire makeshift defensive line from the east. With no available reserves, all Malinovsky could do was order his forces to stand firm along the Sal and Manych Rivers and urge Kolomiets's army to employ all of its available reserves, primarily its two fresh tank brigades, to counterattack and close the gap.

Before 51st Army could organize a counterattack, however, List's panzers resumed their southward lunge on 26 July. Even though Kolomiets's forces fought XXXX Panzer Corps' 3rd Panzer Division to a standstill along the Sal River, to the west 16th and "GD" Motorized Divisions of III Panzer Corps thrust southward and southeastward toward the Manych River from their bridgehead over the Don, collapsing 12th and 37th Armies' remaining defenses and scattering their divisions to the winds. Hörnlein's "GD" Division advanced 10 kilometers southward along the eastern bank of the Don by day's end, capturing Bogaevskaia (Ashinov), less than 8 kilometers north of the lower Manych River, and forcing Grechko's 12th and Kozlov's 37th Armies to fall back in disorder.[8] At the same time, the panzer grenadiers of Henrici's 16th Motorized Division fanned out to the south and southeast, reaching the northern bank of the Manych River near the villages of Svoboda, Sporny, and Novoselevka, 30, 40, and 55 kilometers east of the Don, respectively.

Once along the Manych, Henrici's troops faced the remnants of 37th Army's 2nd Guards Rifle, 74th, 230th, and 295th Rifle Divisions and 51st Army's 110th Cavalry Division. All of these formations were either retreating southward and eastward or attempting to dig in along the river line. The 16th Motorized Division's 156th Panzer Grenadier Regiment managed to seize a crossing near Svoboda and erect a bridge; the division's 165th Motorcycle Battalion also captured a crossing at Novoselevka. However, an assault by the division's 116th Panzer Battalion at Sporny faltered in the face of heavy artillery fire, forcing the panzers to withdraw. When Henrici's forces resumed a full-scale assault on 27 July, the Soviets blew up a nearby dam across the river, flooding the river valley and wiping out the bridge farther downriver at Svoboda. Not until dawn on 28 July was Henrici's division able to break 37th Army's grip on the river's southern bank and seize the village of Karakashev, 2 kilometers south. By day's end the division also managed to capture the village of Veselyi, merging its three bridgeheads into one.[9] By this time, the Germans could observe the Soviet forces pulling back toward the south.

While "GD" and 16th Motorized Divisions solidified their hold on the middle and lower Manych River, to the northeast Geyr's XXXX Panzer Corps finally broke its stalemate with Kolomiets's 51st Army along the Sal River. On 27 July the main body of Mack's 23rd Panzer Division pushed south across the Don at Nikolaevskaia, deploying on 3rd Panzer Division's left and permitting Breith to concentrate his entire 3rd Panzer along the Sal at Orlovka. Mack's advance struck 51st Army's 110th Cavalry and 302nd Rifle Divisions, forcing them to recoil eastward north of the Sal toward the Sal River village of Bol'shaia Martinovka, 12 kilometers east of Orlovka.[10]

In accordance with Malinovsky's orders, Kolomiets then organized a series of sharp counterstrokes. The first was near the village of Krepianka, several kilometers north of Bol'shaia Martinovka, at 1500 hours on 28 July, with an operational group consisting of 115th Cavalry Division and the fresh 135th Tank Brigade under the command of Major General Boris Andreevich Pogrebov, commander of North Caucasus Front's separate cavalry corps.[11] When this counterattack achieved modest success, the next morning Kolomiets struck Mack's forces at the village of Arbuzov, just north of the crossing over the Sal River at Bol'shaia Martinovka, with the combined forces of 302nd Rifle and 110th Cavalry Divisions and 135th and 155th Tank Brigades. Although Mack's panzers managed to preempt Kolomiets's assault and capture the bridge at Bol'shaia Martinovka, an intense fight ensued, with both sides claiming victory. While the Germans claimed to have destroyed 77 T-34 tanks during close-in fighting, the 51st Army reported destroying or damaging 60 German tanks in two days of fighting. General Pogrebov also perished during the struggle.[12]

Kolomiets soon arrived to direct 51st Army's operations in person and managed to prevent Mack's 23rd Panzer Division from advancing any farther east. Still, Breith's 3rd Panzer Division took advantage of the situation to resume its southward advance. Thrusting southward from Orlovka on the Sal with two *kampfgruppen* (von Liebenstein and Westhoven), Breith's armor on 28 July brushed aside 51st Army's 91st Rifle Division and advanced up to 20 kilometers by day's end. It reached the village of Buddenovskaia, 12 kilometers north of the key crossing over the Manych River at Proletarskaia and only 27 kilometers from its initial objective at Sal'sk.

Adding insult to Malinovsky's injury, by this time List's western pincer finally made its presence known south of the Don River. As it was completing its occupation of Rostov, the forward elements of Ruoff's Seventeenth Army captured crossing sites over the Don River and began transferring forces to the southern bank. Special operations troops from the Brandenburg Regiment captured a foothold on the southern bank of the Don opposite Rostov overnight on 25–26 July. The next day 73rd and 125th Infantry Divisions of Seventeenth Army's XXXXIX Mountain Corps and 198th Infantry and the Slovak Motorized Divisions of V Army Corps expanded the bridgehead to a depth of 5–10 kilometers, seizing the key city of Bataisk from 18th Army. Resuming their advance early on 27 July, XXXXIX Mountain Corps' 73rd and 4th Mountain Divisions fanned out 10 kilometers south and west, captured Kagal'nik, and reached the Kagal'nik River, driving Kirichenko's defending 17th Cavalry Corps and the remnants of Kamkov's 18th Army back to the southern bank.[13]

With crossings over the Don River from Rostov eastward to Aksaiskaia in German hands, on the morning of 28 July V Corps' 198th and 125th Infantry Divisions pushed southward across the Kagal'nik River, routing the Soviet defenders. Meanwhile, XXXXIX Mountain Corps' 73rd, 4th Mountain, and 298th Infantry Divisions struggled with the 17th Cavalry Corps farther west along the Kagal'nik River. During this fight, Herr's 13th Panzer and Steiner's SS "Viking" Motorized Divisions crossed the Don River by day's end with 172 tanks, the former ready to advance southeastward to join the advance by Mackensen's III Panzer Corps and the latter that of Kirchner's LVII Panzer Corps.[14]

Recognizing the mounting danger, Malinovsky, on the night of 27–28 July, had already ordered Kamkov, Grechko, and Kozlov to withdraw the remnants of their 18th, 12th, and 37th Armies back to the southern bank of the Kagal'nik River and Manych Canal and River. However, since 3rd Panzer Division was approaching the Manych at Proletarskaia, and 16th Motorized Division was already across the river farther west, Malinovsky's forces were unable to break contact with the advancing Germans or conduct any sort of orderly withdrawal to new defense lines farther south. As the Germans forced them southward in increasing disorder, the headquarters of Grechko's 12th and Kozlov's 37th Armies lost control of their forces. Lacking any communications with troops, the headquarters did not even know where their own units were located. With the exception of Kolomiets's 51st Army, still fighting to the northeast, and the stout resistance by some of 37th Army's divisions along the Manych, the distraught troops abandoned many positions without a fight. By this time only Grechko's 12th and Kamkov's 18th Armies remained relatively combat-ready, with nine rifle divisions with 300–1,200 bayonets each. Kozlov's 37th Army had four rifle divisions with 500–800 men each, and Ryzhov 56th and 9th and 24th Armies were only shells of their former selves, with headquarters and rear service units but few combat troops.[15]

Thus, by nightfall on 28 July Malinovsky's defenses south of the Don River were a shambles, with part of 18th and all of 12th and 37th Armies in headlong retreat. Only the extreme western portion of his defense line was able to contain XXXXIX Mountain Corps' advance along the lower Kagal'nik River. This line included Kirichenko's 17th Cavalry Corps, with 30 tanks of its attached Maikop Tank Brigade, 56th Army's 385th and 30th Rifle Divisions, and 18th Army's 68th Naval Rifle Brigade.[16]

On 27 July, concerned over Malinovsky's predicament, Major General Vladimir Vasil'evich Tikhomirov, Vasilevsky's deputy in the General Staff, contacted Budenny, commander of North Caucasus Front, inquiring whether Malinovsky's report that the Germans had captured Bataisk was correct and asking, "Where, in your opinion, we must construct a defense in the Northern Caucasus," and "whether or not the Southern and North Caucasus Fronts should be combined?"[17] Budenny, whose chief of staff, Major General Aleksei Innokent'evich Antonov, had sent a lengthy report to the Stavka only hours before, reiterated its contents. He said that North Caucasus Front was capable of performing only a mobile defense with 17th Cavalry Corps and 47th Army, and, given the paucity of forces, it was necessary to combine Southern and North Caucasus Fronts once German forces crossed the Manych River. Thereafter, the only feasible course was to conduct a delaying action to the south and construct a new defensive line along the crest of the Caucasus Mountains and the Terek River eastward to the Caspian Sea. To man this new defensive line, Budenny recommended the *Stavka* assign his *front*'s 47th Army and 1st Separate Rifle Corps, commanded by Major General Grigorii Petrovich Kotov and Colonel Mikhail Mikhailovich Shapovalov, respectively, the mission of defending the ports of Novorossiisk, Anapa, and Tuapse under the Black Sea Fleet's control.[18] In addition, Budenny recommended the *Stavka* form two new reserve armies, with a total of 14–15 rifle divisions, the first to defend the Groznyi region and the second the Ordzhonikidze region.[19]

After Tikhomirov passed Budenny's report to Stalin, early on 28 July the dictator signed a new directive combining Southern and North Caucasus Fronts into a new and expanded North Caucasus Front, with Budenny as commander and Malinovsky and Colonel General I. T. Cherevichenko as his deputies. Headquartered in Armavir, the new *front*'s mission was to "not only halt the further advance of the enemy to the south in their present positions by a stubborn struggle but also recapture Bataisk and restore the situation along the southern bank of the Don River at all costs by active operations." In addition, Budenny was to "allocate part of the force and occupy a line along the southern bank of the Kuban' River from the Krasnodar defensive line to Temizhbekskaia."[20]

Late on 29 July, the *Stavka* approved Budenny's first attempt to improve command and control by splitting his *front* into two separate operational groups, a Don Operational Group operating in the east and a Coastal (Maritime) Operational Group in the west, the former commanded by Malinovsky and the latter by Cherevichenko, Budenny's former deputy.[21] Iakov Timofeevich Cherevichenko was an experienced commander who, before becoming Budenny's deputy, had led Southern Front's 9th Army and Southwestern Front's 21st Army during the summer and fall of 1941 and commanded Southern Front during its successful offensive at Rostov in November and December 1941.[22] Malinovsky's Don Operational Group was responsible for protecting the approaches to Stavropol' with 12th, 37th, and 51st Armies, although the latter was soon transferred to Stalingrad Front. In the western half of his *front*'s sector, Cherevichenko's Coastal Operational Group was to defend the approaches to Krasnodar and the Taman' Peninsula with 18th, 56th, and 47th Armies and 1st Separate Rifle and 17th Cavalry Corps.[23] It also authorized Budenny to defend the Kuban' River line with two rifle brigades of Shapovalov's 1st Separate Rifle Corps.[24]

In accordance with Budenny's recommendation, the *Stavka* on 30 July ordered Trans-Caucasus Front, commanded by Army General I. V. Tiulenev, to construct a defensive line along the Terek River and the approaches to Groznyi and Baku by 7–8 August to back up North Caucasus Front's defenses. Aged 50 in 1942, Ivan Vladimirovich Tiulenev was an experienced commander who had commanded the Trans-Caucasus Military District in 1939–1940 and the prestigious Moscow Military District on the eve of war. After Operation Barbarossa began, he commanded Southern Front during its long withdrawal across southern Ukraine. However, since Stalin questioned Tiulenev's aggressiveness as a *front* commander, the dictator demoted him to command of 28th Army in the *Stavka* Reserve during winter 1942–1943. Stalin relented and reappointed Tiulenev commander of Trans-Caucasus Front in February 1942, a post he would occupy through 1945, in part because of his reputation as an effective force organizer and in part because of his acute knowledge of the region.[25]

Tiulenev was to man his new defensive line with the three rifle divisions and two rifle brigades of General Petrov's 44th Army, plus another three rifle divisions from other *front* forces.[26] The following day the *Stavka* directed Tiulenev to form two new rifle corps, 10th and 11th Guards, and employ them to erect yet another defensive line north of the Caucasus Mountains, this one stretching from Ordzhonikidze eastward through Groznyi to Makhachkala on the Caspian Sea.[27] By 6 August, using elements of the former 3rd Guards Rifle Corps, 10th Guards Rifle Corps, commanded by Major General I. T. Zamertsev, consisted of 5th, 6th, and 7th Guards Rifle Brigades; 11th Guards Rifle Corps, under the command of Major General Konstantin Appolonovich Koroteev, included 8th, 9th, and 10th Brigades.[28] Ivan Terentievich Zamertsev had commanded 255th Rifle Division throughout Operation Barbarossa and 3rd Guards Rifle Corps since 31 June 1942, and Koroteev had commanded Southern Front's 12th Army from October 1942 through April 1942.[29] To underscore the seriousness of the situation, Budenny on 30 July required all of his commanders to read Stalin's 28 July Directive No. 227, the "Not a Step Back!" order, to all of their troops, particularly, the statement, "At all costs, the German occupiers want to seize the Kuban' and the North Caucasus with their oil and other riches."[30]

On 29 July, as if to validate the acute necessity of these prudent defensive measures, List's armor burst southward across the Manych River against only minimal resistance (see Map 74). Despite a shortage of fuel, Breith's 3rd Panzer Division of Geyr's XXXX Panzer Corps captured Proletarskaia on the Sal River and then crossed the Manych River at the widest point, immediately behind a coffer dam. Although the division's first wave crossed safely in the dark, Soviet forces, including an NKVD division and elements of 37th Army, detected the second wave of the crossing:

> The Soviet artillery identified the German strike and hammered the boats with all calibers. . . . Lieutenant Buchmann was in radio contact with the [9th Battery, 75th Panzer Artillery Regiment], which responded with might and main. The Division artillery fired nearly 1200 rounds that morning! . . . The soldiers of the NKVD Division gave nothing up and fought with wild stub-

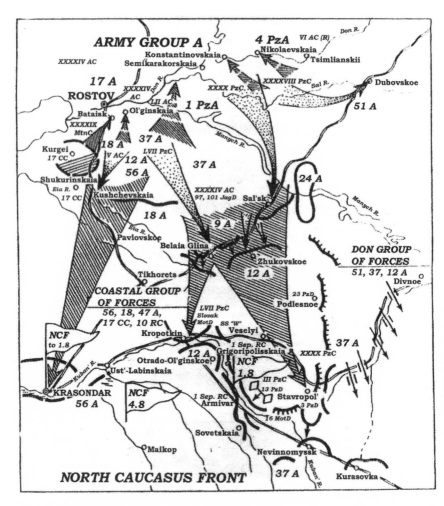

Map 74. Army Group A's advance, 29 July–5 August 1942

bornness. Major Boehm was mortally wounded, and with him fell his adjutant and many other officers and men. This left Senior Lieutenant Tank [commander of 6th Company] in overall charge of the battalion. The 26-year-old officer undertook the command and led the panzer-grenadiers in storming the Russian defenses. As their ammunition ran low, the men fought hand-to-hand, yelling 'hurrah!' . . . The panzer-grenadiers forced their way into the trenches and pushed the enemy out of one position after another.[31]

By morning, the invaders were almost out of ammunition, but a timely *Luftwaffe* attack allowed a few German armored vehicles to drive along the top of the neighboring dam, taking the defenders in their flank. Although Breith's panzers captured bridgeheads across the Manych at and north of Proletarskaia by day's end on 31 July, heavy Soviet resistance prevented them from advancing farther.

Fortunately for List, this was irrelevant, because at dawn on 30 July 13th Panzer Division had thrust eastward from Seventeenth Army's bridgehead south of Bataisk. Advancing headlong toward the southeast with a force of 109 tanks, Herr's panzers traversed well more than 80 kilometers in two days, capturing Sal'sk and another bridgehead across the Srednyi Egorlyk River west of the town and linking up with 3rd Panzer Division along the Manych River south of Proletarskaia. In the wake of Herr's panzers, Steiner's SS "Viking" Motorized Division also thrust southward, capturing a crossing over the Srednyi Egorlyk River near the town of the same name. While Hörnlein's "GD" Division halted to mop up bypassed Soviet forces and then prepare to revert to army group reserve, Henrici's 16th Motorized Division closed up to 13th Panzer's rear at Sal'sk.[32]

After 13th Panzer Division's tanks linked up with those of 3rd Panzer Division at Sal'sk on 31 July, the next day List reorganized the panzer corps of Kleist's First Panzer Army, leaving XXXX, III, and LVII Panzer Corps intact but transferring XXXXVIII Panzer and IV Army Corps to Hoth's Fourth Panzer Army in accordance with Hitler's 30 July decision (see below).[33] Once this reorganization was complete, First Panzer Army was positioned to begin its rapid exploitation to the south.

While List was reorganizing his eastern pincer for its final drive toward Armavir and the Maikop oil fields, his western pincer, Ruoff's Seventeenth Army, was expanding its offensive southward toward Krasnodar. Steiner's SS "Viking" Division made a spectacular advance toward the Srednyi Egorlyk River to the east, despite temperatures up to 40 degrees Centigrade (104 degrees Fahrenheit). To exploit this success, 198th, 125th, and 73rd Infantry Divisions of Seventeenth Army's V Corps pushed steadily southward from the Kagal'nik River on 30 July and, against diminishing resistance, smashed through the defenses of Kamkov's 18th Army along the Eia River by day's end on 1 August, capturing bridgeheads at and east of Kushchevskaia from 18th Army's 216th Rifle Division.[34] To the west, XXXXIX Mountain Corps' 298th Infantry and 4th Mountain Divisions finally overcame the defenses of Kirichenko's 17th Cavalry Corps along the lower Kagal'nik River and pushed forward to the Eia River west of Kushchevskaia. Ruoff's order no. 89, dated 30 July, subordinated 298th Infantry Division to Romanian I Army Corps and ordered XXXXIX Mountain and V Army Corps to advance southward to secure the Taman' and Krasnodar regions.

With First Panzer and Seventeenth Armies' forces safely across the Manych, Kagal'nik, Eia, and Srednyi Egorlyk Rivers, List's penetration battle was over, and the way was open for the exploitation operation. At this point, from Hitler's and List's perspectives, the most important unanswered question was how far their forces could sustain their exploitation.

Command Decisions and Opposing Forces

In the very midst of List's penetration operation, new strategic realities—specifically the unexpected resistance Paulus's Sixth Army was encountering in its advance toward Stalingrad—caused Hitler to alter his offensive plan. Deciding on 30 July that Paulus's drive required assistance, Hitler the next day directed Hoth to wheel the bulk of Fourth Panzer Army northeastward toward Stalingrad (see Map 75). As a sop to List, however, the Führer directed Hoth to transfer Geyr's XXXX Panzer Corps headquarters, together with its 3rd and 23rd Panzer Divisions, to the control of Kleist's First Panzer Army. The ensuing loss of Hoth's panzer army left List with no choice but to alter his offensive plan. Abandoning his planned encirclement at Tikhoretsk, he instead ordered Kleist's First Panzer and Ruoff's Seventeenth Armies to advance due south toward Maikop and Krasnodar, respectively.

The resubordination of Fourth Panzer Army to Army Group B left List with only limited resources to occupy this vast territory (see Table 22).[35]

Thus, on 1 August Kleist's First Panzer Army disposed of XXXX, III, and LVII Panzer Corps, each with mobile divisions, supported by XXXXIV and LII Army Corps, with two infantry divisions apiece. Although still imposing on paper, First Panzer Army now consisted of only ten divisions (12 after 13 August), including three panzer and two motorized divisions. By mid-August, further weakening Kleist's army, OKH transferred 22nd Panzer and "GD" Motorized Divisions, which also constituted the army group's reserve, to Army Group B and the West, respectively. This left Kleist with a force of roughly 350 tanks with which to conquer an area almost as large as France.[36]

Kleist's revised offensive plan required Mackensen's III Panzer Corps, deployed in his army's center, to attack southward through Armavir with its 13th Panzer and 16th Motorized Divisions to capture the Maikop region and its nearby oil fields and refineries. Protecting Mackensen's left flank, 23rd and 3rd Panzer Divisions of Geyr's XXXX Panzer Corps, with their own left flank secured by LII Corps' 370th and 111th Infantry Divisions, were to advance southeastward through Stavropol' to capture the Piatigorsk and Kislovodsk regions near the headwaters of the Terek River. On Mackensen's right flank, SS "Viking" and the Slovak Motorized Divisions of Kirchner's LVII Panzer Corps were to thrust due southward across the Kuban' River at Kropotkin and then advance west of Maikop to split Soviet forces in the Maikop region from those in Krasnodar to the west. Once Maikop and Stavropol' were in Kleist's hands, his forces were to advance southeastward parallel to the eastern foothills of the Caucasus Mountains to seize Nal'chik and Mozdok, cross the Terek River, and capture Grozny, the coast of the Caspian Sea near Makhachkala, and, ultimately, Baku.

While Kleist's panzers advanced on their deep objectives, during the first phase of its exploitation Ruoff's reinforced Seventeenth Army (*Armeegruppe*

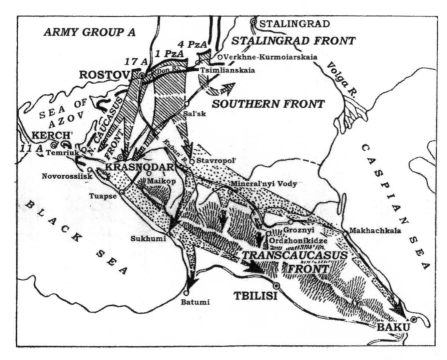

Map 75. Army Group A's revised plan, August 1942

Ruoff) was to capture Krasnodar and the eastern coast of the Black Sea, including Novorossiisk, the high passes through the western Caucasus Mountains, and
Tuapse. With Romanian Third Army's I Army Corps and Cavalry Corps protecting its right flank from east of Krasnodar to the coast of the Sea of Azov, Seventeenth Army's V Corps (ultimately with 9th, 73rd, 125th, and 198th Infantry
Divisions) was to capture Krasnodar and, subsequently, seize the eastern coast
of the Black Sea and the Soviet Black Sea Fleet's base at Novorossiisk.

Castling to Seventeenth Army's left (eastern) flank, XXXIX Mountain Corps
(ultimately with 1st and 4th Mountain and Romanian 2nd Mountain Divisions)
was to assault the high passes at the western end of the Caucasus Mountains and
capture Sukhumi before late September snows closed the passes. Meanwhile,
XXXIV Corps' 97th and 101st Jäger Divisions, transferred to Seventeenth Army
from Kleist's panzer army, were to advance through the western Caucasus Mountains from the region south of Maikop to Tuapse on the Black Sea coast. Thus, during its exploitation XXXIX Mountain Corps was to transfer 9th and 73rd Infantry
Divisions to V Corps for its assault on Krasnodar and 298th Infantry Division to
Romanian Third Army's I Army Corps for its advance into the Taman' Peninsula.

In addition, List's army group included the three divisions of the Italian Alpine

Table 22. Organization of Army Group A, 1–13 August 1942

ARMY GROUP A—Field Marshal Wilhelm List
 First Panzer Army—Colonel General Ewald von Kleist
  XXXX Panzer Corps—General of Panzer Troops Leo *Freiherr* Geyr von
  Schweppenburg
   23rd Panzer Division—Major General Erwin Mack (to 26 August) and
   Lieutenant General Hans Wilhelm *Freiherr* von Boineburg-Lengsfeld
   (to 26 December)
   3rd Panzer Division—General of Panzer Troops Hermann Breith
  III Panzer Corps—Lieutenant General Eberhard von Mackensen
   16th Motorized Division—General of Panzer Troops Sigrid Henrici
   13th Panzer Division—General of Panzer Troops Traugott Herr
  XXXXIV Army Corps—General of Artillery Maximilian de Angelis
   101st Jäger Division
   97th Jäger Division
   Walloon Battalion 373
  LVII Panzer Corps—General of Panzer Troops Friedrich Kirchner
   SS "Viking" Motorized Division—SS Lieutenant General Felix Steiner
   Slovak Mobile Division
  LII Army Corps—General of Infantry Eugen Ott
   111th Infantry Division
   370th Infantry Division
   Grossdeutschland Motorized Division (Army group reserve by 13 August)—
   General of Infantry Walter Hörnlein
  XXXXIX Mountain Corps (from *Armeegruppe* Ruoff on 12 August)
   1st Mountain Division
   4th Mountain Division
   Romanian 2nd Infantry Division
 Armeegruppe Ruoff (*Seventeenth Army*)—Colonel General Richard Ruoff
  V Army Corps—General of Infantry Wilhelm Wetzel
   198th Infantry Division
   125th Infantry Division
   73rd Infantry Division (by 12 August)
   9th Infantry Division (by 12 August)
  XXXXIX Mountain Corps—General of Mountain Troops Rudolf Konrad (to First
  Panzer Army on 12 August)
   73rd Infantry Division (to V Army Corps by 12 August)
   9th Infantry Division (to V Army Corps by 12 August)
   4th Mountain Division
   1st Mountain Division
  Romanian Third Army—General Petre Dumitrescu
   Romanian I Army Corps—General Mihail Racovita
    Romanian 2nd Mountain Division (to XXXXIX Mountain Corps by
    12 August)
    298th Infantry Division
   Romanian Cavalry Corps
    Romanian 5th Cavalry Division
    Romanian 6th Cavalry Division
    Romanian 9th Cavalry Division (by 12 August)
   Romanian II Army Corps
 Eleventh Army (diverted to the Leningrad region)—Colonel General Fritz-Erich von
 Manstein
  Group Mattenklott (XXXXII Army Corps)
   Romanian VII Army Corps
    Romanian 10th Infantry Division
   132nd Infantry Division

Table 22. Continued

           46th Infantry Division
           Romanian 19th Infantry Division
           Romanian 18th Infantry Division
           Romanian 8th Cavalry Division
           Romanian 3rd Mountain Division
      XXX Army Corps (being withdrawn)
           24th Infantry Division
           72nd Infantry Division
           28th Infantry Division
      LIV Army Corps
           50th Infantry Division
  Reserve
      Italian Alpine Corps (diverted to Army Group B in late August)
           4th Alpine Division Cuneense
           3rd Alpine Division Julia
           2nd Alpine Division Tridentina (by 13 August)
      Romanian 9th Cavalry Division (to Romanian Cavalry Corps by 12 August)
      "Grossdeutschland" Motorized Division (withdrawing after 13 August)
  Army Group Rear Area Command A
      454th Security Division
      445th Security Division
      4th Security Regiment

Source: Hoorst Boog, Werner Rahn, Reinhard Stumpf, and Bernd Wegner, *Germany and the Second World War, Volume 4: The Global War* (Oxford: Clarendon Press, 2001), 1030.

Corps and at least a portion of Manstein's Eleventh Army in the Crimea. However, when Paulus's Sixth Army encountered unexpected resistance on the approaches to Stalingrad in mid-August, OKH transferred the Italian Alpine Corps to Army Group B late in the month. Then, when Hitler decided to redeploy the bulk of Eleventh Army to the Leningrad region, this left List with only one infantry division (46th) from the Eleventh. Complicating List's task, when OKH decided to redeploy Romanian Third Army northward to protect Army Group B's left flank in early September, List was left with only Seventeenth Army and First Panzer Army to accomplish Hitler's ambitious objectives.

With Southern Front's defenses in the North Caucasus shattered by 1 August, Budenny and his masters in Moscow faced even more imposing challenges. As a result of the measures the *Stavka* undertook to restore defenses in the Caucasus region in late July, including rear service forces and tens of thousands of disorganized stragglers, Budenny's North Caucasus Front officially by 1 August fielded roughly 300,000 troops, to which were soon added 216,000 reinforcements from the former North Caucasus and the Trans-Caucasus Fronts. This brought the total strength of Red Army forces in the entire Caucasus region to 516,100 men, plus 87,100 sailors subordinate to the Black Sea Fleet and Azov Flotilla (see Table 23).[37] However, since the bulk of 56th, 18th, 12th, and 37th Armies' forces were no longer combat effective, Budenny's *front* was able to offer only token resistance to List's initial exploitation.

Table 23. Organization of Soviet Forces in the Caucasus Region on 1 August 1942

NORTH CAUCASUS FRONT—Marshal of the Soviet Union S. M. Budenny
    Coastal (Maritime) Operational Group—Colonel General Ia. T. Cherevichenko
        47th Army—Major General G. P. Kotov
            32nd Guards and 77th Rifle Divisions and 103rd Rifle Brigade
            126th Separate Tank Battalion
        56th Army—Major General A. I. Ryzhov
            30th, 339th, and 349th Rifle Divisions and 76th Naval Rifle Brigade
            151st and 158th Fortified Regions
        18th Army—Major General F. V. Kamkov
            216th, 236th, 353rd, 383rd, and 395th Rifle Divisions and 16th Rifle and
                68th Naval Rifle Brigades
        1st Separate Rifle Corps—Colonel M. M. Shapovalov
            83rd Naval Rifle and 139th Rifle Brigades
        17th Cavalry Corps (4th Guards on 27 August)—Major General N. Ia. Kirichenko
            12th, 13th, 15th, and 116th Cavalry Divisions
        69th Fortified Region
    Don Operational Group—Colonel General R. Ia. Malinovsky
        12th Army—Major General A. A. Grechko
            4th, 31st, 176th, and 261st Rifle Divisions, 109th Rifle Regiment (74th Rifle
                Division), and 81st Naval Rifle Brigade
        37th Army—Major General P. M. Kozlov
            2nd Guards, 74th, 230th, 275th, 295th, and 347th Rifle Divisions
            41st Motorized Rifle Brigade
        51st Army — Major General T. K. Kolomiets (transferred to the Stalingrad Front
          on 31 July but temporarily in the group's sector)
            91st, 138th, 157th, and 302nd Rifle Divisions
            110th and 115th Cavalry Divisions
            135th and 155th Tank Brigades (en route with 104 KV tanks)
            125th Separate Tank Battalion
            14th Tank Corps (remnants) (1,612 men and 15 tanks)—Major General
                N. N. Radkevich
        136th, 138th, and 139th Tank and 21st Motorized Rifle Brigades
        5th Guards, 2nd, 15th, 63rd, and 140th Tank Brigades and the Special Motorized
          Rifle Brigade
        62nd and 75th Separate Tank Battalions
    Front subordinate:
        9th Army (reorganizing)—Major General F. A. Parkhomenko
            51st, 81st, 106th, 140th, 242nd, 255th, 296th, and 318th Rifle Divisions
            30th Cavalry Division
             18th and 19th Destroyer Brigades
            132nd Separate Tank Battalion
        24th Army—Major General V. N. Martsenkevich and Major General D. T.
          Kozlov (in August) (headquarters only)
        4th Air Army—Major General of Aviation K. A. Vershinin
            216th, 229th, and 265th Fighter, 218th Fighter-Bomber, 219th Bomber, and
                230th Assault Aviation Divisions
            8th Guards and 136th Close Bomber and 647th, 762nd, and 889th Mixed
                Aviation Regiments
            217th Fighter Aviation Division (forming)
        5th Air Army—Lieutenant General of Aviation S. K. Goriunov
            132nd Bomber, 236th and 237th Fighter and 238th Assault Aviation
                Divisions
            267th Fighter, 763rd Light Bomber, and 742nd Reconnaissance Aviation
                Regiments
        8th Sapper Army—Colonel I. E. Salashchenko

Table 23. Continued

        11th, 23rd, 24th, 25th, 26th, 28th, 29th, and 30th Sapper Brigades
        (with 19 construction battalions)
     Front strength—74 tanks and 230 combat aircraft

Trans-Caucasus Front—Army General I. V. Tiulenev
        44th Army—Major General I. E. Petrov
            223rd, 414th, and 416th Rifle Divisions
            9th and 10th Rifle Brigades
        46th Army—Major General V. F. Sergatskov and Major General of Artillery K. N.
          Leselidze (on 23 August)
            3rd Mountain Rifle Corps—Major General of Artillery K. N. Leselidze
                9th and 20th Mountain Rifle Divisions
            389th, 392nd, 394th, and 406th Rifle Divisions and 156th Rifle Brigade
            63rd Cavalry Division
            51st Fortified Region
            12th Separate Tank Battalion
        45th Army—Lieutenant General F. N. Remezov
            61st, 89th, 151st, 402nd, 408th, and 409th Rifle Divisions
            55th Fortified Region
            151st Tank Brigade
     Front subordinate:
            417th Rifle Division, 3rd Rifle Brigade, and Separate Parachute Assault Battalion
            52nd and 191st Tank Brigades

Source: Boevoi sostav Sovetskoi armii, Chast 2 (ianvar'–dekabr' 1942 goda) [Combat composition of the Soviet Army, Part 2 (January–December 1942)] (Moscow: Voenizdat, 1966), 150–151.

Because Budenny's armies were too weak to do more than delay and degrade the German advance, the *Stavka* had ordered Tiulenev's Trans-Caucasus Front to defend the Terek River, gateway to the refineries of Grozny, the Caspian Sea coast at Makhachkala, and the Caucasus Mountains, with its 44th Army, two new rifle corps, and whatever other forces it could muster from its 45th and 46th Armies.[38]

The commanders of Trans-Caucasus Front's three armies and single rifle corps were all experienced generals, particularly General Petrov, whose exploits at Odessa and Sevastopol' are covered above. Vasilii Fadeevich Sergatskov, 43 years old when assigned command of 46th Army and distinguished by his shock of jet-black hair, was the least experienced commander of the three. Although he led a rifle regiment in the 1920s and a rifle division and corps in the 1930s, he was a senior professor at the Voroshilov General Staff Academy before war began and became deputy commander of Western Front's 28th and 30th Armies during Operation Barbarossa.[39] His counterpart in 45th Army, Fedor Nikitich Remezov, was two years older than Sergatskov and had far more experience, having commanded the Trans-Baikal and Orel Military Districts before the war. After Operation Barbarossa began, Remezov headed 13th Army during the battle of Smolensk, the North Caucasus Military District in September and October 1941, 56th Separate Army during its victory over First Panzer Group at Rostov in November–December 1941, and the Southern Ural Military District prior to reappointment to army command.[40] The last of the three was the Georgian-born

Konstantin Nikolaevich Leselidze, commander of 3rd Mountain Rifle Corps, an artilleryman by trade who distinguished himself as chief of artillery for Western Front's 50th Army during the battle for Moscow.[41]

As for the *front*'s commander, Marshal of the Soviet Union Budenny was another warhorse from the Russian Civil War who had previously commanded the entire North Caucasus Main Direction (Axis) Command, a super-*front* or provisional theater of military operations (TVD) headquarters, before becoming commander of the North Caucasus Front during the summer crisis. Although personally courageous and popular with his frontline troops, Budenny was as ineffectual as his contemporary Timoshenko. Instead, the command climate behind the Soviet front once again relied on fear. Josef Stalin, himself an Ossetian from the endangered region, suspected with some justification that the various minority groups of the Trans-Caucasus might favor the German invaders over the Great Russian oppressors. The Soviet dictator unleashed Lavrenti Beriia, People's Commissar for Internal Affairs, to repress any disaffection. When Malinovsky protested, Beriia threatened to arrest him, and the general was undoubtedly glad when he was reassigned in late August to command one of the reserve armies committed at Stalingrad. Behind him, Beriia's NKVD troops murdered or deported thousands of Chechens, Tartars, Volga Germans, Ingushes, and other minorities. Small wonder, therefore, that Stalin's fear became self-fulfilling, with the Germans receiving passive and, in some instances, armed support from the peoples they encountered.[42]

ARMY GROUP A'S EXPLOITATION TO STAVROPOL', MAIKOP, AND KRASNODAR, 1–15 AUGUST

The Initial Exploitation, 1–5 August

List's army group began its exploitation on 1 August (see Map 74). On the army group's left wing, Kleist's First Panzer Army advanced southward with Mackensen's III and Kirchner's LVII Panzer Corps heading toward Armavir and Geyr's XXXX Panzer Corps toward Stavropol' to protect the army group's left flank. Simultaneously, V Army and XXXXIX Mountain Corps of Ruoff's Seventeenth Army pressed southward toward Krasnodar from their bridgehead across the Eia River east and west of Kushchevskaia. Leading III Panzer Corps' attack, Herr's 13th Panzer Division pushed 15–20 kilometers southward from Sal'sk, capturing the town of Peschanokopskoe. In 13th Panzer's wake, Henrici's 16th Motorized Division moved into the Sal'sk region. On III Panzer Corps' left, Breith's 3rd Panzer Division of Geyr's XXXX Panzer Corps advanced 15 kilometers east of Sal'sk, capturing crossings over the Egorlyk River, while Mack's 23rd Panzer Division left part of its forces north of the Sal River to contain Kolomiets's 51st Army and used the remainder of its forces, together with XXXXIV Army Corps' 101st and 97th Jäger Divisions, to liquidate the bypassed remnants of Grechko's 12th and Kozlov's 37th Armies south of the Sal and Manych Rivers in First Panzer Army's rear. On III Panzer Corps' right, LVII Panzer Corps' SS "Viking" Motorized Division, with the Slovak Motorized Division in its wake, pushed 15 kilometers south of the Srednyi Egorlyk River and seized the village of Belaia Glina, 10 kilometers northeast of Tikhoretsk and halfway to the Kropotkin on the Kuban' River.

With Soviet resistance melting away, Kleist's armored divisions accelerated their exploitation on 2 August. Advancing almost 100 kilometers in two days in the vanguard of Mackensen's III Panzer Corps, Herr's 13th Panzer Division captured Armavir on the Kuban' River on 3 August after a sharp fight. Well to its rear, 16th Motorized Division hastened forward on 13th Panzer's path, joining Herr's panzers on 4 August. In the process, Henrici's panzer grenadiers captured Colonel Shapovalov, commander of 1st Separate Rifle Corps, and many of his troops. On III Panzer Corps' left, the lead division of Geyr's XXXX Panzer Corps, Breith's 3rd Panzer, reached the northern outskirts of Stavropol', 60 kilometers to the east, and seized the city from 37th Army on 5 August after a two-day struggle. Protecting XXXX Panzer Corps' long left flank, despite recurring fuel shortages, Mack's 23rd Panzer Division employed small *kampfgruppen* to erect a long panzer screen stretching from east of Proletarskaia on the Manych River southward to just northeast of Stavropol'. On III Panzer Corps' right flank, SS "Viking" Division of Kirchner's LVII Panzer Corps reached the Kuban' River near Grigoripolisskaia, 35 kilometers northwest of Armavir, on 3 August. On its right, the Slovak Motorized Division reached the northeastern approaches to Kropotkin on the Kuban' River on the panzer corps' right flank. While Steiner's SS "Viking" Division fanned out along the river's northern bank, the Slovak Division occupied Kropotkin on 5 August, driving the newly identified 1st Separate Rifle Corps and 318th Rifle Division south of the river.[43]

As Kleist's panzers penetrated deeply to Armavir and Stavropol', Ruoff's Seventeenth Army, with Romanian Third Army moving forward to protect its right (western) flank along the coast of the Sea of Azov, attacked southeastward from the Eia River. XXXXIX Mountain Corps' 73rd Infantry Division and V Army Corps' 198th and 125th Infantry Divisions managed to advance up to 20 kilometers south of the Eia River at and east of Kushchevskaia. Still, continued stout resistance by Kirichenko's 17th Cavalry Corps and remnants of Kamkov's 18th and Ryzhov's 56th Armies west of the town held up the mountain corps' right. However, the arrival of 1st Mountain and 9th Infantry Divisions restored the momentum of Ruoff's advance. By 5 August, his reinforced V Corps pushed southward 20–30 kilometers, while reconnaissance detachments from 1st and 4th Mountain and 73rd, 9th, 125th, and 198th Infantry Divisions pushed forward another 10 kilometers, capturing Tikhoretsk and penetrating to within 80 kilometers of Krasnodar.[44]

The Soviet Reaction

As List's forces began their exploitation, Budenny kept the *Stavka* informed of the deteriorating situation and dispatched continuous requests for assistance. For example, on 1 August he described the situation in his *front* as "difficult" and said the enemy had already captured Sal'sk, Peschanokopskoe, Kushchev-skaia, and Aleksandrovka and was advancing toward Armavir and Tikhoretsk. He reported that the weak remnants of 37th, 12th, and 18th Armies were attempting to establish defenses along the Kuban' River, and he was in the process of rein-forcing his defenses at Armavir and westward along the Kuban' River to Kropotkin with 1st Separate Rifle Corps, 2,000 officers from the Uriupinsk Infantry School, and four machine gun–artillery battalions from 151st Fortified Region. However, he asserted he had no forces to protect the Terek River front east of Armavir. Finally, Budenny declared he was defending the line from the Taman' Peninsula eastward to Krasnodar with 47th Army's 77th Rifle Division, 103rd Rifle Brigade, and 32nd Guards Rifle Division.[45] Shortly thereafter, the *Stavka* approved Budenny's decision to dispatch 32nd Guards to Krasnodar and, recalling the desperate measures it took in summer 1941, authorized him to raise three new divisions from People's Militia to reinforce his defenses.[46]

Late on 3 August, with his defenses being overrun by three panzer corps and more than 200 tanks, Malinovsky asked permission to withdraw his Don Oper-ational Group back to the line of the Kuban' River. The *Stavka* agreed, assigning his group responsibility for defending Armavir, even though the city fell to 13th Panzer the same day.[47] Protected by rear guards, Kozlov then withdrew the rem-nants of his shattered 37th Army east and south of Stavropol'. To the west, Grechko's 12th Army also retired southwestward across the Kuban' west of Armavir. On 2 August, after being ordered forward from the coast of the Black Sea, Shapovalov's 1st Separate Rifle Corps tried to establish defenses east of Grigoripolisskaia but was preempted by SS "Viking" Division and forced to with-draw westward across the Kuban' River. Over the next two days, the corps was routed in the Armavir region by the advancing 13th Panzer and 16th Motorized Divisions, losing its commander and many of its troops.

Alarmed by the speed at which its defenses in the Caucasus were collapsing, the *Stavka* on 5 August took further measures to bolster its defenses, first by sending Budenny a dire warning: "In connection with the enemy's desire to seize Maikop by operating from the Armavir region and subsequently reach the Black Sea coast at Tuapse, it is necessary to protect the Maikop region and the Maikop-Tuapse road immediately, resolutely, and at all costs to deny the enemy the opportunity of reaching the Black Sea coast from the Armavir-Maikop axis."[48]

The *Stavka* then ordered Tiulenev's Trans-Caucasus Front to reinforce its defenses north of the mountains with 89th Rifle Division and 52nd Tank Brigade from Erevan, the capital of the Armenian Republic, and prepare to deploy most of his *front*'s forces to the north.[49] Finally, it ordered the North Caucasus Military District headquarters to form the new 66th Army and man it with forces already located in the Terek River valley and additional forces from Trans-Caucasus Front. Commanded by Lieutenant General Vladimir Nikolaevich Kurdiumov, the military district's commander, and headquartered in Ordzhonikidze, the army was to defend the Terek Valley with eight newly formed rifle divisions.[50] Later the same day, the *Stavka* reminded Budenny he was responsible for defending the Caucasus Mountain line west of the Urukh River, which flowed northward from the mountains to the Kuban' River just east of Armavir. To maintain communications with Malinovsky's Don Operational Group, it ordered him to hold firmly to the railroad line from Armavir eastward to Prokhladnyi, a key railroad center on the Terek River west of Mozdok, and expel German forces already south of the Kuban' River west of Armavir.[51]

Late on the evening of 6 August, Vasilevsky and Lieutenant General Sergei Matveevich Shtemenko in the Red Army General Staff contacted Tiulenev by secure teletype to determine what measures the Trans-Caucasus Front commander had taken. Tiulenev reported he had dispatched 89th Rifle Division and 52nd Tank Brigade northward, and a special operational group from his staff headed by Major General Grigorii Timofeevich Timofeev, inspector of his *front*'s cavalry, reported the Germans had conducted a parachute assault in the Georgievsk region, east of Piatigorsk.[52] The 66th Army's headquarters, which was collocated with that of 9th Army, sent an NKVD battalion to liquidate the assault. Further, Tiulenev was using 9th Army to gather up all soldiers in the Groznyi and Ordzhonikidze regions, together with Timofeev's group, and the headquarters of 24th Army, with 223rd Rifle Division, was doing the same in the Derbent region to the east, as well as constructing defensive lines.

Vasilevsky then directed Tiulenev to organize a Northern Group of Forces within his *front*, under the command of Lieutenant General Ivan Ivanovich Maslennikov, an NKVD officer and former commander of Kalinin Front's 39th Army, and consisting of Petrov's 44th Army and the reorganized 9th Army, the latter now under Major General Aleksandr Aleksandrovich Khadeev, former commander of 44th and 46th Armies.[53] In addition, Vasilevsky advised Tiulenev to retain one of the three guards rifle corps destined for 9th Army as a strong reserve and informed him his *front* would receive priority distribution of aircraft from the factory in Tbilisi and Lend-Lease tanks sent through Iran.[54]

The Maikop Operation, 7–11 August

However, by this time XXXX Panzer Corps' 3rd Panzer Division had already advanced southward from Stavropol' and captured Nevinnomyssk, a key town on the railroad line 60 kilometers southeast of Armavir and midway between Armavir and the spa town of Mineral'nye Vody (Mineral Water). To the northeast, the same corps' 23rd Panzer Division was racing toward Sergeevskaia, 60 kilometers east of Stavropol'. Thus, Breith's and Mack's panzers had already severed communications between Cherevichenko's Coastal Operational Group, west of Stavropol', and Malinovsky's Don Operational Group, east and southeast of that city. In an attempt to plug this gap, the *Stavka* ordered Budenny to form two small detachments made up of school troops and training forces backed up by 11th NKVD Rifle Division, under General Timofeev's command, to block any German advance eastward along the railroad line to Mineral'nye Vody.[55]

By capturing Armavir and Stavropol', Kleist's panzers drove more than 100 kilometers into the center of Budenny's *front*, forcing the remnants of Kolomiets's 51st Army to withdraw eastward, Kozlov's 37th Army to retreat southeastward, and the remnants of Kamkov's 18th and Grechko's 12th Armies to fight a delaying action southwestward toward Maikop. However, neither Kleist's nor Ruoff's armies were able to encircle and destroy any major portion of Budenny's forces north of the Kuban' River. Before Kleist could consolidate his gains, it was necessary to bring the infantry of XXXXIV Corps' 97th and 101st Jäger Divisions forward and protect his left flank with LII Corps' 370th and 111th Infantry Divisions. While the former were still closing on the Kuban' River north of Armavir, the latter were still in the Proletarskaia region far to the north. Driven on by Hitler, even before these forces completed their deployment forward, List unleashed Kleist's panzer corps on a concerted advance deeper into the Caucasus. List's hope was to push First Panzer Army forward through Maikop and then insert XXXXIV Army and XXXXIX Mountain Corps through the Caucasus Mountain to capture Sukhumi and Tuapse, thereby encircling and destroying Budenny's Coastal Group south of the Kuban' River.

To that end, on 7 August XXXX Panzer Corps' 23rd and 3rd Panzer Divisions continued their headlong advance on Kleist's left wing, the former advancing on Mineral'nye Vody from the north and the latter toward the town along the railroad from the west (see Map 76). Geyr's panzer corps faced the weakened remnants of Kozlov's 37th Army and Budenny's two ersatz groups plus 11th NKVD Division. Delivering Kleist's main attack in his panzer army's center, III Panzer Corps' 13th Panzer and 16th Motorized Divisions swung westward from Armavir and captured bridgeheads across the Laba River, a southern tributary of the Kuban' River, at Kurgannaia and Labinskaia, only 40 kilometers east of Maikop, from the remnants of Grechko's 12th Army. On Kleist's right wing to the west, LVII Panzer Corps' SS "Viking" and Slovak Motorized Divisions pushed southward across the Kuban' River, reaching the Laba River north of Maikop and defeating the remnants of 1st Separate Rifle Corps. Although 37th Army's makeshift detachments and 11th NKVD Rifle Division managed to contain 3rd and 23rd Panzer Divisions for two days in heavy fighting on the approaches to Mineral'nye Vody, Breith's 3rd Panzer bypassed the town from the southwest and captured Piatigorsk on 9 August and Cherkessk, 48 kilometers south of the railroad line and 80 kilometers west of Piatigorsk, on 10 August.[56]

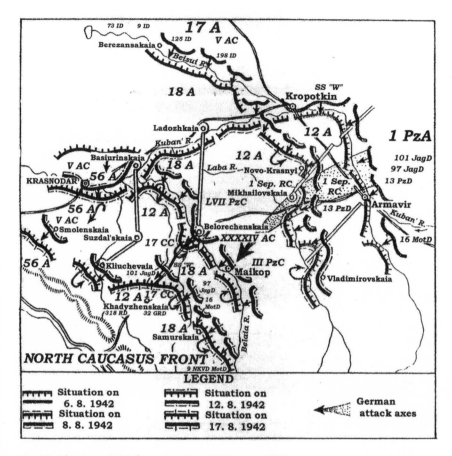

Map 76. The Armavir-Maikop operation, 6–17 August 1942

To the west, the combined forces of III Panzer Corps' 13th Panzer and 16th Motorized Divisions and LVII Panzer Corps' SS "Viking" Motorized Division converged on Maikop from the east and north, capturing the city and its adjacent oil fields on 9 and 10 August. Hitler was overjoyed at the news, but subsequent reports indicated that the defenders had destroyed most of the wellheads and storage facilities and removed key components from the refineries. Indeed, for several nights in early August, Mackensen's III Panzer Corps had guided its advance by marching toward the flames rising from Maikop.[57]

On 11 August, immediately after capturing the city, III Panzer Corps' 13th Panzer and 16th Motorized Divisions and LVII Panzer Corps' SS "Viking" Division dispatched small *kampfgruppen* southward into the valleys leading into the depth of the High Caucasus Mountains, while the Slovak Motorized Division protected Kleist's right flank. Kleist then moved XXXXIV Army Corps' 97th and

101st Jäger Divisions forward into assembly areas at and west of Maikop and ordered the two light divisions, supported by small *kampfgruppen* from the SS "Viking" and 16th Motorized Divisions, to penetrate through the passes in the western Caucasus and capture Tuapse.

Farther south, XXXX Panzer Corps' 3rd Panzer Division clung firmly to Piatigorsk and also sent a *kampfgruppe* southward into the mountain from Cherkessk, while one regiment of 23rd Panzer Division completed clearing Mineral'nye Vody of its persistent defenders. The remainder of Mack's panzer division manned a screen protecting the southern half of Kleist's long left flank northward to east of Stavropol'. Still farther north, LII Army Corps' 370th and 111th Infantry Divisions finally relieved 23rd Panzer's stay-behind forces on First Panzer Army's left flank, and the advance guard of 111th Infantry Division reached Elista, the only sizeable town in the region, on 12 August.[58]

Because Kleist's deep advance pushed Grechko's 12th and Kozlov's 37th Armies apart and severed all ground communications between them, Budenny subordinated Grechko's army to Cherevichenko's Coastal Operational Group, leaving Malinovsky's Don Group with only 37th Army.[59] Ominously, on 10 August the *Stavka* warned Budenny, "In connection with the existing situation, the most basic and dangerous thing for the North Caucasus Front and the Black Sea coast at this moment is the axis from Maikop to Tuapse," adding:

> With the arrival of the enemy in the Tuapse region, 47th Army and all of the *front*'s forces located in the Krasnodar region could be cut off and end up as prisoners. . . . Immediately push 32nd Guards Rifle Division forward and, with it, together with 236th Rifle Division, occupy three-four lines in depth from Maikop to Tuapse, and, at all costs, you are personally responsible for letting the enemy through to Tuapse.
>
> Withdraw 77th Rifle Division from the Taman' immediately and employ it to reinforce the defense at Novorossiisk, leaving the defense of the Taman' Peninsula to coastal units of the Black Sea Fleet.[60]

Because the only army remaining in Malinovsky's Don Operational Group was Kozlov's 37th, the *Stavka* effectively abolished his operational group on 11 August, subordinating 37th Army and Maslennikov's Northern Group of Forces to Tiulenev's Trans-Caucasus Front. It directed Tiulenev to withdraw the shattered army for rest and refitting.[61] The following day he reported on the parlous conditions in Southern Front's and North Caucasus Front's surviving force:

> Based on a visit to the units, I determined [there is] exceptional chaos and disorder in the withdrawal of the defeated units of the former Southern and North Caucasus Fronts. The withdrawing subunits do not know the direction of their movement, and, furthermore, no one knows his combat mission. As a result, I unexpectedly discovered crowds of unarmed personnel in various

populated points, who explained their state by explaining they had not succeeded in organizing. There is complete disdain for camouflage and discipline among them. I have taken measures to withdraw 4,500 *tankists* [tank crews] without equipment from various tank brigades, 40 aviation service support battalions, and 8th Sapper Army—up to 28,000 men—and the remnants of other units back behind the front.[62]

However, on the positive side, Trans-Caucasus Front described the measures it had taken to regroup its forces and establish a viable defense in a 13 August entry in its daily combat journal:

The forces of the Trans-Caucasus Front, while conducting a forced regrouping during the 10–12 days from the day the *front* commander reached his decision for a defense (30 July 1942), concentrated in a new defensive line along the southern bank of the Terek River and along the Urukh River by 10 August 1942, protected it along the entire front, and, first and foremost, carried out engineer work, while continuing its improvement. Simultaneously, reserves consisting of 89th, and 417th Rifle Divisions, 52nd Tank Brigade, and 44th and 52nd Guards-Mortar Regiments and others were brought forward to the Groznyi and Ordzhonikidze regions and designated to organize counterattacks on possible routes the enemy might appear.

In addition, nine rifle brigades (60th, 62nd, 107th, 131st, 19th, 57th, 84th, 119th, and 256th) and 10th Guards Rifle Corps, consisting of 5th, 6th, and 7th Guards Rifle Brigades, part of whose forces had already reached the Khasav-Iurt region, were dispatched from the *Stavka*'s reserve and were already en route to the Trans-Caucasus Front. During this period the *front* commander conducted immense organizational work. . . .

If only 9th and 10th Rifle Brigades had initially defended along the lower course of the Terek River on 1 August, then by 12 August 10th and 9th Rifle Brigades, 389th Rifle Division, 11th Guards Rifle Corps, 151st Rifle Division, and 392nd Rifle Division were already defending here. The 89th Rifle Division, 52nd Tank Brigade, and 44th Guards-Mortar Regiment were concentrated in the Groznyi region. The 417th Rifle Division and 44th Guards-Mortar Regiment were concentrated in the Ordzhonikidze region.

In this period 8 rifle divisions withdrawn from the North Caucasus Front and 10 mortar battalions and several tank brigades and separate tank battalions were deployed for urgent replenishment. Simultaneously, separate small subunits and rear service units were deployed for extensive reorganization.

All of the *front*'s command and control organs worked to support the newly organized defenses and did not give the enemy the opportunity to penetrate through them.

It is now possible to declare openly that the missions assigned to the command in the telegraph transmissions from the chief of the Red Army's General

Staff on 29 July and the *Stavka's* directive of 30 July concerning the defense of the Terek and Urukh River have been fulfilled.[63]

Finally, on 16 August Tiulenev reported to the NKVD that his *front* had completed all measures necessary to construct defensive lines to protect the approaches to the Trans-Caucasus region, including the provision of a labor force, trucks and tractors, and necessary supervision for the work and had deployed two rifle brigades from Baku to defend the Makhachkala Defensive Region.[64]

The Krasnodar and Kuban' Operations, 12–15 August

As Kleist's panzer corps were capturing Stavropol', Piatigorsk, and Maikop, to the west Ruoff's Seventeenth Army, now reinforced by Romanian forces on its right flank, accelerated its advance on Krasnodar (see Map 77). Ruoff reorganized his army on 5 August, transferring XXXXIX Mountain Corps' 73rd and 9th Infantry Divisions to V Army Corps and ordering the mountain corps to shift eastward into the sector of XXXX Panzer Corps' 3rd Panzer Division near Cherkessk, where it was to advance southward through the high passes of the Caucasus west of Mount Elbrus, the highest peak in the mountains, to Sukhumi on the Black Sea coast. Now consisting of four infantry divisions (198th, 125th, 9th, and 73rd), V Corps was to converge on Krasnodar from the north and east, capture the city, and then swing westward in concert with Romanian Third Army to capture the Taman' Peninsula and Novorossiisk.

Opposite advancing V Corps, Cherevichenko's Coastal Operational Group defended the city's approaches with four weak divisions from Ryzhov's 56th and Kamkov's 18th Army, supplemented by the Krasnodar People's Militia Rifle Division.[65] The final assault by V Corps broke into Krasnodar, the oil refinery capital of the Kuban' River region, on 10 August.[66] Once in the city, however, Ruoff's infantry encountered the first significant resistance of the operation when 56th Army's 30th Rifle Division defended the city's northeastern suburb of Pashkovskaia with great determination, counterattacking German 308th Infantry Regiment with *Katiushas*, tanks, and even air support. Then, after evacuating as many troops as possible, the defenders blew up the bridge over the Kuban' River in the very face of the German advance. This effort forced the Germans to wait two days and cross the river in assault boats. The German consolidation in the area was not complete until 15 August.[67]

With Stavropol', Piatigorsk, Maikop, and Krasnodar under his control, List began formulating a plan to eliminate all Soviet forces from the region north of the Caucasus Mountains, in particular the Taman' Peninsula and the northern foothills of the Caucasus, and create conditions for First Panzer Army to pursue its deep objectives in the Mozdok, Ordzhonikidze, and Groznyi regions and at Baku beyond (see Map 78).

Before embarking on these operations, however, List ordered Kleist to

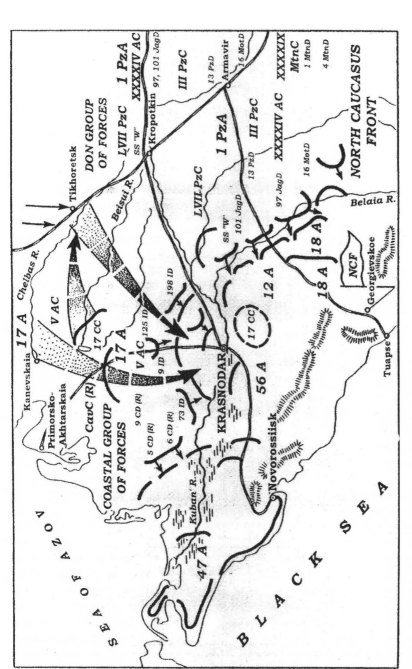

Map 77. The Krasnodar-Kuban' operation, 12–15 August 1942

employ General Maximilian de Angelis's XXXXIV Army Corps, supported by armor from Kirchner's LVII and Mackensen's III Panzer Corps, to conduct a rapid surprise advance through the western Caucasus Mountains to Tuapse on the Black Sea coast.[68] List's plan called for two groups to conduct the attack, Henrici's 16th Motorized and the 97th Jäger Divisions penetrating into the mountain from the region south of Maikop, and Steiner's SS "Viking" Motorized and 101st Jäger Divisions doing so along two axes from the Belorechenskaia region northwest of Maikop. Henrici's panzer grenadiers, supported by infantrymen from 97th Jäger Division, were to thrust westward from Abadsechskaia and Dachovskaia, 20–30 kilometers south of Maikop, to reach Samurskaia and Lazarevskaia on the Black Sea coast. Steiner's SS motorized troops, accompanied by infantry from 101st Jäger Division, were to advance from Belorechenskaia toward Tuapse, the former via Apsheronskii and Neftegorsk, and the latter through Khadyshenskii and Navaginskaia. If successful, this bold thrust would encircle Ryzhov's 56th Army in the Novorossiisk region.[69]

Following the guidance he received from the *Stavka* on 10 August, Budenny the next day began reinforcing his defenses along the Maikop-Tuapse axis. First, he ordered Kirichenko to shift 17th Cavalry Corps southeastward from the Krasnodar region and occupy defenses on the western bank of the Pshish River to block any German advance from the region northwest of Maikop. Grechko's 12th Army, reinforced by part of Kamkov's 18th Army, was to man defenses southwest of Maikop to prevent German forces from reaching and penetrating the Caucasus Mountains along the two roads leading through the mountains to Tuapse and Lazarevskaia. Finally, after ships of the Black Sea Fleet transported it from Novorossiisk to Tuapse, 32nd Guards Rifle Division was to occupy defenses near the villages of Navaginskaia and Pshish along the upper Pshish River to block German movement through the passes along the two mountain roads.[70]

Supported by Kleist's panzers, de Angelis's infantrymen began their assault on 12 August (see Map 79). In the south, 16th Motorized and 97th Jäger Divisions managed to capture Samurskaia by 15 August, but heavy Soviet counterattacks halted them near Rozhet and forced the Germans to withdraw to Samurskaia. To the north, SS "Viking" and 101st Jäger Divisions captured Belorechenskaia from 18th Army's 383rd Rifle Division and 17th Cavalry Corps' 12th Cavalry Division on 12 August. Advancing in two columns, SS "Viking" and 101st Jäger Divisions, supported by *kampfgruppen* from Herr's 13th Panzer and Henrici's 16th Motorized Divisions operating out of Maikop, pushed southward rapidly up the mountain valleys. They captured Khadyshenskii and reached 32nd Guards Rifle Division's defenses at Navaginskaia by day's end on 13 August. The next day Herr's *kampfgruppe* captured Apsheronskii, and one day later, after overcoming strong resistance, Henrici's *kampfgruppe* captured Neftegorsk. However, facing stiffening resistance and fresh counterattacks, de Angelis's drive ended by 18 August, bogged down in the mountains and well short of its ultimate objectives. In the words of one German account:

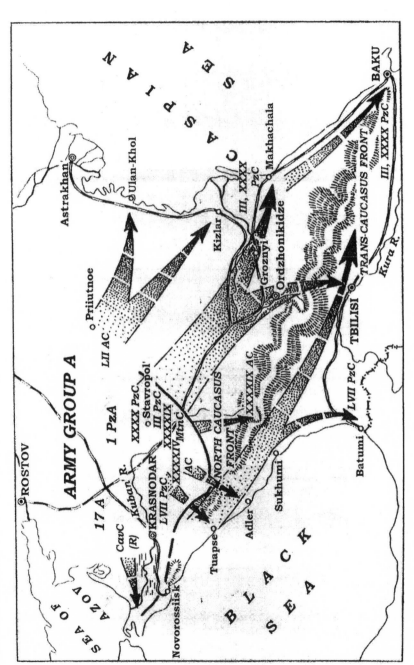

Map 78. Army Group A's revised plan, mid-August 1942

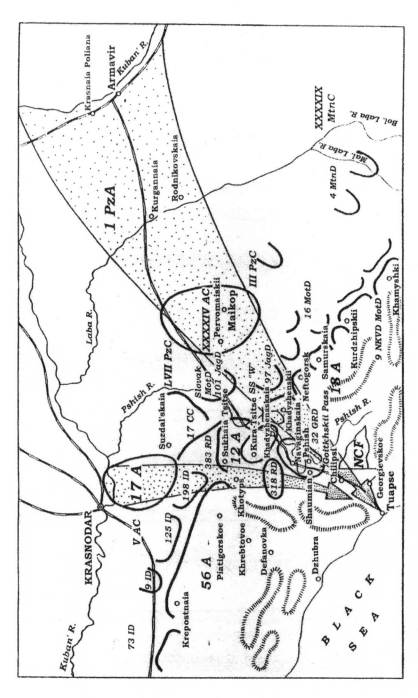

Map 79. The Tuapse operation, 12–28 August 1942

The attack began on 18 August. However, the plan fell apart at the Khady-shenskaia railroad station. The attack of the 101st Jäger Division stalled at the tunnel. The commander of the "Black Sea Group," General I. Y. Petrov, had deployed his best division in this area on the previous day because the key to the pass lay there. The Soviet 32nd Guards Rifle Division made the Würt-temburgers of the 101st Jäger Division pay for every meter of ground. Even the outflanking attack failed. . . . The attempt to cross the mountains using routes Nr. 3 and 4 [to Lazarevskaia and Adler, to the south] was abandoned.[71]

In the wake of this fighting, North Caucasus Front severely criticized Kirichenko's 17th Cavalry Corps and Kamkov's 18th Army for failing to halt the German advance short of the mountains. However, this criticism proved unjusti-fied in light of the cavalry corps' stellar performance in helping stop the German advances short of the Black Sea coast. As a reward for its contributions, the *Stavka* awarded Kirichenko's cavalry corps the designation of 4th Guards on 28 August.[72]

With the imminent fall of Krasnodar and Maikop and additional disasters impending along his entire front, on 13 August Budenny informed Stalin about the condition of his *front*'s forces and defenses:

1. At the moment the North Caucasus and Southern Fronts were combined in accordance with *Stavka* directive no. 170534 of 28 July 1942, the armies of the North Caucasus Front were operating [as follows]: 51st Army on the right wing of the front along the Don River, while in heavy fighting in the region southeast of Nikolaevskaia; 47th Army was holding on to the Taman' Penin-sula; and the armies of the former Southern Front were included in the North Caucasus Front at a time when they were continuing to withdraw southward from the Don River and occupying the greater part of the front. It is necessary to point out that there is no continuous front at this time. After abandoning Rostov, the armies were retreating in disorder, and individual units were con-ducting a fighting withdrawal, but the majority of the forces fled from the front in a demoralized state.

   The 12th and 18th Armies, which have a total of nine rifle divisions, each with about 300–1,200 bayonets, have still preserved their relative combat capability. The 37th Army has four rifle divisions, each with about 500–800 bayonets, and there were only force headquarters and rear service units in 56th, 9th, and 24th Armies. No more than 15 tanks remained at that time, predominantly light [models]. Thus, the total number of bayonets in all of the armies of the former Southern Front reached only 12,000 bayonets.

   Reinforcing artillery remained fully intact, and divisional artillery was pres-ent in 12th and 18th Armies, but the remaining [armies] had losses of up to 50 percent or more.

   There are 126 operating aircraft remaining in the air forces, including 42 night [aircraft].

There are no *front* reserves, excluding 17th Cavalry Corps, which was being employed on the *front's* left wing.

This state of the *front's* forces and the absence of communications led to disruption of fulfillment of the *Stavka's* directive concerning the restoration of positions along the Don River, and the Military Council assigned the mission to stop the further enemy advance along the Sal'sk, Srednyi Egorlyk, and Kushchevskaia line.

However, the forces did not even fulfill this limited mission, since, having lost their combat capability under the attacks of enemy tanks and aircraft, they continued retreating to the south while conducting delaying actions.

The chief reason for not fulfilling the *Stavka's* directives and for the subsequent withdrawal, which led to the abandonment of the Kuban', was the complete absence of tanks and motorized units in the *front,* the weakness of the aviation, the extreme exhaustion and paucity of the infantry, the absence of reserves, and the weak command and control of the forces and communication with them on the part of the weak newly formed *front* staff. These circumstances, along with the presence of the enemy's large tank forces and superiority in aircraft, accorded the enemy significant superiority, permitting him to reach our flanks and, at times, preempt our units at their intended defense lines, first by penetrating them with some tanks and then by widening the penetration. Despite the fact that the continuous front is now weak, the forces are fighting, but most of them remain weak because, as soon as the enemy penetrates the front somewhere with tanks, panic seizes the units closest to the penetration, and the units begin to retreat after some fighting.

Exploiting his superiority in tanks, the enemy races far forward and unexpectedly approaches this or that place, by doing so demoralizing not only the units but also the headquarters and even individual members of the *front's* staff, who frequently resolve missions by proposing new [defensive] lines, that is, new retreats instead of organizing battles. . . .

Overall, the *front's* armies on 12 August have:

18th Army—about 6,000 bayonets,
12th Army—about 3,000 bayonets,
56th Army—about 4,500 bayonets, and
47th Army—about 11,000 bayonets.
Total—about 24,500 bayonets.

Excluding the arrivals from 9th and 37th Armies, the artillery relatively intact includes 377th, 380th, 368th, 374th, and 1157th Army Artillery Regiments, 1195th, 31st, and 547th Howitzer Artillery Regiments, 530th and 521st Antitank Artillery Regiments, and two mortar regiments. The heavy artillery regiments, as well as the antitank artillery regiments, have 50–70 percent of their equipment but cannot be considered combat ready. The mortar units have all of their equipment. The antiaircraft artillery is relatively intact, with 24 antiaircraft batteries present.

Frontal aviation consists of units of former 5th Air Army. The 6th Air Army of the former Southern Front withdrew completely to the Trans-Caucasus Front, together with Group Malinovsky. On 11 August it had:

— All operable aircraft of former 5th Air Army—94 aircraft, including 15 Il-2, 9 DB 3, 9 SB, 15 I-15, 4 Iak-1, 11 LaGG-3, 16 I-16, 1 Pe-2, 5 R-5, and 7 U-2.
— Inoperable—89.

The North Caucasus Front has no tanks at all.

From the above, it is apparent that the *front*'s forces and weaponry are few and even inadequate for fortifying the line of the Belaia River, the Kuban' River at Krasnodar, and the Taman' Peninsula.

The *front*'s chief mission is to defend the axes to Tuapse and Novorossiisk resolutely. Therefore, it is necessary to resolve [this mission] by means of a solid defense of the mountain defiles that protect Tuapse and Novorossiisk. . . .

Budenny, Kaganovich, Antonov[73]

As early as 16 August, Kleist began withdrawing III Panzer Corps' 16th Motorized and 13th Panzer Divisions from the mountains southwest of Maikop for rest and refitting before committing them deeper into the Caucasus. Ultimately, Herr's 13th Panzer moved southeastward with III Panzer Corps headquarters and joined the ongoing advance of Geyr's XXXX Panzer Corps toward Groznyi. After Henrici's 16th Motorized Division remained in the region east of Stavropol' for about a week, OKH on 23 August transferred it to Army Group B, assigning it the mission of protecting the gap between Weichs's and List's army group in the Kalmyk Steppe. Two days later, Henrici's division moved eastward to begin mobile screening operations in the Elista region. Thereafter, de Angelis's XXXXIV Corps made several more attempts to push forward along the Tuapse road in late August, only to see every attack fail. However, by this time the center of gravity of List's operations had shifted decisively to Seventeenth Army's advance on Novorossiisk in the west and, more important, to the advance by Kleist's panzer spearheads into the Terek River region.

ARMY GROUP A'S ADVANCE TO THE CAUCASUS MOUNTAINS, 16 AUGUST–11 SEPTEMBER

Despite intermittent Soviet resistance, Army Group A achieved considerable success during the first three weeks of its offensive. After mid-August, however, a combination of factors, including Army Group A's overextended supply lines, recurring shortages of fuel, the difficult semimountainous terrain, and ever-stiffening Soviet resistance significantly slowed the army group's advance. Exacerbating these factors, the insatiable demands by Paulus's Sixth Army for additional troops and air support sapped the strength of List's army group, leaving it with fewer resources to accomplish its ambitious mission. The three-division Italian Alpine Corps, for example, arrived in mid-August but soon received orders to reinforce the defenses on Army Group B's left wing northwest of Stalingrad. In response to the demands of other fronts (see below), "GD" Motorized and 22nd Panzer Divisions, as well as most of the available air support, also departed from Army Group A in mid-August. They were followed near the end of the month by 16th Motorized Division.

Faced with these reductions, List reorganized his army group on 17 August, effective the following day, by transferring LVII Panzer and XXXXIV and XXXXIX Mountain Corps to *Armeegruppe* Ruoff and leaving Kleist's First Panzer Army with III and XXX Panzer and LII Army Corps. The German mountaineers of General Konrad's XXXXIX Mountain Corps fulfilled a lifetime dream by planting a swastika flag on the summit of Mount El'brus, the highest peak in the Caucasus Mountain range, on 21 August. Still, in light of the future difficulties Kleist's panzers would experience, this feat would prove to be little more than a propaganda victory.[74]

After the 17 August reorganization, List ordered Kleist's First Panzer Army to advance southeastward parallel to the Caucasus Mountains. The objective was to seize the Terek River valley, the key cities of Ordzhonikidze and Groznyi, the mountain passes across the eastern Caucasus, and ultimately Baku with Geyr's XXXX Panzer Corps and, later, Mackensen's III Panzer Corps. At the same time, he directed *Armeegruppe* Ruoff to accomplish a series of tasks. Romanian Third Army's Cavalry Corps, reinforced by German 298th and 46th Infantry Divisions, the latter attacking from the Crimea, were to clear Soviet forces from the Eisk region and Taman' Peninsula. Meanwhile, Seventeenth Army's V Army Corps would capture Novorossiisk, while XXXXIV Army, XXXXIX Mountain, and LVII Panzer Corps seized the passes through the Caucasus Mountains and the Black Sea ports of Tuapse and Sukhumi.[75] Thus, beginning after mid-August, Hitler required List's army group to conduct three major operations in the Caucasus region: first Kleist's advance into the Terek River valley; second Ruoff's offensive to seize the Taman' Peninsula and Novorossiisk; and third an attack by Ruoff's mountain troops to seize the high passes through the Caucasus Mountains. List's most formidable challenge was to orchestrate all three thrusts simultaneously.

The Mozdok Operation, 16–31 August

Kleist began the most important of these operations on 16 August when 23rd and 3rd Panzer Divisions of Geyr's XXXX Panzer Corps advanced southeastward from the Mineral'nye Vody and Piatigorsk regions (see Map 80). Mack's panzers seized

Georgievsk and advanced to within 30 kilometers of Prokhladnyi, on the Baksan River 50 kilometers west of Mozdok; farther west, Breith's panzers reached Baksan, on the same river, 20 kilometers north of Nal'chik, situated in the northern foothills of the Caucasus Mountains. On Kleist's right wing, Mackensen's III Panzer Corps began withdrawing Herr's 13th Panzer Division and Henrici's 16th Motorized Division from the Maikop region to rest and refit and then reinforce XXXX Panzer Corps' advance. A week later, however, OKH ordered Henrici's panzer grenadiers to redeploy northeastward to the Elista region, releasing LII Army Corps' 370th and 111th Infantry Divisions so that they could move south and support XXXX Panzer Corps' advance toward the Terek River.

To the southeast, Maslennikov's Northern Group of Forces seemed ill-prepared to halt First Panzer Army's advance before it breached the Baksan and Terek River lines. By this time, Maslennikov's group consisted of 37th, 9th, and 44th Armies, later backed up with another new army, the 24th (subsequently renumbered 58th). These three armies defended a front of about 420 kilometers. On Maslennikov's left wing, Kozlov's 37th Army, which had just withdrawn from the Malka River, 30 kilometers southeast of Piatigorsk, manned defenses along the Baksan River from north of Nal'chik to just west of Prokhladnyi with under-strength 2nd Guards, 275th, 392nd, 295th, and 11th NKVD Rifle Divisions and no armor whatsoever. In Maslennikov's center, 9th Army, commanded by Major General V. N. Martsenkevich after Khadeev fell ill, defended the sector along the Terek River from Prokhladnyi eastward past Mozdok with 151st, 176th, and 389th Rifle Divisions, 11th Guards Rifle Corps' 8th, 9th, and 10th Guards Rifle Brigades, 62nd Naval Rifle Brigade, and 36th and 42nd Armored Train Battalions.[76] On Maslennikov's right wing, Petrov's 44th Army defended the Terek River line from east of Mozdok to the Caspian Sea coast north of Makhachkala with 414th, 416th, and 223rd Rifle Divisions and 9th, 10th, 256th Rifle, and 84th Naval Rifle Brigades, supported by 44th Separate Tank Battalion, 66th Separate Armored Train Battalion, and 17th and 18th Separate Armored Trains.[77]

Maslennikov's reserves included 10th Guards Rifle Corps (4th, 5th, 6th, and 7th Guards Rifle Brigades), 89th, 347th, and 417th Rifle Divisions, 52nd Tank Brigade (with 46 tanks), and 249th, 258th, and 563rd Separate Tank Battalions (equipped with a mixture of British and American Lend-Lease tanks).[78] As formidable as his Northern Group seemed on paper, many of its formations were woefully understrength. The 417th Rifle Division fielded only 500 rifles, and other rifle divisions and brigades had neither machine guns nor artillery. Because Maslennikov's group had only 105 tanks to oppose the roughly 350 tanks fielded by XXXX and III Panzer Corps, the defenders were fortunate to mount any defense at all. Behind these troops, 90,000 civilians worked frantically to erect antitank defenses at Makhachkala and Baku.[79] This was the force Kleist's XXXX Panzer Corps encountered as it began its push eastward across the arid steppe into the foothills of the Caucasus Mountains.

Tiulenev assigned Maslennikov's Northern Group its specific combat missions

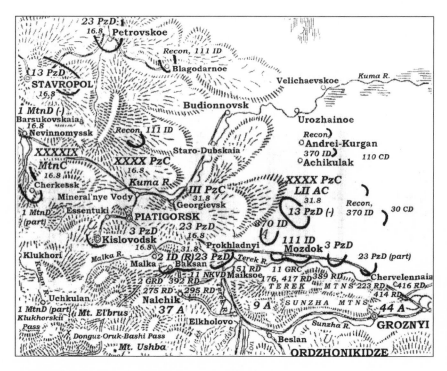

Map 80. The Mozdok operation, 16–31 August 1942

on 16 August. Maslennikov pointed out that the enemy had pushed the main forces of its XXXX Panzer Corps (one motorized and one panzer division) into the gap between the school forces and 37th Army, with at least one panzer division advancing deep along the Piatigorsk axis. He therefore predicted these forces would advance toward Prokhladnyi and Maiskoe. To counter this threat, Tiulenev ordered the Northern Group commander to:

1. Prepare a short night attack against the enemy's flank and rear from Novo-Pavlovskoe toward Mar'inskaia on 16 August 1942 to capture and destroy his crossings in the Kuba region and from Kyzburun-1 toward Malka with an analogous mission.
2. Conduct the attack at night, completing the operation before first light. A secret movement of the forces into their jumping-off positions is necessary for success. Maneuver at night must be simple—conduct the attack along well-identified lines, if possible, not opening fire until the enemy has detected our movement.[80]

However, the impetuous assault by Kleist's panzers preempted Tiulenev's orders. Attacking from the Georgievsk and Piatigorsk regions on 18 August, 23rd and 3rd Panzer Divisions brushed aside the forces of Kozlov's 37th Army defending along the Malka River and lunged southeast, with Mack's panzers reaching the outskirts of Prokhladnyi, and Breith's the northern outskirts of Baksan. There the two panzer divisions, reinforced on 20 August by Romanian 2nd Mountain Division, fought a two-day battle with Kozlov's forces defending the Baksan River line.

Meanwhile on 18 August, racing forward to join XXXX Panzer Corps' advance, III Panzer Corps' 13th Panzer Division seized the crossing over the Kuma River at Voronzova-Aleksandrovskoe, 40 kilometers northeast of Georgievsk, after a short but sharp fight against the forward security elements of Martsenkevich's 9th Army. As 3rd and 23rd Panzers engaged Kozlov's forces along the Baksan River, the panzers of Herr's 13th Panzer Division swung eastward and then southward in a wide arc in an attempt to reach and cross the Terek River east of Mozdok—thereby outflanking Martsenkevich's army from the west—and capture Mozdok. A reconnaissance party from Herr's panzer division reached the Terek River at Ishcherskaia, 30 kilometers east of Mozdok, on 23 August.[81] After passing its sector along the Baksan River to Romanian 2nd Mountain Division on 22 August, Breith's 3rd Panzer Division also regrouped its forces eastward through the rear of Mack's 23rd Panzer Division, crossed the Lenin Canal north of the city, and reached the northern bank of the Terek River in the Mozdok region late on 23 August. There it began preparations to assault the city's defenses during the evening in conjunction with an attack by Herr's panzers farther to the east.[82]

When Breith's forces reached the outskirts of Mozdok, the city was defended by a small detachment from 9th Army, a student regiment from the Rostov Artillery School, and 26th Reserve Rifle Brigade, supported by several armored trains.[83] To their rear, the Terek River was 100–250 meters wide and extremely swift. After several assaults on the city with two *kampfgruppen* (Liebenstein and Westhoven) failed on 24 August, Breith's forces captured the city in a more carefully organized attack on 25 August.[84] However, by this time Martsenkevich had reinforced his 9th Army's defenses along the southern bank of the Terek River opposite Mozdok with three rifle brigades from Koroteev's 11th Guards Rifle Corps, which were able to contain the German assault on the northern bank. The next day, the forward elements of Herr's 13th Panzer Division seized a bridgehead across the Terek River at Ishcherskaia, downriver from Mozdok, from 9th Army's 389th Rifle Division.

After capturing Mozdok and the bridgehead at Ishcherskaia, Kleist transferred 13th Panzer Division to XXXX Panzer Corps on 25 August. Thereafter, 3rd and 13th Panzer Divisions, joined on 27 August by the main body of 23rd Panzer Division, took over responsibility for the Terek River sector from Prokhladnyi eastward past Mozdok, leaving III Panzer Corps controlling Romanian 2nd Mountain Division at the town of Baksan to the west and part of 23rd Panzer Division in the Prokhladnyi region. The same day, 13th Panzer Division shifted part of its forces farther east along the Terek River and seized a bridge-head at Naurskaia after an intense fight, providing it with two footholds on the river's southern bank.[85] Stay-behind elements of 23rd Panzer Division captured Prokhladnyi from 9th Army's 151st Rifle Division on 25–26 August. However, 23rd Panzer commander, General Mack, was killed, along with other officers on his staff, while conducting an inspection at the front and was replaced by General Boineburg-Lengsfeld, the division's former commander who had been relieved after the Reichel Affair.[86] By this time, after more than a week of confused fight-ing, Kleist's First Panzer Army had come to a virtual standstill.

During the ensuing week, Kleist worked frantically to end the stalemate by massing his forces so that they could renew their advance from Mozdok across the Terek River and southward toward Ordzhonikidze. In his army's center, 370th and 111th Infantry Divisions of General Ott's LII Army Corps, which reached the Mozdok region after a thoroughly exhausting march southward from the Elista region, relieved 3rd Panzer Division. During the first week of Sep-tember, the two infantry divisions conducted operations to seize bridgeheads across the Terek River south of Mozdok. Once relieved, Breith regrouped his panzer division eastward along the northern bank of the Terek River, joining the forward elements of 23rd and 13th Panzer Divisions, which were stretched out along the northern bank as far east as Naurskaia, with reconnaissance parties reaching as far east as north of Groznyi. Kleist then ordered Herr's 13th Panzer to move into concentration areas north of Mozdok and, once LII Corps' infantry had captured bridgeheads across the Terek River, attack southward from those bridgeheads toward Ordzhonikidze. To the west, Boineburg-Lengsfeld's 23rd Panzer Division was to reassemble its forces south of Prokhladnyi and prepare to attack southward along the Terek River valley toward Ordzhonikidze. Given the scattered nature of First Panzer Army's forces and persistent fuel shortages, Kleist's forces were unable to mount a concerted drive south until 11 September. In the interim, intense fighting took place in the Mozdok region as Ott's LII Corps struggled to seize the necessary bridgehead against near-constant Soviet counterattacks (see below).[87]

On 22 August, while XXXX Panzer Corps was advancing on Mozdok, Hitler intervened by depriving Army Group A of one of its vital mobile divisions, dis-rupting List's plans and dispositions. Concerned about a possible Soviet coun-terattack force concentrating west of Astrakhan', Hitler detached Henrici's 16th Motorized Division from III Panzer Corps to screen the army group's left flank. Although this permitted List to send the two infantry divisions of LII Corps southward to assist Kleist's panzers, 16th Motorized Division's movement to its new base at Elista, in the Kalmyk Steppe 250 kilometers east of Rostov, further strained Army Group A's logistics. In fact, in order to move Henrici's motorized division to Elista, Kleist had to drain the tanks of a panzer division—and, compli-cating his task, the motorized division also reverted to Army Group B's control.

Over the next several months, 16th Motorized Division pushed motorized patrols a further 200 kilometers east and southeast to the outskirts of Astrakhan' and the Caspian Sea. A number of Cossacks and exiled Ukrainians provided the German patrols with paramilitary support, and these patrols occasionally interdicted railroad lines between the Caucasus and the European Soviet Union. Yet the impossible scale of the mission assigned to a single division is a clear reflection of the inadequate forces available to Army Group A.[88]

Reorganization of Soviet Defenses

The *Stavka* reacted quickly to the danger posed by German panzers advancing into the Prokhladnyi and Mozdok regions. First, on 23 August it ordered Tiulenev to form a new 24th Army to defend the Makhachkala region. Commanded by Major General Vasilii Afanas'evich Khomenko, former deputy head of the Moscow Defense Zone, the army would consist of 328th, 337th, and 317th Rifle Divisions, the Makhachkala NKVD Rifle Division, and 3rd Rifle Brigade.[89] However, on 27 and 28 August the *Stavka* countermanded this order, instead forming 24th Army in the region north of Stalingrad and renaming Khomenko's army the 58th.[90]

Then, on 1 September the *Stavka* combined the North Caucasus and Trans-Caucasus Fronts into a single Trans-Caucasus Front, effective 4 September. This directive reorganized the former North Caucasus Front into the Black Sea Group of Forces under Trans-Caucasus Front's control. It simultaneously ordered the hapless Budenny to return to Moscow, retained Tiulenev as *front* commander, and appointed Cherevichenko as commander of the Black Sea Group of Forces.[91] Two days later, on the advice of its representative, Beriia, the *Stavka* relieved 9th Army's commander, Martsenkevich, for dereliction of duty and replaced him with Major General Konstantin Apollonovich Koroteev, who had commanded Southern Front's 12th Army during the Rostov offensive in November and December 1941. Major General Ivan Pavlovich Roslyi, former commander of Trans-Caucasus Front's 4th Rifle Division during Operation Barbarossa, replaced Koroteev as commander of 11th Guards Rifle Corps.[92]

Once the *Stavka*, Tiulenev, and Maslennikov completed reorganizing defenses along the Baksan and Terek Rivers, Trans-Caucasus Front's Northern Group of Forces consisted of 37th, 9th, and 44th Armies deployed in first echelon from west to east along a 420-kilometer front, backed up by 58th Army forming in the Makhachkala region in second echelon, and supported by 176 combat aircraft subordinate to Lieutenant General of Aviation Konstantin Andreevich Vershinin's 4th Air Army.[93] On Maslennikov's left wing opposite III Panzer Corps' 23rd Panzer and Romanian 2nd Mountain Divisions, Kozlov's 37th Army defended the sector along the Baksan River with its 2nd Guards, 275th, 392nd, and 295th Rifle and 11th NKVD Rifle Divisions. Kozlov's mission was to hold the river line and prevent the Germans from advancing southward to Nal'chik. In Maslennikov's center opposite LII Army Corps' 370th and 111th Infantry and 13th Panzer Divisions, Koroteev's 9th Army occupied the southern bank of the Terek

River from south of Prokhladnyi eastward to northwest of Groznyi. The 9th controlled 151st, 176th, 389th, and 417th Rifle Divisions, 62nd Naval Rifle Brigade, and 8th, 9th, and 10th Guards Rifle Brigades of Roslyi's 11th Guards Rifle Corps. Koroteev's mission was to hold the Terek River line east and west of Mozdok.

On Maslennikov's right wing opposite 3rd Panzer Division and LII Corps' screening force on Kleist's left flank, Petrov's 44th Army manned defenses along the southern bank of the Terek River from northwest of Groznyi northeastward to Kizliar. Petrov's army included 223rd, 414th, and 416th Rifle Divisions, 30th and 110th Cavalry Divisions, and 9th, 10th, 60th, 84th, and 256th Rifle Brigades. The two cavalry divisions and three armored trains patrolled the railroad from Kizliar northward to Astrakhan'. Maslennikov's sizeable reserves, consisting of 5th, 6th, and 7th Guards Rifle Brigades of Zamertsev's 10th Guards Rifle Corps, 89th and 347th Rifle Divisions, 52nd Tank Brigade, and 249th and 258th Separate Tank Battalions, were concentrated in the depths along the Ordzhonikidze and Groznyi axes.[94] In addition, the *Stavka* transferred Kirichenko's 4th Guards Cavalry Corps from the mountains north of Tuapse and subordinated it to Maslennikov's group, replacing it with 328th and 408th Rifle Divisions from 45th and 58th Armies. Kirichenko's cavalry corps was to operate against the forces on the Germans' extended left flank in the Kalmyk Steppe south of Elista.

By virtue of these measures, by 1 September Maslennikov's forces outnumbered Kleist's in terms of manpower, although Kleist's forces were still superior by a factor of greater than two-to-one in tanks. However, Maslennikov mistakenly distributed his forces unevenly across the entire front, leaving only one rifle division and two rifle brigades with 45 tanks to protect the Mozdok-Malgobek axis against a German attack force of two panzer divisions and one infantry division with 191 tanks.[95] Because of *Stavka's* careful marshalling of forces, however, any further advance by Kleist's armor would be no cakewalk.

The Novorossiisk and Taman' Operations, 19 August–11 September

As Kleist's panzer spearheads pressed on toward Mozdok, Nal'chik, and beyond, *Armeegruppe* Ruoff resumed its advance on 19 August. Seventeenth Army's V Corps delivered the *armeegruppe's* main effort against the port city of Novorossiisk, and Romanian Cavalry Corps, supported by one German and one Romanian division attacking from the Crimea, conducted a secondary attack farther west to clear Soviet forces from the Taman' Peninsula (see Map 81).

Ruoff's offensive plan called for General Wilhelm Wetzel's V Army Corps to play a vital role in the operation. The corps' 125th and 198th Infantry Divisions were to press southward from the Krasnodar region toward the crest of the western Caucasus Mountains, while the corps' 9th and 73rd Infantry Divisions, with 64 tanks and assault guns, later joined by the 125th Infantry Division, swung westward along the railroad line through Abinskaia and Krymskaia to assault

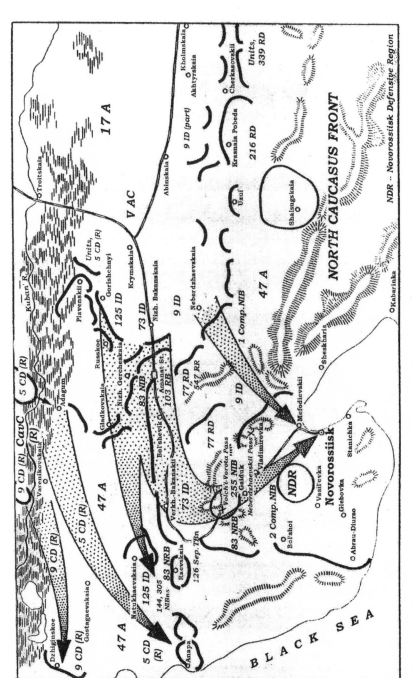

Map 81. The Novorossiisk–Taman' operation, 19 August–11 September 1942

Novorossiisk from the north. Farther west, 5th, 6th, and 9th Cavalry Divisions of General Racovita's Romanian Cavalry Corps were to cross the Kuban' River between Krasnodar and the river's mouth at Temriuk and advance on the port of Anapa on the Black Sea coast. Farther west, German 46th Infantry and Romanian 3rd Mountain Divisions of XXXXII Mountain Corps (from Eleventh Army) were to cross Kerch' Strait from the Crimea and advance southward and eastward, the former to capture Taman' city and the latter to link up with Romanian cavalry after they crossed the Kuban' River.[96] An experienced commander, Wetzel had led his corps since 12 January 1942.

After German forces captured Krasnodar on 15 August, Coastal Operational Group's 18th, 12th, and 56th Armies began withdrawing southward toward the foothills of the western Caucasus Mountains. At the same time, the *Stavka* assigned responsibility for defending the Taman' region to the Black Sea Fleet's ground force of several naval rifle battalions and ordered Kotov's 47th Army to shift its forces eastward to defend Novorossiisk. As a result, the *Stavka* disbanded Cherevichenko's Coastal Operational Group on 17 August because it was no longer a coherent body. By this time, Kamkov's 18th, Grechko's 12th, and Ryzhov's 56th Armies were conducting a fighting withdrawal into new defenses along the crest of the High Caucasus Mountains south of Krasnodar and Maikop to protect the approaches to Tuapse. As 47th Army withdrew to defenses protecting the approaches to Novorossiisk, a 40-kilometer-wide gap formed between the 47th and 56th Army on its right, isolating the former in the Novorossiisk region.

Determined to hold firm to its vital naval base, the *Stavka* on 18 August established the Novorossiisk Defensive Region (NDR). Consisting of seven distinct defensive sectors, it encompassed the entire Taman' Peninsula, the region south of the Kuban' River and west of the Krymskaia River, and the Novorossiisk region. This order assigned Kotov's 47th Army responsibility for the NDR's defense, with Vice Admiral Sergei Georgievich Gorshkov, commander of the Azov Military Flotilla (and commander of the Soviet Navy after 1956), as his deputy. Kotov's forces included his own 47th Army, 56th Army's 216th Rifle Division, naval infantry forces subordinate to the Black Sea Fleet, and the Azov Military Flotilla, supported by a mixed aviation group consisting of 237th Aviation Division and aircraft from the Black Sea fleet.[97] Kotov's 47th Army consisted of 77th and 216th Rifle Divisions, 103rd Rifle, 83rd Naval Rifle, and 1st Mixed Naval Infantry Brigades, and 126th Separate Tank Battalion, with 36 tanks, for a total force of roughly 15,000 men. With these forces, Kotov's NDR was to "prevent the enemy from penetrating into Novorossiisk from the ground and the sea."[98] Although sapper and construction forces were to build fortifications throughout the defensive region, in particular in and around the city, most of this work was incomplete when German forces began their offensive.

By day's end on 19 August, Kotov had allocated specific forces to defend each of the NDR's seven defensive sectors:

- 1st Sector—216th Rifle Division deployed in the Shapsugskaia region, 20 kilometers northeast of Novorossiisk, to protect the northeastern approaches to Novorossiisk;
- 2nd Sector—1st Mixed Naval Infantry Brigade deployed in the Neberdzhaevskaia region, 18 kilometers north of Novorossiisk, to defend the northern approaches to Novorossiisk;
- 3rd Sector—77th Rifle Division and 547th Rifle Regiment deployed in the Verkhne-Bakanskii region, 21 kilometers northwest of Novorossiisk, to protect the Volch'i Vorota Pass, 18 kilometers north of Novorossiisk;
- 4th Sector—83rd Naval Rifle Brigade, first defending the Taman' coast and, after 21 August, deployed in the Krymskaia, Kievskoe, and Gladkovskaia region south of the Kuban' River, 18–30 kilometers west of Abinskaia, backed up by 126th Separate Tank Battalion;
- 5th Sector—144th and 35th Separate Naval Infantry Battalions and 40th Separate Gun Artillery Battalion defending the Kurka River from Krasnyi Oktiabr' to Kalabatka, northeast of the mouth of the Kuban' River;
- 6th Sector—Novorossiisk Naval Base contingent defending the Black Sea coast from Fal'shivyi Gelendzhik, 30 kilometers east of Novorossiisk through Novorossiisk to Anapa, 50 kilometers west of Novorossiisk; and
- 7th Sector—Kerch' Naval Base contingent, with 305th Separate Naval Infantry Battalion and two batteries of 40th Separate Gun Artillery Battalion protecting the coast of the Taman' Peninsula.[99]

Serving as a forward security force for 1st, 2nd, 4th, and 5th Sectors, 103rd Rifle Brigade deployed company- to battalion-size outposts from Abinskaia, 36 kilometers northeast of Novorossiisk, northward to Troitskoe on the Kuban' River, with its main force at Abinskaia.

The forces of *Armeegruppe* Ruoff began their offensive on 19 August, when 9th and 73rd Infantry Divisions of V Corps pushed westward from the Krasnodar region toward Abinskaia, capturing several villages but failing to push 103rd Rifle Brigade out of Abinskaia. Simultaneously, Romanian Cavalry Corps' 5th, 6th, and 9th Cavalry Divisions captured Troitskoe from one of 103rd Rifle Brigade's company outposts but failed to secure the railroad station at Krymskaia by an attack from the march. Frustrated in its drive toward the south, Romanian 5th Cavalry Division then wheeled westward along the northern bank of the Kuban' River and advanced toward Temriuk on the coast of the Sea of Azov, capturing Krasnyi Oktiabr' from 144th Separate Naval Infantry Battalion and pushing westward 10 kilometers to Kurchanskaia, 10 kilometers from Temriuk.

Lacking significant reserves, the Azov Military Flotilla formed a mixed infantry battalion of 500 men to defend Kurchanskaia and, together with naval gunfire, halted 5th Cavalry Division's advance, inflicting heavy losses on the Romanians. Romanian Cavalry Corps responded by conducting a general assault with its 9th Cavalry Division, which, after heavy fighting, forced 144th and 305th

Major General Petr Mikhailovich Kozlov, commander of 37th Army

Major General Trofim Kalinovich Kolomiets, commander of 51st Army

Major General Aleksandr Ivanovich Ryzhov, commander of 56th Army

Major General Nikolai Iakovlevich Kirichenko, commander of 17th (4th Guards) Cavalry Corps

Major General Grigorii Petrovich Kotov,
commander of 46th Army

Major General Vasilii Fadeevich
Sergatskov, commander of 46th Army

Major General Konstantin Nikolaevich
Leselidze, commander if 46th Army

Major General Fedor Nikitich Remezov,
commander of 45th Army

Major General Feofan Agonovich
Parkhomenko, commander of 9th Army

Naval Infantry Battalions to abandon Temriuk and withdraw westward and southward by day's end on 23 August.[100]

When V Army Corps resumed its assaults on Krymskaia on 21 August, Kotov deployed 83rd Naval Rifle Brigade and 126th Separate Tank Battalion, supported by the "Death to German Occupiers" Armored Train, into the region. However, V Corps' 9th Infantry Division overcame 103rd Rifle and 83rd Naval Rifle Brigades' defenses at Abinskaia and Krymskaia by late on 21 August, forcing the two brigades to fall back toward the Mikhailovskii, Babicha, Kabardinskii, Neberdzhaevskaia, and Volch'i Vorota Passes, 7–15 kilometers north of Novorossiisk.[101] Gorshkov then raised several special naval detachments, which, with 142nd Separate Naval Infantry Battalion, deployed forward to defend the passes as ships of the Black Sea Fleet prepared to provide fire support. To the east, V Corps' 73rd Infantry Division captured Neberdzhaevskaia Station and Nizhne-Bakanskii, 12 kilometers north of Novorossiisk, from 103rd Rifle Brigade on 23 August after a two-day fight, permitting German artillery to fire on the port and city of Novorossiisk.[102]

Farther west, after determining that the Soviets were withdrawing the bulk of their forces from the Taman' Peninsula to reinforce Novorossiisk, Romanian Cavalry Corps accelerated its advance and ultimately captured the port of Anapa on 1 September. The same day, German 46th Infantry Division and Romanian 3rd Mountain Division crossed Kerch' Strait and, several days later, captured Taman'.

Faced with an imminent German advance on Novorossiisk, Budenny and Kotov on 25 August moved forcefully to reinforce its defenses by forming the new 255th Naval Infantry Brigade from sailors of the Black Sea Fleet. Commanded by Lieutenant Colonel D. V. Gordeev and consisting of three naval infantry battalions, the brigade was to defend the Neberdzhaevskaia-Novorossiisk road and adjacent heights, while Kotov raised another unnumbered ersatz naval infantry battalion and sent it to reinforce the defenses at Anapa to the west.[103]

Not content to remain passive, in accordance with Kotov's orders, 77th Rifle Division launched a counterattack against a regiment of V Corps' 125th Infantry Division, which had just reinforced 73rd Infantry Division in the Neberdzhaev-skaia sector, on 25 August. Although this assault recaptured the railroad station, 77th Rifle Division was ultimately forced to withdraw first to its jumping-off positions, then even farther to the rear, after suffering heavy losses.[104] After reinforcing 73rd and 9th Infantry Divisions with the entire 125th Infantry Division, Ruoff's forces resumed their offensive on 29 August, this time along two converging axes (Nizhne-Bakanskii and Neberdzhaevskaia), with support provided by about 50 assault guns from 249th Assault Gun Brigade.

Although the defending 83rd Naval Rifle Brigade parried 9th Infantry Division's assault along the eastern axis to Neberdzhaevskaia, 73rd and 125th Infantry Divisions forced 103rd Rifle Brigade to withdraw 3–5 kilometers along the Nizhne-Bakanskii axis.[105] By this time, the Romanian cavalry was advancing toward Anapa, cutting off 47th Army's forces defending the Novorossiisk region from the naval infantry defending the Taman' Peninsula and forcing the Azov Flotilla to evacuate as many of these forces as possible to Novorossiisk by sea.[106]

Faced with this deteriorating situation, the *Stavka* undertook vigorous measures to shore up the defenses around Novorossiisk. First, on 30 August Moscow reiterated its previous orders demanding Kotov's army defend Novorossiisk "at all costs."[107] Then, on 1 September it reorganized forces in the Caucasus region, transforming North Caucasus Front (and its 12th, 18th, 47th, and 56th Armies) into the Black Sea Group of Forces under Cherevichenko and assigning the group to Tiulenev's Trans-Caucasus Front (see above). In the wake of this transformation, Kotov's army, now reinforced by 318th Rifle Division from the new *front*'s reserve, was to hold firm to Novorossiisk, in particular, the defense line passing through Neberdzhaevskaia and Verkhne-Bakanskii north and northwest of the city.[108] In addition, before relinquishing command of his *front,* Budenny on 1 September reinforced Kotov's army with 16th Rifle Brigade, two battalions of its 81st Naval Rifle Brigade, and a separate naval infantry regiment from Grechko's 12th Army.[109]

Wetzel's V Corps began its final assault on Novorossiisk's defenses on 1 September with 9th, 73rd, and 125th Infantry Divisions attacking southward along the Neberdzhaevskaia, Verkhne-Bakanskii, and Raevskii axes toward the passes north and northwest of Novorossiisk. Kotov's army defended with its 255th Naval Infantry Brigade protecting the Neberdzhaevskaia axis, 83rd Naval Infantry Brigade and 16th Naval Infantry Battalion, backed up by 77th Rifle Division and 103rd Rifle Brigade, defending the Verkhne-Bakanskii axis and the Volch'i Vorota Pass, and 144th and 305th Naval Infantry Battalions defending the Raevskii axis northwest of the city.[110] During this fight, the advancing 9th Infantry Division encircled part of 255th Naval Infantry Brigade. 73rd Infantry Division did likewise to 77th Rifle Division and 103rd Rifle Brigade in the Volch'i Vorota Pass, although Russian sources claim most of the encircled forces were able to fight to freedom.

On 7 September, after six days of heavy fighting, during which Grechko replaced Kotov as 47th Army commander, V Corps' three infantry divisions finally penetrated into the northern portion of the city, capturing the railroad station and the port facilities. Not until 10 September, however, was this corps formally able to announce the city was under its control.[111] The day before, Grechko had ordered the Black Sea Fleet to remove its ships from the port to safer bases farther south. Thereafter, fierce and costly fighting continued in the factory and industrial districts adjacent to the city's suburbs until 26 September. However, after reaching the cement factory south of the city on 11 September, the front line did not budge from that spot until late December, when the Germans began abandoning the Kuban' region.

Despite its inherent weaknesses, Kotov's army had managed to conduct a resolute defense of the city and port of Novorossiisk, forcing Ruoff to reinforce V Corps with the bulk of the Romanian forces subordinate to his *armeegruppe*. Although his forces finally captured the city, the German effort was slow and costly and prevented List from shifting any forces from the Novorossiisk sector to reinforce the more vital drives across the Caucasus Mountains and deeper into the oil-rich regions with troops, supplies, and air support. By Soviet count, Ruoff's forces lost 14,000 men, 47 tanks, and 95 guns and mortars in the German offensive against Novorossiisk, although Kotov's army undoubtedly suffered far heavier casualties.[112] At least in part, the difficulties involved in capturing Novorossiisk also adversely affected the efforts by Seventeenth Army's XXXXIV Army and XXXXIX Mountain Corps during their twin advances across the Caucasus Mountains toward Tuapse and Sukhumi on the Black Sea coast by diverting forces, including 125th Infantry Division, from the effort.

The Battle for the Caucasus Mountain Passes, 16 August–September

As the infantry of Wetzel's V Army Corps struggled to capture the Taman' Peninsula and Novorossiisk, and Kleist's panzers maneuvered forward into Mozdok, General Konrad's XXXXIX Mountain Corps, after regrouping its 1st and 4th Mountain Divisions and Romanian 2nd Mountain Division into the Cherkessk region, stunned Budenny's North Caucasus Front with a sudden thrust into the mountains to the south (see Map 82). Rudolf Konrad, who was assigned command of his mountain corps on 19 December 1941 at age 50, was an experienced general who had been chief of staff of XVIII Army Corps and of Second Army from 1938 through 1940, a liaison officer to the *Luftwaffe* commander in 1940–1941, and commander of 7th Mountain Division during Operation Barbarossa.[113]

By day's end on 16 August, Konrad's mountain troops had reached Klukhori

Pass, which at the time was defended by only two Soviet rifle companies from 394th Rifle Division's 815th Regiment.[114] This position threatened the road to the port of Sukhumi and therefore the entire Soviet defense north of that point along the Black Sea coast.[115] Still farther northwest, LVII Panzer Corps' SS "Viking" and Slovak Motorized Divisions remained south of Maikop, supporting the ongoing efforts by 97th and 101st Jäger Divisions of Seventeenth Army's XXXXIV Army Corps to penetrate through the mountains to the Black Sea coast at Tuapse.

Trans-Caucasus Front entrusted 46th Army with the task of defending the central sector of the Caucasus Mountains, in particular the roads leading through the mountain passes to Sukhumi and Ochemchiri. Commanded by Major General Vasilii Fadeevich Sergatskov until 27 August and Lieutenant General Konstantin Nikolaevich Leselidze thereafter, 46th Army on 1 August consisted of 9th and 20th Mountain Rifle Divisions of Leselidze's 3rd Mountain Rifle Corps, 389th, 392nd, 394th, and 406th Rifle Divisions, 155th Rifle Brigade, 63rd Cavalry Division, 51st Fortified Region, 12th Separate Tank Battalion, and four armored train battalions. In late June 1942, Trans-Caucasus Front had instructed 46th Army to protect the passes through which the Ossetian and Sukhumi Military Roads ran through the High Caucasus Mountains and also required the army to defend the adjacent Black Sea coast.[116] Finally, to shore up 46th Army's defenses, 7th NKVD Rifle Division also operated in the army's sector.

Because 46th Army had insufficient forces to defend the 275-kilometer-wide mountain front, and its senior commanders believed many of the mountain passes were impassable for military forces, they neglected to construct adequate defenses therein. The few sapper forces available in this region were unable to build necessary fortifications by mid-August. 3rd Mountain Rifle Corps' 9th and 20th Mountain Divisions and 394th Rifle and 63rd Cavalry Divisions, which were responsible for defending the passes, kept their main forces on the western slopes and dispatched only small detachments lacking adequate knowledge of the terrain forward into the mountains. In addition, the army failed to conduct necessary reconnaissance in the mountains and had poor communications with and control over its forces. Making matters worse, Trans-Caucasus Front neglected the defenses in the mountain passes, and the *Stavka* focused its attentions on the Terek River sector, shifting forces and reinforcements to that region instead of the mountains. As a result, by mid-August most of the passes were defended by company- and battalion-size forces; some had no defenses at all.[117]

Another major reason for the initial German success in this region, and the slow development of effective Soviet defensive planning, was the interference in operational planning by Stalin's henchman Lavrenti Beriia. Acting as a representative of the *Stavka*, Beriia frequently disrupted the smooth operations of the North Caucasus and Trans-Caucasus Fronts by questioning and often changing the *front* and army commanders' decisions.

Only after 10 August did the *front* and *Stavka* begin to pay adequate attention

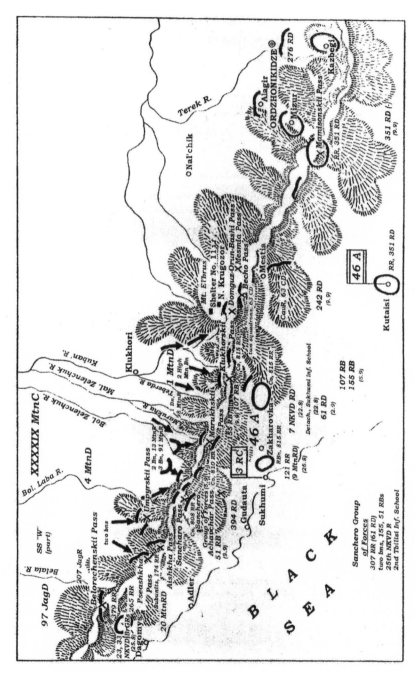

Map 82. The battle for the Caucasus Mountain passes, 16 August–September 1942

to the dangers of a German advance through the mountains. At that time, besides reinforcing their garrisons in the passes, 20th Mountain and 394th Rifle Divisions increased the depth of their defenses in the passes by sending platoon- and company-sized reconnaissance detachments up to 20 kilometers forward of the passes. At the same time, the *front* ordered 46th Army to form ten detachments numbering 50–150 men each from reserve and local NKVD troops capable of operating in the mountains separate from the army's main forces. However, the army was slow in implementing this order. Because they were inexperienced in mountain operations, when deployed forward these detachments failed to conduct reconnaissance and organize all-around defenses, instead operating in weak linear formations.

As late as 16 August, the day after a battalion of 394th Rifle Division's 815th Regiment was engaged by the advancing Germans along the approaches to Klukhori Pass, 46th Army reported, "The situation at the front is unchanged."[118] In fact, the news of this encounter did not reach army headquarters until 17 August. Similar incidents occurred throughout this sector when, from 17 August through 9 September, German forces either preempted 46th Army by occupying several passes or routed small detachments defending other passes in the sector from Mount El'brus westward to the Umpyr Pass and sent forces 10–25 kilometers west of Klukhori and Sancharo Passes to threaten Sukhumi.

On 12 August OKW had subordinated Konrad's XXXXIX Mountain Corps to Seventeenth Army and assigned it the mission of capturing the passes through the central and eastern portion of the High Caucasus Mountains and Mount El'brus. According to Konrad's plan, on the corps' left wing, 1st Mountain Division was to seize the passes at the headwaters of the Teberda and Kuban' Rivers, while its left flank battalion secured the Baksan River valley and Mount El'brus. On the corps' right wing, 4th Mountain Division was to capture the passes at the headwaters of the Bol'shaia Laba River. The divisions were to lead the advance with small mobile advanced detachments, employing trucks during the initial advance and, thereafter, pack animals to transport equipment.[119]

Shifting rapidly southeastward, the forward elements of the two mountain divisions reached the Cherkessk region by 11 August; 1st Mountain Division reached the town of Mikoian Shakhar, the gateway to the mountains on Teberda River south of Cherkessk, the following day, encountering only feeble resistance. Thrusting forward without delay, 1st Mountain Division's advanced detachments captured the town of Teberda, 30 kilometers south of Mikoian Shakhar, on 14 August after a short fight, Klukhori Pass on 17 August, and Khotiu-Tai Pass and Mount El'brus from 19 through 21 August, virtually without a fight.[120] This thrust encountered and overcame elements of 1st Battalion, 815th Regiment, of 46th Army's 394th Rifle Division. Pushing into the mountains from the east, also in advanced detachment configuration, 4th Mountain Division's forces thrust southward along the Bol'shaia Laba River valley toward Klukhori, Khotiu-Tai, Nakhar, and Naur Passes from 18 to 22 August.[121]

Initially, Sergatskov's 46th Army reinforced its defenses west of Klukhori Pass with 3rd Battalion of 815th Regiment, 394th Rifle Division's training battalion, detachments from the Sukhumi Infantry School, and 7th NKVD Division. These forces reached the area on 22 August, in sufficient time to halt the German advance 10–12 kilometers west of the pass. Because these forces were strong enough to contain the German advance but too weak to drive it back, Sergatskov rushed reinforcements to the region. By 26 August these included 3rd Battalion of 394th Rifle Division's 810th Regiment and 9th Mountain Rifle Division's 121st Regiment. Although these forces successfully parried several thrusts by 1st Mountain Division, subsequent counterattacks failed because the Soviet troops conducted them frontally.[122]

By the beginning of the last week of August 1942, the sudden advance by the German mountain troops had finally galvanized the *Stavka* and the *front* into forming a more rational plan of defense in the key mountain region. Alarmed by news of the Germans' preemptive advance, Tiulenev himself on 19 August traveled to Sukhumi, where he remained until 28 August, organizing the defenses of the already lost passes in person, in particular at Klukhori Pass. The following day the *Stavka* issued a blistering directive criticizing the *front*'s and army's efforts and demanding Tiulenev take immediate action to organize credible defenses along the crest of the High Caucasus Mountains, focusing primarily on the Georgian, Ossetian, and Sukhumi Military Roads and the passes they traversed.[123] Tiulenev then assigned responsibility for defending each road and its associated passes to specific 46th Army forces. He also ordered his air forces to constantly reconnoiter these roads and passes and directed the *front*'s 27th Engineer Brigade to erect obstacles and barriers along the roads and adjacent to the approaches to the passes. To ensure better control over the defending forces, Tiulenev instructed 46th Army headquarters to displace to Sukhumi, reinforced Sergatskov's army with 61st Rifle Division from 45th Army (in the deep rear), and directed Sergatskov to organize special detachments to operate independently along specific mountain axes.

Once these measures took effect, Sergatskov's forces defended as follows:

- East of the Georgian Military Highway and the Krestovyi Pass—16 detachments made up of rifle companies, machine gun and mortar platoons, and sapper squads formed from reserve units and military schools;
- Krestovyi Pass—the *front*'s junior lieutenants course;
- Ossetian Military Road—351st Rifle Division;
- El'brus axis and nearby passes—242nd Mountain Division;
- Klukhori and Marukh Passes and the Sukhumi Military Road—394th Rifle Division;
- Sancharo Pass—51st Rifle Brigade; and
- Pseashkha and Belorechenskii Passes—20th Mountain Rifle Division.[124]

In turn, each of these forces organized special company- and battalion-size mountain detachments to reinforce key threatened sectors, as well as mobile platoon- and company-sized sapper and engineer detachments to forestall maneuver along the roads and mountain paths by German forces. Once Beriia ceased his interference, on 27 August the *Stavka* relieved Sergatskov of command for "not being able to cope with his work," replacing him with General Leselidze, commander of 3rd Rifle Corps.[125] By this time, a considerable portion of 46th Army was actively defending the Caucasus Mountains, albeit more often than not on the western slopes.

After organizing a more coherent defense along and west of the crest of the High Caucasus Mountains during the last week of August, 46th Army's forces slowly stabilized their defenses, all the while fending off repeated assaults and probing attacks by the two German mountain divisions across the entire front. The most threatening attack took place along the Sukhumi Military Road and the approaches to the vital Marukh Pass. After commencing operations on 2 September, Group Eisgruber (1st Battalion of 1st Mountain Division's 98th Regiment and 2nd High Mountain Battalion) assaulted 394th Rifle Division's defenses at the pass on 5 September and captured the pass from the rifle division's 808th and 810th Regiments on 7 September. In response, Leselidze reinforced 394th Rifle Division with three battalions from 155th and 107th Rifle Brigades and the 2nd Tbilisi Infantry School. However, a counterattack by these forces on 9 September failed to dislodge the Germans, as did three more counterattacks in October.[126]

Farther west, Group Stettner (2nd Battalion, 13th Regiment, and 3rd Battalion, 91st Regiment) of 4th Mountain Division attacked the company-sized defenses from 394th Rifle Division's 808th Regiment and a mixed detachment from 7th NKVD Rifle Division at Sancharo Pass on 25 August, capturing the pass. To counter this thrust, 46th Army created the Sancharo Group of Forces made up of 61st Rifle Division's 307th Regiment, two battalions of 155th and 51st Rifle Brigades, 25th NKVD Border Guards Regiment, a mixed NKVD Regiment, and a detachment from the 2nd Tbilisi Infantry School. The army ordered the group to recapture the pass.[127]

Meanwhile, another detachment from 2nd Battalion, 13th Regiment, 4th Mountain Division, attacked toward the nearby village of Pskhu on 29 August, only to be halted by the approaching mixed NKVD Regiment. When a subsequent attempt to encircle and destroy this German force failed, the Sancharo Group mounted an even stronger assault on the pass on 6 September. It recaptured Pskhu but failed to take the pass. Ultimately, it took until 20 October for the Sancharo Group to recapture Sancharo Pass.[128]

The 46th Army's defense of the Umpyr Pass was a bit more skillful. Initially, in heavy fighting on 28 August, two companies of 20th Mountain Rifle Division managed to fend off an assault by two battalions of 4th Mountain Division. However, 4th Mountain then organized an enveloping attack from the valleys of the Umpyr and Bol'shaia Laba Rivers and captured Umpyr Pass on 31 August but failed to seize Pseashkha Pass. Thereafter, 20th Mountain Rifle Division's 174th Regiment managed to hold the Germans at bay.[129]

Finally, farther west, from 20 through 25 August, 20th Mountain Rifle Division's 379th Regiment fought with elements of 97th Jäger Division's 207th Regiment along the approaches to Belorechenskii Pass south of Maikop. During this fighting, 46th Army reinforced this sector with 23rd and 33rd NKVD Border Guards Regiments, which, in heavy counterattacks after 25 August, drove the *jägers* back from the mountain crests by 10 October.[130]

By the end of the first week of September, the forces of Leselidze's 46th Army had regained the initiative in the High Caucasus and succeeded in driving German forces back toward the passes, reaching the western end of Klukhori Pass by midmonth. Thereafter, a combination of Soviet offensive action to recapture the lost mountain passes and the approaching winter snows frustrated all hopes the Germans harbored for reaching the Black Sea coast and Georgia beyond. As one German account noted:

> From mid- to the end of September, the Soviets increased the pressure against the defenses on the high ridges. Several forward positions had to be given up. Then, after many days of rain and fog, the mountain winter arrived. Combat operations froze in the frost and snow. Based on the weather conditions in the high mountains, the German leadership [command] came up with a new plan:
>
> 1. The main ridges could be defended with fewer troops.
> 2. Therefore, half of the forces of XXXXIX Mountain Corps could be freed up to break through to Tuapse.
> 3. The breakthrough would be into the Caucasus Forest [southwest of Maikop], where winter would not arrive until five weeks later.
>
> In accordance with this plan, battalions from the two mountain divisions were marched into the Caucasus Forest, so that there were practically only two gebirgsjäger regiments holding the entire corps front.[131]

Although the bold thrust by the two divisions of Konrad's XXXXIX Mountain Corps came close to achieving its objectives, once again rapid action by the *Stavka* and Trans-Caucasus Front averted disaster—albeit narrowly. Skillfully mimicking armor tactics in the steppe by maneuvering small mobile detachments through narrow valleys and mountain defiles, the German mountain troops achieved spectacular feats by reaching and capturing many of the vital Caucasus passes. Once 46th Army reacted forcefully, however, the defenders proved that, by exploiting similar terrain factors, equally determined small forces could check the advancing German forces. However successful the German troops were in capturing these passes, such feats were irrelevant unless they could sustain their operations to the Black Sea coast. By mid-September, it was clear they could not.[132]

THE NORTHERN FLANK

Voronezh Déjà Vu

While Army Group B battered itself to pieces at Stalingrad and Army Group A fell a few battalions short of total success in the Caucasus, Army Groups Center and North were beset with their own problems. As illustrated in Chapters 5 and 6, during July both sides had planned limited offensives in these areas to straighten out front lines. Tactically, neither side achieved its goals, and the Red Army suffered additional defeats. In the broader operational and strategic context, however, a series of Soviet attacks from late July through August helped strain German troop strength and logistics to the breaking point, tying down precious divisions at a time when they were desperately needed near Stalingrad. As such, these operations were important precursors to the ultimate Soviet victory at Stalingrad. Moreover, the very existence of such attacks—however unsuccessful—calls into question the traditional German view that the Red Army deliberately avoided decisive engagement in sectors other than Stalingrad and the Caucasus during summer 1942.

If perseverance alone ensured success, then Briansk and Voronezh Fronts would be the champions of the German-Soviet conflict. The series of counterstrokes and counterattacks the Red Army launched around Voronezh in early July continued almost without pause through late September. General Chibisov, deputy commander of Briansk Front, had already failed in July to break through around Voronezh—that is, the northern shoulder of the entire German advance for 1942. In early August, however, the *Stavka* provided Briansk Front with new forces, blending 4th Reserve Army with survivors of Chibisov's former operational group to create a resurrected 38th Army under Chibisov's command. The new 38th Army was a powerful formation, combining six rifle divisions and seven rifle brigades with an imposing array of four tank and one cavalry corps (1st, 2nd, 7th, and 11th Tank and 8th Cavalry) fielding a total force of more than 400 tanks.[133]

On 3 August the *Stavka* directed that Chibisov's army would attack southward along the western bank of the Don River on 8 August. Simultaneous thrusts by Cherniakhovsky's 60th and Popov's 40th Armies of Voronezh Front would support Chibisov by attacking westward across the Don north and south of Voronezh to link up with Chibisov's forces west of the city. As before, the goal was to seize Voronezh and destroy the so-called German Zemliansk Grouping, which consisted of VII Army Corps' 340th, 385th, 387th, 168th, 57th, 75th, and 323rd

Infantry Divisions.[134] However, the *Stavka's* real intent in ordering this offensive was to relieve pressure on its 4th Tank Army, which was attempting to defend Stalingrad Front's final lodgment in the northeast sector of the Great Bend of the Don River by tying down German forces and their forces the Voronezh region.

To accomplish these tasks, Chibisov formed three shock groups, each consisting of a tank corps with a rifle division, two rifle brigades, and additional artillery either attached to the group or under the army's operational control (see Map 83). Each tank corps commander was to control both his own armor as his exploitation force and an assault force of infantry, infantry support tanks, artillery, and sappers. On Chibisov's right (western) wing, Rotmistrov's 7th Tank Corps fielded 173 tanks, controlled 240th Rifle Division and two rifle brigades, and was supported by seven artillery and four guards-mortar regiments. This corps was to deliver 38th Army's main attack southward through Malaia Vereika and, finally, Zemliansk, cutting off the retreat of the four German infantry divisions that defended the salient located in the front northwest of Voronezh. Simultaneously, on Rotmistrov's left, Lazarev's 11th Tank Corps with 98 tanks, supported by 237th Rifle Division and two rifle brigades, was to attack in the center. Katukov's veteran 1st Tank Corps, with 108 tanks plus 167th Rifle Division and one rifle brigade in support, was to advance on the left. Lazarev's and Katukov's shock groups were to converge on Zemliansk from the northeast and east. Colonel Lunev's reinforced 8th Cavalry Corps, with three cavalry divisions and two rifle brigades, was to tie down German forces on Chibisov's right flank and screen the advance during the exploitation.[135]

This formidable concentration of forces, supported by additional attacks from Voronezh Front to the east, should have been sufficient to crush the three German infantry divisions in the area, especially considering that all available panzer forces had been siphoned off to support other operations. Unfortunately for the Soviets, Chibisov's August offensive suffered the same problems that plagued his previous efforts. The five days (3–7 August) initially allocated for preparation proved woefully inadequate to mount such an operation given the limited experience and logistical support of the force and the continued *Luftwaffe* interdiction of supply lines. Although Rokossovsky as *front* commander won a postponement, the operation was nonetheless ill-prepared when it stepped off on 12 August.

After a brief but intense 13-minute artillery preparation, Chibisov's shock groups managed to penetrate the Germans' first defensive positions, advancing up to 1.5 kilometers into the carefully constructed German defensive web before bogging down. Repeated attempts to revive the offensive on 13 August failed when the Germans brought up fresh infantry reserves and pounded Chibisov's forces with an intense aerial bombardment. Nor did Chibisov's shock groups prove capable of coordinating tanks and infantry skillfully enough to break the stalemate. For example, when 104th Rifle Brigade of Katukov's shock group

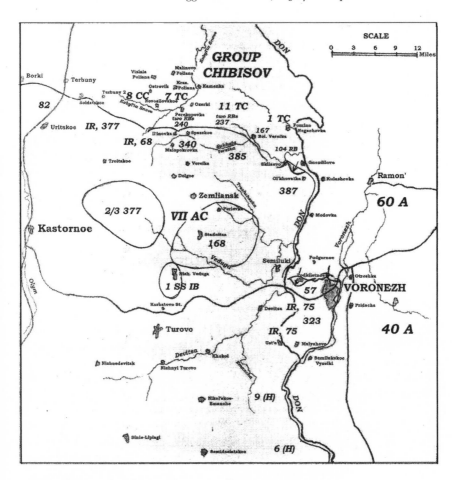

Map 83. The Briansk and Voronezh Fronts' offensive, 12–15 August 1942

bogged down, an inexperienced tank brigade commander, sent to support the infantry, blundered into battle without reconnaissance and suffered heavy losses. In another instance, a tank detachment was unable to eliminate the German strongpoint in Kaver'e, east of Zemliansk, because the tanks trying to clear the village were unsupported by infantry.[136] Because the attacks by Cherniakhovsky's 60th and Popov's 40th Armies on German defenses at and east of Voronezh also failed, the *Stavka* ordered Rokossovsky to halt his futile offensive late on 15 August.[137]

The most that can be said for its August offensive was that the *Stavka* had learned not to continue attacks that had obviously failed. After ordering Rokossovsky's forces to cease their offensive, the *Stavka* withdrew two of his three tank corps (7th and 2nd) into its reserve to rest and refit, while Chibisov's remaining forces dug in to defend their slender gains.[138] In addition to failing to attract German reserves from elsewhere on the front, Rokossovsky's offensive certainly did not deter German Sixth Army's further advance since Paulus unleashed a massive assault against 4th Tank Army's defenses in the northeast sector of the Great Bend on 15 August. More ominous for Paulus, on 30 August the *Stavka* also withdrew Katukov's 1st Tank Corps into its reserve, assigning it, together with 26th Tank Corps and 119th Rifle Division, to its reorganized 5th Tank Army, which Stalin kept under his direct operational control.[139] The next time the Germans would encounter 5th Tank Army and its 1st Tank Corps would be 19 November—to their everlasting regret.

The Struggle for the Rzhev Salient, 30 July–23 August

As the forces of Army Groups A and B thrust deep into the Great Bend and the Caucasus in southern Russia during July and August, Stalin and his advisers could not shake their belief that the Germans would eventually resume their offensive against Moscow. Therefore, the Red Army kept many of its most capable units in Kalinin and Western Fronts, which had the task of defending Moscow against Field Marshal Guenther von Kluge's Army Group Center. In May and July 1942, for example, Kluge's army group had launched a series of limited operations to reduce and disperse major Soviet forces isolated within several large pockets behind its front lines during the fighting the previous winter. The May offensive, code-named Operation Hannover, eliminated General P. A. Belov's Cavalry Group and cooperating airborne forces from the Viaz'ma region in Army Group Center's rear west of Moscow.[140] The June offensive, Operation Seydlitz, liquidated the salient occupied by Kalinin Front's 39th Army and 11th Cavalry Corps in Army Group Center's rear area northwest of Viaz'ma.[141] Thereafter, Kluge's low-priority units waited anxiously on the defensive.

Two hundred kilometers west-northwest of Moscow lay Rzhev, a vital road and rail center on the northern bank of the Volga River, which was defended by German Ninth Army. General of Panzer Troops Heinrich-Gottfried von Vietinghoff commanded Ninth Army temporarily while its commander, General Walter Model, was on convalescent leave from wounds received during Operation Seydlitz.[142] Rzhev, situated at the northern tip of a salient jutting northeastward from the Smolensk region through Viaz'ma, was the anchor and pivot point between Army Groups Center and North. The city was also located at the boundary between Kalinin and Western Fronts, commanded by General Ivan Stepanovich Konev and General G. K. Zhukov.[143] Because Rzhev was so close to Moscow, the *Stavka* considered Rzhev and adjacent salient to form a dagger aimed at Moscow. Thus, Stalin placed Zhukov, his most trusted fighter, in command of the vital Western Front.

Therefore, on 16 July the *Stavka* authorized Western and Kalinin Fronts to conduct an offensive to eliminate part of the salient, to distract German attention and forces from their thrust toward Stalingrad, and in response to Zhukov's belief that the Moscow axis was the most decisive. The *Stavka's* directive ordered the armies on the right wing of Zhukov's *front*, in combination with those on the left wing of Konev's *front*, to smash Army Group Center's defenses at the northeastern extremity of the Rzhev-Viaz'ma salient. Specifically, Zhukov's and Konev's shock groups were "to clear the enemy from the territory in the Rzhev and Zubtsov regions north of the Volga River and the Zubtsov, Karmanovo, Pogoreloe, and Gorodishche regions east of the Vazuza River, capture Rzhev and Zubtsov, and reach and firmly consolidate positions [in bridgeheads] along the Volga and Vazuza Rivers."[144]

Kalinin Front's 30th Army, commanded by Lieutenant General Dmitrii Danilovich Leliushenko and supported by Major General Vasilii Ivanovich Shvetsov's 29th Army on its left, was to assault Ninth Army's defenses north and northeast of Rzhev on 28 July, capture the city, and drive German forces south of the Volga River.[145] Three days later, 31st and 20th Armies of Zhukov's Western Front, commanded by Major General Vitalii Sergeevich Polenov and Lieutenant General Maks Andreevich Reiter, respectively, supported by Major General Andrei Lavrent'evich Getman's and Major General Mikhail Dmitrievich Solomatin's 6th and 8th Tank Corps and Major General Vladimir Viktorovich Kriukov's 2nd Guards Cavalry Corps, were to penetrate Ninth Army's defenses north and south of Pogoreloe-Gorodishche and exploit westward to capture bridgeheads over the Vazuza River northeast and east of Sychevka and southward to capture Karmanovo.[146] As they attacked, the two shock groups would catch German forces defending north and east of Zubtsov in a massive pincer and destroy them before they could withdraw back across the Volga and Vazuza Rivers.

After delaying the start of the operation for several days to complete necessary preparations, the two *fronts* began the so-called Rzhev-Sychevka offensive with a rippling series of attacks from north to south, seeking to collapse German defenses around the Rzhev salient (see Map 84).[147] Konev's Kalinin Front began its operation with a 90-minute artillery bombardment at 0630 hours on 30 July, after which 30th and 29th Armies assaulted southward toward Rzhev. Lulled by a number of seemingly pointless Soviet troop concentrations during past encounters, the Germans were caught off-guard. Konev's initial attack tore through the understrength defenders but began to bog down as the local German commanders recovered from the surprise and as Vietinghoff dispatched reserves to the region.

Six days after Kalinin Front's initial assault, Zhukov's forces went into action at dawn on 4 August, when, after a strong artillery and air preparation, Polenov's 31st and Reiter's 20th Armies commenced their assault in the Pogoreloe-Gorodishche sector. Advancing in a 30-kilometer-wide sector, the two armies penetrated the German defenses and advanced up to 25 kilometers by day's end on 5 August. This penetration created suitable conditions for Zhukov to commit

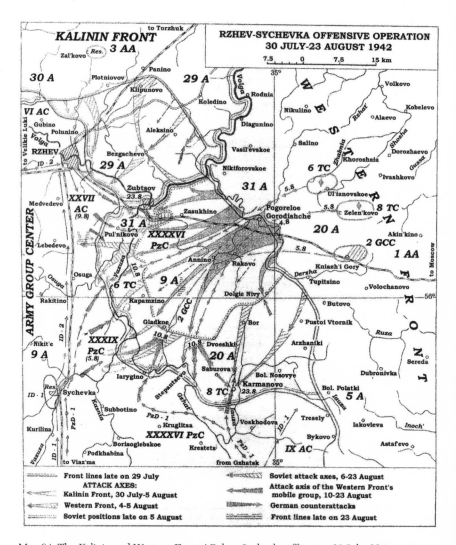

Map 84. The Kalinin and Western Fronts' Rzhev-Sychevka offensive, 30 July–23 August 1942

his *front*'s mobile group, 6th and 8th Tank and 2nd Guards Cavalry Corps, for their exploitation toward Sychevka, 55 kilometers south of Rzhev.[148] Late on 5 August, the *Stavka* gave Zhukov control over both *fronts* to ensure closer coordination.[149]

Zhukov's mobile group, which was commanded by his deputy *front* commander, Major General Ivan Vasil'evich Galanin, consisted of roughly 600 tanks, more than half of them KV-1s and T-34s.[150] This mobile group went into action on 6 August, advancing more than 50 kilometers by day's end through the remnants of the already shattered German 161st Infantry Division.[151] In addition, Zhukov committed the fresh 8th Guards Rifle Corps to reinforce his advancing mobile forces, whose mission was to force the Vazuza and Gzhat' Rivers on 6 August and capture the Osuga and Sychevka line on 7 August to sever the Rzhev-Viaz'ma railroad line and split German Ninth Army in two.[152] Zhukov's powerful assault decimated 161st Infantry Division and carved an immense gap between 2nd Panzer and 36th Motorized Divisions of Ninth Army's XXXXVI Panzer Corps, which were defending the army's right wing north of Karmanovo, and 14th Motorized Division of the army's VI Army Corps, which was defending east of Rzhev.[153] By nightfall on 6 August, Zhukov's armored spearheads were halfway to the Vazuza, contained only by 5th Panzer Division, which Vietinghoff had deployed forward to block any Soviet advance to the river.[154]

Although Hitler was focused on Stalingrad and the Caucasus, he reacted promptly to this threat, using forces previously programmed for a local counteroffensive. The 1st, 2nd, and 5th Panzer Divisions, together with 78th and 102nd Infantry Divisions and XXXIX Panzer Corps headquarters, went to Kluge with the stipulation they counterattack against the Soviet penetration from the south. However, the situation was so critical that they could not be massed for the typical panzer counterattack. Instead, Vietinghoff fed in the units piecemeal as they arrived by rail.[155] Although the German front held north of Rzhev and east of Zubtsov, it collapsed to the south, leaving the Sychevka axis unprotected and vulnerable to the advance by Zhukov's mobile group.

Needing more reinforcements, Kluge went to Hitler's headquarters on 7 August. There, however, he was surprised to learn that both Halder and Hitler believed that the Soviet offensive had run its course. Rather than reinforcing Ninth Army's defense, Hitler proposed going over to the offensive. Operation *Wirbelwind* (Whirlwind) was an existing plan to shorten the front of Army Group Center by eliminating the Soviet salient jutting westward at Kirov, about 200 kilometers south of Rzhev (see Map 85). The original plan called for Fourth Army to attack southward toward Mosal'sk at the same time that Second Panzer Army advanced northward through Ul'ianovo, on the Zhizdra River. These converging attacks would pinch off and defeat 10th and 16th Armies on Western Front's southern wing, thereby (presumably) diverting Soviet efforts away from Rzhev. Unfortunately, most of Fourth Army's units earmarked for this attack had already been diverted to the defense of Rzhev. Thus, when Kluge told his army commanders to launch *Wirbelwind* immediately, Colonel General Gotthard Heinrici, commander of Fourth Army, replied that he lacked the forces to carry it out.[156]

At Kluge's insistence, *Wirbelwind* went forward anyway, although rain delayed it until 11 August. But without the forces initially assigned to it, this offensive accomplished very little. 11th and 9th Panzer Divisions, which led the attack for Colonel General Rudolf Schmidt's Second Panzer Army, encountered the elab-

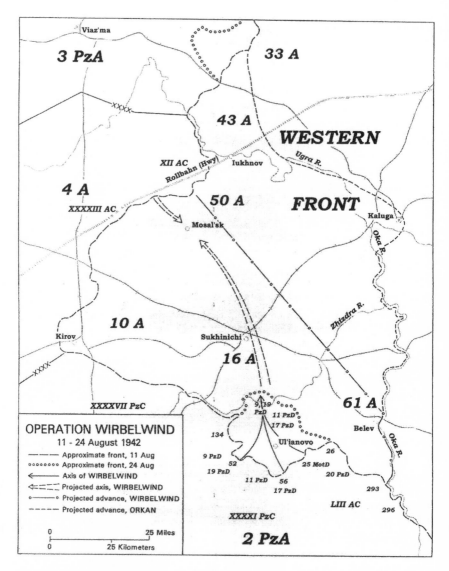

Map 85. Operation *Wirbelwind*, 11–24 August 1942

orate defensive fortifications erected by 16th Army, now commanded by General
I. K. Bagramian, the Southwestern Main Direction Command's chief of staff during the disastrous battle for Khar'kov in May (see Chapters 2 and 3).[157] The German attack did surround forward regiments of three rifle divisions, but 9th and
19th Panzer Divisions ran into difficulties when they crossed the Zhizdra River.[158]

While the Germans continued to grind against the Kirov salient, Zhukov pressed the offensive in the Rzhev area. On 11 August, in order to clear the southern flank of his attack on Sychevka, he redirected Reiter's 20th Army and Solomatin's 8th Tank Corps, joined by Major General Ivan Ivanovich Fediuninsky's neighboring 5th Army near Gzhatsk, against the town of Karmanovo.[159] This attack, although it finally succeeded on 23 August, greatly depleted the striking power of the Soviet force. Meanwhile, on 13 August Zhukov unleashed another surprise farther south. Lieutenant General Mikhail Semenovich Khozin's 33rd Army, reinforced to a total of 90,000 men and 400 tanks, attacked in the Voria River valley, threatening the southern flank of Third Panzer Army, including the rail center of Viaz'ma.[160]

That same day, Model, who had returned from sick leave to command the threatened Ninth Army, persuaded Hitler to promise him 9th Panzer and 95th Infantry Divisions when those units could be extracted from the failed attack by Second Panzer Army. In the interim, however, neither Model nor Kluge had any operational reserves to meet new threats. During a 14 August telephone conversation with Halder, Kluge painted a "very grave picture" of the situation. Reluctantly, 72nd Infantry Division, en route from the Crimea to Leningrad, was diverted to Smolensk, and trains carrying "GD" Motorized Division were also directed to Sychevka. These two divisions began to arrive on 17 August, but Hitler retained operational control of "GD," which he did not wish to see tied down in a defensive operation.[161]

This left the corps commanders of Ninth and Third Panzer Armies to halt Zhukov without any outside aid. On 15–16 August, the German 31st Infantry Division conducted a local counterattack into the southern flank of Khozin's 33rd Army, slowing the Soviet advance and preventing a complete breakthrough. Khozin tried repeatedly to break free into the German rear but finally failed. During 25–28 August, elements of 18th Panzer and 98th Infantry Divisions cut off and destroyed the spearheads of 33rd Army's last effort in an encirclement battle on the road to Gzhatsk. Konev, who by this time had succeeded Zhukov in command of Western Front, reluctantly brought the battle to a close, although the fighting around Rzhev went on until 24 September.[162]

The Zhizdra River Operation, 23–29 August

As Zhukov's Rzhev-Sychevka offensive slowly ground to a halt in late August, expiring entirely in early September, the *Stavka* shifted its attention to the south. Here the Red Army not only absorbed the Germans' *Wirbelwind* offensive but actually launched its own offensive built around another of its newly formed tank armies. On 15 August, the *Stavka* appointed Lieutenant General Prokofii Logvinovich Romanenko, commander of 3rd Tank Army, as deputy commander of Western Front. This gave Romanenko authority to control his own forces as well as those of 16th and 61st Armies in a coordinated counterstroke against the eastern flank of Second Panzer Army's *Wirbelwind* penetration along the Zhizdra River.[163]

Zhukov's offensive plan for the so-called Zhizdra or Kozel'sk offensive required the armies on his *front*'s left wing, Bagramian's 16th, Belov's 61st, and Romanenko's 3rd Tank, to destroy the Germans' entire *Wirbelwind* force along the Zhizdra River by converging attacks from the region south of Kozel'sk (see Map 86). Belov's army, spearheaded by Romanenko's reinforced tank army, was to attack from the Belev region southeast of Kozel'sk, cross the Vytebet' River, and capture Ul'ianovo in the German grouping's rear. Bagramian's 16th Army, led by Major General Aleksei Vasil'evich Kurkin's 9th and Major General Vasilii Gerasimovich Burkov's 10th Tank and General Viktor Kirillovich Baranov's 1st Guards Cavalry Corps, was to attack from the region southwest of Kozel'sk, smash German defenses along the Zhizdra River, and link up with 61st Army at Ul'ianovo to encircle the defending German force.[164]

Once assembled, Romanenko's 3rd Tank Army included its own 12th and 15th Tank Corps, commanded by Major General Semen Il'ich Bogdanov and Major General Vasilii Alekseevich Koptsov, respectively, and Major General of Tank Forces Dmitrii Karpovich Mostovenko's reinforcing 3rd Tank Corps, for a total of about 610 tanks; in addition, 9th and 10th Tank Corps supporting Bagramian's 16th Army fielded roughly 100 tanks.[165] These forces faced 134th, 52nd, 56th, and 26th Infantry, 11th, 17th, 9th, and 20th Panzer, and 25th Motorized Divisions of Second Panzer Army's XXXV Army and XXXXI Panzer Corps, with a combined force of roughly 200 tanks and assault guns.[166] In four frantic days (15–19 August), 3rd Tank Army moved to Kozel'sk by rail, detrained, and prepared to conduct its first attack since its formation. Romanenko devised an impressive plan, with three shock groups built around his three tank corps. Each of the shock groups included, in addition to the tank corps itself, a rifle division and nondivisional artillery support—the same pattern exhibited at Voronezh.[167]

Yet again, however, another Soviet offensive foundered because units lacked planning, air superiority, cohesion, and experience. The attack began at 0615 hours on 22 August, but the Soviet forces rapidly bogged down. Forests and swamps, minefields, careful German defensive planning, and active *Luftwaffe* intervention all took their toll on the inexperienced tank corps. The three shock groups achieved advances of no more than 5 kilometers. Romanenko had slightly more success on 23 August, when he committed the veteran 1st Guards Motorized Rifle Division to continue the attack against Koptsov's 15th Tank Corps in the center of 3rd Tank Army's assault. This division pushed German 25th Motorized Division back another 4 kilometers, further reducing the German salient, but again ground to a halt on 25 August. Romanenko regrouped his forces and attacked yet again on 2–3 September, with similar dismal results. In the end, Western Front had unquestionably defeated Operation *Wirbelwind* but otherwise achieved very little in comparison to the large number of forces committed. In the process, Zhukov's forces lost as many as 500 of the 700 tanks committed in this bloody confrontation.[168]

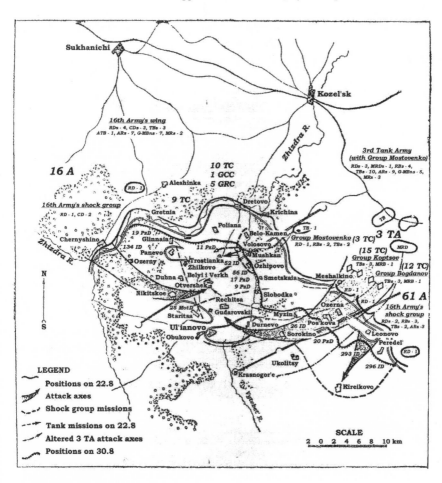

Map 86. The Western Front's Zhizdra offensive, 23–29 August 1942

The Battle for the Demiansk Pocket, August 1942

In his guidance to the *Stavka* and his *front* commanders the previous spring, Stalin had directed them to launch several limited offensives all along the front from the Crimea north to Leningrad. Although these operations were spectacular failures, they set a pattern for summer operations. So while German Army Groups A and B conducted Operation Blau and Army Group Center was hard-pressed at Rzhev, Army Group North faced a series of persistent if unproductive Soviet attacks. Although details varied, the objective was always the same: to pinch off German Sixteenth Army's II Army Corps, which was defending a salient around Demiansk, south of Lake Il'men' and east of Staraia Russa and, in the process, weaken German attempts to seize Leningrad. The Demiansk salient had been formed in January 1942 when Northwestern Front encircled II Army Corps in the region during the Red Army's winter offensive.

Lieutenant General Pavel Alekseevich Kurochkin, commander of Northwestern Front, attempted this feat twice, in attacks beginning on 5 May and 17 July.[169] During the first offensive, the Germans counterattacked (Operation Seydlitz) and managed to carve out a narrow corridor connecting their main forces in the Staraia Russa region, with II Corps defending the Demiansk salient. During the second offensive in July, Kurochkin attempted to sever the Germans' so-called Ramushevo corridor and isolate and crush the Demiansk salient with assaults by his *front*'s 11th and 27th Armies but failed in this task after a week of intense fighting.[170] As in May, the offensive failed largely because the attackers lacked sufficient artillery support to penetrate the German defenses; therefore, they accomplished little other than to inflict a few casualties on the defenders.[171]

To maintain pressure on the corridor and attached salient, the *Stavka* ordered Kurochkin to plan a third offensive, using only Lieutenant General Vasilii Ivanovich Morozov's 11th Army to attack the northern side of the Ramushevo corridor.[172] His first plan for such an attack was so poorly received that it earned him a written rebuke from Stalin and Vasilevsky, who dispatched Marshal Timoshenko to supervise preparation of the new effort. The *Stavka*'s new plan called for converging assaults against the corridor with 11th Army from the north and Lieutenant General Vladimir Zakharovich Romanovsky's 1st Shock Army from the south (see Map 87).[173] As a result, the new offensive did not begin until 10 August, by which time the Germans had formed a special headquarters (Corps Group Knobelsdorff) and built additional defenses to protect the corridor. Poor weather and ammunition shortages further weakened Kurochkin's chances; in ten days of fighting, 1st Shock Army advanced only a few hundred meters into the German defenses, which included 3rd SS *"Totenkopf"* [Death's Head] Motorized Division.[174]

THE FLANK BATTLES: AN ASSESSMENT

A decade after the war, Colonel General Kurt Zeitzler, Halder's successor as chief of the German General Staff, summarized the standard staff explanation for the failure of Operation Blau:

> Military objectives must always correspond to the forces and other means available for their attainment. From a purely tactical point of view it is not enough simply to reach an objective: consolidation upon the objective is also essential. If this is not achieved, the forces involved will have overreached themselves, and the offensive operation, no matter how attractive the target, will contain within itself and from its beginning the germ of failure if not of actual defeat.

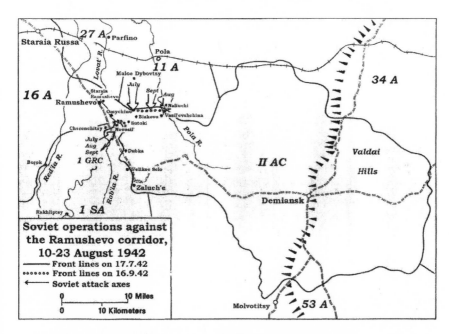

Map 87. The Northwestern Front's Demiansk offensive, 10–21 August 1942

The first objective, Stalingrad, lay nearly three hundred miles [480 kilometers] beyond the front line that existed in the spring of 1942; the Caucasus was even farther away, over three hundred and fifty miles [560 kilometers] distant. . . . Being some three hundred and fifty miles apart, the two operations must diverge.[175]

There is much truth in this statement, although it is worth noting that the Red Army and Red Air Force had to operate over the same vast distances, with poor communications, and in pursuit of divergent objectives much like their German counterparts. Certainly the German reach—the strategic ability to advance against the slowly maturing Soviets and the ability to sustain their advance, supply the troops, and consolidate on their far-flung objectives—exceeded their capacity.

Given his personal direction of the campaign, Hitler must bear a large measure of responsibility for this dispersed effort—the constant shifting of air and ground assets between the Crimea, Stalingrad, and the Caucasus, not to mention Western Europe and Leningrad. Yet at the time, many if not most of his subordinates were as optimistic as the Führer. Even Franz Halder, who expressed many doubts in his diary and apparently during his briefings, remarked on 30 July, "The enemy is running for dear life and will be in the northern foothills of

Field Marshal Wilhelm von List, commander of Army Group A (center), meeting with his commanders in Rostov, late July 1942

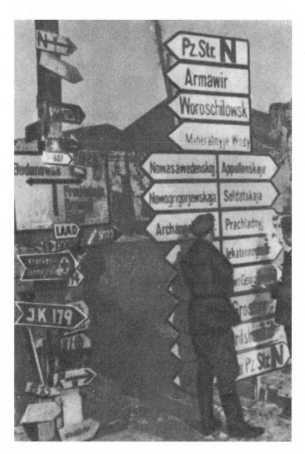

German road signs pointing into the Caucasus region, August 1942

Red Army infantry in the foothills of the Caucasus, August 1942

Red Army artillery in the northern Caucasus, August 1942

Soviet naval infantry in combat in Novorossiisk, August 1942

Novorossiisk and its harbor, August 1942

Red Army Infantry defending the foothills of the Caucasus Mountains, August 1942

Red Army counterattack in the northern Caucasus, August 1942

Red Army infantry in the High Caucasus

Red Army reinforcements along military roads through the High Caucasus, August 1942

A German cemetery in the Caucasus Mountains

the Caucasus a good piece ahead of our armor."[176] Under the circumstances, Stalingrad appeared to be an opportunity to force the Soviets to stand and fight, as well as to inflict a propaganda and psychological victory. Even if Germany had been capable of accomplishing victory given these circumstances, however, the battle for Stalingrad was an improvised event that distracted from the original objective of Operation Blau—the Caucasus oil fields. Whether or not the objective of taking the oil fields was ever attainable, it certainly could not be achieved with 16 to 18 divisions while the rest of the available ground and air forces were concentrated farther north.

It is in this context—the possibility (indeed probability) that the *Wehrmacht* was already stretched to the breaking point—that one must evaluate the Soviet offensives outside the Stalingrad region. By this standard, the repeated Soviet offensives on the Voronezh shoulder were abject failures, squandering Soviet resources without retaking ground or attracting an equivalent German response. The same could be said for the Demiansk offensives south of Leningrad: Army Group North easily contained Kurochkin's feeble efforts, and the German counteroffensives in the area were mounted with purely local forces.

One could argue, hypothetically, that the Voronezh and Demiansk operations prevented the Germans from withdrawing even more units from quiet sectors. But playing "might-have-been" is a dangerous game: There is no objective method for evaluating such a hypothesis. By the same token, there is no way to assess whether the same Soviet assets might have achieved an earlier or more decisive victory if they were concentrated at Stalingrad.

Thus, only the Soviet operations against Army Group Center, and especially the Rzhev-Sychevka Offensive of 30 July–23 August, contributed to the self-inflicted overextension of the *Wehrmacht* in 1942. In a few instances, one can even identify German units that were distracted from other missions. For example, 9th and 11th Panzer Divisions, which departed Voronezh in late July, were tasked with spearheading Operation *Wirbelwind* in August rather than being used against designated priorities such as Leningrad, Stalingrad, and the Caucasus. More important still, based on the progress his forces made during the Soviet August offensive at Rzhev and Sychevka, Zhukov remained convinced of the absolutely vital importance of the Moscow axis and, if provided with larger forces, that Western Front could have achieved far more spectacular success. As Zhukov later recorded in his memoirs:

With one or two more armies at our disposal [in the Rzhev-Sychevka operation] we could have combined with the Kalinin Front under General I. S. Konev and defeated the enemy not only in the Rzhev area but the entire Rzhev-Vyazma German force and substantially improved the operational situation in the whole Western strategic direction. Unfortunately, this real opportunity was missed by the Supreme Command.[177]

Thereafter, Zhukov considered his Rzhev-Sychevka offensive as a dress rehearsal for an even grander operation once Stalin provided him with additional armies—which the dictator would do by November.

In addition, for the Soviets, the Rzhev-Sychevka and *Wirbelwind* operations also represented early experiments in large unit mechanized operations. Galanin's improvised mobile group east of Sychevka and Romanenko's 3rd Tank Army at Kozel'sk are forgotten reminders of the painful process by which the Red Army learned to conduct the type of sophisticated mobile operations that dominated the second half of the German-Soviet conflict.

Regardless of the degree to which the Soviet offensives actually tied down German resources, they compounded the psychological strain on Hitler and the German military command. Such pressure, in turn, made it more difficult for staff officers to voice doubts to the Führer, and it encouraged Hitler to mistrust (and ultimately dismiss) his most experienced subordinates. Whether these psychological effects were worth the enormous cost in Soviet blood and matériel remains an entirely subjective judgment.

CHAPTER 10

Conclusions: German Strategic Misconceptions

Given the ideologies, geopolitics, and economics involved, it was probably inevitable that National Socialist Germany and the Soviet Union would fight a war to the death during the 1940s. In the short term, therefore, Adolf Hitler was undoubtedly correct to attack in 1941, when the Red Army and Red Air Force were still in transition in regard to equipment, organization, doctrine, and leadership.

But even if we accept these premises, the German civilian and military leadership, while planning Operation Barbarossa in 1941, made fundamental errors in logistics and force planning, and they repeated the same errors while planning Operation Blau the following year. Logistically, the *Wehrmacht* was a disjointed combination of units—some were mechanized, but the vast majority depended on human and animal power. Such an organization, for all its tactical excellence, was unlikely to be able to conduct a sustained campaign over the vast distances and poor communications structure of European Russia.

In November 1940, the OKH quartermaster general, Major General Edouard Wagner, had briefed General Halder, his chief, about logistical calculations for the coming campaign. Wagner estimated the army had sufficient fuel to advance to a maximum depth of only 500–800 kilometers, with enough food and ammunition for a 20-day operation. After that, Wagner concluded, the army would have to pause for several weeks for resupply and would be dependent on the inadequate Soviet road and rail networks for any further penetration.[1] Wagner's predictions were fulfilled in every detail and, in some cases, were actually too optimistic in predicting German operational depth. The armored spearheads had to pause time and again during the invasion so that supplies and infantry units could catch up. These pauses not only cost operational momentum but also allowed large numbers of bypassed Red Army soldiers to escape and fight another day.

Hitler and his generals were aware of the logistical limitations, but their proposed solution was to destroy the Red Army in a series of sprawling encirclement operations in the western Soviet Union, after which a much smaller German force would advance into the Soviet heartland to mop up and occupy ground. Thus, Operation Barbarossa required the three army groups of the *Wehrmacht's* Eastern Army—North, Center, and South—to advance eastward simultaneously along three strategic axes and to destroy the Red Army between the Soviet Union's western borders and the Dvina and Dnepr Rivers. Thereafter, the invaders would have to sustain an advance of great depth—from 800 to more than 1,000 kilometers—and ultimately capture the cities of Leningrad, Moscow, and Rostov.

However, this solution was based on the assumption that the Red Army was of fixed size and could be defeated in a short, decisive war. Instead, the Germans encountered an enemy dedicated to a war of attrition, fielding a force that was able to generate new units as quickly as the Germans shattered the old ones. Not only was the Soviet population far larger than that of Germany, but a larger proportion of that population had undergone peacetime military training, including millions of older Soviet men who were conscripted before Germany restored its own compulsory service in 1935.

By 31 December 1941, for example, the Soviet Armed Forces had already lost at least 4.5 million men in combat—including 3.1 million dead, captured, or missing in action—yet was still able to field a force of more than 4.2 million men. During the harrowing six months to start the war, 23 Soviet armies and some 200 divisions were severely damaged or destroyed outright by the German juggernaut. Yet during the same six-month period, the Soviet Union raised a staggering total of 55 new armies, 53 of which were deployed to meet the blitzkrieg bearing down on the western Soviet Union, and almost 200 new divisions and hundreds of separate rifle and tank brigades, which, with almost 100 divisions shifted from within the Soviet Union, increased the Red Army's strength in the West to about 592 divisional equivalents. Such numbers far exceeded the 300-division force that the Germans, in planning for Operation Barbarossa, estimated the Soviet Union could field. Many of the new Soviet units were short on training and equipment, to be sure, but they continued to retard and weaken the invader.[2] This force generation was only one aspect of the Soviets' typically ruthless mobilization of society and industry at a time when Hitler continued to avoid similar measures in the fatherland because such sacrifices might be unpopular.

As the course of the early war indicated, the tasks Hitler assigned to his *Wehrmacht* in 1941 far exceeded its capabilities. After losing almost 4,000 tanks and assault guns and suffering more than 800,000 casualties (fully one-quarter of its original manpower strength) during the first six months of the German invasion, Hitler's armies were finally defeated outside Leningrad, at the gates of Moscow, and in the Rostov region during November and December 1941.

During the planning of Operation Blau in spring 1942, even after Germany suffered unprecedented defeats during late fall 1941 and winter 1941–1942, Hitler and most of the *Wehrmacht*'s officers and men remained confident that their still impressive military machine could prevail. To do this, however, in 1942 they had to inflict a crippling defeat on the Red Army and then seize regions economically vital to the Soviet Union's survival. In the Führer's view, this meant conquering lands within the Great Bend of the Don River, together with the lower reaches of the Volga River, and the oil fields north and south of the Caucasus Mountains. The seizure of these objectives, Hitler reasoned, would sever the most important route for Lend-Lease equipment reaching the Soviet Union from the Western Allies and deprive the Soviet Union of vital fuel supplies.

To achieve these objectives, Hitler concentrated the bulk of the *Wehrmacht's* combat strength in Army Group South, operating along the southern strategic axis. He ordered Bock's army group to conduct a surprise offensive, shatter and destroy Soviet forces in southern Russia, and then exploit eastward to capture Stalingrad and the Caucasus. To reach these objectives, the *Wehrmacht* and the armies of its Axis allies would have to advance eastward along not one, not two, but ultimately three strategic axes—toward the Don River at Voronezh, southward along the Don River to the Volga River at Stalingrad, and into and through the Caucasus region—sustaining operations to depths of 200 to 1,100 kilometers. Understanding it was necessary to employ a full army group along each strategic axis, Hitler deliberately split Army Group South into two parts (Bock's Army Group A and List's Army Group B) and ordered the former to advance toward the Don River and Stalingrad on the Volga River, the latter to reach deep into the Caucasus. Yet by late August it was apparent that even this expedient had failed, forcing Hitler to acknowledge tacitly that his two army groups were too weak to operate along all three strategic axes. He reluctantly committed several satellite armies to shore up his overextended front lines.

As they planned Blau, Hitler and his military planners took care to avoid mistakes they had made in Barbarossa. They were convinced the Red Army had survived catastrophic defeats in 1941 because of the Soviet Union's immense mobilization potential and the weakness of its road and rail networks. This weakness, exacerbated by the difficult terrain and harsh Russian weather, strained German logistics beyond the breaking point and prevented the Wehrmacht from sustaining military operations to necessary depths. Thus, instead of conducting a seamless advance in accordance with Operation Barbarossa the year before, after mid-July 1941 the Wehrmacht had advanced in fits and starts—offensive bursts of 100–160 kilometers lasting 10 days punctuated by periodic 7- to 10-day pauses to rest, reorganize, and replenish fuel and ammunition—and by improvising ad hoc operations to take advantage of opportunities when and where they arose. Even so, Hitler concluded, the Red Army had barely staved off total defeat.

The architects of Blau sought to remedy these problems in four key aspects. First, by incorporating preliminary operations such as Wilhelm and Fridericus into the plan, they attempted to replicate what surprise had achieved in 1941. By destroying at least two of Southwestern Front's forward-deployed armies, preliminary German operations would tear an immense hole in the Red Army's strategic defenses in the southern Soviet Union, severely weaken its defending forces, outflank Southwestern and Southern Fronts, and then subject each *front* to defeat in detail. Second, given the millions of men the Red Army raised and fielded in 1941 and the roughly 7.5 million casualties (including almost 4 million dead, captured, and missing) it had suffered in 1941 and the first six months of

1942, German planners could scarcely imagine the Soviets fielding anywhere near the 53 armies they had raised and fielded in 1941. Third, the rapid advance by German forces concentrated along one and then two strategic axes would certainly negate the impact of whatever reserves the Soviets were able to raise and employ. Fourth, by conducting the offensive in several distinct stages (Blau I and II, preceded by Wilhelm and Fridericus), the German planners hoped to catch the Soviets wrong-footed and fragment the Red Army's defending forces and confuse them as to the Wehrmacht's ultimate objectives, again subjecting each defending Red Army *front* to defeat and destruction.

Fortuitously for German planners, Stalin committed a major strategic blunder that played into the Wehrmacht's hands. German deception plans (such as Operation Kremlin) convinced Stalin that Moscow would remain Hitler's preeminent strategic objective during summer 1942. Transfixed by the presumed importance of the Moscow axis, Stalin stubbornly insisted that the Red Army concentrate a major portion of its operating armies and its strategic reserves along that axis. Compounding his error, Stalin directed the Red Army to conduct two simultaneous large-scale offensive operations along the southern axis to divert German attention and forces away from Moscow. This decision played into Hitler's hands, leading to catastrophic Red Army defeats at Khar'kov and in the Crimea in May 1942. During the subsequent victories in Wilhelm and Fridericus in June, Army Group South exploited its May successes and seized jumping-off positions for the Blau offensives. In turn, by eliminating three armies, weakening three more, and tearing more than 300,000 soldiers from the ranks of the Red Army's Southwestern and Southern Fronts, these operational successes set up the catastrophic strategic defeats those two *fronts* would experience in July.

ANTECEDENTS

As Hitler intended, the Wehrmacht's victories at Khar'kov and in the Crimea in May and June, and during Operations Wilhelm and Fridericus II in June, did much to restore German confidence and morale. Given the poor performance of Soviet forces in May and June 1942, the Germans had every reason to expect a series of easy victories leading to their ultimate goals: Stalingrad and the Caucasus oil fields. The danger for the Germans, however, lay not in defeat on the battlefield but in trying to go too far too quickly with too little. By attempting to seize everything at once, Germans would allow it all to slip through their fingers and permitted the Red Army to escape and fight another day. Most German staff officers and commanders understood the limits under which they worked. Even in Army Group South, the German divisions had never recovered completely from the losses suffered during the previous winter. Moreover, the vast distances and logistical problems of Operation Blau were almost as crippling as during Operation Barbarossa the previous summer.

In short, although Operations Wilhelm and Fridericus II demonstrated that German forces could still seize territory and inflict staggering tactical defeats on the Red Army, it remained to be seen whether—as at Khar'kov and in the Crimea—the Wehrmacht would be able to destroy their opponents completely at the operational and strategic levels. Much like the British fighting the Continental Army during the American Revolution, even though the Wehrmacht might win every battle it could not win the war as long as the opponent remained in the field.

Soviet commanders might console themselves with such thoughts, but they were far from confident about the outcome of the looming German offensive. The fall of the Crimea, the failure of the Khar'kov offensive, and the easy German victories in subsequent operations only reinforced a nagging Soviet sense of inferiority. Moreover, as late as the last week in June 1942, the Soviets were still massed in the wrong places. Stalin and Vasilevsky continued to expect that the main summer offensive would lunge toward Moscow, an expectation illustrated by the allocation of their best general, Zhukov, and 10 field armies to the Western Front. This error was compounded by the destruction of many of Timoshenko's armies in the south during May and June, which forced the defenders to commit less-capable, less-trained units, including the new tank armies, to premature battle. It was going to be a difficult summer for both sides—long, hot, and insufferably fatal. As late as 27 June 1942—by which time Hitler had stitched together an imposing body of Axis forces in the southern Soviet Union—it remained to be seen whether or not Stalin's prudent precautionary measures would prove adequate to forestall a second summer of spectacular Wehrmacht victories.

BLAU I AND II

Despite Hitler's careful planning of Operation Blau, from its very beginning many of the same successes and failures the Germans had experienced in 1941 were repeated—and for many of the same reasons. Once again, the Germans achieved strategic surprise, this time by striking toward the economic resources of the Caucasus rather than the political capital in Moscow. Likewise, the recently rebuilt panzer divisions rolled across the landscape against what seemed at the highest levels to be minor resistance. Yet despite the Wehrmacht's initial dramatic advances, it became increasingly difficult for the Germans to sustain momentum given the twin challenges of distance and the growing Soviet military competence. Thus, by late July the German Army was subject to the same fits and starts experienced in 1941.

Beyond this, however, the most perplexing dilemma facing the Wehrmacht throughout its advance in 1942 was its vulnerable left flank, which lengthened inexorably as Army Groups A and B sped eastward toward the Don and Volga Rivers, Stalingrad, and, ultimately, the Caucasus. This inherent and daunting problem was complicated by two additional factors. First, the Red Army was qualitatively far superior to what it had been in 1941 and continued to improve at a rapid pace during 1942. By contrast, the Wehrmacht had been unable to replace completely the material and personnel losses of 1941, so it was understrength even at the start of its grueling Blau campaign. Second, while it is true that some green Soviet units crumbled in the face of the superbly executed blitzkrieg, others gave a good account of themselves. Indeed, the surprising skill of the Soviet soldiers and at least some of their leaders was chiefly responsible for the sometimes slow progress of the German spearheads and for their failure to repeat the huge prisoner hauls of the previous year. From army group commanders down to the most junior *landser*, the Germans in the field were aware that the Soviets were constantly counterattacking and often inflicting heavy casualties on the invaders. Thus, long before November 1942, when 13th Panzer Division would become encircled at Gizel', at the western gates of Ordzhonikidze, and Sixth Army trapped at Stalingrad, selected Soviet units and commanders had demonstrated the ability to imperil German units.

This increased Soviet effectiveness was often invisible to Hitler and his immediate military advisers, who consistently and with increasing vitriol blamed field commanders for the slow rates of advance and failure to destroy their enemies. Thus, the Soviet defense, however uneven and sometimes amateurish, not only slowed the German advance but also contributed to Hitler's frustration toward and ultimate break with his most skilled commanders.

Despite these problems, Hitler and Bock considered Blau I to be a resounding success. Attacking with three panzer corps, *Armeegruppe* Weichs and Paulus's Sixth Army advanced up to 200 kilometers eastward in 15 days, shattering the Southwestern Main Direction's defenses, encircling and destroying most of Briansk Front's 40th and Southwestern Front's 21st Armies, and seizing assigned objectives in the Voronezh region and along the western bank of the Don River. After demolishing six Soviet tank corps with more than 600 tanks on the road to Voronezh, once near the city, Weichs's and Paulus's forces defeated 5th Tank Army (with another 600 tanks) and fought two more Soviet tank corps to a stalemate in nine days of fighting northwest and east of the city.

Taken by surprise and with their communications disrupted, neither Golikov's Briansk Front nor Timoshenko's Southwestern Front could react quickly enough to stave off initial disaster and stabilize the situation before the Germans seized their designated objectives. Energized by the new threat in the Voronezh region, Stalin reacted vigorously, first by ordering his forward forces to conduct a resolute defense along successive lines rather than abandoning the field to the Germans, and second by committing his new 5th Tank Army and 3rd, 5th, 6th, and 7th Reserve Armies to action to contain the German advance and drive it back with powerful counterstrokes. However, the same command and control problems affecting his lower-level commands prevented him from doing so in time to undo the damage already done.

Although successful for the Germans, the intense fighting in the Voronezh region posed a new dilemma to Hitler. First, the Führer demanded that Weichs and Paulus complete the encirclements called for in Blau I. At the same time, however, he insisted that Army Group South—now split into Bock's Army Group A and List's Army Group B—begin Blau II on schedule. Impatient with the "diversion" at Voronezh, Hitler ordered Bock to release the bulk of Hoth's Fourth Panzer Army from that region so that it could cooperate with the advance of Army Group A's First Panzer Army deeper into the Donbas region to complete the second encirclement.

In terms of speed and depth, the Wehrmacht's advance during Blau II was as impressive as in Blau I. In slightly less than one week, the advancing pincers of the two army groups virtually crippled Southwestern Front's 21st, 28th, and 38th Armies and Southern Front's 9th Army and were in position to envelop and destroy most, if not all, Soviet forces in the Donbas region. Caught wrong-footed again, the *Stavka* ordered the armies of its two *fronts*, now reinforced by 57th and 24th Armies, to continue to defend the eastern Donbas region, once again along successive lines identified in Moscow. However, bypassing the Rossosh' and Millerovo region, XXXX Panzer Corps of Army Group B's Fourth Panzer Army cut off Southwestern Front's 28th and 38th Armies' routes of withdrawal to the east, largely because of the *Stavka*'s stand-fast orders. Simultaneously, First Panzer Army's III and XIV Panzer Corps of Army Group A thrust eastward north of Voroshilovgrad, forcing Southern Front's 9th and 37th Armies to withdraw eastward in disorder toward the region south of Millerovo.

In the wake of this disaster, Stalin formed a new Stalingrad Front from the remnants of Southwestern Front and incorporating the new 62nd, 63rd, and 64th Armies to protect the approaches to Stalingrad. He directed the *front* to erect defenses along the Don and Chir Rivers, particularly in the Great Bend of the Don River. In the meantime, Stalin ordered Malinovsky's Southern Front to rescue the forces encircled in the Millerovo region and to man new defenses from Millerovo southward to Rostov. The Wehrmacht's rapid advance, however, rendered such measures irrelevant. Unable to escape and join Southern Front, the remnants of Southwestern Front's 28th, 38th, and 57th Armies instead fled eastward across the Don, leaving Southern Front's shattered 9th, 24th, and 37th, 12th, 18th, and 56th Armies, now backed up by the North Caucasus Front's 51st Army, to defend the Mius River line and the approaches to Rostov.

ALTERED PLANS

Elated over his recent victories but concerned lest the Soviets in the eastern Donbas region escape, Hitler on 12 July fundamentally altered his plans for the third stage of Operation Blau. Instead of attacking due east toward the ultimate objective of Blau III—Stalingrad—the Führer decided to unleash his panzers southeastward toward the lower Don River and Rostov to destroy Soviet forces in that region. When Bock objected, Hitler replaced him with Weichs. Leaving Paulus's Sixth Army to protect the Don River front with its infantry, Hoth's Fourth Panzer Army, now under Army Group A's control and with all three of Army Group B's panzer corps, advanced southeastward toward Rostov during 17–24 July in cooperation with Kleist's First Panzer Army advancing from the west. This joint thrust outflanked and defeated the Southern Front armies defending the approaches to Rostov, captured the city, and propelled Army Group A's forces to the lower Don River. This left Southern Front no choice but to withdraw in disorder to new defenses along the lower Don.

Hitler's bold gambit decimated Southern Front's 9th, 12th, 18th, 24th, 37th, and 56th Armies but permitted roughly one-third of those forces to escape, albeit in disorder, southward through Rostov. This occurred because the follow-on infantry divisions of Army Groups A and B were too few in number to contain and swallow up the massive Soviet forces bypassed and encircled by the advancing panzer and motorized divisions. Although the gambit succeeded strategically, the Rostov "diversion" shifted the center of gravity of Operation Blau away from Stalingrad, thereby undermining the intent of Blau III. This, in turn, confronted Hitler with yet another strategic dilemma: whether to continue his advance into the Caucasus, resume his march toward Stalingrad, or, as the audacious Führer ultimately decided, to attempt both operations simultaneously.

Hitler's Directive No. 45, issued on 23 July, ordered Army Group B's Sixth Army, now including two panzer corps (XIV and XXIV), to thrust eastward through the Great Bend of the Don and across the river to capture Stalingrad, and Army Group A, with three panzer corps (XXXX, XXXXVIII, and III) of Fourth and First Panzer Armies and Seventeenth Army's infantry, bolstered by LVII Panzer Corps, to exploit southward into the Caucasus to seize the oil resources at Maikop and Baku. The armies on Army Group B's left wing were to defend an ever-lengthening front along the Don River. Thus, the directive required two army groups to operate along three separate strategic axes—the Voronezh region, toward Stalingrad, and into the Caucasus—rather than two. Although risky because it violated the long-standing precept that one army group should be responsible for one strategic axis, this strategy was reasonable to the Führer because the Soviets' strategic defenses seemed in so dilapidated a state.

Actually, Hitler might have overcome the inherent difficulties in Directive No. 45—albeit with great difficulty—if Army Group A had unquestioned priority for scarce supplies and combat power. Instead, Stalingrad, a city barely mentioned in the original Führer Directive No. 41 of 5 April 1942, came to dominate the entire campaign. The result was more than a major diversion of troops and supplies away from the original objective of the Caucasus oil fields. While complicating Sixth Army's operations along the approaches to Stalingrad, ultimately the city itself became a black hole that absorbed German attention, supplies, and blood in a tactical environment where the combat groups of Chuikov's defending

62nd Army would neutralize or counter most of the tactical and technical advantages of their German counterparts.

THE ADVANCE TO STALINGRAD

On the road toward Stalingrad, the twin pincers of Paulus's Sixth Army recorded notable successes in the Great Bend of the Don River by the end of July despite frequent Soviet counterattacks. While its northern pincer, XIV Panzer Corps, succeeded in penetrating the defenses on 62nd Army's right wing and pushed forward 50 kilometers toward Kalach-on-the-Don, its southern pincer, XXIV Panzer Corps, pressed 64th Army back and seized a bridgehead across the Chir River southwest of Kalach. However, the cumulative effects of tenacious Soviet resistance by the new 1st and 4th Tank as well as 62nd and 64th Armies, punctuated by frequent Soviet counterstrokes, combined with chronic German fuel shortages to halt Paulus's advance enticingly short of Kalach. This prompted Paulus to inform Hitler that, unless reinforced, he would be unable to cross the Don River and penetrate eastward to Stalingrad. Hitler realized reinforcements would be available only if and when he revised his campaign plan.

Therefore, incrementally from 17 July through 31 July, Hitler provided Paulus with his required reinforcements, first with 16th Panzer and 3rd and 60th Motorized Divisions by 22 July, second with 24th Panzer Division on 25 July, and finally with XXXXVIII Panzer Corps of Hoth's Fourth Panzer Army on 28 July—with orders to advance on Stalingrad from the southwest. By employing these forces, Paulus was able to clear Soviet forces from the Great Bend in multiple offensive impulses (on 17 and 23 July and 8 and 15 August) rather than the "single bound" envisioned in Hitler's directive, thereby repeating the problems of 1941. This more costly method of stop-and-start offensive operations was necessitated not only by recurring shortages of fuel and ammunition but also by the increasing weakness of Paulus's army relative to the opposition.

While Sixth Army was at long last destroying the Soviet bridgehead west of the Don and capturing Kalach, Hoth's Fourth Panzer Army launched its spectacular advance to the Abganerovo region. By 11 August, however, Hoth's forces also bogged down against intensifying resistance by Soviet 64th Army. This forced Sixth Army to conduct another offensive, this time to clear 4th Tank Army from the northeast corner of the Great Bend so that Paulus's army could cross the Don and begin the long-awaited final advance on Stalingrad. However, even after Sixth Army accomplished this task, Hoth required additional reinforcements, this time 24th Panzer Division, before he could join Sixth Army's drive on the city.

Soviet resistance to Sixth Army during its advance to the Don River proved far heavier than anticipated and far more damaging to Paulus's army than previous histories have recorded. Paulus never had the overwhelming force necessary to conduct the glorious advance into Stalingrad. Instead, he had to prepare and execute four separate deliberate attacks just to break through to the city. Even when his army's XIV Panzer Corps finally reached the Volga on 23 August, Soviet counterattacks cut off the spearhead and threatened to overwhelm most of the corps. Thus, after destroying or severely damaging three Soviet armies (21st, 28th, and 38th) in July and three more (62nd and 1st and 4th Tank) in the first half of August, at midmonth Paulus's army still faced five Soviet armies (63rd, 21st, 1st Guards, 4th Tank, and 62nd). With Red armies reappearing, seemingly from Soviet graveyards, across the entire front, and with Sixth Army's rate of advance steadily falling from 55 to 70 kilometers per day in July to less than 10 kilometers per day by mid-August, there was no reason to assume the advance over the remaining 70 kilometers to the Volga River and Stalingrad would be any easier.

Although Paulus's army exacted a terrible cost from the opposing Red Army forces, attrition decimated his own forces as well. 24th Panzer Division, for example, was a superb implement of mechanized maneuver warfare, but it began the campaign with only a limited number of infantry and other "dismounted" forces and was slowly destroyed in the ambushes and skirmishes of urban combat. Nor were the infantry units, which bore the brunt of the urban combat, more fortunate. Consider, for example, Lieutenant Adelbert Holl, an officer in 2nd Battalion, 276th Infantry Regiment, 94th Division, who was wounded early in 1942. By the time he rejoined his unit in Stalingrad on 23 September, every company in the battalion had lost two commanders killed or wounded, making an experienced officer like Holl a precious commodity to maintain unit effectiveness. In the ensuing months, during which Holl was wounded twice more, his unit was loaned out at various times to the weakened 24th and 16th Panzer Divisions, where the infantrymen felt they were being sacrificed by their unfamiliar new masters.[3] (In fairness, a poll of their Soviet counterparts would undoubtedly have reflected the same sense of being sacrificed.) The net result of this costly and drawn-out campaign, even before reaching the city, was to bleed and gradually immobilize Sixth Army, fixing it in one costly battle after another while the Soviets prepared their counteroffensive to destroy it.

Nevertheless, within days after reaching the Don, on 23 August Sixth Army's XIV Panzer Corps struck eastward toward the Volga River, carving a narrow corridor between the Don and the Volga and cutting off 62nd Army from Stalingrad Front's main forces to the north. When Paulus's army linked up with Hoth's Fourth Panzer Army west of Stalingrad on 3 September, the two armies finally isolated 62nd and 64th Armies in the city and a narrow belt of land stretching southward along the eastern bank of the Volga. The two German armies had killed, wounded, or captured tens of thousands of Red Army soldiers and destroyed as many as 400 Soviet tanks during their drive to the Don and Volga Rivers, raising the Soviets' gruesome casualty count to well more than 300,000 soldiers and 1,000 tanks since mid-July. Now, however, Sixth and Fourth Panzer

Armies faced the task of eliminating the remnants of 62nd and 64th Armies and seizing Stalingrad city itself or, more likely, occupying its ruins.

The triumphal three-day dash by Wietersheim's XIV Panzer Corps from the Don to the Volga during the second half of August erased all memories of Sixth Army's failure to reach Kalach in a single bound during the second half of July. However, instead of seizing the northern half of Stalingrad in a coup de main, as Paulus had hoped, when Wietersheim's armor reached the Volga it began a struggle for survival against counterattacking Soviet forces; this foreshadowed the fighting to come. Wietersheim's dramatic losses—up to 500 men per day—set the pattern for, at best, victory in a deadly war of attrition and, at worse, nothing more than a stalemate. Adding insult to injury, even after Paulus's and Hoth's armies destroyed Soviet 1st Tank Army and severely damaged 4th Tank, 62nd, and 64th Armies, the Soviets fielded four new armies in reinforcement (1st Guards, 24th, 66th, and 28th). Compounding Weichs's problems, while Paulus and Hoth fought for Stalingrad proper they also had to fend off constant Soviet counterstrokes north and south of the city and defend their long left wing along the Don River to the northwest.

Thereafter, to free up German forces for the decisive fight inside the city, Army Group B had no choice but to insert Hungarian, Italian, and finally Romanian forces to defend the Don River flank. During August and September, even though bolstered by German forces detached from Sixth Army, these forces endured repeated assaults by Stalingrad Front's 63rd, 21st, and 1st Guards Armies, which ultimately captured vital bridgeheads on the Don's southern bank near Serafimovich and Kletskaia, bridgeheads the Germans neglected to eradicate. The loss of these bridgeheads and the failure to retake them underscored the reality by late August that Army Group B was stretched too thin—a grim reality that would become graver still by November. In short, the fighting during July and August clearly demonstrated that Paulus's Sixth Army lacked the strength necessary to accomplish its assigned missions. As it cannibalized forces from other sectors to generate combat power for the urban fight inside Stalingrad, it increasingly had to rely on sheer willpower and persistence to accomplish Hitler's demands.

Thus in early September Hitler—his appetite whetted by the Wehrmacht's summertime victories—believed he was about to reap the full rewards that Blau had promised. Within the astonishingly brief period of two weeks, the forces of Bock's Army Group B advanced eastward up to 150 kilometers, savaged Southwestern Front's defenses east of Kursk and Khar'kov, decimated its armies, and forced their remnants to withdraw precipitously to the Don River. In just six more weeks of fighting, the army group's forces raced eastward another 350 kilometers, reached and fortified the mighty Don River line from Voronezh southward to Stalingrad's northwestern approaches, cleared Soviet forces from the Great Bend of the Don, and lunged eastward to the western bank of the Volga River north of Stalingrad. By 3 September the army group's forces immobilized 62nd Army inside Stalingrad and relegated 64th Army to a seemingly irrelevant bridgehead south of the city. By early September, this ostensibly seamless advance of up to 500 kilometers convinced Hitler that, once he issued orders to attack, Army Group B's Sixth and Fourth Panzer Armies were ideally poised to march triumphantly into Stalin's namesake city.

On Army Group B's left, List's Army Group A, by employing skillful maneuver, was able to advance up to 250 kilometers in just more than two weeks of fighting, envelop Southern Front, force its armies to withdraw pell-mell to the supposed safety of the lower Don River, and capture Rostov and the crossings over the lower Don. This advance tore open a northern gateway directly into the Caucasus. Although dismayed by the army groups' pitifully small bag of prisoners, the elated Führer nonetheless unleashed List's army group on an exhilarating advance southward toward the High Caucasus Mountains and the Baku oil fields beyond. During the ensuing six weeks of fighting, List's forces advanced up to 400 kilometers, capturing Krasnodar, Novorossiisk, and Mozdok and reaching the crest of the High Caucasus Mountains and the Baksan and Terek Rivers. Because List's forces proved able to sustain an advance of up to 650 kilometers in little more than two months of seemingly desultory fighting, Hitler believed the 80-kilometer advance on Ordzhonikidze and Groznyi in September would be child's play. And once those two cities fell into List's hands, the road to Baku, although it stretched southward another 400 kilometers, seemed wide open.

Thus, by early September the Führer had every reason to believe that both Stalingrad and Baku were his for the taking. After attacking a Red Army force of 16 armies defending a front of roughly 600 kilometers on 28 June, Army Groups A and B in two short months of fighting had defeated 13 armies (40th, 21st, 28th, 38th, 9th, 12th, 37th, 18th, 56th, 24th, 57th, and 1st and 5th Tank), demolishing most of them outright, and crippled 3 others (62nd, 64th, and 4th Tank). Even though the *Stavka* managed to field 24 additional armies (from north to south, 13th, 38th, 60th, 40th, 6th, 63rd, 21st, 4th Tank, 24th, 1st Guards, 66th, 62nd, 64th, 57th, 51st, 28th, 44th, 58th, 9th, 37th, 46th, 18th, 56th, and 47th) to oppose the 2 German army groups by early September, these forces manned tenuous defenses stretching more than 2,000 kilometers from Voronezh on the Don southward through Stalingrad and the Caucasus and westward to the Black Sea. As formidable as this force appeared on paper, 12 of these armies were partially refurbished versions of previously destroyed armies; the remainder were freshly mobilized and renumbered reserve armies commanded by experienced officers but manned largely by green conscripts and older reservists. Compounding the *Stavka*'s defensive dilemma, its seven armies defending the Caucasus were fighting in partial isolation, cut off from supply bases to the north and largely dependent for survival on Lend-Lease supplies delivered by the Western Allies through Iran.

Lost amid this depressing mosaic of abject Soviet defeat during summer 1942 were three far more positive aspects of the Red Army's defense that, although often keenly appreciated by many lower-level German combat commanders in the field, remained largely obscure to higher German commands and to most historians who have since described these operations. Masked by the *Wehrmacht's* many brilliant successes during that summer, ultimately these factors would foreshadow far greater difficulties that advancing German forces would encounter come autumn.

First, conventional wisdom maintains that, as early as the first week of Operation Blau, Stalin willfully ordered his forces in southern Russia to withdraw from harm's way, thereby avoiding the disastrous losses the Red Army had suffered in summer 1941. As proof, historians cite the lamentably small bag of prisoners the advancing Wehrmacht succeeded in taking during the summer. This is self-evidently incorrect. Archival documents now indicate that from the very beginning of Blau and, indeed, throughout the operation, Stalin reacted far more forcefully and belligerently than previously concluded. Rather than ordering his forces to withdraw to avoid encirclement by the advancing Germans, Stalin insisted that they defend as far forward as possible and, when that strategy failed, conduct rigorous defensive operations along successive lines. Although this strategy did indeed result in the encirclement and near destruction of entire armies, many if not most of the soldiers escaped to fight another day simply because German forces were too weak in infantry to police them.

Second, and as a corollary to the first factor, conventional wisdom would argue that the *Stavka* willfully abandoned the Donbas region and the Great Bend of the Don River so as to preserve its forces and contain the German onslaught along more defensible lines, principally the Don and Volga Rivers. It then chose to conduct a resolute defense only after 62nd and 64th Armies were pinned down inside and south of Stalingrad. This conclusion is also self-evidently wrong. In reality, from the very beginning of and, indeed, throughout Operation Blau, Stalin ordered his operating *fronts* in southern Russia to organize and conduct ever-larger counteractions to blunt the German spearheads and drive them back. These began with 5th Tank Army's abortive counterstroke in the Voronezh region in early July, continued with 1st and 4th Tank Armies failed counterblows in the Great Bend (together with renewed offensives by Briansk and Voronezh Fronts in the Voronezh region) in late July, and culminated with Stalingrad Front's vigorous counterstrokes in late August and early September to restore communications between the armies isolated in Stalingrad city and those operating between the Don and Volga Rivers to the northwest. Stalin's vigorous countermeasures to thwart Blau also included numerous offensives, counterstrokes, and local attacks conducted by Northwestern, Kalinin, and Western Fronts in the Demiansk, Kalinin, Rzhev, Zhizdra, and Bolkhov regions—fully two-thirds of the entire German-Soviet front. By attacking across such a wide sector, he was able to distract and weaken the German offensive.

Third, conventional wisdom would also assert that, even though the *Stavka* indeed managed to mobilize fresh forces during summer 1942, most of the armies that slowed, halted, and ultimately defeated the German juggernaut in Operation Blau were the same ones that had escaped destruction by withdrawing time and again during the summer. This conclusion is also mistaken. As indicated above, fully half of the 25 Soviet armies that opposed Army Groups A and B in early September 1943 were entirely new armies raised and fielded in a mobilization effort that, in comparison, dwarfed the scope of the 1941 mobilization. In addition, as many as 50 percent, and perhaps more, of the soldiers who filled up these refurbished armies were also a product of this mobilization. Therefore, as with Operation Barbarossa the year before, the German High Command during Operation Blau woefully underestimated the *Stavka's* capacity to raise and field fresh armies to replace those that had been destroyed.

Although the Germans failed to recognize these three factors in early September 1942, and most historians have overlooked them since, collectively they decided the fate of Operation Blau. If they did not foreshadow the coming German defeat by early in September, they certainly confirmed it in two months.

The Experiences of the Commanders of Tank Armies and Tank Corps assigned to Briansk, Southwestern, Southern, and Crimean Fronts and the *Stavka* Reserve from 1 May to 1 July 1942 and Stalingrad Front on 1 August 1942

BRIANSK FRONT
1st Tank Corps (1 May)

Major General Mikhail Efimovich Katukov (born 17 September 1900–died 8 June 1976). Major General, 10 November 1941, Lieutenant General, 18 January 1943, Colonel General, 10 April 1944, and Marshal of Tank Forces, 1959. Twice Hero of the Soviet Union (23 September 1944 and 6 May 1945). Mogilev Infantry Course (1922), *"Vystrel'"* Officers Course (1927), Stalin Mechanization and Motorization Academy (1935), and Voroshilov Academy (1951). Commander, platoon, company, and training battalion (1922–1937), chief of staff, 45th Mechanized Corps (1937–1939), commander, 5th Light Tank (134th Mechanized) Brigade, 25th Tank Corps (1939) (Poland), commander, 38th Light Tank Brigade (20 July 1940), commander, 20th Tank Division, 9th Mechanized Corps (28 November 1940–29 August 1941), commander, 4th (1st Guards) Tank Brigade (8 September 1941–2 April 1942), commander, 1st Tank Corps (31 March–18 July 1942), commander, 3rd Mechanized Corps (18 September 1942–30 January 1943), commander, 1st (1st Guards) Tank Army (30 January 1943–1945), commander, 1st Mechanized Army (1945–1948), chief of Tank and Mechanized Forces, Group of Soviet Occupation Forces, Germany (GSOFG) (1949–1951), General-Inspector, Ministry of Defense Main Inspectorate (1955–1963), and Group of General Inspectors (retirement) (1963).

Colonel (Major General, 3 May 1942) Vasilii Vasil'evich Butkov (19 September 1942) (born 29 December 1900–died 24 June 1981). Lieutenant General, 7 June 1943 and Colonel General, 1958. Hero of the Soviet Union (19 April 1945). Moscow Combined Military School (1926), Engel's Military-Political Course, Leningrad (1928), Frunze Academy (1937), and Voroshilov Academy (1954). Commander, platoon, battery, political officer, and battalion (1922–1934), chief of staff, 13th Mechanized Brigade (1937–1940), chief of staff, 17th Tank Division (June 1940–May 1941), chief of staff and deputy commander, 5th Mechanized Corps (May–August 1941), assistant chief of staff, Red Army's Main Armored Directorate (August 1941–8 September 1942), commander, 8th Tank Corps (8–14 September 1942), commander, 1st Tank Corps (19 September 1942–11 May 1945), commander, Tank and Mechanized Forces, Special (Konigsberg), North Caucasus, and Moscow Military Districts (1946–1950), commander, 3rd Guards Mechanized Army (1950–1953), General-Inspector of Tank Forces, Ministry of Defense (1954–

1955), 1st deputy commander, Moscow Military District (1955–1958), Senior Adviser, Czech Peoples' Army (1958–1959), Representative, Warsaw Pact in Czechoslovakia (1959–1961), retired (1961).

4th Tank Corps (1 May)

Major General Vasilii Aleksandrovich Mishulin (born 26 April 1900–died 26 April 1967). Major General, 24 July 1941 and Lieutenant General, postwar. Hero of the Soviet Union (24 July 1941). 37th Tikhoretsk Infantry Course (1923), Political Preparation Course (1928), Frunze Academy (1936), and Voroshilov Academy (1944). Commander, squad and company and political officer (1922–1936), chief of staff, 29th Mechanized Regiment, 29th Cavalry Division (1936–1937), commander, special-designation motorized armored regiment, reorganized as 8th Motorized-Armored Brigade, 57th Special Corps (1938–1939) (Khalkhin Gol), commander, 57th Tank Division, 29th Mechanized Corps (11 March–1 September 1941), 1st deputy chief, Main Auto-Armored Directorate (September 1941–January 1942), commander, tank group (23rd, 26th, 27th Tank Brigades) (October–December 1941), deputy commander, Kalinin Front's Tank and Mechanized Forces (January–31 March 1942), commander, 4th Tank Corps (31 March–18 September 1942), relieved for "weak control of his forces"(October 1942), commander, 173rd Separate Tank Brigade, 3rd Tank Army (12 October 1942–19 June 43), commander, 3rd Tank Corps (1 April–4 July 1944), commander, Tank and Mechanized Forces, 10th Guards Army (September 1944–May 1945), commander, Tank and Mechanized Forces, Tavria and Eastern Siberian Military Districts (1945–1953), retired (June 1953).

Major General Andrei Grigor'evich Kravchenko (18 September 1942) (see 2nd Tank Corps, 5th Tank Army, below). Commander, 4th (5th Guards) Tank Corps (18 September 1942–24 January 1944), commander, 6th Guards Tank Army (20 January 1944–September 1953), assistant commander, Far Eastern Military District for Tank Weaponry (January 1954–October 1955), retired (October 1955).

16th Tank Corps (1 July)

Major General Mikhail Ivanovich Pavelkin (born 14 September 1900–died 15 May 1955). Major General, 4 June 1940 and Lieutenant General, 19 April 1945. Department of Military Commissars, Higher School for Command Cadre (1923), Leningrad Armored Course (KUKS) (1931), Stalin Military Academy of Mechanization and Motorization (1937), and Voroshilov Academy (1948). Assistant commissar, 1st and 3rd Workers' Brigades, Donets Workers' Army (1921), political worker, 453rd Regiment, 51st Perekop Rifle Division (1922–1923), commissar, 12th Auto-Armored Battalion, 2nd Cavalry Corps (October 1927–November 1930), commander, 33rd Tank Battalion, Caucasus Red Army (June 1932–July 1933), commander, 36th Tank Battalion, 36th Trans-Baikal Division, Trans-Baikal Group of Forces (Front in March 1935) (July 1933–February 1936), commander, 6th Mechanized (8th Light Tank) Brigade, 20th Tank Corps (September 1937–November 1940) (Khalkhin Gol), deputy commander, 5th Mechanized Corps (November 1940–11 March 1941), commander, 29th Mechanized Corps (11 March–7 May 1941), commander, Auto-Armored Forces, Far Eastern Front, Trans-Caucasus Military District, and Crimean Front (7 May 1941–April 1942), chief, Gorki Tank Center (April–June 1942), commander, 16th Tank Corps (1 June–14 September 1942), chief, Molotov Auto-Armored Center (October 1942–June 1943), deputy chief for formations, Kosterov Tank Laager (June 1943–September 1944), chief, Khar'kov Tank Laager (September 1944–January 1945), commander, Tank and Mechanized Forces, 3rd Ukrainian Front (January–May 1945), deputy commander, Tank and Mechanized Forces, Southern Group of Forces (SGF), Hungary (June 1945–March 1947), commander, Tank and Mechanized Forces, Kiev Military District (June 1948–February 1951), Senior military adviser, tank and mechanized forces, Czech Peoples' Army (February 1951–1955), retired (January 1955).

Major General of Technical Forces Aleksei Gavrilovich Maslov (15 September 1942) (born 25 February 1901–died 21 February 1968). Major General, 4 June 1940. Infantry Course (1921), *"Vystrel'"* Officers Course (1926), Frunze Academy (1934), and Chemical Defense Academy (1937). Commander, platoon, 24th Nizhegorodskaia and 9th Ufa Rifle Divisions (1921–1922), commander, company, assistant battalion commander, 100th Rifle Regiment, and political worker, 102nd Rifle Regiment, 34th Rifle Division (1923–1934), chief of staff and deputy for training, Saratov Armored School (1934–1937), chief of staff, 107th Rifle Division (1939–1940), chief of staff, 9th Mechanized Corps (1940–19 July 1941), commander, 9th Mechanized Corps (19 July–September 1941), chief of staff, 38th Army (September–24 December 1941), commander, 38th Army (24 December 1941–20 February 1942), chief of staff, 28th Army (March–April 1942), commander, 9th Tank Corps (April–May 1942), deputy commander for Tank Forces, 5th Army (May–September 1942), commander, 16th Tank Corps (15 September 1942–24 February 1943), deputy chief, Red Army's Main Directorate for Guards-Mortar Units (April 1943–1944), chief, Red Army's Directorate for the Supply and Repair of Combat and Transport vehicles (1944–1945), commander, Armored and Mechanized Forces, L'vov Military District (1945–1947), commander, 23rd Mechanized and 3rd Guards Divisions (1947–1949), chief, Higher Officers School (1949–1957), retired (1957).

17th Tank Corps (1 July)

Major General Nikolai Vladimirovich Feklenko (born October 1901–died 12 October 1951). Major General, 4 June 1940, and Lieutenant General, 5 November 1943. Stavropol' Political Workers Course (1922), Military-Political School (1925), Cavalry officers Improvement Course (1928), Mechanization and Motorization Academy (1933), and Voroshilov Academy (1949). Political worker, commander, cavalry squadron, and chief of regimental school (1921–1930), commander, mechanized regiment, 5th Cavalry Division (1933), commander, 7th Motorized Armored Brigade (1936–1938), commander, 57th Special Rifle Corps (8 September 1938–16 June 1939) (Khalkhin-Gol), commander, 14th Heavy Tank Brigade (1939–1940), commander, 15th Tank Division, 8th Mechanized Corps (June 1940–11 March 1941), commander, 19th Mechanized Corps (11 March–15 August 1941), commander, 38th Army (15 August–22 September 1941), relieved , 22 September 1941, commander, Stalingrad Military District (November 1941–May 1942), deputy commander, Red Army's Main Auto-Armored Directorate (May–June 1942), commander, 17th Tank Corps (19 June–1 July 1942), chief, Tula and Stalingrad Armored Centers (July 1942–July 1943), commander, Tank and Mechanized Forces, Steppe Front (July–December 1943), chief, Red Army Directorate for the Formation of Armored and Mechanized Forces (December 1943–May 1946), staff officer and commander, Red Army Tank and Mechanized Forces (May–September 1946), commander, Tank and Mechanized Forces, Belorussian and Carpathian Military Districts (September 1946–April 1950), staff officer and commander, Red Army Tank and Mechanized Forces (October 1950–July 1951), retired (July 1951).

Colonel (Major General, 3 May 1942) Ivan Petrovich Korchagin (2 July 1942) (born 24 August 1898–died 24 July 1951). Lieutenant General, 18 January 1943. Hero of the Soviet Union (17 October 1943). 5th Moscow Warrant Officers School (1916), *"Vystrel'"* Officers Course (1927), and Voroshilov Academy (1947). Commander, companies, 312th Infantry and 258th Reserve Regiments (1917), commander, company and battalion, Gorokhovetsk Rifle Regiment, 7th Separate Brigade (August 1918–May 1919), commander, battalion, 501st Railroad Regiment (1920), deputy chief of staff, 101st Rifle Brigade (January–June 1921), chief of staff, 1st and 2nd Turkestan Rifle Regiments, Central Asia (September 1922–December 1924), chief of staff, 4th Turkestan Rifle Regiment, commander, 5th Turkestan Rifle Regiment, 2nd Rifle Division (December 1924–January 1927), commander, 3rd Turkestan Rifle Regiment, 1st Mountain Rifle Division (January 1927–November 1930) (Basmachi insurgency), chief of staff, 56th Rifle Division, Leningrad Military District (November 1930–February 1935), senior staff officer, Leningrad Military District (February 1935–November 1936), commander, 31st Mechanized Brigade, 7th Mechanized Corps (November 1936–August 1937), repressed in August 1937 but released in February 1940, chief of infantry, 121st Rifle Division, 24th Rifle Corps (February–June 1940), deputy commander, 17th Tank Division, 5th Mechanized Corps (June 1940–March 1941), commander, 17th Tank Division, 5th Mechanized Corps (1 March–28 August 1941), commander, 126th Tank Brigade (17 August–October 1941), encircled and destroyed at Viaz'ma, commander, 36th Tank Brigade (6–29 December 1941), chief, 7th Department (*Aerosanyi* Forces), Red Army Main Auto-Armored Directorate (29 December 1941–2 July 1942), commander, 17th Tank Corps (2–20 July 1942) (see 18th Tank Corps below).

Colonel (Major General, 14 October 1942) Boris Sergeevich Bakharov (21 July 1942) (born 10 September 1902–died 16 July 1944). Combined International Military School (1926), Frunze Academy (1932), and Leningrad Armored School (1932). Political worker, company, 20th Rifle Division (August 1926–May 1929), staff officer, 4th Mechanized Brigade (May 1932–May 1936), commander, training battalions, 10th and 18th Mechanized Brigades, Belorussian Military District (May 1936–October 1938), chief, Auto-Armored Forces, Khar'kov Military District (October 1938–November 1939), commander, 52nd Separate Light Tank Brigade, Khar'kov Military District (November 1939–March 1941), commander, 50th Tank Division, 25th Mechanized Corps (11 March–17 September 1941), commander, 150th Tank Brigade (18 September 1941–15 June 1942), chief of staff, 17th Tank

Corps (15 June–21 July 1942), commander, 17th Tank Corps (21 July–6 August 1942), commander, 18th Tank Corps (11 September–16 July 1943), deputy commander, 9th Tank Corps (July–2 September 1943), commander, 9th Tank Corps (2 September 1943–16 July 1944), killed in action in the Belorussian operation.

Colonel (Major General, 10 November 1942) Pavel Petrovich Poluboiarov (7 August 1942) (born 16 June 1901–died 17 September 1984). Lieutenant General, 23 March 1943, Colonel General, postwar, and Marshal of Tank Forces, 1962. Hero of the Soviet Union (29 May 1945). Tula Infantry Command Course (1920), School for Higher Command Cadre of Armored Forces (1920) Leningrad Armored School (1926), Stalin Academy of Mechanization and Motorization (1928), and Voroshilov Academy (1941). Commander, platoon, 3rd Auto-Motorized Regiment (October 1926–October 1927), commander, training platoon, 12th Auto-Armored Battalion (October 1927–December 1929), commander, auto-armored battalion, 45th Rifle Division (December 1929–April 1931), chief of staff, tank training regiment (April–November 1931), staff officer, Auto-Armored Forces, Ukrainian Military District (May 1931–November 1934), commander, Tank and Mechanized Forces, Trans-Baikal Military District (November 1938–June 1940) (Khalkhin-Gol), deputy commander, Tank and Mechanized Forces, 17th Army (June–November 1940), commander, Tank and Mechanized Forces, Leningrad Military District (January–March 1941), commander, Tank and Mechanized Forces, Baltic Special Military District and Northwestern Front (March 1941–March 1942), deputy commander, Tank Forces, Kalinin Front (March–August 1942), commander, 17th (4th Guards) Tank Corps (7 August 1942–11 May 1945), commander, 5th Guards Tank Army (April 1945–June 1946), commander, 5th Guards Mechanized Army (June 1946–March 1949), 1st deputy commander, Soviet Army's Tank and Mechanized Forces (March 1949–January 1954), chief, Soviet Army Tank Forces (May 1954–May 1969), retired into Group of General Inspectors (May 1969).

24th Tank Corps (Southern Front, 1 May, Briansk Front, 1 July)
Major General Vasilii Mikhailovich Badanov (born 26 December 1895–died 1 April 1971). Major General, 28 December 1941 and Lieutenant General, 26 December 1942. Chuguev Military School (1916), Officers Improvement Course (KUKS) (1927, 1931, and 1932), Military Academy of Mechanization and Motorization (1934), and Voroshilov Academy (1950). Staff officer, regiment and division of Cheka and OGPU Forces (1922–January 1930), chief, machine gun course, Saratov Commanders' School (January 1930–May 1931), commander, separate tank battalion, Saratov Armored School (May 1931–1932), assistant chief, Military Auto-Technical School, Baltic Special Military District (1932–January 1940), chief, Poltava Military Auto-Technical School (January 1940–March 1941), commander, 55th Tank Division, 25th Mechanized Corps, Western and Central Fronts (11 March–10 August 1941), commander, 12th Tank Brigade (2 September 1941–16 March 1942), deputy commander, 56th Army (16 March–19 April 1942), commander, 24th (2nd Guards) Tank Corps (19 April 1942–25 June 1943), commander, 4th Tank Army (25 June 1943–29 March 1944), seriously wounded in the Proskurov-Chernovitsy operation in March 1944, chief, Training Directorate, Red

Army Main Directorate for the Formation and Combat Training of Tank and Mechanized Forces (August 1944–June 1946), commander, Tank and Mechanized Forces, Central Group of Forces (June 1946–1949), chief, Soviet Army Directorate for Training Tank and Mechanized Forces (July 1950–1953), retired (1953).

SOUTHWESTERN FRONT

13th Tank Corps (1 July)

Major General Petr Evdokimovich Shurov (born 5 January 1897–died 2 July 1942). Major General, 4 June 1940. Saratov Infantry School (1919), "*Vystrel*" Officers Course (1928), Leningrad Armored School (1932), and Stalin Academy of Mechanization and Motorization (1936). Commander, platoon, 194th Malouzensk and 6th Tula Rifle Regiments (1919), commander, company and battalion and deputy commander, regiment (1920), chief, Sestroretsk garrison (1921) (suppressed Kronshtadt mutiny), commander, battalion, and deputy commander, 51st and 33rd Rifle Regiments (1923–1924), chief of staff, 29th Rifle Regiment, 10th Rifle Division (October 1924–October 1927), deputy commander, 10th Rifle Regiment, 4th Turkestan Rifle Division (November 1929–March 1930) (Basmachi insurgency), commander, 31st Rifle Regiment, 11th Rifle Division (March 1930–June 1932), chief of school, 11th Mechanized Corps (August 1932–August 1934), commander, 19th Mechanized Brigade, 11th Mechanized Corps (August 1934–August 1936), chief, Ural Armored School (October 1936–August 1940), repressed but exonerated and released in 1936, deputy General Inspector, Red Army's Auto-Armored Forces (August 1940–November 1941), assistant commander, Auto-Armored Forces, Western Front (November 1941–January 1942), commander, Stalingrad Tank Training Center (January–May 1942), commander, 13th Tank Corps (23 May–2 July 1942), fatally wounded in action in the Novyi Oskol region (July 1942).

Colonel Trofim Ivanovich Tanaschishin (17 July 1942) (born 31 January 1903–died 31 March 1944). Major General, 7 December 1942 and Lieutenant General on 30 August 1943. Budenny Cavalry School (1928) and Leningrad Armored School (KUKS) (1931 and 1935). Physical training instructor, various military commissariats (1921–1924), commander, platoon, 52nd and 54th Cavalry Regiments, 9th Cavalry Division (September 1928–May 1931), commander, armored train and motorized detachment, Moscow Proletarian Rifle Division (May–October 1931), commander, separate mechanized squadron, 11th Cavalry Division (October 1931–April 1932), commander, 11th Mechanized Regiment and tank squadron and deputy chief of staff, regiment, 11th Cavalry Division (April–November 1934), deputy chief of staff, chief of staff, and commander, 11th Mechanized Regiment, 11th Cavalry Division (May 1935–June 1938), staff officer, 1st Tank Brigade, Belorussian Special Military District (June 1938–April 1940), assistant chief of staff, 21st Tank Brigade, Western Special Military District (April–June 1940), chief of supply, 4th Tank Division, 6th Mechanized Corps (July 1940–March 1941), commander, 60th Tank Regiment, 30th Tank Division, 14th Mechanized Corps (March–August 1941), commander, 36th Separate (1st Guards) Motorcycle Regiment, 5th Army, Western Front (August–December 1941), commander, 36th Tank Brigade, Moscow Military District and 22nd Tank Corps (30 December 1941–15 July 1942), commander, 13th Tank Corps (17 July 1942) (see 13th Tank Corps, 1st Tank Army, below).

14th Tank Corps (Stavka Reserve, 1 June, Southwestern Front, 1 July)
  Colonel (Major General, 13 May 1942) Nikolai Nikolaevich Radkevich (born
  22 February 1904–died 4 June 1982). Lieutenant General, 1954. Petrograd Higher
  Military Auto-Armored School (1923), Stalin Academy of Mechanization and Motorization (1937), and Voroshilov Academy (1941 and 1949). Instructor and platoon
  leader, 5th Red Banner Army (1921–January 1925), commander, cavalry platoon
  (January 1925–October 1926), commander, tank platoon and training company,
  Leningrad Armored School (October 1926–May 1932), commander, tank forces,
  Moscow Officers Course (KUKS) (May 1932–1933), chief of staff and commander,
  5th Tank Brigade (1937–June 1938), chief, 1st Department, Western Special Military District's Auto-Armored Directorate (June 1939–October 1940), commander,
  63rd Reserve Tank Regiment (June–August 1941), commander, 121st Tank Brigade
  (1 August 1941–15 June 1942), commander, 14th Tank Corps (16 June–30 September 1942), commander, 11th Tank Corps (8 June–21 October 1943), commander,
  Tank and Mechanized Forces, Far Eastern Front and Military District (October
  1943–April 1948), commander, Tank and Mechanized Forces, Central Group of
  Forces (May 1949–December 1950), 1st deputy and deputy chief, Soviet Army
  Main Armored Directorate (December 1950–July 1954), senior adviser, Tank and
  Mechanized Forces, Hungarian Peoples' Army (July 1954–November 1956), mili-
  tary attaché to Czechoslovakia (March 1957–March 1959), retired (March 1959).

Reorganized into *6th Mechanized Corps*, 30 September 1942
  Major General Semen Il'ich Bogdanov (26 September 1941) (born 29 August
  1897–died 12 March 1960). Lieutenant General, 7 June 1943, Colonel General,
  24 April 1944, and Marshal of Tank Forces, 1 June 1945. Twice Hero of the Soviet
  Union (11 March 1944 and 6 April 1945). Northern Front's Warrant Officers
  School (1917), Higher Military-Pedagogical School (1923), *"Vystrel'"* Officers
  Course (1930), Stalin Academy of Mechanization and Motorization (1936). Com-
  mander, platoon, company, and battalion (1918–1928), assistant commander, 134th
  Rifle Regiment (1928–1930), commander, 134th Rifle Regiment (October 1930–
  May 1932), commander, 134th Mechanized Brigade (May 1932–October 1935),
  commander, 9th Mechanized Brigade (January 1937–May 1938), repressed 1 May
  1938 but released in October 1939, commander, 29th Mechanized Division, 6th
  Mechanized Corps (1940), commander, 32nd Light Tank Brigade (December
  1940–March 1941), commander, 30th Tank Division, 14th Mechanized Corps (11
  March–30 June 1941), commander, Tank and Mechanized Forces, Moscow Mili-
  tary District (July–October 1941), commander, Mozhaisk Fortified Region and
  deputy commander, 5th Army (October 1941–May 1942), commander, 12th Tank
  Corps (19 May–7 September 1942), commander, 6th (5th Guards) Mechanized
  Corps (26 September 1942–25 February 1943), commander, 9th Tank Corps (11
  March–24 August 1943), commander, 2nd Guards Tank Army (9 September 1943–
  23 July 1944), hospitalized with wounds, commander, 2nd Guards Tank Army (7
  January 1945–10 June 1947), commander, Tank and Mechanized Forces, Group
  of Soviet Occupation Forces, Germany (June 1947), 1st deputy commander and
  commander, Soviet Army's Tank and Mechanized Forces (1947–1953), commander,
  7th Mechanized Army (April 1953–May 1954), chief, Military Academy of
  Armored Forces (1954–1960), retired (1956).

21st Tank Corps (1 May)

Major General Grigorii Ivanovich Kuz'min (born 2 January 1895–died 28 May 1942). Major General, 9 November 1941. Leningrad Instructor-Inspector Course (1919), Petrograd 2nd Military School of Physical Culture (1923), *"Vystrel'"* Officers Course (1931), and Moscow Motor-Mechanized Officers Improvement Course (1932). Commander, platoon, 2nd Red Banner Reserve Regiment (September–October 1918), commander, company, 52nd Rifle Regiment, Northern Front (May–September 1919), captured by British forces but escaped (September–October 1919), commander, company, 15th Rifle Regiment, Western Front (1920) (Polish War), commander, company, 15th and 5th Rifle Regiments, Moscow Military District (1920–January 1922), commander, platoon and company and chief of regimental school, 251st Rifle Regiment, 84th Rifle Division (May 1924–1931), commander, battalion, *"Vystrel'"* School (1931–1932), chief of staff, training mechanized regiment, Stalin Academy of Mechanization and Motorization (December 1933–February 1937), chief of staff, deputy commander, and temporary commander, 10th Mechanized Brigade, Belorussian Military District (February 1937–December 1939), deputy commander, 43rd Motor Transport Brigade (December 1939–October 1940), deputy commander, 11th Tank Division, 2nd Mechanized Corps (October 1940–March 1941), commander, 11th Tank Division, 2nd Mechanized Corps (1 March–27 August 1941), reorganized into 132nd (4th Guards) Tank Brigade (27 August 1941–19 April 1942), and commander, 21st Tank Corps (19 April 1942–28 May 1942). Killed in action during the battle for Khar'kov.

Destroyed at Khar'kov in May and disbanded in June 1942

22nd Tank Corps (1 May)

Colonel (Major General, 13 May 1942) Aleksandr Aleksandrovich Shamshin (born 25 August 1908–died 23 September 1972). Stalin Nizhegorodskaia Infantry School (1931), Moscow Officers Improvement Course (KUKS) (1932), and Frunze Academy (1938). Joined Red Army in September 1928. Commander, platoon, 12th Rifle Regiment, 4th Rifle Division (March 1931–October 1932), commander, tank platoon and company and chief of operations, 3rd Training Tank Brigade (October 1932–May 1935), chief of staff, 42nd Tank Brigade, Far East (September 1938–June 1939), teacher, Stalin Academy of Mechanization and Motorization(June 1939–October 1940), chief of staff, 39th Tank Brigade (October 1940–March 1941), chief of staff, 39th Tank Division, 16th Mechanized Corps (March–September 1941), commander, 34th Motorized Rifle Brigade (September 1941–April 1942), commander, 22nd Tank Corps (3 April–30 August 1942) (see 22nd Tank Corps, 4th Tank Army, below).

23rd Tank Corps (1 May)

Major General Efim Grigor'evich Pushkin (born 28 January 1899–died 11 March 1944). Major General, 27 March 1942 and Lieutenant General, 18 January 1943. Hero of the Soviet Union (9 November 1941). Orel Cavalry Course (1919), 16th Army's cavalry course (1921), and Leningrad Auto-Armored School (1932). Commander, platoon and squadron, 2nd Taman' and 17th Cavalry Regiments (1919–1920) (Polish War), commander, squadron, 17th Cavalry Regiment, Turkestan Front (1921–1923) (Basmachi insurgency), commander, squadron, chief, regimental school, and chief of staff, 52nd Cavalry Regiment (July 1925–May 1932), chief of staff, 14th Mechanized Regiment, 14th Cavalry Division (September 1932–October 1938), commander, 32nd Tank Division, 4th Mechanized Corps (February–July 1941), commander, 8th Tank Division (July–September 1941), commander, 130th Tank Brigade (September 1941–March 1942), simultaneously, commander, Group of Forces, Southern Front (January–February 1942), deputy commander, 18th Army (March–April 1942), commander, 23rd Tank Corps (12 April–4 June 1942), destroyed in battle for Khar'kov, deputy commander, Tank Forces, Southwestern Front (4 June–August 1942), deputy commander, 4th Tank Army (August–29 November 1942), commander, 23rd Tank Corps, second formation (29 November 1942–11 March 1944). Killed in action in the Ukraine.

Colonel (Major General, 21 July 1942) Abram Matveevich Khasin (5 June 1942) (born 17 January 1899–died 12 April 1967). Khar'kov Artillery Course (1919), Moscow Artillery Command Cadre Course (1920), Antiaircraft Artillery Officers Improvement Course (KUKS) (1930), Officer Improvement Course (KUKS), Dzerzhinsky Military-Technical Academy (1932), and Stalin Academy of Mechanization and Motorization (1936). Commander, platoon, 3rd Revolutionary Army (1918–1919), commander, battery, 13th Army (1920–1921), commander, platoon, and assistant commander, battery, 2nd Light Artillery Battalion, 30th Rifle Division (March 1921–April 1922), commander, battery, Sevastopol' Fortress (April 1922–September 1923), various artillery staff and command positions in Sevastopol' (September 1923–June 1927) and 121st Artillery Regiment, Ural Military District (June 1927–March 1930), commander, separate tank battalion, 90th Rifle Division (January 1937–May 1938), deputy commander and commander, 9th Mechanized Brigade, Leningrad Military District (May 1938–January 1940), commander, 11th Reserve Tank Regiment (January–July 1940), commander, 25th Tank Regiment, 163rd Motorized Rifle Division, 1st Mechanized Corps (July 1940–1 September 1941), commander, 1st (6th Guards) Tank Brigade, 56th Army (1 September 1941–15 June 1942), commander, 23rd Tank Corps (5 June–25 August 1942) (see 23rd Tank Corps, 4th Tank Army, below).

Major General Aleksei Fedorovich Popov (30 August 1942) (see 11th Tank Corps below). Commander, 23rd Tank Corps (30 August–15 October 1942), and commander, 2nd (8th Guards) Tank Corps (16 October 1942–9 May 1945).

Lieutenant Colonel Vasilii Vasil'evich Koshelev (16 October 1942) (born 19 July 1908–died 14 October 1992). Major General of Tank Forces, 15 September 1943. Lenin Political Officer Improvement Course (1938), Improvement Course (KUKS) at the Stalin Academy of Mechanization and Motorization (1941), Short Course at the Voroshilov Academy (1942), and Voroshilov Academy (1948). Conscripted in 1930. Political worker, 4th Turkestan Cavalry Division (December 1932–1936), received Order of Lenin (1936), commander, squadron, 4th Mechanized Battalion, and armored train squadron, 18th Mountain Cavalry Division (April 1938–May 1940), commander, 33rd Armored Train Battalion, 18th Mountain Cavalry Division (May 1940–September 1941) (Iranian border), staff officer, General Staff (January–March 1942), General Staff representative to 23rd Tank Corps

(May–October 1942), chief of staff, 23rd Tank Corps (October 1942–February 1943), temporary commander, 23rd Tank Corps (16 October–28 November 1942), deputy commander and commander, 2nd (8th Guards) Tank Corps (February 1943–June 1945), reorganized as 8th Guards Tank Division (June 1945–January 1947), chief, Tashkent Tank School (March 1949–March 1950), chief of staff, 4th Guards Mechanized Army (March 1950–May 1953), chief, Saratov Tank School (May 1953–December 1957), department chief, Soviet Army Directorate for Combat Training (December 1957–August 1958), deputy chief, Soviet Army's Directorate for Combat Training (August 1958–March 1968), retired (March 1968).

SOUTHERN FRONT
24th Tank Corps (1 May, Briansk Front, 1 July)
STAVKA RESERVE
7th Tank Corps (Kalinin Front, 1 May, 1 June, *Stavka* Reserve, 1 July)
Colonel (Major General, 21 July 1942) Pavel Alekseevich Rotmistrov (born 6 July 1901–died 6 April 1982). Lieutenant General, 29 December 1942, Colonel General, 20 October 1943, and Chief Marshal of Tank Forces in 1962. Doctor of Military Science (1956) and professor of Military Science (1958). Hero of the Soviet Union (7 May 1965). 3rd Smolensk Infantry School for Red Commanders (1921), 1st Combined Military School (1924), Frunze Academy (1931), and Voroshilov Academy (1953). Political worker, 149th and 51st Rifle Regiments (1919–1921) (Kronshtadt mutiny), commander, platoon and company, and assistant battalion commander, 31st Rifle Regiment, 11th Rifle Division, Leningrad Military District (1924–1928), chief of staff section, 36th Trans-Baikal Rifle Division and Separate Red Banner Far Eastern Army (1931–July 1937), commander, 63rd Rifle Regiment, 21st Rifle Division (July–October 1937), teacher, tactics department, Stalin Academy of Mechanization and Motorization (December 1937–1939), commander, tank battalion, and chief of staff, 35th Light Tank Brigade (1939–December 1940) (Finnish War), deputy commander, 5th Tank Division, and chief of staff, 3rd Mechanized Corps, Baltic Special Military District (December 1940–early September 1941) (escaped from Minsk encirclement), commander, 8th (3rd Guards) Tank Brigade (14 September 1941–26 April 1942), commander, 7th (3rd Guards) Tank Corps (17 April 1942–22 February 1943), commander, 5th Guards Tank Army (22 February 1943–August 1944), deputy chief, Soviet Army Tank and Mechanized Forces (August 1944–June 1945), commander, Tank and Mechanized Forces, Group of Soviet Occupation Forces, Germany (June 1945–May 1947), commander, Tank and Mechanized Forces, Far East (May 1947–April 1948), chief of the tank and mechanized forces and strategy and operational art faculties, Voroshilov Academy (August 1948–April 1964), assistant Minister of Defense of the USSR for Training (April 1964–June 1968), retired into the Ministry of Defense's Group of Inspectors (June 1968).

Reorganized as 3rd Guards Tank Corps on 29 December 1942
18th Tank Corps (1 July)
Colonel (Major General, 3 May 1942) Ivan Danilovich Cherniakhovsky (born 26 March 1906–died 18 February 1945). Lieutenant General, 14 February 1943, Colonel General, 5 March 1944, and Army General, August 1944. Twice

Hero of the Soviet Union (17 October 1943 and 29 July 1944). Kiev Artillery School (1928) and Stalin Academy of Mechanization and Motorization (1936). Commander, platoon, political officer, and deputy commander and commander, battery (1928–1931), chief of staff and commander, 1st Tank Battalion, 8th Mechanized Brigade (1936–May 1938), commander, 9th Separate Light Tank Brigade (May 1938–June 1940), deputy commander, 2nd Tank Division, 3rd Mechanized Corps (June 1940–March 1941), commander, 28th Tank Division, 12th Mechanized Corps, Baltic Special Military District (Northwestern Front) (11 March–27 August 1941), commander, 241st Rifle Division (13 December 1941–15 June 1942), commander, 18th Tank Corps (15–25 July 1942), commander, 60th Army (25 June 1942–April 1944), commander, Western Front (April 1944), and commander, 3rd Belorussian Front (14 April 1944–18 February 1945). Killed in action in the East Prussian operation.

Major General Ivan Petrovich Korchagin (26 July 1942) (see 17th Tank Corps above). Commander, 18th Tank Corps (26 July–10 September 1942), commander, 2nd (7th Guards) Mechanized Corps, 3rd Guards Tank Army (8 September 1942–May 1945), commander, 7th Guards Mechanized Corps (Division) (May 1945–May 1946), commander, Tank and Mechanized Forces, Southern Group of Forces (April 1947–February 1948), commander, 8th Mechanized Army (February 1948–September 1950), deputy chief, Ministry of Defense Main Auto-Tractor Directorate (April–July 1951), died (July 1951).

Colonel (Major General, 14 October 1942) Boris Sergeevich Bakharov (11 September 1942) (born 10 September 1902–died 16 July 1944). Combined International Military School (1926), Frunze Academy (1932), and Leningrad Armored Officers Improvement Course (KUKS) (1932). Company and regimental political officer, 59th Regiment. 20th Rifle Division (1924–1929), staff officer, 4th Mechanized Brigade (May 1932–May 1936), commander, training battalion, 10th and 18th Mechanized Brigades (May 1936–October 1938), commander, Auto-Armored Forces, Khar'kov Military District (October 1938–November 1939), commander, 52nd Light Tank Brigade (November 1939–March 1941), commander, 50th Tank Division, 25th Mechanized Corps, Kiev Special Military District (11 March–17 September 1941), commander, 150th Tank Brigade (18 September 1941–15 June 1942), chief of staff, 17th Tank Corps (June–July 1942), commander, 17th Tank Corps (21 July–6 August 1942), commander, 18th Tank Corps (11 September 1942–25 July 1943), 9th Tank Corps (2 September 1943–16 July 1944). Killed in action in the Belorussian operation.

25th Tank Corps (1 July)

Major General Petr Petrovich Pavlov (born 12 January 1898–died 4 September 1962). Major General, 3 May 1942. Novocherkassk Cavalry Officer Improvement Course (KUKS) (1929), Leningrad Armored School (1932), and Voroshilov Academy (1947). Commander, platoon and separate cavalry squadron (1918–1919), commander, squadron, 23rd and 24th Separate Cavalry Regiments (January 1923–February 1925), commander, squadron, deputy chief of staff, regiment, and chief of regimental school, 19th Manych Cavalry Regiment (February 1925–December

1928), deputy chief of staff, 19th Manych Cavalry Regiment (September 1929–November 1930), staff officer, 4th Leningrad Cavalry Division (November 1930–May 1931), chief of regimental school, 23rd Sal'sk Cavalry Regiment (May–November 1931), teacher, Nizhegorodskaia Tank School (March 1932–July 1937), deputy commander, 38th Light Tank Brigade, Kiev Special Military District (January 1939–8 August 1940), deputy Inspector-General, Red Army Tank Forces (8 August–10 September 1940), commander, 38th Light Tank Brigade (10 September 1940–March 1941), commander, 41st Tank Division, 22nd Mechanized Corps (11 March–9 September 1941), deputy commander, 46th Tank Brigade, 4th Army, Volkov Front (9 September 1941–February 1942), deputy commander, Armored Forces, 59th Army (February–13 July 1942), commander, 25th Tank Corps (13 July 1942–15 March 1943), wounded and captured in the Donbas operation and prisoner-of-war in Germany (March 1943–April 1945), released by Americans and repatriated into the Soviet Union, "filtration" process by NKVD organs (May 1945–March 1946), chief, Soviet Army Directorate for Armored and Mechanized Forces (March–May 1947), deputy commander, Tank and Mechanized Forces, 36th Guards Rifle Corps (May 1947–June 1950), retired (June 1950).

5th Tank Army (Briansk Front, 2 July, *Stavka* Reserve, late July)
Major General Aleksandr Il'ich Liziukov (born 26 March 1900–died 23 July 1942). Major General, 10 January 1942. Hero of the Soviet Union (5 August 1941). Smolensk Artillery Course for Command Cadre (1919), Leningrad Armored School (1923), and Frunze Academy (1927). Teacher, Leningrad Armored Officer Improvement Course (KUKS) and Military-Technical Academy (1922–January 1933), commander, 3rd Separate Tank Battalion, and Separate Heavy Tank Regiment, Moscow Military District (January 1933–1934), commander, 6th Separate Heavy Tank Brigade (March 1936–1937), repressed in 1938 but released in 1940, deputy commander, 36th Tank Division, 17th Mechanized Corps (March–June 1941), chief of staff, Borisov Garrison (June–July 1941), chief of staff and commander, Operational Group Borisov at Orsha on the Dnepr River (mid-July 1941), commander, 1st Red Banner Moscow Motorized Rifle (Tank) Division, 2nd formation (18 August–22 September 1941), reorganized into 1st Guards Moscow Motorized Rifle Division on 22 September 1941, commander, 1st Guards Moscow Motorized Rifle Division (22 September–30 November 1941), deputy commander, 20th Army (30 November–31 December 1941), commander, 2nd Guards Rifle Corps (31 December 1941–4 April 1942), reorganized into 2nd Tank Corps in April 1941, commander, 2nd Tank Corps (15 April–28 May 1942), commander, 5th Tank Army (5 June–15 July 1942), commander, 2nd Tank Corps (15 July 1942) (see 2nd Tank Corps below).

2nd Tank Corps (*Stavka* Reserve, 1 May, Briansk Front, 1 June, 5th Tank Army, 1 July)
Colonel Semen Petrovich Mal'tsev (28 May 1942) (born 7 April 1901–died 6 February 1943). Infantry School (1931), Stalin Academy of Mechanization and Motorization (1936), and Voroshilov Academy (1941). Joined the Red Army in September 1922. Political worker, company and regimental school, 3rd Auto-Motorized Regiment (March 1925–November 1927), instructor, propaganda section, 23rd Rifle Division, Ukrainian military District (November 1927–January 1931), military

commissar, Balakleia Artillery Depot No. 29 and Balakleia Factory (January 1931–February 1933), staff officer, 8th Separate Mechanized Brigade (January–November 1937), commander, tank battalion, 8th Mechanized Brigade (November 1937–June 1939), assistant commander, 8th Mechanized Brigade (June–November 1939), chief of staff, 11th Tank Corps and 9th Tank Division (July 1941–March 1942), commander, training battalion, Red Army reserve (March–May 1942), chief of staff, 2nd Tank Corps (May 1942), commander, 2nd Tank Corps (28 May–9 June 1942), died in combat (6 February 1943).

Major General Ivan Gavrilovich Lazarev (10 June 1942) (born 7 January 1898–died 27 September 1979). Major General, 4 June 1940 and Lieutenant General, 7 June 1943. Petrograd Soviet Artillery Course (1918), Higher Artillery School for Command Cadre (1922), and Frunze Academy (1929). Commander, battery (1918–1919), commander, battery, assistant chief of staff, artillery regiment, and teacher, Stalin Academy of Mechanization and Motorization (1922–1935), commander, 16th (22nd Light Tank) Mechanized Brigade (1935–1939), deputy commander and commander, 1st Mechanized Corps, Leningrad Military District (December 1940–11 March 1941), commander, 10th Mechanized Corps (11 March–20 July 1941), commander, Luga Operational Group (20 July–early August 1941), repressed but released in August, commander, Narva, Slutsk-Kolpino Groups of Forces (August 1941), commander, 55th Army (1 September–17 November 1941), deputy General-Inspector, Main Auto-Tank Directorate and assistant commander, Northwestern Direction Main Command for Tank Forces (December 1941–May 1942), commander, 2nd Tank Corps (10 June–1 July 1942), commander, 11th Tank Corps (22 July 1942) (see 11th Tank Corps below).

Major General Aleksandr Il'ich Liziukov (see 5th Tank Army above) (15–23 July 1942). Killed in action in the Voronezh region on 23 July 1942.

Colonel (Major General, 21 July 1942) Andrei Grigor'evich Kravchenko (23 July 1942) (born 18 November 1899–died 18 October 1963). Lieutenant General, 7 June 1943, and Colonel General, 13 September 1944. Twice Hero of the Soviet Union (10 January 1944 and 8 September 1945). Poltava Military Infantry School (1923), Frunze Academy (1928), and Voroshilov Academy (1949). Commander, company and battalion, chief of staff, regiment, and instructor, Leningrad (KUKS) and Saratov Armored Schools (1922–1936), chief of staff, 173rd Rifle Division (May 1939–June 1940) (Finnish War), chief of staff, 16th Tank Division, 2nd Mechanized Corps (June 1940–March 1941), chief of staff, 18th Mechanized Corps (March–August 1941), commander, 31st Tank Brigade, Western Front (9 September 1941–10 January 1942), commander, Tank Forces, 61st Army (February–March 1942), chief of staff, 1st Tank Corps (March–2 July 1942), commander, 2nd Tank Corps (2 July–13 September 1942), commander, 4th Tank Corps (18 September 1942) (see above).

Major General Abram Matveevich Khasin (14 September 1942) (born 17 January 1899–died 12 April 1967) (see below). Commander, 2nd Tank Corps (14 September–15 October 1942), chief, Tambov Tank Center and chief, Red Army

Directorate for the Formation and Combat Training of Tank and Mechanized Forces (January–August 1943), commander, 8th Mechanized Corps (9 August 1943–10 January 1944), deputy commander, Leningrad and 2nd Baltic Front's Armored and Mechanized Forces (March 1944–May 1945), staff duty, Red Army's Tank and Mechanized Forces (October 1945–June 1946), commander, 19th Mechanized Division, Southern Group of Forces (June–November 1946), retired (June 1946).

11th Tank Corps (Briansk Front, 1 June, 5th Tank Army, 1 July)
Major General Aleksei Fedorovich Popov (born 30 March 1896–died 12 October 1946). Major General, 4 June 1940, and Lieutenant General in 1943. 112th Artillery Brigade's Training Command (1916), Petrograd Cavalry Course for Red Commanders (1918), Taganrog 6th Normal Command Cavalry School (1924), Novocherkassk Red Army Cavalry Officers Improvement Course (KUKS) (1929), and the Leningrad Armored Course for the Improvement of Red Army Command Cadre (1939). Commander, detachment, platoon, and squadron, 1st Saratov Cavalry Regiment, 2nd Cavalry Division (1919–1920), commander, platoon, regimental school, and squadron, 25th Amur Regiment, 5th Cavalry Division (September 1922–October 1928), deputy chief of staff and chief of staff, 28th Taman' Regiment, 5th Cavalry Division (September 1929–May 1932), chief of staff and commander, 5th Mechanized Regiment, 5th Cavalry Division, Ukrainian and Kiev Special Military Districts (May 1932–July 1938), chief, Tank and Mechanized Forces, 1st Red Banner Army (July 1938–March 1941), commander, 60th Tank Division, 30th Mechanized Corps and then separate 30th Tank Division (11 March 1941–20 January 1942), chief, Cheliabinsk Tank Center (January–May 1942), commander, 11th Tank Corps, 5th Tank Army (19 May–21 July 1942), commander, 23rd Tank Corps (30 August–15 October 1942), commander, 2nd (8th Guards) Tank Corps (16 October 1942–9 May 1946), deputy commander, 9th Mechanized Army (9 May–September 1946), fell ill in September and died (October 1946).

Major General Ivan Gavrilovich Lazarev (22 July 1942) (see 2nd Tank Corps above). Commander, 11th Tank Corps (22 July 1942–7 June 1943), commander, 20th Tank Corps (7 July 1943–9 May 1945), deputy commander, 8th Mechanized Army, Carpathian Military District (June 1945–August 1947), chief, Tank and Mechanized Forces faculty, Lenin Military-Political Academy (August 1947–February 1958), retired (February 1958).

STALINGRAD FRONT (1 August)
1st Tank Army (26 July, disbanded, 6 August)
Major General of Artillery Kirill Semenovich Moskalenko (born 11 May 1902–died 17 June 1985). Major General, 4 June 1940, Lieutenant General, 19 January 1943, Colonel General, and Marshal of the Soviet Union in 1955. Khar'kov Combine Officers School (1922), Artillery Officer Improvement Course (KUKS) (1928), and Dzerzhinsky Military Academy (1939). Twice Hero of the Soviet Union (23 October 1943 and 21 February 1978). Commander, artillery platoon, battery, and battalion, 6th Chongar Cavalry Division (1922–March 1933), chief of staff and commander, cavalry-artillery regiment, Separate Cavalry Division, Trans-Baikal

Group of Forces, Far Eastern Army (March 1933–1935), chief of artillery, 23rd Mechanized Brigade, Coastal Group, Separate Red Banner Far Eastern Army (1935–November 1936), commander, rifle regiment, 133rd Mechanized Brigade, 2nd Mechanized Corps, Kiev Military District (November 1936–1938), chief of artillery, 51st Perekop Rifle Division (June 1939–May 1940) (Finnish War), chief of artillery, 35th Rifle Corps (May–September 1940) (Bessarabia), chief of artillery, 2nd Mechanized Corps, Odessa Military District (September 1940–May 1941), commander, 1st Motorized Antitank Artillery Brigade, 5th Army, Kiev Special Military District (May–September 1941), commander, 15th Rifle Corps, 5th Army, Southwestern Front (September–early December 1941), commander, Cavalry-Mechanized Group, 13th Army (December 1941), temporary commander, 6th Army (mid-December 1941–12 February 1942), commander, 6th Cavalry Corps (12 February–5 March 1942), commander, 38th Army (5 March–26 July 1942), commander, 1st Tank Army (26 July–August 1942), commander, 1st Guards Army (August–October 1942), commander, 40th Army (October 1942–October 1943), commander, 38th Army (October 1943–May 1945), commander, army (June 1945–1948), commander, Moscow PVO (Air Defense) Region and District (1948–1953), commander, Moscow Military District (1953–1960), commander, Strategic Rocket Forces and Deputy Minister of Defense (1960–1962), Chief Inspector, USSR Ministry of Defense and deputy Minister of Defense (1962–1983), retired into Group of General Inspectors (1983).

13th Tank Corps

Colonel (Major General, 7 December 1942) Trofim Ivanovich Tanaschishin (see 13th Tank Corps above). Commander, 13th Tank (4th Guards Mechanized) Corps (17 July 1942–31 March 1944), killed in action in the Odessa operation.

28th Tank Corps (formed 13 July 1942)

Colonel (Major General, 4 August 1942) Georgii Semenovich Rodin (born 19 November 1897–died 6 January 1976). Lieutenant General, 7 June 1943. Orel Infantry Course (1919), Rostov Officers Course (1923), *"Vystrel'"* Officers Course (1925), and Course for the Technical Improvement of Red Army Command Cadre (1934). Commander, platoon, 32nd Reserve Regiment, 219th Kotel'nikovskii Regiment, 55th Infantry Division (1916–1917), commander, platoon and company and assistant chief of reconnaissance, Orel Infantry Course, Reserve and Composite Orel Regiments, 9th Kuban' Army, and 2nd Rifle Regiment, 18th Kuban' Army (1918–1921), commander, platoon, assistant commander, company, and deputy battalion commander, 2nd, 115th, and 65th Rifle Regiments, 9th Army (1921–December 1926), deputy commander and commander, 234th Rifle Regiment, (December 1930–December 1933), commander, separate tank battalion and chief of Armor, 25th Rifle Division (December 1933–April 1938), commander, 27th Tank Battalion, 21st Tank Brigade, Belorussian Special Military District (May 1939–January 1940) (Poland), commander, 24th Tank Regiment, 24th Tank (former Motorized Cavalry) Division (January–December 1940) (Finnish War), commander, 23rd Separate Light Tank Brigade (December 1940–March 1941), commander, 47th Tank Division, 18th Mechanized Corps (11 March–7 October 1941), wounded in action, commander, 142nd Tank Brigade (7 October 1941–29 January 1942), commander, 52nd Tank Brigade (March–June 1942), commander, 28th (4th Mechanized) Tank Corps (13 July–10 October 1942), commander, Tank and Mechanized Forces, Southwestern Front (10 October 1942–March 1943), commander, 30th (10th Guards) Tank Corps (28 March 1943–15 March 1944), relieved for poor performance, commander, 6th Training Tank Brigade (25 April 1944–May 1945), chief, Belorussian Tank Center (June 1945–July 1946), retired (July 1946).

Reorganized as *4th Mechanized Corps*, 10 October 1942

Major General Vasilii Timofeevich Vol'sky (11 October 1942) (born 22 March 1897–died 22 February 1946). Major General, 4 June 1940, Lieutenant General, 7 February 1943, and Colonel General, 26 October 1944. Frunze Academy (1926), Officers Improvement Course (KUVNAS) (1929), and Tank Officers Improvement Course (KUKS) (1930). Political worker and regimental and division commissar (1919–1920), commander, cavalry squadron and regiment (1921–1929), commander, mechanized regiment and 32nd Separate Mechanized Brigade (the first in the RKKA) (1930–1932), staff officer, Red Army Directorate of Mechanization and Motorization (1932), 6th Separate Mechanized Brigade (1932), assistant chief, Stalin Academy of Mechanization and Motorization (May 1939–1941), deputy commander, Auto-Tank Forces, 21st Army (June–July 1941), deputy chief, Auto-Tank Forces, Southwestern Front (July–September 1941), assistant General-Inspector, Auto-Tank Forces (January–April 1942), deputy commander, Tank Forces, Crimean and North Caucasus Fronts (April–October 1942), commander, 4th (3rd Guards) Mechanized Corps (11 October 1942–3 January 1943), ill March–June 1943, deputy commander, Red Army Tank and Mechanized Forces (June 1943–August 1944), commander, 5th Guards Tank Army (August 1944–March 1945), removed from command due to ill health and hospitalized (March 1945–February 1946), and died (22 February 1946).

4th Tank Army (1 August, reorganized as 65th Army, 22 October)

Major General Vasilii Dmitrievich Kriuchenkin (born 13 January 1894–died 10 June 1976). Major General, 6 April 1940 and Lieutenant General, 28 June 1943. Kiev Combined School (1923), Officers Improvement Course (KUKS) (1926), Cavalry Officers Improvement Course (KUKS), Frunze Academy (1941), and Voroshilov Academy short course (1943). Commander, platoon and squadron, and deputy commander and commander, cavalry regiment (1918–1920), chief of regimental school, deputy commander and commander, cavalry regiment (1921–1938), commander, 14th Cavalry Division, 5th Cavalry Corps, Kiev Special Military District (10 June 1938–28 November 1941), commander, 5th (3rd Guards) Cavalry Corps (28 November 1941–3 July 1942), commander, 28th Army (3 July–1 August 1942), commander, 4th Tank Army (1 August–22 October 1942), commander, 69th Army (March 1943–April 1944), commander, 10th Army (April 1944), commander, 33rd Army (April–July 1944), relieved from command due to poor health, staff officer, Military Council, 1st Belorussian Front (December 1944–January 1945), deputy commander, 61st Army (January–February 1945), deputy commander, 1st Belorussian Front (March–May 1945), deputy commander, Don Military District (June 1945–1946), retired (1946).

22nd Tank Corps
Major General Aleksandr Aleksandrovich Shamshin (see 22nd Tank Corps above). Commander, 22nd Tank (5th Mechanized) Corps (3 April–30 August 1942), commander, 9th Tank Corps (19 October 1942–10 March 1943), chief, Red Army Directorate for the Combat Training of Tank and Mechanized Forces (April–December 1943), commander, 3rd Tank Corps, 2nd Tank Army (17 December 1943–28 February 1944), commander, Tank and Mechanized Forces, Volga Military District (September 1944–July 1946), deputy commander, 27th Mechanized Division (July 1946–November 1948), tactics teacher, Stalin Academy of Tank Forces (November 1948–May 1957), retired (May 1957).

Reorganized as *5th Mechanized Corps*, 2 November 1941
Major General Mikhail Vasil'evich Volkov (2 November 1942) (born 25 March 1895–died 23 June 1969). Lieutenant General, 5 November 1943. 2nd Peterhof Warrant Officers School (1916), Moscow Infantry Course (1925), Frunze Academy (1935), Voroshilov Academy short course (1942), and Voroshilov Academy (1950). Commander, company, 62nd Reserve Regiment (1917), wounded 1917 and 1918, commander, company, 1st and 9th Volga Rifle Regiments (May–December 1919), chief of logistics, 10th Volga Rifle Regiment (December 1919–May 1920), instructor, 80th Infantry Machine Gun School and command courses, 27th Ivanovo-Voznesensk and 11th Stalin Nizhegorodskaia Infantry Schools (May 1920–May 1928), commander, battalion, and chief of staff, 52nd Rifle Regiment, 18th Rifle Division, and chief of staff and commander, 50th Rifle Regiment, 17th Rifle Division, Moscow Military District (May 1928–May 1935), section chief, 17th Rifle Division (May 1935–May 1937), under NKVD investigation (May 1937–November 1938), assistant chief of staff, 77th Azerbaijani Mountain Rifle Division (November 1938–February 1940), chief of staff, 63rd Mountain Rifle Division (February–June 1940), section and department chief, Trans-Baikal Military District (June 1940–August 1941), 52nd Rifle Regiment, 18th Rifle Division, 77th Mountain Rifle Division (9 October 1941–2 March 1942), commander, 5th (9th Guards) Mechanized Corps (2 November 1942–20 June 1945), commander, 9th Guards Mechanized Division (20 June 1945–January 1948), assistant commander, 5th Guards Mechanized Army (January 1948–April 1949), deputy chief, Soviet Army Directorate for Combat Training and commander, Soviet Army Tank and Mechanized Forces (December 1949–August 1957), chief of the military faculty, All-Union State Institute of Cinematography (August 1957–August 1959), and retired (August 1959).

23rd Tank Corps
Major General Abram Matveevich Khasin 23rd Tank Corps (5 June–25 August 1942). Commander, 2nd Tank Corps, 5th Tank Army (14 September 1942) (see 2nd Tank Corps above).

Sources: N. I. Nikoforov et al., ed., *Velikaia Otechestvennaia voina 1941–1945 gg.: Deistvuiushchaia armiia* [The Great Patriotic War, 1941–1945: The operating army] (Moscow: Animi Fortitudo, Kuchkovo pole, 2005); *Komandarmy. Voennyi biograficheskii slovar'* [Army commanders. A military-biographical dictionary] (Moscow: Institute of Military History, Russian Federation's Ministry of Defense, 2005 "Kuchkovo pole," 2005); *Komkory. Voennyi biograficheskii slovar'* [Corps commanders. A military-biographical dictionary] (Moscow: Institute of Military History, Russian Federation's Ministry of Defense, "Kuchkovo pole," 2006); *Komandovanie korpusnogo i divizionnogo zvena Sovetskikh Vooruzhennykh Sil perioda Velikoi Otechestvennoi voiny, 1941–1945 gg.* [Commanders at the corps and division level in the Soviet Armed Forces in the period of the Great Patriotic War, 1941–1945] (Moscow: Frunze Military Academy, 1964); Evgenii Drig, *Mekhanizirovannye korpusa RKKA v boiu: Istoriia avtobronetankovykh voisk Krasnoi Armii v 1940–1941 godakh* [Mechanized corps of the RKKA in battle: A history of the Auto-armored forces of the Red Army in 1940–1941] (Moscow: Transkniga, 2005); I. I. Kuznetsov, *Sud'by general'skie* [The generals' fates] (Irkutsk: Irkutsk University, 2002); and David M. Glantz, *Red Army Command Cadre (1941–1945), Volume 1: Direction, Front, Army, Military District, Defense Zone, and Mobile Corps Commanders* (Carlisle, PA: Self-published, 2002) and *Volume 2: Profile in Command at Main Direction, Front, Army, and Corps Level* (Carlisle, PA: Self-published, 2004).

Notes: All generals are "of tank forces" unless otherwise indicated.

Abbreviations

In addition to specific abbreviations listed below, the following are generally used:

JSMS	*Journal of Slavic Military Studies*
TsAMO	*Tsentral'nyi arkhiv Ministerstva Oborony* [Central Archives of the Ministry of Defense]
TsPA UML	*Tsentral'nyi partiinyi arkhiv Instituta Marksizma-Leninizma* [Central Party Archives of the Institute of Marxism and Leninism]
VIZh	*Voenno-istoricheskii zhurnal* [Military-historical journal]
VV	*Voennyi vestnik* [Military herald]

Prologue: Along the Sukhaia Vereika River, 23 July 1942

1. For a detailed description of 5th Tank Army and the Soviet counteroffensives at Voronezh, see David M. Glantz, *Forgotten Battles of the German-Soviet War (1941–1945), Vol. 3: The Summer Campaign (12 May–18 November 1942)* (Carlisle, PA: Self-published, 1999), 11–84; and Maksim Kolomiets and Aleksandr Smirnov, "Boi v izluchine Dona, 28 iiunia–23 iiulia 1942 goda" [The battle in the bend of the Don, 28 June–23 July 1942], in *Frontovaia illiustratsiia*, 6–2002 [Front illustrated, 6–2002].

2. The German Army, to avoid confusion, routinely used the Roman numeral XXXX instead of conventional XL when designating its army or panzer corps numbered 40 through 49 on its operational and tactical documents and accompanying maps. Therefore, they used XXXXIII rather than XLIII, XXXXVIII instead of XLVIII, and so forth. This study accepts and follows this German practice.

3. M. E. Katukov, *Na ostrie glavnogo udara* [At the point of the main attack] (Moscow: Voenizdat, 1976), 163–164, provides the conventional account of Liziukov's death. Then commanding 1st Tank Corps, which was supporting Liziukov's 2nd Tank Corps, Katukov asserts that scouts from his tank corps located Liziukov's body and buried it with honors near the village of Sukhaia Vereika on 25 July. This account, however, now appears to have been apocryphal. Exploiting the records of 1st and 2nd Tank Corps, Briansk Front, and the German divisions and corps involved in the battle, I. Iu. Sdvizhkov reconstructs the actual circumstances of Liziukov's death in the articles, "Kak pogib i gde pokhoronen general Liziukov?" [How did General Liziukov perish and where was he buried?], in *Voenno-istoricheskii arkhiv* [Military-historical archives], 9, 81 (2006): 149–165, and 10, 82 (2006): 39–56. According to Sdvizhkov, Katukov and others concocted the false account of Liziukov's death, and the incorrect date of 25 July, to assuage Stalin's fears that, like Liziukov's former com-

mander, Vlasov, who surrendered his 2nd Shock Army to the Germans in July 1942 and later collaborated with them by forming the Russian Liberation Army (ROA) in Hitler's service, the 2nd Tank Corps' commander deserted to the Germans. Sdvizhkov's painstaking research indicated Liziukov indeed perished in battle and not as a traitor.

Chapter 1: The *Wehrmacht*

1. For the state of the Red Army in 1941, see David M. Glantz, *Stumbling Colossus: The Red Army on the Eve of World War* (Lawrence: University Press of Kansas, 1998), esp. 26–41, 258–260; and David M. Glantz, *Colossus Reborn: The Red Army at War, 1941–1943* (Lawrence: University Press of Kansas, 2005), esp. 135–369.

2. Franz Halder, *The Halder War Diary, 1939–1942* (Novato, CA: Presidio Press, 1988), 506.

3. Ibid., 521.

4. Klaus Reinhardt, *Moscow—The Turning Point: The Failure of Hitler's Strategy in the Winter of 1941–1942*, trans. Karl Keenan (Oxford, UK, & Providence, RI: Oxford University Press, 1992), 367–368. This discussion of the *Wehrmacht*'s recovery is drawn heavily from Reinhardt.

5. Ibid., 369–370. This total included 4,262 antitank guns, 5,990 mortars, 1,942 howitzers, and 1,411 infantry support guns.

6. David M. Glantz and Jonathan M. House, *When Titans Clashed: How the Red Army Stopped Hitler* (Lawrence: University Press of Kansas, 1995), 301; and (although older) Earl F. Ziemke and Magna E. Bauer, *Moscow to Stalingrad: Decision in the East* (Washington, DC: Center of Military History, United States Army, 1987), 294.

7. George E. Blau, *The German Campaign in Russia: Planning and Operations, 1940–1942*, Department of the Army Pamphlet No. 20–261a (Washington, DC: Department of the Army, 1955), 120.

8. Reinhardt, *Moscow—The Turning Point*, 381–387.

9. Albert Speer, *Inside the Third Reich*, trans. Richard and Clara Winston (New York: Macmillan, 1970), 193–220. On the *Luftwaffe*'s losses and reconstruction, see Williamson Murray, *Luftwaffe* (Baltimore: Nautical & Aviation, 1985), 92–106.

10. Ziemke and Bauer, *Moscow to Stalingrad*, 177, 293–295; Halder, *The Halder War Diary*, 613–615; and Timothy A. Wray, *Standing Fast: German Defensive Doctrine on the Russian Front during World War II, Prewar to March 1943* (Ft. Leavenworth, KS: Combat Studies Institute, 1986), 112–113.

11. Horst Boog, Werner Rahn, Reinhard Stumpf, and Bernd Wegner, *Germany and the Second World War, Volume VI: The Global War*, trans. Ewald Osers, John Brownjohn, Patricia Crampton, and Louise Willmot (Oxford, UK: Clarendon Press, 2001), 965, shows *Luftwaffe* strength at its peak on 20 June 1942. Based on older data, Ziemke and Bauer, *Moscow to Stalingrad*, 296, and Murray, *Luftwaffe*, 112–119, assert that the *Luftwaffe* fielded 2,750 aircraft in the East at the beginning of the summer campaign.

12. Walter J. Spielberger and Uwe Feist, *Panzerkampfwagen IV: "Workhorse" of the German Panzertruppe* (Berkeley: Feist Publications, 1968), 5. On the larger problems of the German tank park, see Richard L. DiNardo, *Germany's Panzer Arm* (Westport, CT: Greenwood Press, 1997), 15–17. For a more thorough survey of German tanks, see Thomas L. Jentz, *Panzertruppen* (Atglen, PA: Schiffer Publishing, 1996).

13. Blau, *German Campaign in Russia*, 131.

14. Alexander Statiev, "Ugly Duckling of the Armed Forces: Romanian Armour, 1919–1941," *Journal of Slavic Military Studies* (hereafter *JSMS*) 12, 2 (June 1999): 225–240. On the poor preparation of the Romanian Army, see the same author's "When an Army Becomes 'Merely a Burden': Romanian Defense Policy and Strategy (1918–1941)," *JSMS* 13, 2 (June 2000): 67–85. For details on the Romanian Army, see Mark Axworthy, Cornel Scafes, and Cristian Craciunoiu, *Third Axis Fourth Ally: The Romanian Armed Forces in the European War, 1941–1945* (London: Arms and Armour Press, 1995), esp. 43–73.

15. Halder, *Halder War Diary*, 611–612; and Ziemke and Bauer, *Moscow to Stalingrad*, 291–292.

16. Joel S. A. Hayward, *Stopped at Stalingrad: The Luftwaffe and Hitler's Defeat in the East, 1942–1943* (Lawrence: University Press of Kansas, 1998), 4, 9.

17. Ibid., 2–11 and 19–20, provide a masterful discussion of Germany's petroleum problems.

18. As evidence of this fact, the *Luftwaffe*, in September and October 1941, conducted extensive reconnaissance over the entire Caucasus region and Stalingrad, using aerial photography to prepare maps showing key objectives in both regions keyed to newly devised grid schemes. See volume 2 (forthcoming) of this study.

19. Blau, *The German Campaign in Russia*, 109–118.

20. On Case Blue, see ibid., 121–124; and Paul Carell, *Stalingrad: The Defeat of the German 6th Army*, trans. David Johnston (Atglen, PA: Schiffer Publishing, 1993), 14–23.

21. For the full text of Directive No. 41, see *Sbornik voenno-istoricheskikh materialov Velikoi Otechestvennoi voiny, Vypusk 18* [Collection of materials of the Great Patriotic War, Issue 18] (Moscow: Voenizdat, 1960), 257–262. Prepared by the Military-Historical Department of the General Staff's Military-Scientific Directorate and classified secret. Hereafter cited as *SVIMVOV*, with appropriate issue number and page(s).

22. Ibid. See also Hugh R. Trevor-Roper (ed.), *Blitzkrieg to Defeat: Hitler's War Directives, 1939–1945* (New York, Chicago: Holt, Reinhart and Winston, 1964), 117.

23. *SVIMVOV*, 18, 259.

24. This analysis is based on ibid., 119; Blau, *The German Campaign in Russia*, 122–123; and Ziemke and Bauer, *Moscow to Stalingrad*, 289–290.

25. *SVIMVOV*, 18, 259.

26. Ibid.

27. Ibid., and Trevor-Roper, *Blitzkrieg to Defeat*, 119.

28. For a description of Operation *Kreml* and German documents associated with the deception operation, see Operatsiia *"Kreml'"* [Operation Kremlin], *Voenno-istoricheskii zhurnal* [Military-historical journal] (*VIZh*), 8, 1961, 9–90.

29. *SVIMVOV*, 18, 258.

30. Ziemke and Bauer, *Moscow to Stalingrad*, 322.

31. For a discussion of this dilemma, see David M. Glantz, *The Strategic and Operational Impact of Terrain on Military Operations in Central and Eastern Europe* (Carlisle, PA: Self-published, 1998).

32. See Boog, et al., *Germany and the Second World War, Volume VI*, 962.

33. Geoffrey Jukes, *Hitler's Stalingrad Decisions* (Berkeley: University of California Press, 1985), 7.

34. Walter Goerlitz, *Paulus and Stalingrad: A Life of Field-Marshal Friedrich Paulus with Notes, Correspondence, and Documents from His Papers*, trans. R. H. Stevens (New York: Citadel Press, 1963), 42.

35. Halder, *The Halder War Diary*, 669–671.

36. On Bock, see "Ritterkreuzträger Fedor von Bock," from website *Die Generale des Heeres* at http://balsi.de/Homepage-Generale/Heer/Heer-Startseite.htm; and Konstantin Zalessky, *Vermacht: Sukhoputnye voiska i Verkhovnoe komandovanie* [The *Wehrmacht*: Ground forces and the High Command] (Moscow: Iauza, 2005), 55–56. After Hitler relieved him of command of Army Group B in July 1942, Bock retired from military service. The field marshal died in May 1945, along with his wife and daughter, when the vehicle in which they were riding was destroyed in a British bombing raid.

37. On List, see "Ritterkreuzträger Wilhelm List," in *Die Generale des Heeres*, and Zalessky, *Vermacht*, 273–275.

38. On Richthofen, see Hayward, *Stopped at Stalingrad*, esp. 70–73; and Helmut Heiber and David M. Glantz, *Hitler and His Generals: The Military Conferences, 1942–1945* (New York: Enigma Books, 2002), 829. After commanding the Fourth Air Fleet at Stalingrad, Richthofen, promoted to the rank of field marshal on 17 February 1943, went on to command Second Air Fleet in Italy from June 1943 through August 1944. Afflicted by a brain ailment, he underwent brain surgery in August 1944 and died of complications from the surgery on 12 July 1945.

39. On Hoth, see Heiber and Glantz, *Hitler and His Generals*, 938; and Zalessky, *Vermacht*, 151–153. After Operation Blau, Hoth commanded Fourth Panzer Army during the battle for Kursk and its harrowing withdrawal behind the Dnepr River. Relieved of command on 10 December 1943, Hoth remained unemployed until assigned as "Commander, Erzigebirge" shortly before war's end. Sentenced at Nurnberg to 15 years' imprisonment, Hoth was released on parole in 1954 and died in 1979.

40. See the essay by Richard Carver in Correlli Barnett (ed.), *Hitler's Generals* (New York: Grove Weidenfeld, 1989), 221–246, "Schwerterträger Erich von Manstein," in *Die Generale des Heeres*, and Zalessky, *Vermacht*, 284–287. Manstein's own memoirs, *Lost Victories*, trans. Anthony G. Powell (Chicago: Henry Regnery, 1958), 261–386, blame Hitler for all the failures of the Stalingrad campaign. While commanding Army Groups Don and South from 1942 through March 1944, Manstein was the architect of the counteroffensive in the Donbas region and Khar'kov, which restored German strategic defenses in southern Russia in the wake of the disaster at Stalingrad and the failed Kursk offensive (Operation Citadel) of July 1943. Thereafter, he tried to employ "elastic" mobile defenses to contain Red Army offensives in Ukraine until Hitler replaced him on 30 March 1944. Arrested at war's end and sentenced by a British court in Hamburg to 18 years' imprisonment, Manstein was paroled in 1952 and died in 1973. Manstein is considered by many as the most outstanding senior *Wehrmacht* leader during World War II. On Manstein's involvement in war crimes, see Marcel Stein, *Field Marshal Von Manstein: The Janus Head/A Portrait* (Solihull, UK: Helion, 2007).

41. Samuel W. Mitcham Jr., in Barnett (ed.), *Hitler's Generals*, 249–263; Heiber and Glantz, *Hitler and His Generals*, 896–897; and Zalessky, *Vermacht*, 240–242. After the German defeat at Stalingrad, Kleist commanded First Panzer Army, until relieved by Hitler on 31 March 1944, and then retired. Arrested by the Gestapo after the plot against Hitler's life in July 1944, Kleist was exonerated, only to be rearrested by the Western Allies after war's end and transferred to Soviet control, where he died in prison camp, reportedly of malnutrition.

42. This account is based largely on the sympathetic biography by Goerlitz, *Paulus and Stalingrad*. See also Samuel Mitcham's analysis in Barnett (ed.), *Hitler's Generals*,

361–373, "Eichenlauträber Friedrich Paulus," in *Die Generale des Heeres*; and Zalessky, *Vermacht*, 325–327.

43. Goerlitz, *Paulus and Stalingrad*, 21–28, 35.

44. After his capture at Stalingrad, Paulus at first refused to join the Free Germany League of German officers, which was formed under Soviet auspices to conduct propaganda on behalf of their captors. In August 1944, however, after the failed plot against Hitler and the death of Paulus's son in Italy, he joined the organization and began broadcasts aimed at overthrowing Hitler's regime. Tried at Nurnberg, Paulus was imprisoned in the Soviet Union, released to return to East Germany in 1953, and died of cancer in 1957.

45. On Weichs, see Zalessky, *Vermacht*, 81–83. After the German defeat at Stalingrad, Weichs commanded Army Group B until 14 February 1943, when the army group was disbanded, assigned to the OKW's control for employment in the West, and ultimately disbanded in July 1943. Weichs then commanded Army Group F in the Balkans from August 1943 through October 1944, during which his forces were repeatedly accused of committing atrocities against partisans and civilians in the region. After rejecting Weichs's assignment as commander of Army Group Vistula in January 1945, Hitler disbanded his Army Group F in March 1945 and retired him from active service. Arrested and imprisoned by war crimes tribunals in 1945, Weichs was released in 1947 due to failing health; he died in 1954.

46. On Ruoff, see "Ritterkreuzträger Richard Ruoff," in *Die Generale des Heeres*, and Zalessky, *Vermacht*, 374–375. After the battle for Stalingrad, Ruoff commanded Seventeenth Army until June 1943, when he ended his active service and reverted to the reserves. Ruoff died in 1967.

47. On Wietersheim, see Zalessky, *Vermacht*, 100. After his relief, Wietersheim occupied no further command position in the army. At war's end, he was serving as a common soldier in Germany's ragtag *Volksturm* (People's Militia).

48. On Stumme, see "Ritterkreuzträger Georg Stumme," in *Die Generale des Heeres*; and Zalessky, *Vermacht*, 530. Stumme died in October 1942 during the fighting against British Eighth Army at El Alamein.

49. On Geyr, see "Ritterkreuzträger Leo *Reichsfreiherr* Geyr von Schweppenburg," in *Die Generale des Heeres*; and Zalessky, *Vermacht*, 496–497. After Geyr served a brief stint commanding LVIII Panzer Corps and Panzer Group West in the Western theater from August 1943 through June 1944, Hitler appointed Geyr General-Inspector of the German Army's panzer forces. Tried and imprisoned after war's end, Geyr was pardoned in 1947 and died in 1974.

50. On Kempf, see Heiber and Glantz, *Hitler and His Generals*, 860, "Eichenlaubträger Werner Kempf," in *Generale des Heeres*; and Zalessky, *Vermacht*, 232–233. After commanding XXXXVIII Panzer Corps during the Stalingrad campaign, Kempf commanded an *Armeegruppe* bearing his name during the fighting at Khar'kov and Kursk in 1943 and, thereafter, Eighth Army to August 1944, the Armed Forces of the Ostland (Eastland) Commissariat (an antipartisan command) until the end of 1944, and the High Command in the Vosges Mountains (France), until he reverted to the OKW's reserve in December 1944. Surviving the war, Kempf died in 1964.

51. On Mackensen, see Heiber and Glantz, *Hitler and His Generals*, 873–874, "Eichenlaubträger Eberhard von Mackensen," in *Generale des Heeres*; and Zalessky, *Vermacht*, 281–282. Mackensen commanded First Panzer Army throughout most of 1943.

Along with Manstein, the commander of Army Group South, Mackensen brilliantly orchestrated the army group's counteroffensive in the Donbas region in February 1943 and, in July, the army group's ill-fated advance to Prokhorovka during the battle for Kursk. In the wake of the *Wehrmacht's* defeat at Kursk and during its retreat to the Dnepr River, Hitler recalled Mackensen to the West, where he took command of the new Fourteenth Army in Italy. In command in Italy, Mackensen conducted a skillful defense of the peninsula, including the strenuous and nearly successful defenses against the Allied amphibious landing at Anzio. Replaced by General Joachim Lemelsen in June 1944, Mackensen retired, only to be arrested and imprisoned by Allied war crimes tribunals in 1945. Released in 1952, Mackensen died in 1969.

52. On Kirchner, see Heiber and Glantz, *Hitler and His Generals*, 1075–1076; and Zalessky, *Vermacht*, 238–239. Kirchner was never promoted to army command, in part because his panzer corps failed to break through to Stalingrad and rescue its garrison in December 1942. With brief interruptions, Kirchner commanded LVII Panzer Corps to war's end and, after avoiding the dragnet of postwar war crimes trials, died in 1960.

53. More on Breith in Heiber and Glantz, *Hitler and His Generals*, 1064; "Schwertträger Hermann Breith," in *Generale des Heeres*; and Zalessky, *Vermacht*, 63–64. After Operation Blau ended, Breith commanded III Panzer Corps from January through October 1943, participating in the climactic battle for Kursk and the harrowing German retreat to the Dnepr River and, with brief interruptions, III Panzer Corps to war's end. During the final two years of the war, Breith's panzer corps led the attempted relief of the two German corps encircled in the Cherkassy pocket in February 1944, First Panzer Army's escape from the Kamenets–Podolsk pocket in April 1944, and the seesaw struggles for Romania, Hungary, and Austria in 1944 and 1945. Tried and imprisoned briefly after war's end, Breith was released in 1947 and died in 1964.

54. On Balck, see Heiber and Glantz, *Hitler and His Generals*, 1074–1075; "Brillantenträger Hermann Balck," in *Generale des Heeres*; and Zalessky, *Vermacht*, 35–37. After the German defeat at Stalingrad, Balck's 11th Panzer Division distinguished itself by holding off counterattacking Red Army forces along the Chir River in December 1942 and in the Donbas and Khar'kov regions in February and March 1943, where it played a major role in containing the Red Army's ambitious winter offensive. Recognized as a superb panzer specialist, Balck commanded, in succession, the famed *Grossdeutschland* Motorized Division from March to August 1943, when it took part in the climactic battle for Kursk; XIV, XXXX, and XXXXVIII Panzer Corps during the fighting in Ukraine in late 1943 and 1944; and Fourth Panzer Army, Army Group G, and *Armeegruppe* Balck in the intense and complex fighting in the Balkans and Hungary in late 1944 and 1945. Imprisoned on two occasions after war's end, Balck was finally released in 1948 and died in 1982.

55. On Hube, see Heiber and Glantz, *Hitler and His Generals*, 798; "Brillantenträger Hans-Valentin Hube," in *Generale des Heeres*; and Zalessky, *Vermacht*, 478–479. After escaping the Stalingrad cauldron via aircraft in January 1943, Hube rose to command a new XIV Panzer Corps as Group Hube in Sicily and then returned to the Eastern Front as commander of First Panzer Army in November 1943. Thereafter, Hube led the panzer army in Army Group South's trying struggle in Ukraine in early 1944, during which he orchestrated its harrowing escape from the Kamenets-Podolsk pocket in April. Ironically, Hube perished in an aircraft accident on 21 April while en route to the Führer's lair in Berchtesgaden, where he was to receive command of new Army Group North Ukraine.

56. See Zalessky, *Vermacht*, 470–471. After recovering from wounds he received dur-

ing the battle for Ordzhonikidze, Herr distinguished himself in command of LXXVI Panzer Corps during the Italian campaign in 1943 and led Fourteenth Army in the same theater in 1944. Wounded once again in late 1944, Herr recovered to command Tenth Army until war's end. Imprisoned briefly after the war, he was released in 1948 and died in 1976.

57. On Heim, see "Ritterkreuzträger Ferdinand Heim," in *Generale des Heeres*. Unlike many of his colleague division and corps commanders, Heim survived the war and died in 1977.

58. Though many sources assert that General Boineburg-Lengsfeld did not return to service, the website *Axis Fact Book–Des Heeres* (http://www.axishistory.com/index .php?id=30) indicates that Hitler restored the general to command of 23rd Panzer Division on 26 August, and Boineburg-Lengsfeld retained this posting until 26 December 1942. For confirmation, see Wilhelm Tieke, *The Caucasus and the Oil: The German-Soviet War in the Caucasus, 1942/43*, trans. Joseph G. Welsh (Winnipeg: J.J. Fedorowicz, 1995), 236, which identifies Boineburg-Lengsfeld as commander, 23rd Panzer Division, on 11 November 1942.

59. On Hörnlein, see Heiber and Glantz, *Hitler and His Generals*, 763. After commanding *Grossdeutschland* Motorized Division through the remainder of 1942, Hörnlein commanded the division throughout 1943, when it played a significant role in the battle for Kursk, and most of 1944. Thereafter, Hörnlein led LXXXII and XXVII Army Corps until war's end.

60. Wray, *Standing Fast*, 113.

61. Omar Bartov, *The Eastern Front, 1941–1945: German Troops and the Barbarization of Warfare* (New York: St. Martin's Press, 1986), 51, 66, and passim.

Chapter 2: The Red Army

1. For a thorough description of the Soviet force regeneration program, see Glantz, *Colossus Reborn*, 135–369.

2. The Soviets classified divisions and brigades of various types as formations (soedinenii) and all types of regiments as units (*chasti*). Forces below regimental level, such as battalions, companies, and platoons, were considered subunits (*podrozdelenii*).

3. See Glantz, *Colossus Reborn*, 180–184, 201–206, for the operating strengths of rifle divisions and brigades.

4. Pavel A. Belov, *Za nami Moskva* [Behind us, Moscow] (Moscow: Voenizdat, 1963); David M. Glantz, *A History of Soviet Airborne Forces* (London: Frank Cass, 1994), 104–227, which describes the joint operation of Belov's cavalry corps and 4th Airborne Corps in detail; and *Soviet Documents of the Use of War Experience, Volume Three: Military Operations 1941 and 1942*, trans. Harold S. Orenstein (London: Frank Cass, 1993), 27–61.

5. Iu. P. Babich and A. G. Baier, *Razvitie vooruzheniia i organitzatsii Sovetskikh sukhoputnykh voist v gody Velikoi Otechestvennoi voiny* [Development of the armament and organization of the Soviet ground forces in the Great Patriotic War] (Moscow: Frunze Academy, 1990), 42–43.

6. See Alexander Hill, "British 'Lend Lease' Tanks and the Battle for Moscow, November–December 1941—A Research Note," *JSMS*, 19, 2 (June 2006): 289–294. The

British supplied the Red Army with 361 tanks, primarily Matilda and Valentine models, by 31 December 1941. These supplemented the 2,819 T-34 and KV tanks produced by Soviet industry during the second half of 1941.

7. For all aspects of Fedorenko's program, see Glantz, *Colossus Reborn*, 218–236.

8. See also O. A. Losik, *Stroitel'stvo i boevoe primenenie Sovetskikh tankovykh voisk v gody Velikoi Otechestvennoi voiny* [The Formation and combat use of Soviet tank units in the years of the Great Patriotic War] (Moscow: Voenizdat, 1979).

9. Babich and Baier, *Razvitie vooruzheniia*, 44–45; and Glantz, *Colossus Reborn*, 228.

10. Glantz, *Colossus Reborn*, 230–231.

11. Steve Zaloga and Peter Sarson, *T-34/76 Medium Tank, 1941–1945* (London: Osprey/Reed Publishing, 1994), esp. 17–23.

12. David M. Glantz, *The Role of Intelligence in Soviet Military Strategy in World War II* (Novato, CA: Presidio Press, 1990), 42–48.

13. On the strategic debate, see S. M. Shtemenko, *The General Staff at War, 1941–1945*, bk. 1, trans. Robert Daglish (Moscow: Voenizdat, 1985), 60–72; David M. Glantz, *Kharkov 1942: Anatomy of a Military Disaster* (Rockville Center, NY: Sarpedon, 1998), 21–30; and documents in V. A. Zolotarev, ed., "*Stavka* VGK: Dokumenty i materialy 1942" [The *Stavka* VGK: Documents and materials of 1942], in *Russkii arkhiv: Velikaia Otechestvennaia*, 16 (5–2) [The Russian archives: The Great Patriotic [War], 16 (5–2)] (Moscow: "TERRA," 1996), 146–199. Hereafter cited as Zolotarev, "*Stavka* 1942," with appropriate page(s).

14. Oleg Rzheshevsky, "Boris Mikhailovich Shaposhnikov," in Harold Shukman, ed., *Stalin's Generals* (London: Weidenfeld & Nicolson, 1993), 229; and N. I. Nikoforov, et al., ed., *Velikaia Otechestvennaia voina 1941–1945 gg.: Deistvuiushchaia armiia* [The Great Patriotic War, 1941–1945: The operating army] (Moscow: Animi Fortitudo, Kuchkovo pole, 2005), 300–301. After suffering a heart attack, Shaposhnikov would serve as deputy commissar of defense to June 1943 and chief of the Academy of the General Staff until his death in March 1945.

15. Ibid., 221.

16. In addition to his memoir, A. M. Vasilevsky, *Delo vsei zhizni* [Life's work] (Moscow: Politizdat, 1983), see Geoffrey Jukes, "Alexander Mikhailovich Vasilevsky," in Shukman, *Stalin's Generals*, 275–285; and Nikoforov, *Velikaia Otechestvennaia voina 1941–1945 gg.*, 288–291. As chief of the General Staff and Deputy Commissar of Defense, Vasilevsky would play a significant role planning and supervising the Stalingrad counteroffensive (Operation Uranus), the winter offensive of 1942–1943, the battle for Kursk and subsequent summer offensive of 1943, the offensive in the Ukraine and Crimea in early 1944, where he was wounded, and the Belorussian offensive (Operation Bagration) in summer 1944. When General Cherniakhovsky, commander of 3rd Belorussian Front, died in February 1945, Vasilevsky took command of his *front* and completed the operation, after which he was appointed Deputy Supreme High Commander to Stalin and a member of the *Stavka*. Vasilevsky capped his wartime career when, as Supreme High Commander of Forces in the Far East, in essence a theater commander, he orchestrated the destruction of the Japanese Kwantung Army in the Manchurian offensive of August and September 1945. After war's end Vasilevsky became minister of the USSR's Armed Forces in 1949 and 1st Deputy Minister of Defense of the USSR in 1953, a post he relinquished at his own request in 1956. Although in semiretirement due to poor health, he figured sig-

nificantly in the reorganization of the Soviet Army during the late 1950s before retiring in 1957. Vasilevsky died in 1977.

17. Zhukov is the subject of numerous biographies; see the most recent in Nikoforov, *Velikaia Otechestvennaia voina 1941–1945 gg.*, 293–296. Zhukov served as representative of the *Stavka* in many of the Red Army's most important offensives to war's end, including the failed Operation Polar Star in February 1943 against German Army Group North in the Leningrad region, the battle for Kursk in the summer of 1943, and the struggle in Ukraine during the winter of 1943–1944, when in March he would take command of 1st Ukrainian Front after its commander, Vatutin, was killed by Ukrainian partisans. During the summer of 1944 he helped plan and supervised the Belorussian offensive, and during 1945, as commander of 1st Belorussian Front, he led the advance through Poland, the destruction of German forces in Pomerania, and the final assault on Berlin in April and May. After the war ended, Zhukov served as commander of the Group of Soviet Occupation Forces in Germany and commander of the Soviet Armed Forces and Deputy Minister of Defense of the USSR in 1945 and 1946 and in virtual "exile" as commander of the Odessa and Ural Military Districts from 1946 to 1953. Stalin's death in 1953 permitted Zhukov to return to Moscow, where he became Minister of Defense of the USSR in 1957 and was responsible for reorganizing the Soviet Armed Forces during the new nuclear age. Intimately involved in the politics revolving around N. S. Khrushchev's rise and fall as Soviet leader from 1960 to 1964, Zhukov retired in the 1960s and died in 1974.

18. Most Soviet sources written after 1964 also credit Zhukov with planning the Stalingrad counteroffensive, although many sources prior to that date accord credit for doing so to Vasilevsky and Eremenko. Certainly, as Deputy Supreme Commander, Zhukov indeed played a considerable role in all *Stavka* strategic planning. See volume 3 (forthcoming) of this study for the historiographical debate about planning the counteroffensive.

19. G. Zhukov, *Reminiscences and Reflections*, vol. 2 (Moscow: Progress Publishers, 1985), 72–73.

20. A. M. Vasilevsky, *Delo vsei zhizni* [Life's work] (Moscow: Izdatel'stvo politicheskoi literatury, 1983), 183–185. These offensives were to take place in the Crimea, the Khar'kov region, along the L'gov-Kursk and Smolensk axes, and in the Demiansk and Leningrad regions.

21. See Viktor Anfilov, "Semen Konstantinovich Timoshenko," in Shukman, *Stalin's Generals*, 239–253; and "Timoshenko, Semen, Konstantinovich," Sovetskaia Voennaia Entsiklopediia v vos'mi tomakh, 8 [Soviet military encyclopedia in eight volumes, 8] (Moscow: Voenizdat, 1980), 43–44. Hereafter cited as *SVE* with appropriate volume and page(s). See the most recent biography of Timoshenko in Nikoforov, *Velikaia Otechestvennaia voina 1941–1945 gg.*, 282–284. During the latter stages of Operation Blau, Stalin removed Timoshenko from command of Stalingrad Front in October 1942, assigning him instead to command the Northwestern Front. After his *front* liquidated the German Demiansk salient in early 1943 but failed in its more ambitious offensive to defeat Army Group North (Operation Polar Star), Stalin relieved him as *front* commander in March but retained him as a representative of the *Stavka*. During the last 18 months of war, Timoshenko served in this capacity in the Leningrad region up to November 1943, in the Baltic region in early 1944, and in the Balkans in August and September 1944. After war's end, Timoshenko commanded the Baranovichi, South Urals, and Belorussian Military Districts from 1946 through 1960. Stalin's old warhorse retired in 1960 and died in 1970.

22. During the Barvenkovo-Lozovaia offensive (18–31 January 1942), Southwestern and Southern Fronts' 6th, 9th, 57th, and 37th Armies seized a large salient on the western bank of the Northern Donets River south of Khar'kov to employ as a launching pad for subsequent offensive operations.

23. Organized as a *troika* [threesome] to assist the commanders at direction, *front*, and army levels, the Military Council consisted of the commander and his commissar and chief of staff.

24. The other was A. Kh. Babadzhanian, a tank brigade and tank corps commander.

25. See M. M. Kozlov, ed., *Velikaia Otechestvennaia voina 1941–1945: Entsiklopediia* [The Great Patriotic War, 1941–1945: An encyclopedia] (Moscow: "Sovetskaia entsiklopediia," 1985), 73, hereafter cited as Kozlov, *VOV*, with appropriate page(s); and I. N. Rodionov, ed., *Voennaia entsiklopediia v vos'mi tomakh, 1* [Military encyclopedia in eight volumes, 1] (Moscow: Voenizdat, 1997), 1: 337–338. Hereafter cited as *VE*, with appropriate volume and page(s).

26. Nikoforov, *Velikaia Otechestvennaia voina 1941–1945 gg.*, 304–306. After the Khar'kov disaster, Stalin appointed Bagramian to command Western Front's 16th Army, which he led throughout Operation Blau, and, after it was redesignated 11th Guards Army, figured prominently during the Orel counteroffensive in July–August 1943. Elevated to command 1st Baltic Front in November 1943, he led this *front* in its unsuccessful attempts to defeat German Army Group Center in Belorussia in the winter of 1943–1944 but redeemed himself in summer 1944 when his forces finally collapsed German defenses in Belorussia, capping their success with the liberation of Riga the ensuing fall. He ended his wartime career by commanding the Zemland Group of Forces and serving as deputy commander of 3rd Belorussian Front during the struggle for Konigsberg. After war's end, Bagramian commanded the Baltic Military District to 1954, when, largely because of his wartime association with Khrushchev, he became a deputy minister of defense in 1955, chief of the Voroshilov General Staff Academy in 1956, and Deputy Minister of Defense of the USSR and chief of the Rear of the Soviet Armed Forces in 1958. Bagramian retired in 1968, wrote one of the best wartime memoirs, and died in 1982.

27. Glantz, *Kharkov 1942*, 24–26.

28. K. S. Moskalenko, *Na iugo–zapadnom napravlentii* [On the southwestern axis], vol. 1 (Moscow: Nauka, 1969), 176–177.

29. The 22 March estimate of the Southwestern Direction is reprinted as an appendix to Glantz, *Kharkov 1942*, 252–255.

30. I. Kh. Bagramian, *Tak shli my k pobeda* [As we went on to victory] (Moscow: Voenizdat, 1977), 54–67.

31. Zolotarev, "*Stavka* 1942," 152.

32. Ibid., 171–172.

33. Ibid., 173–174.

34. Ibid., 174.

35. On Soviet planning for their offensives in the summer and fall of 1942, see also A. N. Grilev, "Nekotorye osobennosti planirovaniia letne–osennei kampanii 1942 goda" [Some features of planning for the 1942 summer–autumn campaign], *VIZh*, 9 (September 1991): 4–11.

36. The 10 April 1942 plan of the Southwestern Direction is reproduced as Appendix 3 in Glantz, *Kharkov 1942*, 256–258.

37. Ibid., 31–32.

38. Nikoforov, *Velikaia Otechestvennaia voina 1941–1945 gg.*, 541–546 and V. A. Zolotarev, ed., *Velikaia Otechestvennaia voina 1941–1945, Kniga 1: Surovye ispytaniia* [The Great Patriotic War, bk. 1: A harsh education] (Moscow: Nauka, 1998), 325.

39. On 1 December 1941, the Red Army was equipped with 5,908 tanks, 57,031 guns and mortars, 874 multiple rocket launchers (*Katiusha*), 10,017 combat aircraft (6,346 operational), 311,555 vehicles (235,162 trucks), and 1,287,641 horses. A GKO decree dated 7 March 1942 recorded a total strength of 9,597,802 personnel, with 4,663,697 at the front and 397,978 in hospitals. A similar decree dated 5 May indicated a total strength of 8,950,000, with 5,449,898 at the front and 414,400 in hospitals. See Central Party Archives of the Institute of Marxism and Leninism (*TsPA UML*), *fond* [collection] (f.). 644, *opis* [subgroup] (op.) 1, *delo* [file] (d.), 23, *listy* [leaf, pages] (ll.) 127–129 and f. 644, op. 1, d. 33, ll. 48–50.

40. Zolotarev, *Velikaia Otechestvennaia voina*, bk. 1, 325.

41. The actual armored strength of Axis forces in the south was no more than 2,000 tanks and assault guns by 1 May 1942.

42. *Boevoi sostav Sovetskoi armii, Chast' 2 (Ianvar'–dekabr' 1942 goda)* [Combat composition of the Soviet Army, pt. 2 (January–December 1942)] (Moscow: Voenizdat, 1966), 93.

43. For Golikov's qualified warnings, see *Stumbling Colossus*, 241, 244.

44. *Komandarmy. Voennyi biograficheskii slovar'* [The Great Patriotic [War]. Army commanders. Military-bibliographical dictionary] (Moscow: Institute of Military History, Russian Federation's Ministry of Defense, OOO "Kuchkovo pole," 2005), 48–50. In Operation Blau, Golikov led Briansk Front during its retreat to the Don River and 1st Guards Army during the intense fighting northwest of Stalingrad in August and September 1942. He then served as deputy commander of Northwestern Front in September and October and, briefly, as chief of the Red Army's Main Intelligence Directorate in October and commanded Voronezh Front from October 1942 through March 1943. After the counteroffensive by Manstein's Army Group South crushed his *front* in March 1943, producing the infamous Kursk "Bulge," Stalin removed Golikov from command, assigning him to key Ministry of Defense and General Staff positions to war's end. Reflecting Stalin's favor of his reliable general, Golikov commanded a mechanized army in East Germany from 1950 through 1956 and served as chief of the Armored Academy and Soviet Army's Main Political Directorate before retiring in 1962. Surviving to age 80, Golikov died in 1980.

45. Ibid., 139–141. Malinovsky presided over his *front*'s near total destruction during Operation Blau but survived the embarrassment to command 66th Army's during its many counterattacks in the Kotluban' region northwest of Stalingrad from August into October 1942 and powerful 2nd Guards Army from October 1942 to February 1943, when his army played a pivotal role blocking German attempts to relieve its Sixth Army encircled in Stalingrad. Thereafter, Stalin appointed Malinovsky to command Southern Front in February 1943 and Southwestern Front in March 1943. Malinovsky commanded Southwestern (renamed 3rd Ukrainian in October 1943) and 2nd Ukrainian Fronts until war's end. Because he planned and conducted most of the Red Army's most significant victories in Ukraine and southeastern Europe, Stalin appointed Malinovsky command of Trans-Baikal Front during the Manchurian campaign against the Japanese Kwantung Army in August and September 1945. After remaining in the Far East as Supreme High Commander from 1947 to 1953 and commander of Far East Military District from 1953 to 1956, Malinovsky returned to Moscow in March 1956 to become commander of Soviet

Ground Forces and 1st Deputy Minister of Defense of the USSR and, in October 1957, Minister of Defense of the USSR, a post he held until his death in 1967.

46. Ibid., 95–96. Prior to Operation Blau, Kozlov fell from Stalin's favor when Manstein's Eleventh Army attacked and overcame Crimean Front's defenses at Kerch' and drove its three armies off the peninsula and across the Kerch' Strait to the Taman' Peninsula in the western Caucasus region. Stalin, who understood that his personnel representative, Mekhlis, bore considerable blame for the defeat, retained Kozlov as commander of 6th and 9th Reserve Armies throughout the summer of 1942 and 24th Army after its conversion from 9th Reserve Army in August 1942. Kozlov then led 24th Army during its bloody struggles in the Kotluban' region during September 1942 and, after a brief stint on Voronezh Front's staff, served as representative of the *Stavka* during the Red Army's Ostrogozhsk–Rossosh', Voronezh–Kastornoe, and Khar'kov offensives in January–March 1943. Once again discredited when his forces were defeated in the Khar'kov region in March 1943, Kozlov spent the remainder of the war as deputy commander of Trans-Baikal Front, where he remained during the Manchurian campaign in August and September 1945. After war's end, he was deputy commander of the Trans-Baikal Military District. Never fully regaining Stalin's favor, Kozlov died in 1967.

47. I. I. Kuznetsov, *Sud'by general'skie: Vysshie komandnye kadry Krasnoi Armii v 1940–1953 gg.* [The fates of the generals: The higher command cadre of the Red Army in 1940–1953] (Irkutsk: Irkutsk University Press, 2002).

48. *Komandarmy. Voennyi biograficheskii slovar'*, 185–186. Like several other army commanders of 1942, Pukhov commanded his army to war's end, performing competently in the battles of Kursk in 1943, in the Ukraine in 1943 and 1944, and in Poland and along the road to Berlin in late 1944 and 1945. During this period, he also became a Hero of the Soviet Union for his army's contributions to the victory at Kursk. After the war, Pukhov commanded 13th Army and the Odessa, North Caucasus, Western Siberian, and Siberian Military Districts before becoming chief adviser to the Romanian Army in 1957, a position he occupied at the time of his death in 1958.

49. Ibid., 165–167. Advancing German forces encircled and nearly destroyed Parsegov's 40th Army in July 1942, prompting Stalin to relieve him of command and to assign him to the Far East, where he became deputy commander of Far Eastern Front's artillery and, later, deputy commander and chief of artillery of 2nd Far Eastern Front during the Manchurian offensive against Japanese forces in August and September 1945. After war's end, Parsegov commanded the artillery in several military districts and, later, became a department head at the Kalinin Artillery Academy before his death in 1964.

50. Ibid., 51–53. Gordov commanded 21st Army until June 1942, when, in the midst of Operation Blau, Stalin assigned him as commander of the new Stalingrad Front. When he failed to halt the German advance short of Stalingrad, Stalin in August removed him from his post, replacing him with A. I. General Eremenko. Thereafter, Gordov commanded Western Front's 33rd Army from October 1942 through April 1944 and 1st Ukrainian Front's 3rd Guards Army from April 1944 through May 1945. For his army's outstanding performance in Poland and the battle for Berlin, Gordov also became a Hero of the Soviet Union. After war's end, Gordov commanded the Volga Military District until his retirement in 1947. Arrested, tried, and convicted of treason by Stalin's courts, Gordov was executed in 1950 but rehabilitated posthumously in 1956.

51. Ibid., 202–203. In the wake of the disastrous Khar'kov offensive in May 1942, during which Riabyshev was accused of losing control of his forces, he was relieved of com-

mand and reverted to the *Stavka*'s control. After attending the Voroshilov General Staff Academy in 1943, Riabyshev returned to the field army as commander of 3rd Reserve Army, deputy commander of 3rd Guards Army, commander of 3rd Army, and briefly commander of 3rd Guards Army. In January 1944 and at his own request, Riabyshev was assigned as a corps commander in 3rd Guards, 5th Shock, and 70th Armies, posts he would occupy until war's end.

52. Ibid., 153–155. Moskalenko commanded 38th, 1st Tank, 1st Guards, and 40th Armies during Operation Blau and 38th Army, once again, from October 1943 through war's end. While in command, his army figured prominently in many of the Red Army's most important victories in the Ukraine, Poland, and Czechoslovakia. After war's end, Moskalenko commanded at the army level through 1948, the Moscow Military District's PVO (Air Defense) Forces from 1948 through 1953, and, after helping thwart an attempted coup by Beriia's NKVD in the wake of Stalin's death in 1953, the Moscow Military District; he became Marshal of the Soviet Union and Deputy Minister of Defense of the USSR in 1955. After retiring in 1962, Moskalenko wrote one of the best of the memoirs penned by wartime Red Army generals; he died in 1985.

53. Ibid., 54–56. Gorodniansky's military career ended abruptly in late May 1942 when he perished during the battle for Khar'kov.

54. Ibid., 174–175. Like his counterpart Gorodniansky, Podlas was killed in action during the intense fighting in the Barvenkovo-Lozovaia bridgehead south of Khar'kov in late May 1942.

55. Ibid., 241–242. Kharitonov survived the Khar'kov disaster of May 1942 and commanded 6th Army throughout Operation Blau and the Red Army's counteroffensive in the winter of 1942–1943. However, he died of an illness in May 1943, shortly after his army was encircled and largely destroyed in the Donbas region in February and March 1943 by Manstein's counterattacking Army Group South.

56. Ibid., 129–131. Lopatin was appointed to command 9th Army in June 1942, shortly before Operation Blau began. However, after the advancing Germans decimated his army during the initial stage of Blau, the *Stavka* assigned Lopatin command of 62nd Army in Timoshenko's new Stalingrad Front. When Lopatin failed to live up to Stalin's expectations during the fighting in the Great Bend of the Don River in late July and early August, General Eremenko, Stalingrad Front's new commander, replaced Lopatin with General Chuikov. After serving in a variety of staff positions in Moscow, Lopatin returned to the field to command Northwestern Front's 34th and 11th Armies from October 1942 through March 1943 and Kalinin Front's 20th Army in September 1943. After serving as deputy commander of 1st Baltic Front's 43rd Army from September 1943 to July 1944, Lopatin, at his own request, reverted to corps command, leading 43rd Army's 13th Guards Rifle Corps during the East Prussia operation in January and February 1945 and Trans-Baikal Front's 2nd Separate Rifle Corps during the Manchurian offensive in August and September 1945. After war's end, Lopatin graduated from the Voroshilov General Staff Academy in 1947 and served as assistant commander of Trans-Baikal Front's 7th Guards Army and commander of 13th and 9th Rifle Corps before his retirement in 1954; he died in 1965.

57. Ibid., 57–59. Grechko commanded Southern Front's 12th Army during its harrowing retreat into the northern Caucasus region in July and August 1942 and 47th Army during its defense of Novorossiisk in September. Because of the significant role he played in the defense of the Caucasus, Grechko headed 56th Army from January through Octo-

ber 1943, served as deputy commander of Voronezh Front in October 1943, and commanded 1st Guards Army from December 1943 through war's end. During the last two years of the war, Grechko's armies performed with distinction during most of the Red Army's offensive operations in Ukraine, Poland, and Czechoslovakia. Grechko continued his meteoric rise after war's end, serving as commander of the Kiev Military District, 1st Deputy Minister of Defense of the USSR and, simultaneously, commander of the Soviet Army's Ground Forces in November 1957, and Minister of Defense of the USSR in 1967 before his retirement in the early 1970s and death in 1976.

58. Ibid., 88–89. After the initial phases of Operation Blau, Kamkov commanded North Caucasus Front's 18th Army during its defense of the northern Caucasus region and Trans-Caucasus Front's 47th Army during its defense of the Black Sea port and naval base at Tuapse in October 1942. After being relieved of command and placed under the *front's* and *Stavka's* control in January 1943, supposedly for his questionable performance as army commander, Kamkov returned to field duty with his beloved cavalry in February 1944. He then served as deputy commander of 2nd Ukrainian Front's Cavalry-Mechanized Group, fighting with distinction in the Korsun'-Shevchenkovskii encirclement operation in January and February 1943, in the Red Army's dramatic advance across Ukraine during the spring and summer of 1944, in the destruction of German Army Group South Ukraine during the Iasi-Kishinev offensive in Romania in August 1944, and in the Debrecen and Budapest offensives in Hungary in fall 1944. Returned to Stalin's favor, Kamkov ended the war in command of 1st Guards Cavalry-Mechanized Group's famous 4th Guards Cossack Cavalry Corps, which liberated Austria and southern Czechoslovakia in March and April 1945. After war's end, Kamkov commanded 4th Guards Cavalry Corps, taught at the Frunze Academy through 1946, commanded 3rd Guards and 4th Guards Cavalry Corps through November 1949, and ended his military career as deputy commander of the North Caucasus Military District, a position he occupied when he died in 1951.

59. Ibid., 250. Relieved of command in July 1942, Tsyganov became deputy commander of the Moscow Military District for Education and Training until his death from illness in June 1944.

60. Ibid., 98–99. Disgraced by the performance of his 44th Army during the Kerch' disaster in May 1942, Kolganov was reduced in rank to colonel in June and assigned as deputy chief of staff of Briansk Front in late summer, deputy commander of 48th Army in September 1942, and commander of 42nd Rifle Corps from June 1943 to war's end. Although unsuccessful as an army commander, largely because of meddling by Mekhlis, Stalin's notorious commissar henchman, Kolganov performed well as a deputy army and corps commander in the battle for Kursk and the Chernigov-Pripiat offensive in 1943 and during the Belorussian and East Prussian offensives in 1944 and 1945. After war's end, Kolganov served as commander, 53rd Rifle Corps, deputy chief of training of the Soviet Ground Forces in 1946, adviser to the Romanian Army in 1948, attaché to Bucharest in December 1949, and deputy chief of the Frunze Academy in 1952 before retiring in 1964; he died in 1981.

61. Ibid., 133–134. L'vov perished on 11 May 1942 when *Luftwaffe* aircraft bombed his army's command post during German Eleventh Army's offensive to recapture the Kerch' Peninsula.

62. Ibid., 255–257. Although his military career went into a virtual tailspin after the Kerch' disaster in May 1942, the resolute Cherniak managed to serve in combat through-

out the remainder of the war. Reduced in rank to colonel, he commanded 10th Reserve Army's 306th Rifle Division from June through December 1942, when he was wounded in action. After recovering from his wounds, he served as deputy commander of 39th Army's 5th Guards Rifle Corps in April 1943 and commander of 3rd Shock Army's 32nd Rifle Division in June 1943, only to be relieved of command once again in August for "not fulfilling orders to penetrate the defenses." Despite Cherniak's previous misfortunes, the NKO restored him to command in October 1943, this time as commander of 65th Army's 162nd Rifle Division, which he led with distinction in the Gomel'–Rechitsa offensive during November 1943, for which his division received the Order of the Red Banner. Wounded once again during Belorussian Front's Kalinkovichi offensive in January 1944, Cherniak returned to field duty in March to command 41st Rifle Division, first under 65th Army's control and, to war's end, under 69th Army's control, performing credibly in the Lublin-Brest, Vistula-Oder, and Berlin offensives. After war's end, Cherniak occupied several minor staff positions in several military districts until he retired in 1958. A true survivor of the war, Cherniak died in 1976 at age 78.

63. Ibid., 172. After escaping from Sevastopol' shortly before its surrender, Petrov commanded Trans-Caucasus Front's 44th Army from August to October 1942, the same front's Black Sea Group of Forces to May 1943, and the North Caucasus Front from May 1943 to November 1943. However, because he quarreled with Stalin's henchman, Mekhlis, he was reduced in rank from army general to colonel general in March 1944 and assigned command of 2nd Belorussian Front's 33rd Army. Always indomitable, Petrov rose once again to command 4th Ukrainian Front from August 1944 to March 1945. Although Petrov distinguished himself during the struggle for the Carpathian Mountains, interference by Stalin's commissars resulted in his relief and reassignment as chief of staff of 1st Ukrainian Front to war's end. Exiled after the war to command the Turkistan Military District, Petrov returned to Moscow after Stalin's death to become 1st Assistant Chief Inspector of the Soviet Army in 1954, chief of the army's Main Training Directorate, and 1st Deputy Commander of the Soviet Army's Ground Forces before his death in 1958.

64. For a more detailed description of the Red Army soldier, see Glantz, *Colossus Reborn*, 536–608.

65. For examples of ethnic friction, see Waling T. Gorter-Gronvik and Mikhail N. Suprun, "Ethnic Minorities and Warfare at the Arctic Front, 1939–1945," *JSMS* 13, 1 (March 2000): 127–142.

66. See details on the nature and scale of women's participation in the war effort in Glantz, *Colossus Reborn*, 551–554. Women soldiers also manned 1st Women's Rifle Brigade in Moscow, an organization formed to train snipers for service throughout the field army.

Chapter 3: Preliminaries, April–June 1942

1. V. A. Zolotarev, ed., *Velikaia Otechestvennaia voina 1941–1945, kniga 1: Surovye ispytaniia* [The Great Patriotic War, 1941–1945, book 1: A harsh education] (Moscow: Nauka, 1998), 331 (hereafter cited as *VOV*). The *Stavka* formed the Crimean Front on 28 January, including in it roughly half of Caucasus Front's forces, and tasked it with defending the Kerch' Peninsula and attacking westward to relieve Separate Coastal Army,

then besieged in Sevastopol' by Manstein's Eleventh Army. For details on these operations, see David M. Glantz, *Combat Chronology and Documents on the Battle for the Crimea, Volume 1: 9 September–31 December 1941* (Carlisle, PA: Self-published, 2008).

2. *Boevoi sostav Sovetskoi armii*, 2: 67.

3. Shtemenko, *Soviet General Staff at War*, bk. 1, 69. General Vechnyi survived to head the Red Army General Staff's Department for the Exploitation of War Experience, which was responsible for collecting and publishing many studies of wartime military operations for the betterment of the Red and Soviet Army in the future.

4. For details on Crimean Front's failed offensives and the subsequent German offensive, see David M. Glantz, *Forgotten Battles of the Soviet-German War (1941–1945), Volume 2: The Winter Campaign (5 December 1941–April 1942)* (Carlisle, PA: Self-published, 1999), 118–154; A. A. Volkov, *Kriticheskii prolog: Nezavershennye frontovye nastupatel'nye operatsii pervykh kampanii Velikoi Otechestvennoi voiny* [Critical prologue: Incomplete front offensive operations of the initial campaign of the Great Patriotic War] (Moscow: AVIAR, 1992), 128–143; *Soviet Documents on the Use of War Experience, Volume 3: Military Operations, 1941–1942*, trans. Harold S. Orenstein (London: Frank Cass, 1993), 122–161; V. V. Beshanov, *God 1942—"Uchebnyi"* [The Year 1942—Educational] (Minsk: Harvest, 2002), 130–191; Aleksei Isaev, *Kratkii kurs Istorii Velikoi Otechestvennoi voiny: Nastuplenie Marshala Shaposhnikova* [A short course in the history of the Great Patriotic War: The offensives of Marshal Shaposhnikov] (Moscow: "IAUZA" "EKSMO," 2005), 276–284; Shtemenko, *Soviet General Staff at War*, bk. 1, 68–70; Manstein, *Lost Victories*, 233–235; and Hayward, *Stopped at Stalingrad*, 68–85.

5. B. I. Nevzorov, "Mai 1942–go: Ak Monai, Enikale" [May 1942: Ak Monai and Enikale], *VIZh*, 8 (August 1992): 33.

6. Volkov, *Kriticheskii prolog*, 131.

7. Axis forces which fought at Kerch' included XXX Army Corps' 28th Jäger, 50th, 132nd, and 170th Infantry Divisions and 22nd Panzer Division and XXXXII Army Corps' German 46th Infantry Division and Romanian 10th and 19th Infantry and 8th Cavalry Divisions, subordinate to Romanian VII Army Corps.

8. Ziemke and Bauer, *Moscow to Stalingrad*, 262–263.

9. Hayward, *Stopped at Stalingrad*, 68–70, 85.

10. This account of the actual assault on Kerch' is based primarily on Carell, *Stalingrad*, 25–29.

11. Quoted in Shtemenko, *Soviet General Staff at War*, bk. 1, 69–70. See other caustic exchanges between Stalin and the *Stavka* and Kozlov in Zolotarev, "*Stavka* 1942," 196, 198–199.

12. See Zolotarev, *VOV*, 1: 332; Hayward, *Stopped at Stalingrad*, 84–85; and Werner Haupt, *Army Group South: The Wehrmacht in Russia, 1941–1945*, trans. Joseph G. Welsh (Atglen, PA: Schiffer Press, 1998), 112–114. Officially, the Soviet casualty toll at Kerch' amounted to 176,566 soldiers, including 162,282 killed, mortally wounded, or missing in action (captured), and 14,284 wounded or sick. Kozlov's *front* also lost 347 tanks, 3,476 guns and mortars, and 400 aircraft. See G. F. Krivosheev, ed., *Grif sekretnosti sniat: Poteri vooruzhennykh sil SSSR v voinakh, boevykh deistviiakh, i voennykh konfliktakh* [The classification secret is removed: The losses of the USSR's Armed Forces in wars, combat operations, and military conflicts] (Moscow: Voenizdat, 1993), 224.

13. David M. Glantz, *Kharkov 1942: The Anatomy of a Military Disaster* (Rockville Center, NY: Sarpedon, 1998), 42–43.

14. See Chapter 5 in this volume for Kriuchenkin's biographical sketch.

15. Glantz, *Kharkov 1942*, 44–48, 51–52. Although details remain sketchy about Bobkin's military career, he was born in 1894, joined the Red Guards in 1917 and Red Army in 1918, and received the Order of the Red Banner for his service in the Civil War. Bobkin graduated from the Leningrad Higher Cavalry School in 1925, where he earned praise from his instructor, I. Kh. Bagramian, for being a superb cavalry tactician. Thereafter, he served in cavalry forces before and during Operation Barbarossa and was appointed assistant commander for cavalry of Southwestern Front in early 1942. Born in 1898, Noskov fought as a private in the tsar's army during World War I, joined the Red Army in 1918, and fought in cavalry units on the western and southern fronts during the Civil War. A 1932 graduate of the Budenny Cavalry School, the Red Army's Command Course (KUKS) in 1932, and the Frunze Academy in 1941, Noskov served in cavalry units during the 1920s and 1930s, rising to command 9th Cavalry Division's 52nd Cavalry Regiment from December 1938 through December 1940 and serve as deputy commander of 150th Rifle Division from December 1940 through the outbreak of war. Appointed to command 6th Army's 26th Cavalry Division in July 1941, he led his divisions during Southern Front's fighting withdrawal across Ukraine during the summer of 1941 and during Southwestern Front's defense of the Donbas region that fall. He was assigned command of 6th Cavalry Corps in February 1942. Wounded and captured during the battle for Khar'kov, Noskov spent the rest of the war in German captivity. After his release from imprisonment in May 1945 and NKVD "filtration" to ensure his loyalty to the Soviet Union, Noskov graduated from the Voroshilov Academy in 1947, served as deputy commander of 5th Guards Army until July 1951, 16th Guards Mechanized Corps until February 1952, and 17th Rifle and 119th Mountain Rifle Corps until his retirement in 1954. Noskov died in 1960. For further details, see *Komkory. Voennyi biograficheskii slovar'*, 74–75, and Aleksander A. Maslov, *Captured Soviet Generals: The Fate of Soviet Generals Captured by the Germans, 1941–1945* (London: Frank Cass, 2001), 71–73, 95–96.

16. Beshanov, *God 1942*, 212–214.

17. Ibid., 51–56.

18. Ibid., 51, 54.

19. For a complete description of the battle, see Glantz, *Kharkov 1942*; David M. Glantz, *Atlas and Survey: The Soviet Khar'kov Offensive, 12–29 May 1942* (Carlisle, PA: Self-published, 1998); Andrei Galushko and Maksim Kolomiets, "Boi za Khar'kov v mae 1942 god" [The battle for Khar'kov in May 1942], in *Frontovaia illiustratsiia*, 6–2000 [Front illustrated, 6–2000] (Moscow: "Strategiia KM," 1999); Beshanov, *God 1942*, 220–238; and Isaev, *Kratkii kurs*, 321–354.

20. Zhukov, *Reminiscences and Reflections*, 2: 75.

21. Bock, quoted in Ziemke and Bauer, *Moscow to Stalingrad*, 273.

22. Antony Beevor, *Stalingrad: The Fateful Siege: 1942–1943* (New York: Viking, 1998), 65; Glantz, *Kharkov 1942*, 126–128; and, on the transfer of aircraft, Hayward, *Stopped at Stalingrad*, 82–83.

23. Halder, *The Halder War Diary*, 616–617; and Ziemke and Bauer, *Moscow to Stalingrad*, 275–278.

24. The counterattack by III Motorized Corps is summarized in Eberhard von Mackensen, *Vom Bug zum Kaukasus: Das III. Panzerkorps im Feldzug gegen Sowjetrussland 1941/42* (Neckargemünd: Kurt Vowinkel Verlag, 1967), 68–75.

25. Galushko and Kolomiets, "Boi za Khar'kov," 73; and Isaev, *Kratki kurs*, 352–353.

26. On the Soviet command debate, see Zhukov, *Reminiscences and Reflections*, 2: 76–77; Shtemenko, *The Soviet General Staff at War*, bk. 1, 72–774; and Ziemke and Bauer, *Moscow to Stalingrad*, 279–282. For Paulus's reaction, see Goerlitz, *Paulus and Stalingrad*, 56.

27. See the directives associated with the formation and deployment of these reserve forces in Zolotarev, "*Stavka* 1942," 210–250.

28. "Letter, Stalin to the Military Council of the Southwestern Front, 26 June 1942," quoted in Glantz, *Kharkov 1942*, 225.

29. Bagramian, *Tak shli my k pobeda* [As we went on to victory], 131.

30. Beshanov, *God 1942*, 240.

31. For details on Briansk Front's planned offensives, see "Boevye deistviia voisk Brianskogo i Voronezhskogo frontov letom 1942 na Voronezhskom napravlenii" [The combat operations of the forces of the Briansk and Voronezh Fronts along the Voronezh axis in the summer of 1942], in *SVIMVOV, Vypusk 15* (Moscow: Voenizdat, 1955).

32. Beshanov, *God 1942*, 240.

33. Blau, *The German Campaign in Russia*, 140.

34. Ibid., 140–141; and Beevor, *Stalingrad*, 69–70.

35. *Boevoi sostav Sovetskii armii*, 3: 106; and Isaev, *Kratkii kurs*, 288–289.

36. Beshanov, *God 1942*, 192; and Isaev, *Kratkii kurs*, 288.

37. Isaev, *Kratkii kurs*, 289.

38. Carell, *Stalingrad*, 38–39, 44; and Hayward, *Stopped at Stalingrad*, 90–91.

39. Alex Buchner, *Sewastopol: Der Angriff auf die stärkste Festung der Welt 1942* (Friedberg: Podzun-Pallas-Verlag, 1978), 109–110; Isaev, *Kratkii kurs*, 289–290; and Beshanov, *God 1942*, 195.

40. On the siege artillery at Sevastopol, see Buchner, *Sewastopol*, 110–113; Ziemke and Bauer, *Moscow to Stalingrad*, 309; Hayward, *Stopped at Stalingrad*, 91–92; and Carell, *Stalingrad*, 43. As many as 35,000 of the city's inhabitants endured the siege in the city proper.

41. For details on the final battle for Sevastopol', see G. I. Vaneev, S. L. Ermash, I. D. Malakhovsky, S. T. Sakhno, A. F. Khrenov, *Geroicheskaia oborona Sevastopolia 1941–1942* [The heroic defense of Sevastopol' 1941–1942] (Moscow: Voenizdat, 1969); E. A. Ignatovich, *Zenitnoe bratstvo Sevastopolia* [The antiaircraft brotherhood of Sevastopol'] (Kiev: Politicheskoi literatury Ukrainy, 1986); A. Dukachev, *Kurs na Sevastopol'* [The path to Sevastopol'] (Simferopol': "Tavriia," 1974); S. G. Gorshkov, *Na Iuzhnom flange, osen' 1941 g.–vesna 1944 g.* [On the southern flank, fall 1941–spring 1944] (Moscow: Voenizdat, 1989); G. I. Vaneev, *Chernomortsy v Velikoi Otechestvennoi voine* [Black Sea sailors in the Great Patriotic War] (Moscow: Voenizdat, 1978); *Krasnoznamennyi Chernomorskii Flot* [The Red Banner Black Sea Fleet] (Moscow: Voenizdat, 1987); *SVIMVOV*, issue 14 (Moscow: Voenizdat, 1954), 88–114; N. M. Zamiatkin, F. D. Vorob'ev, *Oborona Sevastopolia* [The defense of Sevastopol'] (Moscow: Voenizdat, 1943); and Buchner, *Sewastopol*.

42. This description of LIV Corps' attack is quoted in Haupt, *Army Group South*, 121.

43. Ziemke and Bauer, *Moscow to Stalingrad*, 312.

44. See the evocative accounts in Carell, *Stalingrad*, 44–49.

45. Ziemke and Bauer, *Moscow to Stalingrad*, 316–318.

46. Haupt, *Army Group South*, 123–124.

47. Ziemke and Bauer, *Moscow to Stalingrad*, 319–321; and Manstein, *Lost Victories*, 248–258.

48. Isaev, *Kratkii kurs*, 302.

49. Beshanov, *God 1942*, 210.

50. See German planning maps and documents for Wilhelm and Fridericus II in "'Friedericus, 1' Anlagenmappe 1 zum KTB Nr. 8, PzAOK 1, Ia, 27 Mar–14 May 1942," *PzAOK 1, 25179/3*, in NAM T-313, Roll 5.

51. I. Ia. Vyrodov, ed., *V srazheniiakh za Pobedu: Boevoi put' 38-i armii v gody Velikoi Otechestvennoi voyny 1941–1945* [In battles for the Fatherland: The combat path of the 38th Army in the Great Patriotic War, 1941–1945] (Moscow: Nauka, 1974), 120. 5th Tank Army's destination, Efremov, was 200 kilometers north of Voronezh in the rear of Briansk Front. The concentration areas of 4th and 16th Tank Corps, Novyi Oskol and Kastornoe, were 140 kilometers southwest and 100 kilometers west of Voronezh, respectively.

52. K. S. Moskalenko, *Na iugo–zapadnom napravlenii* [Along the southwestern axis] (Moscow: "Nauka," 1969), 1: 224. Because of the limited space within the Staryi Saltov bridgehead, the tank brigades of 22nd Tank Corps had to fight as separate entities in support of 28th and 38th Armies' first echelon rifle divisions during the battle for Khar'kov.

53. For details on the opposing tank strength, see Jentz, *Panzertruppen*, 236–239.

54. See the daily situation maps in "Ia, Lagenkarten zum KTB 12, May–Jul 1942," *AOK 6, 22855/Ia*, in NAM T-312, Roll 1446.

55. Moskalenko, *Na iugo–zapadnom napravlenii*, 1: 226–227. This counterattack was supposed to be a part of a larger counterstroke to be conducted by all of 22nd Tank Corps, 162nd and 278th Rifle Divisions, and 3rd and 156th Tank Brigades, all under the command of Major General N. A. Novikov, Moskalenko's chief of armored and mechanized forces. However, the counterstroke failed because of poor command and control, and the attacking forces suffered heavy losses.

56. Ziemke and Bauer, *Moscow to Stalingrad*, 316.

57. See "Notes of conversations by direct line of the Supreme High Commander and the deputy chief of the General Staff with the High Command of the Southwestern Direction," in Zolotarev, "*Stavka 1942*," 247.

58. Ibid.

59. Ibid.

60. Ibid., 249.

61. See Liziukov's biography in Chapter 4 of this volume.

62. Ibid.

63. See *Stavka* directive no. 170454, dated 0145 hours 17 June 1942, in ibid., 251.

64. See *Stavka* directives nos. 994068, 994069, and 994070, all dated 2210 hours 20 June 1942, in ibid., 255–256.

65. See *Stavka* directive no. 170458, dated 0235 hours 21 June, in ibid., 258.

66. The name Fridericus appears in several spellings. Both Fridericus and Friedericus are used in German operational documents. Here we adhere to the spelling Fridericus, which Earl Ziemke used in his seminal works about the Soviet-German War.

67. Ziemke and Bauer, *Moscow to Stalingrad*, 317–318; and Halder, *The Halder War Diary*, 623–624.

68. See the daily situation maps in "Ia, Lagenkarten zum KTB 12, May–Jul 1942,"

AOK 6, 22855/Ia, in NAM T-312, Roll 1446; and "Lagenkarten Pz. AOK 1, Ia (Armee–Gruppe v. Kleist), 1–29 Jun 1942," *PzAOK 1, 24906/12*, in NAM T-313, Roll 35.

69. Born in 1898, Nikishov served as an enlisted soldier during the World War and, after joining the Red Guards in December 1917 and the Red Army in 1918, was a political officer at the battalion and regimental level during the Civil War. A 1927 graduate of the Frunze Academy and a graduate of the General Staff Academy in 1937, Nikishov commanded a battalion in the 1920s and a regiment in the 1930s before being posted as chief of staff of the North Caucasus Military District in 1939 and the Northwestern Front's 9th Army in January 1940. After planning and supervising this army's successful operations during the second stage of the Finnish War, for which his army received the Order of the Red Banner, Nikishov became, in succession, chief of staff of the North Caucasus Military District in April 1940, chief of staff of the Red Army Air Force in August 1940, and chief of staff of the Leningrad Military District in March 1941. During Operation Barbarossa, Nikishov was chief of staff of the new Northern Front, with special responsibility for the Karelian axis. In January 1942, he was appointed chief of the 5th Sapper Army's 4th Department for Fortified Regions and, in February, chief of the Southwestern Front's Department for Fortified Regions. The NKO exploited Nikishov's work in erecting the Southwestern Front's defenses by appointing him as deputy commander of 9th Army in June 1942. See *Komandarmy. Voennyi biograficheskii slovar'*, 158–159.

70. Beshanov, *God 1942*, 247; and *Boevoi sostav Sovetskoi armii*, 2: 106. The 9th Guards Rifle Division joined Moskalenko's army on 11 June 1942, 81st Rifle Division was transferred to 9th Army on 13 June, and 277th Rifle Division reverted to *front* reserve the same day.

71. *Boevoi sostav Sovetskoi armii*, 2: 105; and "Feindlagenkarten, PzAOK 1, Ic, 31 May–28 Jun 1942," *PzAOK 1, 24906/23*, in NAM T-313, Roll 37.

72. Born in 1893, Parkhomenko fought in the tsar's army during the World War, joined the Red Army in 1918, and commanded a cavalry squadron and regiment during the Civil War. A 1924 graduate of the Taganrog Cavalry School, a Cavalry Officers' Course (KUKS) in 1929, and the Frunze Academy in 1930, Parkhomenko led cavalry regiments in the 1920s and 22nd Cavalry Division in 1936 before being caught up in Stalin's military purges and imprisoned as an "enemy of the people" in 1937. More fortunate than most of his counterparts, Parkhomenko was exonerated and rehabilitated in 1940 and assigned command of 4th Cavalry Division in spring 1940 and 210th Motorized Division in March 1941. After the Barbarossa invasion, he led this division throughout the summer and early fall of 1941, fighting in the battle for the Dnepr and in the Smolensk region in July and August and against Guderian's Second Panzer Group during its southward thrust toward Kiev in September. Thereafter, he commanded 1st Cavalry Corps during the Southern Front's offensive in the winter of 1941–1942 and was assigned command of 5th Cavalry Corps in July 1942. After leading his corps during the defense of the Donbas region in July and early August, Parkhomenko commanded 9th Army briefly in late August and then served as deputy commander of 24th Army during its defense in the Stalingrad region during the fall. In the wake of Operation Blau, he commanded the Far Eastern Front's 18th Cavalry Corps from March 1943 to March 1944 and served as deputy commander of 125th Rifle Corps and 70th Army during the 2nd Belorussian Front's many offensives from March 1944 through war's end, ending his wartime career by participating in the Berlin offensive during April and May 1945. After war's end, Parkhomenko was

deputy commander of the Central Group of Forces' (CGF) 43rd Army until his retirement in 1954 and death in 1962. For further details, see *Komandarmy. Voennyi biograficheskii slovar'*, 168–169.

73. Ziemke and Bauer, *Moscow to Stalingrad*, 318–319.

74. Wolfgang Werthen, *Geschichte der 16. Panzer–Division 1939–1945* (Friedberg: Podzun-Pallas Verlag, 1958), 96.

75. For more on Beloborodov's illustrious career, see *Komandarmy. Voennyi biograficheskii slovar'*, 22–24. After commanding 39th and 5th Guards Armies during the postwar, Beloborodov capped his career as commander of the Moscow Military District from 1963 to 1968 before retiring in 1968. The author of one of the best wartime memoirs, Beloborodov died in 1990 at age 87.

76. Trevori-Roper, *Blitzkrieg to Defeat*, 120.

77. The best account of the Reichel affair is Carell, *Stalingrad*, 50–57.

78. See *SVIMVOV*, Issue 15, 123. In part, the compromised order read:

"After Operation Wilhelm, which is being conducted in the Volchansk region and has as its mission reaching the general line of Efremovka and Malo Mikhailovka, the following mission is planned for XXXX Motorized Corps in Operation "Blau:" As part of Sixth Army, XXXX Motorized Corps will encircle and destroy enemy forces northeast of Belgorod. It will penetrate the enemy front between the Volch'ia and Nezhegol' Rivers, capture bridgeheads on the Oskol River in the Volokonovka and Novyi Oskol sector by swift attacks, and turn its units east of the Oskol River in the direction of Staryi Oskol to block an enemy withdrawal eastward from the region northeast of Belgorod.

The corps' main forces will capture line of dominating terrain northeast of Volokonovka in preparation for an offensive to the south or southeast or to hold the encirclement front.

Adjacent forces:

Fourth Panzer Army, moving its main forces from the Kursk region toward Voronezh, will seize Staryi Oskol using part of its forces, where XXXX Motorized Corps should close the encirclement front with it.

VIII Army Corps, clearing the enemy out of forest on the northern bank of the Nezhegol' River, will advance in a more northeasterly direction of XXXX Motorized Corps' left.

Hungarian Second Army, advancing south or southeast, will clear the territory of surrounded enemy units."

79. Carell, *Stalingrad*, 56–57; and Wilhelm Keitel, *In the Service of the Reich*, trans. David Irving (New York: Stein and Day, 1966), 178.

80. Shtemenko, *Soviet General Staff at War*, bk. I, 79–80.

81. See *Stavka* directive no. 170461, dated 0200 hours 23 June 1942, in Zolotarev, "*Stavka* 1942," 262. Born in 1893, P. M. Kozlov was a veteran of World War I and the Civil War who graduated from the Frunze Academy in 1926, commanded a rifle regiment, served as chief of staff of 14th Army, and headed a department at the General Staff Academy in the 1920s and 1930s. After war began in June 1941, Kozlov served as chief of Rear Services in Southern Front's 56th Army and commanded an operational group in the same army from November 1941 through March 1942, when he became deputy commander of 18th Army at age 49. Thereafter, Kozlov commanded 37th, 9th, and 47th Armies from June 1942 until August 1943, when he was relieved of command for exer-

cising poor command and "permitting" too many casualties in his army, and 77th Rifle Corps until his death from illness on 17 April 1944. For additional details, see *Komandarmy. Voennyi biograficheskii slovar'*, 96–97.

82. See *Stavka* directive no. 170462, dated 0345 hours 25 June 1942, in ibid., 263.

83. See *Stavka* directive no. 994076 and 170466, dated 26 June and 2020 hours on 28 June 1942, respectively, in ibid., 264–265.

84. See *Stavka* directive no. 170465, dated 2025 hours 28 June 1942, in ibid., 266.

Chapter 4: Punch and Counterpunch, Blau I, 28 June–12 July 1942

1. The region within this rectangle is largely unchanged today, except for numerous dams and associated lakes along the rivers and several new highways added to the road network. Although improved, the rail system is also essentially unchanged.

2. Born in 1897, Khaliuzin was a cavalry veteran of World War I and the Civil War who, after transferring to the infantry, commanded a rifle regiment in the 1920s, 96th Rifle Division from 1937 to March 1941, and the Orel Military District's 33rd Rifle Corps from March 1941 through the outbreak of the Soviet-German War. After the war began, Khaliuzin led 28th Army's 36th Rifle Corps during the heavy fighting in the Roslavl' region south of Smolensk in July and August 1941 and served as chief of staff of 13th Army and Briansk Front in September and October 1941. After surviving the infamous Briansk encirclement in October, Khaliuzin was given command of 48th Army in May 1942 at age 45. He went on to lead the army until relieved of command in February 1943, probably because of his army's poor performance during the offensive against the German Orel salient. Khaliuzin, who was promoted to lieutenant general in 1944, spent the remainder of the war as chief of staff of 61st Army and then commander of 89th Rifle and 9th Guards Rifle Corps. He ended his military career by serving as assistant commandant of the Frunze Academy from 1949 through 1953 and retired in 1953. He died in 1975. Ignored by Soviet-era encyclopedias, his biography can now be found in *Komandarmy. Voennyi biograficheskii slovar'*, 239–240.

3. Ibid., 64–66. Danilov, born in 1897, was also a veteran of World War I and the Civil War who joined the Red Army in 1918. A 1924 graduate of the *"Vystrel'"* Officers Course, the Frunze Academy in 1931, and the General Staff Academy in 1939, after serving in low-level command and higher-level staff positions during the interwar years, Danilov commanded 49th Rifle Corps during the Finnish War of 1939–1940 and was appointed chief of the Kiev Special Military District's PVO (Air Defense) forces in July 1940, a position he occupied when Operation Barbarossa began. Thereafter, Danilov served as chief of staff of Briansk Front's 21st Army in October 1941 and as the army's commander in June 1942. In Operation Blau's wake, Danilov commanded 12th Army from May to November 1943 and 17th Army in the Far East through war's end, leading the latter with distinction during the Manchurian offensive in August–September 1945. After war's end Danilov commanded 17th Army and a rifle corps and then was chief adviser to the North Korean People's Army before retiring in 1968; he died in 1981.

4. "Boevye deistviia voisk Brianskogo i Voronezhskogo frontov letom 1942 na Voronezhskom napravlenii," in *SVIMVOV, Vypusk* 15, 127.

5. See *Stavka* directives nos. 170464 and 170465, dated 2020 and 2025 hours 28 June 1942, in Zolotarev, "*Stavka* 1942," 265–266.

6. See *Stavka* directives nos. 1035010 and 170467, dated 2130 hours 28 June and 0045 hours 29 June 1942, in ibid., 266.

7. *SVIMVOV, Vypusk* 15, 128.

8. Ibid.

9. Ibid.

10. Carell, *Stalingrad*, 58–59; Ziemke and Bauer, *Moscow to Stalingrad*, 333; and Ferdinand von Senger und Etterlin, *Die 24. Panzer–Division vormals 1. Kavallerie-Division 1939–1945* (Neckargemünd: Kurt Vowinckel Verlag, 1962), 71–74. The attack on *Grossdeutschland* Division's 2nd Regiment is described in Helmuth Spaeter, *The History of the Panzerkorps Grossdeutschland*, vol. 1, trans. David Johnston (Winnipeg: J. J. Fedorowicz, 1992), 323–324.

11. *SVIMVOV, Vypusk* 15, 129.

12. Ibid.

13. See Zolotarev, "*Stavka* 1942," 268–272, for the entire discussion.

14. Ibid., 271.

15. Ibid., 272–276; and Glantz, *Forgotten Battles*, 3: 17–21.

16. "Boevye rasporiazhenie i boevye doneseniia shtaba 28 Armii (12.5–12.7.1942)" [Combat orders and combat reports of the headquarters of the 28th Army (12.5–12.7.42)], in *TsAMO*, f. 382, op. 8452, ed. khr. 37, l. 53.

17. *SVIMVOV, Vypusk* 15, 130.

18. See Maksim Kolomiets and Aleksandr Smirnov, "Boi v izluchine Dona, 28 iiunia–23 iiulia 1942 goda" [The battle in the bend of the Don, 28 June–23 July 1942], in *Frontovaia illiustratsiia, 6-2002* [Front illustrated, 6-2002] (Moscow: "Strategiia KM," 2002), 71–73.

19. Ibid., 26–28.

20. *TsAMO*, f. 382, op. 8452, ed. khr. 37, l. 55.

21. Ibid., 56.

22. See the discussions between the *Stavka* and Golikov in Zolotarev, "*Stavka* 1942," 272–279; and *SVIMVOV, Vypusk* 15, 131–132.

23. *SVIMVOV, Vypusk* 15, 132.

24. Specifically, XXIX Corps' 168th and 75th Infantry Divisions and VIII Corps' 389th Infantry Division.

25. Moskalenko, *Na iugo–zapadnom napravlenii*, 1: 251.

26. Shurov was wounded near the village of Shevtsovo but died the next day en route to a hospital. The two dead brigade commanders were Major P. I. Turbin (full name still unknown) of 20th Motorized Rifle Brigade and Major General Anatolii Alekseevich Aseichev of 85th Tank Brigade. See Kolomiets and Smirnov, "Boi v izluchine Dona," 33.

27. See *Stavka* directives nos. 170471–170474, dated 2 July 1942, in Zolotarev, "*Stavka* 1942," 280–282.

28. See *Stavka* directive no. 994089, dated 0520 hours 2 July 1942, in ibid., 282.

29. *SVIMVOV, Vypusk* 15, 134.

30. Born in 1896, Lunev fought as a battalion commander in the tsar's army during World War I, joined the Red Army in 1918, rose to command a cavalry squadron in the Civil War, and took part in the suppression of the Kronshtadt mutiny in 1921. A 1922 graduate of the Smolensk Combined Military School for Senior Combat Commands, the Leningrad Cavalry School in 1926, and the Red Army's Senior Cavalry Officers Course (KUKS) in 1930, Lunev commanded a battalion during the campaign against the Basmachi

insurgents in central Asia in 1923–1924 and 5th Cavalry Division's 28th Regiment in 1933–1934. He spent six years as chief of Red Army Horse Breeding Centers but was appointed deputy commander of 32nd Cavalry Division in November 1940 and then deputy commander of 5th Mechanized Corps' 219th Motorized Division in the Kiev Special Military District in April 1941. After his unit was reorganized into a rifle division in August, he led it during the struggle for Gomel' in August 1941, where he was wounded in action. When he returned from his convalescence in early September, he commanded 37th Army's 295th Rifle Division until its destruction in the Kiev encirclement. Escaping with 500 of his men, Lunev was accused of "treason under enemy fire," only to be exonerated and appointed to command 8th Cavalry Corps on 28 May 1942 after spending several months in NKVD custody. Lunev commanded his cavalry corps until 9 September 1942, after which he served in rear service staff positions in 3rd, 6th, and 65th Armies until war's end. Lunev retired from the army in 1946 and died in 1962. Largely ignored by Soviet-era books, his biography can be found in *Komkory. Voennyi biograficheskii slovar'*, 68–69.

31. *SVIMVOV, Vypusk* 15, 133.

32. Born in 1902, Popov, who was assigned command of 40th Army at the young age of 39, joined the Red Army in 1920, fought during the final year of the Civil War, and graduated from the "*Vystrel*'" Officers Course in 1925 and the Frunze Academy in 1936. After commanding a battalion in the mid-1930s and serving as chief of staff of a mechanized brigade and 5th Mechanized Corps in 1936 and 1937, Popov became deputy commander of the Far Eastern Military District's 1st Red Banner Army in 1938, an army he commanded in July 1939. As war approached, Popov became commander of the Leningrad Military District in January 1941 and, after war began, of the Northern and Leningrad Fronts, which he led during the intense fighting at the gates of Leningrad in August and September 1941, first under the lackluster supervision of Marshal Voroshilov, and later under the more severe and successful taskmaster, General Zhukov. After the successful defense of Leningrad, the Stavka assigned Popov command of Briansk Front's 61st Army in November 1941 and the same *front*'s 40th Army in June 1942. Popov served as deputy commander of Stalingrad and Southwestern Fronts during the fighting in the Stalingrad region in the fall of 1942 and as commander of the Reserve, Steppe, Briansk, Baltic, and 2nd Baltic Fronts, in succession, from December 1942 through April 1944. He ended his wartime service as chief of staff of the Leningrad and 2nd Baltic Fronts. Promoted to the rank of army general in 1953, Popov ended his distinguished military career by commanding the L'vov and Tavria Military Districts and serving as deputy chief of the Soviet Army's Main Training Directorate. He was 1st Deputy Commander of the Soviet Army's Ground Forces at the time of his death in 1969. For further details on Popov's career, see *Komandarmy. Voennyi biograficheskii slovar'*, 181–182.

33. Spaeter, *Panzerkorps Grossdeutschland*, 1: 351.

34. Ibid., 3: 11–13, and 21; and Ziemke and Bauer, *Moscow to Stalingrad*, 336–337.

35. See *Stavka* directive no. 170475, dated 0030 hours 3 July 1942, in Zolotarev, "*Stavka* 1942," 284.

36. For a complete breakdown of 5th Tank Army's organizational structure and strength, see Kolomiets and Smirnov, "Boi v izluchine Dona," 41.

37. Baranov, who was born in 1901, served in various staff and lower-level command positions in cavalry units during the 1920s and 1930s before he was appointed to command 5th Cavalry Division in March 1941. He led the division throughout all of Operation Barbarossa; after the division received the honorific designation of 1st Guards on 26

December 1941, he led it during the winter campaign of 1941–1942 when it took part in the deep raid conducted by General Belov's famous 1st Guards Cavalry Corps into German Army Group Center's rear area between Viaz'ma and Smolensk. Surviving this audacious but costly venture, Baranov was assigned command of the guards cavalry corps in May 1942, when Belov moved up to command of 60th Army, and led the cavalry corps to war's end, reaching the rank of lieutenant general. After the war, Baranov commanded 1st Guards Cavalry and 14th Rifle Corps and graduated from the Voroshilov General Staff Academy before retiring in 1953. One of the Red Army's most famous wartime cavalry leaders, Baranov died in 1970. For further details on his career, see the website "The Generals of World War II," at http://www.generals.dk/general Baranov/Viktor_Kirillovich/ Soviet_Union.html.

38. M. E. Katukov, *Na ostrie glavnogo udara* [At the point of the main attack] (Moscow: Voenizdat, 1976), 133.

39. See *Stavka* directives nos. 170479–170481, dated 0430 hours 4 July 1942, in Zolotarev, "*Stavka* 1942," 288–289.

40. See *Stavka* directives nos. 994092 and 994096, dated 3 and 6 July 1942, in ibid., 285, 290. Romanenko, with General Liziukov, was one of the first two generals the *Stavka* selected to command its tank armies. Born in 1897, Romanenko fought as a warrant officer in World War I, joined the Red Army in 1918, and took part in the Russian Civil War when he led partisan units and later commanded a cavalry squadron, regiment, and brigade in Budenny's famous 1st Cavalry Army. Romanenko's star rose quickly in the Red Army's cavalry arm and, after 1937, in its fledgling mechanized force as he graduated from Cavalry School in 1925, the Officer Improvement Course in 1930, and the Frunze Academy in 1933. He commanded a regular army cavalry regiment in the 1920s and 11th Mechanized Brigade in 1937. He punctuated his field service with a stint as assistant department chief in the Red Army's Directorate for Motorization and Mechanization. After "volunteering" as an adviser to the Republican government during the Spanish Civil War (1936–1939), for which he was awarded the Order of Lenin, Romanenko returned to the Soviet Union, where he commanded 7th Mechanized Corps during the Finnish War (1939–1940), 1st Mechanized Corps after its formation in June 1940, and Trans-Baikal Front's 17th Army, where he was situated when Operation Barbarossa began. Romanenko served in the Far East until May 1942, when the Stavka brought him back to the West, assigning him command of the new 3rd Tank Army. After commanding 3rd Tank Army on the fringes of Operation Blau, particularly in the failed counterstroke along the Zhizdra axis in August 1942, Romanenko took command of a reorganized 5th Tank Army in early November 1942, which achieved lasting fame by spearheading the Red Army's successful counteroffensive at Stalingrad. Transferred to command 2nd Tank Army in February 1943, he led this army during Central Front's unsuccessful offensive to capture Orel and Briansk in February and March 1943, and 48th Army under Briansk, Central, and 1st and 2nd Belorussian Fronts throughout the rest of 1943 and 1944, playing a prominent role in the battle of Kursk and the Red Army's offensives to liberate Belorussia in fall 1943 and 1944. After departing field command in December 1944, supposedly because of deteriorating health, Romanenko, now a colonel general, commanded the Eastern Siberian Military District from 1945 to 1947 and died in March 1949. For further details, see *Komandarmy. Voennyi biograficheskii slovar'*, 195–196.

41. Kolomiets and Smirnov, "Boi v izluchine Dona," 42.

42. Born in 1895, Vorozheikin fought in World War I, joined the Red Army in 1918,

and served as deputy chief of staff of a rifle brigade during the Civil War. A 1933 graduate of the Zhukovsky Air Academy, he was serving as commander of the Volga Military District's air forces when war began in 1941. After leading an aviation division during June and July 1941 and Central Front's air forces in August, Vorozheikin served as chief of staff of the Red Army's Air Force from August 1941 through March 1942. Thereafter, he commanded a shock aviation group from March through May 1942 and was 1st deputy commander of the Red (later Soviet) Army's Air Force from May 1942 through 1946, simultaneously serving as *Stavka* coordinator of the air forces participating in numerous successful offensive operations. After the war, Vorozheikin commanded air armies in 1946 and 1947 and was a faculty head at the Zhukovsky Air Academy from 1953 until his retirement in 1959. Vorozheikin died in 1974. For further details see *VE*, 2: 272.

43. For details on this fighting, see also A. I. Goloborodov, "Kontrudar 5-i tankovoi armiii pod Voronezhem" [The 5th Tank Army's counterstroke at Voronezh], *Voennaia mysl'* [Military thought] 4 (April 1993): 42–48. Hereafter cited as *VM* with appropriate volume, date, and page(s).

44. The 53rd and 160th Tank Brigades of Kravchenko's 2nd Tank Corps lagged behind because their tanks became mired in the mud of the Kobyl'ia Snova River.

45. Kolomiets and Smirnov, "Boi v izluchine Dona," 44. For additional details on this and other battles in the Voronezh region, see Pavel A. Rotmistrov, *Stal'naia gvardiia* [Steel guards] (Moscow: Voenizdat, 1984), 116; and Glantz, *Forgotten Battles*, 3: 30–34.

46. See *Stavka* directive no. 170483, dated 2100 hours 7 July 1942, in Zolotarev, "Stavka 1942," 291–292.

47. Born in 1892, Chibisov was a junior officer in the tsar's army during World War I, joined the Red Army in 1918, and commanded a platoon, company, battalion, and regiment during the ensuing Civil War. A 1935 graduate of the Frunze Academy, Chibisov occupied a variety of command and staff positions during the interwar years, including command of a rifle division in 1937 and a rifle corps in 1938 and service as chief of staff of the Leningrad Military District and Northwestern Front's 7th Army during the Finnish War in 1939–1940. After serving as deputy commander of the Leningrad Military District from July 1940 through year's end, Chibisov was appointed commander of the Odessa Military District in January 1941, a post he occupied when Operation Barbarossa began. For Chibisov's accomplishments in mobilizing the military district for war and, later, helping organize the defense of Odessa, the NKO appointed him deputy commander of Briansk Front in September 1941. After his brief stint as commander of Briansk Front during July 1942, Chibisov commanded 38th Army from August 1942 to November 1943, 3rd Shock Army until April 1944, and 1st Shock Army until June 1944, when he became chief of the Frunze Academy, a post he occupied until March 1949. Chibisov then served as deputy commander of the Belorussian Military District before retiring in 1954. He died in 1959. For further details, see *Komandarmy, Voennyi biograficheskii slovar'*, 258–259. For Kharitonov's biography, see Chapter 2 in this volume.

48. See *Stavka* directive no. 170483, dated 2100 hours 7 July 1942, in Zolotarev, "Stavka 1942," 291–292. Antoniuk, who was born in 1895, fought in World War I, joined the Red Guards in 1917 and the Red Army a year later, and commanded a regiment, brigade, and the Mozyr' Group of Forces during the Russian Civil War. A graduate of courses at the RKKA Academy in 1921 and 1924, Antoniuk commanded 4th Turkestan, 5th Vitebsk, and 3rd Crimean Rifle Divisions from 1924 through 1930 and then taught at the Frunze Academy in 1930 and 1931. Continuing his meteoric career, he served as

commander and commissar of 8th Rifle Corps from 1931 to 1937 and of the Siberian Military District from June 1937 to August 1938, when he was suddenly caught up in the dragnet of Stalin's military purges. More fortunate than most of his counterparts, Antoniuk escaped the spurious charges and was exonerated and returned to the faculty of the Frunze Academy. During the last two years of peacetime, he served as chief and later as inspector-general of Red Army Infantry; after war began, he was instrumental in raising and fielding new formations and personnel replacement for the Red Army. Dispatched to the front in August 1941, Antoniuk commanded 7th Army's Petrozavodsk Operational Group, which halted the Finnish Army's advance north of Lake Ladoga and, in September 1941, 48th Army, which tried but failed to halt the German juggernaut toward Shlissel'burg on the southern shore of Lake Ladoga, a thrust that began the siege of the city of Leningrad. Thereafter, Antoniuk led an operational group in Leningrad Front's 54th Army during several failed attempts to raise the siege of Leningrad and served on Leningrad Front's staff before being appointed to command 60th Army in July 1942. In the midst of Operation Blau, Antoniuk was appointed to command 2nd Reserve Army in September 1942 but was replaced before that army went into action. Subsequently, in succession, Antoniuk served as deputy commander of Steppe, Baltic, and 2nd Baltic Fronts throughout the remainder of the war. Continuing as a deputy military district commander after war's end, Antoniuk retired in 1947 and died in 1961. Also neglected in Soviet-era sources, Antoniuk's biography is now found in *Komandarmy, Voennyi biograficheskii slovar'*, 13–14.

49. See *Stavka* directives nos. 1035033 and 994101, dated 7 and 8 July 1942, in Zolotarev, "*Stavka* 1942," 292–294.

50. The 11th Tank Corps employed 63 KV-1 and "Matilda" [British] tanks and 60 T-60s.

51. The 11th Tank Corps reportedly destroyed 15 German tanks at a cost of eight of its own.

52. Glantz, *Forgotten Battles*, 3: 36–37.

53. Kolomiets and Smirnov, "Boi v izluchine Dona," 45. By this time, Liziukov's forces had been reinforced by 22 antitank guns from 2nd Destroyer Division's 3rd Brigade.

54. Ibid., 46.

55. Ibid.

56. Ibid.

57. Katukov, *Na ostrie glavnogo udara*, 160–162.

58. Glantz, *Forgotten Battles*, 3: 48–52.

59. See *Stavka* directive no. 170511, dated 0405 hours 15 July 1942, in Zolotarev, "*Stavka* 1942," 309–310.

60. See *Stavka* directive no.170507, dated 1740 hours 13 July 1942, in ibid., 308.

61. See *Stavka* directive no.170509, dated 14 July 1942, in ibid., 309.

62. See Richard Woff, "Konstantin Konstantinovich Rokossovsky," in Shukman, *Stalin's Generals*, 177–196; and Rokossovsky's now unexpurgated memoir, *Soldatskii dolg* [A soldier's duty] (Moscow: "GOLOS," 2000).

63. Iu. D. Zakharov, *General armii Vatutin* (Moscow: Voenizdat, 1985); and David M. Glantz, "Nikolai Fedorovich Vatutin," in Shukman, *Stalin's Generals*, 287–298.

64. Klaus Gerbet, ed., *Generalfeldmarschall Fedor von Bock: The War Diary, 1939–1945*, trans. David Johnson (Atglen, PA: Schiffer Military History, 1996), 512, hereafter referred to as *Bock Diary*.

65. Ibid.

66. Ibid., 513.

67. On the Poltava conference, see Jukes, *Hitler's Stalingrad Decisions*, 35–38; Ziemke and Bauer, *Moscow to Stalingrad*, 337–339; and *Bock Diary*, 512–514.

68. Halder, *The Halder War Diary*, 633–634.

69. *Bock Diary*, 514–515.

70. Ibid., 517.

71. Ibid., 517, 520.

Chapter 5: Blau II, 9–24 July 1942

1. During Operation Barbarossa, after roughly 15 July 1941, German logistical stocks were sufficient to sustain advances of about 125 kilometers over a period of about ten days. Thereafter, German forces had to pause for at least a week to replenish their depleted fuel and ammunition stocks before they could resume offensive operations. The same phenomenon would plague German forces after Blau II.

2. Carell, *Stalingrad*, 65–68. On the fuel shortage, see Friedrich W. von Mellenthin, *German Generals of World War II as I Saw Them* (Norman: University of Oklahoma Press, 1977), 108–109.

3. Track XXXX Panzer Corps' and Sixth Army's daily advances in "Ia, Lagenkarten Nr. 1 zum KTB Nrs. 12–13, May–Jul 1942, Jul–Oct 1942," *AOK 6, 22855/Ia, 23984/Ia,* in NAM T-312, Roll 1146.

4. Born in 1894, Kriuchenkin fought as a noncommissioned officer in the tsar's army during World War I, joined the Red Guards in 1917 and the Red Army in 1918, and commanded a cavalry regiment during the Civil War. A graduate of cavalry courses in 1926 and 1935 and the Frunze Academy in 1941, Kriuchenkin commanded the Kiev Special Military District's 14th Cavalry Division in June 1938, leading it during the Soviet invasion of eastern Poland in September 1939. In Operation Barbarossa, Kriuchenkin's division, subordinate to Kamkov's famous 5th Cavalry Corps, fought gallantly in the harrowing border battles and during Southern Front's prolonged withdrawal eastward across the Ukraine and Donbas region in the summer and fall of 1941. Kriuchenkin was awarded the Order of the Red Banner when he led his cavalrymen's escape from German encirclement on two occasions. Appointed to command 5th Cavalry Corps in November 1941, he led it during the victorious offensive in the winter of 1941–1942, during which his corps earned the designation of 3rd Guards for the role it played in Southwestern Front's victory at Elets in December. After the successful Barvenkovo–Lozovaia offensive in January and February 1942 and the failed Khar'kov operation in May, Kriuchenkin was appointed to command 28th Army. In the wake of Operation Blau, Kriuchenkin commanded 69th, 10th, and 33rd Armies from March 1943 to the fall of 1944, taking part in the battle for Kursk and the Belorussian offensive in the summer of 1944. Although relieved of command on several occasions for both cause and illness, Kriuchenkin ended the war as deputy commander of 61st Army and, later, 1st Belorussian Front. After serving as deputy commander of the Don Military District, Kriuchenkin retired in 1946 and died in 1976. For further details, see *Komandarmy. Voennyi biograficheskii slovar'*, 113–114.

5. *TsAMO*, f. 382, op. 8452, ed. khr. 37, ll. 56. The formal order relieving Riabyshev

of command was issued on 8 July. The same order relieved Riabyshev's chief of staff, Major General N. K. Popol'.

6. Moskalenko, *Na iiugo-zapadnom napravlenii*, 1: 252.

7. Kolomiets and Smirnov, "Boi v izluchine Dona," 58.

8. V. A. Zhilin, ed., *Stalingradskaia bitva: Khronika, fakty, liudi v 2 kn.* [The battle of Stalingrad: chronicles, facts, people in 2 books] (Moscow: OLMA, 2002), 1: 168. Hereafter cited as Zhilin, *Stalingradskaia bitva*, with book number and page(s).

9. Kolomiets and Smirnov, "Boi v izluchine Dona," 60–61, also describes an attempt by Khasin, commander of 28th Army's 23rd Tank Corps, to protect the army's right flank in the Rossosh' region, an action perhaps confused with or supplementing Pushkin's well-documented efforts.

10. Moskalenko, *Na iiugo-zapadnom napravlenii*, 1: 253. The Sixth Army's daily maps confirm Moskalenko's account.

11. The precise date when Martsenkevich replaced Smirnov as 24th Army commander remains unclear. A bit older than most Soviet army commanders, Smirnov was born in 1887, served as a junior officer in the tsar's army during World War I, and joined the Red Army in 1918. During the Russian Civil War, he led a partisan detachment and commanded a company, battalion, and regiment, ending the war as an assistant division commander. A graduate of the Frunze Academy in 1928 and the Lenin Political-Military Academy in 1931, Smirnov taught at a variety of Red Army military schools during the 1920s and commanded the North Caucasus Military District's 22nd Rifle Division in 1931–1932, the Belorussian Military District's 43rd Rifle Division in 1935–1937, and the Khar'kov Military District from April 1938 to April 1940. After serving as inspector-general of Red Army Infantry and chief of the Red Army's Training Directorate on the eve of war, when Operation Barbarossa began, Smirnov was appointed as chief of Southern Front's Rear Services. The *Stavka* assigned him command of 18th Army in February 1942 and, after he served on the Southwestern Main Direction's staff, the ill-fated 24th Army in May 1942. After relieving Smirnov of army command in September 1942, the *Stavka* assigned him to a series of staff positions at *front* level for two years but restored him to army command in February 1944. Thereafter, he commanded Steppe (2nd Ukrainian) Front's 4th Guards Army during its advance across southern Ukraine until April 1944 and the L'vov Military District until war's end. While commanding the L'vov Military District, Smirnov organized and conducted the struggle against Ukrainian nationalist forces in the region. After war's end, Smirnov commanded the Gor'ki Military District in 1945–1946, served as deputy commander of the Moscow Military District for Training until his retirement in 1953, and died in 1964. For further details, see *Komandarmy, Voennyi biograficheskii slovar'*, 213–215.

Martsenkevich, Smirnov's successor in 24th Army, was born in 1896 and joined the Red Army in 1918, fighting in the Civil War as a partisan leader and, ultimately, commanding a battalion and a regiment on the war's eastern, southern, and western fronts. A graduate of the Senior Command Cadre School in 1923 and a course at the Military-Economic Academy in 1937, Martsenkevich commanded a rifle battalion and rifle regiment during the interwar years. He led 7th Army's 173rd Rifle Division during the Finnish War in 1939–1940, for which he was awarded the Order of the Red Banner. As commander of the Odessa Military District's 176th Rifle Division when Operation Barbarossa began, his division fought under Southern Front's 9th Army as it conducted its long and arduous withdrawal eastward across Ukraine and the Donbas region in the summer and fall of 1941. In the wake of this long retreat, his division played a prominent role in Southern Front's successful counteroffensive at Rostov in November and December 1941 and the ensuing winter campaign of 1941–1942. After commanding 24th Army from May to July 1942, he commanded the Trans-Caucasus 9th Army in August during the defensive operations in the Caucasus region. Relieved in September because his army failed to halt German First Panzer Army's advance across the Terek River, Martsenkevich took command of 229th Rifle Division in Volkhov Front's 52nd Army, where he fell seriously ill during the time when his division attempted to force the Volkhov River in fall 1943. Restored to command in June 1944 after attending a course at the Voroshilov Academy, Martsenkevich led 69th Army's 134th Rifle Division during 1st Belorussian Front's Lublin–Brest offensive in July 1944 but was killed in action on 30 July while his division was conducting an assault crossing over the Vistula River at Pulavy south of Warsaw. Posthumously, Martsenkevich was designated a Hero of the Soviet Union in April 1945 for his bravery under fire at Pulavy. For further details, see *Komandarmy. Voennyi biograficheskii slovar'*, 145–146.

12. Moskalenko, *Na iiugo–zapadnom napravlenii*, 1: 253.

13. Ibid., 255.

14. *TsAMO*, f. 382, op. 8452, ed. khr. 37, ll. 432.

15. See ibid., ll. 78–91 for 28th Army's subsequent reports.

16. See *Stavka* directive no. 170490, dated 0115 hours 10 July 1942, in Zolotarev, "*Stavka* 1942," 298.

17. See *Stavka* directives no. 735/up, dated 1245 hours 10 July 1942 and no. 170491, dated 1910 hours 10 July 1942, in ibid., 298–299.

18. Born in 1900, Alekseev joined the Red Army in 1919 and fought on the eastern front during the Civil War. A graduate of Moscow's 1st Combined Command School in 1926, the Leningrad Armored Command Course in 1932, and a command course (KUKS) at the Frunze Academy in 1941, he served as a political worker at regimental level and commanded a company and battalion during the 1920s. After transferring to the Red Army's mechanized and armored forces in the early 1930s, Alekseev led a tankette battalion in 6th Rifle Division and tank battalions in 50th Rifle Division and 20th Light Tank Brigade from 1932 to early 1936. Dispatched to the Far East in April 1936, he commanded a special-designation reconnaissance battalion in 57th Special Corps and, in 1938 and 1939, the corps' 9th Motorized-Armored Brigade and 82nd Rifle Division, which he led during Zhukov's victory over Japanese forces at Khalkhin-Gol in August and September. After receiving the Order of the Red Banner for his exploits in the Far East, Alekseev returned west in 1939 to command 110th Rifle Division during the Finnish War in 1939–1940 and attend the Frunze Academy in 1940–1941. Sent to Trans-Baikal Front in March 1941, he took command of 28th Mechanized Corps' 6th Tank Division. After his division was converted into 6th Guards Tank Brigade and sent west in the fall of 1941, he headed this brigade during Southern Front's victories at Rostov in December and during the Lozovaia–Barvenkovo offensive in January 1942. By now one of the Red Army's most promising young armor officers, Alekseev led 45th Army's and, later, Southern Front's armored and mechanized forces throughout Operation Blau. In the wake of Blau, he commanded 10th Tank Corps in the victory at Kursk in July 1943 but was severely wounded during the Belgorod–Khar'kov offensive in August. Recovering from his wounds, Alekseev led 10th Tank Corps throughout the remainder of 1943, participating in the advance to the Dnepr River and the battle for Kiev in the fall of 1943, and 5th Guards Tank Corps

during its many successful offensives in the Ukraine from January through August 1944. By now a Hero of the Soviet Union, Alekseev was killed in action on 25 August 1944 while leading his corps in the victorious Iasi–Kishinev offensive in Romania. For additional details, see *Komkory. Voennyi biograficheskii slovar'*, 97–98.

19. Zhilin, *Stalingradskaia bitva*, 182.

20. See Moskalenko, *Na iiugo–zapadnom napravlenii*, 1: 256–261, and Vyrodov, *V srazheniiakh za Pobedu*, 132–133.

21. Zhilin, *Stalingradskaia bitva*, 180.

22. Shtemenko, *Soviet General Staff at War*, bk. 1, 84–87.

23. See *Stavka* order no. 170435, dated 0020 hours 11 July 1942, in Zolotarev, "*Stavka* 1942," 300. At the time, 62nd Army consisted of 33rd Guards, 147th, 181st, 184th, 192nd, and 196th Rifle Divisions. As of 10 July, 62nd Army's six rifle divisions numbered 81,000 men. See Aleksei Isaev, *Stalingrad: Za Volgoi dlia nas zemli net* [Stalingrad: There is no land for us beyond the Volga] (Moscow: Iauza, Eksmo, 2008), 12.

24. See *Stavka* directive no. 170495, dated 0215 hours 12 July 1942, in ibid., 302.

25. See *Stavka* directives nos. 994110–994112, dated 0440, 0450, and 0445 hours 12 July 1942, respectively, in ibid., 303–304. As of 10 July, 63rd Army counted 67,000 men and 64th Army 72,800 men, bringing Stalingrad Front's total strength to more than 200,000 men. See Isaev, *Stalingrad*, 12.

26. One of three generals with this last name who commanded Soviet armies during the Soviet–German War, Vasilii Ivanovich Kuznetsov was one of the Red Army's most experienced commanders. Born in 1894, he commanded a regiment during World War I, joined the Red Army in 1918, and led a regiment in the Civil War. A graduate of Warrant Officer's School in 1916, the "*Vystrel'*" Officers Course in 1926, and the Frunze Academy in 1936, Kuznetsov commanded the famous 51st Perekop Rifle Division's 89th Chongar Regiment in the late 1920s and the 51st and 25th Rifle, 2nd Turkestan Rifle, and 99th Rifle Divisions during the first half of the 1930s. Assigned command of 16th Rifle Corps in August 1937, Kuznetsov later led Belorussian Front's Vitebsk Army Group of Forces during the Czech crisis in 1938 and the Western Special Military District's 3rd Army from 1939 through the beginning of Operation Barbarossa. Surviving his army's shattering defeat during the German invasion, Kuznetsov was appointed to command 21st Army, which he led when it was encircled and largely destroyed during the Kiev encirclement of September 1941. Escaping unscathed, Kuznetsov commanded the Khar'kov Military District in October–November 1941, the *Stavka*'s 58th Reserve Army in November, and the newly formed 1st Shock Army, which spearheaded Western Front's counterstroke at Moscow in December 1941. Burnishing his record as a successful fighter, Kuznetsov commanded 1st Shock Army during Northwestern Front's offensive at Demiansk in February 1942, which encircled but failed to destroy German II Army Corps. An audacious and talented general, Kuznetsov led 63rd Army during the heavy fighting in the Stalingrad region and, after serving briefly as Southwestern Front's deputy commander in November 1942, commanded 1st Guards Army from December 1942 to December 1943. Promoted to colonel general in late 1943, he was deputy commander of 1st Baltic Front from December 1943 to March 1944 and led 3rd Shock Army from March 1944 to war's end. During this time, Kuznetsov's armies figured prominently in the liberation of the Donbas region and in the 1st Belorussian Front's climactic offensive against Berlin, which earned for Kuznetsov the title of Hero of the Soviet Union in May 1945. After the war, Kuznetsov commanded 3rd Shock Army in the Group of Soviet Forces Germany (GSFG) from 1945 to 1948 and the Volga Military Dis-

trict from 1953 to 1957 before returning to service on the General Staff and retiring in 1960. Kuznetsov died in 1964. For further details, see *Komandarmy, Voennyi biograficheskii slovar'*, 116–118.

27. One of the Red Army's youngest army commanders, Kolpakchi was 42 years old when he was appointed to command 7th Reserve Army in May 1942. Born in 1899, Kolpakchi was a noncommissioned officer in the tsar's army during World War I but joined the Red Guards in 1917 and took part in the storming of the tsar's Winter Palace in October 1917. During the Civil War, Kolpakchi commanded a company, battalion, and regiment and served as commandant of the Red Army's garrisons at Pskov and Petrograd. A 1928 graduate of the Frunze Academy, Kolpakchi served as commissar of 3rd Turkestan Rifle Division during the interwar years in the struggle against the Basmachi insurgency, commanded another rifle division, and was deputy chief of staff of the Belorussian Military District. After serving as a command adviser to the Republican government during the Spanish Civil War, Kolpakchi commanded the Baltic Special Military District's 12th Rifle Corps and was appointed chief of staff of the Khar'kov Military District on the eve of war. When war began and the Khar'kov Military District became the headquarters of Southern Front's 18th Army, Kolpakchi became the army's chief of staff as it conducted its fighting withdrawal across Ukraine in summer 1941. When Army Group South encircled the army in the Melitopol' region in October 1941, killing its commander, General A. K. Smirnov, Kolpakchi assumed command and led its successful escape. Assigned as assistant commander of Briansk Front in November 1941 and deputy commander of Kalinin Front's 4th Shock Army in January 1942, Kolpakchi led Kalinin Front's special operational group that recaptured the city of Belyi in April 1942. In recognition of this accomplishment, the Stavka assigned Kolpakchi command of 7th Reserve (later 62nd) Army in May 1942. In recognition of his accomplishments, the *Stavka* assigned Kolpakchi command of 7th Reserve Army (later 62nd Army) in May 1942. After leading 62nd Army during the heavy fighting in the Great Bend of the Don River in July and August 1942, Kolpakchi became deputy commander of 1st Guards Army through the remainder of Operation Blau. Transferred to the Western Front in late 1942, he led the *front's* 30th Army in the reduction of the Rzhev salient in February–March 1943 and 63rd Army, once again, from May 1943 through February 1944, when it fought with distinction during the battle for Kursk, the Briansk offensive of August–September 1943, and the Belorussian offensive in fall 1943 and winter 1943–1944. During the final year of the war, Kolpakchi commanded 1st Belorussian Front's 69th Army in the Vistula–Oder and Berlin operations, was promoted to colonel general, and was named a Hero of the Soviet Union. After the war, Kolpakchi commanded the Baku Military District in 1945 and 1946, the Odessa Military District's 40th Army in 1946, the Trans-Baikal Military District's 1st Red Banner Army from 1946 to 1950, and, after attending a course at the Voroshilov Academy, the Northern Military District's 6th Army and the military district itself from 1952 to 1956. Kolpakchi died in an automobile accident in 1961 while serving as chief of the Soviet Army's Main Combat Training Directorate. For further details, see *Komandarmy. Voennyi biograficheskii slovar'*, 99–100.

28. Richard Woff, "Chuikov," in Shukman, *Stalin's Generals*, 67–76.

29. See Chuikov's testimony to a special commission headed by Stalin on the conduct of the war in Alexander O. Chubarian and Harold Shukman, eds., *Stalin and the Soviet–Finnish War, 1939–1940* (London: Frank Cass, 2002), esp. 89–96.

30. Born in 1900, Chuikov served as a cadet in the training detachment of the tsar's

army in Kronshtadt Fortress in 1917 but deserted to join the Red Army in 1918. After taking part in suppressing counterrevolutionary mutinies in Moscow in late 1918, he fought on the southern, eastern, and western fronts during the Civil War, rising to command a regiment. A graduate of the Frunze Academy in 1925 and a course at the Red Army's Academy of Motorization and Mechanization in 1936, Chuikov served as an adviser to the Chinese Army from 1927 to 1929 and as a department chief in the Separate Red Banner Far Eastern Army from 1929 to 1932. After commanding a mechanized brigade from 1936 to early 1938, Chuikov led a rifle corps and the Belorussian Special Military District's Bobruisk Army Group during the Czech crisis in the fall of 1938, the same district's 4th Army during the invasion of eastern Poland in September 1939, and Northwestern Front's 9th Army during the Finnish War in 1939–1940. Chuikov's shaky performance during the Finnish War, when two of his army's divisions were encircled and destroyed by Finnish forces, prompted Stalin to exile him to attaché duty in China in December 1940. After Chuikov spent a year in China, however, the *Stavka* recalled him to the West in 1941, where an automobile accident sidelined him for another year. Despite his previous travails, Chuikov took command of 1st Reserve Army in March 1942 and, after it was renamed 64th Army, led it for a short period in July. As the army's deputy commander, he headed an operational group in August that defended the Don River line and southwestern approaches to Stalingrad. Assigned command of 62nd Army in early September 1942, he led this army (redesignated as 8th Guards in January 1943) to war's end, in the process playing a significant role in the defense of Stalingrad, 3rd Ukrainian Front's advance across Ukraine in winter 1943–1944 and early summer 1944, and 1st Belorussian Front's offensives in Poland and Germany, culminating in the assault on Berlin in April and May 1945. After the war, Chuikov served as 1st deputy commander of GSFG until 1949 and the group's commander to 1953. Surviving Stalin's death in 1953, Chuikov commanded the Kiev Military from 1953 to 1960 and, benefiting from his ties with Khrushchev, the Soviet Union's new leader, became chief of the Soviet Armed Forces and 1st deputy Minister of Defense of the USSR from 1960 to 1964. Chuikov ended his military career as chief of the USSR's Civil Defense and retired into the Soviet Army's Group of General Inspectors before his death in 1982. A two-time Hero of the Soviet Union (March 1944 and May 1945) and the recipient of 18 Red Army honorific medals, Chuikov, symbolically, was buried on Mamaev Kurgan in Stalingrad, at the site of his greatest triumph. For further details, see *Komandarmy. Voennyi biograficheskii slovar'*, 262–264.

31. See *Stavka* directives nos. 170497, 170499, and 170500, dated 12 July 1942, in ibid., 304–306.

32. See *Stavka* directives nos. 1035055, 170501, and 170502, dated 12 July 1942, in ibid., 306–307.

33. See *Stavka* directive no. 170508, dated 0240 hours 14 July 1942, in ibid., 308–309.

34. See *Stavka* directive no. 170513, dated 17 July 1942, in ibid., 312.

35. See *Stavka* directives nos. 170512 and 170515, dated 1525 hours 15 July and 0015 hours 17 July 1942, respectively, in ibid., 310, 312. A Marshal of the Soviet Union since 1935 and the leading member of Stalin's so-called cavalry clique, after joining the Red Army in 1918 Budenny became its most illustrious cavalry general during the Russian Civil War. He commanded 1st and 4th Cavalry Divisions and the famous 1st Cavalry Army in the fighting in the Tsaritsyn, Don, Donbas, and Caucasus regions alongside Stalin, who was then Lenin's and Trotsky's chief commissar in the regions. Born in 1883, Budenny

had received his baptism of fire in the Russo–Japanese War and World War I, when he earned four Georgievskii Crosses and four medals "for bravery." During the Russian Civil War, he led Southern and Southwestern Fronts' cavalry in their most important operations and, in the process, established an enduring close personal relationship with Stalin. As a result, when Stalin consolidated his power as dictator of the Soviet Union in the late 1920s, Budenny's military career also flourished. During the interwar period, Budenny was assistant commander of the RKKA cavalry, a member of the USSR's Revolutionary Military Council, chief of Red Army Cavalry from 1923 to 1937, and commander of the Moscow Military District from 1937 to 1939 and, simultaneously, a member of the Main Military Council of the USSR's Peoples Commissariat of Defense (NKO). Budenny reached the pinnacle of his military career when Stalin appointed him 1st Deputy Minister of Defense of the USSR in August 1940. Only days after the German invasion, Budenny became a charter member of Stalin's first *Stavka*. In the wake of the disastrous battles along the border, Stalin dispatched Budenny to the field, first to command the Group of *Stavka* Reserve Armies in late June and early July, then as deputy commander of Western Front in early July and commander of the Southwestern Main Direction Command in mid-July, and, finally, on the eve of the Kiev encirclement, as commander of the Reserve Front in September. Totally unable to either understand or conduct modern mobile war, Budenny, although removed from command shortly before the disaster occurred, presided over Southwestern Front's catastrophic defeat at Kiev in September 1941 and the Reserve Front's equally tragic defeat in the Viaz'ma encirclement in October 1941. Despite Budenny's lackluster performance, Stalin appointed his favorite to head the North Caucasus Main Direction in April 1942 and North Caucasus Front in May. Finally removed from field command during the latter stages of Operation Blau, Budenny spent the remainder of the war in the largely honorific post of chief of the Red Army's Cavalry, a position he held until 1954. After the war, Budenny also served, simultaneously, as a deputy minister of agriculture of the USSR for cavalry forage and inspector-general of the Ministry of Defense's Cavalry. Budenny died in 1973 at age 90. For further details, see *Komandarmy. Voennyi biograficheskii slovar'*, 32–34.

36. Kolomiets, who was assigned command of 51st Army in July 1942 at age 48, was born in 1894, served as a junior officer during World War I, joined the Red Army in 1919, and fought as a regimental commissar on the southern front during the Civil War. A 1927 graduate of the *"Vystrel'"* Officers Course, the Frunze Academy in 1934, and a course at the Voroshilov Academy in 1941, Kolomiets commanded a rifle regiment and rifle division in the 1920s and 1930s before being appointed to command 32nd Rifle Corps in the Trans-Baikal Military District's 16th Army in November 1939. After Operation Barbarossa began, Kolomiets's corps was transferred to the west with 16th Army in July 1941, but, shortly before 16th Army was encircled and largely destroyed in the battle for Smolensk, the *Stavka* assigned Kolomiets as deputy commander of 51st Army in late July 1941. After commanding 51st Army through Operation Blau, Kolomiets headed 54th Rifle Corps in the 51st and 2nd Guards Armies during 1943 and 1944, leading his corps in the Donbas and Crimean offensives, and, after serving as deputy commander of 57th Army, commanded 2nd Guards Army's 60th Rifle Corps during 3rd Belorussian Front's East Prussian offensive in January and February 1945. After the war, Kolomiets served as deputy commander of 57th and 9th Mechanized Armies before retiring in 1948. He died in 1971. See, *Komandarmy. Voennyi biograficheskii slovar'*, 98–99.

37. Halder, *The Halder War Diary*, 639.

38. *Bock Diary*, 524–525.

39. Ibid., 525.

40. Ibid., 525–526.

41. Ibid., 526.

42. Halder, *The Halder Diary*, 639–640.

43. On Bock's dismissal, see also Jukes, *Hitler's Stalingrad Decisions*, 43; and Ziemke and Bauer, *Moscow to Stalingrad*, 347–348.

44. Salmuth was relieved as commander of Second Army on 4 February 1943 but would return to army command by leading Army Group B's Fifteenth Army during the Allied landings at Normandy in June 1944.

45. Blau, *The German Campaign in Russia*, 148; and Ziemke and Bauer, *Moscow to Stalingrad*, 351.

46. Halder, *The Halder War Diary*, 635; and Jukes, *Hitler's Stalingrad Decisions*, 39.

47. Führer Directive No. 43 is reproduced in Trevor-Roper, *Blitzkrieg to Defeat*, 124–127.

48. Ziemke and Bauer, *Moscow to Stalingrad*, 349–351.

49. Moskalenko, *Na iugo–zapadnom napravlenii*, 1: 259–262. Based on "prisoners captured," on 17 July First Panzer Army identified the remnants of 37th Army's 275th, 295th, 102nd, and 230th Rifle Divisions; 9th Army's 318th, 51st, 140th, 255th, 296th, 278th, and 106th Rifle Divisions and 5th Cavalry Corps' 30th, 34th, and 60th Cavalry Divisions; 38th Army's 277th, 199th, 304th, 300th, 242nd, and 81st Rifle Divisions; 28th Army's 244th Rifle Division; 24th Army's 218th, 335th, and 73rd Rifle Divisions; and the separate 254th and 292nd Rifle Divisions in the Millerovo pocket. See "Feindlagenkarten, PzAOK 1, Ic, 29 Jun–31 Jul 1992," *PzAOK 1, 24906/24*, in NAM T-313, Roll 38.

50. Zhilin, *Stalingradskaia*, 198. Quoting from *Kriegstagebuch der Oberkommandes der Wehrmacht/Wehrmachtfuhrungsstab: 1940–1945, Bd. II* (Frankfurt, 1963).

51. Blau, *The German Campaign in Russia*, 149–150.

52. On XXXX Corps, see Beevor, *Stalingrad*, 78; and Blau, *The German Campaign in Russia*, 150, the prisoner figure.

53. Haupt, *Army Group South*, 156–157.

54. M. M. Povalyi, *Vosemnadtsataia v srazheniia za Rodiny* [The 18th Army in the defense of the Motherland] (Moscow: Voenizdat, 1982), 106–107.

55. Ibid., 108.

56. The two regiments of 18th Army defending Rostov were from its 395th Rifle Division.

57. Povalyi, *Vosemnadtsataia v srazheniia za Rodiny*, 109.

58. Beevor, *Stalingrad*, 79; Haupt, *Army Group South*, 180–181; and Carell, *Stalingrad*, 71–76.

59. The tally of Soviet prisoners of war varies widely according to source. For example, Ziemke and Bauer, *Moscow to Stalingrad*, mention 70,000 taken during Blau I (p. 344), 88,000 by 13 July (p. 348), 21,000 captured by Fourth Panzer Army in the Millerovo region from 13 to 16 July (p. 349), and 83,000 taken by First Panzer Army in its drive to Rostov (p. 356).

60. Aleksei Isaev, *Kogda vnezapnosti uzhe ne bylo* [When there was no surprise] (Moscow: "IAUZA" "EKSMO," 2005), 53–54; Beshanov, *God 1942*, 284; and *Stalingrad:*

Zabytoe srazhenie [Stalingrad: The forgotten battle] (Moscow: AST, 2005), 77. The same sources claim the *Wehrmacht* lost 91,400 men, including more than 19,000 killed and missing in action during the same period.

61. G. F. Krivosheev, ed., *Rossiia i SSSR v voinakh XX veka: Poteri vooruzhennykh sil, Statisticheskoe issledovanie* [Russia and the USSR in wars of the XX Century: Armed Forces losses, a statistical investigation] (Moscow: "OLMA," 2001), 460.

62. For the routine underestimation, see S. A. I'lenkov, "Concerning the Registration of Soviet Armed Forces Wartime Irrevocable Losses, 1941–1945," *JSMS* 9, 2 (June 1996): 440–442, which asserts the Red Army's irrevocable losses were roughly 14.7 million rather than the 8.8 million claimed by official sources. In addition, there are serious discrepancies regarding strengths and losses in Soviet and Russian sources. For example, according to official count, Southern Front, which consisted of 12th, 18th, 37th, and 56th Armies and fielded a total of 522,500 soldiers on 28 June, lost 193,213 personnel between 28 June and 24 July, including 128,460 irreplaceable (killed, captured, or missing) and 64,753 wounded or sick. This meant the *front* should have fielded roughly 390,000 soldiers on 24 July. Yet Isaev, *Kogda vnezapnosti uzhe ne bylo*, 52, states, "The total numerical strength of the Southern Front's armies [12th, 18th, 37th, 56th, and 24th] in this period [25 July] did not exceed 100,000 persons," and Krivosheev, *Grif sekretnosti sniat*, 180, states that Southern Front fielded 300,000 men on 25 July but only 216,100 when it became North Caucasus Front on 28 July, even though it had received reinforcements. Further, Krivosheev, *Grif sekretnosti sniat*, 146, states that the Red Army lost 684,767 soldiers as POWs or MIAs from 1 July to 30 September 1942, at a time when the Red Army suffered most of its losses of this nature in southern Russia. While tending to substantiate the POW loss of 150,000, it also underscores the reality that many Soviet soldiers simply disappeared.

63. See Krivosheev, *Grif sekretnosti sniat*, 179; and Il'ia Moshchansky and Sergei Smolinov, "Oborona Stalingrada: Stalingradskaia strategicheskaia oboronitel'naia operatsiia, 17 iiulia–18 noiabria 1942 goda" [The defense of Stalingrad: The Stalingrad strategic defensive operation, 17 July–18 November 1942], in *Voennaia letopis'*, 6-2002 [Military chronicle, 6-2002] (Moscow: BTV, 2002), 12.

64. Führer Directive No. 45 is reproduced in full in *SVIMVOV, Vypusk* 18, 265–267; and Trevor-Roper, *Blitzkrieg to Defeat*, 129–131. See also Blau, *The German Campaign in Russia*, 152–155, for an analysis.

65. *SVIMVOV, Vypusk* 18, 265. See also Trevor-Roper, *Blitzkrieg to Defeat*, 130.

66. Ibid.

67. Ibid.

68. Ibid., 266.

69. Ibid.

70. Ibid.

71. Ibid.

72. During the advance on Rostov, Kleist's First Panzer Army and Ruoff's Seventeenth Army became thoroughly intermingled across the 125–kilometer front from Konstantinovskaia westward to Rostov and in the depths. The two armies fielded a total of eight infantry, three panzer, and two motorized divisions deployed forward, with III Panzer Corps (14th, and 22nd Panzer and "GD" and 16th Motorized Divisions) on the left, XXXXIV and XXXXIX Mountain Corps in the center, and Group Kirchner (LVII Panzer

Corps, with 13th Panzer and SS "Viking" Divisions and the Slovak Mobile Division) on the right. Another 11 German and six Italian infantry divisions subordinate to V, VI, XI, and XXXXIV Army Corps and XXXXIX Mountain Corps were deploying forward, still clearing the rear area or in the process of reverting to the army group's reserve.

73. These figures assume that a tank corps, three tank brigades, or six tank battalions were equivalent to one panzer division, and two rifle brigades were equivalent to one rifle division.

74. "Lagenkarten, 8 July–5 October 1942," *AOK II, Ia, 2585/207a*, in NAM T-312, Roll 1207. The OKH transferred 11th Panzer Division to Army Group Center's Second Panzer Army after mid-July. *Boevoi sostav Sovetskoi armii*, 2: 146–147. 48th Army consisted of three rifle divisions, two rifle brigades, and one tank brigade; 13th Army of six rifle divisions, three rifle brigades, and one tank brigade; and Group Chibisov of five rifle divisions, two rifle brigades, and one cavalry corps (8th). In addition, one rifle division, five rifle brigades, five tank corps (1st, 2nd, 7th, 11th, and 16th), five tank brigades, one cavalry corps (7th), and one destroyer division were subordinate to Briansk Front. Voronezh Front included 60th Army, with seven rifle divisions, three tank corps (17th, 18th, and 25th), two destroyer brigades, and one fortified region, and 40th Army, with two rifle divisions and one tank brigade opposite the German Second Army.

75. *Boevoi sostav Sovetskoi armii*, 2: 147. The 6th Army consisted of five rifle divisions, two tank corps (4th and 24th), one fortified region, and one destroyer division, while 40th Army deployed two rifle divisions, one rifle brigade, and one tank brigade opposite Hungarian Second Army.

76. See "Ia, Lagenkarten Nr. 1 zum KTB Nr. 13, Jul–Oct 1942," *AOK 6, 23948/1a*, in NAM T-312, Roll 1446. Jentz, *Panzertruppen*, 248, provides 24th Panzer Division's tank strength of 141 tanks. With comparable attrition rates, 16th Panzer Division likely fielded about 70 tanks and 3rd and 60th Motorized Divisions, with roughly 40 tanks each.

77. As of 23 July, 63rd Army consisted of seven rifle divisions, three tank brigades, two separate tank battalions, and one destroyer brigade; 62nd Army of six rifle divisions, one tank brigade, and six separate tank battalions; 64th Army of six rifle divisions, one rifle brigade, one naval rifle brigade, and two tank brigades; 21st Army of 12 rifle divisions, most of them understrength; and 38th and 57th Armies each of four understrength rifle divisions and a destroyer brigade. Another four rifle divisions, four destroyer brigades, one cavalry corps (3rd Guards), five tank brigades, and two separate tank battalions were directly subordinate to the *front*. In addition, 22nd and 23rd Tank Corps were deployed in 21st and 63rd Armies' sectors north of the Don, and 13th and 28th Tank Corps were situated behind 64th Army. See *Boevoi sostav Sovetskoi armii*, 2: 148–149; and Iu. P. Babich, *Podgotovka oborony 62nd Armiei vne soprikosnovaniia s protivnikom i vedenie oboronitel'noi operatsii v usloviiakh prevoskhodstva protivnika v manevrennosti (po opytu Stalingradskoi bitvy)* [The preparation of 62nd Army's defense in close proximity to the enemy and the conduct of the defensive operation in circumstances of enemy superiority in maneuver (based on the experience of the battle of Stalingrad)] (Moscow: Frunze Academy, 1991), for order of battle and Soviet conduct of the operation. Moshchansky and Smolinov, *Oborona Stalingrada*, 8–12, shows a weaker Soviet force of 36 divisions, two tank brigades, and six separate tank battalions. German intelligence records substantiate the larger Soviet force.

78. "Ia, Lagenkarten Nr. 1 zum KTB Nr. 13, Jul–Oct 1942," *AOK 6, 23948/1a*, in

NAM T-312, Roll 1446. Russian sources credit Fourth Panzer Army with 371 tanks as of 1 July. However, attrition had reduced this number significantly. See Maksim Kolomiets and Il'ia Moshchansky, "Oborona Kavkaza (iiul'–dekabr' 1942 goda)" [The defense of the Caucasus (July–December 1942)], in *Frontovaia illiustratsiia*, 2–2000 [Front illustrated, 2–2000] (Moscow: "Strategiia KM," 2000), 5.

79. "Feindlagenkarten, PzAOK 1, Ic, 29 Jun–31 Jul 1942," *PzAOK 1, 24906/24*, in NAM T-313, Roll 38; and "Anlage 3 zum Tatigkeitsbericht, OAK 17, Ic, 20 Jul–25 Jul 1942," *AOK 17, 24411/33*, in NAM T-312, Roll 679. By 25 July, Kleist's First Panzer Army consisted of III Panzer Corps' 14th and 22nd Panzer and "GD" and 16th Motorized Divisions and XXXXIV Army Corps' 101st and 97th Jäger Divisions, backed up by IV Army Corps' 94th and 371st Infantry Divisions, LII Army Corps' 111th and 370th Infantry Divisions, and XI Army Corps' 295th and 76th Infantry Divisions. Ruoff's Seventeenth Army included LVII Panzer Corps' 13th Panzer and SS "Viking" Motorized Divisions; V Army Corps' German 9th, 198th, and 125th Infantry, Romanian 2nd Mountain, and the Slovak Mobile Divisions; XXXXIX Mountain Corps' 73rd and 298th Infantry and 1st and 4th Mountain Divisions; and the Romanian Third Army's Cavalry Corps, with the Romanian 5th and 6th Cavalry Divisions. Finally, 297th and 257th Infantry Divisions were in army or army group reserve. For Soviet strengths, see Kolomiets and Moshchansky, "Oborona Kavkaza," 8. North Caucasus Front's four armies were backed up by one tank corps (14th, which survived the Millerovo encirclement with 13 tanks), a mixed tank group (of three tank brigades and one motorized rifle brigade, with 57 tanks), and two separate tank brigades and two separate tank battalions, with a strength of 123 tanks, for a total strength of about 193 tanks.

80. Kolomiets and Moshchansky, "Oborona Kavkaza," 6.

81. By 25 July 1942, Army Group A's eight mobile divisions had an average of only 54 functioning tanks each. See Blau, *The German Campaign in Russia*, 149–150, 155. Kolomiets and Moshchansky, "Oborona Kavkaza," 5, which does not list the strength of 16th Panzer Division, places First Panzer Army's tank strength, less 22nd Panzer and "GD" Motorized Divisions, at 209 tanks.

82. See *Stavka* directives nos. 170516 and 170519, dated 1610 hours and 1800 hours 17 July 1942, respectively, in Zolotarev, "*Stavka* 1942," 313–314. 1st Tank Army was to form by 28 July and 4th Tank Army by 1 August.

83. See *Stavka* directive no. 994121, dated 18 July 1942, in ibid., 315.

84. See *Stavka* directive no. 170523, dated 1600 hours 21 July 1942, in ibid., 316.

85. See the conversation and *Stavka* directive no. 170524 and order no. 0035, dated 1850 hours 22 July and 22 July 1942, respectively, in ibid., 317–320.

86. See Stavka directives nos. 994124 and 994125, dated 2030 hours 22 July 1942, in ibid., 320–321.

87. Born in 1898, Novikov joined the Red Army in 1918, fought in the Civil War, and, after graduating from cavalry school in 1919, commanded a cavalry regiment in the 1920s. After transferring to the Red Army's mechanized forces in the early 1930s, Novikov commanded 4th Mechanized Regiment and 3rd Mechanized Brigade and served as deputy commander of an operational group during the Finnish War (1939–1940). He then commanded the Trans-Caucasus Military District's 126th Rifle Division and 28th Mechanized Corps' 6th Tank Division before the outbreak of war and 28th Mechanized Corps and 47th and 45th Armies during the first year of war. After Operation Blau, Novikov served

as 4th Tank Army's deputy commander for armored forces and commander of 6th Guards Tank Corps from April 1944 through April 1945 and 7th Guards Tank Corps from April 1945 to war's end. Promoted to lieutenant general in June 1945, Novikov later retired. He died in 1965. For sketchy details on his career, see Drig, *Mekhanizirovannye korpusa RKKA v boiu*, 692–693.

88. See *Stavka* instructions, dated 0225 hours 23 July 1942, in Zolotarev, "*Stavka* 1942," 321.

Chapter 6: The German Advance into the Great Bend of the Don, 23–31 July 1942

1. For details on 16th Panzer Division's advance and battles in the Great Bend of the Don River, see Wolfgang Werthen, *Geschichte der 16. Panzer-Division 1939–1945* (Bad Nauheim, Germany: Podzun-Pallas-Verlag, 1958), 99–103. 3rd Motorized Division's operations are covered by Gerhard Dieckhoff, *3. Infantrie-Division, 3. Infantrie-Division (mot), 3. PanzerGrenadier-Division* (Cuxhaven, Germany: Oberstudienrat Gerhard Dieckhoff, 1960).

2. See "Ia, Lagenkarten Nr. 1 zum KTB Nr. 13, Jul–Oct 1942," *AOK 6, 23948/1a*, in NAM T-312, Roll 1446, for the daily positions of Sixth Army's subordinate formations. 113th Infantry Division engaged and defeated 192nd Rifle Division's forward detachment (1st Battalion, 676th Rifle Regiment, supported by two artillery battalions from 293rd Artillery Regiment and 64th Tank Battalion) at the village of Pronin. See Moshchansky and Smolinov, "Oborona Stalingrada," 9.

3. "Ia, Lagenkarten Nr. 1 zum KTB Nr. 13, Jul–Oct 1942," *AOK 6, 23948/1a*, in NAM T-312, Roll 1446. The estimated strength of Paulus's force is based on roughly 15,000 men per German division.

4. *Boevoi sostav Sovetskoi armii*, 2: 148–149. Moshchansky and Smolinov, "Oborona Stalingrada," 12, also claims that 62nd Army fielded 68,462 men and 64th Army, 34,464 men, for a total of 102,926, as opposed to Paulus's force of 157,700 men. However, this counts only Soviet forces west of the Don River, that is, roughly half of Chuikov's army, and it overstates the strength of Paulus's force of 120,000 men, meaning that German and Soviet forces were at rough parity in terms of manpower. The divisions of Kolpakchi's 62nd Army ranged from a low of 11,428 men in 196th Rifle Division to a high of 12,903 men in 184th Rifle Division, compared to a required (*shtatnyi*) strength of 12,807 men. See Isaev, *Stalingrad*, 26.

5. When Gordov took command of Stalingrad Front, according to Chuikov, the new *front* commander redeployed 112th Rifle Division to Stalingrad's outer defenses and 66th Naval Rifle and 137th Tank Brigades to defenses along the Aksai River on the army's left wing. See Vasili I. Chuikov, *The Battle for Stalingrad*, trans. Harold Silver (New York: Holt, Rinehart and Winston, 1964), 19–20.

6. The forward detachments of Chuikov's 29th and 214th Rifle Divisions occupied their forward positions late on 22 July, and those of the other divisions did so on 23 and 24 July. See Zhilin, *Stalingradskaia bitva*, 232.

7. Werthen, *Geschichte der 16. Panzer-Division*, 99.

8. See Zhilin, *Stalingradskaia bitva*, 228, 232, for the Red Army General Staff's daily

operational summaries for 21 and 22 July and for each day of action thereafter in the sector of Kolpakchi's 62nd Army as well as the remainder of Stalingrad Front's sector. For details on the struggle by Kolpakchi's and Chuikov's forward detachments, see F. Utenkov, "Nekotorye voprosy oboronitel'nogo srazheniia na dal'nykh podstupakh k Stalingradu" [Some questions concerning the defensive battles on the distant approaches to Stalingrad], *VIZh* 9 (September 1962), 34–48.

9. See Werthen, *Geschichte der 16. Panzer-Division*, 99.

10. By this time, 3rd and 60th Motorized and 16th Panzer Divisions had about 140 operational tanks, and 24th Panzer, about 140. See, Jentz, *Panzertruppen*, 48; and Ziemke and Bauer, *Moscow to Stalingrad*, 357.

11. See also V. E. Tarrant, *Stalingrad: Anatomy of an Agony* (London: Leo Cooper, 1992), 39. On aerial resupply, see Hayward, *Stopped at Stalingrad*, 183.

12. Chuikov, *The Battle for Stalingrad*, 17–20. In contrast, see Moshchansky and Smolinov, "Oborona Stalingrada," 9; and Isaev, *Kogda vnezapnosti uzhe new bylo*, 60. On the other hand, K. K. Rokossovsky, ed., *Velikaia bitva na Volge* [Great victory on the Volga] (Moscow: Voenizdat, 1965), 37, the most thorough Soviet account of the campaign, which was published during the same period as Chuikov's memoirs, refers to Chuikov as 64th Army's "temporary" commander during the period between 17 and 23 July.

13. *Boevoi sostav Sovetskoi armii*, 2: 148–149; and Shtemenko, *Soviet General Staff at War*, bk. 1, 89–90.

14. See the full conversation in Zolotarev, "*Stavka* 1942," 321–322.

15. "Ia, Lagenkarten Nr. 1 zum KTB Nr. 13, Jul–Oct 1942," *AOK 6, 23948/1a*, in NAM T-312, Roll 1446.

16. Zhilin, *Stalingradskaia bitva*, 239–240.

17. Ibid., 244.

18. Ziemke and Bauer, *Moscow to Stalingrad*, 357–358.

19. Rokossovsky, *Velikaia pobeda na Volge*, 63.

20. Halder, *The Halder War Diary*, 646.

21. For details on the encirclement battle within the Great Bend, see ibid., 63; and Moshchansky and Smolinov, "Oborona Stalingrada," 15. As of 23 July Tanaschishin's tank corps numbered 157 tanks (94 T-34s and 63 T-70s) and ten armored cars. His corps' 163rd and 169th Tank Brigades fielded 32 T-34 and 21 T-70 tanks and his 166th Brigade, 30 T-34 and 21 T-70 tanks. The corps' 20th Motorized Rifle Brigade, which Tanaschishin considered not combat-ready, had only 857 of its required 3,258 riflemen. See Isaev, *Stalingrad*, 33–34.

22. Rokossovsky, *Velikaia pobeda na Volge*, 64–65.

23. Halder, *The Halder War Diary*, 647.

24. Zhilin, *Stalingradskaia bitva*, 1: 252.

25. "Ia, Lagenkarten Nr. 1 zum KTB Nr. 13, Jul–Oct 1942," *AOK 6, 23948/1a*, in NAM T-312, Roll 1446; and Ziemke and Bauer, *Moscow to Stalingrad*, 358. The full German report is found in Zhilin, *Stalingradskaia bitva*, 254. The 3rd Motorized Division claimed destroying 27 Soviet tanks in the fighting.

26. "Ia, Lagenkarten Nr. 1 zum KTB Nr. 13, Jul–Oct 1942," *AOK 6, 23948/1a*, in NAM T-312, Roll 1446.

27. Ziemke and Bauer, *Moscow to Stalingrad*, 358.

28. Halder, *The Halder War Diary*, 647.

29. Rokossovsky, *Velikaia pobeda na Volge*, 66.

30. Ibid., 67.

31. For details on the condition of the tank armies and their subsequent combat performance, see Moskalenko, *Na iugo–zapadnom napravlenii*, 1: 267–287. As of 25 July, Rodin's 28th Tank Corps fielded 208 tanks, including 68, 71, and 69 tanks in its 39th, 55th, and 56th Tank Brigades, respectively. The corps' 32nd Motorized Rifle Brigade numbered 3,147 men and 133 vehicles. See Isaev, *Stalingrad*, 45.

32. Ibid., 272.

33. Zhilin, *Stalingradskaia bitva*, 256. By nightfall on 27 July the intense fighting reduced the tank strength of Tanaschishin's 13th Tank Corps to only 40 operational vehicles (27 T-34s and 13 T-70s). During the day, German aircraft alone destroyed 13 T-34 and 7 T-70 tanks. See Isaev, *Stalingrad*, 48–49.

34. Werthen, *Geschichte der 16. Panzer-Division*, 100. For clarity and consistency here and hereafter, all place-names are rendered in proper Russian transliteration.

35. Halder, *The Halder War Diary*, 648.

36. Zhilin, *Stalingradskaia bitva*, 260.

37. Werthen, *Geschichte der 16. Panzer-Division*, 101.

38. Rokossovsky, *Velikaia pobeda na Volge*, 68.

39. Werthen, *Geschichte der 16. Panzer-Division*, 102.

40. Halder, *The Halder War Diary*, 648.

41. Ibid.

42. Ibid., 69. While Rokossovsky asserts that 66 tanks escaped, Moshchansky and Smolinov, "Oborona Stalingrada," 16, states only 22 tanks did so. The former is probably more accurate.

43. Zhilin, *Stalingradskaia bitva*, 265, 274. Colonel Zhuravlev was seriously wounded during the escape attempt but survived to reach the rank of major general on 22 February 1944. He died in 1976; his biography is still obscure. As of 30 July, 62nd Army reported its 192nd Rifle Division fielded 8,310 men, 184th Rifle Division, 1,196 men, and 33rd Guards Rifle Division, 5,613 men. However, 196th Rifle Division reported losing 2,159 dead, 2,894 wounded, and 2,089 missing in action from 15 July to 1 August, more than 80 percent of its strength. See Isaev, *Stalingrad*, 53.

44. Ibid., 267.

45. Werthen, *Geschichte der 16. Panzer-Division*, 102.

46. Zhilin, *Stalingradskaia bitva*, 271.

47. Halder, *The Halder War Diary*, 649.

48. Rokossovsky, *Velikaia pobeda na Volge*, 69–70. On 29 July, 22nd Tank Corps' 182nd Tank Brigade concentrated 41 tanks (21 T-34s, 8 T-70s, and 12 T-60s) east of Ventsy, but its remaining 25 tanks (11 T-34s, 13 T-70s, and 1 T-60) had already broken down and were left behind. 173rd Tank Brigade managed to assemble 55 tanks (23 T-34s, 19 T-70s, and 13 T-60s) in the Verkhne-Golubaia region, but its remaining 11 tanks (9 T-34s and 2 T-70s) had also broken down. 176th Tank Brigade remained in reserve until 30 July, with 29 operational tanks (19 T-34s, 10 T-70s) and another 19 tanks (13 T-34s and 6 T-70s) that had also broken down. See Moshchansky and Smolinov, "Oborona Stalingrada," 15. When it entered combat on 29 July, Shamshin's 22nd Tank Corps was able to commit only 125 of its 180 tanks into combat, as follows:

Combat Composition of 22nd Tank Corps

Tank Brigade	Type of Tank			
	T-34	T-70	T-60	Total
173rd	32/23	21/19	13/13	65/55
176th	32/19	16/10	—	48/29
182nd	32/21	21/8	13/12	66/41
Total	96/63	58/37	26/25	180/125

See Isaev, *Stalingrad*, citing *TsAMO FR*, f. 220, op. 220, d. 8, ll. 302–303.

By day's end on 1 August, Shamshin's tank corps, now reinforced by 133rd Tank Brigade, numbered only 96 tanks, predominantly light models, as follows:

Tank Brigade	Authorized	Operational	Abandoned on the Battlefield	Destroyed	In Repair
173rd					
T-34	22	9	7	2	9
T-70	21	12	2	1	4
T-60	13	9	—	—	2
Total	66	30	9	3	15
176th					
T-34	32	3	—	—	—
T-70	16	2	—	—	—
Total	48	5	—	—	—
182nd					
T-34	32	7	—	9	—
T-70	16	7	—	5	—
T-60	13	7	—	6	—
Total	61	21	—	20	—
133rd					
KV	40	40	—	—	—
Grand Total	215	96	9	32	15

See Isaev, *Stalingrad*, 62–63, citing *TsAMO RF*, f. 38, op. 11360, d. 120, l. 153.

49. Moshchansky and Smolinov, "Oborona Stalingrada," 16. Officially, Tanaschishin's 13th Tank Corps numbered 9 T-34 and 7 T-70 tanks as of 1 August. It had lost 51 T-34 and 30 T-70 tanks, and another 34 T-34 and 26 T-70 tanks were in various states of disrepair. See Isaev, *Stalingrad*, 54.

50. See *Stavka* directive no. 170535, dated 1645 hours 28 July 1942, in Zolotarev, "Stavka 1942," 331–332.

51. The *Stavka* had previously issued numerous directives to improve cooperation between Southern Front and North Caucasus Front. See *Stavka* directives nos. 170529, dated 1630 hours 23 July 1942, and 170530, dated 1635 hours 23 July 1942, in Zolotarev, "Stavka 1942," 327–328.

52. See *Stavka* directive no. 170534, dated 0245 hours 18 July 1942, in ibid., 330.

53. See also Moskalenko, *Na iugo-zapadnom napravlenii*, 1: 278–280; and Rokossovsky, *Velikaia pobeda na Volge*, 70–71. Although the paper strength of Khasin's 23rd Tank Corps was 178 tanks, as of 27 July Khasin's corps fielded only two brigades with a total of 75 tanks; including 99th Tank Brigade with 17 T-34 and 16 T-70 tanks and 189th Tank Brigade with 26 T-34 and 16 T-70 tanks. The corps' 9th Motorized Rifle Brigade numbered only 1,190 of its required 3,258 riflemen. For details of 23rd Tank Corps' fight, see Isaev, *Stalingrad*, 56–58.

54. Born in 1895, Shumilov served as a noncommissioned officer in the tsar's army during World War I, joined the Red Guards in 1917 and Red Army in 1918, and commanded a company, battalion, and regiment during the Civil War. A graduate of a Command-Political Course in 1924 and the *"Vystrel'"* Officers Course in 1929, Shumilov commanded a rifle regiment in the 1920s and a rifle division in the 1930s before rising to command 8th Army before and during Operation Barbarossa. After commanding 64th Army during Operation Blau, he would command the same army (redesignated as 7th Guards) to war's end and fight in the Red Army's famous victories at Kursk in the summer of 1943 and in Ukraine, Romania, and Hungary in 1944 before ending his wartime career at Vienna in May 1945. After the war, Shumilov commanded 7th Guards Army through 1948 and the Belorussian and Voronezh Military Districts from 1948 until his retirement in 1958. Shumilov died in 1975 at age 80. For further details, see *Komandarmy. Voennyi biograficheskii slovar'*, 272–273.

55. Ziemke and Bauer, *Moscow to Stalingrad*, 363.

56. See *Stavka* directive no. 156595, dated 1930 hours 10 August 1942, in Zolotarev, "*Stavka* 1942," 356–357.

57. Isaev, *Kogda vnezapnosti uzhe ne bylo*, 67. By 1 August 1st Tank Army's armor strength (less 13th Tank Corps, which had joined 4th Tank Army) fell to a total of 123 tanks, as follows:

Force	Tank Strength by Type Tank				
	T-34	T-70	T-60	BT	Total
28th Tank Corps					
55th TB	13	1	—	16	30
39th TB	4	1	10	—	15
Total	17	2	10	16	45
23rd Tank Corps					
56th TB	24	24	—	—	48
99th TB	5	6	—	—	11
189th TB	9	—	3	—	12
20th MRB	7	—	—	—	7
Total	45	30	3	—	78
1st Tank Army					
Grand Total	62	32	13	16	123

See Isaev, *Stalingrad*, 64, citing TsAMO RF, f. 38, op. 11360, d. 120, l. 154.

58. Opposite 4th Tank Army's bridgehead, Sixth Army's VIII Army Corps defended

the sector from Kletskaia on the Don River southeastward to Golubinskii on the Don, 25 kilometers north of Kalach, with its 305th and 113th Infantry Divisions and roughly half of 16th Panzer Division. To the south, VIII Corps' 336th Infantry and 100th Jäger Divisions, and XIV Panzer Corps' 60th and 3rd Motorized Divisions, also supported by elements of 16th Panzer Division, formed a more or less continuous front extending southeastward from the Manoilin region to the Don River, 15 kilometers north of Kalach. See "Ia, Lagenkarten Nr. 1 zum KTB Nr. 13, Jul–Oct 1942," *AOK 6, 23948/1a*, in NAM T-312, Roll 1446.

59. Although German tank losses were significantly lower than those of the Soviets, given the heavy fighting, they were also high. For example, Moskalenko's 1st Tank Army reported destroying or capturing 116 German tanks and 90 guns and killing 14,500 German soldiers during the period 23–30 August. See Moshchansky and Smolinov, "Oborona Stalingrada," 20.

60. Halder, *The Halder War Diary*, 649.

61. Ibid.

62. R. M. Portugal'sky, *Analiz opyta nezavershennykh nastupatel'nykh operatsii Velikoi Otechestvenoi voyny. Vyvody i uroki* [An analysis of the experience of uncompleted offensive operations of the Great Patriotic War. Conclusions and lessons] (Moscow: Izdanie akademii, 1991), 11. See details about this offensive in Glantz, *Forgotten Battles*, 3: 103–114.

63. The 16th Army's assault engaged German 296th and 112th Infantry Divisions defending astride the Zhizdra River north of Zhizdra, and 61st Army attacked 216th and 208th Infantry Divisions' defenses north of Volkhov.

64. Born in 1896, Rokossovsky joined the tsar's army in 1914, fought as a dragoon in World War I, joined the Red Army in 1918, and commanded a cavalry squadron, battalion, and regiment during the Civil War. A graduate of the Leningrad Cavalry School in 1925 and the Frunze Academy in 1929, Rokossovsky commanded 3rd and 5th Separate Cavalry Brigades in the 1920s, participating in the fighting along the Chinese Eastern Railroad in 1929. He then led 7th, 15th, and 5th Cavalry Divisions from 1930 through 1940 before being appointed to command the Kiev Special Military District's 9th Mechanized Corps in November 1940. In the wake of the Barbarossa invasion, Rokossovsky's mechanized corps, despite being equipped with only light and old-model tanks outgunned by their German foes, performed credibly and certainly better than any of its counterpart corps. After helping halt German Army Group Center's panzer juggernaut in August 1941 with his scratch Group Iartsevo, Rokossovsky, now appointed as commander, 16th Army, escaped the Viaz'ma encirclement in October 1941, where his army was destroyed, and, at the head of a new 16th Army, contributed significantly to Western Front's victory in the battle for Moscow and the ensuing winter campaign. Assigned to command Briansk Front in July, Rokossovsky led, in succession, Briansk, Don, Central, Belorussian, 1st Belorussian, and 2nd Belorussian Fronts to war's end, contributing to victories in the Stalingrad, Kursk, Belorussian, East Prussian, and Berlin operations. After war's end, Rokossovsky commanded the Soviet Northern Group of Forces in Poland from 1945 to 1949 and served as Polish minister of national defense from 1949 to 1956 and Deputy Minister of Defense of the USSR from 1956 to 1962 before retiring. He died in 1968. Arguably the most capable of Red Army wartime *front* commanders, but frequently neglected because he was Belorussian rather than Great Russian, Rokossovsky courageously challenged his superiors (such as Zhukov) when necessary and earned the respect of his

subordinates, officers and soldiers alike, for his reluctance to expend lives unnecessarily in search of victory. In return, with a few others like General Batov, one of his protégés, he avoided the "bloody general" sobriquet ascribed to so many Red Army wartime commanders. For further details, see his splendid biography, *Soldatskii dolg* [A Soldier's duty], now published in unexpurgated form, and *Komandarmy. Voennyi biograficheskii slovar'*, 194–195.

65. Born in 1897, Belov was a veteran of World War I who joined the Red Army in 1918. He commanded a cavalry squadron and served as an assistant regimental commander in the Civil War. Educated at the Cavalry Officers School in 1927 and the Frunze Academy in 1933, Belov commanded a cavalry regiment in the 1920s, served as the deputy inspector-general of Red Army Cavalry (to Budenny) in 1932–1933, and commanded 7th Samara Cavalry Division in 1936. Rising quickly in command, he led a mountain rifle division in 1940 and was appointed to command 2nd Cavalry Corps in March 1941. After Operation Barbarossa began, Belov's corps performed well in the intense fighting in Ukraine and, after being transferred to Western Front in the fall, solidified Western Front's defense at Moscow in November and spearheaded its counteroffensive in December 1941 and the ensuing winter offensive of 1941–1942, for which his corps received the honorific designation of 1st Guards. Beginning in February 1942, the five cavalry divisions of Belov's 1st Cavalry Corps penetrated into German Army Group Center's rear area and, in conjunction with elements of 4th Airborne Corps and, later, parts of two other Red Army airborne corps dropped by parachute, tied down elements of seven German divisions for six months before escaping back to the Red Army's front lines in July 1942. Within days, the *Stavka* assigned Belov command of 61st Army, which he led until war's end, taking part in the Red Army's victories at Kursk, the Chernigov-Pripiat, Kalinkovichi, Belorussian, Lublin-Brest, and Vistula-Oder offensives, and the battle for Berlin. A colonel general and Hero of the Soviet Union by war's end, Belov commanded the Don and North Caucasus Military Districts after the war from 1945 to 1948, attended the Voroshilov Academy in 1948, led the Southern Ural Military District from 1948 to 1955, and headed the Soviet Army's Volunteer Organization (DOSAAF) until his retirement in 1960. He died two years later. For further details, see *Komandarmy. Voennyi biograficheskii slovar'*, 24–25. For details about the raid of Belov's cavalry corps, see his superb account, *Za nami Moskva* [Behind us Moscow] (Moscow: Voenizdat, 1963); and David M. Glantz, *A History of Soviet Airborne Forces* (London: Frank Cass, 1994).

66. Born in 1901, Burkov joined the Red Army in 1919 and served as a political worker and commissar in 5th Reserve Regiment and an armored train during the Civil War. A graduate of the Leningrad Military District's Artillery School in 1925 and an officer improvement course at the Kazan' Armored and Mechanized School in 1932, Burkov commanded 4th Armored Train and 2nd Armored Train Battalion in the 1920s before being dispatched to the Far East to command Separate Red Banner Army's Separate Armored Train Battalion. After commanding 8th Mechanized Regiment and 20th Separate Mechanized Brigade from 1936 to 1938, Burkov fell victim to Stalin's military purge, only to be exonerated in May 1939 and assigned command of the Central Asian Military District's 9th Separate Tank Division in June 1940, redesignated as 104th Separate Tank Division in July 1941; Burkov led it during the battle for Smolensk in August 1941, when he was seriously wounded in action. Awarded with the Order of the Red Banner for his bravery at Smolensk, Burkov, after recovering from his wounds, commanded 10th Tank Corps from April 1942 to July 1943. During this period he participated in 16th Army's

offensive along the Zhizdra River in July and August 1942 and the battle for Kursk in July 1943, when he was once again seriously wounded. Thereafter, Burkov served as chief of the Leningrad Armored School's High Officers Course until the end of the war and through 1949. Burkov retired in 1955 and died in 1957. For further details, see *Komkory. Voennyi biograficheskii slovar'*, 2: 113–114.

Born in 1895, Mostovenko fought in World War I, joined the Red Army in 1918, and commanded a battalion and regiment on the southern front during the Civil War. A graduate of the Frunze Academy in 1926 and the armored faculty of the Dzerzhinsky Military–Technical Academy in 1931, Mostovenko commanded a battalion in 45th Rifle Division during the 1920s and served as chief of staff of 75th Rifle Division until his transfer to the Red Army's mechanized forces in 1930. During the ensuing decade, he commanded a tank regiment in the Ural Military District in 1930–1931, served as chief of the Separate Red Banner Far Eastern Army's Armored and Mechanized Forces in 1932–1933, headed the command faculty of the Red Army's Mechanization and Motorization Academy in 1933–1938, and was chief of the Western Special Military District's Armored and Mechanized Forces in 1938–1941. On the eve of Operation Barbarossa, the NKO appointed Mostovenko as commander of the Western Special Military District's 11th Mechanized Corps, which he led during its fierce but futile counterattacks against German forces in the Grodno region during late June and July 1941 before his corps was encircled and destroyed in the Minsk pocket in July. Escaping death at Minsk, Mostovenko became chief of Western Front's Armored Forces and headed a department in the Red Army General Staff during fall 1941 and winter 1941–1942. Assigned command of Western Front's 3rd Tank Corps in spring 1942, he led the corps until September, when he was relieved of command and returned to his former post as chief of the *front's* armored forces. Thereafter, Mostovenko served as chief of Western Front's Armored Forces until the end of the war and, simultaneously, as chief of armor for Polish forces under Soviet command, a post he occupied through 1947. Before retiring in 1954, Mostovenko commanded the Odessa Military District's Armored Forces and was deputy chief of the Soviet Army's Armored and Mechanized Forces Academy. Mostovenko died in 1975. For further details, see *Komkory. Voennyi biograficheskii slovar'*, 2: 235–237.

67. "Nekotorie vyvody po operatsiiam levogo kryla Zapodnogo fronta" [Some conclusions concerning the operations of the Western Front's left wing], *Sbornik materialov po izucheniiu opyta voiny* [Collection of materials for the study of war experience] No. 5 (Moscow: Voenizdat, 1943), 60–75. See also K. K. Rokossovsky, "Soldatskii dolg" [A soldier's duty], *VIZh* 2 (February 1990): 52, for his criticism of the operation and his front commander, Zhukov, as well.

68. The 11th Panzer Division, which had been in Second Army's reserve through 18 July, began redeploying to Army Group Center's sector on 20 July.

69. See *Stavka* directive no. 170516, dated 1630 hours 17 July 1942, in Zolotarev, "*Stavka* 1942," 313–314.

70. The 340th and 284th Rifle Divisions cooperated with 11th and 7th Tank Corps, 237th and 167th Rifle Divisions with 2nd Tank Corps, with 193rd Rifle Division in second echelon. 104th Rifle Brigade protected the shock group's left flank, and Katukov's 1st Tank Corps prepared to exploit the penetration.

71. For example, 284th Rifle Division was an experienced and effective force; Colonel N. F. Batiuk had been in command since February 1942. Yet 237th Rifle Division had

just completed its formation in Novosibirsk *oblast'* on 13 July, after which it was deployed straight to the front.

72. Jentz, *Panzertruppen*, 241.

73. Glantz, *Forgotten Battles*, 3: 55.

74. For details, see I. Iu. Sdvizhkov, "Kak pogib i gde pokhoronen general Liziukov?" [How did General Liziukov perish and where was he buried?], in *Voenno-istoricheskii arkhiv* [Military-historical archives] 9, 81 (2006): 149–165, and 10, 82 (2006): 39–56.

75. Ibid., 56.

76. Korchagin relinquished command of 17th Tank Corps to Colonel B. S. Bakharov on 20 July, but the former replaced General Cherniakhovsky on 26 July when Cherniakhovsky took over command of 60th Army.

77. For details on 9th Panzer Division's struggle, see Carl Hans Hermann, *Die 9. Panzerdivision, 1939–1945* (Friedberg: Podzun-Pallas-Verlag, 2004).

78. See Sdvizhkov, "Kak pogib i gde pokhoronen general Liziukov?" for an accurate account of Liziukov's death reconstructed on the basis of both Soviet and German archival records. Prior to Sdvizhkov's research, Liziukov's colleague, General Katukov, commander of 1st Tank Corps, had concocted an account of Liziukov's death that solved the mystery, emphasized the bravery of 2nd Tank Corps' commander, and answered Stalin's concerns that Liziukov had defected to the Germans. According to Katukov, *Na ostrie glavnogo udara*, 163–164:

On 25 July Liziukov sat in a tank and personally drove the combat vehicle into the attack to breach the enemy's defense around the village of Sukhaia Vereika and withdraw his tank brigade from encirclement. Simultaneously, 1st Tank Corps' 1st Guards Tank Brigade went over to the attack. One must realize that this attack was conducted without proper preparation and necessary cover. I repeat, we had no opportunity to do this.

I followed the course of the attack from my command post with considerable emotion. A Hitlerite battery greeted the tanks with furious fire. Apparently, the Germans had anticipated the direction of the attack and had brought heavy artillery forces forward to this region. Our tanks burst into flame, one after another. The tank which Liziukov was located in broke out far forward. But it was as if he was stumbling against invisible obstacles and standing motionlessly in front of the Hitlerites' foxholes. Shells were exploding all around, and the paths of tracer bullets were crisscrossing around him.

The tank was motionless. Now no doubt remained but that it had been knocked out. Furthermore, after failing to achieve success, the remaining tanks were withdrawing to the rear. The commander's tank remained the only one in enemy occupied territory.

I asked to be put through to V. M. Gorelov, the commander of 1st Guards [Tank] Brigade.

"Organize a local counterattack! Dispatch a tank group forward, cover them with fire, and pay attention to the enemy. Evacuate Liziukov's tank from the battlefield at all costs."

Soon, under cover from our fire, a small group of tanks managed to approach the enemy's foxholes. One of these tanks took Liziukov's tank in tow and dragged it out from under the [enemy's] fire.

The circumstances of Liziukov's death became well known from the account of a driver-mechanic who, although wounded, managed to reach the rear safely. It turned out that Liziukov's tank was knocked out by a direct hit from an armor piercing shell. Major General Liziukov ordered the crew to abandon the tank. The first to crawl out through the top hatch was the radioman, but he was disposed of by a burst of automatic weapons fire. Liziukov abandoned the tank safely but could not manage a step, since shells were exploding all around him . . .

Liziukov's body, with a smashed skull and dressed in overalls and ordinary jackboots (he never dressed in other clothing), was carried to the rear. With heavy heart, we buried the respected general in a cemetery close to the village of Sukhaia Vereika. We buried him with full military honors.

Katukov had met with Stalin on 17 September 1942 to discuss other matters. During that meeting, which took place after General A. A. Vlasov had surrendered his 2nd Shock Army and defected to the German side in July, Stalin asked Katukov whether Liziukov, who had served as deputy commander of General Vlasov's 20th Army the year before, had also surrendered to the Germans. Katukov said no and, to honor his friend, later included his apocryphal account of 2nd Tank Corps' commander death in his memoirs.

79. This pocket extended from the Lebiazh'e region, 7 kilometers northeast of Zemliansk northeastward to Bol'shaia Vereika, 18 kilometers northeast of Zemliansk.

80. See Rolf Stoves, *Die Gepanzerten und Motorisierten Deutschen Grossverbande, 1935–1945* (Friedberg, Germany: Podzun-Pallas-Verlag, 1986), 84, 174.

81. V. A. Zolotarev, ed., *Russkii arkhiv: Velikaia Otechestvennaia [voina]: Prikazy narodnogo komissara oborony SSSR, 22 iiunia 1941 g.–1942, T. 13 (2-2)* [The Russian archives: The Great Patriotic [War]: Orders of the People's Commissariat of Defense of the USSR, 22 June 1941–1942, vol. 13 (2-2)] (Moscow: "TERRA," 1997), 276–278. Hereafter cited as Zolotarev, "NKO 1941–42," with appropriate page(s). This order, which was signed by Stalin, was entitled "Order No. 227 Concerning Measures for Strengthening Discipline and Order in the Red Army and Preventing Unauthorized Retreat from Combat Positions."

82. Ibid.

83. Ibid.

84. Ibid., 278–279.

85. Ibid.

86. Ibid.

87. Ibid.

88. See Shtemenko, *Soviet General Staff at War*, bk. 1, 102–104, 107.

89. For additional orders related to Order No. 227, see P. N. Lashchenko, "Prodiktovan surovoi neobkhodimost'iu" [Severe measures are dictated], *VIZh* 8 (August 1988): 76–80.

90. The Red Army General Staff's daily summary for 25 July reported, "The 229th RD repelled attacks by up to two enemy infantry regiments supported by tanks against Hills 126.0, 158.3, and 153.3. Nine enemy tanks were destroyed." The next day it added, "Beginning on the morning of 26 July, 229th RD was fighting a stubborn defensive battle with up to one and one half enemy infantry divisions and 80 enemy tanks. By 1600 hours, the enemy captured the regions of the Derbentsevo and Trenoshkina *Balkas*. The division's forces are conducting a fighting withdrawal to the east across the Chir River." Completing the story on 27 July, it reported, "229th RD conducted a fierce battle with the

enemy, suffered heavy losses, and withdrew to the left bank of the Chir under intense pressure, where it occupied defenses along the Kaz. [abbreviation unclear] (2 kilometers north of Dmitrievka State Farm), Bol'shaia Osinovka, and Staromaksimovskii line. The 112th RD and 137th TB occupied defenses in the Marker 85.3, Trekhtubochnaia *Balka*, and Verkhne-Chirskaia sector on the right bank of the Don River. After fighting in the Nizhne-Chirskaia region, 66th Naval Rifle Brigade and 121st TB withdrew to the left bank of the Don River, where they occupied defenses along the Zimovskii and Lake Prorva line. The brigades suffered losses of up to 50 percent." See Zhilin, *Stalingradskaia bitva*, 248, 252, and 254.

91. Chuikov, *Battle for Stalingrad*, 30–38. The quotation is from Senger und Etterlin, *Die 24. Panzer-Division*, 96.

92. Rokossovsky, *Velikaia pobeda na Volge*, 71.

93. Ibid.

94. Ibid., 71–72.

Chapter 7: Endgame in the Great Bend of the Don, 1–19 August 1942

1. Halder, *The Halder War Diary*, 646.

2. Ibid.

3. Ibid.

4. Ibid.

5. Ibid.

6. Ziemke and Bauer, *Moscow to Stalingrad*, 364.

7. Ibid.

8. Halder, *The Halder Diary*, 649–650.

9. Ziemke and Bauer, *Moscow to Stalingrad*, 365.

10. Blau, *The German Campaign in Russia*, 156–157.

11. For the changing organization of Sixth and Fourth Panzer Armies, see "Ia, Lagenkarten Nr. 1 zum KTB Nr. 13, Jul–Oct 1942," *AOK 6, 23948/1a*, in NAM T-312, Roll 1446.

12. See *Stavka* directive no. 994129, dated 28 July 1942, in Zolotarev, "*Stavka* 1942," 331.

13. See *Stavka* directive no. 994131, dated 1920 hours 29 July 1942, in ibid., 333.

14. See *Stavka* directives nos. 170539 and 170541, dated 2300 hours 30 July 1942 and 1345 hours 31 July 1942, respectively, in ibid., 335–337. 51st Army had been transferred to North Caucasus Front in late July.

15. See *Stavka* directive no. 170524, dated 1940 hours 31 July 1942, in ibid., 337.

16. See unnumbered *Stavka* directive, dated 2 August 1942, in ibid., 338–339.

17. *Boevoi sostav Sovetskoi armii*, 2: 148–149.

18. See, for example, Joachim Lemelsen, et al., *29. Division: 29. Infanteriedivision, 29. Infanteriedivision (mot), 29. Panzergrenadier-Division* (Bad Nauheim, BRD: Podzun Verlag, 1960), 192–193; and, although sketchy, Rolf Grams, *Die 14. Panzer-Division 1940–1945* (Bad Nauheim, BRD: Verlag Hans-Henning Podzun, 1957), 50–51.

19. S. M. Sarkis'ian, *51–ia Armiia* [51st Army] (Moscow: Voenizdat, 1983), 81.

20. Zhilin, *Stalingradskaia bitva*, 277.

21. Rokossovsky, *Velikaia pobeda na Volge*, 75. The 38th Rifle Division numbered only 1,685 men on 25 July. See Isaev, *Stalingrad*, 84.

22. Born in 1894, Tolbukhin, who was assigned command of 57th Army at age 46, had commanded a battalion in the tsar's army during the World War. After joining the Red Army in 1918, he was chief of staff of a rifle division and an army on the southern and western fronts during the Civil War. A two-time graduate of the "*Vystrel*'" Officers Course in 1927 and 1930 and the Frunze Academy in 1934, Tolbukhin served as chief of staff of a rifle division and rifle corps and commanded a rifle division in 1937. Appointed chief of staff of the Trans-Caucasus Military District in July 1938, he was occupying that post when Operation Barbarossa began. He then served as chief of staff of the same military district through August 1941 and the Trans-Caucasus, Caucasus, and Crimean Fronts until his appointment to head 57th Army, which he commanded throughout Operation Blau. Thereafter, Tolbukhin commanded the Southern and 4th and 3rd Ukrainian Fronts from March 1943 to war's end, leading them to victory after victory in Ukraine in 1943–1944 and in the Iasi-Kishinev, Belgrade, Budapest, Balaton, and Vienna offensive operations in 1944 and 1945. After the war, Tolbukhin commanded the Soviet Southern Group of Forces in Hungary from 1945 to 1947 and, thereafter, the Trans-Caucasus Military District until his death in 1949. For further details, see *Komandarmy. Voennyi biograficheskii slovar'*, 225–226.

23. Ibid. See also Lemelsen, et al., *29.Division*, 194.

24. For further details, see Grams, *Die 14. Panzer-Division*, 50.

25. Zhilin, *Stalingradskaia bitva*, 282.

26. Rokossovsky, *Velikaia pobeda na Volge*, 76.

27. The personnel strengths of 138th and 157th Rifle Divisions were 4,200 and 1,500 men, respectively. See ibid., 77. For an account in English of the operations of Chuikov's operational group, see Chuikov, *The Battle for Stalingrad*, 44–56.

28. Ibid.

29. See *Komandarmy. Voennyi biograficheskii slovar'*, 70–71; and Grachev, ed., *VE*, 3: 165.

30. A. I. Eremenko, *Stalingrad: Zapiski komanduuishchevo frontom* [Stalingrad: The notes of a *front* commander] (Moscow: Voenizdat, 1961), 38–39.

31. Disagreement exists over the actual timing of Stalin's decision to split Stalingrad Front. In his memoirs, Eremenko asserts that Stalin made the decision on the evening of 2–3 August, after extensive consultations with the General Staff. However, Vasilevsky, in *Delo vsei zhizni* [A life's work] (Moscow: Politizdat, 1983), 210, claims, "On 5 August the *Stavka* decided to divide the Stalingrad Front into two separate *fronts*—Stalingrad and Southeastern," without mentioning the disagreement between Eremenko, the General Staff, and Stalin. Vasilevsky's most recent biography, A. Ia. Sukharev, ed., *Marshal A. M. Vasilevsky—strateg, polkovodets, chelovek* [Marshal A. M. Vasilevsky—strategist, military leader, and the man] (Moscow: Sovet Veteranov knigoizdaniia, 1998), 151, and Rokossovsky, *Velikaia bitva na Volge*, 78, also assert that the directive was issued on 5 August. However, newly released documents indicate that the *Stavka* issued two directives, the first at 0530 hours on 4 August to its main directorates and the second at 0415 hours on 5 August to its two new *front* commanders.

32. See *Stavka* directive no. 170554, dated 0415 hours 5 August 1942, in Zolotarev, "*Stavka* 1942," 342–343. The first directive, *Stavka* directive no. 994140, dated 0530 hours 4 August 1942, in ibid., reads:

The *Stavka* of the Supreme High Command orders:

1. Form the Southeastern Front command by 9 August 1942.
2. Deploy the Southeastern Front command on the base of 4th Tank Army's command [headquarters] and station it in the Stalingrad region.
3. Colonel General Comrade Eremenko, A. I., is appointed commander of the Southeastern Front, Major General Comrade Zakharov, G.F.,—as the chief of staff of the *front*, effective when he is freed of his duties as the deputy chief of staff of the North Caucasus Front.
4. The chief of the Main Cadre Directorate and the chiefs of the NKO's main directorates will fill out the Southeastern Front command with missing commanders and command cadre by 9 August according to tables of organization and equipment [*shtati*] Nos. 02/210, 02/208, 02/165-6, and 010/1-B. Dispatch the command personnel (the chiefs of department, directorates, and force branches) by aircraft so that they arrive at their designated positions by 6 August.
5. The chief of the Main Directorate for the Formation and Manning of the Red Army [GLAVUPROFORM] will issue orders concerning the formation of necessary rear service units and service installations for the *front* command.
6. The chief of the Red Army's Main Signal Directorate will dispatch 42nd Separate Signal Regiment and 36th Separate Radio Battalion from the Stalingrad Front to the control of the Southeastern Front commander by 9 August; and the remaining signal units—in accordance with separate orders.
7. The chief of the Red Army's rear will allocate necessary rear service units and installations at the expense of reserve and surpluses from other *fronts* and place them at the disposal of the Southeastern Front's commander by 9 August.

Report fulfillment. [signed] Vasilevsky

33. See Moskalenko, *Na iugo–zapadnom napravlenie*, 1: 258–259, for Moskalenko's perspectives on these changes.

34. See *Stavka* directive no. 994144, dated 0450 hours 5 August 1942, in Zolotarev, "*Stavka* 1942," 345.

35. See *Stavka* directive no. 1036004, dated 5 August 1942, in ibid., 348.

36. Rokossovsky, *Velikaia pobeda na Volge*, 78–79.

37. See *Stavka* directive no. 170562, dated 2300 hours 9 August 1942, in Zolotarev, "*Stavka* 1942," 354.

38. This and subsequent descriptions of Operational Group Chuikov's defense is found in Chuikov, *Battle for Stalingrad*, 44–49.

39. Grams, *Die 14. Panzer-Division*, 50–51.

40. Zhilin, *Stalingradskaia bitva*, 304.

41. The IV Army Corps' 371st Infantry Division remained well to the rear, blocking the remainder of Kolomiets's 51st Army from returning north to rejoin its parent army.

42. See the detailed daily reports about 157th and 138th Rifle Divisions' struggle in Zhilin, *Stalingradskaia bitva*, 317, 322.

43. Ibid., 349. Chuikov, *Battle for Stalingrad*, 54, asserts this withdrawal began on 17 August. German maps indicate a withdrawal halfway back to the Myshkova River by 13 August but no change in the sector thereafter until 64th Army initiated its general withdrawal back to Stalingrad proper.

44. Chuikov, *Battle for Stalingrad*, 50–53.

45. See *Stavka* directive no. 170556, dated 1630 hours 6 August 1942, in Zolotarev, "*Stavka* 1942," 349.

46. Moshchansky and Smolinov, "Oborona Stalingrada," 28. Lemelsen, et al., 29. *Division*, 195, identified 6th Guards, 254th, and 13th Tank Brigades and 15th Guards, 204th, and 38th Rifle Divisions among the counterattacking Soviet forces. The 13th Tank Corps reported its strength on 8 August as follows:

13th Tank Brigade	11 T-34s
6th Guards Tank Brigade	10 T-34s
254th Tank Brigade	6 T-34s and 4 T-70s
Total	27 T-34s and 4 T-70s

See Isaev, *Stalingrad*, 94.

47. Moshchansky and Smolinov, "Oborona Stalingrada," 25.

48. The 14th Panzer Division's armor strength fell from about 100 tanks on 1 August to 24 tanks on 10 August. At this time 29th Motorized Division fielded 26 tanks.

49. For additional details on the fighting, see Moshchansky and Smolinov, "Oborona Stalingrada," 28–30. When 13th Tank Brigade reached Tinguta Station on 5 August, it fielded 44 T-34 tanks and its motorized rifle battalion was at full strength. After fighting with 14th Panzer Division's forces near 74 km Station on 6 and 7 August, the brigade's tank strength fell sharply to 22 armored vehicles. Thereafter, with 38th Rifle Division, the tank brigade defended the approaches to Tinguta Station. See Isaev, *Stalingrad*, 90.

50. Lemelsen, et al., 29. *Division*, 194–195.

51. Moshchansky and Smolinov, "Oborona Stalingrada," 29. The 29th Motorized Division suffered 1,911 casualties, including 371 killed and 66 missing in action during August, most of them during the fighting in the Abganerovo region. It had already suffered 1,553 losses in July, including 278 dead and 22 missing. This meant the division had lost up to 15 percent of its strength, principally in its combat units. During August 14th Panzer Division suffered 1,515 casualties, including 395 dead and 19 missing, added to their equally heavy losses in July. See George W. S. Kuhn, *Ground Forces Casualty Rate Patterns: The Empirical Evidence, Report FP703TR1* (Bethesda, MD: Logistics Management Agency, September 1989), in attached tables derived from German archival records of specific *Wehrmacht* divisions.

52. See also "Ia, Lagenkarten Nr. 1 zum KTB Nr. 13, Jul–Oct 1942," *AOK 6, 23948/1a,*. in NAM T-312, Roll 1446.

53. Zhilin, *Stalingradskaia bitva*, 325.

54. Ibid., 328, 336–337, and 342. The full report on 10 August read, "The 214th RD was defending a line from the grove east of Lipovskii to Novoaksaiskii; 138th RD occupied defenses from Chausovskii to Novoaksaiskii; 157th RD completely cleared the enemy from the right bank of the Aksai and was defending the line from Novoaksaiskii to Chikov; 29th RD defended the line from Chikov to Antonov; and 118th Fortified Region fought with an enemy force of up to an infantry regiment."

55. Ibid., 344.

56. After losing 59 tanks in the two days of fighting near 74 km Station and Abganerovo, Southeastern Front fielded 64 tanks on 12 August (all in Shumilov's 64th Army), with another 99 tanks being repaired. This included 26 tanks (24 T-34s and 2 T-

70s) in 13th Tank Corps' 6th Guards, and 13th and 254th Tank Brigades, 22 KV tanks in 133rd Tank Brigade, and 16 T-34 tanks in 6th Tank Brigade. See Moshchansky and Smolinov, "Oborona Stalingrada," 29.

57. See the appropriate daily situation maps in "Ia, Lagenkarten Nr. 1 zum KTB Nr. 13, Jul–Oct 1942," *AOK 6, 23948/1a*, in NAM T-312, Roll 1446.

58. For example, 16th Panzer Division's 2nd Panzer Regiment (Group Sieckenius) fielded 120 tanks, 24th Panzer Division, 138 tanks, and 3rd and 60th Motorized Divisions, roughly 40 tanks apiece. See Werthen, *Geschichte der 16 Panzer-Division*, 103; and Jentz, *Panzertruppen*, 248.

59. Hayward, *Stopped at Stalingrad*, 183–185.

60. See also Rokossovsky, *Velikaia pobeda na Volge*, 86. Rokossovsky also provides a detailed and accurate description of the battle west of Kalach, although he underestimates the scale of 62nd Army's defeat.

61. For details, see Werthen, *Geschichte der 16. Panzer-Division*, 103–104. The attacking force included *Kampfgruppe* Siekenius, made up of most of the division's 2nd Panzer Regiment, and *Kampfgruppen* Lattmann, Reinisch, and Krumpen, formed from 64th and 79th Panzer Grenadier Regiments and elements of 16th Panzer Jägt (Hunter) Battalion, 16th Panzer Artillery Regiment, and minimal tank support.

62. Ibid., 103.

63. For details on 24th Panzer Division's advance to Kalach, see Senger und Etterlin, *Die 24. Panzer-Division*, 105–107. The division reported capturing 7,760 Soviet soldiers, including 150 officers, and destroying or capturing 81 tanks, 91 artillery pieces, 110 antitank and 8 antiaircraft guns, 197 grenade launchers, and 149 antitank rifles during its advance.

64. Zhilin, *Stalingradskaia bitva*, 316–317.

65. Werthen, *Geschichte der 16. Panzer-Division*, 104.

66. Zhilin, *Stalingradskaia bitva*, 322.

67. The forces of 62nd Army encircled west of Kalach included 33rd Guards Rifle Division's 91st Regiment, 147th, 181st, and 229th Rifle Divisions (which reported strengths of 9,575, 11,142, and 5,419 men, respectively, on 5 August), the Krasnodar School, 555th, 508th, 881st, 1185th, and 1252nd Antitank Regiments, and 645th, 650th, and 651st Separate Tank Battalions. The encircled forces totaled roughly 28,000 men, and lost weaponry included 157 field and 67 antitank guns, 17 T-34 tanks, 39 T-60 tanks, and 354 motor vehicles. The 33rd Guards Rifle Division's 84th and 88th Regiments escaped to rejoin 4th Tank Army. The 399th and 131st Rifle Divisions, which were transferred from 1st Tank to 6th Army on 6 August with 12,322 and 6,279 men, respectively, escaped eastward across the Don River, where they manned new defenses on the river's eastern bank together with 54th Fortified Region and the remnants of 23rd and 28th Tank Corps. By 20 August 62nd Army reported that its divisions that managed to escape eastward across the Don River totaled about 3,700 men, including:

33rd Guards Rifle Division	48 men
147th Rifle Division	171 men
181st Rifle Division	28 men
229th Rifle Division	278 men
112th Rifle Division	3,376 men

See Isaev, *Stalingrad*, 67–68, 74–75, citing *TsAMO RF*, f. 220, op. 220, d. 71, ll. 141, 171.

68. Ibid., 328, 336, 342.

69. Maps dated 10–12 August 1942, in "Ia, Lagenkarten Nr. 1 zum KTB Nr. 13, Jul–Oct 1942," *AOK 6, 23948/1a*, in NAM T-312, Roll 1446. See also Zhilin, *Stalingradskaia bitva*, 344, quoting the OKW summary dated 12 August 1942. Other Western sources, such as Ziemke and Bauer, *Moscow to Stalingrad*, 384, cite a figure of almost 50,000 prisoners.

70. Werthen, *Geschichte der 16. Panzer-Division*, 104.

71. Zhilin, *Stalingradskaia bitva*, 343, quoting an OKW bulletin dated 12 August 1942. This bulletin substantiates the claim in Werthen, *Geschichte der 16. Panzer-Division*, 104, that 16th Panzer Division captured 8,300 Soviet troops and destroyed 275 enemy tanks and 298 enemy guns, raising the total number of enemy tanks destroyed since 22 June 1941 to 1,000.

72. Jentz, *Panzertruppen*, 248.

73. Rokossovsky, *Velikaia pobeda na Volge*, 96. Born in 1902, Malenkov entered the Red Army as a political worker and served as commissar in a cavalry brigade during the Civil War. After graduating from Moscow's Bauman Higher Technical School in 1925, he worked in the apparatus of the Communist Party Central Committee until 1930, allying himself with Stalin in his struggle to seize total power within the party. Rising quickly in party leadership organs, all the while helping create Stalin's "cult of personality," Malenkov by 1939 was appointed as secretary of the Communist Party's Central Committee, a post he held until 1953. During the war Malenkov was a member of Stalin's State Defense Committee (GKO), which exercised oversight over the war's conduct; as a lieutenant general in the Red Army, he represented the GKO in the field during the battles for Leningrad, Moscow, Stalingrad, and Kursk. From August 1943 to war's end, he served as head of the Council of People's Commissars' Committee for the Reconstruction of the Economy in Regions Liberated from Nazi Occupation. After the war ended, Malenkov was deputy chairman of the USSR's Council of Ministers through 1953, playing a lead role in Stalin's purges associated with the so-called Leningrad Affair (the Doctor's Plot). After Stalin's death in 1953, Malenkov shared power with Khrushchev and Bulganin by serving as chairman of the USSR's Council of Ministers. However, Khrushchev slowly maneuvered him from power, finally expelling him from the Communist Party's Central Committee and Presidium of the Supreme Soviet in 1961 for "fractional activities in anti-Party groups." Removed from all of his official posts, Malenkov retired in 1961; he died in 1988. For further details, see *VE*, 4: 537.

Novikov, one of the Red Army's most famous air force commanders, was born in 1900, joined the Red Army in 1919, and fought in the Civil War. A graduate of the *"Vystrel'"* Officers Course in 1922 and the Frunze Academy in 1930, Novikov led Northwestern Front's air forces during the Finnish War in 1939–1940. After the Soviet-German War began, he commanded Northern and Leningrad Fronts' air forces throughout Operation Barbarossa. For Novikov's effective work in the successful defense of Leningrad, the *Stavka* appointed him overall commander of the Red Army's Air Force, a post he occupied through war's end and, simultaneously, as deputy People's Commissar of Defense for Aviation in 1942–1943. In addition to reorganizing the Air Force, primarily through the formation of air armies and corps, Novikov also served as a Stavka representative, coordinating the air forces in the battles for Stalingrad and Kursk and during the Red Army's strategic offensive in Manchuria in August–September 1945, in the process becoming Main Marshal of Aviation and a two-time Hero of the Soviet Union. Novikov was suddenly purged by Stalin in 1946 and sentenced to five years' imprisonment for "treason" and "anti-Party activity." However, he was released and rehabilitated after Stalin's death in 1953 and served as commander of the strategically important long-range aviation until 1955. After occupying a series of lesser posts, Novikov retired in 1956; he died in 1976. For further details, see *VE*, 5: 493–494.

74. See *Stavka* directive no. 170566, dated 2050 hours 13 August 1942, in Zolotarev, "*Stavka* 1942," 360.

75. Rokossovsky, *Velikaia pobeda na Volge*, 97. One of the Red Army's most famous air army commanders, Rudenko was born in 1904 and rose to command 16th Air Army in September 1942 at age 38. Too young to participate in World War I or the Civil War, Rudenko joined the Red Army in 1923 and graduated from the Kachinsk Pilots School in 1927 and the RKKA Academy in 1932. Rising through aviation squadron, regiment, and brigade command during the 1930s, Rudenko commanded Western Front's 31st Aviation Division during Operation Barbarossa and 61st Army's air forces during the battle for Moscow in December 1941. After commanding Volkhov Front's air forces and 1st Aviation and 7th Shock Aviation Groups during the winter offensive of 1941–1942, Rudenko was appointed to command Southwestern Front's air forces in June 1942 and 16th Air Army in September. He led 16th Air Army to war's end, in the process rising to the rank of lieutenant general and becoming a Hero of the Soviet Union. During the last three years of war, he served in the battles for Stalingrad and Kursk and the Belorussian, Vistula-Oder, and Berlin offensives. After the war ended, Rudenko commanded his air army and the Soviet Army's Airborne Forces before becoming chief of the Air Forces' Main Staff in 1949. Rudenko continued to occupy senior positions in the Red Air Force until his retirement in 1973; he died in 1990. For further details, see *VE*, 7: 288.

76. Ibid., 99–100.

77. For the situation and problems in 1st Guards Army, see Moskalenko, *Na iugo–zapadnom napravlenii*, 1: 294–298. The army's 39th and 40th Guards Rifle Divisions unloaded at Ilovlia Station by day's end on 13 August, 37th and 38th Guards Rifle Divisions on 14–15 August, and only 40th Guards reached the Kremenskaia bridgehead in time to participate in the battle.

78. See *Stavka* directive no. 170569, dated 0420 hours 15 August 1942, in Zolotarev, "*Stavka* 1942," 362, which contains instructions as to how 62nd Army was to rescue its encircled divisions.

79. Rokossovsky, *Velikaia pobeda na Volge*, 100–102. See also *Stavka* directive no. 170568, dated 2140 hours 14 August 1942, in Zolotarev, "*Stavka* 1942," 361.

80. Additionally, 64th Army was to, "Dig your tanks into the ground on all dominating terrain along the external defensive line. Protect the withdrawal of the army's forces from the Aksai line with strong rear guards, which will remain along the Aksai to defend the territory between the river and the [external] defensive line. Retain in army reserve 29th Rifle Division in the Verkhne-Tsaritsynskii and Zety regions, 138th Rifle Division in the Eriko-Krepinskii and State Farm '*Krep*'' [Strength] region, and 13th Tank Corps (with 52 tanks) in the region southeast of Tinguta Station."

81. Specifically, 57th Army was to, "Organize a middle defensive line in the Varvarovka, Ivanovka, and Chapurniki sector [25–30 kilometers southwest and south of Stalingrad] with four divisions. To prevent the enemy from reaching the Volga southeast of Raigorod, 36th Guards Rifle Division's 108th Guards Rifle Regiment will defend the defiles between Lakes Sarpa, Tsatsa, Barmantsak, and Malyi Derbety, fortifying these

against attack along all likely armored axes from the west. Form the army in two echelons, with up to two divisions in first echelon and four divisions in second."

82. Specifically, 8th Air Army was to, "Support the detraining of 1st Guards Army's forces at Log and Ilovlia Stations. Aircraft must protect the Kachalinskaia and Ilovlia regions, the crossing sites over the Don in the Novo–Grigor'evskaia and Trekhostrovskaia sector, and its concentration areas in Perekopskaia, Kamyshinka, Kisliaki, and Nizhnyi Akatov [in 4th Tank Army's bridgehead]."

83. In addition, the Volga Military Flotilla was to, "Lay mines in the Volga from Stalingrad to Astrakhan'. The Astrakhan' Naval Base of the Caspian Flotilla will become operationally subordinate to the Volga Military Flotilla beginning on 8 August."

84. All subordinate armies established their auxiliary command posts on key terrain along the front lines, where they also served as the army commander's observation posts.

85. Rokossovsky, *Velikaia pobeda na Volge*, 103.

86. Ibid., 104. A combat load was enough ammunition to last a given force for "x" number of days, with the x equaling about two days of fighting. One refill of fuel allowed vehicles and tanks to travel a distance equivalent to its fuel consumption rate, e.g., so many kilometers per liter. These figures reflected stocks in army warehouses and did not include ammunition and fuel on hand in the forces themselves (which was significantly lower).

87. Ibid., 105.

88. See "Ia, Lagenkarten Nr. 1 zum KTB Nr. 13, Jul–Oct 1942," *AOK 6, 23948/1a*, in NAM T-312, Roll 1446.

89. See Werthen, *Geschichte der 16. Panzer-Division*, 105.

90. "Ia, Lagenkarten Nr. 1 zum KTB Nr. 13, Jul–Oct 1942," *AOK 6, 23948/1a*, in NAM T-312, Roll 1446.

91. Ibid.; and *Boevoi sostav Sovetskoi armii*, 2: 148–149. The formations of Kriuchenkin's 4th Tank Army reported the following personnel and weapons strengths on 14 August:

18th Rifle Division	8,724 men
184th Rifle Division	3,950 men
192nd Rifle Division	4,965 men
205th Rifle Division	8,374 men
321st Rifle Division	7,544 men
343rd Rifle Division	8,677 men
182nd Tank Brigade	36 tanks (10 T-34s, 6 T-70s, and 20 T-60s), about 20 operational.

See Isaev, *Stalingrad*, 78.

92. See "Ia, Lagenkarten Nr. 1 zum KTB Nr. 13, Jul–Oct 1942," *AOK 6, 23948/1a*, in NAM T-312, Roll 1446; and Rokossovsky, *Velikaia pobeda na Volge*, 99. The 22nd Tank Corps had concentrated all of its 20 operational tanks (7 T-34s, 4 T-70s, and 9 T-60s) in its 182nd Tank Brigade. See also Moshchansky and Smolinov, "Oborona Stalingrada," 18.

93. Zhilin, *Stalingradskaia bitva*, 353–354.

94. Rokossovsky, *Velikaia pobeda na Volge*, ibid., 113. These reinforcements included 646th and 647th Separate Tank Battalions (with about 25 tanks), 57th Guards-Mortar Regiment, 156th and 331st Artillery Regiments, and 468th, 612th, 737th, and 738th Antitank Artillery Regiments.

95. Werthen, *Geschichte der 16. Panzer-Division*, 104–105.

96. Zhilin, *Stalingradskaia bitva*, 365.

97. See "Ia, Lagenkarten Nr. 1 zum KTB Nr. 13, Jul–Oct 1942," *AOK 6, 23948/1a*, in NAM T-312, Roll 1446. See a more detailed description of this short two-day battle in Rokossovsky, *Velikaia pobeda na Volge*, 113–115.

98. Moshchansky and Smolinov, "Oborona Stalingrada," 30–31.

99. Rokossovsky, *Velikaia pobeda na Volge*, 114.

100. Werthen, *Geschichte der 16. Panzer-Division*, 105.

101. Zhilin, *Stalingradskaia bitva*, 373.

102. Ibid.

103. For further details, see Moskalenko, *Na iugo–zapadnom napravlenii*, 1: 296–298; and I. M. Chistiakov, ed., *Po prikazu Rodiny: boevoi put' 6-i gvardeiskoi armii v Velikoi Otechestvennoi voine* [By order of the Motherland; The combat path of 6th Guards Army in the Great Patriotic War] (Moscow: Voenizdat, 1971), 18–20, which describes 21st Army's role in this fighting.

104. For a brief description of 3rd Motorized Division's fight, see Dieckhoff, *3. Infanterie-Division*, 192–193, which asserts the division captured 1,775 prisoners and destroyed 288 enemy tanks, 92 guns, 93 grenade launchers, 116 machine guns, and 34 vehicles since 9 August. This brought the division's tally of destroyed tanks to 400 since 31 July.

105. Rokossovsky, *Velikaia pobeda na Volge*, 114–115.

106. Werthen, *Geschichte der 16. Panzer-Division*, 105.

107. Ibid., 115–116. The formation of Kriuchenkin's 4th Tank Army reported the following strengths on 20 August:

18th Rifle Division	1,281 men
184th Rifle Division	676 men
192nd Rifle Division	1,238 men
321st Rifle Division	4,356 men

See Isaev, *Stalingrad*, 80.

108. Ibid., 116–117.

109. See "Ia, Lagenkarten Nr. 1 zum KTB Nr. 13, Jul–Oct 1942," *AOK 6, 23948/1a*, in NAM T-312, Roll 1446.

110. Rokossovsky, *Velikaia pobeda na Volge*, 117.

111. Jentz, *Panzer truppen*, 248.

112. Grams, *Die 14. Panzer-Division*, 51.

Chapter 8: The German Advance to the Volga River,
20 August–2 September 1942

1. Quoted in full in Heinz Schröter, *Stalingrad* (New York: Ballantine, 1958), 24; and Haupt, *Army Group South*, 161. See also Zhilin, *Stalingradskaia bitva*, 386.

2. Schröter, *Stalingrad*, 24; and Zhilin, *Stalingradskaia bitva*, 387. At this stage of the offensive, Paulus' "conservative" approach is understandable, since he, better than anyone, understood the state of his forces and the difficulties they were likely to encounter.

3. Schröter, *Stalingrad*, 24–25.

4. Ibid., 26–27; and Zhilin, *Stalingradskaia bitva*, 387–388.

5. Schröter, *Stalingrad*, 27. For details of the fight on the Soviet side, see 4th Tank Army's daily reports for 19–22 August in Zhilin, *Stalingradskaia bitva*, 384, 383–384, 395, 400, 406, and 411. Contrary to the German war correspondent's account, while they inflicted heavy casualties on the two German divisions, the Soviet forces were not able to crush the bridgehead. Dispatched to 62nd Army by the *Stavka*, 98th Rifle Division numbered 11,689 men on 15 August. See Isaev, *Stalingrad*, 102.

6. Werthen, *Geschichte der 16. Panzer-Division*, 106.

7. For details on this attack, see Zhilin, *Stalingradskaia bitva*, 309, 315, and 321. The 6th Army's 25th Guards, 174th, and 309th Rifle Divisions, supported by 24th Tank Corps and 1st Destroyer Division, conducted the attack against the Hungarian 7th Infantry Division.

8. Glantz, *Forgotten Battles*, 3: 66–74.

9. Rokossovsky, *Velikaia pobeda na Volge*, 119.

10. Ibid. Dispatched to 62nd Army from the *Stavka's* reserve, 87th Rifle Division had 11,429 men on 15 August. See Isaev, *Stalingrad*, 102.

11. Rokossovsky, *Velikaia pobeda na Volge*, 120. These included 1158th, 1105th, and 1103rd Gun Artillery Regiments and 398th and 651st Antitank Artillery Regiments.

12. Ibid., 120–121.

13. All of 22nd Tank Corps' tanks (roughly 20) were still assigned to its 182nd Tank Brigade.

14. Rokossovsky, *Velikaia pobeda na Volge*, 122.

15. Schröter, *Stalingrad*, 28.

16. Zhilin, *Stalingradskaia bitva*, 406.

17. Ibid., 410.

18. The casualty figures are from Tarrant, *Stalingrad: Anatomy*, 51.

19. Zhilin, *Stalingradskaia bitva*, 417.

20. Werthen, *Geschichte der 16. Panzer-Division*, 106.

21. Hayward, *Stopped at Stalingrad*, 188. The Soviets counted more than 2,000 German aircraft sorties against the city.

22. Werthen, *Geschichte der 16. Panzer-Division*, 106.

23. Ibid., 107. These antiaircraft guns were assigned to 1st and 5th Batteries of 2nd PVO Corps Region's 1077th Antiaircraft Artillery Regiment. See Rokossovsky, *Velikaia pobeda na Volge*, 127.

24. Werthen, *Geschichte der 16. Panzer-Division*, 107.

25. Ibid., 106–107; and Carell, *Stalingrad*, 124–125.

26. Werthen, *Geschichte der 16. Panzer-Division*, 107.

27. For details, see Langermann, *3. Infanterie-Division*, 94–96.

28. Schröter, *Stalingrad*, 28.

29. Ibid.

30. Moshchansky and Smolinov, "Oborona Stalingrada," 32.

31. This force included 27th Guards, 84th, and 298th Rifle Divisions from the *Stavka* Reserve and 62nd Army's 35th Guards Rifle Division and 169th Tank Brigade.

32. Rokossovsky, *Velikaia pobeda na Volge*, 124.

33. Ibid., 125–126, provides details about the complex redeployment of 62nd Army's and 4th Tank Army's forces from 21 to 23 August.

34. Ibid., 132.

35. As of 23 August General Kravchenko's 2nd Tank Corps fielded a total of 183 tanks, subdivided as follows:

Brigade	KVs	T-34s	T-70s	T-60s	Total
26th TB	—	37	5	23	65
27th TB	—	42	5	24	71
148th TB	15	—	5	27	47
Total	15	79	15	74	183

General Khasin led 23rd Tank Corps until 30 August, when he was replaced by General A. F. Popov, who had commanded 11th Tank Corps during the July fighting in the Voronezh region. On 23 August Khasin's tank corps consisted of one tank brigade, the 189th, because 62nd Army had transferred the corps' 56th and 99th Tank Brigades to other sectors and its 9th Motorized Rifle Brigade was in the process of reorganizing. Therefore, when Khasin's corps was directed to support 2nd Tank Corps, its 189th Tank Brigade consisted of 43 operational tanks (22 T-34s, 16 T-70s, and 5 T-60s), with another seven tanks in disrepair (4 T-34s, 2 T-70s, and 1 T-60). See Isaev, *Stalingrad*, 108–110, citing *TsAMO RF*, f. 38, op. 11360, d. 77, l. 31.

36. Rokossovsky, *Velikaia pobeda na Volge*, 132.

37. Ibid., 133.

38. Zhilin, *Stalingradskaia bitva*, 418–419.

39. Werthen, *Geschichte der 16. Panzer-Division*, 107–108.

40. Schröter, *Stalingrad*, 31.

41. Werthen, *Geschichte der 16. Panzer-Division*, 109.

42. Ziemke and Bauer, *Moscow to Stalingrad*, 87.

43. See Schröter, *Stalingrad*, 31; and Werthen, *Geschichte der 16. Panzer-Division*, 110–111, for the details of Hube's predicament and 16th Panzer Division's fight to month's end.

44. Zhilin, *Stalingradskaia bitva*, 438.

45. See *Stavka* Directive No. 994170, dated 2015 hours 24 August 1942, in Zolotarev, "*Stavka* 1942," 372–373.

46. Born in 1890, Kalinin served as a warrant officer in the tsar's army before and during World War I, joined the Red Army in 1918, and, after serving as a commissar, rose to become a brigade commander and deputy chief of the Volga Military District's forces during the Civil War. A graduate of an officer cadre improvement course in 1928 and the Lenin Political-Military Academy in 1930, Kalinin led a rifle division and was deputy chief of staff of the Ukrainian Military District in the 1920s. Rising rapidly in the 1930s, primarily due to his unquestioned political reliability, he commanded a rifle division and rifle corps in the 1930s and, after serving as deputy commander of the Siberian Military District and Kiev Special Military District, headed the Siberian Military District from 1938 through the last two years of peace. Deployed westward in May and June 1941 at the head of 24th Army, which he raised, after war began Kalinin led the 24th during Western Front's defense of Smolensk in July and early August. More fortunate than his army, which would be encircled and destroyed at Viaz'ma in October 1941, Kalinin became assistant

commander of Western Front in August. In November the *Stavka* exploited Kalinin's organizational skills by appointing him commander of the Volga Military District, a post he occupied when summoned to form 66th Army in August 1942. After his replacement by Malinovsky in late August, Kalinin headed the Volga Military District once again until March 1944, when he took command of the Khar'kov Military District. Misfortune caught up with Kalinin in June 1944 when he was relieved of command and arrested on unspecified but likely spurious political charges. Dismissed from the army in 1946, he received a sentence of 25 years' imprisonment in 1951. Upon Stalin's death in 1953, the courts exonerated Kalinin within several months, and although the army retired him from service the following year, it restored his rank and pension. A survivor of the Germans as well as Stalin, Kalinin died in 1975. For further details, see *Komandarmy. Voennyi biograficheskii slovar'*, 87–88.

47. Rokossovsky, *Velikaia pobeda na Volge*, 134. Born in 1891, Kovalenko served as the deputy inspector-general of the Red Army's Infantry before the Soviet–German War and commanded 242nd Rifle Division throughout Operation Barbarossa. After organizing and leading a special operational group during Stalingrad Front's attempt to liquidate XIV Panzer Corps' corridor northwest of the city, Kovalenko was appointed the *front's* chief of staff on 10 September 1942. Although he ultimately rose to the rank of lieutenant general, other details about his wartime career and postwar service remain obscure. Kovalenko died in 1980.

48. Ibid.

49. Ibid. Born in 1899, Shtevnev commanded 15th Tank Division's 55th Light Tank regiment in 1939–1940 and 7th Mechanized Corps, 15th Tank Division, from June 1940 until the Barbarossa invasion. Assigned as deputy chief of Southern Front's Armored and Mechanized Forces two days after the invasion, he occupied this post until appointed chief of Stalingrad Front's Armored and Mechanized Forces in late July 1942. Thereafter, Shtevnev served as commander of 38th Army's Armored and Mechanized Forces from January to May 1943 and of 1st Ukrainian Front's Armored and Mechanized Forces until his death from German fire on 29 January 1944 during the Korsun'-Shevchenkovskii offensive. For further details about his career and death, see Drig, *Mekhanizirovannye korpusa RKKA v boiu*, 700, and Maslov, *Fallen Soviet Generals*, 201–202.

50. Zhilin, *Stalingradskaia bitva*, 421. See the Red Army General Staff's account of Group Kovalenko's temporary success, in ibid., 417.

51. Rokossovsky, *Velikaia bitva na Volge*, 136–137.

52. Ibid., 137–138.

53. Ibid., 138.

54. Ibid., 140. As of 20 August, Pavelkhin's 16th Tank Corps numbered 6,217 men, 178 tanks (24 KV, 82 T-34, and 72 T-60 models), 12 76mm field guns, three 45m antitank guns, and six 37mm antiaircraft guns. During the fighting on 26 August, Pavelkhin's corps lost 27 tanks, as follows: 107th Tank Brigade—12 KV tanks, including 5 burned; 109th Tank Brigade—13 T-34 tanks, including 7 burned; and 164th Tank Brigade—2 tanks missing in action. By 29 August 16th Tank Corps fielded 47 operational tanks, as follows: 107th Tank Brigade—4 KVs and 7 T-60s; 109th Tank Brigade—6 T-34s and 9 T-70s; and 164th Tank Brigade—13 T-34s and 8 T-60s. Mishulin's 4th Tank Corps, whose strength was close to that of 16th Tank Corps on 20 August, suffered comparable losses. Kravchenko's 2nd Tank Corps, with 26th and 27th Tank Brigades, lost 28 men killed and 97 wounded and

26 tanks (24 T-34s, 1 T-70, and 1 T-60) destroyed in the fighting on 24 August. After being reinforced by 56th Tank Brigade on 25 August and 99th Tank Brigade (with 50 T-34s) on 26 August, it lost 6 tanks from 56th Brigade on 25 August and 27 tanks on 26 August, including 18 T-34s in 99th Brigade, 3 T-34s in 26th Brigade, and 6 T-34s and 1 T-70 in 27th Brigade. See Isaev, *Stalingrad*, 115–116, 118–119, 121, citing *TsAMO RF*, f. 3414, op. 1, d. 24, l. 5ob.

55. Werthen, *Geschichte der 16. Panzer-Division*, 109.

56. See *Stavka* directive no. 170588, dated 0355 hours 26 August 1942, in Zolotarev, "*Stavka* 1942," 373.

57. See *Stavka* directive no. 994171, dated 2320 hours 27 August 1942, in ibid., 374.

58. G. Dërr, *Pokhod na Stalingrad* [The march on Stalingrad] (Moscow: Voenizdat, 1957), 48. This is a translation, of General Major A. D. Hans von Doerr, *Der Feldzug nach Stalingrad : Versuch eines operativen Überblickes* (Darmstadt, Germany: E. S. Mittler und Sohn GmbH, 1955).

59. For details about the fighting from 27 to 29 August, see the Red Army General Staff's daily operational summaries for these days, in Zhilin, *Stalingradskaia bitva*, 428, 433–434, 438, 443–444, 449, and 458. After being reinforced by 315th Rifle Division on 27 August, on 28 August 2nd Tank Corps' 26th and 27th Tank Brigades received 21 T-70 tanks as replacements for their previous losses. This allowed 27th Brigade to employ 47 tanks (12 T-34s, 20 T-70s, and 15 T-60s) in its assault toward Opytnoe Pole State Farm the next day. After failing to link up with 16th Tank Corps' forces, which were attacking from the north, Kravchenko's tank corps went over to the defense on 30–31 August. The 62nd Army disbanded Shtevnev's group on 1–2 September. See Isaev, *Stalingrad*, 116.

60. Ibid., 449.

61. Ibid., 444.

62. Werthen, *Geschichte der 16. Panzer-Division*, 109.

63. Ibid., 110. This account also provides a vivid description of the Russian assault on and capture of Rynok by 16th Panzer Division's motorcycle battalion and the successful defense north of Spartanovka by 64th Grenadier Regiment's 2nd and 3rd Battalions.

64. Ibid.

65. See "Ia, Lagenkarten Nr. 1 zum KTB Nr. 13, Jul–Oct 1942," *AOK 6, 23948/1a*, in NAM T-312, Roll 1446.

66. Rokossovsky, *Velikaia bitva na Volge*, 142.

67. For the complete message, see *Stavka* Instructions No. 170585, dated 0515 hours 25 August 1942, in Zolotarev, "*Stavka* 1942," 373.

68. Rokossovsky, *Velikaia bitva na Volge*, 143–144.

69. Rokossovsky, ibid., incorrectly maintains that the Germans actually cut the railroad line when, in fact, they were about 2 kilometers to its north.

70. Ibid., 144.

71. See Zhukov, *Reminiscences and Reflections*, 2: 88–89.

72. For details on 24th Panzer Division's mission and subsequent operations, see Jason D. Mark, *Death of the Leaping Horseman: 24. Panzer-Division in Stalingrad, 12th August–20th November 1942* (Sydney, Australia: Leaping Horsemen Books, 2003), 14–44.

73. Jentz, *Panzertruppen*, 248, provides 24th Panzer Division's strength. The 14th Panzer had fielded 24 tanks on 12 August but probably more than doubled its strength thereafter.

74. See *Boevoi sostav Sovetskoi armii*, 2: 172. Tanaschishin's 13th Tank Corps consisted of 13th, 254th, and 133rd Tank, 6th Guards Tank, and 38th Motorized Rifle Brigades.

75. Rokossovsky, *Velikaia pobeda na Volge*, 99–100.

76. *Boevoi sostav Sovetskoi armii*, 2: 172.

77. Mark, *Death of the Leaping Horseman*, 19, indicates that 24th Panzer Division fielded 5 command tanks and 28 Pz. II, 30 Pz. III short, 23 Pz. III long, 5 Pz. IV short, and 3 Pz. IV long tanks. This pioneering book is the most detailed study published to date on the operations of any German division during the battle for Stalingrad.

78. Ibid., 36, shows the division's 24th Panzer and 21st and 26th Panzer Grenadier Regiments with ration strengths of 2,411, 1,875, and 1,943 men, respectively, while their combat actual strength was 1,385, 1,418, and 1,531 men, respectively.

79. On 20 August 57th Army reported to the General Staff that it was being attacked by "an infantry division and 150 tanks." See Zhilin, *Stalingradskaia bitva*, 401.

80. Ibid., 147; and "Ia, Lagenkarten Nr. 1 zum KTB Nr. 13, Jul–Oct 1942," *AOK 6, 23948/1a*, in NAM T-312, Roll 1446.

81. See Mark, *Death of the Leaping Horseman*, 30–33, for details.

82. Zhilin, *Stalingradskaia bitva*, 407.

83. Rokossovsky, *Velikaia pobeda na Volge*, 147. These supporting regiments were 738th, 500th, 612th, 1188th, 499th, and 665th Antitank Artillery Regiments.

84. For details on Hoth's change in strategy, see Mark, *Death of the Leaping Horseman*, 49.

85. Zhilin, *Stalingradskaia bitva*, 412.

86. Ibid., 418, 428. The letter "K" in the report refers to a similar capital letter "K" in a place-name on tactical and operational maps of the region. Red Army unit commanders and operations officers often used the letters on these maps as reference points.

87. Mark, *Death of the Leaping Horseman*, 53–54.

88. Ibid., 58. These included 15 Pz. II, 10 Pz. III long, 23 Pz. III short, 2 Pz. IV long, and 3 Pz. IV short tanks.

89. By 25 August 24th Panzer Division had increased its tank strength to 83 vehicles, including 27 Pz. II, 30 Pz. III short, 22 Pz. III long, 2 Pz. IV short, and 2 Pz. IV long tanks. See ibid., 61.

90. Rokossovsky, *Velikaia pobeda na Volge*, 149.

91. Mark, *Death of the Leaping Horseman*, 62.

92. Ibid., 64.

93. Ibid., 150; and "Ia, Lagenkarten Nr. 1 zum KTB Nr. 13, Jul–Oct 1942," *AOK 6, 23948/1a*, in NAM T-312, Roll 1446.

94. Mark, *Death of the Leaping Horseman*, 67. This included 12 Pz. II, 25 Pz. III short, 15 Pz. IV long, 2 Pz. IV short, and 3 Pz. IV long tanks.

95. Ibid., 71–72. Specifically, since 28 June 24th Panzer Division had suffered 2,601 casualties, reducing 21st Grenadier Regiment's strength by 36.4 percent, 26th Grenadier Regiment's by 28 percent, and 24th Panzer Regiment's by 9.3 percent. By 26 August the panzer regiment fielded only a single weak panzer battalion.

96. Ibid., 69.

97. Rokossovsky, *Velikaia pobeda na Volge*, 150.

98. Mark, *Death of the Leaping Horseman*, 79, records that 24th Panzer Division fielded 13 Pz. II, 18 Pz. III short, 16 Pz. IV long, and 2 Pz. IV long tanks. See ibid., 82–91,

for a vivid and detailed account of 24th Panzer Division's advance, which Mark accurately describes as an "armored stampede." That night 24th Panzer reported capturing 700 prisoners, 5 tanks (2 of these heavy), 18 guns, 6 "Stalin Organs" (*Katiushas*), six antiaircraft guns, and over 50 antitank rifles. See ibid., 91.

99. Zhilin, *Stalingradskaia bitva*, 451.

100. Ibid., 458.

101. Rokossovsky, *Velikaia pobeda na Volge*, 151.

102. See *Stavka* directive no. 994186, dated 0745 hours 31 August 1942, in Zolotarev, "*Stavka* 1942," 381. Gerasimenko was born in 1900, joined the Red Army in 1918, and fought as a machine-gunner and assistant platoon leader on the north Caucasus and southern fronts during the Civil War. A 1927 graduate of the Minsk Combined Military School and the Frunze Academy in 1931, Gerasimenko commanded a battalion in the 1920s and was chief of staff of a rifle division and commander of 8th Rifle Corps during the 1930s. Assigned command of the Volga Military District in July 1940, when war began Gerasimenko raised and led Western Front's 21st Army in late June and July 1941 and the same *front's* 13th Army during the battle for Smolensk in July. After a short period under NKO control in Moscow, from September 1941 to his appointment as 28th Army commander in September 1942, Gerasimenko served as deputy commander of the Reserve Front and, after its destruction in the Viaz'ma encirclement in October, as assistant chief of the Red Army's Rear Services and commander of the Stalingrad Military District. In the wake of Operation Blau, Gerasimenko's 28th Army fought under the Stalingrad, Southern, and 4th Ukrainian Fronts until December 1943, participating in offensive operations to liberate the Donbas region and the Crimea. Relieved of command in December 1943, Gerasimenko commanded the Khar'kov and Kiev Military Districts until war's end. After commanding the Kiev Military District to October 1945 and serving as deputy commander of the Baltic Military District, Gerasimenko retired in 1953; he died in 1961. For further details, see *Komandarmy. Voennyi biograficheskii slovar'*, 42.

103. Mark, *Death of the Leaping Horseman*, 94. This included 11 Pz. II, 15 Pz. III short, 12 Pz. III long, 1 Pz. IV short, and 2 Pz. IV long tanks. 24th Panzer Division reported capturing 3,500 prisoners, 10 aircraft, 39 guns, 10 tanks, and 17 antitank guns, 6 antiaircraft guns, 78 mortars, 100 antitank rifles, and 7 "Stalin organs" [*Katiushas*] from 24 to 30 August.

104. Ibid., 107–108.

105. Zhilin, *Stalingradskaia bitva*, 462, 469, and 473–474.

106. Rokossovsky, *Velikaia pobeda na Volge*, 152.

107. "Ia, Lagenkarten Nr. 1 zum KTB Nr. 13, Jul–Oct 1942," *AOK 6, 23948/1a*, in NAM T-312, Roll 1446.

108. Mark, *Death of the Leaping Horseman*, 108.

109. Ibid., 108–109.

110. Moshchansky and Smolinov, "Oborona Stalingrada," 36, provides a detailed breakdown of the front's tank strength by type and unit as of 31 August.

111. Mark, *Death of the Leaping Horseman*, 111.

112. Ziemke and Bauer, *Moscow to Stalingrad*, 388–391; and Carell, *Stalingrad*, 129–131.

113. Rokossovsky, *Velikaia pobeda na Volge*, 133.

114. Rokossovsky, *Velikaia pobeda na Volge*, 153.

115. Hayward, *Stopped at Stalingrad*, 187–189.

116. Von Hardesty, *Red Phoenix: The Rise of Soviet Air Power, 1941–1945* (Washington, DC: Smithsonian Press, 1982), 91–93.

117. See detailed reports on the German bombing raids, in Zhilin, *Stalingradskaia bitva*, 469–470, 474, and 481.

118. Rokossovsky, *Velikaia pobeda na Volge*, 122.

119. Pliev, who was born in 1903, joined the Red Army in 1922 and graduated from the Leningrad Cavalry School in 1926, the Frunze Academy in 1933, and the General Staff Academy in 1941. After serving on the faculty of the Krasnodar Cavalry School from 1926 to 1930, he was chief of operations of 5th Cavalry Division and an adviser to the Mongolian People's Army from 1936 to 1938. Pliev then commanded a regiment in 6th Cavalry Division during the invasion of eastern Poland in September 1939. During Operation Barbarossa, Pliev led Western Front's 50th Cavalry Division on audacious raids into German Army Group Center's rear during the battle for Smolensk in August 1941 and then figured prominently in the defense of Moscow in fall 1941, for which his division was awarded with the honorific designation of 3rd Guards. Elevated to command 2nd Guards Cavalry Corps in December 1941, Pliev led this corps during the winter campaign of 1941–1942, 5th Guards Cavalry Corps from April to July 1942, 3rd Guards Cavalry Corps from July 1942 through November 1943, and 4th Guards Cavalry Corps from November 1943 through November 1944. During this extended period, his corps played a prominent role in the battle for Stalingrad and subsequent offensive operations in the Donbas region, eastern Ukraine, Romania, and Hungary. Pliev then led 1st Guards Cavalry-Mechanized Group during the conquest of Hungary and Austria in 1944–1945, twice receiving the honorific title Hero of the Soviet Union. Pliev capped his wartime career by forming and leading Trans-Baikal Front's Soviet-Mongolian Cavalry-Mechanized Group during the Manchurian offensive of August–September 1945. After the war, Pliev commanded the Southern Group of Forces' 9th Mechanized Army in 1945–1946, 13th and 4th Armies from 1947 to 1955, and, as a full army general, the North Caucasus Military District from 1958 to 1968. During this period, he also commanded the Group of Soviet Forces Cuba from 1960 to 1962, playing a key role in the missile crisis. Pliev, arguably the Soviet Union's most famous cavalry general, retired in 1968 and died in 1979. For further details, see Pliev's many books and memoirs and *VE* 6: 410.

120. "Ia, Lagenkarten Nr. 1 zum KTB Nr. 13, Jul–Oct 1942," *AOK 6*, 23948/1a, in NAM T-312, Roll 1446.

121. Zhilin, *Stalingradskaia bitva*, 400.

122. Ibid., 411.

123. Rokossovsky, *Velikaia pobeda na Volge*, 129.

124. Zhilin, *Stalingradskaia bitva*, 422.

125. Ibid., 433.

126. Ibid., 442–443.

127. Rokossovsky, *Velikaia pobeda na Volge*, 129.

128. Halder, *The Halder War Diary*, 661–662.

129. Ibid., 663.

130. Rokossovsky, *Velikaia pobeda na Volge*, 122.

131. "Ia, Lagenkarten Nr. 1 zum KTB Nr. 13, Jul–Oct 1942," *AOK 6*, 23948/1a, in NAM T-312, Roll 1446. See also Rolf Stoves, *Die 22. Panzer-Division, Die 25. Panzer-Division, Die 27. Panzer-Division, und die Die 233. Reserve-Panzer-Division* (Friedberg, Germany: Podzun-Pallas-Verlag, 1985), 34–35.

132. For day-by-day details on the progress of this battle, see Zhilin, *Stalingradskaia bitva*, 411, 417, 427, 433, and 438; and Moskalenko, *Na iugo-zapadnom napravlenii*, 1; 303–307.

133. Zhilin, *Stalingradskaia bitva*, 421.

134. Schröter, *Stalingrad*, 33.

Chapter 9: The Struggle on the Flanks, 25 July–11 September 1942

1. For details on German plans and operations, see Ziemke and Bauer, *Moscow to Stalingrad*, 367; Wilhelm Tieke, *The Caucasus and the Oil: The German-Soviet War in the Caucasus 1942/43*, trans. Joseph G. Welsh (Winnipeg: J. J. Fedorowicz, 1995). The order of battle of German forces is found in "Lagenkarten. Anlage 9 zum Kriegstagebuch Nr. 3, AOK 17, Ia., 31 Jul–13 Aug 1942," *AOK 17. 24411/19*, in NAM T-312, Roll 696; and "Ia, Lagenkarten Pz AOK 1, 1–31 Aug 1942," *Pz AOK 1, 24906/14*, in NAM T-313, Roll 36.

2. *SVIMVOV* 18, 265; and Trevor-Roper, *Blitzkrieg to Defeat*, 130.

3. Erickson, *The Road to Stalingrad*, 378.

4. Zolotarev, *VOV*, 1: 370. According to A. A. Grechko, *Bitva za Kavkaz* [The battle for the Caucasus] (Moscow: Voenizdat, 1973), 53–54, on 25 July the strength of the Southern Front's armies were as follows: 51st Army—4 rifle divisions and 1 cavalry division, with 40,000 men; 37th Army—17,000 men; 12th Army—3 rifle divisions, with 17,000 men; 18th Army—3 rifle divisions and 1 rifle brigade, with 20,000 men; 56th Army—5 rifle divisions and 3 rifle brigades, with 18,000 men. See the larger figures in Krivosheev, *Grif sekretnosti sniat*, 180.

5. Born in 1895, Kirichenko served as a junior officer in the Russian Army during World War I, joined the Red Army in 1918, and commanded a cavalry regiment and brigade on the southern front during the Civil War. A graduate of two Red Army command courses in the 1920s and the army's Motorization and Mechanization Academy in 1934, Kirichenko commanded a cavalry brigade in the late 1920s, served in the General Staff's Intelligence Directorate for four years during the 1930s, and commanded a rifle division and 26th Mechanized Corps from 1938 to 1941. After the Barbarossa invasion, Kirichenko's corps fought in the Vitebsk and Smolensk regions until its dissolution in August 1941. Thereafter, Kirichenko commanded 38th Separate Cavalry Division and North Caucasus Front's 17th Cavalry Corps during the winter of 1941–1942 and throughout Operation Blau, when his corps earned the designation of 4th Guards Cavalry for its solid performance against Kleist's First Panzer Army. Kirichenko commanded 51st and 12th Armies briefly during the latter stages of Blau and, once again, 4th Guards Cavalry Corps during the Red Army's counteroffensive in the Caucasus region and subsequent offensive operations in the Donbas region in 1943–1944. Appointed chief of the Red Army's Higher Cavalry School in November 1944, Kirichenko remained in this post until 1946, retired in 1949, and died in 1973. For further details, see *Komandarmy. Voennyi biograficheskii slovar'*, 90–92.

6. Track the movements of First Panzer Army's forces from 25 July to 1 August in "Feindlagenkarten, Pz AOK Ic, 29 Jun–31 Jul 1992," *Pz AOK 1, 24906/24*, in NAM T-313, Roll 38; "Ia, Lagenkarten Pz AOK 1, 1–31 Aug 1942," *Pz AOK 1, 24906/14*, in NAM T-313, Roll 36; and Tieke, *The Caucasus and the Oil*, 29–35.

7. The 51st Army employed 138th, 91st, and 157th Rifle Divisions in its counterattack at Tsimlianskaia. See Sarkis'ian, *51-ia Armiia*, 75.

8. For details see, Hans-Joachim Jung, *The History of Panzerregiment Grossdeutschland*, trans. David Johnson (Winnipeg: J. J. Fedorowicz, 2000), 20.

9. Tieke, *The Caucasus and the Oil*, 29–32.

10. Ibid., 34; and Sarkis'ian, *51-ia Armiia*, 77–78.

11. Born in 1898, Pogrebov joined the Red Army in 1918 and commanded a machine-gun group and cavalry regiment on the southern front during the Civil War. A 1927 graduate of the Red Army's Cavalry School and the Frunze Academy in 1938, Pogrebov commanded a cavalry brigade and division in the 1920s and 1930s. After Operation Barbarossa began, Pogrebov commanded the air forces of the Reserve Front's 24th Army during the battle for Smolensk in July–August 1941 and served as chief of the Red Army Air Force Academy's command cadre faculty throughout the fall of 1941. Appointed to lead 61st Army's 7th Cavalry Corps in December 1941, Pogrebov spearheaded Briansk Front's counteroffensive in the Orel region during the winter offensive of 1941–1942. Pogrebov led North Caucasus Front's separate cavalry corps before his death during Operation Blau. For further details, see *Komkory. Voennyi biograficheskii slovar', v 2-kh tomakh* [Corps commanders—A military-biographical dictionary, in two volumes] (Moscow: Kuchkovo Pole, 2006), 2: 80–81.

12. Carell, *Stalingrad*, 85–86; Haupt, *Army Group South*, 187; and Sarkis'ian, *51-ia Armiia*, 77–78. Although Carell claims that a "Russian tank corps" tried to ambush 23rd Panzer Division, 51st Army's 135th and 155th Tank Brigades caused much of the damage to the panzer division.

13. See "Lagenkarten. Anlage 9 zum Kriegstagebuch Nr. 3, AOK 17, Ia., 31 Jul–13 Aug 1942," *AOK 17. 24411/19*, in NAM T-312, Roll 696.

14. Tieke, *The Caucasus and the Oil*, 23–24.

15. Grechko, *Bitva za Kavkaz*, 60.

16. Ibid., 76–77.

17. See the full conversation in Zolotarev, "*Stavka 1942*," 329. Born in 1897, Tikhomirov, before becoming Vasilevsky's deputy, had served as chief of staff of 47th Rifle Corps and Northwestern Front's 34th Army and commanded a rifle regiment and brigade during Operation Barbarossa. In the wake of Operation Blau, he led 93rd Guards Rifle Division from April 1943 until his death from illness in January 1944.

18. Born in 1902, Kotov joined the Red Army in 1919 and rose to head a machine-gun command on the southern front during the Civil War. A graduate of the Moscow Machine Gun Course in 1921, Kotov also graduated from a command cadre course in 1927 and the Frunze Academy in 1936. After commanding a company and battalion in the 1920s, he became deputy chief of staff of Far Eastern Front in 1938 and its chief of operations during the battle with Japanese forces at Khalkhin-Gol in August and September 1939 and chief of staff of Northwestern Front's 8th Army during the Finnish War in 1939–1940. When Operation Barbarossa began, Kotov was teaching at the Frunze Academy. Before assuming command of 47th Army in May 1942, Kotov commanded 163rd Rifle Division throughout Operation Barbarossa and served as chief of staff of Crimean Front's 51st Army during its disaster at Kerch' in May 1942. Replaced by General Malinovsky as commander of 47th Army in September 1942, Kotov led Trans-Caucasus Front's 44th Army during the defense of the Caucasus region in fall 1942 but was severely wounded in the fighting along the Terek River in December. After recovering from his

wounds, Kotov served as deputy commander of 58th and 46th Armies from January to December 1943 and led 37th and 57th Armies' 6th Guards Rifle Corps from December 1943 to November 1944. Tragically, after leading his corps in most of the Red Army's most famous offensives in Ukraine and Romania, Kotov perished on 7 November 1944 when his headquarters was bombed by U.S. aircraft in the region southwest of Belgrade, Yugoslavia. For further details, see *Komandarmy. Voennyi biograficheskii slovar'*, 109–110; and, regarding the circumstances of his death, A. A. Maslov and David M. Glantz, "How and Why Did the Americans Kill Soviet General Kotov?" *JSMS* 11, 2 (June 1998): 142–171.

Shapovalov, who was born in 1898, served as a cavalryman in the tsar's famous 9th Cavalry Division during World War I and rose to command a cavalry squadron in Budenny's 1st Cavalry Army during the Russian Civil War and the Polish War of 1920. A 1919 graduate of the Moscow Cavalry School, the Higher School for Senior Command Cadre in Khar'kov in 1922, the Higher Military-Chemical School in Moscow in 1928, and the Frunze Academy in 1941, Shapovalov headed chemical subunits in the 651st Cavalry Regiment and Colonel G. K. Zhukov's 9th Crimean Cavalry Division before becoming chief of the Vladivostok Fortified Region's chemical service in 1937. Arrested in the fall of 1937 for being a member of an "anti–Soviet military fascist plot," Shapovalov spent eight months in an NKVD prison before being released and appointed, first as chief of the Sevastopol' Artillery School in 1938, and then as a student at the Frunze Academy in 1941. Upon graduation, Shapovalov commanded 45th Army's 320th Rifle Division in the Crimea from August 1941 to June 1942 and then headed the 1st Guards Rifle Corps from July to August 1942. He was captured in early August by the German 16th Motorized Division during the fight for Armavir. In captivity, Shapovalov cooperated with the German *Abwehr* by serving as chief of the operations department of its Special Headquarters (Sonderstab) "R" in Warsaw, Poland, in 1943 and by serving as commandant of a special camp for Red Army prisoners of war in Torun', Poland, in 1944. Beginning in December 1944, Shapovalov assisted General A. A. Vlasov, former commander of Soviet 2nd Shock Army, in organizing the Russian Liberation Army, which consisted of former Red Army POWs in Hitler's service, and commanded the army's 3rd Infantry Division in 1945. Shapovalov was killed by Czech partisans on 8 May 1945. For additional details, see *Komkory. Voennyi biograficheskii slovar'*, 1: 623–624; and Maslov, *Captured Soviet Generals*, 192–196.

19. See North Caucasus Front report no. 4198, dated 0751 hours 27 July 1942, in Zolotarev, "*Stavka* 1942," 530–532.

20. See *Stavka* directive no. 170534, dated 0245 hours 28 July 1942, in ibid., 330.

21. See *Stavka* directive no. 156400, dated 1730 hours 29 July 1942, which approved Budenny's decision to create the two operational groups, in ibid., 332.

22. Born in 1894, Cherevichenko served in the tsar's army during World War I, joined the Red Army in 1918, and fought as a junior cavalry officer during the Civil War. Graduating from the Leningrad Cavalry School in 1924 and the Lenin Political-Military Academy in 1931 and Frunze Academy in 1935, Cherevichenko commanded a cavalry regiment and division during the 1920s, 3rd Cavalry Corps during the 1930s, and the Odessa Military District on the eve of Operation Barbarossa. Assigned command of Southern Front's 9th Army shortly after war began, Cherevichenko skillfully orchestrated his army's fighting withdrawal eastward across Ukraine during the summer of 1941, avoiding encirclement and destruction on several occasions. After Southwestern Front and its 21st, 5th, 6th, 37th, and 26th Armies were destroyed in the disastrous Kiev encirclement

in September 1941, the *Stavka* selected Cherevichenko to command a new 21st Army, which halted the German advance east of Belgorod in October. Assigned command of Southern Front in late October, Cherevichenko planned and conducted the successful counteroffensive at Rostov in November and December 1941 before receiving command of Briansk Front in late December. However, after his forces failed to defeat Second Panzer Army in the Orel region during the Red Army's offensive in the winter of 1941–1942, the *Stavka* assigned Cherevichenko as deputy commander of the Crimean and North Caucasus Fronts throughout the spring of 1942 and most of Operation Blau. After the German defeat at Stalingrad, Cherevichenko commanded the Khar'kov Military District in 1943 and 1944 but returned to the field to lead 3rd Shock Army's 7th Rifle Corps during the climactic assault on Berlin in April 1945. After war's end, Cherevichenko commanded a rifle corps in the Soviet Group of Occupation Forces in Germany until 1948, served as deputy commander of the Tavria Military District until his retirement in 1950, and died in 1976. For additional information, see *Komandarmy. Voennyi biograficheskii slovar'*, 252–253.

23. For details on Red Army operations, see A. A. Grechko, *Bitva za Kavkaz* [The battle for the Caucasus] (Moscow: Voenizdat, 1973). Relevant documents are in V. A. Shapovalov, ed., *Bitva za Kavkaz v dokumentakh i materialov* [The battle for the Caucasus in documents and materials] (Stavropol': Stavropol' State University, 2003).

24. See *Stavka* directive no. 156400, dated 1730 hours 29 July 1942, in Zolotarev, "*Stavka* 1942," 332.

25. *VE*, 8: 163.

26. See *Stavka* directive no. 170536, dated 0417 hours 30 July 1942, in Zolotarev, "*Stavka* 1942," 333–334.

27. See *Stavka* directive no. 994139, dated 0305 hours 31 July 1942, in ibid., 336.

28. The 5th, 6th, 7th, and 9th Brigades were dispatched from Moscow to Ordzhonikidze and Makhachkala, 10th Brigade was formed from 4th Reserve Airborne Brigade in Ordzhonikidze, and 11th Brigade was formed from 4th Maneuver Airborne Brigade in Groznyi.

29. Born in 1899, Zamertsev joined the Red Army in 1920, graduated from several command cadre courses, and commanded at platoon, company, and battalion levels during the 1920s and 1930s. He led the famous 51st Perekop Rifle Division's 287th Regiment during the Finnish War in 1939–1940 and 81st Fortified Region during the 18 months preceding Operation Barbarossa. Assigned to command the Odessa Military District's 255th Rifle Division shortly after the German invasion, he led this division during the fighting withdrawal of Southern Front's 6th Army across Ukraine in the summer and fall of 1941 and during the successful Barvenkovo-Lozovaia offensive in the winter of 1941–1942. After escaping from the Khar'kov encirclement in May 1942, Zamertsev led 3rd (later 10th Guards) Rifle Corps during North Caucasus Front's defensive operations in late summer 1942. Although relieved from command in September 1942 for "failing to accomplish his assigned missions," Zamertsev was restored to corps command a month later and, thereafter, led 9th and 11th Rifle Corps during Southwestern (3rd Ukrainian) Front's successful offensives in Ukraine and Romania in 1943 and early 1944. Once again removed from corps command in April 1944 "for cause," Zamertsev led 8th Guards Army's 57th Guards Rifle Division during 1st Belorussian Front's Vistula-Oder offensive in January 1945 and its assault on Berlin in April 1945. After war's end, Zamertsev commanded 57th Guards Rifle, 19th Guards Mechanized, and 88th Guards Rifle Divisions

from 1945 to 1947, graduated from the Voroshilov Academy in 1948, and served as deputy commander of 14th and 15th Armies and commander of 15th Army and the Turkestan Military District before his retirement in 1969; he died in 1981. For further details, see *Komkory. Voennyi biograficheskii slovar'*, 1: 212–214.

Koroteev, who at age 38 was appointed to command 55th Rifle Corps in March 1941 and 12th Army in October 1941, was one of the youngest generals in the Red Army to command a corps and army. Born in 1903, Koroteev served as a private in the Russian Army during World War I, joined the Red Army in 1918, and commanded a platoon and company during the Civil War. After attending several tactical level schools in the 1920s, Koroteev graduated from the *"Vystrel'"* Officers Course in 1926 and commanded 27th Rifle Division during the invasion of eastern Poland in September 1939 and the Finnish War in 1939–1940. Appointed commander of the Kiev Special Military District's 55th Rifle Corps in March 1941 after it was assigned to 18th Army, he led his division during Southern Front's harrowing withdrawal across Ukraine in summer 1941. After serving as chief of 18th Army's rear, Koroteev was appointed commander of Southern Front's 12th Army, which he led during the *front*'s successful counteroffensive at Rostov in November and December 1941, and then became the *front*'s deputy commander. During the defense of the Caucasus region in late summer and fall 1942, Koroteev commanded, in succession, 9th Army's 11th Guards Rifle Corps during August and September and 9th Army during the Trans-Caucasus Front's successful defense of Ordzhonikidze in October and November. Thereafter, Koroteev commanded 18th, 9th, 37th, and 52nd Armies to war's end, participating in the Red Army's victories in Ukraine, Romania, Poland, Germany, and Czechoslovakia. A Hero of the Soviet Union by war's end, after the war Koroteev commanded an army, graduated from the Voroshilov Academy in 1947, commanded the Trans-Baikal Military District through 1951, and served as deputy commander of the North Caucasus Military District until his death in 1953. For additional details, see *Komandarmy. Voennyi biograficheskii slovar'*, 104–105.

30. Grechko, *Bitva za Kavkaz*, 61.

31. *Geschichte der 3. Panzer-Division, Berlin–Brandenburg 1935–1945* (Berlin: Verlag der Buchhandlung Gunter Richter, 1947), 308.

32. For details on this fighting from the German perspective, see Tieke, *The Caucasus and the Oil*, 34–36.

33. Ibid., 37; "Feindlagenkarten, PzAOK Ic, 29 Jun–31 Jul 1992," *PzAOK 1, 24906/24*, in NAM T-313, Roll 38; and "Ia, Lagenkarten Pz AOK 1, 1–31 Aug 1942," *PzAOK 1, 24906/14*, in NAM T-313, Roll 36.

34. For details of 17th Cavalry Corps' and 18th Army's defenses, see Grechko, *Bitva za Kavkaz*, 78.

35. See also Ziemke and Bauer, *Moscow to Stalingrad*, 367–371; Haupt, *Army Group South*, 182–183; and Blau, *The German Campaign in Russia*, 158–161.

36. As of early July, the tank strengths of First Panzer Army's panzer and motorized divisions were as follows: 3rd Panzer Division—164 tanks, 13th Panzer Division—103 tanks, 23rd Panzer Division—138 tanks, 16th Motorized Division—53 tanks, SS "Viking" Motorized Division—53 tanks, and the Slovak Mobile Division—53 tanks, for a total of about 550 tanks. However, about 100 of these tanks were Pz. II models and command tanks, and attrition since mid-July had reduced this total to about 350 tanks. See Maksim Kolomiets and Il'ia Moshchansky, "Oborona Kavkaza, iiul'–dekabr' 1942 goda" [Defense of the Caucasus, July–December 1942], in *Frontovaia illiustratsiia*, 2–2002 [Front illus-

trated, 2–2002] (Moscow: OOO "Strategiia KM," 2002), 8. Jentz, *Panzertruppen*, 251, provides the strength of 13th Panzer Division, which decreased from a high of 129 tanks on 29 July to 80 on 26 September 1942.

37. *Boevoi sostav Sovetskoi armii*, 2: 150–151; and Grechko, *Bitva za Kavkaz*, 67–68.

38. Zhukov, *Reminiscences and Reflections*, 2: 81; Ziemke and Bauer, *Moscow to Stalingrad*, 367–370; and Erickson, *The Road to Stalingrad*, 377.

39. Born in 1898, Sergatskov served as a noncommissioned officer during World War I, joined the Red Army in 1918, and fought extensively as a detachment, battalion, and regimental commander during the Civil War. Graduating from the *"Vystrel'"* Officers Course in 1927 and the Voroshilov Academy in 1941, Sergatskov commanded the Trans-Baikal Military District's 94th, 40th, and 57th Rifle Divisions and taught at the Frunze and Voroshilov Academies in the late 1930s and led the Baltic Special Military District's 63rd Rifle Corps in 1939–1940. After serving as chief of Rear Services in the Reserve Front's 28th Army and Kalinin Front's 30th Army during the winter of 1941–1942, Sergatskov was assigned command of Trans-Caucasus Front's 46th Army in April 1942 and led his army during the defense of the Caucasus until relieved in late August, a victim of one of Stalin's political henchmen, Lavrenti Beriia. Although reduced to command 37th Army's 351st Rifle Division, Sergatskov redeemed himself and was assigned command of 47th Army's 3rd Rifle Corps from January to March 1943, 56th Army's 22nd Rifle Corps from April to October 1943, and 11th Guards Rifle Corps through January 1944, when poor health forced him to give up his field command and become chief of the Frunze Academy's tactics faculty from January 1944 through 1951. Sergatskov ended his military career as adviser to the Albanian People's Army before his retirement in 1961; he died in 1975. For further details, see *Komandarmy. Voennyi biograficheskii slovar'*, 209–210.

40. Born in 1896, Remezov joined the Red Army in 1918 and commanded a company and battalion during the Civil War. A 1932 graduate of the Frunze Academy, Remezov commanded a rifle regiment in 1931, 45th Rifle Division in 1937, the Zhitomir Army Group during the Czech crisis in 1938, and the Trans-Baikal and Orel Military Districts from July 1939 to the outbreak of war in June 1941. Appointed to command Western Front's 13th Army in early July 1941, Remezov led his army during the heavy fighting along the Dnepr River in July and in the Smolensk region during August. Dispatched in early September to command the North Caucasus Military District, Remezov was instrumental in mobilizing and training fresh divisions and brigades for the Red Army, including 56th Army, which he commanded in October 1941 and led to victory in the Rostov counteroffensive in November 1941 and the winter offensive of 1941–1942. Appointed to command the Southern Ural Military District in early 1942, Remezov once again proved effective in raising and training new Red Army formations. As commander of Trans-Caucasus Front's 45th Army from April 1942 through war's end, Remezov performed the vital mission of protecting the Soviet Union's borders with Turkey and Iran and ensuring that Lend-Lease routes through Iran remained open. Remezov completed his military career as a faculty head at the Frunze Academy, deputy chief of the Dzerzhinsky Military Academy, and deputy commander of the Moscow Military District before his retirement in 1959; he died in 1990. For further details, see *Komandarmy, Voennyi biograficheskii slovar'*, 190–191.

41. Born in 1903, Leselidze, a Georgian by nationality, joined the Red Army in 1921 and graduated from the Georgian Military School in 1922, the Tiflis Artillery School in 1925, and the Command Cadre Improvement Course in 1929. After playing a prominent

role in the consolidation of Soviet power in Georgia during the early 1920s, Leselidze served in a variety of artillery assignments at regimental and division levels before becoming chief of a rifle corps' artillery in the Belorussian Special Military District in February 1941. After the Barbarossa invasion, he served as chief of 2nd Rifle Corps' artillery and then chief of 50th Army's artillery during the defense of Tula in November 1941 and the Red Army counteroffensive at Moscow from December 1941 through April 1942. Appointed commander of 47th Army's 3rd Rifle Corps in July 1942, Leselidze's outstanding performance in the defense of the High Caucasus Mountains earned him command of, first, 47th Army, which he led during the winter campaign of 1942–1943, and, later, 18th Army, which spearheaded 1st Ukrainian Front's offensives in the Ukraine during late 1943 and 1944. Wounded during the later stages of the Zhitomir–Berdichev offensive, Leselidze, arguably one of the most famous and talented Georgian officers in the Red Army, died on 21 February 1944 and was posthumously designated as a Hero of the Soviet Union. For additional details, see *Komandarmy, Voennyi biograficheskii slovar'*, 128–129.

42. Shukman, *Stalin's Generals*, 64–65, 119–120; and Erickson, *The Road to Stalingrad*, 378–379.

43. Track Army Group A's daily progress in "Lagenkarten. Anlage 9 zum Kriegstagebuch Nr. 3, AOK 17, Ia., 31 Jul–13 Aug 1942," *AOK 17. 24411/19*, in NAM T-312, Roll 696; and "Ia, Lagenkarten Pz AOK 1, 1–31 Aug 1942," *PzAOK 1, 24906/14*, in NAM T-313, Roll 36.

44. Tieke, *The Caucasus and the Oil*, 27–28, 83.

45. See Zolotarev, "*Stavka* 1942," 533.

46. See *Stavka* directive no. 170544, dated 1630 hours 1 August 1942, in ibid., 338.

47. See *Stavka* directive no. 170548, dated 1705 hours 3 August 1942, in ibid., 340.

48. Grechko, *Bitva za Kavkaz*, 80.

49. See *Stavka* directive no. 170553, dated 0445 hours 5 August 1942, in Zolotarev, "*Stavka* 1942," 344. See Tiulenev's report no. 587/op to the chief of the General Staff on 4 August noting the German success and proposing to reinforce the defenses in the Caucasus Mountains, in Shapovalov, *Bitva za Kavkaz v dokumentakh*, 135–136. See the conversation between the deputy chief of the General Staff and the chief of staff of the Trans-Caucasus Front regarding the *Stavka*'s 5 August order, in ibid., 138–139.

50. See *Stavka* directive no. 170555, dated 0445 hours 5 August 1942, in Zolotarev, "*Stavka* 1942," 344. The 66th Army was to include 271st, 276th, 317th, 319th, 320th, 328th, 337th, and 351st Rifle Divisions, raised in Makhachkala, Derbent, and Baku.

51. See *Stavka* directives no. 170551 and 170552, dated 0600 and 0615 hours 5 August 1942, in ibid., 346–347.

52. Born in 1900, Timofeev joined the Red Army in 1918 and commanded a cavalry squadron and regiment during the Civil War. Graduating from the Frunze Academy in 1934 and the Voroshilov Academy's command course in 1939, Timofeev commanded 25th Cavalry Division's 98th Regiment in 1937, 12th Cavalry Division in 1939, and the North Caucasus Military District's 103rd Motorized Division from March 1941 through the outbreak of war in June. During Operation Barbarossa, Timofeev's motorized division fought under the Reserve Front's 24th Army during its defense of Smolensk in July 1941, after which the NKO assigned Timofeev command of Leningrad Front's 27th Separate Cavalry Division, which took part in the defense of Tikhvin in October. Although relieved of command for "failing to fulfill his assigned mission," Timofeev redeemed himself by com-

manding a grenadier brigade with distinction during the fighting along the Volkhov River in the winter of 1941–1942. Assigned command of the Kalinin Front's 11th Cavalry Corps in January 1942, Timofeev led it on its spectacular five-month raid into German Army Group Center's rear area north of Viaz'ma. However, when the ever-feisty Timofeev criticized his *front* commander, Konev, for unnecessarily "wasting" his cavalry corps on senseless missions, the NKO relieved Timofeev of command in May 1942, instead assigning him as inspector-general of Trans-Caucasus Front's cavalry, a post he occupied to March 1944. Thereafter, Timofeev served as deputy commander of 15th Cavalry Corps in Iran but returned to field command in March 1945 as deputy commander of the famous 4th Guards Kuban' Cossack Cavalry Corps, which spearheaded 2nd Ukrainian Front's offensive in western Hungary and Czechoslovakia in March and April 1945. Restored to corps command, Timofeev led 4th Guards Cavalry during the Prague offensive in May 1945. Ever challenging his superiors, Timofeev spent the postwar years as military commissar of the Ul'ianovo and Voronezh Military Commissariats before retiring in 1951; he died in 1954. For further details, see *Komkory. Voennyi–biograficheskii slovar'*, 2: 88–89.

53. Unlike most of his counterpart army commanders, Maslennikov was among those senior Red Army generals who emerged from the ranks of the NKVD. Born in 1900, Maslennikov joined the Red Army in 1918 and commanded a cavalry squadron and brigade during the Civil War. Educated at the Red Army's Novocherkassk Cavalry School in 1926 and the Frunze Academy in 1935, Maslennikov transferred to the NKVD's border guards' forces in 1928. He commanded a border guards' cavalry regiment in the late 1920s, served as chief of training for NKVD Security Forces in the Georgian, Azerbaijan, and Belorussian Republics during the 1930s, and became Deputy People's Commissar for Internal Affairs (NKVD) in 1939. Assigned to field duty along with many other NKVD officers shortly after the German invasion, Maslennikov commanded Western Front's 29th Army during the battle for Smolensk in July–August 1941, defended the Kalinin region in October and November 1941, and, assigned command of 39th Army in December, led it during the Western and Kalinin Front's counteroffensive at Moscow in December and the ensuing winter campaign in 1941–1942. After Maslennikov recovered from wounds he received when his army was encircled and nearly destroyed by the Germans in July 1942, the *Stavka* in August appointed him commander of Trans-Caucasus Front's Northern Group of Forces, which defended the Mozdok and Ordzhonikidze regions in the fall and conducted a counteroffensive in the Caucasus region in December. After the Northern Group was reorganized into a new North Caucasus Front under Maslennikov's command in late January 1942, it liberated the Krasnodar regions and isolated German forces in the Taman' region. Thereafter, Maslennikov, who had earned a reputation as a superb organizer and resolute fighter, served as deputy commander of Volkhov and Southwestern (3rd Ukrainian) Fronts from May through December 1943, commander of Leningrad Front's 42nd Army from December 1943 through March 1944, and commander of 3rd Baltic Front to May 1945. He capped his military career by serving as deputy commander of Vasilevsky's Far Eastern Command during the Manchurian offensive in August–September 1945. After war's end, Maslennikov commanded the Baku and Trans-Caucasus Military Districts from 1945 to 1947, where he helped quash rebellions among the civil population, and served as a senior commander of USSR's Internal Security Forces through 1954. Suffering from an incurable illness, Maslennikov committed suicide in April 1954. For further details, see *Komandarmy, Voennyi biograficheskii slovar'*, 146–147.

Born in 1894, Khadeev served as a junior officer in the Russian Army during World

War I, joined the Red Guards in 1917 and Red Army in 1918, fought in the Civil War, and took part in suppressing the Kronshtadt mutiny against Lenin's Bolshevik government in 1921. Graduating from the Higher Military–Pedagogical School in 1922 and the Frunze Academy in 1929, Khadeev led at every level from platoon to corps during the interwar years, including command of 138th Rifle Division during the Finnish War in 1939–1940 and the Trans-Caucasus Military District's 40th Rifle Corps from March 1941 to the outbreak of the war. After Khadeev's corps spent the first few months of the war securing the Iranian border, the *Stavka* reorganized it into 44th Army in August 1941 and assigned it first to the Trans-Caucasus Front and, in October 1941, to the North Caucasus region. Assigned to Trans-Caucasus Front's Northern Group of Forces in December 1941 and now under Khadeev's command, 46th Army was responsible for defending the central portion of the High Caucasus Mountains. However, because of Khadeev's deteriorating health, in April 1942 the NKO assigned him as deputy commander of Trans-Caucasus Front for the Formation of Forces, a position he occupied throughout the remainder of the war. After war's end Khadeev served briefly as commander of the Tbilisi Military District but retired in late 1945; he died in 1957. For further details, see *Komandarmy. Voennyi biograficheskii slovar'*, 239.

54. Ibid., 350–351. See also *Stavka* directive no. 994147, dated 0028 hours 8 August 1942, in ibid., 352. Because he fell ill, Khadeev commanded 9th Army only briefly and was soon replaced by Major General Martsenkevich.

55. Grechko, *Bitva za Kavkaz*, 74. The detachments included the Rostov Artillery, Poltava Tractor, Novocherkassk Cavalry, and Ordzhonikidze Infantry Schools, motorized rifle and mortar battalions formed from officers assigned to the "*Vystrel*'" Officers Course, 12th Motorized Rifle Training Regiment, and 36th and 41st Armored Train Battalions, with a total of four armored trains.

56. Piatigorsk was defended by 11th NKVD Rifle Division's 26th Border Guards Regiment. See the report by the chief of staff of Trans-Caucasus Front to the deputy chief of the General Staff concerning the fall of Prokhladnyi in Shapovalov, *Bitva za Kavkaz v dokumentakh*, 140.

57. Mackensen, *Vom Bug zum Kaukasus*, 91–93; Carell, *Stalingrad*, 83–85; Hayward, *Stopped at Stalingrad*, 157–159; and Ziemke and Bauer, *Moscow to Stalingrad*, 370. For a Soviet description of the deliberate destruction, see Grechko, *Bitva za Kavkaz*, 85.

58. To track First Panzer Army's movements in this period, see "Ia, Lagenkarten Pz AOK 1, 1–31 Aug 1942," *PzAOK 1, 24906/14*, in NAM T-313, Roll 36; and Tieke, *The Caucasus and the Oil*, 50–65.

59. Grechko, *Bitva za Kavkaz*, 85.

60. See *Stavka* directive no. 170564, dated 1955 hours 10 August 1942, in Zolotarev, "*Stavka* 1942," 357.

61. See *Stavka* directive no. 170565, dated 11 August 1942, in ibid., 358.

62. See "A report by the commander of the Trans-Caucasus Front to the deputy chief of the General Staff," dated 12 August 1942, in Shapovalov, *Bitva za Kavkaz v dokumentakh*, 141. Born in 1895, Kurdiumov fought as a battalion commander during World War I, joined the Red Army in 1918, and commanded a battalion and brigade in the Civil War. A 1925 graduate of the Frunze Academy, Kurdiumov served as military attaché to Estonia and Lithuania in 1929 and 1930 and commanded the famous 25th Chapaev Rifle Division in the early 1930s and the Leningrad Military District's 1st Rifle Corps in 1935–1936. After serving as deputy chief and chief of Red Army Combat Training from 1937 to 1939,

Kurdiumov became deputy commander of 8th Army and commander of 15th Army during the Finnish War of 1939–1940. On the eve of Operation Barbarossa, Kurdiumov was the Western Special Military District's assistant commander for logistics, a post he held until November 1941. In recognition of his organizational talents, the *Stavka* in November 1941 appointed Kurdiumov commander of the Southern Ural and North Caucasus Military Districts and, when the Germans invaded the Caucasus region in August 1942, deputy commander of the Trans-Caucasus Front for the Formation and Filling Out of Forces. Thereafter, Kurdiumov occupied similar posts in the North Caucasus and Siberian Military Districts to war's end, playing a significant role in the Red Army's mobilization efforts. After the war, Kurdiumov served as commander of the Western Siberian Military District through 1947 and as deputy chief inspector of Soviet ground forces before his retirement in 1957; he died in 1970. For further details, see *Komandarmy, Voennyi biograficheskii slovar'*, 123.

63. See entries from Trans-Caucasus Front's combat journal, dated 13 August 1942, in ibid., 145–146.

64. See the complete message in ibid., 150. See subsequent reports and conversations between the Northern Group of Forces, 8th Sapper Army, and the NKVD from 19 to 23 August concerning the state of the defenses around Groznyi and Ordzhonikidze in ibid., 153–163.

65. These forces included 56th Army's 30th, 339th, and 349th Rifle Divisions and 18th Army's 216th Rifle Division.

66. For details on the fighting in Krasnodar, see Grechko, *Bitva za Kavkaz*, 80–81; and Tieke, *The Caucasus and the Oil*, 83–85.

67. Haupt, *Army Group South*, 185–187; and Carell, *Stalingrad*, 91–93.

68. Born in 1889 in Austria, de Angelis served in artillery assignments during World War I and the interwar years. He then commanded 76th Infantry Division from 1938 through 1941, leading his division during the French campaign of 1940 and all of Operation Barbarossa. While commanding XXXXIV Army Corps from February 1942 to April 1944, he also served briefly as deputy commander of the new Sixth Army created to replace Paulus's Sixth Army, destroyed at Stalingrad. After commanding Sixth Army's successful defense of the Dnestr River line in Romania from April to June 1944, de Angelis led Second Panzer Army during its defense of Yugoslavia and Austria from July 1944 through May 1945. Captured by the Americans shortly after the war ended, de Angelis was extradited to Yugoslavia in 1946 and turned over to the Russians as a prisoner of war. Released from prison camp in 1955, de Angelis returned to Germany, where he died in 1974. On de Angelis, see "Ritterkreuzträger Maximilian de Angelis," from website *Die Generale des Heeres* at http://balsi.de/Homepage-Generale/Heer/Heer-Startseite.htm; and Heiber and Glantz, *Hitler and His Generals*, 1111–1112.

69. For details on the Tuapse operation, see Tieke, *The Caucasus and the Oil*, 68–82; and Grechko, *Bitva za Kavkaz*, 86–88.

70. Grechko, *Bitva za Kavkaz*, 86.

71. Tieke, *The Caucasus and the Oil*, 77.

72. Grechko, *Bitva za Kavkaz*, 86–87.

73. See the complete report in "From report no. 65 by the Military Council of the North Caucasus Front to the Supreme High Commander [Stalin] and deputy chief of the General Staff," dated 13 August 1942, in Shapovalov, *Bitva za Kavkaz v dokumentakh*, 142–144.

74. Ziemke and Bauer, *Moscow to Stalingrad*, 372–375; and on the strategic demand for German forces, see Jukes, *Hitler's Stalingrad Decisions*, 52–54.

75. For German planning, see Tieke, *The Caucasus and the Oil*.

76. Confusion exists over who actually commanded 9th Army during late August 1942. While Soviet and Russian military encyclopedias assert that Major General K. A. Koroteev commanded the army beginning on 1 September, they fail to mention either Khadeev or Martsenkevich as its commanders. Koroteev, who led 11th Guards Rifle Corps until 1 September, assumed command of 9th Army after Martsenkevich's relief.

77. *Boevoi sostav Sovetskoi armii*, 2: 173–174.

78. The 249th Separate Tank Battalion fielded 9 British Mk-111 Valentine and 20 American M-3 tanks, 258th Separate Tank Battalion fielded 8 Valentines and 20 M-3s, and 563rd Separate Tank Brigade fielded 16 Mk-III and 14 M-3 tanks. See Kolomiets and Moshchansky, "Oborona Kavkaza," 19.

79. Grechko, *Bitva za Kavkaz*, 109–110; Kolomiets and Moshchansky, "Oborona Kavkaza," 17–18; and Shtemenko, *Soviet General Staff at War*, bk. 1, 123–124, 127.

80. "Combat order no. 0490/op of the Trans-Caucasus Front," dated 16 August 1942, in Shapovalov, *Bitva za Kavkaz v dokumentakh*, 150–151.

81. Mackensen, *Vom Bug zum Kaukasus*, 96–97.

82. See "Ia, Lagenkarten Pz AOK 1, 1–31 Aug 1942," *PzAOK 1, 24906/14*, in NAM T-313, Roll 36.

83. Grechko, *Bitva za Kavkaz*, 112. For a more complete description of the Northern Group of Forces' defensive plans, see the Northern Group of Forces' operational directives no. 036 and 037, dated 1400 hours 23 August 1942, to its subordinate forces, in Shapovalov, *Bitva za Kavkaz v dokumentakh*, 163–169.

84. Tieke, *The Caucasus and the Oil*, 124.

85. Ibid., 138–142.

86. Ibid.

87. For details on this fighting see Tieke, *The Caucasus and the Oil*, 149–162.

88. Ziemke and Bauer, *Moscow to Stalingrad*, 375; and Carell, *Stalingrad*, 101–109.

89. See *Stavka* directive no. 170580, dated 1347 hours 23 August 1942, in Zolotarev, "*Stavka 1942*," 371–372. See Trans-Caucasus Front's order no. 0137/op, dated 29 August 1942, which criticized Maslennikov's defensive measures along the Terek River, in Shapovalov, *Bitva za Kavkaz v dokumentakh*, 182–183. Born in 1899, Khomenko joined the Red Army in 1918 and served as regimental commander and division commissar during the Civil War. A 1928 graduate of the Frunze Academy, Khomenko commanded a regiment in the struggle against the Basmachi insurgency in central Asia during the early 1920s and a cavalry brigade in the 1930s. After transferring to the NKVD's forces in 1935, Khomenko became chief of staff of NKVD Border and Internal Security Forces in the Leningrad Military District until November 1940, deputy chief of the NKVD's Border Guards' Forces in the Moldavian and Ukrainian Republics from November 1940 through June 1941, and then deputy commander of the Kiev Special Military District for Rear Area Security through the outbreak of war. When the *Stavka* formed its Front of Reserve Armies in early July 1941, it assigned senior NKVD officers, including Khomenko, as command cadre in most of the front's armies. Khomenko commanded 30th Army in Western Front's struggle in the Smolensk region in July and August 1941 and in Kalinin Front's defense of the Rzhev and Kalinin regions during the fall of 1941. As a reward for his army's outstanding performance at Kalinin, Khomenko was appointed deputy commander

of the Moscow Defense Zone by the *Stavka* in December 1941 and commander of the new 24th (later renamed 58th) Army in the Groznyi region in August 1942. Thereafter, Khomenko commanded 58th and 44th Armies throughout the ensuing struggle for the Caucasus and 44th Army as it advanced westward across the Donbas region during Southern Front's offensives in 1943. Khomenko perished on 9 November 1944 when, while pursuing German forces into the Crimea, his vehicular convoy mistakenly wandered into the Germans' rear area and he was struck and killed by German machine gunfire. For further details, see *Komandarmy. Voennyi biograficheskii slovar'*, 246–247. The exact circumstances of Khomenko's death are found in Maslov, *Fallen Soviet Generals*, 114–117. Always suspicious of his generals, Stalin initially presumed that Khomenko had defected to the Germans.

90. The *Stavka* directive creating 58th Army was no. 989233. See Grechko, *Bitva za Kavkaz*, 114; and Kolomiets and Moshchansky, "Oborona Kavkaza," 19.

91. See *Stavka* directive no. 170596, dated 1440 hours 1 September 1942, in Zolotarev, "*Stavka* 1942," 386, and the *Stavka*'s discussion of prospective candidates for command of the new Trans-Caucasus Front with its representative, Beriia, in Shapovalov, *Bitva za Kavkaz v dokumentakh*, 185–186.

92. See *Stavka* directive no. 170598, dated 0250 hours 3 September 1942, in Zolotarev, "*Stavka* 1942," 387. A full copy of Beriia's often acerbic report of the state of the Northern Group of Forces and its armies is in Shapovalov, *Bitva za Kavkaz v dokumentakh*, 189–193. Born in 1920, Roslyi joined the Red Army in 1924 and graduated from the "*Vystrel*'" Officers Course in 1937 and the Frunze Academy in 1939. After commanding a battalion in 1936, Roslyi led 123rd Rifle Division's 245th Regiment during the invasion of eastern Poland in September 1939. During the Finnish War in 1939–1940, Roslyi's division spearheaded the assault by Northwestern Front's 7th Army on the Mannerheim Defense Line and performed so well that the NKO annointed Roslyi with the title of Hero of the Soviet Union. Assigned command of the Trans-Caucasus Military District's 4th Rifle Division in April 1940, Roslyi's forces secured the Turkish border during the first year of the war but were deployed northward to defend the High Caucasus Mountains in August 1942. In recognition of his division's resolute defense, the Trans-Caucasus Front assigned Roslyi, now age 40, to command 9th Army's new 11th Guards Rifle Corps in September 1942. After skillfully leading his corps during the battles for Mozdok and Ordzhonikidze in October and November 1942, Roslyi became deputy commander of 58th Army during the initial phases of Trans-Caucasus Front's counteroffensive and commanded 46th Army during the Krasnodar offensive in the winter of 1942–1943 and 9th Rifle Corps during the offensive to reduce German defenses on the Taman' Peninsula. Subsequently, Roslyi commanded 28th Army's 9th Rifle Corps during the Belorussian offensive in the summer of 1944 and the East Prussian, Berlin, and Prague offensives in 1945. After the war, Roslyi graduated from the Voroshilov Academy in 1948, commanded 16th Guards Rifle Corps until 1957, retired in 1961, and died in 1980. For further details, see *Komandarmy. Voennyi biograficheskii slovar'*, 199–200.

93. Born in 1900, Vershinin joined the Red Army in 1919, fought in the Civil War, and took part in suppressing the Kronshtadt mutiny in 1921. After serving in rifle forces during the 1920s, Vershinin transferred to the fledgling Red Air Forces in 1930, graduated from the Zhukovsky Air Academy in 1932 and the Miasnikov 1st Pilots School in 1935, and became, in succession, assistant chief of the Red Army's Higher Aviation Course for the Improvement of Flight Crews in August 1938 and chief of the school in May 1941.

In the wake of the Barbarossa invasion, Vershinin commanded Southern Front's air forces from September 1941 to May 1942, playing a significant role in supporting the front's counteroffensive at Rostov in November and December 1941 and the ensuing winter campaign in 1941–1942. In command of 4th Air Army from May 1942 to war's end, and also commander of Trans-Caucasus Front's air forces, Vershinin made significant contribution to the front's successful defense of the Caucasus in the fall of 1942 and the offensives it conducted in the winter of 1942–1943 and spring of 1943, when his air forces swept the *Luftwaffe* from the skies over the Kuban' region. After the war, Vershinin became commander of the Soviet Army's Air Forces and Deputy Minister of Defense of the USSR from 1945 through 1969, interrupted by a stint as commander of PVO Strany (National Air Defense) from 1953 to 1957. Arguably one of the Soviet Union's most prominent air force generals, Vershinin retired in 1969 and died in 1973. For further details, see *Komandarmy. Voennyi biograficheskii slovar'*, 367–368.

94. Grechko, *Bitva za Kavkaz*, 115.

95. V. F. Mozolev, "Mozdok–Malgrobekaia operatsiia 1942" [The Mozdok–Malgrobek operation, 1942], in *VE*, 5: 196.

96. Tieke, *The Caucasus and the Oil*, 87.

97. See *Stavka* directive no. 170575, dated 1945 hours 18 August 1942, in Zolotarev, "*Stavka* 1942," 367.

98. Grechko, *Bitva za Kavkaz*, 128–129. See also I. S. Shiian, *Ratnyi podvig Novorossiiska* [Feat of arms at Novorossiisk] (Moscow: Voenizdat, 1977), 35–52, for details on the fighting during August and early September.

99. Grechko, *Bitva za Kavkaz*, 133; and Shiian, *Ratnyi podvig*, 37–38.

100. Grechko, *Bitva za Kavkaz*, 133–134; and Mark Axworthy, Cornel Scafes, and Cristian Craciunoiu, *Third Axis Fourth Ally: The Romanian Armed Forces in the European War, 1941–1945* (London: Arms and Armour, 1995), 82.

101. See details on 126th Separate Tank Battalion's role in this fighting in Kolomiets and Moshchansky, "Oborona Kavkaza," 31. By 22 August the battalion lost 30 of its 36 T-26 light tanks.

102. Shiian, *Ratnyi podvig*, 41–42. For a German perspective, see Tieke, *The Caucasus and the Oil*, 88–89.

103. Shiian, *Ratnyi podvig*, 43. The 255th Naval Rifle Brigade consisted of 14th, 322nd, and 142nd Naval Infantry Battalions.

104. Ibid.; Tieke, *The Caucasus and the Oil*, 88–89. According to Grechko, *Bitva za Kavkaz*, 136, 47th Army's commissar, Brigade Commissar I. P. Abramov, was killed during 77th Rifle Division's counterattacks.

105. For details, see Grechko, *Bitva za Kavkaz*, 137–138.

106. Ibid., 139. According to Grechko, the Azov Flotilla evacuated over 6,000 men to Novorossiisk, later forming them into four naval infantry battalions for the defense of the city.

107. See *Stavka* directive no. 170595, dated 30 August 1942, in Zolotarev, "*Stavka* 1942," 379. This directive also subordinated the Black Sea Fleet to Tiulenev's Trans-Caucasus Front, effective 1 September, and required Budenny to hold Tuapse at all costs.

108. Shiian, *Ratnyi podvig*, 46–47.

109. Ibid., 47. See North Caucasus Front's report no. 0089, dated 2 September 1942, in which Budenny describes the measures he undertook to defend Novorossiisk, in Shapovalov, *Bitva za Kavkaz v dokumentakh*, 193–199.

110. The only Soviet tank unit involved in this fighting was 126th Separate Tank Battalion, with six T-26 and three BT-7 tanks (two in disrepair). See Kolomiets and Moshchansky, "Oborona Kavkaza," 32.

111. See Tieke, *The Caucasus and the Oil*, 95, for details on the final assault. See Shiian, *Ratnyi podvig*, 49–54, and Grechko, *Bitva za Kavkaz*, 142–154, for details on the fighting through 26 September. See Trans-Caucasus Front directive no. 006, dated 1230 hours 6 September 1942, and Beriia's vitriolic report on 47th Army's defense of Novorossiisk, in Shapovalov, *Bitva za Kavkaz v dokumentakh*, 204–209.

112. "Novorossiiskaia operatsiia 1942" [The Novorossiisk operation 1942], in *VE*, 5: 501.

113. Born in 1891, Konrad commanded 100th Mountain Regiment in 1935–1936, served as chief of operations of Second Army and chief of staff of XVIII Army Corps and Second Army from 1936 to 1940, and commanded 7th Mountain Division in 1941. Thereafter, he commanded XXXXIX Mountain Corps from late 1941 through 1944 and the Margarethen area and LXVIII Army Corps to war's end. Interned briefly after war's end, Konrad died in 1964. For a sketchy biography, see the website Axis Fact Book—*Des Heeres* at http://www.axishistory.com/index.

114. See the detailed report by 394th Rifle Division's 808th Regiment about its actions in August and September in Shapovalov, *Bitva za Kavkaz v dokumentakh*, 239–244.

115. On the mountain advance, see Tieke, *The Caucasus and the Oil*, 99–118; Ziemke and Bauer, *Moscow to Stalingrad*, 370; and Shtemenko, *Soviet General Staff at War*, bk. 1, 123.

116. These included the Khotiu-Tai and Nakhar Passes along the upper valley of the Kuban' River west of Mount El'brus, the Klukhori and Dombai-Ul'gen Passes at the headwaters of the Teberda River, the Marukh, Naur, and Achavchar Passes at the headwaters of the Marukha and Bol'shoi Zelenchuk Rivers, the Sancharo, Umpyr, Aishkha, and Pseashkha Passes at the headwaters of the Bol'shaia Laba River, and the Belorechenskii Pass along the Upper Belaia River. These passes are often designated by the adjectival forms of their spelling, such as Klukhorskii (Klukhori), Marukhskii (Marukh), and Naurskii (Naur).

117. Grechko, *Bitva za Kavkaz*, 154–155.

118. Ibid., 156.

119. Tieke, *The Caucasus and the Oil*, 101.

120. Ibid., 105–106.

121. Ibid., 107–108. See the description of 394th Rifle Division in the Klukhori Pass in Shapovalov, *Bitva za Kavkaz v dokumentakh*, 152–153.

122. Grechko, *Bitva za Kavkaz*, 163.

123. See *Stavka* directive no. 170579, dated 2350 hours 20 August 1942, in Zolotarev, "*Stavka* 1942," 369–370. See also Beriia's messages to the *Stavka* regarding the defense of the mountain passes in Shapovalov, *Bitva za Kavkaz v dokumentakh*, 199–200.

124. Grechko, *Bitva za Kavkaz*, 160–162.

125. See *Stavka* directive no. 994172, dated 2330 hours 27 August 1942, in Zolotarev, "*Stavka* 1942," 375. The *Stavka* also reinforced Leselidze's army with a regiment of student officers (1,200 men) from the Krasnodar Military School to defend the Black Sea coast. See exchanges of messages between 46th Army and Trans-Caucasus Front on 27 and 28 August and orders criticizing the army's defense, in Shapovalov, *Bitva za Kavkaz v dokumentakh*, 175–182, 187–189.

126. Grechko, *Bitva za Kavkaz*, 164–165; and Tieke, *The Caucasus and the Oil*, 110–111.

127. Grechko, *Bitva za Kavkaz*, 165–166; and Tieke, *The Caucasus and the Oil*, 112–113.

128. Grechko, *Bitva za Kavkaz*, 166; and Tieke, *The Caucasus and the Oil*, 112–114.

129. Grechko, *Bitva za Kavkaz*, 166–167; and Tieke, *The Caucasus and the Oil*, 108–109.

130. See additional messages and orders pertaining to 46th Army's fight in the mountain passes during the first half of September in Shapovalov, *Bitva za Kavkaz v dokumentakh*, 219–222, 227–229.

131. Tieke, *The Caucasus and the Oil*, 117.

132. See insightful comments on the opposing tactics in Grechko, *Bitva za Kavkaz*, 167–169.

133. For further details on the fighting around Voronezh in August, see Glantz, *Forgotten Battles*, 3: 66–74.

134. See 38th Army's specific mission in I. Ia. Vyrodov (ed.), *V srazheniiakh za Pobedu* [In battles for victory] (Moscow: Voenizdat, 1974), 135–136.

135. Glantz, *Forgotten Battles*, 3: 67–68.

136. For details, see Katukov, *Na ostrie glavnogo udara*, 166–168.

137. See *Stavka* directive no. 156675, dated 1850 hours 15 August 1942, in Zolotarev, "*Stavka* 1942," 363.

138. See *Stavka* directives nos. 994165 and 1036030, dated 16 August 1942, in ibid., 364, 366.

139. See *Stavka* directive no. 994176, dated 0300 hours 30 August 1942, in ibid., 376–377.

140. For details on Operation Hannover, see David M. Glantz, *A History of Soviet Airborne Forces* (London: Frank Cass, 1994), 145–228.

141. For details on Operation Seydlitz, see Glantz, *Forgotten Battles*, pt. 3, 130–149.

142. Born in 1887, Vietinghoff commanded 1st Grenadier Brigade from 1935 to 1938 and 5th Panzer Division during the Polish campaign in 1939. Thereafter, he led XIII Army Corps in 1939 and 1940 and Second Panzer Group's XXXXVI Motorized Corps during Operation Barbarossa. After serving as acting commander of Ninth Army during the Rzhev–Sychevka offensive in the winter of 1941–1942, Vietinghoff commanded Fifteenth Army in France in 1942 and Tenth Army during the defense of Italy in 1943 and 1944. Shuffled to and fro during the last year of the war, he served as commander in chief, South–West, commander of Army Group Kurland, and commander in chief, Army Group Italy, to war's end. Vietinghoff died in 1952. For a very brief biography, see the website Axis Fact Book—*Des Heeres* at http://www.axishistory.com/index.

143. Born in 1897, Konev, excepting Marshal Zhukov, was arguably the most famous Red Army *front* commander during the Soviet-German War. A junior officer in the Russian Army during World War I, Konev joined the Red Army in 1918 and fought in the Far East during the Civil War. A 1934 graduate of the Frunze Academy, Konev served as military commissar in 17th Rifle Corps and 17th Rifle Division in the 1920s and commanded a regiment, division, and corps, 2nd Red Banner Army, and the Trans-Baikal and North Caucasus Military Districts during the interwar years. Shortly before the Barbarossa invasion, Konev led his 19th Army westward, first to the Kiev region, then, after 22 June, northward to the Vitebsk and Smolensk regions, where his army was decimated in the

heavy fighting. Konev then commanded Western Front during the disastrous Viaz'ma encirclement in October and Kalinin Front throughout the defense of Moscow in the fall of 1941 and the Red Army's subsequent Moscow counteroffensive from December 1941 through April 1942. Konev's *front* conducted offensive operations in the Rzhev region during August and September 1942 and the failed Operation Mars in November and December 1942. Protected throughout his career by his mentor, Zhukov, Konev commanded Western, Northwestern, Steppe (2nd Ukrainian), and 1st Ukrainian Fronts throughout the remainder of the war, leading the Red Army's unsuccessful offensive into Romania in April and May 1944 but playing a significant role in the Red Army's victories in Ukraine and eastern Poland in 1944 and the Vistula–Oder and Berlin offensives in 1945. After the war, Konev commanded the Soviet Central Group of Forces in Czechoslovakia from 1946 to 1950 and served as Supreme High Commander of Soviet Ground Forces, 1st Deputy Minister of Defense of the USSR, and Supreme High Commander of the Warsaw Pact's forces through 1956. A favorite of Stalin during the postwar years, in part as a counterweight to Zhukov, with whom he frequently quarreled in his memoirs, Konev's star faded after Khrushchev's rise to political power. Konev retired in 1960 and died in 1973. For further details, see *Komandarmy. Voennyi biograficheskii slovar'*, 101– 102; and Konev's memoirs, *Zapiski komanduiushchego frontom* [Notes of a *front* commander] (Moscow: "GOLOS," 2000), which, although now published in unexpurgated form, like other biographies of the general, largely ignore his military service prior to 1943, probably because of his prewar record as a commissar and his association with many military defeats in 1941 and 1942.

144. See *Stavka* directive no. 170514, dated 2200 hours 16 July 1942, in Zolotarev, "*Stavka* 1942," 311–312.

145. Born in 1901, Leliushenko joined the Red Army in 1919 and fought as a cavalryman in Budenny's 1st Cavalry Army during the Civil War. Graduating from the Cavalry School for Red Commanders in 1927 and the Frunze Academy in 1933, Leliushenko commanded 4th Cavalry Division's 21st Regiment in the 1920s and, after transferring to the Red Army's mechanized forces in the early 1930s, served as a staff officer in the experimental 1st and 13th Mechanized Brigades in the mid-1930s. Leliushenko then commanded a tank regiment and brigade in 1938 and 1939, which he led during the invasion of eastern Poland in September 1939, and 39th Separate Tank Brigade, which he commanded successfully during the Finnish War in 1939–1940, also earning the honorific title of Hero of the Soviet Union. After leading the elite 1st Proletarian Moscow Motorized Rifle Division in 1940 and early 1941, Leliushenko was appointed commander of the Leningrad Military District's 21st Mechanized Corps in March 1941, which he led during Northwestern Front's defense of the Baltic region in the summer of 1941. Assigned as deputy chief of the Red Army's Main Armored Directorate in August 1941 and chief of the Directorate for the Formation and Manning of Armored Forces shortly thereafter, Leliushenko was instrumental in abolishing the Red Army's mechanized corps and creating separate tank brigades and battalions in their stead. During Operation Typhoon, the German drive on Moscow in October 1941, Leliushenko commanded 1st Guards Rifle Corps' famous defense in the Orel and Tula regions in October and November, 5th Army's defense of Mozhaisk in November, and 30th Army during the Moscow counterstroke in December and the subsequent counteroffensive during the winter of 1941–1942. By now recognized as one of the army's foremost "fighting" generals, Leliushenko commanded 1st Guards Army during the climax of Operation Blau, 3rd Guards Army during the Red

Army's offensives in 1943 and 1944, and 4th (Guards) Tank Army during the final year of the war, when his tank army played a significant role in 1st Ukrainian Front's successful offensives in Poland and the climactic assault on Berlin in April and May 1945. After the war, Leliushenko commanded 4th Mechanized Army and served as chief of GSFG's Armored Forces from 1945 through the early 1950s and commanded several military districts before retiring in 1964. A prolific memoir writer, Leliushenko died in 1987. For additional details, see *Komandarmy, Voennyi biograficheskii slovar'*, 127–128.

Born in 1898, Shvetsov joined the Red Army in 1919 and served as a combat engineer during the Civil War. Graduating from the Leningrad Military School in 1923 and courses at the Frunze Academy in 1929 and 1931, Shvetsov taught at various Red Army Schools, including the Frunze Academy, in the 1920s and 1930s and was assigned command of the Siberian Military District's 133rd Rifle Division in September 1939. Deploying westward with 24th Army in May and June 1941, after the German invasion Shvetsov's division played a leading role in the Reserve Front's victory at El'nia in August and September 1941. After surviving his army's encirclement and destruction in the Viaz'ma region in October 1941, Shvetsov commanded Kalinin Front's 29th Army from December 1941 through September 1942, participating in the battle for Moscow and once again surviving his army's near destruction by German Army Group Center in February 1942. After the *Stavka* relieved him of army command for "tolerating mistakes" during the Rzhev-Sychevka offensive in August and September 1942, Shvetsov became deputy commander of 3rd Shock Army. After recovering from wounds received during his army's victory over German forces at Velikie Luki in February 1943, Shvetsov commanded 4th Shock Army from May to December 1943, Western and Leningrad Front's 21st Army from February to July 1944, and the same *fronts'* 23rd Army until war's end. After the war, Shvetsov commanded 23rd Army to 1948 and 25th and 39th Armies in the Far East until 1955; he died in 1958 while serving as 1st deputy commander of the Baltic Military District. For further details, see *Komandarmy, Voennyi biograficheskii slovar'*, 268–269.

146. Born in 1901, Polenov joined the Red Army in 1918 and fought as a junior officer in the Civil War. Graduating from the *"Vystrel'"* Officers Course in 1931 and the Frunze Academy in 1938, Polenov served in NKVD's Border Guards units during the 1920s and 1930s, rising to command a border guards' detachment when Operation Barbarossa began. Along with many other NKVD officers assigned as cadre for the Red Army's new wave of reserve armies, Polenov commanded 243rd Rifle Division in Western Front's 31st Army in July 1941 and led a special operational group that subsequently delayed Third Panzer Group's advance northwest of Moscow in October and November 1941. After Polenov's division participated in recapturing Kalinin during Western Front's Moscow counteroffensive in December 1941, the NKO promoted him to lieutenant general in January 1942 and appointed him deputy commander of 29th Army. Despite the encirclement and near destruction of his army in February and March 1942, Polenov escaped to take command of 31st Army in April. Thereafter, Polenov commanded 31st, 5th, and 47th Armies through June 1944 and 2nd Shock Army's 108th Rifle Corps from August 1944 to war's end. After the war, Polenov commanded 108th Rifle Corps to 1948 and served in a variety of senior positions in military districts until his retirement in 1958 and death in 1968. For additional details, see *Komandarmy. Voennyi biograficheskii slovar'*, 175–176.

Born in 1886, Reiter rose to the rank of colonel in the Russian Army during World War I, joined the Red Army in 1919, commanded a rifle regiment in the Civil War and Polish

War, and participated in the suppression of the Kronshtadt mutiny in 1921. A 1935 graduate of the Frunze Academy, Reiter led a rifle brigade in the early 1920s and 2nd Amur and 36th Rifle Divisions during the struggle with Chinese forces for possession of the Chinese Eastern Railroad in 1929. During the 1930s, he commanded the Siberian Military District's 73rd Rifle Division and served as a department chief in the Red Army's Combat Training Directorate. After the German Barbarossa invasion, Reiter became chief of Central and Briansk Fronts' Rear from August through December 1941 but was severely wounded during the latter's successful offensive at Elets in December. Returning to the field in January 1942, Reiter headed the North Caucasus Military District, served as deputy commander of Western Front in February, and became commander of Western Front's 20th Army in March. His army spearheaded Western Front's Pogoreloe–Gorodishche offensive in August and September, after which Reiter commanded Briansk Front when it destroyed the Hungarian Second Army and severely damaged the German Second Army during the Voronezh offensive in January 1943. In the wake of the winter campaign, the *Stavka* appointed Reiter as commander of a new Reserve Front in March 1943, which, after being transformed into the Steppe Military District and, later, the Steppe Front, figured prominently in the Red Army's victory at Kursk in July 1943. In failing health, Reiter relinquished his command in July 1943 to become deputy commander of Voronezh Front and, in September 1943, commander of the Southern Ural Military District through 1946. Reiter ended his military career as chief of the *"Vystrel'"* Officers School, a position he occupied at the time of his death in 1950. For further details, see *Komandarmy, Voennyi biograficheskii slovar'*, 189–190.

Born in 1903, Getman joined the Red Army in 1924, commanded a rifle platoon and company in the 1920s, and, after graduating from the Red Army's Academy of Mechanization and Motorization in 1937, was assigned to 7th Mechanized Corps as temporary commander of its 31st Brigade. Transferred to the Far East in 1939, Getman served as deputy commander of 1st Separate Red Banner Army's 2nd Separate Tank Brigade during the battle with Japanese forces at Khalkhin-Gol in September 1939. He then led the army's 45th Light Tank Brigade and 17th Mechanized Corps' 27th Tank Division from November 1940 to March 1941 before becoming chief of staff of Far Eastern Front's 30th Mechanized Corps in March 1941. Appointed to command 112th Tank Division, which the *Stavka* transferred to the West in September 1941, Getman led the division during Western Front's defeat of Second Panzer Army in the Tula region in December 1941 and during the Red Army's subsequent offensive in the winter of 1941–1942. Recognizing his success at Moscow, the *Stavka* selected Getman to command its new 6th Tank Corps in April 1942. Thereafter, Getman commanded the 6th (11th Guards) Tank Corps until August 1944, always under the control of Katukov's 1st (1st Guards) Tank Army, and then served as Katukov's deputy to war's end. During the last two years of the war, Getman's corps and tank army participated in the battle for Kursk, the struggle for bridgeheads across the Dnepr River, and in many of the Red Army's victories in Ukraine and Poland in 1944, culminating with its assault on Berlin in April 1945. After the war, Getman headed the Ural and Trans-Caucasus Military Districts' armored forces until 1949, served as chief of staff and, later, commander of the Soviet Army's Armored and Mechanized Forces until 1954, and then led a separate mechanized army and 1st Separate Army through 1958. Getman ended his active military career as commander of the Carpathian Military District before retiring in 1964. Honored as a Hero of the Soviet Union in 1965, Getman died in 1987. For further details, see *Komkory. Voennyi biograficheskii slovar'*, 1: 125–126.

Born in 1894, Solomatin fought as a junior officer in the tsar's army during World War I, joined the Red Army in 1918, and rose to regimental command during the Civil War, when he was twice wounded in action. Graduating from the *"Vystrel'"* Officers Course in 1927 and the Frunze Academy in 1930, Solomatin commanded a rifle regiment and taught at the *"Vystrel'"* Officers Course and at a motor-mechanization course in the 1920s. He commanded Separate Red Banner Army's 59th Rifle Division and, later, its armored and mechanized forces during the first half of the 1930s. Although falsely accused and arrested by Stalin's security forces in October 1938, Solomatin was exonerated in April 1939 and was appointed, in succession, as deputy commander of the Kiev Special Military District's 25th Tank Corps in April 1939, commander of 2nd Mechanized Corps' 15th Motorized Division in March 1940, and commander of 24th Mechanized Corps' 45th Tank Division in March 1941. During the Barbarossa invasion, decisive action by Solomatin's division, which permitted Southern Front's 6th and 12th Armies to escape encirclement in western Ukraine, earned Solomatin the Order of the Red Banner. After his division, together with Southern Front's 6th and 12th Armies, was encircled and largely destroyed by the advancing Germans in the Uman' region in August 1941, Solomatin led 28 survivors on a harrowing 20–day escape back to Red Army lines. Returning to the Red Army's ranks in October, Solomatin commanded Western Front's 145th Tank Brigade, which cooperated with General Belov's 1st Guards Cavalry Corps in its successful defeat of German Second Panzer Army in the Tula region during the Moscow counteroffensive in December 1942. After recovering from wounds he received during this offensive, Solomatin led Western Front's 8th Tank Corps during the Pogoreloe–Gorodishche offensive in August and September 1942 and Kalinin Front's 1st Mechanized Corps during Operation Mars in November and December 1942. In the latter offensive, he once again led the survivors of his corps from German encirclement, for which he received the Order of Kutuzov, 2nd Degree. Thereafter, Solomatin commanded 1st Mechanized Corps until February 1944, participating in the Red Army's victories at Belgorod–Khar'kov in August 1943, the race to the Dnepr River in September 1943, and the struggle in the Ukraine during the winter of 1943–1944. After serving a brief stint as deputy chief of the Red Army's Armored and Mechanized Forces from February to August 1944, Solomatin commanded 5th Guards Tank Army during the latter stages of the Belorussian offensive and became chief of staff of the Red Army's Armored and Mechanized Directorate in September 1944, a post he occupied to war's end. Simultaneously, from March through August 1945, he served as chief of armored and mechanized forces in the Far East in preparation for the ensuing offensive in Manchuria. After the war, Solomatin commanded the Belorussian Military District's 5th Mechanized Army through March 1946, when, in failing health, he was reassigned as senior faculty chief at the Voroshilov and Frunze Academies. Solomatin retired due to illness in 1959; he died much later, in 1986. For further details, see *Komandarmy. Voennyi biograficheskii slovar'*, 297–298.

Born in 1897, Kriukov was a veteran of World War I, joined the Red Guards in 1917 and Red Army in 1918, and fought on the southern front during the Civil War. Completing the Leningrad Cavalry School in 1924 and the Frunze Academy in 1932, Kriukov commanded a cavalry squadron and served on the staff of cavalry regiments and divisions in the 1920s and headed 4th Cavalry Division's 20th Regiment in the 1930s. Kriukov commanded 306th Rifle Regiment from February 1940 until March 1941 and the Leningrad Military District's 8th Cavalry Brigade and 198th Motorized Rifle Division from March 1941 to the outbreak of war. Operating under the Northern (later Leningrad) Front's 54th

Army during the first six months of war, Kriukov's division defended the Volkhov region in August and September 1941, helped defend Tikhvin in October 1941, and spearheaded the Red Army offensive that drove German forces back to the Volkhov River by late November. Because of these successes, the *Stavka* appointed Kriukov to command Western Front's 10th Cavalry Corps in January 1942 and Briansk Front's 2nd Guards Cavalry Corps in March. Thereafter, Kriukov led 2nd Guards Cavalry until war's end, participating in many of the Red Army's most famous victories in Belorussia, Poland, and Germany. After 1945, Kriukov commanded a cavalry and rifle corps and served as chief of the Budenny High Cavalry School before being caught up and arrested during Stalin's final purges in November 1942. Although stripped of his rank and placed under house arrest until August 1953, Kriukov was freed shortly after Stalin's death, rehabilitated, and restored to his military duties. After graduating from the Voroshilov Academy in 1954, Kriukov served as deputy chief of the Military–Judicial Academy for Tactics and Combat Training, retired in 1957, and died in 1959. For further details, see *Komkory. Voennyi biograficheskii slovar'*, 2: 65–66.

147. For further details on this operation, see Ziemke and Bauer, *Moscow to Stalingrad*, 240–254; Horst Grossman, *Rzhev: The Cornerstone of the Eastern Front*, unpublished, trans. Joseph G. Welsh, from the German, *Rshew: Eckpfeiler der Ostfront (unterveranderter Nachdruck)* (Bad Nauheim, BRD: Podzun-Verlag, 1962); Nikolai Belov and Tat'iana Mikhailova, *Rzhev, Rshew 1942. Bitva za vysotu, Die Schlacht um Höhe 200* [Rzhev 1942. The battle for Hill 200] (Tver, 2000), which covers 30th Army's assault in detail; and A. M. Sandalov, *Pogoreloe-Gorodishchenskaia operatsiia: Nastupatel'naia operatsiia 20-i armii Zapadnogo fronta v avguste 1942 goda* [The Pogoreloe-Gorodishche operation: The offensive operation of the Western Front's 20th Army in August 1942] (Moscow: Voenizdat, 1960).

148. Glantz, *Forgotten Battles*, 3: 153–157; and Ziemke and Bauer, *Moscow to Stalingrad*, 400. See the OKH's perception of the offensive in Halder, *The Halder War Diaries*, 649, 653.

149. Telephonic order from Vasilevsky, 5 August 1942, quoted in Zolotarev, "*Stavka* 1942," 347–348.

150. Born in 1899, Galanin joined the Red Army in 1919, fought as a common soldier in the Civil War, and took part in the suppression of the Kronshtadt mutiny in 1921. Finishing the "*Vystrel*'" Officers Course in 1931 and the Frunze Academy in 1936, Galanin rose steadily through the ranks of the infantry to command the Trans-Baikal Military District's 57th Rifle Division during the battle against Japanese forces at Khalkhin-Gol in August and September 1939 and the Kiev Special Military District's 17th Rifle Corps from June 1940 through the outbreak of the Soviet-German War, when he became a member of Zhukov's clique. After war began, Galanin's corps participated in the fighting withdrawal of Southern Front's 18th Army eastward across the Ukraine, escaping encirclement and destruction at Uman' and Nikolaev. He then commanded 18th Army during its defense of the Donbas region from August through November 1941 and Volkhov Front's 59th Army during its defense of Tikhvin and subsequent counteroffensive in the winter of 1941–1942. Transferred to Zhukov's Western Front in April 1942, Galanin commanded a special army operational group in 16th Army in April and May, served as deputy commander of the *front*'s 33rd Army in June and July, and became deputy commander of Voronezh Front in August. At the climax of Operation Blau, the *Stavka* assigned Galanin command of Don Front's 24th Army in October 1942. After leading 24th Army

during the Stalingrad counteroffensive, Galanin commanded 70th Army during the battle for Kursk in July–August 1943, 4th Guards Army during the advance to the Dnepr and battles in eastern Ukraine from September 1943 through January 1944, and 53rd Army during the Red Army's advance through Ukraine, Romania, and Hungary to war's end. After the war, apparently because it was dissatisfied with his performance as an army commander, the Ministry of Defense appointed Galanin deputy commander of a rifle corps. Galanin retired from military service in 1946 and died in 1958. For further details, see *Komandarmy. Voennyi biograficheskii slovar'*, 39–40.

151. Sandalov, *Pogorelo-Gorodischchenskaia operatsiia*, 74.

152. N. M. Ramanichev and V. V. Gurkhin, "Rzhevsko–Sychevskie operatsii 1942" [The Rzhev–Sychevka operation 1942], *VE*, 7: 233.

153. See the daily situation in "Feindlage maps and overlays, AOK 9, Ic/A.O., 1–31 Aug 1942," *AOK 9, 27970/5, Pt. II*, in NAM T-312, Roll 304.

154. For details on 5th Panzer Division's fight, see Anton Detlev von Plato, *Die Geschichte der 5. Panzerdivision 1938 bis 1945* (Regensberg, Germany: Walhalla u. Praetoria Verlag, 1978), 230–240.

155. Halder, *The Halder War Diaries*, 653–654; and Ziemke and Bauer, *Moscow to Stalingrad*, 402–403.

156. Born in 1886, Heinrici earned fame during the Soviet-German War as the *Wehrmacht*'s most accomplished defensive specialist. After serving in World War I as a brigade adjutant during the battle for Verdun, Heinrici commanded 13th Infantry Regiment in the early 1930s, 16th Infantry Division from 1937 to 1940, an infantry corps in the French campaign in 1940, and XXXXIII Army Corps during preparations for the invasion of England (Operation Sea Lion) and throughout the first year of Operation Barbarossa. Heinrici began building his reputation when his corps conducted a stout defense against numerically superior Soviet forces during the Red Army's Moscow counteroffensive and ensuing offensive in the winter of 1941–1942. Succeeding to command of Army Group Center's Fourth Army in January 1942, Heinrici led this army through 1944, skillfully conducting defensive operations westward along the Viaz'ma, Smolensk, and Mogilev axes. After his army was finally destroyed in the Red Army's offensive in Belorussia during the summer of 1944, Heinrici commanded First Panzer Army during its defense of the Carpathian region in late 1944 and Army Group Vistula in its defense of the Oder River line and Berlin in April and May 1945. Imprisoned by the Allies, Heinrici was released in 1948 and died in 1971. For further details, see "Schwerterträger Gotthard Heinrici," from website *Die Generale des Heeres* at http://balsi.de/Homepage-Generale/Heer/Heer-Startseite.htm; and the website Axis Fact Book—*Des Heeres* at http://www.axishistory.com/index.

157. Born in 1886, Schmidt served in World War I and, after the war, commanded 13th Infantry Regiment in 1934–1935 and served as Quartermaster III on the *Reichswehr*'s staff from 1935 to 1937. Schmidt received his baptism of fire in command of 1st Panzer Division during the Polish campaign in September 1939 and, thereafter, led XXXIX Motorized Corps during the French campaign of 1940 and the same corps during Army Group North's advance on Leningrad during Operation Barbarossa. His corps isolated Soviet forces in Leningrad by capturing the fortress town of Shlissel'burg in early September 1941. After being defeated in the Tikhvin region in October and November 1941, Schmidt commanded Second Army in late 1941 and Second Panzer Army from January 1942 to July 1943. Outspoken criticism of Hitler cost Schmidt this command in mid-July

1943, ostensibly for evacuating the Orel salient. Thereafter, he spent the remainder of the war inactive in the OKW's reserve. Found and arrested by Soviet counterintelligence agents in Wismar in 1947, Schmidt was imprisoned in Soviet POW camps until his release in 1956. In ill health due to his harsh captivity, Schmidt died in 1957. For further details, see the website Axis Fact Book—*Des Heeres* at http://www.axishistory.com/index; and Zalessky, *Vermacht*, 514–515.

158. Ziemke and Bauer, *Moscow to Stalingrad*, 403–404; and "Nekotorye vyvody po operatsiiam levogo kryla Zapodnogo fronta" [Some conclusions regarding the operations on the left wing of the Western Front], *SMPIOV* (Moscow: Voenizdat, 1943), 5: 68.

159. Born in 1900, Fediuninsky joined the Red Army in 1919 and fought as a private in the Civil War. Graduating from the "*Vystrel*'" Officers Course in 1931 and the Voroshilov Academy a decade later, Fediuninsky also participated in the struggle against Chinese forces along the Chinese Eastern Railroad in 1929. He became one of Zhukov's favorites when he led 36th Motorized Rifle Division's 24th Regiment during the victory over Japanese forces at Khalkhin-Gol in August and September 1939. After commanding the Trans-Baikal Military District's 82nd Motorized Rifle Division from November 1940 to June 1941, Fediuninsky headed 5th Army's 15th Rifle Corps during Southwestern Front's defense of the western Ukraine in the initial stages of Operation Barbarossa. Summoned by Zhukov to the Leningrad region, Fediuninsky led, in succession, 32nd Army (August–September 1941), 42nd Army (September–October 1941), and 54th Army (October 1941–April 1942) and, after a short stint as deputy commander of the Volkhov and Briansk Fronts, 11th Army (June–December 1943) and 2nd Shock Army from December 1943 to war's end. While in command, Fediuninsky's forces played significant roles in the defense of Leningrad during the summer and fall of 1941, the counteroffensives in the Leningrad and Volkhov regions in 1942, the fight to conquer the Baltic region in 1944, and the Berlin offensive of April–May 1945. Despite Zhukov's fall from grace after war's end, Fediuninsky commanded the Arkhangel'sk Military District from 1946 to 1947 and 7th Guards Army from 1948 to 1951 before becoming deputy commander of GSFG from 1951 to 1954. Fediuninsky ended his career commanding the Trans-Caucasus and Turkestan Military Districts from 1954 to 1965, retired as a member of the Ministry of Defense's Group of General Inspectors in 1965, and died in 1977. For additional details, see *Komandarmy. Voennyi biograficheskii slovar'*, 232–233.

160. For details, see Glantz, *Forgotten Battles*, 3: 156–159. Born in 1896, Khozin fought as a noncommissioned officer in the Russian Army during World War I, joined the Red Army in 1918, and commanded a battalion, regiment, and brigade during the Civil War. Graduating from the Frunze Academy in 1925 and the Lenin Political-Military Academy in 1930, Khozin commanded 34th, 36th, and 18th Rifle Divisions and 1st Rifle Corps in the 1920s and 1930s and served as chief of the Frunze Academy from 1939 to 1941. Considered by Stalin as one of his most experienced and politically reliable generals, Khozin was chief of the Front of Reserve Armies' Rear and chief of staff of Leningrad Front's Rear from August to October 1941. He commanded 54th Army in October 1941 and Leningrad Front and Volkhov Group of Forces from October 1941 through April 1942. During this period, he led 54th Army during its victory at Tikhvin and the *front* in its unsuccessful attempts to raise the siege of Leningrad in the winter of 1941–1942. While commanding Western Front's 33rd and then 20th Army from June 1942 until February 1943, his forces participated in the Pogoreloe-Gorodishche offensive in August–September 1942 and the unsuccessful Operation Mars in November and December 1942.

Assigned command of Northwestern Front's Special Operational Group Khozin in early 1943, he helped plan Zhukov's failed Operation Polar Star against German forces defending Leningrad in February but managed to eliminate the enemy-occupied salient in the Demiansk region by March. Relieved in early 1944 for "inefficiency in command," Khozin ended the war as commander of the Volga Military District. After the war, Khozin was a faculty member of several Soviet Army schools, retired in 1963, and died in 1979. For further details, see *Komandarmy. Voennyi biograficheskii slovar'*, 244–246.

161. The quotation is from Halder, *The Halder War Diaries*, 657. See also Ziemke and Bauer, *Moscow to Stalingrad*, 406–407.

162. Glantz, *Forgotten Battles*, 3: 159–167.

163. See Chapter 4 in this volume for Romanenko's biography.

164. Glantz, *Forgotten Battles*, 3: 118. Born in 1901, because he served in the fledgling tank service of the tsar's army during World War I, Kurkin became the Red Army's senior armor specialist in the 1920s and 1930s. After joining the Red Army in 1918 and commanding an armored train in Ukraine during the Civil War, Kurkin graduated from the Red Army's Mechanization and Motorization Academy in 1935 and the Voroshilov Academy in 1941. During the interwar years he headed the Khar'kov Military District's 4th Heavy Tank Regiment and the Kiev Special Military District's 17th Tank Brigade during the 1930s and 2nd Tank Brigade during the invasion of eastern Poland in September 1939. When the Red Army fielded its new mechanized corps in the two years preceding the war, Kurkin commanded 3rd Mechanized Corps' 5th Tank Division from June 1940 to January 1941 and the corps itself throughout the first three months of Operation Barbarossa, in the process escaping intact from the Minsk encirclement. After his corps was disbanded in August 1941, Kurkin served as deputy commander of Leliushenko's 1st Guards Rifle Corps during its defense of Orel and Tula in October 1941 and, in November, was appointed to command the corps and then the short-lived 26th Army. Assigned command of 9th Tank Corps in May 1942, he led this corps through October 1942, participating in many of Western Front's offensives to disrupt Operation Blau. From late October 1943 to the end of the war, Kurkin served as either deputy commander or commander of the armored and mechanized forces in the Steppe, 2nd Ukrainian, and Trans-Baikal Fronts. In the process, he played a significant role in raising and fielding armored forces employed in the battle of Kursk, in operations in the Ukraine, Romania, Hungary, and Austria, and, finally, in the Red Army's offensive in Manchuria in August and September 1945. After 1945, Kurkin served as inspector-general of the Soviet Army's Armored and Mechanized Forces until his death in 1948. For additional details, see *Komandarmy. Voennyi biograficheskii slovar'*, 123–124. See Chapter 4 in this volume for Baranov's biographical sketch.

165. See Chapter 2 in this volume for Bogdanov's biographical sketch. Born in 1904 and, ultimately, one of the Red Army's youngest tank corps commanders, Koptsov joined the Red Army in 1918 and fought on the southern front during the Civil War. A graduate of a military-political course in 1929 and an armored officers' course in Leningrad in 1931, Koptsov served in 2nd Red Banner Army in 1939, was a political worker in 1st Pacific Ocean Rifle Division in 1930, and commanded a battalion in 1st Tank Regiment in 1932–1933. In August–September 1939, he led a tank battalion in 6th Mechanized Brigade during the victory by Zhukov's 1st Army Group over Japanese forces at Khalkhin–Gol, for which he received the title of Hero of the Soviet Union for his bravery. During the final two years of peace, Koptsov commanded a battalion in 8th Red Banner Light Tank

Brigade from July 1938 to November 1940 and the brigade itself until his appointment as deputy commander of 21st Mechanized Corps' 46th Tank Division in March 1941. During Operation Barbarossa, Koptsov commanded this tank division during the intense struggle in the Baltic and Pskov regions in the summer of 1941 and 6th (7th Guards) Tank Brigade during the Reserve and Western Fronts' defense along the Viaz'ma and Moscow axes in the fall of 1941 and during Western Front's counterstroke at Moscow in December and ensuing offensive in the winter of 1941–1942. Elevated to command 3rd Tank Army's 15th Tank Corps in May 1942, Koptsov at age 38 led his corps until February 1943, participating in many Red Army counterstrokes during Operation Blau and spearheading Voronezh Front's Khar'kov offensive in February 1943. Seriously wounded in late February 1943, when his corps, together with all of 3rd Tank Army, was encircled and destroyed during Army Group South's counteroffensive in the Donbas and Khar'kov regions, Koptsov was evacuated from the battlefield but died on 3 March. For further details, see *Komkory. Voennyi biograficheskii slovar'*, 2: 141–142.

166. Ibid., 122–124; A. M. Zvartsev, ed., *3-ia gvardeiskaia tankovaia armiia* [The 3rd Guards Tank Army] (Moscow: Voenizdat, 1982), 19–20.

167. *SMPIOV*, 5: 70–71.

168. Glantz, *Forgotten Battles*, 3: 122–129; and Zvartsev, *3-ia gvardeiskaia tankovaia*, 19–24.

169. Born in 1900, Kurochkin joined the Red Army in 1918 and fought on the northern and northwestern fronts during the Civil War. Graduating from the Red Army's Higher Cavalry School in 1923, the Frunze Academy in 1932, and the Voroshilov Academy in 1940, Kurochkin led a cavalry battalion and regiment during the Polish War in 1920–1921, served as chief of staff of cavalry regiment and division during the 1920s, and commanded a cavalry regiment and division in the 1930s. In September 1939, he was 2nd Cavalry Corps' chief of staff during the Red Army's invasion of eastern Poland, and in March 1940 he commanded Northwestern Front's 28th Rifle Corps when it conducted its daring assault on the Finnish city of Vyborg across the frozen surface of the Gulf of Finland. After commanding the Trans-Baikal Military District's 1st Army Group in 1940–1941, Kurochkin headed the Orel Military District until the Barbarossa invasion. He then led Western Front's 20th and 43rd Armies during the battle for Smolensk before being transferred to Northwestern Front in August 1941. There Kurochkin served, first, as *Stavka* representative, then later as *front* commander and deputy commander, as well as commander of the *front*'s 11th and 34th Armies through June 1943. During his tenure in front and army command, Kurochkin planned and executed all of the mainly unsuccessful offensives against German II Corps' salient at Demiansk until the Germans finally evacuated the salient in February–March 1943. Thereafter, Kurochkin served as deputy commander of 1st Ukrainian Front from December 1943 through February 1944, headed 2nd Belorussian Front during its unsuccessful offensive at Kovel' from February to April 1944, and led 1st Ukrainian Front's 60th Army during its successful operations in western Ukraine, Poland, and Czechoslovakia up to war's end. Although his career was often fraught with defeats, Kurochkin became a Hero of the Soviet Union in 1945 for his skilled leadership of 60th Army. After the war, Kurochkin commanded the Kuban' Military District, served as deputy commander of GSFG, and ended his career as deputy chief of the Voroshilov Academy, chief of the Frunze Academy, and in senior posts in the Warsaw Pact Armed Forces. Kurochkin retired in 1970 and died in 1989. For further details, see Nikoforov, *Velikaia Otechestvennaia voina 1941–1945 gg.*, 329–330.

170. Glantz, *Forgotten Battles*, 3: 178.

171. G. I. Berdnikov, *Pervaia udarnaia* [The First Shock] (Moscow: Voenizdat, 1985), 106.

172. Born in 1897, Morozov served as a noncommissioned officer in the tsar's army during World War I, joined the Red Army in 1918 and led a company, battalion, and regiment in the Kuban' region during the Civil War. A graduate of the Red Army's "*Vystrel*'" Officers Course in 1923, the Officers Improvement Course in 1925, and the Lenin Political-Military Academy in 1937, Morozov commanded a rifle regiment, division, and corps before his appointment to head the Baltic Military District's 11th Army in 1940. Once Operation Barbarossa began, Morozov's army, although decimated in the first few days of fighting, conducted an effective fighting withdrawal, in the process conducting a counterstroke in the Sol'tsy region in late July that damaged German 8th Panzer Division and delayed Army Group North's advance on Leningrad by two weeks. Forced to withdraw eastward toward the Valdai Hills, Morozov's army also spearheaded Northwestern Front's counterstroke at Staraia Russia in mid-August, which further delayed Army Group North's advance and, perhaps, prevented the Germans from capturing Leningrad. Morozov then commanded Northwestern Front's 11th and 1st Shock Armies in their numerous assaults against German defenses around the Demiansk salient from late 1942 to April 1943 and, still later, Briansk Front's 63rd Army during its assaults against the Germans' Orel salient in April and May 1943. Worn out by his arduous field service, Morozov served continuously as chief of the Red Army's Directorate for Training Armed Forces Rifle Units from May 1943 to 1953, retired in 1962, and died in 1964. For further details, see *Komandarmy. Voennyi biograficheskii slovar'*, 151–152.

173. See *Stavka* directive no. 170546, dated 0220 hours 2 August 1942, in Zolotarev, "*Stavka* 1942," 339; and Kurochkin's operational plan, in ibid., 534–538. Born in 1896, Romanovsky served as a junior officer in the Russian Army during World War I, joined the Red Army in 1918, and commanded a company, battalion, and armored train on the eastern and southern fronts during the Civil War. Graduating from the Lenin Political-Military Academy in 1931 and the Frunze Academy in 1935, Romanovsky led special designation detachments suppressing insurrections in Iakutia in 1924–1925 and began his political–military career by serving as political worker and commissar in 3rd Verkhne-Udinsk Rifle Regiment and 1st Pacific Ocean Rifle Division during the late 1920s. During the 1930s Romanovsky served as military commissar in the Leningrad Military District's 105th Rifle Regiment, led 10th and 11th Turkestan Rifle Regiments, and was deputy commander of 2nd Separate Red Banner Army in the Far East. On the eve of war, he headed the Western Special Military District's 10th Army from July 1940 to March 1941, when he was appointed assistant commander of the Volga Military District. After Operation Barbarossa began, Romanovsky commanded the Arkhangel'sk Military District from June 1941 through April 1942, mobilizing and fielding the 28th and 29th Armies and many separate rifle divisions and brigades, while defending the vital coast of the White Sea. Dispatched to field duty in April 1942, Romanovsky headed Northwestern Front's 1st Shock Army from May–December 1942, when he led his army in all of its futile assaults against the Demiansk salient. In command of Volkhov and Leningrad Fronts' 2nd Shock Army from December 1942 to January 1944, he presided over his army's defeat and near destruction at Siniavino in the summer of 1942 but redeemed himself when his army helped crack the siege of Leningrad in January 1943. Thereafter, Romanovsky was deputy commander of 4th Ukrainian Front during its operations in the Dnepr River bend from

January to March 1944 and commanded Leningrad Front's 42nd Army during its failed attempts to penetrate the Germans' Panther Defense Line at Pskov and Ostrov in March 1944, the same front's 67th Army during the offensives into the Baltic region from March 1944 to March 1945, and 2nd Belorussian Front's 19th Army as it cleared German forces from the Danzig region from March to May 1945. Romanovsky commanded the Voronezh Military District in 1945–1946, the Central Group of Forces' 4th Guards Army in 1947–1948, and the North Caucasus and Don Military Districts in 1948 and 1949. Romanovsky completed his military career as chief of the Voroshilov and Frunze Academies, retired in 1959, and died in 1967. For further details, see *Komandarmy. Voennyi biograficheskii slovar'*, 196–197.

174. Glantz, *Forgotten Battles*, 3: 180–188; and Berdnikov, *Pervaia udarnaia*, 109.

175. Zeitzler in Friedin and Richardson, *The Fatal Decisions*, 132.

176. Halder, *The Halder Diaries*, 649.

177. G. Zhukov, *Reminiscences and Reflections*, 2: 86.

Chapter 10: Conclusions: German Strategic Misconceptions

1. Horst Boog, et al., *Germany and the Second World War, Vol. 4: The Attack on the Soviet Union*, trans. Dean S. McMurry, Ewald Osers, and Louise Wilmot (Oxford, UK: Clarendon Press, 2001), 118–131, 174–177.

2. David M. Glantz, "Soviet Mobilization in Peace and War, 1924–1942: A Survey," *JSMS* 5, 3 (September 1992): 345–352. For a general discussion of Soviet force generation, see Glantz, *Stumbling Colossus*, 205–232.

3. Adelbert Holl, *An Infantryman in Stalingrad: From 24 September 1942 to 2 February 1943*, trans. Jason D. Mark and Neil Page (Sydney, Australia: Leaping Horseman Books, 2005), 2–5, 125, 187.

Selected Bibliography

Abbreviations

JSMS	*Journal of Slavic Military Studies*
TsAMO	*Tsentral'nyi arkhiv Ministerstva Oborony* [Central Archives of the Ministry of Defense]
TsPA UML	*Tsentral'nyi partiinyi arkhiv Instituta Marksizma-Leninizma* [Central Party Archives of the Institute of Marxism and Leninism]
VIZh	*Voenno-istoricheskii zhurnal* [Military-historical journal]
VV	*Voennyi vestnik* [Military herald]

Primary Sources

Combat Journals [*Kreigstagebuch*]: German Sixth Army, in National Archives Microfilm (NAM) series T-312, Roll 1453.
Combat Journals [*Zhurnal boevykh deistvii*]: Soviet
    62nd Army, September-November 1942
    95th Rifle Division
    112th Rifle Division
    138th Rifle Division (*138-ia Krasnoznamennaia strelkovaia diviziia v boiakh za Stalingrada*) [138th Red Banner Rifle Division in the battle for Stalingrad].
    284th Rifle Division
    308th Rifle Division
    37th Guards Rifle Division
    39th Guards Rifle Division
    10th Rifle Brigade
    42nd Rifle Brigade
    "Anlage 3 zum Tatigkeitsbericht, AOK 17, Ic, 20 Jul–25 Jul 1942." *AOK 17, 24411/33*.
National Archives Microfilm (NAM) series T-312, Roll 679.
"Boevye deistviia voisk Brianskogo i Voronezhskogo frontov letom 1942 na Voronezhskom napravlenii" [Combat operations of the forces of the Briansk and Voronezh Fronts along the Voronezh axis in the summer of 1942], in *Sbornik voenno-istoricheskikh materialov Velikoi Otechestvennoi voiny, Vypusk 15* [Collection of military-historical materials of the Great Patriotic War, Issue 15]. Moscow: Voenizdat, 1955.
"Boevye rasporiazhenie i boevye doneseniia shtaba 28 Armii (12.5–12.7.1942) [Combat orders and combat reports of the headquarters of the 28th Army (12.5–12.7.42)]. *TsAMO, Fond* [collection] (f.) 382, *opis* [subgroup] (op.) 8452, *ed. khr.* [common file] 37, l. 53.

Boevoi sostav Sovetskoi armii, chast' 2 (Ianvar'-dekabr' 1942 goda) [Combat composition of the Soviet Army, part 2 (January-December 1942)]. Moscow: Voenizdat, 1966.

Dushen'kin, V. V., ed. *Vnutrennye voiska v Velikoi Otechestvennoi voine 1941–1945 gg.: Dokumenty i materially* [Internal troops in the Great Patriotic War, 1941–1945: Documents and materials]. Moscow: Iuridicheskaia literatura, 1975.

"Feindlagenkarten, PzAOK 1, Ic, 31 May–28 Jun 1942." *PzAOK 1, 24906/23.* National Archives Microfilm (NAM) series T-313, Roll 37.

"Feindlagenkarten, PzAOK 1, Ic, 29 Jun–31 Jul 1992." *PzAOK 1, 24906/24.* National Archives Microfilm (NAM) series T-313, Roll 38.

"'Friedericus, 1' Anlagenmappe 1 zum KTB Nr. 8, PzAOK 1, Ia, 27 Mar–14 May 1942." *PzAOK 1, 25179/3.* National Archives Microfilm (NAM) series T-313, Roll 5.

GKO [State Defense Committee] Decrees, *TsPA UML.* f. 644, op. 1, *delo* [file] (d.), 23, *listy* [leaf, pages] (ll.) 127–129 and f. 644, op. 1, d. 33, ll. 48–50.

"Ia, Lagenkarten Nr. 1 zum KTB Nr. 13, Jul-Oct 1942. *AOK 6, 23948/1a.* National Archives Microfilm (NAM) series T-312, Roll 1446.

"Ia, Lagenkarten zum KTB 12, May-Jul 1942." *AOK 6, 22855/Ia.* National Archives Microfilm (NAM) series T-312, Roll 1446.

Kommandovanie korpusnovo i divizionnogo svena Sovetskikh vooruzhennykh sil perioda Velikoi Otechestvennoi voiny 1941–1945 g. [Commanders at the corps and division level in the Soviet Armed Forces in the period of the Great Patriotic War, 1941–1945]. Moscow: Frunze Academy, 1964.

Kriegstagebuch der Oberkommandes der Wehrmacht/Wehrmachtfuhrungsstab: 1940–1945, Bd. II. Frankfurt, 1963.

"Lagenkarten Pz. AOK 1, Ia (Armee-Gruppe v. Kleist), 1–29 Jun 1942." *PzAOK 1, 24906/12.* National Archives Microfilm (NAM) series T-313, Roll 35.

"Lagenkarten, 8 July–5 October 1942." *AOK II, Ia, 2585/207a.* National Archives Microfilm (NAM) series T-312, Roll 1207.

"Lagenkarten. Anlage 9 zum Kriegstagebuch Nr. 3, AOK 17, Ia., 31 Jul–13 Aug 1942." *AOK 17. 24411/19.* National Archives Microfilm (NAM) series T-312, Roll 696.

"Lagenkarten Pz AOK 1, Ia, 1–31 Aug 1942." *PzAOK 1, 24906/14.* National Archives Microfilm (NAM) series T-313, Roll 36.

"Lagenkarten PzAOK 1, Ia, 1–30 Sep 1942." *PzAOK 1, 24906/15.* National Archives Microfilm (NAM) series T-313, Roll 36.

"Lagenkarten PzAOK 1, Ia, 1–31 Oct 1942." *PzAOK 1, 24906/16.* National Archives Microfilm (NAM) series T-313, Roll 36.

"Lagenkarten zum KTB. Nr. 5 (Teil III.), PzAOK 4, Ia, 21 Oct–24 Nov 1942." *PzAOK 4, 28183/12.* National Archives Microfilm (NAM) series T-313, Roll 359.

"Nekotorye vyvody po operatsiiam levogo kryla Zapodnogo fronta" [Some conclusions concerning the operations of the Western Front's left wing]. *Sbornik materialov po izucheniiu opyta voiny, No. 5* [Collection of Materials for the Study of War Experience, No. 5]. Moscow: Voenizdat, 1943.

Sbornik materialov po izucheniiu opyta voiny, No. 4 (Ianvar'–fevral' 1943 g.) [Collection of materials for the exploitation of war experiences, no. 4]. Moscow: Voenizdat, 1943.

Sbornik materialov po izucheniiu opyta voiny, No. 6 (Aprel'–mai 1943 g.) [Collection of materials for the exploitation of war experiences, no. 6]. Moscow: Voenizdat, 1943.

Sbornik voenno-istoricheskikh materialov Velikoi Otechestvennoi voiny, Vypusk 14 [Collection of materials of the Great Patriotic War, Issue 14]. Moscow: Voenizdat, 1954.

Sbornik voenno-istoricheskikh materialov Velikoi Otechestvennoi voiny, Vypusk 15 [Collection of materials of the Great Patriotic War, Issue 15]. Moscow: Voenizdat, 1955.

Sbornik voenno-istoricheskikh materialov Velikoi Otechestvennoi voiny, Vypusk 18 [Collection of materials of the Great Patriotic War, Issue 18]. Moscow: Voenizdat, 1960.

Shapovalov, V. A., ed. *Bitva za Kavkaz v dokumentakh i materialov* [The battle for the Caucasus in documents and materials]. Stavropol': Stavropol' State University, 2003.

Zhilin, V. A., ed. *Stalingradskaia bitva: Khronika, fakty, liudi v 2 kn.* [The battle of Stalingrad; chronicles, facts, people in 2 books]. Moscow: OLMA, 2002.

Zolotarev, A. M., ed. "General'nyi shtab v gody Velikoi Otechestvennoi voiny: Dokumenty i materially, 1942 god" [The General Staff in the Great Patriotic War: Documents and materials, 1942]. In *Russki arkhiv: Velikaia Otechestvennaia [voina]*, 23 (12–2) [The Russian archives: The Great Patriotic (War), vol. 23 (12–2)]. Moscow: "TERRA," 1999.

———. Prikazy narodnogo komissara oborony SSSR, 22 iiunia 1941 g. – 1942 [Orders of the People's Commissariat of Defense of the USSR, 22 June 1941–1942]. In *Russkii arkhiv: Velikaia Otechestvennaia [voina]*, 13 (2–2) [The Russian archives: The Great Patriotic (War), vol. 13 (2–2)]. Moscow: "TERRA," 1997.

———. "*Stavka* VGK: Dokumenty i materialy 1942" [The *Stavka* VGK: Documents and materials, 1942]. In *Russkii arkhiv: Velikaia Otechestvennaia [voina]*, 16 (5–2) [The Russian archives: The Great Patriotic (War), vol. 16 (5–2)]. Moscow: "TERRA," 1996.

Secondary Sources: Books

Abramov, Vsevolod. *Kerchenskaia katastrofa 1942* [The Kerch catastrophe 1942]. Moscow: "IAUZA" "EKSMO," 2006.

Afanas'ev, N. I. *Ot Volgi do Shpree: Boevoi put' 35-i gvardeiskoi strelkovoi Lozovskoi Krasnoznamennoi, ordena Suvorova i Bogdan Khmel'nitskogo divizii* [From the Volga to the Spree: The combat path of the 35th Guard Lozovaia, Red Banner, and Orders of Suvorov and Bogdan Khmel'nitsky Rifle Division]. Moscow: Voenizdat, 1982.

Anfilov, Viktor. "Semen Konstantinovich Timoshenko." In *Stalin's Generals*, ed. Harold Shukman, 239–254. London: Weidenfeld & Nicolson, 1993.

Axworthy, Mark, Cornel Scafes, and Cristian Craciunoiu. *Third Axis Fourth Ally: The Romanian Armed Forces in the European War, 1941–1945*. London: Arms and Armour Press, 1995.

Babich, Iu. P. *Podgotovka oborony 62nd Armiei vne soprikosnovaniia s protivnikom i vedenie oboronitel'noi operatsii v usloviiakh prevoskhodstva protivnika v manevrennosti (po opytu Stalingradskoi bitvy)* [The preparation of 62nd Army's defense in close proximity to the enemy and the conduct of the defensive operation in circumstances of enemy superiority in maneuver (based on the experience of the battle of Stalingrad]. Moscow: Frunze Academy, 1991.

Babich, Iu. P., and A. G. Baier. *Razvitie vooruzheniia i organitzatsii Sovetskikh sukhoputnykh voist v gody Velikoi Otechestvennoi voiny* [Development of the armament and organization of the Soviet ground forces in the Great Patriotic War]. Moscow: Frunze Academy, 1990.

Bagramian, I. Kh. *Tak shli my k pobeda* [As we went on to victory]. Moscow: Voenizdat, 1977.

Barnett, Correlli, ed. *Hitler's Generals*. New York: Grove Weidenfeld, 1989.

Bartov, Omar. *The Eastern Front, 1941–1945: German Troops and the Barbarization of Warfare*. New York: St. Martin's Press, 1986.

Batov, P. I. *V pokhodakh i boiakh* [In marches and battles]. Moscow: "Golos," 2000.

Beevor, Antony. *Stalingrad: The Fateful Siege: 1942–1943*. New York: Viking, 1998.

Belov, Nikolai, and Tat'iana Mikhailova. *Rzhev, Rshew 1942. Bitva za vysotu, Die Schlacht um Höhe 200* [Rzhev 1942. The battle for Hill 200]. Tver, 2000.

Belov, Pavel A. *Za nami Moskva* [Behind us, Moscow]. Moscow: Voenizdat, 1963.

Berdnikov, G. I. *Pervaia udarnaia* [The First Shock (Army)]. Moscow: Voenizdat, 1985.

Beshanov, V. V. *God 1942—"Uchebnyi"* [The Year 1942—Educational]. Minsk: Harvest, 2002.

Bitva pod Stalingradom, chast' 1: Strategicheskaia oboronitel'naia operatsiia [The battle at Stalingrad, part 1: The strategic defensive operation]. Moscow: Voroshilov Military Academy, 1953.

Bitva za Stalingrad [The battle for Stalingrad]. Volgograd: Nizhne-Volzhskoe knizhnoe izdatel'stvo, 1973.

Blau, George E. *The German Campaign in Russia: Planning and Operations (1940-1942)*. Department of the Army Pamphlet No. 20–261a. Washington, DC: Department of the Army, 1955.

Blizoniuk, A. M. *Na bastionakh Sevastopolia* [In the bastions of Sevastopol']. Minsk: "Polymia," 1985.

Boog, Horst, Jurden Forster, Joachim Hoffmann, et al. *Germany and the Second World War*, Vol. 4: *The Attack on the Soviet Union*. Trans. Dean S. McMurry, Ewald Osers, and Louise Wilmot. Oxford, UK: Clarendon Press, 2001.

Bradley, Dermot, Karl-Friedrich Hildebrand, and Markus Rövekamp. *Die Generale des Heeres 1921–1945*. Osnabruk: Biblio Verlag, 1993.

Buchner, Alex. *Sewastopol: Der Angriff auf die stärkste Festung der Welt 1942*. Friedberg: Podzun-Pallas Verlag, 1978.

Carell, Paul. *Stalingrad: The Defeat of the German 6th Army*. Trans. David Johnston. Atglen, PA: Schiffer Publishing, 1993.

Chistiakov, I. M. *Sluzhim otchizne* [In service to the Fatherland]. Moscow: Voenizdat, 1975.

———, ed. *Po prikazu Rodiny: boevoi put' 6-i gvardeiskoi armii v Velikoi Otechestvennoi voine* [By order of the Motherland; The combat path of the 6th Guards Army in the Great Patriotic War]. Moscow: Voenizdat, 1971.

Chuikov, Vasili I. *The Battle for Stalingrad*. Trans. Harold Silver. New York: Holt, Reinhart and Winston, 1964.

Craig, William. *Enemy at the Gates: The Battle for Stalingrad*. New York: Reader's Digest Press, 1973.

Demin, V. A., and R. M. Portugal'sky. *Tanki vkhodiat v proryv* [Tanks enter the penetration]. Moscow: Voenizdat, 1988.

Dërr, G. *Pokhod na Stalingrad* [The march on Stalingrad]. Moscow: Voenizdat, 1957.

Dieckhoff, Gerhard. *3. Infantrie-Division, 3. Infantrie-Division (mot), 3. Panzer-Grenadier-Division*. Cuxhaven, Germany: Oberstudienrat Gerhard Dieckhoff, 1960.

DiNardo, Richard L. *Germany's Panzer Arm*. Westport, CT: Greenwood Press, 1997.

Dragunsky, D. A., ed. *Ot Volgi do Pragi* [From the Volga to Prague]. Moscow: Voenizdat, 1966.

Dukachev, A. *Kurs na Sevastopol'* [The path to Sevastopol']. Simferopol': "Tavriia," 1974.

Eremenko, A. I. *Stalingrad: Uchastnikam Velikoi bitvy pod Stalingradom posviatshchaetsia* [Stalingrad: A participant in the great battle at Stalingrad dedicates]. Moscow: AST, 2006.

———. *Stalingrad: Zapiski komanduuishchevo frontom* [Stalingrad: The notes of a *front* commander]. Moscow: Voenizdat, 1961.

Erickson, John. *The Road to Stalingrad: Stalin's War with Germany, Vol. 1.* New York: Harper & Row, 1975.

Friedin, Seymour, and William Richardson, eds. *The Fatal Decisions.* New York: William Sloane Associates, 1956.

Galushko, Andrei, and Maksim Kolomiets. "Boi za Khar'kov v mae 1942 god" [The battle for Khar'kov in May 1942]. In *Frontovaia illiustratsiia* [Front illustrated]. Moscow: "Strategiia KM," 1999.

Gehlen, Reinhard. *The Service: The Memoirs of General Reinhard Gehlen.* Trans. David Irving. New York: World Publishing, 1972.

Gerbet, Klaus, ed. *Generalfeldmarschall Fedor von Bock: The War Diary, 1939–1945.* Trans. David Johnson. Atglen, PA: Schiffer Military History, 1996.

Geroi Sovetskogo Soiuza, tom 1 [Heroes of the Soviet Union, vol. 1]. Moscow: Voenizdat, 1987.

Geschichte der 3. Panzer-Division, Berlin-Brandenburg 1935–1945. Berlin: Verlag der Buchhandlung Gunter Richter, 1947.

Glantz, David M. *Atlas of Operation Blau: The German Advance on Stalingrad, 28 June–18 November 1942.* Carlisle, PA: Self-published, 1998.

———. *Colossus Reborn: The Red Army at War, 1941–1943.* Lawrence: University Press of Kansas, 2005.

———. *Forgotten Battles of the Soviet-German War (1941–1945), Vol. 2: The Winter Campaign (5 December 1941–April 1942).* Carlisle, PA: Self-published, 1999.

———. *Forgotten Battles of the German-Soviet War (1941–1945), Vol. 3: The Summer Campaign (12 May–18 November 1942).* Carlisle, PA: Self-published, 1999.

———. *A History of Soviet Airborne Forces.* London: Frank Cass, 1994.

———. *Kharkov 1942: Anatomy of a Military Disaster.* Rockville Center, NY: Sarpedon, 1998.

———. *Red Army Command Cadre (1941–1945), Volume 1: Direction, Front, Army, Military District, Defense Zone, and Mobile Corps Commanders.* Carlisle, PA: Self-published, 2002.

———. *The Role of Intelligence in Soviet Military Strategy in World War II.* Novato, CA: Presidio Press, 1990.

———. *The Strategic and Operational Impact of Terrain on Military Operations in Central and Eastern Europe.* Carlisle, PA: Self-published, 1998.

———. *Stumbling Colossus: The Red Army on the Eve of World War.* Lawrence: University Press of Kansas, 1998.

———. "Nikolai Fedorovich Vatutin." In *Stalin's Generals.* Ed. Harold Shukman, 287–300. London: Weidenfeld & Nicolson, 1993.

Glantz, David M., and Jonathan House. *When Titans Clashed: How the Red Army Stopped Hitler.* Lawrence: University Press of Kansas, 1995.

Goerlitz, Walter. *Paulus and Stalingrad: A Life of Field-Marshal Friedrich Paulus with notes, correspondence, and documents from his papers.* Trans. R. H. Stevens. New York: The Citadel Press, 1963.

Golikov, F. I. "V Oborona Stalingrada" [In the defense of Stalingrad]. In *Stalingradskaia epopeia* [The Stalingrad epoch]. Ed. A. M. Samsonov. Moscow: "Nauka," 1968.

Gorshkov, S. G. *Na Iuzhnom flange, osen' 1941 g.–vesna 1944 g.* [On the southern flank, fall 1941–spring 1944]. Moscow: Voenizdat, 1989.

Grams, Rolf. *Die 14. Panzer-Division 1940–1945.* Bad Nauheim, BRD: Verlag Hans-Henning Podzun, 1957.

Grechko, A. A. *Bitva za Kavkaz* [The battle for the Caucasus]. Moscow: Voenizdat, 1973.

———. *Battle for the Caucasus.* Moscow: Progress Publishers, 1971.

———. ed. *Istoriia Vtoroi Mirovoi voiny 1939–1945 v dvenadtsati tomakh, tom piatyi* [History of the Second World War in twelve volumes, vol. 5]. Moscow: Voenizdat, 1975.

Grin'ko, A. I. *Kogda goreli kvartaly: Chasti NKVD v ulichnykh boiakh za Voronezh* [When the houses burned: Units of the NKVD in the street fighting for Voronezh]. Moscow: Voenizdat, 1987.

Grin'ko, A. *V boiakh za Voronezh* [In the battles for Voronezh]. Voronezh: Tsentral'nyo-Chernozemnoe Knizhnoe Izdatel'stvo, 1985.

Grossman, Horst. *Rzhev: The Cornerstone of the Eastern Front.* Unpublished trans. by Joseph G. Welsh from the German, *Rshew: Eckpfeiler der Ostfront (unterveranderter Nachdruck).* Bad Nauheim, BRD: Podzun-Verlag, 1962.

"Gurov Kuz'ma Akimovich." In *Voennaia Entsiklopediia v vos'mi tomakh, 2* [Military encyclopedia in eight volumes, vol. 2]. Ed. P. S. Grachev, 534. Moscow: Voenizdat, 1994.

Halder, Franz. *The Halder War Diary, 1939–1942.* Novato, CA: Presidio Press, 1988.

Hardesty, Von. *Red Phoenix: The Rise of Soviet Air Power, 1941–1945.* Washington, DC: Smithsonian Press, 1982.

Haupt, Werner. *Army Group South: The Wehrmacht in Russia, 1941–1945.* Trans. Joseph G. Welsh. Atglen, PA: Schiffer Press, 1998.

Hayward, Joel S. A. *Stopped at Stalingrad: The Luftwaffe and Hitler's Defeat in the East, 1942–1943.* Lawrence: University Press of Kansas, 1998.

Hermann, Carl Hans. *Die 9. Panzerdivision, 1939–1945.* Friedberg: Podzun-Pallas-Verlag, 2004.

Holl, Adelbert. *An Infantryman in Stalingrad: From 24 September 1942 to 2 February 1943.* Trans. Jason D. Mark and Neil Page. Sydney, Australia: Leaping Horseman Books, 2005.

Ignatovich, E. A. *Zenitnoe bratstvo Sevastopolia* [The antiaircraft brotherhood of Sevastopol']. Kiev: Politicheskoi literatury Ukrainy, 1986.

Isaev, Aleksei. *Kogda vnezapnosti uzhe ne bylo* [When there was no surprise]. Moscow: "IAUZA" "EKSMO," 2005.

———. *Kratkii kurs Istorii Velikoi Otechestvennoi voyny: Nastuplenie Marshala Shaposhnikova* [A short course in the history of the Great Patriotic War: The offensives of Marshal Shaposhnikov]. Moscow: "IAUZA" "EKSMO," 2005.

———. *Stalingrad: Zabytoe Srazhenie* [Stalingrad: The forgotten battle]. Moscow: AST, 2005.

Istoricheskii podvig Stalingrada [The historical victory at Stalingrad]. Moscow: "Mysl'," 1985.

Iushchuk, I. I., *Odinnatsatyi Tankovyi Korpus v boiakh za Rodinu* [The 11th Tank Corps in combat for the Motherland]. Moscow: Voenizdat, 1962.

Jentz, Thomas L. *Panzertruppen*. Atglen, PA: Schiffer Publishing, 1996.

Jukes, Geoffrey. *Hitler's Stalingrad Decisions*. Berkeley, CA: University of California Press, 1985.

————. "Alexander Mikhailovich Vasilevsky." In *Stalin's Generals*. Ed. Harold Shukman, 275–286. London: Weidenfeld & Nicolson, 1993.

Jung, Hans-Joachim. *The History of Panzerregiment Grossdeutschland*. Trans. David Johnson. Winnipeg, Canada: J. J. Fedorowicz, 2000.

Katukov, M. E. *Na ostrie glavnogo udara* [At the point of the main attack]. Moscow: Voenizdat, 1976.

Kazakov, M. I. *Nad kartoi bylykh srazhenii* [There were battles on the maps]. Moscow: Voenizdat, 1965.

Kehrig, Manfred. *Stalingrad: Analyse und Dokumentation einer Schlacht*. Stuttgart: Deutsche Verlag-Anstalt, 1974.

Keilig, Wolf. *Die Generale des Heeres*. Bad Nauheim: Podzun-Pallas, 1983.

Keitel, Wilhelm. *In the Service of the Reich*. Trans. David Irving. New York: Stein and Day, 1966.

Kobyliansky, Isaak. *From Stalingrad to Pillau: A Red Army Artillery Officer Remembers the Great Patriotic War*. Lawrence: University Press of Kansas, 2008.

Kolomiets, Maksim, and Aleksandr Smirnov. "Boi v izluchine Dona, 28 iiunia–23 iiulia 1942 goda" [Battle in the bend of the Don, 28 June–23 July 1942]. In *Frontovaia illiustratsiia* [Front illustrated]. Moscow: "Strategiia KM," 2002.

Kozlov, M. M., ed. *Velikaia Otechestvennaia voina 1941–1945: Entsiklopediia* [The Great Patriotic War, 1941–1945: An encyclopedia]. Moscow: "Sovetskaia entsiklopediia," 1985.

Kolomiets, Maksim, and Il'ia Moshchansky. "Oborona Kavkaz (iiul'–dekabr' 1942 goda)" [The defense of the Caucasus (July–December 1942)]. In *Frontovaia illiustratsiia* [Front illustrated]. Moscow: "Strategiia KM," 2000).

Krasnoznamennyi Chernomorskii Flot [The Red Banner Black Sea Fleet]. Moscow: Voenizdat, 1987.

Krivosheev, G. F., ed. *Grif sekretnosti sniat: Poteri vooruzhennykh sil SSSR v voinakh, boevykh deistviiakh, i voennykh konfliktakh* [The classification secret is removed: The losses of the USSR's armed forces in wars, combat operations, and military conflicts]. Moscow: Voenizdat, 1993.

————. *Rossiia i SSSR v voinakh XX veka: Poteri vooruzhennykh sil, Statisticheskoe issledovanie* [Russia and the USSR in wars of the XX Century: Armed Forces losses, a statistical investigation]. Moscow: "OLMA," 2001.

————. *Soviet Casualty and Combat Losses in the Twentieth Century*. London and Mechanicsburg, PA: Schiffer Books, 1997.

Krylov, N. I. *Stalingradskii rubezh* [The Stalingrad line]. Moscow: Voenizdat, 1984.

Kuhn, George W. S. *Ground Forces Casualty Rate Patterns: The Empirical Evidence, Report FP703TR1*. Bethesda, MD: Logistics Management Agency, September 1989.

Kuz'min, A. V., and I. I. Krasnov. *Kantemirovtsy: Boevoi put' 4-go gvardeiskogo tankovogo Kantemirovskogo ordena Lenina Krasnoznamennogo korpusa* [The men of Kantemirovka: The combat path of the 4th Guards Kantemirovka Order of Lenin Red Banner Tank Corps]. Moscow: Voenizdat, 1971.

Laskin, I. A. *Na puti k perelomu* [On the path to the turning point]. Moscow: Voenizdat, 1977.

Lebedenko, P. P. *V izluchine Dona* [In the bend of the Don]. Moscow: Voenizdat, 1965.

Lebedev, Ia. A., and A. I. Maliutin. *Pomnit dnepr-reka: Vospominaniia veteranov 193-i strelkovoi Dneprovskoi ordena Lenina, Krasnoznamennoi, ordena Suvorova i Kutuzova divizii* [Remember the Dnepr River: Recollections of veterans of the 193rd Dnepr order of Lenin, Red Banner, and orders of Suvorov and Kutuzov Rifle Division]. Minsk: "Belarus'," 1986.

Lemelsen, Joachim, et al. *29. Division: 29. Infanteriedivision, 29. Infanteriedivision (mot), 29. Panzergrenadier-Division.* Bad Nauheim, BRD: Podzun-Verlag, 1960.

Liudnikov, I. I. *Doroda dlinoiu v zhizn'* [The long road in life]. Moscow: Voenizdat, 1969.

Losik, O. A. *Stroitel'stvo i boevoe primenenie Sovetskikh tankovykh voisk v gody Velikoi Otechestvennoi voiny* [The Formation and combat use of Soviet tank units in the years of the Great Patriotic War]. Moscow: Voenizdat, 1979.

Mackensen, Eberhard von. *Vom Bug zum Kaukasus: Das III. Panzerkorps im Feldzug gegen Sowjetrussland 1941/42.* Neckargemünd: Kurt Vowinkel Verlag, 1967.

Manstein, Erich von. *Lost Victories.* Trans. Anthony G. Powell. Chicago: Henry Regnery, 1958.

Mark, Jason D. *Death of the Leaping Horseman: 25. Panzer-Division in Stalingrad, 12th August–20th November 1942.* Sydney, Australia: Leaping Horseman Books, 2003.

———. *Island of Fire: The Battle for the Barrikady Gun Factory in Stalingrad, November 1942–February 1943.* Sydney, Australia: Leaping Horseman Books, 2006.

Martynov, V., and S. Spakhov. *Proliv v ogne* [The straits in flames]. Kiev: Izdatel'stvo politicheskoi literatury Ukrainy, 1984.

Maslov, Aleksander A. *Fallen Soviet Generals.* London: Frank Cass, 1998.

McCroden, William. *The Organization of the German Army in World War II: Army Groups, Armies, Corps, Divisions, and Combat Groups, in five volumes.* Draft manuscript, unpublished and undated.

Mellenthin, Friedrich W. von. *German Generals of World War II As I Saw Them.* Norman: University of Oklahoma Press, 1977.

Mirzoian, Suren. *Stalingradskoe Zarevo* [The Stalingrad conflagration]. Erevan: Izdatel'stvo "Anastan," 1974.

Morozov, I. K. "Na iuzhnom uchaske fronta" [In the *front*'s southern sector]. In *Bitva za Volge* [The battle for the Volga]. Stalingrad: Knizhnoe izdatel'stvo, 1962.

Moshchansky, Il'ia, and Sergei Smolinov. *Oborona Stalingrada: Stalingradskaia strategicheskaia oboronitel'naia operatsiia, 17 iiulia–18 noiabria 1942 goda* [The defense of Stalingrad: The Stalingrad strategic defensive operation, 17 July–18 November 1942]. In *Voennaia Letopis'* [Military chronicle]. Moscow: BTV, 2002.

Moskalenko, K. S. *Na iugo-zapadnom napravlenii* [On the southwestern axis], vol. 1. Moscow: "Nauka," 1969.

Mozolev, V. F. "Mozdok-Malgrobekaia operatsiia 1942" [The Mozdok-Malgrobek operation, 1942]. In *Voennaia entsyklopediia v vos'mi tomakh, 5* [Military encyclopedia in eight volumes, vol. 5]. Ed. I. N. Sergeev, 196–197. Moscow: Voenizdat, 2001.

Müller, Rolf-Dieter, and Gerd R. Ueberschar. *Hitler's War in the East, 1941–1945: A Critical Assessment.* Providence, RI, Oxford, UK: Berghahn Books, 1997.

Muratov, Viktor. *The Battle for the Caucasus.* Moscow: Novosti Press, 1973.

Murray, Williamson. *Luftwaffe.* Baltimore: Nautical & Aviation Publishing Company of America, 1985.

Neidhardt, Hanns. *Mit Tanne und Eichenlaub: Kriegschronik der 100. Jäger-Division vormals 100. leichte Infanterie-Division.* Graz-Stuttgart: Leopold Stocker Verlag, 1981.

"Novorossiiskaia operatsiia 1942" [The Novorossiisk operation 1942]. In *Voennaia entsiklopediia v vos'mi tomakh,* 5 [Military encyclopedia in eight volumes, vol. 5]. Ed. I. N. Sergeev, 501–502. Moscow: Voenizdat, 2001.

Plato, Anton Detlev von. *Die Geschichte der 5. Panzerdivision 1938 bis 1945.* Regensberg: Walhalla u. Praetoria Verlag, 1978.

Portugal'sky, R. M. *Analiz opyta nezavershennykh nastupatel'nykh operatsii Velikoi Otechestvennoi voiny. Vyvody i uroki* [An analysis of the experience of uncompleted offensive operations of the Great Patriotic War. Conclusions and lessons]. Moscow: Izdanie akademii, 1991.

Pospelov, P. N. *Istoriia Velikoi Otechestvennoi voiny Sovetskogo Soiuza 1941–1945 v shesti tomakh, tom vtoroi* [History of the Great Patriotic War, 1941–1945, in six volumes, vol. 2]. Moscow: Voenizdat, 1961.

Povalyi, M. M. *Vosemnadtsataia v srazheniia za Rodiny* [The 18th (Army) in the defense of the Motherland]. Moscow: Voenizdat, 1982.

Ramanichev, N. M., and V. V. Gurkin. "Rzhevsko-Sychevskie operatsii 1942 [The Rzhev-Sychevka operation 1942]. In *Voennaia entsyklopediia v vos'mi tomakh,* 7 [Military encyclopedia in eight volumes, vol. 7]. Ed. S. B. Ivanov, 233–234. Moscow: Voenizdat, 2003.

Reinhardt, Klaus. *Moscow—The Turning Point. The Failure of Hitler's Strategy in the Winter of 1941–1942.* Trans. Karl Keenan. Oxford, UK, Providence, RI: Oxford University Press, 1992.

Rokossovsky, K. K. *Soldatskii dolg* [A soldier's duty]. Moscow: "GOLOS," 2000.

———, ed. *Velikaia bitva na Volge* [Great victory on the Volga]. Moscow: Voenizdat, 1965.

Rotmistrov, Pavel A. *Stal'naia gvardiia* [Steel guards]. Moscow: Voenizdat, 1984.

Rzheshevsky, Oleg. "Boris Mikhailovich Shaposhnikov." In *Stalin's Generals.* Ed. Harold Shukman, 217–232. London: Weidenfeld & Nicolson, 1993.

Samchuk, I. A. *Trinadtsataia gvardeiskaia* [The 13th Guards]. Moscow: Voenizdat, 1971.

Samsonov, A. M. *Stalingradskaia bitva* [The battle for Stalingrad]. Moscow: "Nauka," 1983.

———, ed. *Stalingradskaia epopeia* [Stalingrad epic]. Moscow: "Nauka," 1968.

Sandalov, A. M. *Pogoreloe-Gorodishchenskaia operatsiia: Nastupatel'naia operatsiia 20-i armii Zapadnogo fronta v avguste 1942 goda* [The Pogoreloe-Gorodishche operation: The offensive operation of the Western Front's 20th Army in August 1942]. Moscow: Voenizdat, 1960.

Sarkis'ian, S. M. *51-ia Armiia* [The 51st Army]. Moscow: Voenizdat, 1983.

Schröter, Heinz. *Stalingrad.* New York: Ballantine, 1958.

———. *Stalingrad: ". . . bis letzten Patrone."* Lengerich: Kleins Druck- und Verlagsanstalt, n.d.).

Senger und Etterlin, Ferdinand von. *Die 24. Panzer-Division vormals 1. Kavallerie-Division 1939–1945.* Neckargemünd: Kurt Vowinckel Verlag, 1962.

Shiian, I. S. *Ratnyi podvig Novorossiiska* [Feat of Arms at Novorossiisk]. Moscow: Voenizdat, 1977.

Shtemenko, S. M. *The General Staff at War, 1941–1945*, book 1. Trans. Robert Daglish. Moscow: Voenizdat, 1985.

Slepyan, Kenneth. *Stalin's Guerrillas: Soviet Partisans in World War II.* Lawrence: University Press of Kansas, 2006.

Smol'nyi, M. K. *7000 kilometrov v boiakh i pokhodakh: Boevoi put' 161-i strelkovoi Stanislavskoi Krasnoznamennoi ordena Bogdana Khmel'nitskogo divizii 1941–1945 gg.* [7000 kilometers in combat and marches: The combat path of the 161st Stanislav Red Banner order of Bogdan Khmel'nitsky Rifle Division, 1941–1945]. Moscow: Voenizdat, 1982.

Soviet Documents on the Use of War Experience, Volume Three: Military Operations 1941 and 1942. Trans. Harold S. Orenstein. London: Frank Cass, 1993.

Spaeter, Helmuth. *The History of the Panzerkorps Grossdeutschland*, vol. 1. Trans. David Johnston. Winnipeg: J. J. Fedorowicz Publishing, 1992.

Speer, Albert. *Inside the Third Reich.* Trans. Richard and Clara Winston. New York: Macmillan, 1970.

Spielberger, Walter J., and Uwe Feist. *Panzerkampfwagen IV: "Workhorse" of the German Panzertruppe.* Berkeley, CA: Feist Publications, 1968.

Stalingradskaia epopeia: Vpervye publikuemye dokumenty, rassekrechennye FSB RF [Stalingrad epoch: Declassified documents of the Russian Federation's FSB published for the first time]. Moscow: "Evonnitsa-MG," 2000.

Stoves, Rolf. *Die Gepanzerten und Motorisierten Deutschen Grossverbande, 1935–1945.* Friedberg: Podzun-Pallas-Verlag, 1986.

———. *Die 22. Panzer-Division, Die 25. Panzer-Division, Die 27. Panzer-Division, und die Die 233. Reserve-Panzer-Division.* Friedberg: Podzun-Pallas-Verlag, 1985.

Sukharev, A. Ia., ed. *Marshal A. M. Vasilevsky—strateg, polkovodets, chelovek* [Marshal A. M. Vasilevsky – strategist, military leader, and the man]. Moscow: Sovet Veteranov knigoizdaniia, 1998.

"Tactics of Mobile Units. Operations of the 5th SS Panzergrenadier Division Wiking at Rostov and the Maikop Oilfields (Summer 1942)." Heidelberg, Germany: Foreign Military Studies Branch, Historical Division, Headquarters, United States Army Europe. In OCMH MS # D-248.

Tarrant, V. E. *Stalingrad: Anatomy of an Agony.* London: Leo Cooper, 1992.

Tieke, Wilhelm. *The Caucasus and the Oil: The German-Soviet War in the Caucasus 1942/43.* Trans. Joseph G. Welsh. Winnipeg: J. J. Fedorowicz, 1995.

"Timoshenko, Semen, Konstantinovich." In *Sovetskaia Voennaia Entsiklopediia v bos'mi tomakh, 8* [Soviet military encyclopedia in eight volumes, 8]. Ed. N. V. Ogarkov, 43–44. Moscow: Voenizdat, 1980.

Tiulenev, I. V. *Krakh operatsii "Edel'veis"* [The defeat of Operation Edelweiss]. Ordzhonikidze: Izdatel'stvo "Ir," 1975.

Trevor-Roper, Hugh R., ed. *Blitzkrieg to Defeat: Hitler's War Directives, 1939–1945.* New York, Chicago: Holt, Reinhart and Winston, 1964.

Two Hundred Days of Fire: Accounts by Participants and Witnesses of the Battle of Stalingrad. Moscow: Progress Publishers, 1970.

Utkin, Anatolii. *Sorok vtoroi god [1942].* Smolensk: "Rusich," 2002.

Vaneev, G. I. *Chernomortsy v Velikoi Otechestvennoi voine* [Black Sea sailors in the Great Patriotic War]. Moscow: Voenizdat, 1978.

Vaneev, G. I., S. L. Ermash, I. D. Malakhovsky, S. T. Sakhno, and A. F. Khrenov. *Geroi-cheskaia oborona Sevastopolia 1941–1942* [The heroic defense of Sevastopol' 1941–1942]. Moscow: Voenizdat, 1969.

Vasilevsky, A. M. *Delo vsei zhizni* [Life's work]. Moscow: Izdatel'stvo politicheskoi literatury, 1983.

Venkov, B. S., and P. P. Dudinov. *Gvardeiskaia doblest': Boevoi put' 70-i gvardeiskoi strelkovoi glukhovskoi ordena Lenina, dvazhdy krasnoznamennoi, ordena Suvorova, Kutuzova i Bogdana Khmel'nitskogo divizii* [Guards valor: the combat path of the 70th Guards Glukhov, Order of Lenin and order of Suvorov, Kutuzov and Bogdan Khmel'nitsky Rifle Division]. Moscow: Voenizdat, 1979.

Vider, Ioakhim. *Stalingradskaia tragediia: Za kulisami katastrofy* [The Stalingrad tragedy: Behind the scenes of a catastrophe]. Trans. A. Lebedev and N. Portugalov. Moscow: IAUZA, EKSMO, 2004.

Voennaia entsiklopediia v vos'mi tomakh, 1 [Military encyclopedia in eight volumes, vol. 1]. Ed. I. N. Rodionov. Moscow: Voenizdat, 1997.

Volkov, A. A. *Kriticheskii prolog: Nezavershennye frontovye nastupatel'nye operatsii pervykh kampanii Velikoi Otechestvennoi voiny* [Critical prologue: Incomplete front offensive operations of the initial campaign of the Great Patriotic War]. Moscow: AVIAR, 1992.

Volostnov, N. I. *Na ognennykh rubezhakh* [In firing positions]. Moscow: Voenizdat, 1983.

Vyrodov, I. Ia., ed. *V srazheniiakh za Pobedy: Boevoi put' 38-i armii v gody Velikoi Otechestvennoi voiny 1941–1945* [In battles for the Fatherland: The combat path of the 38th Army in the Great Patriotic War, 1941–1945]. Moscow: "Nauka," 1974.

Warlimont, Walter. *Inside Hitler's Headquarters, 1939–1945*. Trans. R. H. Barry. Novato, CA: Presidio, 1964.

Werthen, Wolfgang. *Geschichte der 16. Panzer-Division 1939–1945*. Bad Nauheim: Podzun-Pallas-Verlag, 1958.

Wijers, Hans J. *The Battle for Stalingrad: The Battle for the Factories, 14 October–19 November 1942*. Heerenveen, The Netherlands: Self-published, 2003.

Woff, Richard. "Chuikov." In *Stalin's Generals*. Ed. Harold Shukman, 67–76. London: Weidenfeld & Nicolson, 1993.

———. "Rokossovsky." In *Stalin's Generals*. Ed. Harold Shukman, 177–198. London: Weidenfeld & Nicolson, 1993.

Wray, Timothy A. *Standing Fast: German Defensive Doctrine on the Russian Front During World War II, Prewar to March 1943*. Fort Leavenworth, KS: Combat Studies Institute, 1986.

Zakharov, Iu. D. *General armii Vatutin*. Moscow: Voenizdat, 1985.

Zaloga, Steve, and Peter Sarson. *T-34/76 Medium Tank, 1941–1945*. London: Osprey/Reed Publishing, 1994.

Zamiatkin, N. M., and F. D. Vorob'ev. *Oborona Sevastopolia* [The defense of Sevastopol']. Moscow: Voenizdat, 1943.

Zhadov, A. S. *Chetyre goda voiny* [Four years of war]. Moscow: Voenizdat, 1978.

Zhukov, G. *Reminiscences and Reflections*, vol. 2. Moscow: Progress Publishers, 1985.

Ziemke, Earl F. *Stalingrad to Berlin: The German Defeat in the East*. Washington, DC: United States Army Office of the Chief of Military History, 1968.

Ziemke, Earl F., and Magna E. Bauer. *Moscow to Stalingrad: Decision in the East*. Washington, DC: Center of Military History United States Army, 1987.

Zolotarev, V. A., ed. *Velikaia Otechestvennaia voina 1941–1945, Kniga 1: Surovye ispytaniia* [The Great Patriotic War, bk. 1: A harsh education]. Moscow: "Nauka," 1998.

Zvartsev, A. M., ed. *3-ia gvardeiskaia tankovaia armiia* [The 3rd Guards Tank Army]. Moscow: Voenizdat, 1982.

Secondary Sources: Articles

Anoshkin, V., and N. Naumov. "O stabilizatsii fronta oborony na Iuzhnom strategicheskom napravlenii letom 1942 goda" [About the stabilization of the defensive front on the southern axis in the summer of 1942]. *VIZh* 10 (October 1982): 18–24.

Bondar', M. M. "4-ia Istrebitel'naia Brigada v boiakh pod Kastornym" [The 4th Destroyer Brigade in the battles for Kastornoe]. *VIZh* 7 (July 1986): 49–54.

Brusin, G., and G. Nekhonov. "Oborona ostrova Zaitsevskii" [The defense of Zaitsevskii Island]. *VIZh* 3 (March 1964): 113–117.

Danilov, F. "Bitva za Kavkaz" [The battle for the Caucasus]. *VIZh* 7 (July 1967): 117–123.

Glantz, David M. "Soviet Mobilization in Peace and War, 1924–42: A Survey." *JSMS* 5, 3 (September 1992): 345–352.

Goloborodov, A. I. "Kontrudar 5-i tankovoi armiii pod Voronezhem" [The 5th Tank Army's counterstroke at Voronezh]. *Voennaia mysl'* [Military thought], 4 (April 1993): 42–48.

Gorter-Gronvik, Waling T., and Mikhail N. Suprun. "Ethnic Minorities and Warfare at the Arctic Front, 1939–1945." *JSMS* 13, 1 (March 2000): 127–142.

Grilev, A. N. "Nekotorye osobennosti planirovaniia letne-osennei kampanii 1942 goda" [Some features of planning for the 1942 summer-autumn campaign]. *VIZh* 9 (September 1991): 4–11.

Gurkin, V. "'Dom Pavlova'—symbol doblesti i geoistva sovetskikh voinov" ["Pavlov's House"—a symbol of the valor and heroism of Soviet soldiers]. *VIZh* 2 (February 1963): 48–54.

———. "214-ia strelkoviai diviziia v bitva na Volge" [The 214th Rifle Division in the battle for the Volga]. *VIZh* 7 (July 1964): 97–100.

Gurkin, V. V. "Liudskie poteri Sovetskikh Vooruzhennykh sil v 1941–1945 gg.: Novye aspekty" [Personnel losses of the Soviet Armed Forces in 1941–1945: New aspects]. *VIZh* 2 (March-April 1999): 2–13.

Gurkin, V. V., and A. I. Kruglov. "Oborona Kavkaza. 1942 god" [The defense of the Caucasus. 1942]. *VIZh* 10 (October 1942): 11–18.

Hayward, Joel. "Hitler's Quest for Oil: The Impact of Economic Considerations on Military Strategy, 1941–1942." *The Journal of Strategic Studies*, 18, 4 (December 1995): 94–135.

Hill, Alexander. "British 'Lend Lease' Tanks and the Battle for Moscow, November-December 1941 – A Research Note." *JSMS*, 19, 2 (June 2006): 289–294.

I'lenkov, S. A. "Concerning the Registration of Soviet Armed Forces Wartime Irrevocable Losses, 1941–1945." *JSMS* 9, 2 (June 1996): 440–442.

Il'in, P. "Boi za Kalach-na-Donu" [The battle for Kalach-on-the-Don]. *VIZh* 10 (October 1961): 70–81.

Isaev, S. I. "Vekhi frontovogo puti" [Landmarks of a front path]. *VIZh* 10 (October) 1991: 24–25.

Istomin, V. "Inzhenernye voiska v bitve za Kavkaz" [Engineer troops in the battle for the Caucasus]. *VIZh* 10 (October 1963): 86–90.

Kahn, David. "An Intelligence Case Study: The Defense of Osuga, 1942." *Aerospace Historian* 28, 4 (December 1981): 242–252.

Kazakov, M. "Na Voronezhskom napravlenii letom 1942 goda" [On the Voronezh axis in the summer of 1942]. *VIZh* 10 (October 1964): 27–44.

Kharitonov, A. "Na gornykh perevalakh Kavkaza" [In the mountain passes of the Caucasus]. *VIZh* 7 (August 1970): 57–59.

Khar'kov, A. "Sovetskoe voennoe iskusstva v bitva za Kavkaz" [Soviet military art in the battle for the Caucasus]. *VIZh* 3 (March 1983): 21–28.

Khar'kov, V. "112-ia strelkovaia diviziia v Bitva za Stalingradom" [The 112th Rifle Division in the battle for Stalingrad]. *VIZh* 3: (March 1980): 36–43.

Kuz'michev, I. V. "Shtafniki" [Penal troops]. *Serzhant* [Sergeant] 14 (2006): 25–34.

Lashchenko, P. N. "Prodiktovan surovoi neobkhodimost'iu" [Severe measures are dictated]. *VIZh* 8 (August) 1988: 76–80.

Loskutov, Iu. "Boevye deistviia 308-i strelkovoi divizii 10–25 sentiabria 1942 goda" [Combat operations of the 308th Rifle Division 10–25 September 1942]. *VIZh* 8 (August 1982): 40–48.

Luchinsky, A. "Na tuapinskom napravlenii" [On the Tuapse axis]. *VIZh* 11 (November 1967): 69–75.

Muriev, D. "Kontrudar pod g. Ordzhonikidze" [The counterstroke at Ordzhonikidze]. *VIZh* 11 (November 1967): 125–128.

"Nakanune Stalingradksoi bitvy" [On the eve of the battle for Stalingrad]. *VIZh* 8 (August 1982): 27–31.

Nevzorov, B. I. "Mai 1942-go: Ak Monai, Enikale" [May 1942: Ak Monai and Enikale], *VIZh* 8 (August 1992): 32–42.

Nikiforov, V. "Sovetskaia aviatsiia v bitva za Kavkaz" [Soviet aviation in the battle for the Caucasus]. *VIZh* 8 (August 1971): 11–19.

"Operatsiia '*Kreml*'" [Operation Kremlin], *VIZh* 8: (August 1961): 9–90.

"Operatsiia neispol'zovannykh vozmozhnostei" [Operations of unfulfilled opportunities]. *VIZh* 7 (July 1965): 117–124.

Parot'kin, I. "O plane letnei kampanii Nemetsko-Fashistskogo komandovaniia na Sovetsko-Germanskom fronte v 1942 godu" [Concerning the summer campaign of the German-Fascist command on the Soviet-German front in 1942]. *VIZh* 1 (January 1961): 31–42.

Poplyko, F. "Geroi bitvy za Kavkaz" [Heroes of the battle for the Caucasus]. *VIZh* 3 (February 1983): 57–60.

Rokossovsky, K. K. "Soldatskii dolg" [A soldier's duty]. *VIZh* 2 (February 1990): 47–52.

Runov, V. "Ot oborony—k reidu" [From defense—to a raid]. *VV* [Military herald] 5 (April 1991): 42–46.

Sdvizhkov, I. Iu. "Kak pogib i gde pokhoronen general Liziukov?" [How did General Liziukov perish and where was he buried?], *Voenno-istoricheskii arkhiv* [Military-historical archives] 9, 81 (2006): 149–165, and 10, 82 (2006): 39–56.

Shtykov, N. "V boiakh za platsdarmy na Verkhnem Donu" [In combat for the bridgeheads on the upper Don]. *VIZh* 8 (August 1982): 32–39.

Statiev, Alexander. "The Ugly Duckling of the Armed Forces: Romanian Armour 1919–41." *JSMS* 12, 2 (June 1999): 225–240.

————. "When an Army Becomes 'Merely a Burden': Romanian Defense Policy and Strategy (1918–1941)." *JSMS* 13, 2 (June 2000): 67–85.

Sverdlov, F. "Boi u Volga i na Kavkaze (Sentiabr' 1942 goda)" [The battle on the Volga and in the Caucasus (September 1942)]. *VV* 9 (September 1992): 35–36.

————. "Prichiny neudach (Oktiabr' 1942 goda)" [The reasons for the failures (October 1942)]. *VV* 10 (October 1992): 49–52.

Utenkov, F. "Nekotorye voprosy oboronitel'nogo srazheniia na dal'nykh podstupakh k Stalingradu" [Some questions concerning the defensive battles on the distant approaches to Stalingrad], *VIZh* 9 (September 1962): 34–48.

Vasilevsky, A. "Nekotorye voprosy rukovodstva vooruzhennoi bor'boi letom 1942 goda" [Some questions on the direction of the armed struggle in the summer of 1942]. *VIZh* 8 (August 1965): 3–10.

————. "Nezabyvaemye dni" [Unforgettable days]. *VIZh* 10 (October 1965): 13–24.

Zaitsev, V. "Stalingrad – Sud'ba moia" [Stalingrad—My fate]. *Na boevom postu—Zhurnal Vnutrennykh voisk* [At the combat post—Journal of Internal Forces] 2 (February 1992): 3–8.

Index

Abadsechskaia, 426
Abganerovo, 278–279, 285–290, 302–303, 305, 318–319, 364–365, 481, 556n51
Abganerovo Station, 288–289, 306, 366–367, 370–371, 556n56
Abinskaia, 438, 441, 444
Abramov, 353
Abramov, Brigade Commissar I. P., 581n104
Abwehr (German counterintelligence), 25
Achavchar Pass, 582n116
Adler, 429
Aidar River, 122, 171, 173–176, 179, 181, 184
Air Fleet [*Luftflotte*], German, Fourth, 20, 111
Air Force, Red Army, 149, 292, 382–383
Aishkha Pass, 582n116
Akatov, 325–328, 331–333
Akatov bridgehead (16–18 August 1942), battle for, 325, 327
Akatovka, 337–338, 343
Akimovskii, 313, 331
Aksai, 279–280, 285, 287, 289, 306, 559n80
Aksai River, 167, 278–280, 285–286, 288–290, 306, 543n5, 556n54
Aksaiskaia, 404
Aleksandrovka, 418
Alekseev, Maj. Gen. Vasilii Mikhailovich, 182
biographical sketch, 534–535n18
Alekseevka (Donbas region). *See* Nikolaevka
Alekseevka (Stalingrad region), 378
Alexandria, 345
Altsynkhuta, 307
Anapa, 195, 406, 440–441, 444–445
Andreev, Col. A. G., 51
Andreevka, 378
Angern, Lt. Gen. Günther von, 27
Anna, 151
Anna Rebrikovskaia, 180–181
Antoniuk, Lt. Gen. Maksim Antonovich, 139, 151, 154, 253–256, 405
biographical sketch, 530–531n48
Antonov, 556n54
Antonov, Lt. Gen. A. I., 431

Apell, Lt. Gen. Wilhelm von, 27, 275, 317, 390
Apsheronskii, 426
Arbuzov, 404
Arctic Sea, 47
Arensdorff, Maj. Gen. Hans Adolf von, 27
Armavir, 207, 245, 406, 409–410, 416–420
Armed Forces, German. See *Wehrmacht*
Armed Forces, Soviet
strength, 1 December 1941, 46
strength, 1 May 1942, 46
Armenia, 418
Armies, Finnish, 8
Armies, German
Army of Lapland, 17, 110
First Panzer, 7, 17, 21, 25–26, 31, 55, 59–60, 77, 81, 85, 90, 98–99, 101, 103, 112–113, 115, 117, 125, 157–159, 163, 165, 167–170, 176–177, 183–185, 190, 192, 194–200, 201–203, 205, 208, 210–212, 214–215, 219, 225, 250, 271, 277, 345, 397, 399–404, 407, 409–410, 412–413, 416–417, 419–422, 424, 426, 431–436, 438, 479–480, 539n49, 539n59, 540n72, 542n81
armored strength, 28 June 1942, 119
armored strength, early and mid-July 1942, 573n36
armored strength, 15 August 1942, 410
composition, 23 July 1942, 208
composition, 25 July 1942, 542n79
composition, 1–13 August 1942, 412
Second, 17, 22–23, 110, 126, 158–159, 163, 165, 192, 208–210, 212, 217, 251, 253–257, 259–262, 453–454, 550n68
composition and armored strength, 23 July 1942, 208–209
Second Panzer, 17, 53, 58, 110, 125, 248, 251, 459, 461–462, 451n74
Third Panzer, 17, 110, 461
Fourth, 17, 110, 459

offensive *under* Operations, Soviet
military
Martsenkevich, Maj. Gen. Vladimir Nikolae-
vich, 401, 414, 433, 435, 437, 577n54
biographical sketch, 178, 533–534n11,
579n76
Marukh (Marukhskii) Pass, 450–451, 582n116
Marukha River, 582n116
Maslennikov, Lt. Gen. Ivan Ivanovich, 51, 419,
433–434, 437–438
biographical sketch, 419, 576n53
Maslov, Maj. Gen. of Technical Forces Aleksei
Gavrilovich, 65, 67–68
biographical sketch, 489
Mattenklott, Lt. Gen. Franz, 75, 114, 412
Mechetka River, 218, 348
Medova, 183
Mekenziia, 87
Mekhlis, Lev Zakharovich, 62, 74, 77, 264
Melo-Kletskii, 304, 309–310, 314, 324
Meretskov, Army General K. A., 51, 110
Meshkovskaia, 184, 192
Middle East, 11
Migulinskaia, 183, 187
Mikhailovskii, 444
Mikoian Shakhar, 449
Military Academy of Motorization and Mecha-
nization, Soviet, 56
Military councils, Soviet, 514n23
Military districts, Soviet
Baltic Special, 62
Belorussian (Special), 41, 60–61
Central Asian, 63
Kalinin, 57
Khar'kov, 41
Kiev Special, 39, 41, 43, 53, 55, 57–61, 155
Leningrad, 38, 56, 100
Moscow, 38, 59–60, 63, 407
North Caucasus, 41, 57, 407, 415, 419
Odessa, 58, 151
Orel, 415
Southern Ural, 415
Stalingrad, 279, 307, 375
Trans-Baikal, 415
Trans-Caucasus, 55, 62–63, 407
Turkestan, 57
Volga, 38, 57, 345–346, 353
Western Special, 61
Military highways, Soviet
Georgian, 207, 450
Ossetian, 207, 447, 450
Sukhumi, 447, 450–451

Military Management Academy, Soviet, 56
Millerovo, 14–15, 124, 163, 170, 181–183, 184,
186, 190–192, 194, 197–200, 202, 214–
216, 272, 479
Mineral'nye Vody, 419–420, 422, 432
Minina, 374
Minsk, 3, 23
Mishulin, Maj. Gen. Vasilii Aleksandrovich, 64,
66–68, 97–98, 111, 128, 131, 132, 136,
139, 345, 351, 564n54
biographical sketch, 488
Mius River, 55, 60, 167–170, 177, 195, 199,
202, 214–215, 479
Mobilization, Soviet Armed Forces, 474
Model, General of Panzer Troops, Walter, 17,
456, 461
Mokraia Mechetka River, 218, 336, 338, 340,
342, 344–345, 351
Mokryi Log *Balka*, 310
Monastryrshchina, 183
Morozov, Maj. Gen. I. S., 51
Morozov, Lt. Gen. Vasilii Ivanovich, 51, 464
biographical sketch, 593n172
Morozov *Balka*, 367
Morozovsk, 196, 199, 219, 283
Morozovskaia (Morozovskaya), 190–191
Mosal'sk, 459
Moscow, 3–5, 10, 15–16, 20, 25, 34, 37, 39–41,
44, 77–78, 84–85, 103–105, 126, 129,
139, 142, 148, 156, 164, 266, 339, 363,
413, 456–457, 471, 474, 477, 572n28
Moscow, Battle for (October 1941–January
1942), 155–156, 187
Moscow counteroffensive. *See* Operations, So-
viet military
Moskalenko, Maj. Gen. of Artillery (Lt. Gen.)
Kirill Semenovich, 45, 52, 55, 65–66,
68, 78, 81, 90, 96, 100–102, 111, 138,
141, 172–179, 181–185, 188, 197–198,
213, 220, 229–233, 236, 239, 246, 266,
284, 303–305, 313–314, 316, 318, 329,
390, 393, 548n59
biographical sketch, 57–58, 500–501,
517n52
Moskovka, 101
Mostki, 174
Mostovenko, Maj. Gen. Dmitri Karpovich,
249, 462
biographical sketch, 251, 550n66
Mozdok, 410, 419, 424, 433, 435–438, 446, 484
Mozdok operation. *See* Operations, German
military